CROSS-BORDER COSMOPOLITANS

▼ ▼ ▼

CROSS-BORDER COSMOPOLITANS

THE MAKING OF A PAN-AFRICAN NORTH AMERICA

▼ ▼ ▼

WENDELL NII LARYEA ADJETEY

THE UNIVERSITY OF NORTH CAROLINA PRESS

Chapel Hill

*This book is published with the assistance of the
Anniversary Fund of the University of North Carolina Press.*

Designed by Rich Hendel
Set in Miller and Transat
by Jamie McKee, MacKey Composition
Manufactured in the United States of America

Cover design by Lindsay Starr

Library of Congress Cataloging-in Publication Data
Names: Adjetey, Wendell Nii Laryea, author.
Title: Cross-border cosmopolitans : the making of a Pan-African North America /
Wendell Nii Laryea Adjetey.
Description: Chapel Hill : The University of North Carolina Press, 2023. |
Includes bibliographical references and index.
Identifiers: LCCN 2022022449 | ISBN 9781469669922 (cloth ; alk. paper) |
ISBN 9781469672113 (paperback) | ISBN 9781469669939 (ebook)
Subjects: LCSH: Black people—North America—History—20th century. | Black
people—Political activity—North America. | Black people—North America—
Social conditions—20th century. | Pan-Africanism. | African diaspora.
Classification: LCC E49.2.B53 A45 2023 | DDC 320.54096—dc23/eng/20220629
LC record available at https://lccn.loc.gov/2022022449

For

Osabu
(Osabu Olaitei, Ogidigidi, Gbègbèètégbèèté,
Katamansu Ta Tsè, Nuunko-Nuunko, Bo chukuò ni Bo nyagãa)

and

Atrékor Wé
for witnessing Osabu's everlasting flame and
in whose hearts and minds Osabu kindled a spirit for
resisting injustice and surviving improbable odds.

Hiao! Hiao! Hiao!

CONTENTS

ILLUSTRATIONS

▼ ▼ ▼

MAPS

TABLES

ACKNOWLEDGMENTS

▼ ▼ ▼

When you hail from neocolonial Africa's laboring masses for whom material security and dignity are too often a mirage, a life in the academy underscores the many hands and good graces that have facilitated your social mobility. When graduating from junior high school is the equivalent of your parents' formal education, because of basic human rights denied them under colonialism and neocolonialism—or when English is not your parental tongue in an English-speaking birth country, let alone your adopted country—it becomes exceptionally difficult to imagine that which is humanly possible. My story, therefore, is a testament to the power of the proverbial African village. African peoples are a cosmopolitan people, so my village included not only Gã loved ones and elders but also kindred spirits from other parts of Africa, the Caribbean, Canada, and the United States, of different shades and backgrounds. Many non-Africans also aided me on my journey.

My debts, indeed, are too many to enumerate. But I try.

The anonymous peer reviewers have been more of a blessing than I anticipated. They vetted the manuscript in a timely manner, found typos, and alerted me to gaps in my writing. Their overall suggestions, critiques, and enthusiasm with the manuscript gave me additional confidence in the project's value. The readers, in fact, encouraged me to write boldly in terms of the manuscript's interventions. It was invaluable for me to receive this type of advice from seasoned historians.

The manuscript would not have made it to peer review in July 2021 if my McGill University colleagues and interlocutors at other institutions had not organized a pivotal workshop for me in May. Lorenz Lüthi, Catherine Lu, Jason Opal, Jim Walker, Joshua Guild, and Russell Rickford read the manuscript closely and provided insightful chapter-by-chapter comments. These six senior scholars, whose research and writing span diverse fields, from global history and theories of political justice to ethnic history and Black Power, brought rich perspectives that complemented the scope and ambition of my manuscript. They inspired me to seize my authorial voice.

I owe a special note of thanks to my colleague Lorenz Lüthi. Since I arrived at McGill in August 2019, Lorenz has gone above and beyond to make me feel welcomed, valued, and supported as an untenured faculty member. His foresight and gentle—yet persistent—reminders that a manuscript workshop would help me immensely and that he would take on the task of organizing one has been one of the defining experiences of my young career in the professoriate. Although he had just completed his own book—an 800-page urtext titled *Cold Wars*—his kindness, selflessness, and professionalism have taught me a significant lesson where academic citizenship is concerned and what it means to hold the title of senior colleague.

Similarly, Catherine Lu has been a steadfast advocate, colleague, and friend. She is also a talented political scientist and institution builder. We discovered that one of her doctoral advisors at the University of Toronto, David A. Welch, was one of my undergraduate champions and mentors and the advisor of my senior thesis on child soldiers in West Africa.

Adelle Blackett is another stalwart. Her wisdom, advocacy, and love for community are inspiring. She is not only a pioneering legal scholar but also one who has had an outsize impact on making the Canadian academy more equitable. Adelle, in fact, is responsible for laying the groundwork that led to McGill recruiting me in December 2018.

My New Haven, Connecticut, dream team remains undefeated. Glenda Gilmore, a master historian—and, frankly, someone who should seriously consider publishing a guidebook on the art of training historians—read every chapter of the manuscript at least twice and provided copious feedback. Her sharp eye for detail and penchant for good writing meant that I received helpful pointers to tighten my prose. She showed patience and poise throughout. G. G. has been a major source of inspiration and mentorship. Gerald Jaynes, an economist by training, is not only a gifted social scientist but also a skillful humanist whose interdisciplinary appreciation of U.S. history and the African American experience helped me see the big picture of this project and piece together what, at times, seemed like disparate threads. Gerry reread chapters and provided thoughtful suggestions. Equally supportive was Matthew Jacobson, who also read parts of the manuscript and shared incisive advice that I, in my inexperience, was only too glad to receive. I have said it once, and I will say it again: M. J. sees U.S. history as a high-definition, three-dimensional process. Enthusiastic support and helpful recommendations for the manuscript also came from Jonathan Holloway and Jay Gitlin. Jonathan identified gaps in my analysis, and Jay's scholarship on French North America gave me ideas on how to formulate a framework of African North America. These scholars not only facilitated my admission to Yale in August 2012 but also ensured, once I arrived in New Haven, my thriving.

At McGill, my colleagues in the Department of History and Classical Studies and other parts of the university have played an integral role in my progress. My previous chair, Jason Opal, ensured that my teaching and service commitments did not delay completion of my manuscript. Jason's wisdom and overall support have been invaluable. My current chair, Kate Desbarats, has also been uplifting. My late colleague Jarrett Rudy embodied kindness and collegiality. Comrades in the Dr. Kenneth Melville McGill Black Faculty and Staff Caucus also deserve praise for their tireless efforts to make McGill a more equitable institution. My students inspire me with their intellect, eagerness to learn, and compassion for humanity.

Other sources of support, such as professional development and archival funding, aided the research of this manuscript and my scholarship at different stages. A grant from McGill's Faculty of Arts acting dean Jim Engle-Warnick provided modest honoraria to the manuscript workshop participants as a token of my appreciation. Start-up research money from McGill allowed me to complete last-minute archival trips and offset research-related expenses. From 2016 to 2019, I enjoyed various fellowships and made progress on my writing at Massey College, University of Toronto; the School of Humanities, Arts, and Social Sciences, and the History Section at Massachusetts Institute of Technology; and Harvard University's Weatherhead Center for International Affairs. I received funding from various benefactors at Yale University, most notably the Graduate School of Arts and Sciences, the Department of History, and the Department of African American Studies. Other research support came from the Social Sciences and Humanities Research Council of Canada; the Pierre Elliott Trudeau Foundation; the Marcus Garvey Foundation; the German Historical Institute and Bosch Foundation Fellowship in Archival Research; and the University of Pennsylvania Social Science and Policy Forum Fellowship in Qualitative and Quantitative Research Methods.

I could not have dreamed of a better publisher for my first book than the University of North Carolina Press. My editor, Brandon Proia, is wise, talented, and empathetic. Brandon was helpful at every stage, reading the manuscript multiple times and providing helpful line edits. His resourcefulness and responsiveness made a demanding process during a global pandemic less challenging and sometimes fun. Countless others at the press deserve enormous praise, too, from marketing and publicity to copy editing to cartography to the arts department.

Archives and knowledgeable archivists throughout the United States, Canada, the Caribbean, and the United Kingdom helped me locate primary sources, and when I could not visit, they scanned materials for me. Securing declassified intelligence documents in a relatively timely manner starting in 2015 from the National Archives and Records Administration's Freedom of Information Act and via Library and Archives Canada's Access to Information and Privacy provided the empirical evidence that substantiates major claims in this book.

I have had the good fortune of meeting leading historians and other scholars who have extended me grace and much support over the past few years. Many commented on parts of my manuscript or complementary works at different stages and offered thoughtful feedback: Malick Ghachem, Kenda Mutongi, Robin Kelley, Winston James, Sarah-Jane Mathieu, Ned Blackhawk, Craig Wilder, Jeff Ravel, Ed Rugemer, Jeff Reitz, Allan Greer, Ted Hewitt, and Christopher Capozzola.

As a Ghanaian Canadian who aspired to pursue doctoral studies in the United States, I corresponded with faculty whose generosity made a real difference in my academic trajectory. Tom Bender, for example, encouraged me to explore fundamental themes in U.S.-Canadian history. I would also like to acknowledge Michele Mitchell, Heather Ann Thompson, Gary Gerstle, Joe McCartin, Marcia Chatelain, Dennis Dickerson, Nico Slate, Maurice Jackson, Danny Walkowitz, and Andrew Needham, to name a few. Although I did not train directly under these senior historians, they have been collegial, generous, and, in many ways, role models of academic excellence and citizenship.

I credit Tera Hunter for introducing me to Joe Trotter. In September 2011, my cousin Bismark (Nii Quaye) and I drove from Toronto to Pittsburgh for me to meet Joe and discuss the doctoral program at Carnegie Mellon University. I was so humbled that a titan in the field agreed to receive me—a stranger, a nobody—like an honored guest. Joe has been such a gentleman, elder, and friend to me. His encouragement and thoughtful feedback on my research are invaluable.

I have admired Michael Gomez from afar for many years. His pioneering work on African peoples in the Atlantic World has influenced my scholarship. Michael's perceptive feedback on my manuscript has made me a better historian. His reassurance and grace remind me that I have much to pay forward in the profession.

I am also thankful for support that I received from Leah Wright Rigueur, Elizabeth Hinton, J. T. Roane, Huewayne Watson, Adom Getachew, Marcus Hunter, Margaret MacMillan, James T. Campbell, Deb Neill, Randall Hansen, David A. Welch, Karolyn Smardz Frost, the late Michael Stein, Akwasi Owusu-Bempah, Holly Guise, Amanda J. Hall, Kaneesha Parsard, Ryan Jobson, Ginny Bales, Ryan Brasseaux, Agustín Rayo, Melissa Nobles,

Tom Sugrue, John Skrentny, Jennifer Allen, Elijah Anderson, David Blight, Rodney Cohen, Michelle Nearon, Elizabeth Alexander, Alicia Schmidt Camacho, Steve Pitti, David Kastan, Jean-Christophe Agnew, Jackie Goldsby, Crystal Feimster, David Austin, C. Arthur Downes, Lascelles "Peabody" Small, Paul Winn, Big Al Barker, the late Romain Pitt, Lennox Farrell, Ato Seitu, Dawn Roach Bowen, Philippe Fils-Aimé, Brenda Paris, Francis McLean, Tim Brodhead, Mary Anne Chambers, Nick Chambers, Neil Seeman, Ian McWhinnie, Morris Rosenberg, Vic Young, John Fraser, Claudia Hepburn, Kris Mohan, Etienne Mashuli, Stephen Peel, Michael Stone, Kofi Appenteng, Stuart Shaw, Joe Kwaofio, Julian Ofori, Sue Ruddick, Penny Von Eschen, Earl Lewis, Ted Gilman, Michèle Lamont, Helen Clayton, and Tim Colton.

My interest in African peoples in the Atlantic World has evolved over the past decade. But, truly, this evolution began over a decade and a half ago. At the University of Toronto, I enrolled in a Caribbean history course that African Canadianist Sheldon Taylor taught. Incidentally, Taylor was my first and only undergraduate Black professor. In his course, I discovered the symbiotic connection between the Caribbean Basin and the North American mainland due to European imperialism, enslavement of Africans, and the circulation of people and ideas in the twentieth century. Another course on African Canadian history and a senior thesis on the founding fathers and chattel slavery in the United States, also with Taylor, crystallized what I knew intuitively but lacked the vocabulary and the deep historiographical training to articulate: that is, diasporic Africans, because of imperialism and colonialism and their organizing against systems of white domination, linked their struggles in the United States, Canada, the Caribbean, and Africa. Furthermore, Taylor introduced me to elders, impressed upon me the import of community, and served as an example of what I could achieve as a first-generation immigrant. He taught me that the Black historian must be a sentinel of Black folk. When revising my manuscript, he shared rare archival material from his private collection and always made time to answer questions and contextualize primary sources or refer me to other interlocutors. He also allowed me to read his book manuscript, which gave me a deeper understanding of Black Toronto's history.

The late Richard Iton, with whom I took an M.A. course at the University of Toronto, sharpened my critiques of U.S. political culture.

The late Robin Winks, an authority on British Commonwealth history, made Black history at Yale a more continental and diasporic enterprise. Although I did not have the pleasure of meeting Winks, his legacy is evident in the world-class advising that I received and the global contours of this book.

My dear friend Jane Anido was one of my biggest cheerleaders. Although she did not live to see this book's publication, her generosity of spirit, steadfastness, and radiant smile helped me immensely on my scholarly journey. I miss you, J. J. My sisters Lizzy and Zaza and the entire Anido Clan keep J. J.'s memory alive.

Many elders made time to share their experiences on and off the record. Their insights gave me a richer appreciation for the struggles and aspirations of African peoples in the Atlantic World, whether in Winston-Salem, North Carolina, in the 1920s or Toronto in the 1930s or the postwar Caribbean or the tumultuous U.S.-Canadian borderlands in the 1960s and 1970s.

I am equally grateful to the individuals, archives, and organizations that granted me permission to reprint images in this book. I would like to extend a special appreciation to Fredrika Newton for granting me permission to reprint a rare image from the *Black Panther* newspaper.

As a child, I could not have imagined writing a book, scholarly or otherwise. Gifted teachers played a decisive role in my academic growth. My fifth-grade teacher, Beverley Kahne Perez, was the first educator to inspire me and to instill in me a love for reading, analysis, and scholastic discipline. Mrs. Perez taught me—a Black boy who had acquired a visceral distaste for school and whom other teachers considered "troublesome"—that I could achieve the improbable when teachers showed me respect and dignity and recognized my talents.

Had it not been for the deep empathy of and support from my guidance counselor, Peter Hinchcliffe, I am unsure how I would have charted a path out of high school, let alone to postsecondary studies. As a teenager from a poor family whose friends had been involved in a gang war for half of my high school years, the last thought on my mind was achieving good grades. Mr. Hinchcliffe was the consummate high school counselor and teacher. (On 30 October 2021, Mr. Hinchcliffe succumbed to cancer. He had fought valiantly. We had not seen each other since 2004. I yearned to reconnect in person and for him to meet my family. May you find perfect peace, Mr. Hinchcliffe.) Thank you, Joanne Filipic, for keeping Mr. Hinchcliffe's memory alive.

The Afrocentric, Black-owned Knowledge Bookstore gifted me my first academic scholarship the summer before freshman year. This modest award gave me a much needed confidence boost. Ms. Alison McLean, who kindly agreed to volunteer and advise my high-school senior essay on transatlantic slavery, recommended me.

As a U of T freshman, Pertia Minott advised me to consider pursuing a Ph.D. I am not entirely sure that I knew the meaning of this abbreviation then or what it entailed. She was the first Canadian of African descent whom I knew with a doctorate, so I discerned that her admonishment was genuine. I told you that my debts are too many to list!

I cannot say enough about African American communities that embraced me and encouraged me over the seven years that I spent in New England and other parts of the country. I felt like a native son, except that I reaped where I had not sown. My dear friends and elders Lisa Monroe, Phyllis and William H. Harris, and Barbara and Curtis Patton know exactly what I mean.

Another source of inspiration are my siblings, cousins, nieces and nephews, godchildren, and all my other brothers and sisters in the 'hood and elsewhere who are struggling, dreaming, and working for a safer and just world.

My elder sister Ivy deserves special recognition. She was the first in our family to attend and graduate from high school and the first to obtain a university degree. She embodies strength, courage, decency, and wisdom, like my elder brother Rudy. He is easily one of the best fathers in the world.

My parents have been our strongest bulwark from the jump. Thank you for everything, Mom and Dad. Your sacrifices and love have brought me to this point. Mom, I cherish your supplications and words of counsel for us. Dad, you are the personification of strength, honor, and justice. You have given me the greatest gift in the world: the blessings of our fathers and foremothers. When faced with improbable odds, my ancestors summoned the Spirit of Osabu—indeed, the Spirit of the Ancient One, the Author of Justice and Life's Mysteries, lè ji Noko yè Djéin—time and time again. They overcame war and famine in the Nile Valley, survived exile in the wilderness, maneuvered hostile nations, and, after their arrival on the Accra Plains in the fifteenth century, resisted the genocidal and seismically disruptive Black Apocalypse—transatlantic slavery. When they founded Teshie as a garrison on the Gulf of Guinea circa 1695 and my patrilineal ancestral war clan Atrékor Wé circa 1696, they imbued both with our credo: "No surrender. No retreat." Throughout my childhood and teenage years—and, honestly, to this very day—I have spent countless hours sitting at my father's feet listening to his deft rendition of Gã narratives. He taught me the meaning of knowledge of history and love of self.

I would be remiss not to acknowledge specifically my kinsmen and kinswomen from Atrékor Wé who also taught me about the art of history. The clan is the braun of Teshie, the pulse of the Klé Musun section (meaning Belly of the Beast; a Gulf of Guinea and Atlantic World riddle), and the heart—or technically the thumb—of the Gã Confederation. They supplemented my dad's teachings, exposing me to sacred and forbidden Gã,

Teshie, and clan knowledge. Yoo'mo Atswei Kpékpélé, for example, brought words from our ancestors. May those words come to pass, and may she have strength and health to enjoy its fruit. It humbles me that my kinsmen and kinswomen's narration of watershed events from centuries ago, including the names of key actors and landmarks, when cross-referenced with the works of professional scholars, often proved more reliable and accurate. They remind me why the scholar or fact finder must always begin at the source, not the periphery, when seeking historical knowledge. My Yale Ph.D. compares not to what they know empirically and in spirit. Their insights are vast; their command encyclopedic. I have learned and grown much from sitting at their feet listening to our ancient battle songs, names of distinguished generals and high priests, tales of the courage and resourcefulness of our foremothers in a highly militarized and violent Atlantic World, and Gã ethics on divinity, sanctity, humanity, and justice—including grounds for just war against enslavers and territorially expansive empires. They showed me, in sum, that knowledge of Black history—yes, the history of African peoples—is necessary to constructing a blueprint for complete emancipation from systems of anti-Black domination, exploitation, and extermination.

My deceased grandparents also deserve recognition. As a little boy, (my grandmother) Yoo'mo Kutorkor was my best friend. We were inseparable. Yoo'mo Atswei Flanta had a brilliant mind. She also had the heart of a warrior. My grandfathers, Nii Okoe Onukpa and Ataa Gbòmò, whom I did not meet in this earthly realm, I honor you.

Last, but certainly not least, I thank Naa Oyoo and Nii Adjei for their love, encouragement, and patience. In their own unique way, they nudged me toward the finish line. Nii Adjei, may you find purpose and fulfillment in adding to the historical record in words and deeds. Indeed, may you, too, cherish the memory of our ancestors and help safeguard the legacy of your ancestral clan Atrékor Wé. For honoring your promise *and* for arriving not a second too late, Daddy is so grateful for and proud of you—you Little Grizzly Bear.

The merits of this book belong to those who helped me on my journey and have entered my African village or bridged theirs to mine as acts of human solidarity. Pardon me for those whom I have forgotten to mention. The demerits of this book, however, are mine alone.

CROSS-BORDER COSMOPOLITANS

▼ ▼ ▼

North America

INTRODUCTION

NORTH AMERICA

A TRANSNATIONAL, GLOBAL ZONE, 1900–1919

"She was a plain-looking little colored girl. Coming from Canada, that rugged land where Apex and Anti-kink are indispensable necessities, but dutiable luxuries, her coarse black hair was 'bad,'" wrote Juanita DeShield of the protagonist in her 1936 short story. Although she concealed her own experience within a sensationalized third-person narrative, the 1934 bus trip from Montreal to New York City that DeShield recounted was real, partly lingering on the physical lineaments of race and difference that she knew intimately. "Her broad flat nose and thick red lips were an unusual complement to her milky-white complexion. Her hands and eyes seemed not to belong to her at all," she admitted. But her eyes, DeShield continued, "large and expressive, registered her every thought, and when she was excited, rolled like Eddie Cantor's."[1] Her disapproval of cosmetic goods that bleached melanated skin and Europeanized African hair—by-products of what the scholar Cedric Robinson would later call "racial capitalism"—not to mention her reference to entertainer Eddie Cantor, who performed in blackface, signified DeShield's acute racial consciousness and awareness of societal contradictions and dehumanization of the Black body.[2]

Born 30 April 1913 in Montreal, Quebec, Juanita Corinne DeShield came of age in North America (Turtle Island), where the diasporic African population had been rapidly intermingling since the turn of the century. Anti-Black racial terrorism, urbanization, industrialization and demand for cheap labor, racial awakening, adventure, and ecological factors pushed and pulled African descendants around the continent. DeShield's community comprised Garveyites and other race-conscious Black people, some Canadian-born, others from the Caribbean Basin and the United States. Her paternal aunt, Anne, belonged to Montreal's Colored Women's Club, a social network and civic bulwark that African American ladies founded circa 1902 when their spouses migrated north to work as sleeping car porters.[3] DeShield's parents and elders provided her with an armor of race pride to blunt the racist and sexist expectations of the dominant society. By her early twenties, as a McGill University undergraduate, DeShield had become a prominent African Canadian youth organizer, pacifist, and anti-fascist cross-border activist. To escape the worst of the Great Depression, the promising intellectual and budding artist moved to Harlem in 1934, where she roomed with relatives, took elocution lessons, wrote about race and militarism, sometimes published, and begrudgingly found work performing domestic chores in the Bronx.[4]

DeShield's reflections on her place within the U.S.-Canadian landmass provide a window into the borderlands, transnational world of diasporic Africans. Hers was a widely shared understanding of marginalization. How do we explain a people whose migrations, labor, family ties, social aspirations, politics, and revolutionary struggle transcended the boundaries of empires and states? How do we reconcile their alienation and emigration from these polities when their presence over generations was foundational to the socioeconomic order? To comprehend this contradictory existence, historians must capture the complexities and multidimensionalities of a people who lived on the borderlands of society, racially subordinated and subjugated, often internally displaced, and unable to enjoy the fruits of citizenship. In the absence of viable African repatriation, many found a home by imagining and forging diasporic and transnational communities that spanned the United States, Canada, the Caribbean Basin, and Africa.[5]

This book maps racial formation and self-determination among North America's mixed Black population of African Americans, African Canadians, and African Caribbean peoples from 1900 to 2000.[6] It provides not only a lexicon that reduces analytical fragmentation, harmonizing the diasporic African experience in the Atlantic World, but also a framework that situates historical actors, ideas, associations, and events within a broad sociopolitical and geographic context. In the words of historians Toyin Falola and Kevin D. Roberts, this project places "micro" analyses into "macro" systems.[7] By examining cross-pollination among African peoples and the ways that they navigated the United States, Canada, the Caribbean, and sometimes Africa, this intervention—the first of its kind—excavates, recovers, and reconstructs the bones and anatomy of African Diaspora and Atlantic World history. A blend of urban, borderlands, transnational, and global history, this spatial body of knowledge is vital to understanding freedom and alternative notions of citizenship, not to mention a North American mentalité that galvanized twentieth-century African anti-colonialism. For Black people of diverse origins in North America, "race"—that is, unity of African peoples, fluidity of borders, and resistance to anti-Black domination, exploitation, and extermination—functioned as a point of reference, bridging mechanism, and rallying cry. This backdrop, which constantly reminded African descendants of their disinheritance and Western cupidity, encouraged serial border crossings and freedom linkages that challenged U.S. and Canadian public and foreign policies predicated on anti-blackness.

Diasporic Africans networked, strategized, created organizations, and led movements while traversing North America and the broader Atlantic World—their cross-border, cosmopolitan corridor. They pursued formal and informal ways of achieving a collective liberation that would also end colonial plunder of Africa and exploitation of the Black masses. The combination of Black people's militant race pride, critiques of imperialism and colonialism, and transatlantic organizing in the twentieth century exposed continental fault lines. Consequently, U.S. and Canadian authorities covertly deployed counterrevolutionary measures in the interwar period and postwar years, particularly the late 1960s through the 1980s, to thwart Black self-determination on the North American mainland, in the Caribbean, and in southern Africa. Considering the worldwide African Diaspora and sheer influence of the Americas on the rise of the Atlantic World, this North American history is, truly, an international and global history of Black self-identification, Black activism, and Black community building and nationhood.

African descendants like DeShield regularly assessed the dynamics that informed their subordination and movement from one racially stratified country to another. Equally important, they appreciated the difficulty of mapping an African conscience and Black body with occasional European traits onto the North American landscape. When Black people in the United States, Canada, and the Caribbean pursued cross-border connections and relocation, they not only imagined freedom but also pushed boundaries— literally and figuratively. Indeed, diasporic Africans moved between—and among—worlds. DeShield, for example, spoke English and French fluently, the languages of social groups that were separate from and hostile to each other in Montreal and antagonistic to her own segregated Black community in the city. Mobility and adaptation became processes that avowed their lineage in the United States, Canada, and the Caribbean. In the nineteenth century, DeShield's forebears plied the North Atlantic off the coast of Newfoundland as Bermudian whalers and seafarers. Before that, some had lived in Santo Domingo (Dominican Republic). Once in Canada, her grandfather George Morris DeShield, like other Black men, helped build the transcontinental railway in the 1880s on which her father would travel as a sleeping car porter in the early 1900s. As the daughter and granddaughter of nation builders with extensive history in North America, DeShield could articulate the unfolding diasporic and transnational logic that shaped the identities of Black people on the continent. And as a descendant of free and enslaved Africans in the Americas, DeShield, according to the late historian Ira Berlin, was an "Atlantic creole" who possessed "linguistic dexterity, cultural plasticity, and social agility."[8]

TOWARD A DISCOURSE OF
NORTH AMERICAN PAN-AFRICANISMS

Since the nineteenth century, African American intellectuals have leaned on the diasporic and transnational to articulate "a different sort of nation-building project," argued historian Robin D. G. Kelley.[9] They believed that internationalizing the Black freedom struggle and writing a collective Black history that restored Africa to its rightful place in human civilizations would mitigate centuries of deracination, facilitate social and physical mobility, strengthen communal bonds, and inspire individual and collective freedom. For diasporic Africans, specifically African North Americans—African Americans, African Canadians, and African Caribbean peoples—this nation-building project was inextricably tied to Pan-Africanisms, a vision that Black people articulated and manifested to different degrees.[10] They looked beyond colonies, unitary states, and empires to forge global Black nationhood.[11] Black people imagined and aspired to create an African World.

This book, as a result, focuses on the twentieth century, an era that witnessed large migrations, frequent border crossings, and seismic developments in local and global Black organizing against imperialism, colonialism, and neocolonialism. This organizing triggered reactionary national and international policies that sought to maintain systems of anti-Black domination. Movements like Marcus Mosiah Garvey's Universal Negro Improvement Association (UNIA) in the 1910s and 1920s, building on turn-of-the-century efforts to establish an autonomous Black cosmos, provided African North Americans and other Black people with a vocabulary, consciousness, political education, and zeal to pursue liberation.[12] Operating within informal and formal structures, transnational actors crisscrossed the U.S.-Canadian border, the Americas, and the Atlantic Ocean during the twentieth century to forge freedom linkages among African peoples. They include African Canadian educator and socialite extraordinaire Beulah Cuzzens; African American founder of African Liberation Day Owusu Sadaukai (Howard Fuller); African Caribbean activist Rosie Douglas, who secured financing for left-leaning African rebel groups in the 1980s and 1990s; and countless workers, hustlers, athletes, musicians, reformists, and revolutionaries.

4 INTRODUCTION

Pan-Africanisms illuminate the racial formation, migrations, community building, and freedom struggles of twentieth-century diasporic Africans who moved among the United States, Canada, and the Caribbean Basin. Sometimes, these African North Americans organized on the African continent, but they fought always for a worldwide community. The uppercase "Pan-Africanism" and lowercase "pan-Africanism" constitute what I call "Pan-Africanisms." The late George Shepperson, pioneering British historian of the African Diaspora, posited that *Pan*-Africanism entailed a formal or "recognizable" movement for national self-determination and cooperation in Africa and its diaspora (or diasporas), such as the watershed 1900 Pan-African Conference or the Pan-African Congresses, which began in 1919.[13] Black studies scholar Kwame Nantambu called this goal "Pan-African nationalism."[14] In other words, Pan-Africanism transcended the ethno-territorial state configuration so common throughout precolonial Africa. It also elevated and integrated aspects of nationalism, sovereignty, and other state principles from the Westphalian model.[15] That Europeans had arbitrarily demarcated the boundaries of African colonies, which newly independent states inherited without addressing long-standing intergroup grievances, imperiled notions of sovereignty and self-determination, essential components of Pan-Africanism.[16] Nonetheless, leading Pan-Africanist statesmen of the twentieth century did not envision the state as the supreme political entity in their formulation of Pan-Africanism, which is why formal Pan-Africanism aspired to achieve a federation or confederation of self-determinative African and diasporic states.[17] For these reasons, I consider (unlike Shepperson and other historians) Marcus Garvey's UNIA—which first showed signs of global promise in 1917 within the U.S.-Canadian borderlands with its petitions to the League of Nations in the 1920s and efforts to establish a United States of Africa that would serve as a beachhead and protector of all Black peoples—an exemplary Pan-African movement.[18] Similarly, African Liberation Day agitation in U.S., Canadian, and Eastern Caribbean cities, which mobilized material and moral support to aid anti-colonial struggles in southern Africa starting in 1972, is another example of Pan-Africanism.

I define *pan*-Africanism as solidarity based on Black racial and cultural consciousness, social mobilization against exploitation and domination, and control over community resources. As an organizing principle, pan-Africanism is less concerned with the creation of self-governing Black states that share power with and partly derive authority from a centralized or decentralized supranational structure. Theorists and rank-and-file activists considered *Pan*-Africanism and *pan*-Africanism not only mutually reinforcing objectives—there was a strong grass-tops and grassroots dynamic—but also necessary worldviews in a centuries-old global order that sought perpetual domination of Black people and exploitation of Africa. In fact, twentieth-century Pan-Africanisms in North America organically synchronized phenomena that scholars call social and cultural history (or history from below) and political and intellectual history (or history from above). As the martyred Guyanese Pan-Africanist intellectual and revolutionary Walter Rodney explained about Pan-Africanisms, "Unity is created in the struggle and is so much the more valid because it is created in struggle."[19]

Pan-Africanisms denote "a language of liberation," observed the writer Aminah Wallace.[20] More than rhetoric, Pan-Africanisms, specifically the orthodox variety, with a revolutionary race-first requisite, demanded racial redemption from the degradation to which imperialism and colonialism reduced Black people in Africa, the Americas, and other jurisdictions where a critical mass of African descendants dwelled.[21] Pan-Africanisms, in fact, predicted a glorious destiny for Black people, because ebony-hued Nilotic Africans and their civilizations in antiquity had no rivals in the known world. Those who influenced Pan-Africanisms' underlining ideas ranged from intellectuals to common folk who treasured African or Black history and understood the genocidal nature of imperialism, colonialism, and other forms of anti-Black intrusions into Africa. On balance, crossing a border in and of itself did not imply "a language of liberation" or *pan-*Africanism.[22] However, awareness of a global Black community in which members could trace their ancestry to Africa, insight that imperialism and colonialism created a common enemy for all Black people, and fighting for liberation and autonomous Black states that would work together constituted Pan-Africanisms. Knowledge that Black people transcended the imaginary borders of empires and states mostly as a legacy of enslavement and conquest in the "New" and Old Worlds also affirmed Pan-Africanisms. According to Audley "Queen Mother" Moore, the Louisiana-born Garveyite and an architect behind the Republic of New Afrika, which African American revolutionaries founded in 1968, "I don't pay those borders no mind at all" where a global Black community is concerned.[23]

Not all historical actors who subscribed to the tenets of Pan-Africanisms explicitly cited this nomenclature when describing themselves or their motivations. Various euphemisms served to evoke the spirit of Pan-Africanisms. Some diasporic Africans, as early as the eighteenth century, began appropriating the noun "Ethiopian" from the King James Bible, which, in ancient Greek, meant a Black person or Africa. This identifier catalyzed the revanchist and messianic movement called Ethiopianism, a prophecy-driven racial

INTRODUCTION

redemption of Africa and its Black inhabitants. Since the nineteenth century, other adherents of Pan-Africanisms spoke of "Africa for the Africans."[24] By the twentieth century—and in addition to Ethiopianism and demands of Africa for the Africans—some used colloquialism to invoke Pan-Africanisms. Barbadian Donald Moore, who immigrated to Canada by way of New York City in 1913 and was a founding member of the Toronto division of the UNIA in 1919, said that British West Indians described *pan*-Africanism as "brothers of the skin."[25]

Most diasporic Africans associated pan-Africanism or pan-Negroism, in part, with a fraternal and sororal racial identity and shared African heritage. Pan-Africanisms, however, meant more than racial consciousness and fleeting camaraderie based on melanin. Put simply, Pan-Africanisms implied that African peoples the world over—many of whom professed a sacred connection to the Creator and ancestral realm, which influenced their outlook on the spiritual, physical, and material—had a responsibility and an inalienable right to organize, retake power from their subjugators, and create self-sufficient, interdependent homes and communities, small and large, local and global. In this vein, Pan-Africanisms encompassed Black Nationalisms and Black Power and overlapped Black Internationalisms.[26] Pan-Africanisms epitomized subtle and at times audacious attempts to resist exploitation and expand the possibilities of Black freedom—dynamic and contested endeavors that evolved generationally.

Twentieth-century Black freedom struggles in North America primarily entailed Pan-Africanisms. And scholars cannot write this history in the fullness of its complexities, let alone grasp the dynamics that helped spark African anti-colonialism, without scrutinizing African North America. Such intervention requires analyses of the ways that African Americans interacted and collaborated with African Canadians and African Caribbean peoples, how these three groups engaged continental Africans, and the importance of geography where borders, transnationalism, and diaspora are concerned. A case in point: Henry Sylvester Williams, the Trinidadian lawyer—who trained at Dalhousie University in Halifax, Nova Scotia, from 1893 to 1895 and was that law school's first Black student—convened from 22 to 24 July 1900 the inaugural Pan-African Conference in London, England. Before crossing the border into Canada, Williams had struggled to find opportunity in New York City around 1891–92. By decade's end, the astute Trinidadian had coined the phrase "Pan-Africanism" and began organizing on a global scale. He soon became the first Black lawyer in South Africa, where his defense of native rights from 1903 to 1905 precipitated the African National Congress. At the 1900 conference, Williams's comrade Jamaican-born

Rev. Henry B. Brown, whom he had befriended during his Canadian sojourn, represented "Lower Canada" (Quebec and parts of Eastern Canada after 1841), serving as vice president and one of thirty delegates.[27] This anti-colonial organizing among African peoples would become more worrisome for the U.S. government and European empires.

The Canadian-born Anna H. Jones, principal of Ohio's Wilberforce University, also attended the 1900 conference. She delivered a lecture titled "The Preservation of Race Individuality." In 1852, Anna Jones's African American father, James Monroe Jones, relocated to Chatham, Canada West (Ontario after 1867), where his daughter was born in 1855. He became a talented artisan who briefly served as a gunsmith for the white revolutionary abolitionist John Brown. In fact, James Monroe was one of the finest gunsmiths in North America. He was among a group of Black delegates who hosted Brown when he visited Chatham in 1858 to plot his raid on Harpers Ferry.[28] Black liberation—whether moderate or revolutionary—was intergenerational, international, and intercontinental.

Other notable African North American delegates contributed to the global 1900 Pan-African Conference in London. One of the first delegates to speak was C. W. French of Saint Kitts, with his presentation "Conditions Favoring a High Standard of African Humanity."[29] Haitian diplomat and intellectual Benito Sylvain attended the conference on behalf of both Haiti and Abyssinia (Ethiopia), whose army had trounced Italian imperial forces at the Battle of Adwa in 1896. Sylvain titled his address "The Necessary Concord to Be Established between Native Races and European Colonists." Participants planned to host Pan-African Congresses biannually, hoping to meet in a European or U.S. city in 1902 and Haiti in 1904 to celebrate the centennial of the founding of Haiti and conclusion of the Haitian Revolution.[30] W. E. B. Du Bois, who was partly of Haitian ancestry, chaired the conference's Committee on the Address. It was on this committee that Du Bois—who, in 1897, touted African American contributions to "Pan-Negroism"—prophesied, "The problem of the twentieth century is the problem of the color-line."[31] Black intellectuals' reflections on global geopolitics and their travels in North America, Africa, and Europe sharpened their analyses of power and exploitation—imperialism, colonialism, capitalism, racial stratification, ethno-racial nationalism, and nation building.

The Pan-African Conference in London demonstrated the endurance of the Atlantic triangle: Africa, the Americas, and Europe. Having studied and traveled in Europe in the late nineteenth century, Williams and Du Bois drew lessons from currents of Pan-Germanism, Pan-Slavism, and Pan-Hispanism—what historian Raymond L. Buell called "pan-nationalism"—emanating from the region.[32] In the wake of the 1884–85 Berlin Conference, a gathering of European powers that further entrenched their colonization of Africa, Black intellectuals saw the handwriting on the wall and interpreted what it foreshadowed for the coming century. As the late Africanist Isidore Okpewho averred, this "Scramble for Africa," which inspired planning of the Pan-African Conference, was a corollary of the Monroe Doctrine, the Antebellum U.S. foreign policy meant to limit European domination of lands in the Americas on which mostly African descendants toiled.[33] Even if they wished to meddle, western Europeans' colonization and plunder of Africa in the 1870s nullified any rebuke of white nationalism's revitalization in the Reconstruction South.[34]

The 1900 conference shaped the trajectory of civil and human rights advocacy in African North America and global Black resistance against imperialism and colonialism. On the mainland, it underscored the fluidity of the U.S.-Canadian border. In 1905, for example, Du Bois and twenty-eight African American men gathered near the iconic Niagara Falls in Fort Erie, Ontario, a terminus of the Underground Railroad less than ten miles from Buffalo, New York. The following year, both men and women organizers converged on Harpers Ferry, West Virginia, where John Brown had led a raid in October 1859 that helped trigger the U.S. Civil War. These discreet meetings—or, as the founders called it, the Niagara Movement—jump-started the National Association for the Advancement of Colored People (NAACP) in 1909. From its inception, the NAACP included a "Pan-African Department," signaling the Niagara Movement's cross-border, continental, hemispheric, and transatlantic aspirations.[35] Thus, when Haiti sought support in 1908 and 1909 to invigorate its Pan-African agenda, Haitian statesman Benito Sylvain fundraised in Canada and the United States. Requesting assistance from African Americans through Du Bois, a torchbearer of Pan-Africanisms, Sylvain affirmed the aspirations of Haitians and their diasporic compatriots: "the *complete* emancipation of our Race."[36] Furthermore, the 1900 Pan-African Conference provided Du Bois with the blueprint for his numerous Pan-African Congresses. He spearheaded the initial one in 1919 at the Paris Peace Conference, which he could not have accomplished without backing from the British Columbia–born Ida Gibbs Hunt, his brilliant anti-imperialist co-organizer. Hunt was of African American parentage and one of the foremost Pan-Africanist women of her generation.[37]

That Black people sought and cultivated connections across the U.S.-Canadian border decade by decade shows that North American Pan-Africanisms pivoted on serial cross-border migrations and belief in the oneness of African peoples to achieve full freedom from white domination.

When Ohioan Joseph Robert Burke "J. R. B." Whitney entered Ontario circa 1909–10, he came, like others before and after, in search of racial progress. Whitney might also have been searching for a new beginning.[38] Despite the racist 1910 Immigration Act, the few thousand African Americans who entered Canada in the 1910s—or the many thousands more whom border officials denied entry—illustrated that the Great Migration's first wave extended beyond the industrial U.S. North. From 1914 to 1919, Whitney, a senior member of Toronto's Prince Hall Freemasons' Eureka Lodge No. 20, was the most influential Race Man in Canada. In an era when the best-educated Black men in Canadian society could find gainful employment only as sleeping car porters, Whitney worked as an administrator for the Northern Ontario Railway. He also owned his Toronto home.[39] In December 1914, Whitney launched the *Canadian Observer*, the national paper of record for the race.[40] Nearly one year later, he exchanged correspondence with the minister of militia and defense, seeking federal authorization to muster an all-Black platoon with a Black captain. "There is nothing in the world to stop them," replied Minister Sam Hughes, that is, except rampant anti-blackness throughout the armed forces and empire.[41] Indeed, Whitney's eloquent editorials, organizing of African Canadians, and ambassadorship to the white establishment helped break the unofficial color bar against Black enlistment in the Great War.[42] Nevertheless, the Canadian Expeditionary Forces, like its U.S. equivalent, remained a Jim Crow fighting unit that tried to relegate most Black servicemen to servile occupations.[43]

Race consciousness and community mobilization during the First World War crystallized ethno-racial nationalisms of sorts in North America. In certain situations, this agitation generated more questions than answers, such as the African Canadian experience.[44] For instance, Whitney occasionally articulated the importance of Black racial pride to white Canadian elites, most notably Sir Edmund Walker, president of the Canadian Bank of Commerce, and fellow high-ranking Freemason.[45] Having heard the grumblings of ethno-racial nationalism among various groups in Canada, which would become more urgent after the war, Whitney tried to prepare African Canadians for a world order on the cusp of seismic shifts. At a one-year anniversary rally for the *Observer*, Walker, an honored guest, cautioned his all-Black audience that group success would take several generations. But he urged them to embrace race pride, because no people or nation, he reasoned, could aspire to organize itself and achieve power without it. Moreover, a race that knew its history and the crucibles that it had overcome—he cited North American slavery—was not only a potent race but also one that was guaranteeing its survival.[46] A reverend of the African Methodist Episcopal

Church in attendance said Walker's words "fell on good soil." The reverend felt "very proud of my people . . . Africans."[47] Why would a scion and sentinel of the British Empire encourage this sentiment—considering the centrality of Black pride, in addition to knowledge of Black and African history—and in doing so fan Black revolutionary flames in the Atlantic World?

Before enjoying prominence as a banking baron in the Montreal–Toronto–New York City–Washington, D.C., corridor and as a fine arts patron at the turn of the century, Walker had come from humble beginnings in rural southwestern Ontario. One of the most skillful financiers in the British Empire, his wide-ranging interests included Black history, as evidenced by his correspondence with Carter G. Woodson and life membership in the Association for the Study of Negro Life and History that Woodson had founded and led starting in 1915.[48] Walker's affinity for exceptional Black men like Whitney and Woodson, however, was not tantamount to a desire for equality among racial and gender groups, especially with African descendants, even when he and fellow imperialists advocated Canada's federation—more like neo-colonization—of the resource-rich British West Indies.[49] Like most white people, Walker was a social Darwinist who believed in the stratification of races.[50] Nonetheless, his rapport with and support of Whitney, but more importantly his unusual candor on the greatness that African peoples could achieve if they organized and harnessed the power of Black pride and Black history, betrayed the prevailing racial, classist, and patriarchal mores of white elites everywhere.

Middle-class Black leaders—Woodson, Whitney, and bourgeois spokespersons, too—did not threaten white elites like Walker. In the post-Emancipation years, some Race Men and Race Women learned to temper their demands for complete liberation with rhetoric that sounded like gradualism, such as at the 1900 Pan-African Conference or in civil rights organizations in the Progressive Era. By 1919, a militant Black populace had gone from seeking a "revolution of thought," which Whitney encouraged in his newspaper to incite a racial awakening in the war years, to calls for actual revolutionary change.[51] This urgency explains why moderate U.S. and Canadian race programs, like the NAACP's, failed to generate the same excitement among the masses as the UNIA's revolutionary agenda. As interracial violence engulfed U.S. cities in what James Weldon Johnson described as the Red Summer of 1919, Whitney returned to his birth country with his newly wedded African Canadian bride, Ada Kelly Whitney. A pioneering educator from Windsor, Ontario, Ada earned her teaching certificate in Detroit circa 1918 and became the first African Canadian school teacher in Windsor. Before leaving Canada in autumn 1919, however, J. R. B.

Whitney secured two letters of recommendation—or notes of safe passage, considering widespread anti-Black violence in the United States—from his prominent friends Sir Edmund Walker and Ontario prime minister Sir William Hearst. The couple settled in New York City—the battleground of the "New Negro"—where they continued their race work, including raising children.[52]

In many ways, the 1900 Pan-African Conference foreshadowed a tumultuous 1919. That year, a fearless New Negro—frustrated by a regression in global Black liberation—fought urban race wars in the United States while shouts of ethno-racial nationalisms thundered in North America, Versailles, Africa, the "Middle East," and Asia. Despite a placid, middle-class, and bourgeois veneer in the early 1900s, Pan-Africanisms in the Atlantic World originated as urgent, revolutionary, emancipatory objectives of the oppressed masses. And as the talisman of revolutionary and emancipatory Pan-Africanisms, Haitians and Haiti have earned a renowned place in the diasporic African imagination. Nowhere in the Americas—or in the known world—have a group of African peoples done more to advance Pan-Africanisms by vanquishing the spell of foreign preponderance over African minds and on African bodies than what enslaved Africans achieved in the French colony of Saint-Domingue from 1791 to 1803. Their resistance culminated in the founding of the Black state of Haiti in January 1804, the first time in human history that a revolution by enslaved persons birthed an independent country. The fourteen-year Rebellion of the Zanj—enslaved Africans—in ninth-century Basra, Iraq, against the Abbasid Caliphate, a global power, came close.[53] That delegates to the 1900 Pan-African Conference planned to commemorate the centennial of the Haitian Revolution in 1904 underscored their appreciation for revolutionary struggle against anti-Black domination. Inspiring this resistance in the twentieth century, notwithstanding most delegates' purported incrementalist rhetoric, was, to use theorist James C. Scott's framework, the "hidden transcript" of the 1900 Pan-African Conference.[54] "No human power can stop the African natives in their social and political development," Haitian diplomat Benito Sylvain assured conference attendees about the fate of Black people globally.[55]

A truly African North American affair with worldwide aspirations, the 1900 Pan-African Conference conveners in general, and Black intellectuals specifically, grasped the propagandist possibilities of history at the turn of the century. Sir Edmund Walker alluded to this premise in his 1915 speech to African Canadians, although he knew not the revolutionary potential of Black pride. For Black leaders, their moral takeaway from the history of African resistance against racial tyranny stressed pivotal events—like the Zanj

J. R. B. Whitney and Ada Kelly Whitney.
Courtesy of Sheldon Taylor.

19th September 1919

Dear Mr Whitney:

I hear that you are
leaving for New York in order to interest
some of your people in advertising in connection with the "Canadian Observer". As I
know that you have worked very hard in connection with this journal and deserve a hearty
support I write this note in order to express
this opinion to you.

I am

Yours faithfully

J. R. B. Whitney, Esq.

154 Jones Avenue

Toronto

Letter from Sir Edmund Walker.
Courtesy of Sheldon Taylor.

Letter from Ontario prime minister Sir William Hearst. Courtesy of Sheldon Taylor.

OFFICE OF
THE PRIME MINISTER & PRESIDENT OF THE COUNCIL
ONTARIO

Toronto, September 22, 1919.

Dear Mr. Whitney,-

        I understand that you are going
to New York in the interests of a group of newspapers in the United States.

        You have done good work in this
country in connection with the "Canadian Observer"
and I wish you success in your new enterprise.

                Yours very truly,

J. R. B. Whitney, Esq.,
Editor "The Canadian Observer"
154 Jones Avenue,
Toronto, Ontario.

Anna H. Jones, class of 1875. Oberlin College Archives.

Rebellion, the Haitian Revolution, and Ethiopia's defeat of Italy at Adwa in 1896, among others—as flashpoints to ignite a new world order.[56] This intellectual tradition, born out of a particular geopolitical milieu, became more apparent when Fascist Italy, in 1935, invaded Ethiopia for the second time in forty years to colonize it. The climate inspired Trinidadian historian C. L. R. James's 1938 masterpiece *The Black Jacobins: Toussaint L'Ouverture and the San Domingo Revolution.* James also published the influential *A History of Negro Revolt* in 1938, which he subsequently updated and reprinted in 1969 as *A History of Pan-African Revolt.*[57] Robin Kelley called these two seminal texts "declarations of war" against Western domination.[58]

STAKES OF THE PROJECT

Regional Pan-Africanisms as a Field of Historical Inquiry

A book on a subject as geographically expansive, personality driven, temporally varied, and conceptually dynamic as Pan-Africanisms can be only a portion, not the totality, of enumerable threads.[59] For these reasons and more, the African Diaspora from a broadly North American perspective merits its own historical field. Research on the making of an African North America generally begins with the geopolitics and imperial rivalries of enslavement, specifically the U.S. Revolutionary War and the War of 1812. Historians have painstakingly shown that these wars led to the relocation of thousands of enslaved and newly emancipated Africans from the United States to Upper Canada (Ontario after 1867), Lower Canada (Quebec after 1867), Nova Scotia, New Brunswick, Prince Edward Island, and Britain's Caribbean colonies.[60] Scholarly interest in this theme peaked with the Underground Railroad into Canada, where historians have deconstructed the lore of British benevolence—soft power—in contrast to U.S. racism and pretensions of republicanism.[61] By the 1850s, whether the leading Pan-Africanist Martin Delany or the indefatigable educator and pioneering publisher Mary Ann Shadd Cary, African Americans envisioned a struggle against racial tyranny that would encircle the United States with beachheads in British North America (Canada after its Confederation in 1867), the Caribbean, and Central America. Shadd might arguably have been the first outspoken nineteenth-century *pan*-Africanist woman in North America, having advocated hemispheric communities of conscientious African-descended peoples.[62]

Several works have heightened my appreciation of diasporic Africans' forced and voluntary migrations, identity formations, lifeways, and resistance in North America. The late Sterling Stuckey's magisterial *Slave Culture*, published in 1987, illustrated a strong nexus between ancestral

African spirituality and mores and what Stuckey described as the emergence of "proto" Pan-Africanisms in the United States and the Americas. Michael Gomez's *Exchanging Our Country Marks* in 1998 and Steven Hahn's *A Nation under Our Feet* in 2003 further illuminated how enslavement crystallized a Black racial identity and a collectivist, political culture from the Colonial and Antebellum South to the early twentieth-century urban North. As Hahn demonstrated, twentieth-century Pan-Africanisms, such as the UNIA, originated from the Great Migration and Underground Railroad. Sarah-Jane Mathieu's *North of the Color Line* in 2010 uncovered how this collectivist spirit aided African American, African Canadian, and African Caribbean sleeping car porters who organized a labor union and established communities across Canada with strong U.S. networks from Reconstruction to the mid-twentieth century. Winston James, doyen of African Caribbean history in the United States, wrote *Holding Aloft the Banner of Ethiopia* in 1998, which detailed Caribbean immigrants' outsize contributions to leftist political organizing and racial awakening in the early twentieth century. Paul Gilroy's *The Black Atlantic* in 1993 linked North American and British diasporic identities and cultures. And Robin Kelley's landmark article "'But a Local Phase of a World Problem,'" published in December 1999, punctuated the end of the millennium with an analytical bang. Kelley posited that the "global vision" of Black history since the nineteenth century is incontrovertible.[63]

For all of these groundbreaking texts that allude to or invoke various forms of Pan-Africanisms in refreshing ways, no book exists to map the scope of Pan-Africanisms in North America. *Cross-Border Cosmopolitans: The Making of a Pan-African North America* takes up that challenge, offering a quasi-revisionist intervention on Black identity, community building, and liberation struggles. This book unearths Pan-Africanisms at the intersections of twentieth-century U.S., Canadian, and Caribbean history, including moments of collaboration on the African continent, illuminating North American and African Diaspora history. The analysis seeks to shift how historians and other scholars synthesize—or harmonize—the experiences of African peoples in the Atlantic World and global African Diaspora. A book on North American and African Diaspora history must take various routes and detours, some of which require layovers in the United States, Canada, the Caribbean, and Africa. As a result, the analysis integrates freedom linkages in these different places and at different times. It ventures what scholars of transnationalism call "interactional history."[64] By examining core themes in twentieth-century U.S. history—race, radicalism, civil rights, immigration, surveillance, and imperialism—under a transnational, diasporic North

American lens, *Cross-Border Cosmopolitans* reframes blackness and refines and enriches our understanding of citizenship (sometimes decoupling it from the Western state) while scrutinizing resistance against colonialism and neocolonialism in the Caribbean and Africa. Washington championed these systems of domination and exploitation, often with Ottawa's direct and indirect support.[65] Indeed, fear of North American Pan-Africanisms incentivized U.S. and Canadian officials to bolster bilateral ties, particularly intelligence cooperation, such as surveilling, censuring, and subverting Marcus Garvey's global organizing in the 1920s, persecuting Black Power militants and Vietnam draft resisters, infiltrating and sabotaging Black radical organizations, and directly and indirectly underwriting counterrevolution in the Eastern Caribbean and southern Africa in the 1970s and 1980s.

A field predicated on Pan-Africanisms in North America decenters African American history from the state while de-exceptionalizing U.S. history. *Cross-Border Cosmopolitans* shines light on the periphery, revealing the ways that Black actors in early twentieth-century North America created the world's first Pan-African zone—a freedom blueprint for the Black cosmos. This continental community of African peoples compelled U.S., Canadian, and colonial governments overseeing the Caribbean to consider what militant Black political organizing and transnational beachheads augured for the Americas, Africa, and Europe. Indeed, Pan-Africanisms in North America sounded the death knell of formal Western colonialism. Historians have made progress chronicling the history of Black Nationalisms, Black Internationalisms, and other dimensions of Black liberation in recent decades. However, the dearth of analyses from a North American perspective elides the ways that twentieth-century global Black liberation movements began within the U.S.-Canadian borderlands as cross-border, continental projects before becoming hemispheric and transatlantic in scope. *Cross-Border Cosmopolitans*, therefore, is a door of return to the diasporic and the hemispheric, the continental and the global.

Adopting a continental framework allows for a deeper understanding and appreciation of North American history. Although long forgotten, embedded in a continental historiography, according to historian Carl Berger, is the "North American Nation."[66] It explains why Canadian financier and Black history enthusiast Sir Edmund Walker described himself as "a citizen of North America" in 1918.[67] By the 1920s and 1930s, this historiographical paradigm elevated the integration of U.S. and Canadian history while overlooking the realities of race and imperialism, central elements in the making of modern North America. The time has arrived to take this call for "continentalist history" further and inspect the boundaries of states and empires by exploring how notions of race, specifically blackness and resistance to white domination, shaped the region and—in the process—remapped the world in the twentieth century.[68] The vital historiographical questions here are not whether North America has "a common history" or whether historians of the Americas can chronicle the past without identifying shared regional threads. In the spirit of the Bolton Theory, both are necessary.[69] More important, however, are how and why did African peoples of diverse nationalities, ethnicities, and origins come together to imagine and create a transnational, cross-border, continental community with transatlantic ties? The impetus for twentieth-century global Black liberation, as a result, emerged out of African North America. Consequently, writing the history of the "North American Nation" without remaining attuned to the symbiotic dynamics of the continent is limiting. The Great Lakes, a natural borderlands zone in North America and point of interchange between the United States and Canada, help anchor the book's analysis. Furthermore, the centuries-long history of African peoples in Nova Scotia, Prince Edward Island, and New Brunswick created opportunities for connections and sometimes conflict with other diasporic Africans from New England and the Caribbean.[70]

Imperfect and often contested, Pan-Africanisms as political, economic, intellectual, and cultural objectives gained traction because of the leadership, critiques, and immense contributions of diasporic Africans in the Americas.[71] For this reason, the Pan-Africanist Ras Makonnen—born George Thomas Griffiths in British Guiana, who lived in the United States as a temporary resident during the Great Depression and tried unsuccessfully to cross the border into Canada in 1932—lamented what he perceived as the one-sidedness of Pan-Africanisms. Makonnen rebuked the African bourgeoisie's "mental treason" for members' refusal to embrace diasporic Africans during the anti-colonial struggle, even though they benefited materially, for example, from U.S. foreign aid. This capital transfer to the African elite, Makonnen argued, amounted to stolen wealth from generations of uncompensated enslaved Africans and their descendants.[72] In other words, those whose forebears had accumulated riches from the capture, trafficking, and enslavement of millions of Africans continued to reap the material benefits generations later, making them more beholden to the imperialists. Hence, Walter Rodney consistently critiqued the selfish, myopic class loyalties of the African (and Caribbean) petty and national bourgeoisie and its members' attempts to extinguish Pan-Africanisms' radical impulse to liberate the masses of Black peasant and proletariat classes.[73] Some scholars describe the material analysis embedded within Pan-Africanisms as "Left Pan-Africanism."[74]

Naming the UNIA's economic program "Black capitalism," as some historians and pundits have done, for example, is a misreading of the empirical evidence. In October 1919 when Garvey visited Newport News, Virginia, to promote and sell stock of the Black Star Line Steamship Corporation—the UNIA's flagship enterprise to transport people and freight among the United States, Canada, the Caribbean, South and Central America, and Africa—he called the corporation "the property of the Negro peoples of the world."[75] In other words, Garvey exuded pride that the masses of Black people, which invariably included UNIA workers, owned the means of production where Black industry was concerned. In this vein, one could argue that Garvey was a race-first revolutionary socialist, not a "Black capitalist." Garvey expressed zero interest in using capital from a few Black shareholders to exploit the masses of Black workers and plunder Africa's abundant raw materials. Rather, he maintained that Black sharecroppers and the growing cadre of industrial workers—the exploited Negro peasant and proletariat classes in the Americas and Africa—must pool their meager resources to sustain Black enterprises that would help transform their material conditions while aiding their revolutionary, self-determinative nationalism and nation building. Whether or not the masses engaged in market logics under the UNIA—buying, investing, selling—was not in and of itself an indication of "Black capitalism." For scholars and laypersons to see a clearer picture of the Black radical tradition and economic dimensions of Pan-Africanisms, the notion of "Black capitalism" in the UNIA and Garveyism warrants serious historical revision.

Scholarly attributions of "Black capitalism" to the UNIA are as misleading as the "nebulous concept of racial unity" proved problematic to Pan-Africanisms, according to historian Wilson Jeremiah Moses.[76] Moses's skepticism of Pan-Africanisms helps explain African elites' willingness to act as if they shared fundamental interests with their white counterparts, despite centuries of Western domination of Africans at home and abroad.[77] Idealism in generic Black racial unity underestimates the powerful appeal of ethnocentrism among humans, which elucidates why some militarized African nations had no misgivings about directly or indirectly assisting Maghrebi, Arabian, and later European enslavers.[78] The apocryphal "curse of Ham" or "curse of Canaan"—the wellspring of anti-Black thought, which has had genocidal implications for African peoples—provided religious justification for adherents of Abrahamic faiths to enslave Black people and wage war on them for millennia. Pan-Africanisms or the pursuit of Black unity and oneness of purpose across different states, ethnicities, religions, and so on to protect Black interests against massive violence and exploitation demanded political education for and steadfast organizing of the masses, not overreliance on melanin. Moses also pointed out the incongruity of nineteenth-century Pan-Africanists, such as Alexander Crummell and Martin Delany, who wanted to Christianize and "civilize" continental Africans in the way that Europeans had tried. The tension between this Western "cultural assimilationism" and African-centered Pan-African nationalism, in addition to centuries of internecine warfare among African ethnic groups, which destabilized the continent and left it vulnerable to conquest by non-Black peoples, illustrated a couple of the various fault lines in the edifice of Pan-African liberation.[79] That postwar African leaders and bourgeoisie, according to Cameroonian writer Elenga M'buyinga, vacillated between aspirational "Pan-Africanism or neo-colonialism" exposes the gulf between rhetoric and reality.[80] The late historian Judith Stein simply dismissed Pan-Africanisms—Garveyism—as "weak" systems of mass mobilization.[81]

For use as organizing principles and tools of analysis, one must employ Pan-Africanisms critically and with nuance. Scholars should resist temptation to render Pan-Africanisms as magic potions that, if unsuccessful, warrant discrediting when the material conditions of African peoples stagnate or regress. In those instances, the issue would not be Pan-Africanisms but imperial forces that wield power directly or indirectly to weaponize a few Black people against the material interests of the Black masses. Scholars should also not use Pan-Africanisms to disavow or supplant the rich ethno-cultural traditions of any group of Black folk, including African Americans, African Caribbean peoples, and African Canadians. Some African Canadian communities, in fact, can trace their lineage to eighteenth- and nineteenth-century U.S. slavery or slavery in Lower and Upper Canada and the Maritime provinces of Nova Scotia and New Brunswick.[82] Like African Americans, African Canadian history precedes the founding of the state. Pan-Africanisms as a framework must not flatten and romanticize other differences based on spirituality, political ideology, class, and gender. Pan-Africanisms or the act of theorizing racial dignity and self-determination beyond borders, for instance, was neither an expression of or desire for "patriarchy" nor an exclusive domain for men to exercise nominal power, as Mary Ann Shadd Cary, Anna H. Jones, Ida Gibbs Hunt, Anna Julia Cooper (who also participated in the 1900 Pan-African Conference), Juanita DeShield, Beulah Cuzzens, Queen Mother Audley Moore, and countless other Black women demonstrated.[83] On the contrary, Pan-Africanisms reified the unique differences among diasporic Africans by illustrating Black actors' conscientious decision to maintain subgroup identity in conjunction with a cosmopolitan character based on African ancestry, racial solidarity, common adversaries, and commitment to Black liberation. It is not coincidental that a Black Muslim movement—the Nation of Islam—emerged from Garveyism, Marcus Garvey's Pan-African ideology. Garveyism propagated "race first" as the most important organizing principle for unifying the Black masses to defeat imperialism and colonialism. It welcomed millions of members into the UNIA whose language, spirituality, nationality, ethnicity, culture, hue, gender, and class reflected the heterogeneity of African peoples.[84]

Adherents of Pan-Africanisms respected that intra-racial differences strengthened the collective. Former sleeping car porter Ralph Budd, an African Canadian whose forebears fled nineteenth-century U.S. slavery in search of refuge in southwestern Ontario, explained that a cosmopolitan racial identity functioned as a bulwark against white domination and exploitation on the North American mainland. "Because even though you have your West Indians, you have your Canadians, and you have your Americans, we are all Black. We have that one thing in common. To the white population, they don't stop to look at the difference. They look at you as Black," Budd explained.[85] Exploiting divisions, on balance, had been a perennial tool of white power, so much that European enslavers maintained meticulous records of Atlantic African ethnicities and their purported characteristics.[86] Moreover, Black immigrants and Black people born in Canada and the United States occasionally chose tribalism to protect class and other parochial interests.[87] Some conflicts notwithstanding, Budd concluded that the "influx" of West Indians provided a much-needed morale boost to African Americans and African Canadians in the pursuit of liberation, regardless of which side of the border they lived and agitated.[88]

While African origins and Middle Passages helped catalyze Pan-Africanisms in the Americas, the right to imagine freedom remained equally decisive.[89] So, too, were resistance to enslavement and the quest to perfect Emancipation—political projects in the Americas that sprung from Pan-Africanisms—as immunity from anti-blackness and exploitation, and pursuit of Black self-determination. Although "controversial and opaque" in its antecedents, according to historian Margaret MacMillan, the concept of self-determination provided African peoples in the twentieth century with a vocabulary to articulate purpose, community, and collective action. Political theorist Adom Getachew explained that postwar Pan-Africanist statesmen "reinvented" self-determination—in their "worldmaking"—to reflect international systems in which imperialism and colonialism denied Black people their humanity.[90] In North America, achieving self-determination, that is, "worldmaking" during bondage and after nominal Emancipation, required Black people to exercise agency with their feet.

Movement and migration, in fact, are essential components of any methodology that seeks to historicize and center Pan-Africanisms in North America. Self-making entailed freedom to travel and relocate, whether during imperial wars in the eighteenth and early nineteenth centuries when enslaved Africans pitted their enslavers against each other to win wartime concessions, or resisting slavery and formulating discourses on emigration from the United States, or twentieth-century circulation of people and ideas. After the U.S. government, for example, imprisoned UNIA president Marcus Garvey on trumped-up charges of mail fraud, subsequently deporting him to Jamaica in December 1927, Garveyites from the United States and Canada leveraged their mobility rights to continue their freedom struggles. Inspired by previous generations of African North Americans, they converged at Port Dalhousie on Lake Ontario every August to commemorate the formal end of chattel slavery in the British Empire and the United States and to celebrate the UNIA's core objectives of Pan-Africanisms. Only twelve miles from the U.S.-Canadian border and thirty-five miles northwest of Buffalo, New York, the strategic location of Port Dalhousie allowed Garveyites, especially those in the United States, to meet their exiled liberator when he visited Canadian cities in the late 1920s and Toronto specifically in 1936, 1937, and 1938 for UNIA International Conventions.

Scholars write about "Pan Africanism based on the *relationship between peoples and nation states* without emphasizing travels or movements" (italics in original), observed the late political scientist Ronald Walters.[91] Central to my formulation of Pan-Africanisms and overall intervention in *Cross-Border Cosmopolitans* are travel and movement, as well as Black actors' interactions with states and empires. As the most effective Pan-Africanist of the twentieth century, Garvey honed his revolutionary politics of "race first" prior to World War I by traveling and working throughout the Caribbean Basin and later the British metropole. Garvey experimented with different organizing techniques while observing the ways that African descendants suffered under Western domination. Countless others in his wake learned from this example and crisscrossed the U.S.-Canadian border, the Americas, and the Atlantic Ocean to forge global Black community and nationhood. So vital was cross-pollination to notions of Black freedom that George Washington Williams—the pioneering nineteenth-century African American historian who, after traveling to Africa in 1890, alerted the world about the slavery and genocide occurring in Belgian king Leopold's Congo Free State—posited that Africans, since antiquity, have been "a cosmopolitan people."[92] Extensive trade routes and syncretic spirituality, among other factors, facilitated cultural exchange. African lifeways that survived Middle Passages and centuries of enslavement retained aspects of their syncretism, penchant for multilingualism, and pluralism largely because the enslaved population had different origins in Africa. Sometimes relocation—or dislocation—continued in the Atlantic World after their arrival.[93] For some, a longing for Africa influenced their migrations and politics.[94]

Pan-Africanisms, indeed, evoked cosmopolitanism. This cosmopolitanism, however, was not tantamount to bourgeois or neocolonial expressions of Black identity and culture that promoted the narrow interests of elites, shortcomings that consistently undermined the credibility and viability of Pan-Africanisms. African North Americans who embraced a race-first, cross-border, cosmopolitan outlook ranged from workers, artists, reformists, and revelers to socialists, communists, and revolutionaries embedded with guerrilla forces fighting for liberation in southern Africa. Despite its cosmopolitanism, Pan-Africanisms, which crystallized because of Black scholars' writings on African ethnology and post-Emancipation self-determination during the long nineteenth century, entailed a national consciousness or "imagined communities" of sorts.[95] Cosmopolitan communities, truly, remained deeply interdependent and universal in espousing an ethic of belonging and mutual respect in the African Diaspora and Africa. Winston James called this phenomenon "Afropolitanism" (one should not confuse it with the jet-setting, consumerist culture of the scions of the African ruling class). James ascribed Afropolitanism to interwar Harlem during its Renaissance.[96]

"Black cosmopolitanism," to borrow the phrase of scholar Ifeoma Nwankwo, required African peoples to choose a side in a world order predicated on race—biologically spurious, yet the most materially consequential variable—to articulate views on race and self-determination and to convert these ideas into praxis.[97] For this reason, Tanzanian president Julius Nyerere explained in 1974 at the Sixth Pan-African Congress in Dar es Salaam, which many North American delegates attended, "We oppose racial thinking. But as long as Black people anywhere continue to be oppressed on the grounds of their color, Black people everywhere will stand together in opposition to that oppression."[98]

One cannot relegate Pan-Africanisms to fascist, chauvinistic, genocidal, supremacist, or Pollyannaish pursuits. Many Black people perceived Pan-Africanisms not as reactionary ideology akin to white nationalism or forms of religious fanaticism but as the means by which they could overcome the impediments of tribalism and global anti-Black violence and exploitation, land on an equal footing, and enjoy the universalism of a human family.[99]

They believed, in other words, that liberation built on Pan-Africanisms would balance the scales of human justice, restoring Africa and its children at home and abroad to their rightful place in world history.

Although proponents of Pan-Africanisms spoke different languages, *Cross-Border Cosmopolitans* focuses mostly on English-speaking North America.[100] This method serves two purposes. First, it adds a layer of commonality and an integrated experience, considering the widespread use of the English language in the Atlantic World. Second—and perhaps more important—it limits the scope of an already ambitious project. For these reasons and others, Mexico is not a focal point in this book. Enslaved and free persons fled the United States to find refuge in Mexico; however, its government's centuries-long campaigns to exterminate, deracinate, and assimilate African Mexicans created hurdles to hemispheric and continental connections.[101] Additionally, the U.S.-Mexican border, much like the Haitian-Dominican border, was a contested, militarized, and often surveilled terrain, far more than the mostly porous U.S.-Canadian border in the twentieth century.[102] Pan-Africanisms, in fact, blossomed in the Spanish-speaking Caribbean and other parts of the Americas, including French-speaking jurisdictions, chiefly Haiti, as revealed by the Haitian Revolution and Benito Sylvain's diplomatic travels to Ethiopia, Canada, and the United States at the turn of the twentieth century.[103] Similarly, Négritude, the literary movement that promoted Black consciousness—its bourgeois orientation, however, prevented substantive critiques of capitalism and imperialism, according to Walter Rodney—sprang from the French Caribbean in the 1930s.[104] Yet, seldom do scholars interpret Black liberation and Black identity in the Americas as phenomena fundamentally rooted in Pan-Africanisms.[105] Considering the vast population of African descendants throughout the Americas—like in Brazil, for example—there is much potential for Pan-Africanisms to illuminate regional and hemispheric history.[106]

Furthermore, studies that have explored twentieth-century freedom linkages in the Americas, particularly North America and its transatlantic connections, consistently overlook Canada's magnetism. Despite anti-Black immigration policies that kept the Black population small, hostility to the few Black people who lived in Canada, and the Canadian government's colonial and quasi-imperial proclivities at home and in the Caribbean, the myth of Canadian progressivism endured. It shaped African Americans' and African Caribbean peoples' ideas on freedom, diaspora, and cross-border solidarity.[107] That Canada was a product of the British Empire meant that it inherited the eighteenth- and nineteenth-century U.S.-British geopolitical rivalry, a competition that was as much about slavery and the place of African peoples in North America as it was about territorial expansion and Indigenous dispossession. North American Pan-Africanisms represent the gateway to a new generation of promising scholarship on the African Diaspora and Atlantic World—hence, it warrants its own field.

ORGANIZATION OF *CROSS-BORDER COSMOPOLITANS*

This social, cultural, intellectual, and political history that spans the Atlantic World unfolds chronologically and thematically, scrutinizing ideas, organizations, practices, events, and a mosaic of micro-biographies as lenses into African North America. Chapter 1—"The Messianic Moment, 1919–1931"— examines the origins of continental Pan-Africanisms and the significance of the early postwar period to global Black liberation. Intractable anti-Black racism, organized massacres of African Americans, the advent of the unapologetic New Negro, and the global rise in ethno-racial nationalisms all lent credence to the idea that a Black deliverer was forthcoming. The chapter resurrects Marcus Garvey, not as a caricature of messianism but as *the* archetypal, revolutionary Black messiah whose massive appeal and revanchist race program in the interwar years foreshadowed U.S. policy toward postwar Black leaders from Malcolm X to Grenada's Maurice Bishop. In this vein, Garvey's messianism and his race-first philosophy are inextricably linked to the ways that European states, often with U.S. support, would later neutralize numerous Pan-Africanist statesmen, such as Patrice Lumumba, Kwame Nkrumah, Eduardo Chivambo Mondlane, Amílcar Cabral, Steve Biko, Thomas Sankara, Chris Hani, and many others. In fact, Malcolm X's assassination on 21 February 1965 counter-subverted the U.S. Black revolution, just as the CIA's overthrow of Kwame Nkrumah on 21 February 1966 felled the African revolution. U.S. intelligence purposely timed these death-blows, irreparably weakening the global Black revolution. Pan-Africanisms, in other words, exposed the "gendercidal" nature of white supremacy and the ways that Western patriarchy achieved counterrevolution.[108]

The messianic moment was neither quixotic nor confined to a marginal section of African North America. It inspired the learned and the lay. The chapter illustrates how the North American UNIA and African American publishers in Canada, such as James Francis Jenkins and Robert Paris Edwards, propagated revanchist and mystical Pan-Africanisms. In addition to the sense of urgency that postwar violence engendered among Black folk, central to the messianic moment, the UNIA, and leading Black newspapers were knowledge of Black history and love of one's self, not opportunistic cultism, which thrived in certain segments of the society.[109] Black people fortified themselves with awareness of an ancient African past and memory of their enslaved ancestors as requisites for racial redemption. Their activism heightened interest in U.S.-Canadian cross-border community building and anti-colonialism in Africa. In sum, the messianic moment marked a resurgence from what historian Rayford Logan called the "nadir" of African American life after Reconstruction.[110] The quasi-religious fervor of the messianic moment reflected an African-oriented spiritualism from the nineteenth century, which helped define the Progressive Era.

As messianism lost some influence during the Great Depression, cross-border connections continued. Chapter 2, "Borderlands Blues, 1930–1950," is about place and space. The chapter explores the ways that African North Americans—such as Beulah Cuzzens; groundbreaking footballer Gillie Heron; the first Black correspondent for the U.S. military daily *Stars and Stripes*, Allan Malcolm Morrison; and many others—in Great Lakes cities imagined freedom and exercised transnational citizenship via serial border crossings or transatlantic travel. Work, freedom linkages, leisure, family reunification, and military service allowed diasporic Africans in the United States and Canada, including those of Caribbean descent, to underscore the centrality of mobility and fluid borders to the African North American experience. Some families also relocated across borders intergenerationally. Chronicling Black life in Great Lakes cities and in the theater of war in Europe, the chapter adds to our understanding of how a transnational people not only bridged borders by linking the United States, Canada, the Caribbean, Africa, and Europe but also crafted family strategies for dignity and economic security, while recasting the freedom struggle against anti-Black racism as a cross-border project. In this process, Pan-Africanisms continued to function as tools of subversion against the preponderance of the United States and the British Empire to restrict Black people's agency.

The post–Second World War period presented opportunities not only to codify Black citizenship but also to make Black activists' aspirations for liberation dependent on Western states. Chapter 3, "Civil Rights or Human Rights? 1950–1967," follows the divergent paths of the freedom movements in the United States and Canada. It focuses on the pivotal contributions that African American sociologist and reformist Daniel Grafton Hill III and his white wife, Donna Hill, played in the advancement of postwar human rights in Canada. After assessing the added constraints of the Cold War and McCarthyism on U.S. race relations, this activist couple immigrated to Canada in 1950, where they supported and then led human rights advocacy at the community and governmental levels. The chapter interprets racism in Canada and the United States through the lens of the "paradox of progress."[111] In the pursuit of postwar human rights, the paradox of progress posits that the volcanic anti-blackness in the United States made Canada, a society that had its own smoldering ashes of racism but few Black people, appear racially temperate. By embracing liberal internationalism and multilateralism and denouncing racism within the British Commonwealth and the United States, Canadian society emerged as an imperfect champion of non-white peoples. The Canadian government, in sum, sought soft power on matters of racial justice to court newly independent, racialized countries and to portray itself as an alternative to a hawkish, racially divided United States.

Activists in the tumultuous 1960s and 1970s tested the limits and boundaries of the state. Chapter 4, "Immigration, Black Power, and Draft Resisters," recovers the radical politics of Caribbean and U.S. immigrants, as well as native-born African Canadians. Before some of these individuals became pioneering senators (Anne Cools, Canada) and prime ministers (Rosie Douglas, Dominica), they stood at the vanguard of Black Power and advocated Pan-Africanisms. The gradual elimination of the white-Canada immigration policy in the mid-1960s helped solidify bonds between diasporic Africans in the United States and Canada. This example was one of several in which Black liberation struggles within the United States quickly spread to the U.S.-Canadian borderlands and then reverberated globally. Drawing on a rich and underutilized collection of Vietnam-era leftist periodicals, the chapter also unearths the stories of African American militants and Black and white Vietnam War draft resisters who resurrected symbolisms of the Antebellum years generally and the Underground Railroad specifically when immigrating to Canada. Because of anti-war activists, Black Power, and other forms of anti-colonial and anti-imperial struggles that transcended borders and elevated Pan-Africanisms, the U.S. and Canadian governments strengthened their intelligence cooperation in the late 1960s.

Indeed, Pan-Africanisms inspired sophisticated counterattacks at every stage. Chapter 5, "The Mind of the State," uses declassified intelligence reports obtained under freedom of information provisions to expose the only known case of cross-border counter-subversion by the U.S. and Canadian intelligence and security services. After Warren Hart, an African American operative for the Federal Bureau of Investigation, founded the Baltimore Black Panther Party in autumn 1968, the U.S. and Canadian governments relocated him to Canada, where he infiltrated law-abiding Black civic organizations and leftist groups. Hart's counter-subversion against Pan-Africanisms took him back and forth across the U.S.-Canadian border and to the Eastern Caribbean. Fearing the potential of a Black Power and Red Power alliance, U.S. and Canadian officials also deputized Hart to sabotage organizing between Black and Indigenous activists.

Counter-subversion and counterintelligence continued into the 1990s, as did resistance to these reactionary forces. Some Black revolutionaries retreated to the Caribbean and Africa in the early 1970s to incite and aid Pan-Africanist socialist transformations. In the process, they engaged in a "back to Africa" of sorts, which harked back to the heyday of the UNIA in the 1920s when Garvey admonished diasporic Africans, prophesying that true freedom and security from anti-Black persecution will elude all Black people until Africa is free from foreign domination and united under one flag.

Chapter 6, "Cold Wars, Hot Wars," examines Washington's efforts to undermine this revolutionary struggle in the Caribbean and southern Africa after U.S. and Canadian intelligence agencies eviscerated the Black Power movement on the mainland. In pursuit of founding a federation or confederation of self-determinative, socialist Pan-African states with strong transatlantic linkages, a generation of Malcolm X disciples became the vanguard of Pan-Africanisms. Under the leadership of African American Owusu Sadaukai—and aided by Antiguan Tim Hector, Grenadian Maurice Bishop, Canadian Brenda Paris, and others—activists initiated African Liberation Day organizing from the 1970s to the 1980s. They traversed North America and sometimes crossed the Atlantic to organize in Africa, ensuring that anti-imperialism, anti-colonialism, and anti-neocolonialism remained the foremost priorities on the African North American liberation agenda.

Reactionary counterrevolution proved unrelenting. This history in the Eastern Caribbean and southern Africa involves the U.S.-Canadian weapons manufacturer Space Research Corp., which tested long-range cannons, shells, and radar units in Barbados and Antigua before smuggling these arms and defense systems to embargoed South Africa in support of U.S. proxies in the region. So, too, was the united front of U.S. and Canadian neo-Nazi and Ku Klux Klan mercenaries who tried to orchestrate coups d'état in Grenada and Dominica. White power paramilitaries, indeed, attempted to counter Black self-determination in North America, but the chief antagonist of Pan-Africanisms was the Central Intelligence Agency. Furthermore, because of Warren Hart's background as a federal agent and experience infiltrating Black revolutionary organizations in the United States, Canada, and the Eastern Caribbean, the arms manufacturer recruited Hart to neutralize its critics in the Caribbean.

Black actors made valiant efforts to overcome state disruption. Pan-Africanisms, however, succumbed to the better organized systems of imperialism, colonialism, and neocolonialism—economic and geopolitical terror that weakened transnational freedom struggles in North America while ravaging the African continent and disorienting the Black masses. Du Bois described the antecedents of this phenomenon in 1897 as the "persistent, relentless, at times covert opposition employed to thwart" the complete self-determination of African peoples.[112] *Cross-Border Cosmopolitans* illustrates, in fact, that "backlash"—as a response against Black progress—is a misnomer, for empires and states sowed the seeds that destroyed Black liberation movements, from the UNIA to Black Power to anti-colonialism, at the beginning of such struggles, not in the middle or at the end. Counter-subversion of Black self-determination, in other words, was often proactive, not reactive. Moreover, the legacy of racial capitalism, explicitly racial caste—that is, the codification of Black subordination and subjugation, white domination, and the stratification of racial groups, which stemmed from seventeenth-century enslavement of Africans in colonial North America—ensured hostility between Black people and U.S. and Canadian societies. "Subordinate citizenship," which is akin to what historian Adriane Lentz-Smith called "stillborn citizenship"—not second-class citizenship—encapsulated the ways that, after nominal Emancipation, diasporic Africans continued to endure the effects of deracination, disinheritance, and dehumanization.[113]

Pan-Africanisms survive even so. Diasporic Africans—despite constant headwinds—relocated, subverted, agitated, and fought to find, reimagine, and build a transnational, global community. *Cross-Border Cosmopolitans* chronicles their hopes and aspirations, struggles and sometimes pyrrhic victories, and quest for a recognized birthright in North America and the broader Atlantic World. It is a work of recovery and an attempt to ingrain within the historical record the stories of some of those men and women— serial border crossers, immigrants, refugees, reformists, and revolutionaries—who dared to imagine and create something bold, borderless, and affirming for Black people.

PART ONE

▼ ▼ ▼

A CREDIT TO MY RACE.

I care not whether books of fame
Doth laud me to the skies,
I seek not golden paths of life
By which I might arise,
But greater than the golden paths
Where fame gives all a place,
I have but a desire to be
A credit to my Race.

I sing,notthat the song may die,
And not its message leave,
I speak,not that the words dissolve
Their mission unachieved.
When my words help my brother live,
And my songs find a place
In his sad heart.Then I will be
A credit to my Race.

Would that my pen,as Moses' staff
Could lead men unto God,
Would that my songs inspire the hearts
Of weary ones that plod,
O could I in the sands of time
My foot-prints leave a trace
Perhaps 'twould help my brother be
A credit to his Race.

Someday my soul must take its flight
Unto the God who gave,
Someday this humble frame of mine
Must rest in a lone grave.
Then may my fellow-man enchance
To view its resting place,
Shed just a tear,and say"He was
A credit to his Race".

Robert Paris Edwards.

Robert Paris Edwards, "A Credit to My Race." Stuart A. Rose Manuscript, Archives, and Rare Book Library, Atlanta.

CHAPTER 1

THE MESSIANIC MOMENT, 1919–1931

▼ ▼ ▼

> *Down with their cheating of childhood*
> *And drunken orgies of war,*
> *down*
> > *down*
> > > *deep down,*
> *Till the devil's strength be shorn,*
> *Till some dim, darker David, a-hoeing of his corn,*
> *And married maiden, mother of God,*
> *Bid the Black Christ be born!*
> —W. E. B. Du Bois, "The Riddle of the Sphynx," 1920

The year 1919 marked the tercentennial of chattel slavery's genesis in English North America. White supremacy may have warped notions of forgiveness, of forbearance, and of the significance of African bondage, but the arrival of this anniversary coincided with a watershed moment for racial consciousness.[1] A resurgence of white power had toppled Reconstruction in the South, ushered in Jim Crow, and triggered an upsurge in Ku Klux Klan and other paramilitary activity among the white masses. In the lead-up to 1919, the category of *New Negro* emerged in recognition of the fact that, when under siege, it was spiritually and morally inexcusable to turn the other cheek. Scholars have pointed out that the idea of a New Negro "was a bold . . . act of language, signifying the will to power, to dare to recreate a race by renaming it."[2] "Race riots"—white supremacist pogroms led by mobs bent on ethnic cleansing—tested the mettle of the New Negro, sparking the 1919 Red Summer.[3]

As early as July, white mobs prowled the streets of Washington, D.C. In pursuit of imaginary Black rapists, they besieged Black men steps from the White House and Capitol. An African American resident who witnessed the spectacle explained that Black civilians responded to the ominous threat by summoning a fighting spirit "buoyed up by deep religious fanaticism" in pursuit of racial martyrdom. For the New Negro, the trauma of past injustices "came before him like ghosts in a dream and he swore by the eternal gods and the best blood of his heart 'They shall not pass.'" Indeed, the bloodlust of the would-be lynchers awoke "the sleeping Demon of Race Consciousness" in ordinary Black folk who "sensed the flavor of the glory of hate and dropped the sting of death into the white man's cup of arrogance." The dramatic prose of this eyewitness account served a significant purpose, even if only rhetorical. The resident concluded that the New Negro, rebirthed in a baptism of unquenchable fire, reached his tipping point in 1919, vowing "eye for eye, tooth for tooth, death for death, and damnation for damnation."[4]

The fear of racial Armageddon extended north, across the U.S.-Canadian border. In the tame streets of Quebec City, panic-stricken French Canadians, bewildered by the carnage of Red Summer, "assailed" a handful of African Canadians with questions about racial violence in Washington, D.C.[5] White Canadians' fear of "race riots" was not overblown. In September 1918, a deadly clash between Black and white spectators at a sporting event in Glace Bay, Nova Scotia, made national headlines.[6] Because interracial violence was possible—even in Canada, although incomparable to the United States—African Canadians who fought in the Great War did so partly because combat experience would equip them with the skills and disposition to protect their families and communities in a racially hostile world. As early as 1919, in fact, Black men in Toronto, like others in the Atlantic World, expressed confidence that their participation in the Great War had produced thousands of battle-hardened citizens who could "combat the outrages" of white supremacy.[7]

In the United States, white supremacists instigated nearly sixty deadly interracial clashes in 1919. Jamaican-born Harlem resident Claude McKay's 1919 sonnet "If We Must Die" captured the fight stance of the New Negro and the dire conditions that inspired dogged resistance to white mob violence.[8] In Chicago, where some of the most ferocious fighting occurred from 27 July to 3 August, African Americans had been stockpiling weapons for weeks. Some had been preparing ever since news broke of the East St. Louis pogrom in 1917.[9]

When the violence began, it seemed as if Chicago's 2.6 million white residents had mobilized against 125,000 African American residents. Some 10,000 of those who resided in the city's Black Belt had fought fiercely against German troops on the Western Front in the 370th Infantry Regiment. After observing their proficiency in killing enemy combatants, the Hun called them "Black Devils." This killer instinct served their community well. When a car full of white joyriders in the downtown Loop district brandished a machine gun, an informal Black militia patrolling the neighborhood allegedly killed the machine gunner and seized the weapon. The getaway driver, a woman, was "severely beaten."[10]

Skirmishes in Chicago resembled guerrilla warfare. An eyewitness described this insurgency as one in which Black women also played an "active" role, sometimes fighting directly or indirectly by inciting Black boys to pelt white mobs with rocks. When a hurled brick struck a policeman, knocking him off his horse at 35th and Wabash, police shot into a crowd of Black bystanders. In response, an unidentified Black man, "incensed by their cowardly act," approached the officers and unloaded a salvo of bullets from an automatic gun. He escaped. The next day, sniper fire struck two mounted officers at 23rd and State. "After these incidents, the behavior of the white officers was splendid," avowed the eyewitness.[11]

In total, fifteen white and twenty-three Black Chicagoans died. Some African Americans believed that the authorities "suppressed the truth" about the white death toll. The eyewitness—whom the Black press called a "brilliant" lawyer with two degrees from Columbia University—cited a white insurance company that processed twenty-seven death claims as a result of the violence.[12] "If death is to be their portion, New Negroes are determined to make their dying a costly investment for all concerned," wrote *Negro World* founding editor Wilfred Domingo in September 1919.[13]

In North America and abroad, economic exploitation of and racial consciousness among the Black masses reached new heights in 1919.[14] Although President Woodrow Wilson's fear that "the American Negro returning from abroad would be our greatest medium in conveying [B]olshevism" proved overblown, a new spirit of militancy was arising.[15] Black intellectuals' rejection of racial essentialism and embrace of social science did not defuse this resurgence.[16] Battle-hardened Black veterans returning from the Western Front refused to kowtow to white power at home. Many fought to defend their honor and neighborhoods during the Red Summer. Anti-blackness— or what Baptist minister and towering intellectual Benjamin Mays called "oppression psychosis"—inspired a new kind of Black solidarity during this period in the United States, Canada, and the Caribbean Basin.[17]

The global nature of the Great War highlighted the cosmopolitanism of Black people and the ways that Black communities aspired to leverage their military service into full citizenship.[18] When members of Toronto's Black community gathered in April 1919 to discuss postwar liberation strategies, one doctor expressed faith in the rule of law but reserved his natural right to "a rebellious spirit," like the "Bolsheviks." State apathy and ethno-racial nationalisms, he pointed out, were the reasons that "other races are looking out for themselves and will never help us."[19] Despite the herculean efforts of Ohio-born J. R. B. Whitney to muster African Canadian troops for the war and their sacrifices on the Western Front, no promising signs emerged in Canada and the British Empire that Black men's contributions to Crown and country would pay social and economic dividends for the race. In Montreal, community members predicated their demands for dignity on the fact that their sons "had shouldered arms" during the war.[20] "Let us show that the Negroes in Canada are entrenched, and willing to fight and kill the Monster Discrimination," said Montreal's Colored Political and Protective Association, which a multiethnic group of Black people founded in 1917. In 1918 and 1919, African Canadians in Ontario and Quebec, mobilizing under the Colored Political and Protective Association and other organizations, launched chapters of the NAACP, signaling a desire for stronger cooperation with their racial kindred across the border.[21]

If the period from the end of Reconstruction in 1877 to the turn of the twentieth century represented a "nadir" for African Americans, then the 1910s and the 1920s symbolized their resurgence, a *messianic moment* of sorts. It was a time of great yearning for a race leader—a deliverer—who would help redeem the African World.[22] Although the Progressive Era pushed the boundaries of interracial cooperation and social reform from the 1890s to the eve of the Great War, the persistence of anti-Black racial terrorism heightened expectations for what one writer called "messianic leadership."[23] It was within this context that Jamaican Marcus Mosiah Garvey, a seasoned organizer and founder of the Universal Negro Improvement Association, a Pan-African nationalist movement, attracted a global following. Starting in mid-1919, Garvey and the UNIA enjoyed a spectacular rise in which he became distinguished as one of the most effective prophets of Black liberation and Garveyism (his movement) as the most meteoric in the history of the Atlantic World.[24] Booker T. Washington's untimely death in November 1915, according to historian Rayford Logan, effectively ended the "Era of Compromise."[25] This opening allowed Garvey, a self-professed disciple of Washington, to outflank a cadre of Black elites and spokespersons, as well as fringe cultish figures in the United States.[26] With postwar global chatter of "self-determination"—however ambiguous, arbitrary, and amorphous a concept—in the background, the messianic moment, indeed, was a time of high expectation for subject peoples and the gifted leaders who would liberate them.[27]

From 1919 to 1931, African North Americans, through word and deed, engaged in cross-border messianic Pan-Africanisms, a corollary of widespread racial terrorism and Black people's reflections on ancient Nilotic civilizations. This prophecy-driven race pride—or Ethiopianism—articulated a shared destiny for diasporic Africans to mitigate racial apathy and subordinate citizenship.[28] The chapter begins with an examination of Black intellectuals' writings on African history and ethnology in the long nineteenth century. This intellectual climate underscored self-determination, informing the messianic and revolutionary dimensions of Garveyism. The final part of the chapter scrutinizes editorials in the Canadian newspaper the *Dawn of Tomorrow*. African Americans James Francis Jenkins—a former student of W. E. B. Du Bois at Atlanta University and later a staff writer for one of Du Bois's short-lived magazines—and poet and composer Robert Paris Edwards launched the *Dawn* in 1923. During Garvey's legal woes and the slow decline of the UNIA, Jenkins and Edwards tried to build on Garvey's movement and foster race pride and cooperation between 20,000 multiethnic Black people in Canada and 10.5 million African Americans. The *Dawn* was an unrivaled exponent of U.S.-Canadian cross-border Black solidarity, global Pan-Africanisms, and twentieth-century messianism.

A messiah, through word and deed, attempts to deliver an afflicted group or chosen people. Hindus have the Kalki; Buddhists have the Maitreya; Christians have the Christ; Jews have the Mashiach; Muslims have the Mahdi. Messianism, according to one historian, is "the perception of a person or group, by itself or by others, as having a . . . God-given role to assert the providential goals of history and to bring about the kingdom of God on earth."[29] Black messianism was both geographically expansive and assertive in its ultimate goals. Because Black people lived under global domination, racial redemption—the Black messiah's calling—had to be transnational and revanchist.[30]

Like previous generations, diasporic Africans in the interwar era embraced the noun "Ethiopia" as a common identifier. In their struggle against anti-Black racism and terror, Ethiopia represented a "Black Zion." It was not only a mystical and messianic metaphor for an imagined promised land but also a prophecy for resistance and racial redemption.[31] Indeed, among civilizations, Ethiopia—Upper Nile or Kush—was alpha and omega. Du Bois called it the "Ancient of Days," a biblical reference to the Creator.[32] Ethiopia symbolized the greatness of the African past, which the ancient Greeks proudly attested in their literature, and the celestial redemption of Africa as prophesied in the Bible. Psalm 68:31 averred, "Princes shall come out of Egypt; Ethiopia shall soon stretch out her hands unto God."[33] For diasporic Africans, a mastery of the Western classics and the Bible not only served to illustrate their capacity for advanced learning but was also a requisite step to uncovering—recovering—their ancient divine lineage.[34] Reclaiming the history of a racial group was one of the cornerstones of racial redemption.[35]

Central to Garveyism, Garvey explained, was the role of history as the "land-mark" and "guide-post" of social movements, nations, and races. History provided direction, instilled purpose, and kindled inspiration.[36]

The lessons of history entailed regeneration, which encouraged self-remaking of a racial group, a paramount notion during the messianic moment. Messianism, whether concerning the collective or the individual, was derived from mythology that privileged a particular lineage.[37] It was partly for this reason that Garvey advocated "African Fundamentalism," admonishing Black people "to create and emulate heroes" and heroines from the race.[38] A master propagandist for the psychic and spiritual eman-cipation of all African peoples, Garvey grasped the import of consecrating prophets and saviors whose legacy could be used to exhort Black liberation. The messianic moment, moreover, was not a metonym for men or manhood, although it allowed some Black men to amplify their prophetic voices as newspaper publishers and organizers of the masses under the banner of racial liberalism, socialism, communism, and Pan-Africanisms.[39] Messianism, in fact, transcended gender, for Harriet Tubman—whom some called Moses, believing that she wore apotropaic paraphernalia while delivering her people from bondage—remained an iconic liberator in North American history.[40]

This messianic moment was an outgrowth of African American millen-nialism—or "Ethiopian millennialism"—after Reconstruction. It reflected a broader subaltern cultural zeitgeist.[41] A similar messianism and spiritualism had undergirded the Ghost Dance movement of the Great Plains and Great Basin in the 1870s and 1890s. Some Native American communities utilized prophetism and mysticism to revive their ancient lifeways and resist colo-nialism. Praying for the resurrection of ancestral shades that would aid the living revealed a deep yearning for messianic salvation and the enduring ways that humans, since time immemorial, tried to reconcile life and the hereafter, the physical and the spiritual, good and evil.[42]

The messianic moment, therefore, reflected a climate in which down-trodden peoples invoked their ancestors and the supernatural to aid their freedom struggles. That African Americans interpreted the U.S. Civil War and (nominal) Emancipation as divine intervention against anti-Black racial tyranny suggests that many continued to wait on the Creator for seismic interventions. Not everyone was awaiting a miracle, however. For years, Black scholars had been laying the groundwork for change in the here and now.

ANCIENT HISTORY AS PROPHECY

The intellectual roots of North American Pan-Africanisms lay in advances that Black scholars made in researching and writing African history in the long nineteenth century. Debates on ethnology, which had preoccupied the attention of Black intellectuals in the nineteenth century and early 1900s, resonated with the New Negro. In 1897, African Americans in Philadelphia founded the American Negro Historical Society. The founding in 1911 of the Negro Society for Historical Research in New York City, which the famed writer John E. Bruce and bibliophile Arturo Schomburg oversaw, championed a Pan-Africanist approach to the study of Black history and Black history as an integral component of global African liberation. Particularly crucial to these pioneering scholars, writers, and organizers were ancient Nilotic civilizations, specifically Ethiopia and "Egypt" (*kmt* or Kemet, land of Black people). As the intellectual historian Franklin L. Baumer observed, "An 'age' or 'period' contains both the fruit of the past and the seeds of the future."[43] The messianic moment of the 1910s and 1920s was no different.

When Mississippi senator and avowed white supremacist James Vardaman stated in February 1914 that Black people were an inferior race, echoing a centuries-old white supremacist fib, he did not anticipate the forceful counterpunch that followed. The "Negro," according to Vardaman, "has never had any civilization except that which has been inculcated by a superior race. . . . When left to himself he has . . . gone back to the barbarism of the jungle." Fifteen months later, Du Bois published his acclaimed book *The Negro*, which preceded by one week the debut box-office hit *The Birth of a Nation*. Although Du Bois cited ancient African history to refute Vardaman's barbs, he understood the difficulty of normalizing the fact that African Americans belonged to a historied people. "That which may be assumed as true of white men," Du Bois cautioned in 1915, "must be proven beyond [doubt] if it relates to Negroes."[44]

Some Black intellectuals saw this Du Boisian challenge as an opportunity to promote race pride. In 1918, thirty-six-year-old George Wells Parker, a graduate of Howard University, published his widely read *Children of the Sun*, a treatise on Nilotic origin of Asian and European civilizations. Ethiopia "wooed civilization and gave birth to nations. Egypt was her first-born," wrote Parker.[45] A native of Omaha, Nebraska, Parker founded in 1917 the Hamitic League of the World—precursor of the African Blood Brotherhood—to inspire national race consciousness and uncover that which had been lost or falsified or concealed concerning the African past. Parker's identification with Ham was subversive. Ham was the son of Noah and alleged progenitor of Africans. Noah, according to an apocryphal myth in Abrahamic scriptures, condemned his Black progeny to servitude. Ham's descendants were neither passive nor damned servants but rather authors of humanity's greatest civilizations.[46]

Alongside his mission to redeem Black history and Black humanity, Parker hoped to redeem the intrinsic worth of Black women. White suffragists in the early twentieth century had tried to convince Black women that their foremost struggle was gender, not race. White women drew this conclusion from national debates on ethnology and the perceived dangers of Black male citizenship.[47] As Parker discerned, the suffragists' strategy was to undermine cooperation between Black men and women, thus disrupting the cohesive push for Black liberation.

Parker sought an antidote to anti-Black womanism in history. He stated that since the beginning of civilization, the Black woman had always been the equal of the Black man, for such was the way of the ancient Ethiopians. African social and gender norms, in fact, could be regarded as more advanced compared with Western societies. White women, after all, were only beginning to emerge from the shadows of their husbands and fathers to claim their political franchise in the wake of the Great War.[48] Despite Parker's attempt to assert the social and cultural equality of Black women, some scholars would describe his pronouncements as "the cult of African moral superiority."[49] Even so, his aim was to prevent gender antagonism between white women and men from dividing Black society.

Parker also alleged that Western thinkers had buried the truth about the advancements of Ethiopian civilization. His work referenced an "American" translator who had committed an egregious act of censorship within the 1802 edition of *Ruins of Empires* by French historian and abolitionist Constantin-François de Chasseboeuf, count de Volney. The omission was perpetrated by none other than Volney's friend and confidant Vice President Thomas Jefferson, who translated the work anonymously. In the 1770s, Volney had visited the Levant and Egypt, retracing the steps of Strabo, Diodorus, Lucian, and Herodotus, intellectuals who commented on the genius of the original Nilotic Black Africans. But his writing was conspicuously abridged. In his original manuscript, he praised the advanced civilization he had unearthed. "There are a people, now forgotten, [who] discovered, while others were yet barbarians, the elements of the arts and sciences. A race of men," wrote Volney, "now rejected from society for their sable skin and [woolly] hair, founded . . . those civil and religious systems which still govern the universe."[50] Jefferson feared the implications of a country founded on racial slavery learning historical truths about Africans, so he deleted this proclamation from the preface.[51]

The censorship to which Parker alluded in 1918 served to substantiate a long-held suspicion among African American intellectuals. It was an article of faith shared by many that white colonizers had always known about the greatness of the African past and had consequently tried to suppress the truth. In a 1917 Omaha public lecture, "The African Origin of the Grecian Civilization," subsequently published under the same title in the *Journal of Negro History*, Parker chided white translators and historians for using modern race prejudice to distort the historical record concerning Black people.[52] For Black intellectuals—purveyors of truth as they saw themselves, and prophets who laid the groundwork for the messianic moment—it was imperative to correct the falsehood that the Black past started with captivity, the Middle Passage, or bondage. Reimagining Black history and correcting the historical record rebuked Western pseudo-scientists and racist historians who claimed that Africans had neither history nor advanced civilization prior to Eurasian contact. To refute this racism, Parker, like his predecessors and contemporaries, leveraged his proficiency in Greek and Latin and training in the Western classics. His endgame was clear: to "quicken the self-consciousness of our race and arouse in it a powerful race pride."[53]

Correcting the historical record was integral to prophetism and messianism, particularly for those who saw cyclical patterns in history. As early as 1767, enslaved Africans appropriated the word "Ethiopian" from Europeans, signaling what one scholar termed "linguistic acculturation" and self-making in the Atlantic World.[54] Those who mastered European notions of literacy used the Bible as proof that ancient Ethiopians had been a mighty and revered people while Europeans lived in a state of backwardness.[55] Diasporic Africans, according to social scientist St. Clair Drake, predicated this "vindicationism" on recovering an ancient African past.[56] Sociologist E. Franklin Frazier made a similar claim in the 1920s, pointing out that Garveyism appealed to the masses because African Americans desired "self-magnification."[57]

There is an extensive body of literature of diasporic Africans tracing the influence of Nilotic kingdoms on Greco-Roman civilizations to inspire a racial renaissance. Before publishing his seminal *The Cushite; or, The Descendants of Ham* in 1893, Rufus Lewis Perry earned a Ph.D. from Kalamazoo Seminary and two honorary doctorates from Simmons College of Kentucky and Wilberforce University. Born in 1834 into slavery in Tennessee, Perry escaped to Windsor, Canada West, in 1852. He read Greek, Hebrew, and Latin. Perry denounced Egyptologists for their "fruitful imagination," that is, the racist Hamitic hypothesis, which attributed the feats of Black men and women to non-Black invaders. He identified abject racism as the reason why diasporic Africans searched for "ancestral greatness" to "kindle in [their] breast a decent flame of pride of race." Speaking for the many direct descendants of ancient Nilotic Africans now living in the Americas,

Perry concluded that it would be "pusillanimous . . . and dishonoring to our ancestors, to be ashamed of either our color or our name."[58] Perry's work complemented African American abolitionist and historian William Wells Brown's 1874 *The Rising Son; or, The Antecedents and Advancements of the Colored Race*. Citing Greek intellectuals' admiration of Ethiopians, Brown argued that Rome acquired its civilization from Greece, which imitated Egypt, an Ethiopian colony.[59]

In 1880, Martin Delany, an indefatigable champion of the race, published *Principia of Ethnology: The Origin of Races and Color, with an Archaeological Compendium of Ethiopian and Egyptian Civilization*. The first African American to interpret Egyptian hieroglyphs, he worked to repudiate surging racism among nineteenth-century Egyptologists and ethnologists who claimed Egypt as a Eurasian civilization and asserted Black inferiority as primordial truth.[60] Citing Lucian, the second-century A.D. Assyrian writer, Delany wrote that the Ethiopians led all others in "wisdom and literature" and that "they invented astronomy and astrology, and communicated those sciences, as well as other branches of learning, to the Egyptians."[61] Doubt over the true identity of ancient Ethiopians and Egyptians persisted, Delany reasoned, because the peoples who subsequently invaded those empires weaponized "spoliation" to erase remnants of the original inhabitants.[62]

An accomplished scholar, Black Nationalist, and pioneering Pan-Africanist to Black people in the United States and Canada, Delany considered racial redemption a process rooted in history and lineage.[63] He pointed out that Africa and Africans played central roles in Christianity: Egypt provided refuge for baby Jesus and his parents; Simon the African helped carry Jesus's cross; and an Ethiopian queen sent a delegation to receive the outlawed Christian faith in Jerusalem shortly after Jesus's crucifixion. This contribution "points to a higher and holier mission designed for that race." Furthermore, Delany considered civilization the corollary of three processes: "revolution, conquest, and emigration." He concluded that revolution could be manifested "morally and peacefully as the coming of the Messiah."[64]

Accompanying Delany's 1880 text were timely works that other Black intellectuals published in the decade. In his 1882 book *The Aims and Methods of a Liberal Education for Africans*, Edward Wilmot Blyden, a founding father of Pan-Africanisms, observed the necessity of studying the Western classics, because the ancient Greeks' reverence for the Ethiopians was evident in the absence of "a sentence, a word, or a syllable disparaging to the Negro." Although mostly correct, Blyden was unaware of the anti-Black writings of Galenus, the first- and second-century Greek physician.[65] Civil War veteran and statesman George Washington Williams's 1883 groundbreaking

History of the Negro Race in America from 1619 to 1880 similarly asserted, "The Negro race antedates all profane history."[66] The father of African American history described the "growing desire" among Black scholars to learn about "the antiquity of the race."[67] By 1905, on the basis of these influential works, African American writer Pauline Hopkins compiled *A Primer of Facts Pertaining to the Early Greatness of the African Race and the Possibility of Restoration by Its Descendants.*[68]

These efforts to harness the liberating potential of Black history were integral to the emergence of Black solidarity in North America at the turn of the century, highlighting the racial ideas that strengthened cross-border linkages among African Americans, African Canadians, and African Caribbean immigrants.[69] In April 1919, for example, Black men and women founded the Colored Literary Association of Toronto, an organization that sought to create a library furnished with books from British colonies and the United States to help members understand the Black past while imagining a Black future.[70] Moreover, the group, which became the Toronto UNIA by December 1919, foresaw that the recovery and propagation of ancient African history would restore racial pride. Mastering and repurposing ancient African history for Black liberation was tantamount, in the words of one scholar, to "a literary Trojan horse."[71]

Excavating the history of the race was as much a scholarly endeavor and an act of self-love as it was an act of prophecy. Black intellectuals and activists could not confront the history of slavery and its aftermath without offering an alternative reality for the future. They turned to their past to seize their future, for as one historian observed, "A prophet issues the warnings and must be ready to reap history's results."[72] More than preoccupation with ancient Nilotic civilizations, the writings of Black intellectuals in the nineteenth and early twentieth centuries foreshadowed a time when history would repeat itself. Soon enough, Black writers' works of history and scholarship would, in turn, become the foundation of a prophetic tradition.

"SIGNS OF THE TIMES"

In his 1906 "A Litany at Atlanta," a reflection on the massacre of unarmed African Americans, which he republished in his 1920 book *Darkwater: Voices from within the Veil*, W. E. B. Du Bois sermonized the deep yearnings of Black folk. Imploring the Creator to avenge the murdered, he wrote, "Great God, deliver us!" "We beseech Thee to hear us, good Lord!" "Bend us Thine ear, O Lord!" In one of his most moving statements, Du Bois illustrated the ways that diasporic Africans held the Creator to account. "Doth not this justice of hell stink in Thy nostrils, O God? How long," asked Du Bois, "shall the mounting flood of innocent blood roar in Thine ears and pound in our hearts for vengeance? Pile the Pale frenzy of blood-crazed brutes, who do such deeds, high on Thine Altar, Jehovah Jireh, and burn it in hell forever and forever!"[73] Du Bois's petition for divine retribution was not a solitary cri de coeur or an isolated cry from the wilderness. Indeed, this sentiment gained traction during the messianic moment. The thirst for revenge among African Americans was as true in 1906 as it was in 1917, in 1919, and throughout the 1920s.

A violent and white supremacist brand of Christianity at the turn of the twentieth century pushed some African Americans away from the white-centered religion of their parents' generation. In their quest for spiritual affirmation, some looked to concurrent developments in African history, applying them to Christianity by embracing the idea that God is Black.[74] This spiritual-racial awakening that Bishop Henry McNeal Turner helped propagate at the end of the nineteenth century had been the norm in the Nile Valley since as early as the Middle Ages. Nilotic Africans inspired Turner, who, along with his nineteenth-century peers, read extensively about Black life in the Nile Valley.[75] According to seventeenth-century German philologist Hiob Ludolf, "The Ethiopians are pleas'd with their own *Blackness*, and prefer it before the *White Colour*." Ludolf, who was known as the "Strabo of Eastern Africa," conducted ethnographic research with the help of the Ethiopian priest Abba Gorgoryos. He observed that those who appeared white among Ethiopians were considered "Pale and Wan" or "Dead Men," for white skin, to many Africans, symbolized leprosy.[76] So proud were the Ethiopians of their ebony phenotype, concluded Ludolf, that they depicted the devil as white-complected. Some West Africans also depicted the devil as white.[77] Nilotic Africans portrayed Christ, the Virgin Mary, and the saints as having a black phenotype.[78]

Ludolf's scholarship shaped Du Bois's outlook on an African-centered, self-affirming Christianity.[79] "Bid the Black Christ be born!" wrote Du Bois in 1920, alluding to messianic racial redemption. His reference to a "dim, darker David," the biblical forefather of the Christ, stressed the importance of lineage to messianism specifically and to prophetism broadly.[80] The prophetic tradition among African Americans was a rhetorical device that helped members of the community address existential matters.[81] One could conceptualize it as a "mission-oriented prophecy," which helped rally Black people to achieve their divine purpose.[82]

The guise of prophet came naturally to Du Bois. Biographer David Levering Lewis pointed out that Du Bois regarded himself as "the avatar of a race whose traveled fate he was predestined to interpret and direct."[83]

He was a leading proponent of the Talented Tenth—the view that a distinguished class of African Americans should lead the race—and members of the Black middle-class in the United States and beyond perceived Du Bois as a deliverer. When an African Canadian from Toronto sent Du Bois birthday cheer in 1918, he thanked the editor of the *Crisis*, the NAACP's official organ, for his "fearless writings" and leadership in behalf of the race. This distant disciple promised to "follow obediently . . . making any sacrifice." He even encouraged Du Bois to globalize the NAACP into a "Pan-African" body, alluding to one of the Niagara Movement's original objectives.[84]

Others "within the veil" needed more convincing of Du Bois's messianic bona fides. In a review of *Darkwater* in 1920, the author wrote that, although Du Bois was a defender of the race, segregation and Jim Crow "forced him to live among [the race], but in spirit he has never been bone of their bone and flesh of their flesh," referring to Du Bois's assertion in *The Souls of Black Folk* that he was thoroughly Black.[85] A prophet and, more important, a messiah must reflect the *volkgeist*. Despite being one of the most prominent African Americans during the messianic moment, Du Bois failed to attract a messianic following, even after the deaths of Henry McNeal Turner—who died in Windsor, Ontario, after abandoning the United States—and Booker T. Washington in 1915 created a spokesperson vacuum. E. Franklin Frazier attributed Du Bois's lack of a mass following to the fact that his race program was too "intellectual" to inspire the masses.[86] Chandler Owen, a prominent socialist, critiqued race leaders, from Du Bois to R. Russa Moton, Washington's successor at Tuskegee. "The hope of the race," Owen prophesied in 1918, rested in "new leaders with a more thorough grasp of scientific education, and a calm but uncompromising courage."[87]

Although Du Bois was a brilliant social scientist, as far as messianic leadership was concerned, he lacked what the masses considered "uncompromising courage."[88] If one lacked Du Bois's scholarly training, what could they achieve if armed with a gift for gab, ingenious capacity to organize Black people, a vision, and "a calm but uncompromising courage"?

Marcus Mosiah Garvey arrived in the United States on 23 March 1916. He visited two-thirds of the country, speaking with sharecroppers, preachers, and other middle-class professionals. In the summer of 1917, he launched the U.S. UNIA in Harlem. After fundraising and evangelizing his gospel of Black liberation, Garvey intended to return home to Jamaica. Factionalism and other organizational setbacks kept Garvey in the United States, though, and from 1918 to October 1919, when he narrowly escaped an assassination, the UNIA recalibrated its mission.[89] Global chatter of self-determination and the bleak racial conditions in the United States convinced Garvey of the need to pursue redemption for diasporic and continental Africans from his new operational base in Harlem.[90]

The sheer destruction wrought by the Great War persuaded Garvey that white men could usher in "an apocalyptic" turn in global affairs.[91] Black people felt the urgency. "Revolution was in the air, and the Negroes were ready for revolution," wrote C. L. R. James, a Trotskyite and pioneering Trinidadian historian of the Haitian Revolution.[92] Historian John Henrik Clarke noted that the "American antecedents" held the key to unlocking the Garvey phenomenon.[93] Journalist Roi Ottley called Garvey "Harlem's first messiah." He averred, "Garvey leaped into the ocean of Black unhappiness at a most timely moment for a savior."[94] St. Clair Drake pointed out that Garvey arrived in the United States "in the fullness of time," and with almost sixty violent clashes in 1919 and postwar disillusionment, African Americans showed their readiness for "racial salvation." In fact, during the First World War, Black clergy remained abreast of "the signs of the times," a biblical reference to the coming of the Messiah.[95] That Garveyism had "apocalyptic overtones," observed Drake, meant that Garvey himself exuded a messianism that complemented the African American religious tradition.[96]

Revelation was key to messianism. Like many messianic figures, Garvey experienced an acute consciousness that convinced him of his divine purpose. Garvey's revelation came to him in the early 1900s as he worked on and toured Caribbean islands, South and Central America, and parts of western Europe. Across all of these places, he witnessed the subordination and subjugation of Black people. He also met African travelers who testified of the terror that colonialism inflicted upon continental Africans. "Where is the Black man's Government?" asked Garvey. "Where is his King and his kingdom? Where is his President, his country, and his ambassador, his army, his navy, his men of big affairs? I could not find them, and then I declared, 'I will help to make them.'" Garvey wrote, "I saw before me . . . a new world of Black men, not peons . . . but a nation of sturdy men making their impress upon civilization and causing a new light to dawn upon the human race. I could not remain in London any more." Having discovered his messianic calling, he explained, "My brain was afire. There was a world of thought to conquer." He boarded a ship at Southampton, England, for Jamaica, where he arrived on 15 July 1914. Garvey's discovery of his life's purpose and abrupt departure from England was either providential or convenient, because two weeks later the world was at war. Five days after returning to Jamaica, he founded the Universal Negro Improvement and Conservation Association and African Communities (Imperial) League.[97]

Although Garvey chose African Americans as his flock—or, more precisely, they embraced him as their shepherd—and the United States as his pasture, he adopted a continental strategy to jumpstart a global movement, inspiring notions of messianic salvation as far away as southern Africa and Australia.[98] On Christmas Day 1919, after Garvey married Amy Ashwood, his first bride and cofounder of the Jamaica UNIA, the newlyweds traveled north from New York City to honeymoon in Canada.[99] They arrived in Montreal on 26 December for two rallies. After a few days, the Garveys traveled to Toronto, where they held three large gatherings at Occidental Hall from 5 January to 7 January. With their ambitious itinerary of romance and advancing racial redemption, the Garveys returned to Harlem having fulfilled at least one of the two: they raised $8,000 from their Canadian sojourn for the UNIA.[100] A groundbreaking study of the UNIA in Montreal revealed that city's and Toronto's invaluable support in sustaining Garveyism in North America.[101]

Garvey's visit in December 1919 was not his first time in Canada or in Montreal. In 1916, Edgerton Langdon, a Montreal resident of Grenadian origin, visited Harlem, and after hearing the recently arrived Garvey speak at St. Mark's Hall, he invited Garvey to Montreal in the winter of 1917. There, Garvey helped to sow the seeds of "race first" in Canada. One year later, Edgerton's niece, twenty-year-old Louise Langdon, emigrated from Grenada to Montreal. Louise, too, became a believer in Garvey's philosophy of race pride and Pan-African self-determination. In 1918 at a "Garvey conference" in Montreal, Louise met African American Earl Little. They married shortly thereafter in May 1919. The union produced seven children, one of whom was Malcolm Little, who, in adulthood, replaced his surname with "X."[102]

From 1919 to 1922, the UNIA's program of racial redemption flooded the Atlantic World. In Canada, more than thirty units sprouted from British Columbia to Nova Scotia. Out of 20,000 Canadians of African descent, one in four held membership in the UNIA.[103] In the United States, 725 units existed in thirty-eight states, and roughly 243 in the Caribbean, Central and South America, Mexico, Africa, the British Isles, India, and Australia. Garvey was a shepherd with a flock in the millions.[104] When he visited the Caribbean in the early 1920s to promote the UNIA, some of his followers described Garvey as "a messiah to the people."[105]

Pan-Africanists in Canada followed the example of the parent body in Harlem. UNIA constitutions vowed "to establish a universal fraternity among the Negro race; to promote a spirit of race pride and love . . . to develop the spirit of independence; to protect Negroes irrespecting [sic] of nationality." They also planned to jump-start Black industry and global commercial interests.[106] The Toronto president, Dr. Abraham Benjamin Thomas, who had in 1919 professed faith in Black Bolshevik-inspired uprising, attended the August 1920 UNIA International Convention at Madison Square Garden in Manhattan, signing "The Declaration of the Rights of the Negro Peoples of the World" (also known as the Negro Declaration of Independence). Montreal's Madame Georgie L. O'Brien and Dr. D. D. Lewis, who was sworn in as the UNIA's surgeon general, were three of the five Canadian signatories.[107] The Negro Declaration of Independence, a fifty-four-point Pan-African manifesto, paralleled the 1776 U.S. Declaration of Independence, the 1789 French Declaration of the Rights of Man and of the Citizen, and the 1804 Haitian Declaration of Independence.

Pan-Africanists in Canada proselytized a growing population of migrants. The demand for sleeping car porters, coal miners, steelworkers, and domestic workers brought Caribbean and African American workers to Canada in the early 1900s.[108] Fearing their permanent residency, the Canadian government enacted various measures to limit Black immigration. In 1914, the superintendent of immigration wrote, "Africans, no matter where they come from are not among the races sought, and, hence, Africans, no matter from what country they come are in common with the uninvited races, not admitted to Canada." A senior official in the Maritimes instructed his subordinates, "Every obstacle is to be put in their way." The 1910 Immigration Act permitted officers at ports of entry to bar Black people, if other measures failed, on grounds that they would "likely become a public charge."[109] Increased Black visibility worried Canadian officials, because it could trigger racial tension in the mostly white country. In 1923, a U.S. commentator, who admired Canada's racist immigration policy, opined that Canada "was much too busy to wish to spend time trying to make [undesirable races] over, and she has not the least intention of letting them try to make her over."[110] Many African Americans, according to one observer, knew that Canada was "fenced off as a white racial reserve."[111]

Entrenched anti-Black racism in Canadian society meant that fewer than 2,400 Caribbean immigrants, many of whom were British subjects and entitled to freedom of mobility in the empire, came to Canada from 1904 to 1932, compared with 88,000 who entered and remained in the United States. Despite restrictive immigration, Caribbean immigrants greatly contributed to the Pan-African renaissance that occurred in interwar Canada. The UNIA helped Caribbean immigrants strengthen their ethnic and racial identities, and the Montreal and Toronto divisions boasted strong Caribbean membership.[112] Canadian-born Black people and African American immigrants in British Columbia, the Prairies, Ontario, Quebec, and the

Maritimes also joined the UNIA. In Nova Scotia, for example, the UNIA enjoyed immense support. The UNIA helped members of the province's 6,000 Black residents—the majority whose forebears sided with the Crown during the U.S. Revolutionary War and the War of 1812, as well as a few hundred Caribbean immigrants—mitigate subordinate citizenship.[113]

Unlike in the United States, traditional working- and middle-class African American uplift strategies in Canada aligned well with Garveyism. Du Bois and Garvey may have been rivals in the United States, but Canada's small Black population compelled disciples to combine the two prophets' strategies of integrationist, bourgeois Pan-Africanisms with militant, Black Nationalist Pan-Africanisms.[114] The UNIA in the United States represented a manifold struggle "and was several movements that faced in multiple directions," according to historian Robert Hill, but Canada's small Black population meant that Pan-Africanisms had less bandwidth for fragmentation.[115]

Garveyites felt confident about the movement's eventual success. Len Johnston, whose parents immigrated to Canada from Jamaica in 1890, argued that Garvey's doctrine had a different application for Pan-Africanists in Canada and the United States. Johnston said, "When you can't get along with the people, you think of going somewhere, such as Africa, where we came from." He added: "And [Garvey's] dream was realized, but it didn't have to be physically done. I don't think he meant for everybody to go back to Africa. I think he meant to know where you come from, be proud of where you come from, and work towards the freedom of Africa."[116] For UNIA boosters throughout Canada, Garvey's vision of Pan-Africanisms was practical enough to recognize that descendants of the enslaved could remain in the diaspora and reap the sacrifices of their forebears, while simultaneously working toward Black liberation in Africa.[117]

Some middle-class Black people in North America, however, dismissed UNIA members as zealots fixated on Africa. "I read a few papers, met a few radicals, but I didn't attend their meetings. . . . I know it was active, quite an active group for some years," said African Canadian Addie Aylestock of the UNIA during the Great Depression. "But I didn't get to know too much about the intricacies, except I knew they . . . were trying to get people to go back to Africa." Aylestock acknowledged, "I didn't get to know much of what was going on then, but my personal idea was that there were so many more opportunities over here. Why would they want to go back to Africa?"[118]

Garvey's detractors took advantage of these misperceptions, spreading false rumors and mischaracterizing his ideas to make him look foolish. One common misinformation frequently trafficked in Canada and the United

States was that Garvey's "back-to-Africa" campaign sought wholescale abandonment of diasporic lands in order to repatriate all Black people.[119] The logic behind the back-to-Africa philosophy was that Garvey believed Black people would never escape racial subordination and subjugation until Africa was free from colonial rule, was united under one flag, and could leverage its vast natural resources to develop economically, militarily, and diplomatically to defend itself and its children in Africa and abroad.

Race consciousness stoked the embers of Pan-Africanisms in the 1920s. Barbadian-born Dudley Marshall recalled feeling a new sense of worth in 1920 when his neighbor, a Black New Orleans woman, showed him a copy of *Negro World*, the UNIA's weekly. After reading Garvey's editorial, Marshall recalled, "That's the first time that I heard a Negro, a Black man that would come forth and speak out sincerely for the rights of his people." In the Toronto division's early years, Marshall stated, "We saved up all the money we could and everybody donated. . . . I know one lady alone, she had $400 in gold and she donated it to Mr. Garvey to carry on the work."[120] Another stalwart, Violet Blackman, peddled "little books" in early 1920s Toronto that practically required her to "beg people" for a donation. "My God, I asked even the streetcar conductor!" she admitted. Blackman, an intrepid woman who performed domestic work, immigrated to Toronto from Jamaica in 1920. She raised $500 for the local UNIA. She even convinced her affluent Anglo-Canadian employers and their neighbors to contribute.[121]

Donating cash like Dudley Marshall or gold like his acquaintance or fundraising aggressively like Violet Blackman in behalf of the UNIA was among Black Canada's many engagements with and support of Pan-Africanism. Because self-determination and anti-colonialism undergirded the UNIA and Pan-Africanisms broadly, a self-help mantra rooted in the principle that ordinary Black people should own the means of production where Black economic development was concerned resonated with the masses. The African Communities League, the UNIA's business arm, launched the Black Star Line (shipping), African Factories Corporation, and Universal Printing House, and *Negro World* propagated the significance of Black agency.

The UNIA's women's auxiliary and Black Cross Nurses gave women opportunities to practice Pan-Africanisms. Many women, indeed, sacrificed to sustain the movement.[122] Despite gendered division of labor, Blackman and other women contributed significantly to local and global Black solidarity and self-determination. The charter empowered women officers, stating that a "Male President" should give "control" over assignments to a "Lady President" who could "exercise better control." Although a Lady President "shall have the right to preside over any meeting called by her on

the approval of the general membership . . . all her reports shall be submitted to the Male President for presentation to the general membership."[123]
Blackman corroborated this protocol: "Though I was the chairlady, anything
I did had to go to the heads, to the president or the treasurer, and then I
would come back [and report] to the committee."[124]

Black women, nevertheless, remained committed to Pan-Africanisms and
their menfolk. However, they demanded one concession for their unwavering
loyalty. Amy Jacques, Garvey's second wife, reminded UNIA men that if
they feared war, "Ethiopia's queens . . . and her Amazons" would deliver the
people.[125] In other words, UNIA women believed in honoring their men,
if Black men appreciated the centrality of achieving a form of racial martyrdom in the pursuit of global Black liberation. This reciprocity entailed
a gendered social contract of sorts.[126] After all, legions of Black men had
eagerly enlisted and died in a "white man's war," which reinforced Western
domination in Africa and its diaspora, so fighting for Black liberation was
non-negotiable, reasoned UNIA women, who foresaw Africa as the ultimate
battleground.[127] Garveyite men not only considered the UNIA their "balm
in Gilead" but also the vehicle to advance a "women's rights" movement
based on the principle of "race first."[128]

"THE SPECTACLES OF ETHIOPIA"

Central to the UNIA's mission was African liberation. "Conscientious spiritual worship," a charter obligation, implored the Creator to play a lead role
in this objective.[129] "Redeem Africa from the hands of those who exploit
and ravish her," Dudley Marshall recalled of the Toronto division's prayer.
"Restore her ancient glory and grant that her oppressed and downtrodden
children at home and in foreign climes may shortly be restored to their
divine inheritance, so that [under] our own vine and fig tree we may gather
to worship thee."[130]

Marcus Garvey understood the cost of African liberation. When he and
his first wife, Amy Ashwood, honeymooned in Canada in December 1919
and January 1920, Garvey predicted that decolonization would be "the
bloodiest of all conflicts."[131] Indeed, the spirit of the times suggested an
imminent bloody clash. "Let Ethiopia throw away her harp and gird on her
sword," an observer pleaded in 1920, "for it is day and the enemy stands
without her gates!"[132]

The UNIA's anthem—"Ethiopia, Thou Land of Our Fathers"—not only
affirmed members' African ancestry and "divine inheritance" but also served
as an official war song. The anthem was one of the first examples of Ethiopianism in Canada.[133] Marshall—who had excelled in school due to his

"terrific memory"—recalled singing the anthem, a "lovely ritual," and other events with great accuracy sixty years later.

Ethiopia, land of our fathers,
The land where the gods love to be
As [storm cloud at] night that gathers
Our armies come rushing to thee.
We must in the fight be victorious
When swords are thrust onward to gleam.
For us will the victory be glorious
[When] led by the red, black and green.

Ethiopia, the tyrant is falling,
Who smote thee upon thy knees,
And thy children are lustily calling
From over the distant seas.
Jehovah, the Great [One], hath heard us,
Has noted our sighs and our tears,
With the spirit of love, He hath stirred us
[To be One] through the coming years.

Oh Jehovah, Thou God of the ages,
Grant [unto our] sons that lead
The wisdom Thou gave to Thy sages,
When Israel was sore in need.
Thy voice through the dim past has spoken,
Ethiopia shall stretch forth her hand,
By Thee shall all fetters be broken
And Heaven bless our dear fatherland.[134]

Barbadian rabbi Arnold Ford coauthored the poem in the United States with Jamaican Benjamin Burrell. The UNIA adopted this poem as its official anthem at the 1920 International Convention at Madison Square Garden. The anthem contained messianic and revanchist prophecy from scripture and references to ancient Greek gods who feasted in Ethiopia.[135] The anthem was a powerful example of interwar Pan-Africanists identifying with and inserting themselves into the Judeo-Christian, Western literary tradition.

After the UNIA's first international convention, the newly elected "Provisional President of Africa"—Marcus Garvey—continued to captivate acolytes with rhetoric of racial redemption. His successor recalled that in 1921, when he listened to his first Garvey speech at a church in Baltimore, the UNIA leader spoke "in a voice like thunder from Heaven."[136] Indeed,

Garvey often tried to inspire the divine. The prophecy of African resurgence in Psalm 68:31 became a recurring motif in his speeches. When a UNIA delegate prepared to attend the 1923 Assembly of the League of Nations in Switzerland, for example, Garvey said to the throngs, "Let us work and pray for . . . when 'Ethiopia shall stretch forth her hands unto God' and our race be lifted from . . . prejudice and injustice to the realm of freedom and true liberty."[137]

The name Ethiopia was one of the most powerful icons of racial redemption during the messianic moment. UNIA aviator Hubert F. Julian christened his would-be transatlantic flight Ethiopia I in 1924 Harlem, three years before Charles Lindbergh traversed the Atlantic. Trinidadian-born Julian claimed to have trained under Canada's First World War ace Billy Bishop. In the 1920s, African American Drusilla Dunjee Houston conducted prodigious research to publish *Wonderful Ethiopians of the Ancient Cushite Empire*. Du Bois often incorporated Nilotic iconography, referencing ancient African civilizations in the *Crisis*.[138]

Scholars call the messianism in the Pan-African movement and Black literary tradition "Ethiopianism." The pioneer of African Diaspora history considered the 1870s to the 1920s the "classical period of Ethiopianism."[139] Despite its historical provenance in scripture and the Greek classics and the virulent anti-Black racism that inspired it, some scholars have dismissed Ethiopianism as "mystical racial chauvinism."[140] According to one historian, the "messianic self-conception, or Ethiopian mysticism," advocates "a cyclical view of history."[141] In other words, literate Christian, Anglicized diasporic Africans believed that "as it was in the beginning, so shall it be in the end," because African resurgence would precipitate Western recession.[142] Pan-Africanists understood that "the divine providence of history" would fulfill Africa's redemption.[143]

Garvey seized any opportunity to propagate the glory of ancient Ethiopia. "We Negroes believe in the God of Ethiopia, the everlasting God—God the Father, God the Son and God the Holy Ghost, the One God of all ages," he professed, notwithstanding that the UNIA welcomed and celebrated members of various religions and creeds. "That is the God in whom we believe, but we shall worship Him through the spectacles of Ethiopia."[144] Furthermore, Garvey's sense of messianic purpose ensured that the UNIA's use of Ethiopian symbolism gave the organization a prophetic appeal. Garvey saw a parallel between Christ's crucifixion and the envy that led to his own persecution by the Black intelligentsia. "We cannot handle Garvey and his Organization, as we have no power, let us go to the State and Federal authorities, and frame him up, let us say he is an anarchist, a seditionist and is speaking against the government," Garvey complained in the third person. "Like the Jews of old, they cry 'Crucify him,' or rather, 'Send him to prison, deport him.'"[145]

If many African descendants perceived Garvey as their deliverer, there were others who saw him as a con man. Du Bois wrote to Canadian officials on multiple occasions in 1920 and 1921, inquiring about the capitalization and officers of the Black Star Line, which the UNIA had incorporated in 1919 to advance economic self-determination.[146] When Garvey's legal woes began in 1922 due to stock sales of the Black Star Line, the UNIA suffered a public relations nightmare. Before knowing that some of his trusted advisors were government agents who had infiltrated the UNIA and sabotaged the Black Star Line, Garvey lamented, "The Negro has no method or system to his dishonesty."[147] The U.S. federal court ultimately convicted Garvey for mail fraud in June 1923. The charges were trumped up but nevertheless marked the UNIA's slow decline.

Garveyism's emphasis on messianic leadership, affiliation with the African Orthodox Church, codified prayers, and "conscientious spiritual worship" resembled a religion, and like a religion, it often passed down from parents to children.[148] Some people deterred their relatives from joining the UNIA. William Aylestock, brother to Addie Aylestock, read about the failings of the Black Star Line. His parents' dislike of Garvey discouraged him from joining the UNIA. A sharp cleavage existed between the pro- and anti-Garvey camps. "If you came up under parents who were Marcus Garvey admirers, you wouldn't . . . dare but not to admire the ground he walked on," said Aylestock. "So I saw that division line. It was not a case of, in my opinion, of your choice, but a case of your parents' choice, what did they believe in."[149] As Garvey receded from the world stage, others soon stepped into the fray of messianic racial redemption.

"DEVOTED TO THE INTERESTS OF THE DARKER RACES"

With Marcus Garvey in legal limbo, other charismatic figures took up the power of prophecy to lead the masses toward racial redemption. Black journalists and newspaper publishers embodied this spirit, even if they did not match Garvey's messianism or disagreed with some of his methods. Decades before joining the UNIA, for example, Ida B. Wells stood out as one such prophetess. Her courageous investigative journalism into lynchings shed light on the politics of misandrist anti-Black terrorism. Her predecessor Mary Ann Shadd Cary described herself as the first Black woman to break the "Editorial Ice" in North America. Journalists such as Wells and Shadd Cary, among others, belonged to a prophetic tradition of Black writers who spoke truth to power.[150] Forgotten newspaper publishers in the interwar years picked up the torch to convene a cross-border readership.

In August 1923, African American expatriate James Francis Jenkins wrote Du Bois, his former professor and employer, seeking moral support from the famed editor of the *Crisis*. He was three weeks from launching a messianic newspaper and hoped that Du Bois might encourage him in his advocacy of race consciousness in Canada. Constrained by his own circumstances of fundraising and competing with other major Black newspapers, Du Bois cautioned Jenkins on the challenges of publishing a race paper.[151] On 14 July 1923, Jenkins and fellow African American Robert Paris Edwards launched the *Dawn of Tomorrow* in London, Ontario. They incorporated Ethiopianism to signal a coming redemption for African descendants in North America. The eight-page weekly, which cost five cents, relied on the Associated Negro Press for most of its content, but the editorials illustrated the salience of cross-border messianic Pan-Africanisms.[152]

The *Dawn's* genesis is a quintessential story about how transnationalism helped African North Americans popularize ideas of race and self-determination. The newspaper's name bears uncanny resemblance to what Du Bois called a "dawning to-morrow" when he reflected on the possibility of interracial harmony in his 1897 American Negro Academy address "The Conservation of Races."[153] Despite the *Dawn's* limited circulation, no North American newspaper rivaled its cross-border Black solidarity. The *Dawn's* founding occurred at a time of immense persecution of the UNIA as the U.S. government brought a baseless charge of mail fraud against Garvey.[154] With the shepherd struck but before his flock could scatter, the *Dawn* appealed to the Pan-Africanisms of Garveyites and their sympathizers, hoping to build on Garvey's messianic movement of race pride and self-determination in North America.

U.S.-Canadian cross-border migration was integral to the Black freedom struggle in North America. James Francis Jenkins was born in Forsyth, Georgia, in August 1884. He completed his preparatory and undergraduate training at Atlanta University, where he studied under Professor Du Bois.[155] Although some of his peers perceived Du Bois as "exacting and impatient," Jenkins enjoyed a close relationship with his teacher, even after graduating.[156] In July 1905, Jenkins was in Chicago working for Du Bois on the publication of a magazine when his mentor and others spearheaded the historic Niagara Movement in Fort Erie, Ontario. No African Canadian participated in the Fort Erie meeting, which culminated in the founding of the NAACP in 1909. It would be conjecture, however, to conclude that Du Bois and his peers rejected African Canadian participation. Widespread racial terrorism and disenfranchisement of African Americans lacked a Canadian equivalent, which reinforced the myth of the "promised land."[157] In fact, one year after the Fort Erie meeting, one of the United States' worst massacres, the Atlanta pogrom, a consequence of the white supremacist canard that Black men rape white women, motivated Jenkins to flee the country.[158] He arrived in the promised land—southwestern Ontario—in 1907.

On 23 June 1914, Robert Paris Edwards arrived in Toronto, five days before an assassin shot and killed Austro-Hungarian royals in Sarajevo. He had worked for several years in New Jersey as a soloist, composer, poet, and youth social worker. A son of enslaved peoples, he grew up listening to Black spirituals at his mother's feet.[159] The state of New Jersey considered Edwards its leading Black poet in 1910, around the time he penned his uplift poem "A Credit to My Race." This ode to blackness reflected "racial destiny," a concept that had messianic dimensions.[160] Starting in June 1915, Edwards was choirmaster of Toronto's First Baptist Church, private messenger to oil magnate Walter C. Teagle during his brief sojourn in Canada, conductor of the Coleridge-Taylor Chorus, and correspondent of the Associated Negro Press.[161] Jenkins found employment as assistant justice of the juvenile court in London, Ontario.

Jenkins and Edwards shared an unwavering commitment to Black liberation. Although adherents of the imperatives of respectability politics and racial integration, they believed in the militance of the New Negro and Marcus Garvey's messianic Pan-Africanisms. Jenkins and Edwards gained an intimate understanding of race relations in Canada after residing there for sixteen years and nine years, respectively, living through the Great War, the rise of ethno-nationalism, and Garveyism. The *Dawn of Tomorrow*, a name reflective of the messianic moment, was "Devoted to the Interests of the Darker Races." This slogan merged two prominent mottos: those of the UNIA's *Negro World*, "A Newspaper Devoted Solely to the Interests of the Negro Race," and of the NAACP's *Crisis*, "A Record of the Darker Races."[162]

When Jenkins and Edwards founded the *Dawn*, African Canadians lacked a national newspaper. They hoped that their paper would serve that purpose and improve on the limited reach of existing African American newspapers in Canadian society. Moreover, they pointed out, "very little news of our people in Canada is found in American publications." This cross-border consciousness was integral to North American Pan-Africanisms. They explained, "Our people in the United States are deprived of a knowledge of important events and intelligent opinions of a progressive people of the same origin, with similar problems, but whom destiny has placed in . . . Canada." Fearing racial fragmentation, the *Dawn*'s editors avowed, "It is also a fact that we, whose lot has fallen in the confines of this great Dominion, need to know each other better." In case readers, white or Black, perceived their inaugural edition as too radical or conformist, Jenkins and Edwards affirmed that Canadian (that is, British) nationalism and Pan-Africanisms shared similarities. They pledged "loyalty to one king, one flag, and one empire," alluding to the UNIA's motto "One God! One Aim! One Destiny!"[163]

The opening sentence of their first editorial paraphrased the last sentence of George Wells Parker's 1917 article "The African Origin of the Grecian Civilization."[164] "It were but yesterday that Ethiopia had made a pilgrimage to the skies to light her candle from the altar-fires of heaven, and had held it aloof throughout the dark ages to brighten the footsteps of all mankind," wrote Jenkins and Edwards. "It were but yesterday that the Africans were a mighty people among all nations of antiquity, because they had contributed much to civilization in days of yore." They referenced Homer's admiration for the "'pious Black men' of Africa" whom the Greek gods favored.[165] "But that were yesterday, and today we find her sons and daughters, not dead, nor dormant, but sleeping. But alas! in their slumber have the spirits of some . . . illustrious forbears appeared to them; has the shade of some long since departed spirit visited them to disturb their peaceful slumber?"[166] This filio-pietistic sentiment is what Casely Hayford, the bourgeois Gold Coast native and Pan-African theorist, encouraged in 1911, writing, "Afro-Americans must bring themselves into touch with some of the general traditions and institutions of their ancestors" to achieve liberation.[167]

For diasporic Africans in the Americas, this plea resonated deeply. Ancestral reverence was a distinct African practice that survived the Middle Passage, although some educated, middle-class Christians in the twentieth century avoided public discussions of this subject. Guyanese intellectual Jan Carew wrote openly about his initiation into the sacred forbidden worlds of his African and Amerindian ancestors, describing the ancestor-focused spiritualism to which Jenkins and Edwards subscribed as "ghosts in our blood."[168] St. Clair Drake called this "ancestor-[veneration], the keystone of West African religion."[169] Asserting the continuity of African spirituality in the Americas, Melville Herskovits considered "the supernatural a major focus of interest."[170] African spirituality did not affect Black people's practice of Christianity.[171] Because Christianity is fundamentally organized around life after death, a phenomenon that affirms African notions of rebirth and the afterlife, it was not antithetical for some Black Christians, such as Jenkins and Edwards, to profess faith in the power of the ancestral or spiritual realm.

Garvey had masterfully invoked the ancestral and spiritual as UNIA leader, even during his imprisonment from 1925 to 1927 at the U.S. penitentiary in Atlanta. "In death," Garvey promised to "be a terror to the foes of Negro liberty." Alluding to the way that enslaved peoples and their West and Central African forebears interpreted natural phenomena, Garvey declared, "If I may come in an earthquake, or a cyclone, or plague, or pestilence, or as God may have me, then be assured that I shall never desert you and make your enemies triumph over you." He explained, "Would I not, like Macbeth's ghost, walk the earth forever for you?" Garvey also promised to recruit ancestors and "bring" to the aid of the living "millions of Black slaves who have died in" Africa, the Atlantic, and the Americas.[172]

Garvey's rhetoric echoed abolitionist Henry Highland Garnet's exhortation of enslaved peoples to seize their freedom by force in 1843. "Awake, awake," Garnet pleaded, "millions of voices are calling you! Your dead fathers speak to you from their graves."[173] "From the graves of millions of my forebears at this hour I hear the cry, and I am going to answer it even though hell is cut loose before Marcus . . . ," Garvey warned.[174] Although Garvey did not originate this dramatic language, African American intellectual Kelly Miller wrote of Garvey's oration, "The magnetic power of his charm and spell seemed never to wane."[175] One Garveyite woman interpreted Garvey's life's work and the conviction with which he communicated as "the outpouring of the pent-up feelings of generations of his ancestors."[176]

When they launched the *Dawn of Tomorrow*, Jenkins and Edwards also drew strength from their ancestors. "Remembering . . . our ancestry and the traditions of our forefathers, we cannot but recall that in the dark days their prayers arose from the canebrakes, the swamps, the everglades, and the cotton fields of the sunny southlands; and the coral islands of the seas, to an omnipotent God for the Dawn of Tomorrow in behalf of their children, yet unborn." They referenced Jews in Jerusalem, Muslims in Mecca, and Buddhists in Beijing who, in supplication, invoked their ancestral lands, patiently awaiting the day of deliverance. Jenkins and Edwards dedicated the *Dawn* to the "memory of those who have gone before" and "lend renewed strength to those of us who are struggling to maintain a place in the sun for posterity."[177] There is no record of others, aside from Garveyites, espousing similar messianic and filiopietistic rhetoric in Canada. In private life, it was not unusual around that time in Canada, however, for some, including a sitting prime minister, to seek assurances from their ancestors in daily affairs. Interest in spiritualism—or the "other world"—transcended race.[178]

As writers, Jenkins and Edwards deserve recognition among the pioneers of African Canadian literature, cultural critics whom one literary scholar described as "refugees, exiles, immigrants, [and] pilgrims." Their writing was neither "subdued" nor "sedate" but unique.[179] Indeed, mapping a genealogy of literary mysticism reveals a clear connection between Du Bois, "a poet of Ethiopianism," and Jenkins, who, after graduating from college, worked as an agent and reporter in 1905 for Du Bois's short-lived publication the *Moon*, a magazine that propagated mysticism.[180] Although a highly regarded social scientist and historian, Du Bois experimented with literary mysticism throughout his career. Transcending gender, his messianic characters defied Western epistemology, integrating elements of African spirituality.[181] The *Dawn*'s editors adopted this literary tradition, modifying it to the circumstances of Black Canada. They acknowledged ancestral reverence, a godly covenant, fulfillment of prophecy, a shared history, and common destiny. Allegiance to the British Crown, the last component of their race politics, was especially feasible for emigrants from the British West Indies. As Pan-Africanists in Canada, Jenkins and Edwards expressed their ideas openly, a right that U.S. officials denied many Black writers.[182]

The *Dawn* was the harbinger of biblical prophecy. "Else what means this turning and tossing; what this simultaneous movement towards race consciousness by these swarthy sons of the sun?" they asked. "It means that Black men and Black women the world over are awakening on the morrow . . . striving in every way and using every fair means to reach the highest standard of citizenship."[183] Their use of "Black" as an adjective for African descendants was still unusual at that time. Newspapers consistently used "Negro" or "Colored."[184] Jenkins and Edwards considered "Black," like Ethiopia, a pan-African term that unified African descendants, regardless of ethnicity or nationality. Black was a badge of honor, for "Ethiopia" in Greek meant one whose face appeared sun-kissed, that is, ebony.

Language has the power to forecast revolution. There was something undeniably revolutionary in the messianic race pride that Jenkins and Edwards afforded to 20,000 African Canadians in a country of 9 million. "We shall see our boys and our girls satisfied with only the best things which this life offers; and then—on tomorrow, 'Ethiopia shall stretch forth her hands unto God,' and she shall come into her own," they wrote. Jenkins and Edwards prophesied that the destiny of Black people was "the handwriting upon the wall. And thus we have chosen our name: The Dawn of Tomorrow." The "handwriting on the wall" idiom meant inevitability. Biblical scholars attributed it to Daniel, the Israelite prophet, who, during the Babylonian captivity, interpreted an ominous and mysterious writing on the wall in the king's court.[185]

Despite its editorial ebullience, some African Canadians feared that the small Black population could not sustain a "race paper."[186] The bourgeois minority that harbored this concern depended on white patronage, desired integration as the gold standard of racial progress, and held conformist political views on race.[187] This branch of the racial uplift movement was excessively class- and color-conscious, resisted a collective approach to social change, and favored instead a model that privileged Black elites who could display a bourgeois racial superiority comparable to white people.[188] Nevertheless, the *Dawn*'s core message of "race first" resonated, for some African Canadians wrote directly to Du Bois to register their appreciation "for [his] building up a mentally rigorous and self-reliant race throughout Pan-Africa."[189]

Although the *Dawn* is an important artifact of Black history in North America, scholars have not remarked on its cross-border messianism. An analysis of Black political activism in Toronto acknowledged the *Dawn*'s import but discounted its Ethiopianism. According to the author, there was no example in Canadian history of Black writers' "expansive yet myopic national libertarian oratorical tradition" that could "arouse political indignation." This assertion elided the revolutionary current of Ethiopianism that Jenkins and Edwards injected into their editorials.[190] Yet, implicit in the UNIA's and Jenkins and Edwards's invocation of Ethiopianism in Canada was the rise of Africa (Black people) and the fall of the West (white people). Had white Canadians understood the *Dawn*'s "hidden transcripts" at the time, many would have considered it sedition.[191]

"ENJOY THE FRUITS OF THE SACRIFICES AND OF THE LABORS OF OUR ANCESTORS"

There was practicality to the messianism espoused in the *Dawn of Tomorrow*. In August 1924, Jenkins cofounded the Canadian League for the Advancement of Colored People (CLACP). Modeled after the NAACP, the CLACP aspired to improve "the industrial, economic, social and spiritual conditions of Negroes."[192] In light of Canada's explicit efforts to keep the Black population as small as possible, Jenkins's collaborative approach to race work meant that the CLACP would pursue Black racial unity while improving African Canadians' socioeconomic standing among white employers and other stakeholders. As a result, the CLACP and the UNIA often joined forces in the 1920s to speak on various issues affecting Black life. Despite some philosophical differences, "Garveyites and CLACP advocates wore the same hat," wrote one historian. Pan-Africanisms as "racial uplift ideology bridged" factions in Canada that otherwise worked against one another in the United States.[193] When the Montreal UNIA, for example, spearheaded its own convention in 1924, Jenkins and Edwards praised the organizers, for they "added zest, zeal, enthusiasm and increased determination to stand by the U.N.I.A. and uphold its principles of unified race consciousness and a redeemed Africa."[194] As editor of the NAACP's *Crisis*, Jenkins's mentor, Du Bois, used his platform to discredit Garvey and the UNIA.

Although the *Dawn's* publication dropped from weekly to biweekly in 1925, as official organ of the CLACP, its editorials continued to address real public policy concerns, such as education, workplace discrimination, and Black brain and muscle drain to the United States.[195] Jenkins and Edwards understood, for example, that 90 percent of Black pupils dropped out of school. Admonishing Black parents, they described this misfortune as "a very sad state of affairs," considering that children of other races remained in school longer. Fearing prolonged racial subordination and subjugation, the *Dawn's* editors warned, "Can we expect them to win the race of life?" Black children must continue their education "until they have crossed over the river Jordan," a promised land metaphor.[196] Employer discrimination, however, meant that educated Black workers struggled. One scholar, writing on Black people in interwar Canada, declared, "The path to Canadian freedom has proved a cul-de-sac."[197]

Jenkins and Edwards placed their faith in education, hoping that it would produce enough well-informed individuals to lead the race. One contributor to the *Dawn* envisioned Black communities in which "race cooperation" permitted "support at all times to our boys and girls who are preparing themselves for professions: our lawyers, doctors, dentists, contractors, manufactures."[198] The emphasis on education as a tool of liberation for all Black children was a recurring theme. Leading nineteenth-century Pan-African theorist Edward Wilmot Blyden underscored the significance of gender egalitarianism in a seminal work on liberal education for African descendants. Blyden averred that Black self-determination would be more robust "when girls receive the same general training as the boys; and our women, besides being able to appreciate the intellectual labors of their husbands and brothers, will be able also to share in the pleasures of intellectual pursuits." He further explained, "We need not fear that they will be less graceful, less natural, or less womanly; but we may be sure that they will make wiser mothers, more appreciative wives, and more affectionate sisters."[199]

Equitable access to education also helped Black people resist racism. Jenkins and Edwards recalled a recruitment speech that they had given at the behest of the government. Most of the attendees were white. After speaking, a spouse of an officer allegedly remarked to Jenkins's mother, "My! What a remarkably brilliant young man. He evidently has a grand education. Canada is no place for him. He should go to the States where he belongs." This sentiment, whether well- or ill-intentioned, was a common refrain for white Canadians, so the *Dawn*'s editors pondered whether "Canada, the promised land, Canada, the haven of runaway slaves . . . is growing callous towards the highest development of our Race?"[200] They rejected the de facto premise that Canada could tolerate Black workers only in servile roles (that is, porters and domestics). They also disputed the false and racist notion that African descendants had no claim to Canada: "The Colored people of the Dominion . . . are 100 percent Canadians." They declared that African Canadians were distinguished "by birth, by patriotism, by culture, and training and by a heritage of more than 200 years of unbroken, unblemished citizenship."[201] A corollary of chattel slavery was that Ethiopia's daughters and sons, whose forebears endured bondage, were not settlers but a unique category of inhabitants or pioneers who had earned an inalienable right to the fruits of diasporic soil.

Conceding Canada to white nation-builders and repatriating to Africa was not an option. When Jenkins and Edwards revisited this long-standing debate in 1926, they concluded that Pan-Africanists in Canada should remain. "Some of us feel more strongly the ties which bind us to America" than to Africa, they confessed. Their reference to "America" described the new hemispheric home of diasporic Africans, which included Canada, a place for which Black people had "labored and fought." They did not use "America" to reinforce a generic United States. Furthermore, most Pan-Africanists in Canada believed that large-scale African repatriation schemes were unfeasible. Besides, western Europeans had already claimed "the best parts" of Africa. "As great as our patriotism is for Africa," they acknowledged, "some of us feel as if we want to remain here and enjoy the fruits of the sacrifices and of the labors of our ancestors," a "natural" claim of white people.[202] For diasporic Pan-Africanists, the dream to reap the fruits of their ancestors' uncompensated labor wedded them to the land, even as they crisscrossed the U.S.-Canadian border in search of an elusive Ethiopia.

Garvey also visited Canada to reap fruits from seeds scattered a decade before, but counterrevolutionary tactics hamstrung him. Less than one year after his deportation from the United States, Garvey arrived in Quebec on 27 October 1928 from a European sojourn aboard the Canadian Pacific Steamship *Empress of Scotland*. His presence troubled U.S. and Canadian authorities, because he planned to instruct 4 million Black Americans to vote against Herbert Hoover.[203] On 31 October, immigration officials summoned

Garvey to an inquiry and slapped a gag order on him, complicating his plans for the upcoming U.S. election. The *Dawn's* editors questioned Canada's commitment to "free speech and real justice." Jenkins and Edwards argued that "imitating our Southern neighbors" would make Canada unsafe. The "roots" of Garveyism "have sunk too deeply into the minds and hearts of Black people to ever be choked out." They predicted that posterity would honor Garvey, because he sparked "the spirit of race consciousness" among "common" folk.[204]

Although few were chosen, other prophets arose during the messianic moment. Some visited Canada to spread their message, such as the mystic Prophet Noble Drew Ali of the Moorish Science Temple. Until he died under mysterious circumstances in 1929, Noble Drew Ali maintained connections with African Americans who had immigrated to Toronto.[205] And no woman during the messianic moment rivaled Laura Adorkor Kofey, a Gold Coast preacher who immigrated to North America circa 1926. Kofey entered the United States from Windsor, Ontario, and became active in the Detroit UNIA. After relocating to Miami, Florida, to further the UNIA's work, she visited Garvey in the Atlanta penitentiary in August 1927. Garvey subsequently denounced Kofey over her unauthorized fundraising, fearing that she was using his name for personal gain. Undeterred, Kofey founded in 1928 the African Universal Church in Jacksonville, which attracted Garveyites interested in her preaching and West African repatriation scheme. On 8 March 1928, an assassin shot and killed Kofey as she delivered a speech in front of a crowd in Miami's Liberty Hall. The martyrdom of the "Warrior Mother of Africa's Warriors of the Most High God" exemplified the personal cost of inspiring racial redemption.[206]

The messianic moment did not continue indefinitely, although various religious sect leaders gained prominence after Garvey's 1927 deportation to Jamaica.[207] The push of Canadian racism and the pull of U.S. employment opportunities in Great Lakes cities intensified before the Great Depression, disrupting the leadership of this messianic movement. Jenkins's associate editor Robert Edwards, though he had criticized the African Canadian brain and muscle drain to the United States, ended up emigrating from Toronto to Buffalo, New York, in September 1928.[208] Relying on a decade of newspaper publishing experience, Edwards, by 1930, became editor of the *Buffalo Recorder* and Syracuse's *Progressive Herald*, papers that served African American communities. His peers also appointed him president of Buffalo's UNIA. New Jersey–born Edwards, driven by a desire to honor his ancestors and be "a credit to his race," honed his politics of Pan-Africanisms in Canada, making lasting contributions to race consciousness during a fourteen-year residency.

Neither the loss of his business partner nor the dog days of the Great Depression could dim Jenkins's optimism. Jenkins kept prophesying that meaningful change for Black people was forthcoming. "But fate is in the habit of playing such peculiar . . . tricks upon us weak humans that it is impossible to predict the future with any certainty," he wrote on 1 October 1930. "Who knows but that ultimately the Canadian colored people will come into their own? Who can say that Ethiopia will not soon stretch forth her hands unto God?"[209] Exactly one month later, the empire of Ethiopia crowned thirty-eight-year-old Ras Makonnen as Haile Selassie I, reviving the millennia-old dynasty that traces its lineage to King Solomon of Israel, the Queen of Sheba, and their son Menelik I. "Look to Africa when a Black king shall be crowned, for the day of deliverance is at hand," Garvey foretold in 1920.[210] Pan-Africanists interpreted this coronation as beginning the fulfillment of a long-awaited biblical prophecy that Ethiopia will "stretch out its hands unto God." Six months later, Canada's Georgia-born prophet of messianic Pan-Africanisms died on 6 May 1931 from complications in surgery.[211] He was forty-six. James Jenkins crossed the River Jordan in death, but he had yearned that Black children would achieve their glory in both life and the hereafter.

Throughout the messianic moment, Black leaders interpreted a glorious ancient African past as prophecy for a long-awaited racial renaissance. African descendants in Canada and the United States, reinforced by their Caribbean compatriots, desired to inaugurate divine redemption, which heightened the sense of anticipation of a deliverer during this period. In pursuit of liberation, leaders from W. E. B. Du Bois to Marcus Garvey appropriated biblical narratives and asserted their lineal ties to ancient Nilotic peoples, embracing the filiopietistic currents inherent in African spirituality, much like their ancestors had done. Through UNIA leaders, divisions, and other spokespersons, such as African American expatriates James Jenkins and Robert Edwards, Black people in Canada localized a global phenomenon. Pan-Africanisms broadly and the UNIA specifically united the Black masses in North America for the first time in the twentieth century. This messianic continental connection created opportunities for cross-border cooperation in the years to come.

Despite Marcus Garvey's meteoric and messianic rise, some historians overlooked his influence, underestimating his movement's reach. One of the first rigorous biographies of Garvey and his movement—Edmund Cronon's *Black Moses*, published in 1955—dismissed Garvey as a pseudo-messiah who led a failed Pan-African movement. In the decades that followed, other historians echoed this sentiment, portraying Garvey's global mission as unworkable, faulty, and doomed.[212] One of the few white figures to recognize Garvey's potential in practical terms was J. Edgar Hoover, head of General Intelligence at the Bureau of Investigation. In 1919, Hoover flagged the organizing prowess of Garvey, calling him "an exceptionally fine orator."[213] Hoover and the U.S. government had no qualms acknowledging that Garvey, to his people, was Moses—a revolutionary Negro messiah, the first such personality of global reach in the Atlantic World. Although many historians underrated Garveyism, the fact that a law enforcement official like Hoover could correctly identify its power bespoke the dangers that aspiring African American male leaders would face if they followed in Garvey's revolutionary footsteps of advocating divinely ordained Pan-Africanisms.

Garvey and Garveyism warrant careful historical revision.[214] In fact, without an accurate depiction of Garvey's true revolutionary and messianic impact on U.S. and global Black politics, analyses of the Black radical tradition will remain incomplete. Despite government sabotage, his bellicose nature, and his controversial ways, such as accepting an audience with the Ku Klux Klan and other white supremacists—which he did because of their frankness on racial segregation and white supremacy and his "uncompromising courage" to defend the inalienable rights of African peoples—Garvey is immortalized for his zealous commitment to global Black liberation.[215] That he predicated his movement on the idea of a Creator who embodies the likeness of Black people further endeared him to the masses, which meant conflict with the "Black Bourgeoisie"—African American elites who, in the words of E. Franklin Frazier, resented the "messianic element" of Garveyism.[216] Marcus Garvey was the most messianic and impactful Black prophet not only of his era but also in the history of the Atlantic World.

The messianic moment, coinciding with the Harlem Renaissance, marked a highpoint in Black liberation. These twin periods of Black self-making set the tone for twentieth-century activism and self-expression. As an elite cultural movement, unlike the racially conservative UNIA, the liberal Harlem Renaissance was an experiment in assimilation and integration. With its white benefactors and Black literati and artists as beneficiaries, the renaissance stood, at times, in contradistinction to "race first." Alain Locke, the renaissance's doyen, lamented the folly of fads in 1929, especially ones driven by whimsical external interests. "There is as much spiritual bondage in these things," Locke mourned, "as there was material bondage in slavery."[217] Dependence on white charity could not produce Black self-determination.

In contrast, ordinary Black folk anointing their own to lead their physical, psychic, material, and spiritual liberation powered the messianic moment. With the deepening of the Great Depression, most Black people needed manna more than a messiah, and for charismatic leaders who met the material needs of their followers, messianism endured.[218] For others, day-to-day liberation played out on the U.S.-Canadian border as cross-border migrations.

CHAPTER 2

BORDERLANDS BLUES, 1930–1950

Growing up with two nationalities and experiencing the racial and cultural dynamics of three regions—the North, the South, and the Caribbean—Gil Scott-Heron, the sensational soul and jazz poet, sang bitterly, "Home is where the hatred is."[1] Lamenting his oikophobia—or fear of home—he sang, "Home is filled with pain; and it might not be a bad idea if I never, never went home again."[2] The son of a Mississippi-born, Chicago-based mother, Scott-Heron was a product of the "Blues People."[3] His father, a Jamaican immigrant, enjoyed a pioneering career as a professional athlete in the 1940s and 1950s, living and working in Great Lakes cities in the United States and Canada, although he struggled to nurture roots in both countries. Scott-Heron used narcotics to escape the deep alienation of what he called "home." Indeed, home to Scott-Heron was an allegory of the United States, the Black ghetto and postindustrialism, broken families, intractable racism, and subordinate citizenship. There is no place like home, unless one is a diasporic African.

Imperialism and colonialism disinherited African peoples. African North Americans struggled to obtain the fruits of citizenship due to the history of forced migration, enslavement, quasi-emancipation, racial terrorism, and formal and informal segregation. This "natal alienation," to borrow historian Orlando Patterson's phrase, compelled diasporic Africans to look beyond the artificial and porous borders of colony, empire, or state to reformulate a language of belonging and rootedness.[4] Cross-border consciousness increased their sense of freedom. Because Black transnationalism stemmed, in part, from alienation and indignity, or what Scott-Heron described as "hatred" at home, those who embraced Pan-Africanisms in North America resisted in meaningful ways the hegemony of the sovereign state to confine Black agency.[5] As partly borderlands, partly colonized peoples, citizenship—that is, the fundamentals of human dignity, or official notions of national identity and allegiance to a sovereign entity—seemed elusive. Cross-border migration or self-exile mitigated, to some extent, the potency of anti-Black racism. Transnationalism became a process through which diasporic Africans, according to historian Robin Kelley, tried to create "a different sort

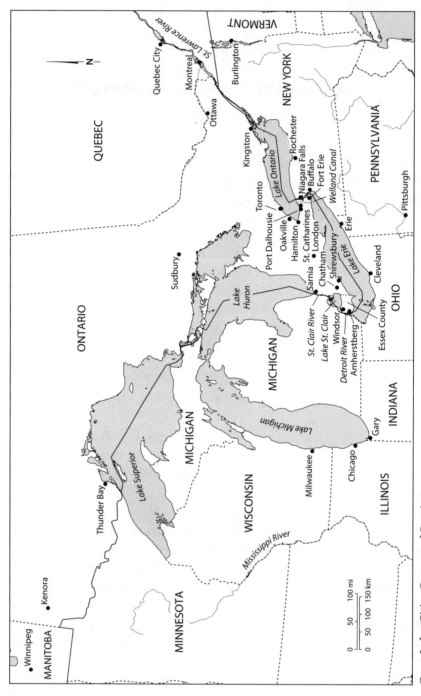

Great Lakes Cities, States, and Provinces

of nation-building project"—indeed, one that would correct their status as a "homeless" racial group that endured "hostile" treatment at home and abroad.[6] Exploring their dislocation, relocation, and rootedness illuminates the social history of how Black people, using Pan-Africanisms, imagined a cross-border, cosmopolitan zone in the Great Lakes region during the 1930s and 1940s. For diasporic peoples whose allegiance to a specific place depended on the ebb and flow of race relations and other socioeconomic and geopolitical forces at a given moment, Black identity functioned as a bridging mechanism.

From the mid-nineteenth to the mid-twentieth century, a group of highly mobile African North Americans practiced interspatial citizenship, that is, racial belonging in the liminal space along an international border. One senior historian with the U.S. Immigration and Naturalization Service (INS) said generational cross-border migration "produced a significant population of either dual citizens or stateless persons."[7] For Black people, this mode of cross-border life amplified Pan-Africanisms, sometimes a bourgeois Du Boisian version or a militant, Black Nationalist Garveyite version but always a universal appreciation of Black solidarity and liberation. They lived, worked, nurtured families, and agitated for full citizenship in the United States and Canada at different moments of their lives, forging a cross-border, continental identity as agents whose "citizenship" transcended both countries, as well as the Caribbean, and sometimes Africa and Europe. In this vein, the Great Lakes region was not simply a U.S.-Canadian border zone but a demilitarized hemispheric and global checkpoint with little surveillance.

Cross-border migration allowed African North Americans whose subordinate citizenship differentiated them from white people, including recently arrived European immigrants, to pursue work, leisure, family reunification, military service, or uplift.[8] This chapter employs biographical vignettes of Beulah Cuzzens, sisters Edith and Edna Mae McGruder, Gilbert "Gillie" Heron, Allan Malcolm Morrison, Daniel Grafton Hill III, and others to demonstrate that, rather than fracture racial identity over large geographical spaces within different international borders, race and mobility facilitated transnational community building and solidarity in North America. Interspatial citizenship strengthened North American Pan-Africanisms in the nexus of Great Lakes cities, states, and Ontario during the 1930s and 1940s.

Moreover, the phenomenon of racial passing—that is, transitioning from one racial group to another to escape social, economic, and political discrimination against a specific group—is a construct that frames border-crossing as quasi-citizenship passing. Although Black people did not disavow their national and ethnic markers, crossing borders allowed Canadians of African descent to "pass" as African Americans, and African Americans to pass as African Canadians. This pan-African solidarity—a testament to the oneness of African peoples—provided some protections against nativism and the presumption that Black people, legally, existed on the fringes of the state.[9] Many Caribbean immigrants, with their heightened consciousness as British subjects and awareness of class and color prejudice, passed as Canadian nationals or U.S. citizens or both.[10] Like racial passing, citizenship passing mirrored what one historian called a "chosen exile."[11] Because passing was a voluntary act of movement and migration (unlike deportation or extradition, which are not the focal points in this chapter), it necessitated transitioning from one sovereign soil to another.[12] In the process, migrants exchanged one identity for an alternative one, sometimes discarding a former identity but always melding aspects of belonging to personal advantage. These adaptive strategies offered short- and long-term benefits but also left people like Gil Scott-Heron and his father grappling with the pain that "home" evoked.

CHRONICLING BORDER CROSSINGS

For North Americans, this "fluid frontier" functioned as the source of rich cross-pollination.[13] Historians have described the Great Lakes region as a "permeable border" and "a zone of cultural mixing and interchange."[14] Others have noted that U.S.-Canadian cross-border migration symbolized "great natural phenomena," perceiving the children of Detroit, Michigan, and Windsor, Ontario, as "eminently capable of allegiance to one country one day and to another the next."[15] Similarly, a Canadian graduate student at the University of Chicago in 1906 observed that "the boundary line is imaginary," because New Yorkers and Ontarians have more in common than Ontarians and Quebeckers.[16] This cross-pollination influenced the ways that African descendants experienced life in Great Lakes cities. For those who practiced interspatial citizenship, cross-border movement, according to one historian, "remained a persistent feature of continental life." Interspatial citizenship, in other words, was the manifestation or praxis of cross-border consciousness. Serial border crossers who engaged in "repeat migration" underscored the extent to which mobility and social and labor market integration in the United States and Canada influenced their life trajectory.[17]

Historians have amply documented the south-north and south-west axes of the Great Migration in the United States.[18] However, an equally important facet worth excavating and documenting is the north-south migration of African Canadians into U.S. cities, such as Detroit, Buffalo, Cleveland, and Chicago in the 1930s and 1940s, not to mention the movement of African Americans who settled in northern cities during the Great Migration only to seek greener pastures in Canada.[19] During its economic boom after the Great War, the United States, having curtailed its reliance on European labor, resembled "a suction pump" on Canada's urban and industrial areas. Some Canadians described this general phenomenon between 1921 and 1929 as the "Great Emigration." In the words of two historians, "Europeans came in and Canadians moved out."[20] In the 1920s, approximately 1.2 million Canadian-born persons resided in the United States, or about 8 percent of Canada's population.[21] Bidirectional border crossings persisted well into the interwar period.

For a time, the permeability of the border threatened the very survival of Canada's small Black population. In 1905, Anderson Ruffin Abbott, the first Canadian-born Black physician and one of eight Black surgeons who served in the U.S. Civil War, wrote, "Our youth evince a strong disposition to cross the border line as soon as they acquire sufficient knowledge and experience to make a living. In this way we [Canada] are impoverished and you [the United States] are correspondingly benefitted." Abbott, a friend of First Lady Mary Todd Lincoln and her husband, President Abraham Lincoln, predicted, "By the process of absorption and expatriation the color line will eventually fade out in Canada."[22] As an integrationist and assimilationist, Abbott foresaw a society with little to no trace of a distinct Black population. Black emigration from Canada and the Canadian government's resistance to Black immigration in the early 1900s lent credence to Abbott's prediction.

Because the methodology for racial classification and the collection of immigration statistics varied from one census to another in Canada and the United States in the early twentieth century, inconsistencies and gaps emerge to thwart the historian. Before 1908, for example, U.S. migrants simply crossed the border into Canada without needing to register with border officials. In subsequent years, Canadian officials required government documentation from U.S. border crossers, although the relatively open border permitted an indeterminable number of migrants to cross from one country to the other without engaging either INS or Canadian immigration officials.[23] Anti-Black sentiments, however, meant that Canadian officials scrutinized and deterred Black cross-border travelers, specifically those who sought residency.[24] Canada's 1910 Immigration Act nearly barred Black immigrants on dubious grounds, such as climatic suitability and other pseudoscientific racial factors, although Canadian officials permitted a few thousand African American and Caribbean sleeping car porters, domestic workers, coal miners, and steelworkers to immigrate to Nova Scotia, Ontario, and Quebec.[25] Furthermore, Canadian census takers consistently underestimated the Black population. Changing and differing notions of racial categories or place of origin, in addition to the itinerant nature of sleeping car porters, complicated the enumeration of the Black population, handicapping the government's ability to maintain accurate statistics.[26]

Rapid nation building at the turn of the twentieth century made Canada a popular destination for U.S. immigrants. Between 1901 and 1931, 2,000,000 U.S. immigrants entered Canada. In 1931, however, only 344,374 appeared in the census, underscoring a trend of return migration to the United States.[27] "If we count all of Canadian stock," wrote Canada's chief statistician in 1937, "perhaps a third of us are south of the line, whilst certainly not more than 1 percent of the Americans are north."[28] As a snapshot in time, decade by decade, census data can reveal only so much. By creating a collage of pan-African micro-biographies, the historian can capture, to some degree, the rich fluidity that characterized life in the U.S.-Canadian borderlands.

Canadians have a long record of seeking employment and maintaining family ties in Great Lakes states and throughout New England. As the most strategic and adjacent border city, Detroit attracted Canadians in droves. In 1930, 94,973 Canadian-born persons resided in Detroit, slightly over 6 percent of the city's population.[29] In Michigan, 1,499 Canadian-born Black people lived in the state, most of whom resided or worked in Wayne County, compared with 376 in Illinois, 459 in Ohio, 866 in New York, and 1,408 in Massachusetts.[30] The larger sum of African Canadians in Massachusetts is attributable to Black folk who had lived in Canadian society for multiple generations or to those whose parents had immigrated to Canada from the Anglophone Caribbean in the early 1900s to work in the coal mines and coke ovens in the Maritimes. Some of their descendants traveled west to Quebec and Ontario, but others went south to New England, New York State, Pennsylvania, Michigan, and other destinations.[31]

All Canadian expatriates fell under one of three categories: naturalized, "having first papers" (that is, initiated the process of naturalization), or alien.[32] The 1930 U.S. Census enumerated only 5,817 Canadian-born Black persons or .45 percent of the total Canadian-born population of 1,286,389 in the country. This sum, which is likely an underestimation, had decreased by roughly a thousand persons since the 1910 census. Their small numbers notwithstanding, Canadian-born Black folk or those with meaningful connections to Canada had an outsize influence on race relations in the United States by 1940. That year, 90 percent of the Canadian-born Black population lived in urban areas, the highest urban concentration among their compatriots in the United States.

In the 1930s and 1940s, most border crossings in the Great Lakes region occurred in the Detroit-Windsor and Buffalo-Niagara-Toronto corridors.

Construction of the Ambassador Bridge in 1929 and the Detroit-Windsor Tunnel in 1930 radically transformed passenger travel in the region, which previously occurred on ferries. By 1931, seventy-one INS inspectors screened passengers on the river ferries and forty-four were assigned to the new tunnel and bridge. From 1901 to 1916, the number of INS agents assigned to the Detroit-Windsor crossing at the foot of Woodward Avenue went from one person to twenty. The astronomical increase of immigration officers by 1931 constituted, in the words of one historian, a "border-crossing culture."[33] On the southwest portion of Lake Ontario, three entry points facilitated passenger crossings in Niagara Falls: Whirlpool Bridge, Honeymoon Bridge, and Rainbow Bridge. In the nearby towns of Queenston, Ontario, and Lewiston, New York, the Queenston-Lewiston Bridge facilitated travel across the border, much like the Peace Bridge in Buffalo, New York.

Border crossings were less stringent and bureaucratic for Canadian and U.S. citizens. Initially, U.S. and Canadian migrants and other British subjects from the Caribbean who wanted to cross the border did not need visas or passports. Workers in Detroit and Windsor and its surrounding areas could obtain Border Crossing Cards or commuter permits if they engaged in frequent border crossings. Over time, this border bureaucratization drew the ire of commuters in Detroit and Windsor, who registered their concerns with elected officials.[34] U.S. nationality quotas, however, meant that foreign-born persons in Canada required visas. In 1927, to curb illegal entry of individuals subject to outright exclusion—such as Chinese migrants— or nationality quotas of the 1924 Immigration Act, the INS, in enforcing Bureau of Immigration General Order No. 86, required all border crossers, including Canadian-born persons, to obtain visas.[35] As a result of General Order No. 86, the classification of Canadian cross-border commuters went from "non-immigrants" to aliens. The INS accepted birth certificates, proof of naturalization, and verification of voting record but not driver's licenses. In some instances, border officials, believing they could discern true U.S. citizens from imposters, accepted membership cards of fraternal orders and other social clubs.[36]

With the coming of the Great Depression, the Canadian government exploited the new economic realities to advance racist policies, making immigration more restrictive. In March 1931, Parliament implemented Order-in-Council PC 695, which limited immigration admissibility, already a prerogative of white people, to U.S. citizens and (white) British subjects, specifically persons who had enough capital to subsist independently, farmworkers, and dependents of Canadian residents.[37] In 1932, for example, George Thomas Griffiths, a budding Pan-Africanist who had emigrated from his native British Guiana to work in Texas, attempted unsuccessfully to cross the border in upstate New York to matriculate at the University of Toronto. He eventually pursued his education at Cornell University.[38] This racist whites-only policy is the reason why an immigration official quipped that "none is too many" in 1939 when asked how many Jewish refugees fleeing Nazi Germany Canada would admit.[39] Despite racist policies that targeted prospective Black, Jewish, and Asian nation builders, Canada stood apart from the United States. Cross-border Black actors who forged a transnational, diasporic community played a significant role in connecting the United States and Canada.

BRIDGING BORDERS

The absence of lynchings in Canada's history was a major reason why it appealed to African American and African Caribbean immigrants. As African American expatriates James Jenkins and Robert Edwards's Pan-Africanisms illustrated in the 1920s, cross-border consciousness was vital to Black liberation in North America. The Black immigrants who came to Canada desired more than safe passage. They intended to stay and nation build—whether this meant coal mining in Nova Scotia, riding the rails from coast to coast as sleeping car porters, homesteading in the Prairies, or working as domestics in urban white households in Montreal and Toronto. Subtle but persistent forms of racism proved insurmountable at times, so with one hand on the plow in the "promised land," some fixed their gaze on the birthplace of Jim Crow, for that was where, paradoxically, opportunity abounded.

For Beulah Cuzzens, Canada was the homeland for which she longed, despite reminders that she was different. Growing up in southwestern Ontario, Cuzzens's proximity to the United States and frequent contact with African Americans from Great Lakes cities transformed her small, parochial region into a cross-border, cosmopolitan corridor for workers, entertainers, revelers, and churchgoers. She attended the African Methodist Episcopal (AME) Church in her town, which proved to be a natural magnet for U.S. bishops, elders, and ministers, many of whom came from Detroit and Cleveland and as far away as Kansas City. These fellow AME congregants allowed her to "hear from the outside world."[40]

Beulah Cuzzens (née Harding) was born to an interracial couple on 27 July 1907 in Chatham, Ontario, an important terminus of the Underground Railroad. Before her Canadian-born parents, Andrew Harding and Sarah Ethel Holmes, a white woman, could marry in Chicago on 2 December 1904, her father had to pass for white.[41] In Canada, however, Harding lived as an African Canadian, and the couple moved to Chatham, where Cuzzens and her seven siblings were born. As an interracial household, Cuzzens's working-class family fought racial prejudice. Although her maternal grandparents "disowned" her mother and her father's family felt "angry" about her parents' union, she said that these challenges "had all been ironed out" prior to her parents having children. Cuzzens's white mother dealt with racism by embracing Chatham's Black church and community. "You look like the race, you joined the race. We became Black children, not half-white, not half-Black. We became Black," Cuzzens recalled.[42]

Cuzzens grew up in a family where race pride meant something practical. She acknowledged, "We were raised in the community to always take pride in our Black family." This sentiment, for Cuzzens, surfaced whenever friends visited their home. "We were just Black and loved it. I can remember, I hate to say this now, because I am grown and mature, but as growing up children we would always do our best when our Black friends came," she confessed. "We had one tablecloth, one or two napkins. If we were going to have company with all our Black friends we'd put on our white tablecloth and put on our best. We didn't do that always for the other race."[43]

As a woman who came of age in the mid-1920s, Cuzzens is representative of what one historian called the "bridging generation." This cohort of resolute African Canadians built on the foundation of previous generations to overcome "the limitations of race and class."[44] With a resilient mother for a role model and a father who pushed her to dream and broaden her geographic horizon, her family positioned Cuzzens to overcome gendered limitations that society placed on her. She completed four years of high school at the Chatham Collegiate Institute and another year of vocational training before moving to London, Ontario, where, in 1926, she matriculated at the teachers college.[45] Cuzzens pursued her education in a society that shrewdly used the color line to push out Black professionals to the United States. As a result, she heeded Jenkins and Edwards's countless admonishments for young Black professionals to acquire education and remain in the country but to forge cross-border connections to advance the race.[46]

Beulah Cuzzens believed in her birthright. But she was also attuned to the realities of the society in which she was born and socialized. "There weren't too many [Black] people well trained at this time in Chatham, but those who did have anything to do at all had to go abroad," which invariably meant U.S. Great Lakes cities. Although Cuzzens welcomed opportunities to spend recreational time in the United States, she resisted the idea that people had to abandon their birth country permanently to plant roots elsewhere. One of her sisters left Chatham to find work as a secretary in a Detroit law firm. "I made up my mind that I was gonna be a school teacher and I was gonna teach and I was gonna do it all in Canada," she recalled. Despite experiencing anti-Black racism, Cuzzens did not succumb to oikophobia: "My first love was Canada, and my first love takes good care of me." Cuzzens successfully completed her degree at the teachers college in 1927, which she partly attributed to working siblings who dispatched her money to offset her six-dollar weekly boarding fee.[47]

If the labor aspirations of Black women like Beulah Cuzzens reveal anything about the staying power of social norms in the late 1920s and early 1930s, then their leisurely activities reveal at least as much about the frailty of gender norms. Although society circumscribed some African Canadian women to church and the household, others, through an assertion of race pride and a transnational consciousness, negotiated and overcame these constraints as they pursued friendships, leisure, and work. When Cuzzens befriended Ann Smith (née Benson), a fellow Black student at the teachers college from nearby Windsor, the two women forged a strong friendship and support system.[48] Smith's three elder sisters taught public school in Cleveland and another sister served on the police force. Cuzzens's and Smith's family ties across the border led to ample social opportunities.

In 1928, Cuzzens worked as a public school teacher in Shrewsbury, Ontario, a small town on the northern shore of Lake Erie, opposite Cleveland. She recalled visiting Cleveland and Detroit on weekends with Smith after a busy week of teaching. On Friday evenings, Cuzzens would commute to Windsor, where Smith taught. "She'd have the programs all laid out: where we were going Friday night [to] Sunday," said Cuzzens. "If I didn't have the right clothes, Ann had them all cut out, she and her aunt, and all I had to do was stand there and let them fit the [hips]." As gainfully employed single women, Cuzzens and Smith had the resources to pursue leisure. As professionals with family connections in U.S. border cities, their networks gave them entry and access to an exciting world of Black entertainers, businesspeople, athletes, and hustlers. "We always had someplace to go in Detroit: dances, theaters, parties. And this is when we met all the people of our time, our contemporaries. We met anybody who was anybody," Cuzzens exclaimed. "We visited the [Paradise] Valley. 'Course my sister had a lot to do with it; she worked in downtown Detroit, and knew all the people downtown, was highly respected."[49] When Cuzzens and Smith began their weekend getaways to Cleveland and Detroit in 1928, the City of Windsor erected a plaque at Riverside Drive and Ouellette Avenue, steps from the Detroit River, proclaiming "HERE THE SLAVE FOUND FREEDOM."[50]

Cuzzens and Smith frequented some of the most iconic spaces in Detroit. Before completion of the Ambassador Bridge and the Detroit-Windsor

Tunnel in November 1929 and November 1930, respectively, the five-cent ferry ride bridging Windsor and Detroit facilitated border crossings in the 1920s and 1930s.[51] Cuzzens and Smith watched Duke Ellington, Earl "Fatha" Hines, Fletcher Henderson, and McKinney's Cotton Pickers perform at the famous Graystone Ballroom. When they went to the Paradise (Valley) Theater, they "knew everybody well enough to go backstage and play cards with them between acts." The vibrant cultural scene in Black Detroit resonated with African Canadians who yearned for the racial solace that a critical mass of Black folk provided. Cuzzens recalled, "That was a nice era in Detroit. Black people were in their own ghetto [Paradise Valley or Black Bottom], but they were working to get out of it and get into this mess we are in now [pseudo-integration]."[52]

Cuzzens considered this period a seminal moment in Black cultural production. "Those were eras, like the Paradise Valley era was also the Joe Louis era for us. You could go down to El Seno or Gold's Drugstore or the Biltmore Hotel or Congo [a social club] . . . rub shoulders with Billie Holiday, Duke Ellington, Earl Hines, Billy Eckstine, Pearl Bailey, Leonard Reed, Ziggy Johnson," she recounted. Whenever these notables crossed the border into southwestern Ontario, Cuzzens also entertained many of them, including Paul Robeson, Joe Louis, and the notorious Jones brothers, who built a policy (that is, lottery where players shake a small tube and winning numbers depend on three digits inside) empire in interwar Chicago.[53] For Black people in Canada, mobility in Great Lakes cities, whether for work or pleasure, tempered the frustration that alienation engendered at home.

Discriminatory practices deepened as the Great Depression took hold in Canada. The 1932 Ottawa Conference or British Empire Economic Conference, for example, emphasized imperial preferences regarding trade and tariffs, but officials made no acknowledgment of Black people's hardships in the empire or immigration restrictions on those in the British West Indies. As a teacher, Cuzzens recalled of the depression, "Things were rather bad. And if either a boy or a girl became trained in any way at all, if you wanted to work, you had to go to the United States." Yet Cuzzens's personal experience countered her belief that one had to immigrate. Cuzzens, who was of a lighter hue, taught in segregated public schools and attended evening professional development classes at Jarvis Collegiate Institute in Toronto in the early 1930s.[54] Still, Windsor resident Hilda Watkins pointed out that her "color was not interviewed for secretarial positions" in Canada. Instead, Watkins found administrative work in the Motor City at a real estate investment firm. "I tried very desperately to find jobs for my business training [in Canada] but was unsuccessful."[55] According to Rella Braithwaite (née

Aylestock), "Some Black women were cook-generals, mother's helpers, chore ladies. It didn't matter how much education or qualifications a Black woman had at that time," Braithwaite explained. "Unless she was very, very light complexion, she just wouldn't be able to obtain any other kind of work. At least, very few did."[56] Despite the economic austerity of the depression, Merze Tate, pioneering African American scholar of international relations who described herself as a "cosmopolitan woman," traveled from Michigan to Montreal in 1931 en route to Europe. Montreal was not only a magnet for African American jazz bands and white revelers but also a way station for Europe-bound tourists from the United States.[57]

Although Montreal was not a Great Lake city, its proximity to the border contributed to its evolution as "Harlem of the north" and "sin city" starting in the 1920s, during the era of U.S. Prohibition. Revelers, musicians, and hustlers trickled into Montreal from the United States. The Black enclave—adjacent to the rail station where Black men (and their families) of U.S., Canadian, and Caribbean origin worked as sleeping car porters—was itself a cosmopolitan corridor within a metropolis. For centuries, indeed, Montreal had been the metropole of the British Empire in the Americas. One of the notable standouts of Black Montreal, Jamaican-born Rufus Rockhead, amassed a sizable fortune bootlegging on his Montreal-Chicago run as a porter. In 1928, Rockhead bought a three-story building in the neighborhood. He obtained a liquor license from the Quebec government in 1931. By 1933, the forces of segregation ensured the ascendance of Rockhead Paradise as one of the hottest jazz joints and after-hours bars in the hemisphere, in addition to Nemderoloc Club ("Coloredmen" in reverse) and the Monte Carlo Grill. Many of the jazz greats whom Beulah Cuzzens befriended in Detroit also performed in Black Montreal. African Canadian jazz bands, such as Myron "Mynie" Sutton's Ambassadors and Charles Winn's Harlem Aces, performed on both sides of the border.[58]

The privations of the Great Depression notwithstanding, community resilience and the pulse of the jazz age kindled the enterprising spirit of Black people. From 1934 to 1938, Edward M. Packwood published the *Free Lance*, a Montreal-based newspaper for "Afro-Canadians," an appellation that Packwood insisted on using instead of "colored," "Negro," or "Black." Packwood designated Montreal-born Juanita DeShield, the pacifist and activist against anti-Black racism who resided in Harlem in 1934, as the paper's U.S. "representative." When a lack of revenue caused the newspaper to fold, Packwood pivoted to tourism, having witnessed white and African American fascination with Montreal's jazz culture and night life. He operated an inn and published his own directory for U.S. tourists. "This was before all the big hotels were here. After they came I couldn't compete any more. I would have liked to see my work develop into a special hotel for people of African descent, not to create segregation, but a place where there would be Afro-Canadian business shops and restaurants." Packwood's wife, Anne Packwood (née DeShield, aunt of Juanita), belonged to the Colored Women's Club of Montreal, which African American women founded in 1902 when their husbands came to Canada to serve as porters on the rails. Anne was a staunch Garveyite, foster mother of scores of orphaned and abused Black children whom the state neglected, and indefatigable defender of her community. She served as secretary of the literary and debating club of the Montreal UNIA.[59]

For African descendants with a cultural heritage and racial consciousness that permeated the Great Lakes region, proximity to friends and family in nearby cities mitigated economic austerity. As the KKK found a toehold in 1930s southwestern Ontario, African Canadians tried to strengthen community institutions. They commemorated their hard-fought battle for emancipation in the British Empire and the United States. Black people in Great Lakes cities rendezvoused annually at Port Dalhousie, a waterfront community in St. Catharines, Ontario, on the first Thursday in August—the designated weekly rest day for domestic workers. "That was one of the big events in the community. . . . Everybody got new things—although it was the depression, we all managed to scrape some money to get new things, get on the boat and dance on the boat. It was like a reunion there," recounted Daniel "Danny" Braithwaite. "We all met with our American counterparts at Port Dalhousie. They came from Buffalo and the surrounding areas."[60] In fact, Robert P. Edwards, the former coeditor of the *Dawn of Tomorrow*, became president of the Buffalo division of the UNIA after returning to the United States in 1928.[61] Members of UNIA branches from upstate New York to Cleveland to Detroit attended the "Big Picnic" in large numbers, many of whom were of Caribbean heritage, adding a welcome flavor. Braithwaite avowed, "They would sell mauby [drink], sugar cakes, and turnovers—things from the West Indies—souse [a stew made with animal by-products, like chitlins], things like this. We had a great time."[62] Black people on the Great Lakes were not a novelty. Like porters on the Pullman trains, the Detroit and Cleveland Navigation Company hired Black bellhops, waiters, and cooks. The boats traveled from Detroit to Windsor, Toronto, Buffalo, and Chicago.

The Emancipation Day and Big Picnic festivities were socially mixed affairs in which women and men participated equally. Women from the Windsor area first spearheaded the Emancipation Day celebration in August 1851 when Mary Bibb, the pathbreaking abolitionist and copublisher of the

Voice of the Fugitive, and other intrepid women in southwestern Ontario founded the Emancipation Day Committee.[63] By 1935, under the auspices of the British-American Association of Colored Brothers, a civic organization that included both men and women from Windsor and Detroit, the grand event attracted African Americans from as far away as Virginia and Kentucky. Black people in Montreal also made the annual pilgrimage. Young and old gathered to commiserate and enjoy an afternoon repast and play softball or baseball. "I would meet my friends from Buffalo. . . . They danced; there was plenty of dancing. There was eating; there was visiting. . . . The people I went with got so wrapped up that we missed the boat and we had to hitchhike back to Toronto," recalled Cuzzens.[64]

Meanwhile, as the Great Depression deepened, African Canadians, especially the professionally trained, resorted to a familiar strategy during economic hardship.[65] Cuzzens sojourned in Detroit from 1931 to 1932, where she worked in the "numbers," the underground African American lottery. With her extensive social network and connections to number runners and policy kings, Cuzzens found ways to subsist. She resumed teaching at the School Section #11 Colchester South in Essex County, Ontario, from 1932 to 1934.[66] Cuzzens spent another year working the numbers in Detroit from 1934 to 1935. She returned to the segregated classroom in 1935 to teach Black students in southwestern Ontario.[67] The following year, Joe Louis, a good friend of Beulah Cuzzens and her husband, Earle, gifted them the boxing gloves that he wore in his title bout against Germany's Max Schmeling. Beulah and Earle, who was born in West Virginia but spent most of his adulthood living and working in the Detroit-Windsor corridor, were also friends with Louis's manager John Roxborough. They all worked in Detroit's numbers industry.[68]

William Nathaniel "Sunnie" Wilson, Paradise Valley impresario, called the numbers—the Black lottery—"the most important source of economic and political power." Wilson recounted an anecdote that a Detroit businessman hotelier—who also ran a numbers operation in the basement of his hotel—shared with him. Every week, the businessman would take cash deposits for the hotel and the numbers operation to the bank. On one occasion, a Chinese man approached him inquiring about the contents of the bag. "I've got Black folks' dreams," the businessman quipped. Soon after that initial encounter, the businessman ran into the Chinese man on the street again. Holding a bag of his own, the Chinese man said, "Chinese people got Black dreams too."[69]

Despite Detroit's dynamism, it was not the only city that attracted Black people looking for gambling dens and a good time.[70] At the turn of the century and before the Great Migration, a popular racetrack in Windsor attracted Detroit's African American working poor.[71] Windsor also provided liquor during Prohibition. Bootleggers dug a tunnel under the Detroit River and "ran whiskey from Canada under the river. They had speed boats on top of the water as decoys," recalled an African American community historian who grew up in Detroit. "The police thought they were chasing the boot-leggers, and the bootleggers were bringing the liquor under the water."[72]

Other African Canadian women with a cross-border consciousness and praxis of interspatial citizenship resembled Beulah Cuzzens. Born in 1914 in Toronto, Edith Gertrude McGruder was a correspondent for the *Chicago Defender*. From Toronto, she contributed to the "Canada" section of the *Defender* starting in the mid-1930s. In the interwar years, the McGruder children and members of the community distributed the *Defender* and other African American newspapers, such as the *Pittsburgh Courier*.[73] The *Defender* served Black communities across the country, and even though Chicago had a 3.5 percent Canadian population (see table 2.5), the "Canada" section demonstrated its outreach to African American expatriates and other Black readers in Canada who could boost the paper's bottom line during the Great Depression. Because the McGruders had relatives on both sides of the border, Edith's family had ample opportunities to engage in cross-border community building and other forms of race work.

Edith McGruder was a trailblazer in her own right. After graduating from the University of Toronto with a B.A. in 1937 and a social work degree in 1939, she played an enormous role as a young interlocutor in Black Toron-to.[74] As a regular contributor to the *Defender*, she informed its readers about social activities, provided updates on the community's wellness, and acknowledged families visiting kin and friends on either side of the border. The intertwined social relations between Black people in U.S. and Canadian Great Lakes cities meant that these community-based reports strengthened interspatial citizenship. The McGruders even celebrated U.S. Thanksgiving annually in Toronto, a sign of their African American and U.S. cultural retention. They provided relatives, travelers, and other passersby a chance to enjoy a U.S.-inspired feast in an African Canadian home.[75]

In 1940, Edith left Toronto for Chicago to work in an administrative capacity for United Charities of Chicago.[76] The forerunner to the United Way, it provided families with social services, welfare, and relief support. She planned to return as a social worker for the Home Service Association, a similar relief organization in Toronto on which she wrote her social work master's thesis in 1942 at Atlanta University.[77] As a former distributor of and contributor to the *Defender*, Chicago seemed a natural fit. She had relatives who lived there. Her father, who worked as a cook on the Canadian National Railway, preferred the Toronto-Chicago run.[78] Because of his itinerant job on the railway, Edith's father, like other porters, had introduced his children to various African American periodicals, including the *Defender*, which helped inspire her interest in journalism.[79]

Edith's younger sister also embraced a cross-border outlook. Edna Mae, born in Toronto on 10 January 1919, completed a B.Sc. at Howard University during the war years before moving to Detroit, where a cousin helped her find work with the Detroit Public Schools. Edith and Edna Mae's parents, Walter Jay McGruder and Charlotte Maude McGruder, were descendants of Underground Railroad families, and the McGruders embodied in every generation their North American, pan-African heritage. Walter, born in Battle Creek, Michigan, and Charlotte, born in Toronto, were committed neither to Canada nor to the United States, encouraging their five children to embrace their transnational, borderlands identity.[80] At birth, the McGruder children received dual status as British subjects and U.S. citizens. In her childhood and youth, Edna Mae and her siblings spent summers at Idlewild, Michigan, the resort town where Black families, celebrities, and intelligentsia vacationed.[81]

Edna Mae's influential Canadian-born grandfather, James Louis McGruder, spent most of his life in Michigan. At Idlewild, "he built the summer house so that we would have somewhere to go and meet different people, thus we would know that there are opportunities out there," she recalled. "He wanted me to go to college and I wanted to go to college. At Idlewild, meeting families from different places inspired me to further my education because they were involved with colleges and inspirational activities."[82] Edna Mae's grandfather and parents emphasized education, encouraging her and her siblings to cultivate Black networks beyond the confines of the small Black community in Toronto. The McGruders provide a window into interspatial citizenship, illustrating the fluidity of citizenship in the Great Lakes region and cross-border linkages that census data could neither capture nor illuminate.

In Detroit, Edna Mae attended Second Baptist Church, where she served on many committees, including the Women's Altar Circle.[83] Although other Canadians of African descent worshipped at Second Baptist, there is no sure way of ascertaining their exact numbers. The church's influential minister, Robert Lewis Bradby, was Canadian. He emigrated from Windsor to Detroit on 29 November 1909.[84] In 1910, he became the pastor of Detroit's Second Avenue Baptist Church, an institution that free and fugitive founders built in 1836. The original structure stood roughly a half mile from the Detroit

River, the natural border that separates the United States and Canada. As a northern refuge point adjacent to the "promised land," Second Baptist, the oldest Black church in the Midwest, aided Underground Railroad fugitives, helping 5,000 cross the river into Canada.[85]

As Bradby was a descendant of African American fugitives who traveled the Underground Railroad to Canada, race shaped his upbringing. He was born in a humble log cabin in Middlemiss, twenty-five miles southwest of London, Ontario, on 17 September 1877 to James Eldridge Bradby and Mary Catherine Rivers, a white woman from Elgin County in southwestern Ontario. His forebears included U.S. freeborn refugees from Virginia who arrived in southwestern Ontario in 1857. Some of his other forebears considered themselves "mulattoes" and others "Indians," including an Ojibway grandmother.[86] Growing up in predominantly white southwestern Ontario gave Bradby skills in social integration, an asset that helped the African Canadian pass as an African American in Detroit.

In his youth, Bradby identified with the African Canadian racial and spiritual milieu. Even though he could have passed for white, he embraced his Black racial heritage. Given the cross-pollination between Black Baptists in the United States and Canada since the mid-nineteenth century, one historian pointed out, "a double consciousness ensued" among border-crossing Black people, which was also multifaceted and mutable.[87] Some pan-Africanists, like Bradby, could not reject the social covenant of race, even when the ability to pass gave them options.

As pastor of a prominent church in Detroit during the Great Migration, Bradby routinely met southern refugees at the train station. His church commissioned a dedicated committee that met and greeted Black passengers aboard trains from the South, providing settlement and integration services. The membership of Second Baptist underwent seismic expansion on the eve of World War II, when it grew from a few hundred to over 4,000 members.[88] Known as the "militant minister" among his flock, Bradby found his congregants coveted jobs at Ford, Chrysler, Dodge, and the Detroit and Cleveland Navigation Company. Some of these workers, like Bradby, came from Canada.[89]

Bradby's influence stemmed, in part, from his friendship with the white U.S. senator James Couzens. Both men spent part of their adolescence in Chatham, Ontario.[90] Couzens had come to Detroit in 1890. An early investor in Ford Motor Company, he became an economic advisor to Henry Ford and implemented the five-dollar daily work wage. One historian considered Couzens the financial and business genius behind the company.[91] Couzens helped Bradby cultivate a personal patronage relationship with Ford executives. Charles Sorensen, a senior executive at Ford Motor Company, invited Bradby to lunch with Henry Ford and other company leaders in 1919. Ford executives wanted an influential Black leader who could help shape Black workers' attitudes regarding industrial work, resolve workplace conflicts among them, and negotiate between Black and white workers on the shop floor. Bradby agreed to recruit "very high type fellows" for the company and to assist management. He also agreed "to acquaint the colored workers with the responsibilities of employment . . . telling them that they should be 'steady workers' so as to prove the worthiness of colored industrial workers."[92] Bradby enjoyed an unprecedented level of access to Ford executives, visiting the plants at will.[93]

In his pulpit, he preached Black home ownership, encouraging flight from the ghetto. While serving as president of the Detroit NAACP in 1925 and 1926, he staunchly supported Dr. Ossian Sweet after a white mob besieged his home, threatening to uproot Sweet for integrating the neighborhood. As a propertied Black Detroiter, Bradby preached "protect your home at all cost," a gospel grounded in self-assertion and pragmatism.[94] By the early 1940s, Bradby's influence began to wane, having reached the pinnacle of his authority as a broker of racial and industrial affairs in Detroit during the previous three decades. His efforts in aiding southern refugees during the Great Migration and in securing Black men coveted industrial jobs illustrate the ways that a pan-African ethic helped working-class Black folk—many of whom had migrated from the South—integrate into urban life in the Great Lakes region. "The history of Detroit," noted Bradby's contemporary, "will never be written without giving Rev. Robert L. Bradby much space."[95]

LOCAL ACTORS, GLOBAL THINKERS

Pan-Africanisms encompassed the local and the global. In fact, the cosmopolitan phenomenon of bridging borders created new frontiers for Pan-Africanisms in North America and the worldwide African community. When Fascist Italy invaded the empire of Ethiopia in December 1934—the second such Italian aggression in forty years—the UNIA's Black Cross Nurses in the United States and Canada partnered with women's groups to collect medical supplies for Ethiopian troops. In Toronto, Black Cross Nurses, who also held leadership on women's committees in the British Methodist Episcopal, African Methodist Episcopal, and First Baptist Churches, mobilized and coordinated efforts.[96] In nearby Windsor, Rev. W. C. Perry of Chatham organized an "Ethiopian Day of Service" from which came the Canadian Friends of Ethiopia. In Montreal, UNIA members chastened "Europeans [who] refused to sell arms to Ethiopians," noting, "Japan reportedly had stepped in to fill the vacuum."[97] Despite this militant language, youth activist Juanita DeShield's uncle Edward M. Packwood, editor of the Montreal-based newspaper the *Free Lance*, tried unsuccessfully to recruit volunteers to fight in Ethiopia. "White students from McGill came," Packwood admitted, "but when I got on the streets my people would tell me: Packwood be careful—you're going to go to jail. But not one came."[98] Steadfast in his Pan-Africanisms, Packwood organized a medical aid fundraiser at Victoria Hall in February 1936, at which African American and local artists, including DeShield, performed.[99]

The geopolitics of European imperialism exacerbated race relations in North America. After Joe Louis pummeled Italy's Primo Carnera in their June 1935 bout, providing a modicum of revenge for the African World, street fights ensued between African Americans and Italian Americans.[100] Louis kept his gloves from this monumental victory, unlike the pair from his loss to Nazi Germany's Max Schmeling in 1936, which he had given to his friends Beulah and Earle Cuzzens. So inflamed were interracial tensions after the Louis-Schmeling fight that three weeks later at the Montreal Forum, during a bout between a Black and a white fighter at the Canadian Olympic boxing trials, a bar refused to sell alcohol to Fred Christie, a Jamaican Canadian. The landmark legal case, *Christie v. York*, went to the Supreme Court of Canada, where the court used "freedom of commerce" in 1939 to uphold racial segregation in Canada.[101]

The liberating ideals of Pan-Africanisms remained a focal point in the mid- to late 1930s. In August 1936 and 1937, Toronto hosted two UNIA international conventions over which Marcus Garvey presided.[102] Garvey's active involvement and presence illustrated his aspiration to use UNIA chapters in Canada to reach his followers in the United States.[103] These two conferences permitted Garvey to enjoy "face-to-face discussions" with African Americans who crossed the border to meet him in Toronto.[104] The Montreal Division helped coordinate the Toronto conferences, seminal events that strengthened Pan-Africanisms after the Great War. In fact, the School of African Philosophy, Garvey's idea to help propagate his race-first ideology, materialized from the 1937 conference, and Garvey subsequently used Toronto to "springboard" his views throughout the African World.[105]

Garvey had not lost his messianic aura when he visited Toronto in 1936 and 1937. Danny Braithwaite and Lenny Johnston, teenagers at that time, recalled listening to Garvey speak at the UNIA Hall in Toronto. Braithwaite—a member of the UNIA Youth Division and whose sister served as Garvey's secretary during the Toronto conferences—remarked, "He was a very dynamic person. I was miles away from him; in fact I used to be way on cloud nine. I was just nothing. When he was speaking, he has a tremendous personality."[106] Johnston remembered, "I saw him when I was a kid. I didn't meet him. He was a strong, thick-necked Black man walking down in front of a whole lot of people. It was quite the sight. To me it was a frightening sight because I had never seen that many Black people."[107]

Garvey toured the Canadian Maritimes in 1937, because the UNIA had nine branches in Nova Scotia alone.[108] An unyielding prophet who aspired to see Black people overcome the invisible scars of bondage, Garvey urged UNIA members in Sydney to seek psychic liberation. "We are going to emancipate ourselves from mental slavery," Garvey insisted, "because whilst others might free the body, none but ourselves can free the mind."[109] Canada and its Black citizens had never been more vital to Garvey's vision of global Black liberation than in the late 1930s when he needed a solid foothold on the North American mainland.

Garvey's Canadian speeches in autumn 1937 sound less controversial, because he did not want to alarm the government. While addressing UNIA members at Menelik Hall, a lodge for sleeping car porters, he said, "We think there is no country more able to help us than Canada. Canada has always played a fair game." Garvey wanted Black communities in Canada to know that they had every right to reap the fruits of Canadian nationhood. "We bore on our shoulders the heavy burden of this civilization. Cane, sugar, rum, cotton, were the industries on which the present civilization was built."[110] Although enslaved Africans in colonial Canada did not produce these commodities, trade and other imperial networks made Britain's North American and Caribbean colonies mutually dependent. Canada directly and indirectly benefited from the enslavement of Africans and British imperialism in the Caribbean well into the twentieth century.

Garvey also highlighted the peaceful disposition of Black folk, a strategy to signify to Canadian authorities, who shadowed his every movement, that his followers were neither subversives nor insurrectionists. "I believe you will find more Bibles and Prayer Books than pistols" among African Canadians, Garvey averred. He also predicted, "So long as Canada is Canada and the Negro lives here, he will be a good citizen."[111] By moderating his rhetoric, Garvey tried to appeal to the better nature of Canadian authorities. He hoped that this strategy would help him visit Canada without state obstruction and also reclaim his once massive following in the United States. Less than three years later, in 1940, Garvey suffered two strokes. The last one proved fatal. He died in London, England, on 10 June. His goal to create an African empire that would protect the interests of all Black people at home and abroad seemed less viable as the storm clouds of war hovered over Europe.

ALWAYS GO BY TUNNEL

Crossing the Border Is Easy

VIA DETROIT-WINDSOR TUNNEL

The First Official Emancipation Day Border Crossing

Twenty-four hours a day, every day of the year the famous Detroit-Windsor Tunnel—the only international vehicular tunnel in the world—is ready to speed your passage across the border. When you use the Tunnel you save time and miles.

PRINTED BY THE WINDSOR DAILY STAR

"Always Go by Tunnel," Windsor Daily Star. *Detroit-Windsor Tunnel LLC.*

Heavyweight champion Joe Louis wore these gloves on 19 June 1936 when he fought Germany's Max Schmeling at New York City's Yankee Stadium. Earle Cuzzens attended. After the bout, Louis and his manager John Roxborough gifted the gloves to Beulah and Earle, their good friends. Gift of Ken Milburn to Smithsonian in memory of Beulah and Earle A. Cuzzens.

Earle A. Cuzzens. Gift of Ken Milburn to Smithsonian in memory of Beulah and Earle A. Cuzzens.

Beulah Cuzzens, circa 1927. Gift of Ken Milburn to Smithsonian in memory of Beulah and Earle A. Cuzzens.

Juanita Corinne DeShield, active member of the Negro Youth Movement and reputed first Canadian-born Black woman graduate of McGill University. A champion debater, she obtained an Honors B.A. in French, graduating at the top of her class, before earning M.A. and Ph.D. degrees in psychology from the University of Montreal. McGill University, 1936.

Military service during wartime—not to mention periods of rivalry among Western empires—complicated notions of citizenship and belonging in North America and the idea of allegiance to the African Diaspora.[112] Although enslaved persons had no claims to the fruits of citizenship, their self-assertion and the ways that they imagined freedom clearly illustrated a sophisticated understanding of alliance—agency that society would ascribe to free, rights-bearing individuals. This phenomenon of war-time agency dates to the U.S. Revolutionary War and the War of 1812, when tens of thousands of enslaved Africans in the United States chose to fight for their enemy's enemy, the British. During the U.S. Civil War, former fugitives from slavery and free Black people in southwestern Ontario returned to fight for the Union army.[113] During the First and Second World Wars, African Americans and African Canadians fought in U.S. and Canadian armed services, principally because North America had common foes in Germany, Italy, and Japan.[114]

Global war against the Axis powers foreshadowed potential advancements in Black rights in North America. Black people, however, discovered that, even as global war accelerated North America's tolerance for group and individual dignity, the boundaries and limits of Black self-assertion remained tightly circumscribed and policed.[115] Young Black men in Toronto, for example, who tried to take two young women visiting from New York City to the Palais Royale dance club in August 1942 could not enter because of their race.[116] In October, African American Earl "Fatha" Hines and his band performed at the Palais Royale. Toronto-born Doug Salmon and his friends were again denied admission to see the jazz icon play. As a result, Salmon, whose Jamaican-born mother was a Garveyite and Black Cross Nurse, led the Race Discrimination Committee's fight against the Palais Royale. A few weeks later, they watched Duke Ellington perform but at a different venue. A community member wrote a letter to the editor, underscoring the point that Black men were fighting for democracy in Europe but banned from entering dance halls "where Black bands were the featured attraction."[117]

Black men's experience in the Great War made some of them reticent to enlist in another global war in which Canadian authorities could humiliate them.[118] Nevertheless, African Canadians began to enlist from coast to coast. When the United Kingdom declared war on Nazi Germany on 3 September 1939, some of the 100,000 Black British subjects who had emigrated from the Caribbean to the United States from 1900 to the eve of the Second World War saw service to the Crown as their pathway to enfranchisement. This wager required them to enlist on Canadian soil. In the early 1940s, hundreds of volunteers emigrated from the Caribbean to enlist in Canada, despite decades of restrictive immigration from majority Black British colonies.[119] Some British West Indians crossed the border from the United States into Canada to enlist in His Majesty's military.

In fact, it was not only British subjects who enlisted in Canada's armed services. A reciprocal induction agreement between the United States and Canada permitted the two countries' respective nationals to serve in each other's militaries.[120] Some have estimated that nearly 30,000 U.S. citizens fought in Canada's military.[121] Before his eighteenth birthday on 12 June 1942, a lanky senior at Phillips Academy at Andover named George H. W. Bush considered enlisting in the Royal Canadian Air Force (RCAF) because one "could get through much faster." The British Commonwealth Air Training Plan made Canada a popular destination for U.S. citizens who wanted to earn their wings. When the United States declared war on the Axis powers in December 1941, over 6,100 U.S. citizens had already joined the RCAF. Nearly 3,800 RCAF-trained pilots had repatriated to U.S. flying services when Bush enlisted in the U.S. Navy in June 1942.[122]

Black men in the United States also sought their wings in the RCAF. Born on 9 April 1922 in Kingston, Jamaica, Gilbert St. Elmo "Gillie" Heron immigrated with his mother and siblings to Cleveland, Ohio, in 1938. They relocated to Detroit the following year. His father, Walter, a planter in Jamaica, and his mother, Lucille Irene Heron, had mixed African and British heritage, which positioned them among the most prominent families on the island.[123] Gillie's patrilineal ancestor Alexander Heron had emigrated from Wigtownshire, Scotland, in 1790 to seek a planter's fortune in Jamaica. Seven years later, Alexander had many enslaved African work gangs cultivating hundreds of acres of land.[124] This exploitation of Black laborers in the Caribbean persisted long after nominal emancipation throughout the British Empire in 1834.[125]

In Detroit, Gillie completed high school and worked for the Cadillac Oil Company from 1941 to 1942. The following year, he apprenticed as an oil cutter but forfeited a generous $180 monthly salary to join the British war effort.[126] As a subject of the Crown, Gillie's birthright beckoned him to answer the call of duty, which required him to leave the United States for British soil. When the twenty-one-year-old crossed the border into Canada, seeking to enlist in the RCAF in the summer of 1943, he wagered that his prodigious athleticism would secure him a coveted spot in an elite unit. A recruitment officer described Gillie, a strong and agile athlete with 20/20 vision, as a "Jamaican who came from the U.S. to enlist. Should make aircrew." Personnel records designated Gillie as an "intelligent" and "well spoken" man. Despite these attributes, the 5′10″, 157-pound enlistee was subjected to opaque bureaucratic jargon intended to preserve a certain racial composition of the Royal Canadian Air Force.[127] According to the enlistment agreement, if the RCAF found a candidate "unsuitable for Aircrew," it could "remuster" the enlistee "to a ground trade or to General Duties or may discharge" him entirely from the armed forces.[128] Military brass perceived opportunities, though, to leverage Gillie's athletic prowess.

Intelligent and in remarkable condition, Gillie made the cut. In a matter of days, Gillie dazzled his peers and superiors during various track and sporting events at Camp Borden—the home base of the RCAF, roughly sixty miles north of Toronto. News coverage of the intramural action called the indomitable athlete "flashy" and the "colored spark."[129] Before joining the RCAF, Gillie had won many accolades dating back to his youth in Jamaica. The 1940 Michigan Welterweight Golden Glove champion had also played on five championship soccer teams. In Jamaica, he had bested Herb McKenley—a future Olympic gold medalist—in school track competition.[130] In fact, Gillie ran the 100-yard dash in 9.9 seconds; boasted 21′10″ in the long jump; and leaped 5′9″ in the high jump. He also excelled in baseball, tennis, basketball, football, and table tennis. At East Technical High School in Cleveland, another prodigious athlete nine years his senior named Jesse Owens had set many records before Gillie could make his mark in the record books.[131] Gillie was a prized RCAF recruit.

Although Gillie declared his intent at the time of his enlistment to return to his budding career as a skilled tradesman and amateur star soccer player rather than remain in Canada's armed forces, his brother Roy had different plans. Roy—who spoke English, Spanish, and Norwegian fluently and read English, French, and Spanish—scored "high" in "mechanical aptitude" and displayed "intelligence" and "alertness." Because he had eighteen months of electrical engineering training from St. Lawrence College, the Detroit technical school founded during the depression, Roy requested that the army place him in the Royal Canadian Corps of Signals. Instead, the army assigned him to the Royal Canadian Electrical and Mechanical Engineers on 30 June 1942, before shipping him out to England in March 1943.[132]

Like his younger brother Gillie, Roy also lived in Great Lakes cities in his youth. During the throes of the Great Depression, his Jamaican parents sent him to Cleveland to live with his maternal aunt, seven years before his mother and siblings joined him. Born on 6 January 1920, Roy came of age during a period of labor turmoil in Jamaica, and, as a high school student in 1937, he joined the Young Communist League.[133] In 1939, he relocated to Detroit with his mother and siblings. While attending night school, Roy drove a truck and worked as a machinist in a tool and die company to support his family. Roy left home in 1940 to work as a seaman on a whaling vessel and subsequently traveled to South America, Asia, and Europe on various ships, where he acquired new languages, uncovered the Black experience in distant environs, and learned practical and complementary knowledge of "instrument mechanics."[134]

As a Caribbean immigrant who spent part of his youth in the U.S. North—Canada's southern shadow—Roy's experience with and understanding of different regimes of color, caste, and class shaped his pan-African sensibilities. Supporting the Allies, he reasoned, was a fight for racial and economic justice. "I did not like what Nazism was doing to people. And being in the [Norwegian] Merchant Marine I could help to a great degree, so I decided to become active. And that's why I came to Canada," he recalled. "I could've joined the American [army], but I couldn't take the American army. Racialism. They had two different armies: A white army and a Black army." In the same interview, Roy recounted experiences in Canada that resembled "racialism," although he downplayed these incidents. "I wanted to join the air force. . . . I wanted to be a pilot, but they told me 'no.' And the navy did not accept people of color in those days, so I went into the army."[135]

Roy's testimony further complicated his claims of U.S. racialism and Canadian cosmopolitanism. "When I took my examination for the army, I got a very high score and I was subject to become an officer, but somehow, it never worked out. But it never worried me at all," he said. "I just went through and did a job I had to do because I know I'm helping this country to achieve a goal and get rid of Nazism and Fascism." In Canada, some African descendants exercised forbearance instead of direct confrontation during the Second World War, hoping that loyalty and service to Crown and country would pay dividends in human and civil rights for the entire community. "I can say I enjoyed my life in the Canadian Army. I had no problems at all to speak of, really; I had no real problems to speak of."[136] For Roy, a true Jim Crow army resembled the U.S. armed forces with its segregated fighting units. Yet systemic discrimination existed throughout Canada's armed forces, limiting the number of African descendants who enlisted in preferred branches, such as the air force, or denying qualified candidates promotion to the officer rank—a policy that directly impacted Roy. Nonetheless, Roy's testimony suggests that it was easier for him to navigate race in wartime Canada than in the United States.

The stonewalling and rejection that Roy experienced echoes the pain that many Black men felt in Canada during the Second World War—a repetition of their experience during the Great War. Toronto-born Leonard Braithwaite remembered that when he visited the local air force office in the summer of 1942, a recruitment officer told him plainly, "No, sorry, we don't take you people." The son of a Barbadian father and Jamaican mother, Leonard was born in October 1923. He endured rejection for six months at the recruitment station. After a routine personnel rotation, a sensible and progressive Ukrainian Canadian replaced the racist recruiting officer. "He told me that . . . Ukrainian people and Polish . . . settlers in the [Canadian Prairies] were treated just the same way, which surprised me." Still, deep-seated anti-blackness in Canadian and U.S. societies denied Black people, unlike eastern Europeans, the benefits of acculturation, ensuring subordinate citizenship. Leonard's struggles notwithstanding, he made air crew in March 1943 but had to serve in a mechanical capacity because of his myopia.[137]

Danny Braithwaite's experience resembled that of his first cousin Leonard Braithwaite. Born to Barbadian parents in Sydney, Nova Scotia, Danny relocated with his family to Toronto at age eight in 1927. He recalled his wartime humiliation. "When I was in the army for that one month [in 1942], they said that you had the option, if you want, from then on to join the air force — any armed service. So I decided I would like to be in the air force, because I had just graduated a few years back with motor mechanics, and I wanted to do aircraft mechanics," said Danny. "I went down, and I was told they were not accepting colored people in the air force. Well, that's it. If I'm not good enough for the air force, I'm not good enough for the army."[138]

Within days, military police apprehended Danny for dereliction of duty. "They took me up to Newmarket [a suburb north of Toronto] the same evening and put me in detention for a few weeks. People wondered where I was; all of a sudden I vanished." When the authorities placed him in the stockade, they denied him his right to call and notify his family and friends until he pleaded that it was his civil right. He finally contacted Rev. Cecil Stewart, a family friend dating back to when the Braithwaites had lived in Nova Scotia and founder of Toronto's Afro-Community Church. The Jamaican-born Reverend Stewart was a Garveyite who had many years of experience navigating racial politics in Canada. He counseled Danny to temper his wartime defiance. "He says I shouldn't antagonize the government at this time. I told him the reason why I didn't sign up in the army. And then I told him that if I could transfer to the air force, I would sign. He said that they would be able to transfer me," Danny recalled. Ultimately, though, the air force denied Danny's transfer. Protesting recruitment bias impacted his reporting to duty, the air force reasoned, which delayed his transfer request. Danny served in the army for two years before his discharge.[139]

Leonard and Danny Braithwaite, the Heron brothers, and other Black men negotiated their sense of place and belonging in wartime North America. The war encouraged some prospective African Canadian enlistees in the United States to return home. Toronto-born Lincoln Alexander, who was also of Caribbean descent, left Toronto in 1936 to live with his mother in Harlem. Three years later, he returned: "We were in New York, but Canadians were being asked to register for the draft, so [Mom] told me I'd better get back to Canada and sign up."[140]

Other Caribbean immigrants in the United States, such as former *Negro World* editor Wilfred Domingo, capitalized on the distraction of the war and returned to Jamaica, where he tried to jump-start self-government on his native island. Nazi Germany's conquest of the Netherlands and control of Vichy France troubled Britain and the United States, because the Nazis could dispossess the Allies of their strategic Caribbean islands. As a result, Franklin D. Roosevelt and Winston Churchill initiated in September 1940 the "destroyers-for-bases deal," an agreement in which the United States transferred fifty naval destroyers to the Royal Navy in exchange for British land and nautical rights. This deal precipitated gradual withdrawal of Britain from the Caribbean. By 1941, colonial authorities charged Domingo with sedition, a time when Britain felt vulnerable to internal discord in its colonies.[141]

Some African Canadians enlisted in the Jim Crow army. The precise number of African Canadians who fought in the U.S. armed forces during the Second World War is hard to ascertain, but many of those who did served with distinction. Allan Malcolm Morrison, for example, left Toronto in 1939 for New York City, the same time that seventeen-year-old Lincoln Alexander left Harlem to enlist in Toronto. Born in November 1916 in Toronto to a Jamaican cricketer, who had arrived in the city in 1914, Morrison, like other African Canadians of his generation, suffered from an unrecognized birthright.[142] His immigration to the United States is but one example of many disenchanted Black people who deserted Canadian society for the land of segregation, since it provided opportunities to advance the race. As a writer interested in Black politics, arts, and letters, Harlem proved an ideal destination for Morrison. With the assistance of two associates in July 1940, he cofounded and published the short-lived *Negro World Digest*, a periodical modeled after *Negro World* and *Negro Digest* but with a mission to showcase the talent of global Black writers. A Marxist and a rising youth leader in Toronto, the Black Mecca offered Morrison a platform to hone his leadership skills in leftist politics and showcase his prowess as a budding storyteller.[143]

U.S. entry into the Second World War gave Morrison an unexpected breakthrough. Enlisting in the army in 1942, he leveraged his journalism experience to climb the ranks. In the theater of war, Morrison used his pen and notepad to fight his two foes: the Nazi war machine and Jim Crow. He had sharpened his advocacy skills as a member of the Canadian Youth Congress in the mid-1930s, around the same time when he had participated in the Negro Youth Movement, a pan-African group of young Canadian leaders that included Juanita DeShield, Grace Price, and Helen Redmon, who emigrated as a child from Chicago to Toronto with her parents, Nathaniel Redmon and Goldie Bishop, in 1913.[144] Members denounced fascism and advocated in behalf of Black communities. Morrison began publishing around 1936 as one of the editors of the short-lived Toronto magazine *Advance*.[145]

After his induction into the U.S. Army, Morrison quickly emerged as a luminary. He initially wrote for Black newspapers at Fort Benning, Georgia, and Fort Huachuca, Arizona, before becoming, in 1943, the first Black correspondent for the military daily *Stars and Stripes*. His fellow journalists considered him "one of the most popular writers." Many GIs became familiar with "his meaty accurate accounts of the warfront," although only a handful knew that he was "a young, shy, bashful Negro reporter." Some white GIs critiqued his reporting as too celebratory of Black GIs, while some Black GIs thought he was some "liberal white" journalist. Nonetheless, his timely pieces on Black troops proved a "great morale-builder" for them.[146]

Sergeant Morrison belonged to a select company. When the Allies invaded occupied France in August 1944, he and seven Black journalists embedded with U.S. forces chronicled the event. The *Chicago Defender*, the *Pittsburgh Courier*, the *Baltimore Afro-American*, and the Associated Negro Press, among others, sent correspondents.[147] Morrison highlighted the bravery of Black soldiers, dealing a direct blow to spurious racial theories. "Showing utter contempt for the 'master race' divisions facing them," wrote Morrison, "U.S. Negro artillerymen firing 155-mm howitzers are blasting German installations and troop concentrations and pounding to pieces the Nazi theory of 'inferior' and 'superior' races."[148] He seized any opportunity to politicize overtly and subtly the intellectual and moral bankruptcy of white supremacy.

Morrison was not the only Canadian making a mark in Uncle Sam's military. The ranks of the 900-plus elite, high-flying Tuskegee Airmen, the nation's first crop of Black fighter pilots, included at least one second-generation African American–African Canadian. Enlisting in the Army Air Corps in 1943, Yenwith Kelly Whitney took on the perilous task of guiding bombers from Italy to Germany. These sorties resembled the aerial protection that the all-Black 99th Fighter Squadron had provided the British 8th Army during the Sicilian-Italian campaign. Completing the single-engine pilot training on 27 June 1944 at the Tuskegee Army Air Field and obtaining the rank of flight officer, Whitney and his colleagues, who successfully finished their training, dubbed themselves the "Lucky Seven."[149] During the war, First Lieutenant Whitney flew a P-51 Mustang in the all-Black 301st Fighter Squadron, completing forty-five successful missions in Italy.[150]

Yenwith Whitney fell in love with airplanes in 1935 as a ten-year-old in the Bronx. "When my mother gave me that [model] airplane, I knew then that I wanted to become a pilot."[151] His boyhood dream was not far-fetched: in 1935, Harlem's Hubert F. Julian—the Trinidadian-born aviator and UNIA icon who allegedly trained in Canada with Billy Bishop, the First World War ace—had repatriated to Ethiopia to lead Haile Selassie's air force in that country's war against Fascist Italy. The Black Eagle, as Julian was affectionately called, became a folk hero to many in New York City and the African World.[152] Aspiring to pilot airplanes or, if necessary, become a fighter pilot in war was more probable than improbable, considering the geopolitics and Pan-Africanisms that shaped Whitney's childhood in New York City.

Born 22 December 1924 in the South Bronx to Ada Kelly Whitney and J. R. B. Whitney, Yenwith Whitney's lineage made him the quintessential African North American. With an Ohio-born father and a mother born in Windsor, Ontario, where his parents wedded on 30 June 1919, the Whitneys had strong ties to the Great Lakes region.[153] J. R. B. Whitney had a powerful network in Toronto with notable friends and benefactors, such as Canadian Bank of Commerce president Sir Edmund Walker. The Canadian press described him as "the clever young editor and publisher."[154] In Toronto, J. R. B. Whitney founded in December 1914 the *Canadian Observer*, the most important national Black newspaper during the Great War. He edited it until June 1919, weeks before he and Ada moved to New York City. Whitney's newspaper forced the Canadian government's hand, first, to permit Black enlistees in April 1916 and, second, to facilitate the mustering of Black troops for a Black battalion.[155] The *Canadian Observer*, in fact, paved the way for African Americans James Jenkins and Robert Edwards to launch their diasporic newspaper the *Dawn of Tomorrow* in July 1923. J. R. B. Whitney also served on the board of the Railway Men's International Benevolent and Industrial Association.[156] His wife, Ada Whitney, was among the first licensed Black educators in Ontario, having earned her certification from Detroit Teachers College circa 1918.[157] While living in Canada, the Whitneys collaborated with the Black press, maintaining business and social links in the United States.

When Ada and J. R. B. Whitney relocated to New York City in 1919, they arrived in time to appear in the 1920 U.S. Census.[158] Although the 1940 U.S. Census listed the family of six as white, the Whitneys were proudly Black, despite Ada's mixed-race appearance.[159] Having lived both in the United States and Canada, the Whitneys exemplified the phenomenon of Black parents who resided, worked, and cultivated a racial identity in one place and had children in another. Rooted in this borderlands and transnational logic was a pan-African sensibility that transcended time, place, and space. It was an aspect of social change that predicated racial liberation on service and sacrifice in behalf of African peoples wherever one was situated.

The couple's commitment to Black racial pride and citizenship—qualities that influenced their four children, especially Yenwith—strengthened in New York City. Catering to the Black press, J. R. B. Whitney utilized his publishing skills and vast network in the industry, serving in the 1920s as the advertising manager of the Associated Negro Press in the agency's Fifth Avenue office.[160] He was a close friend of Associated Negro Press founder Claude Albert Barnett, the Chicago-based Pan-Africanist who visited Africa nearly a dozen times in the 1930s and 1940s.[161] A high-ranking Freemason, Whitney also worked as the business manager of the *Caravan*, the official journal of the Medina Temple No. 19, Ancient Egyptian Arabic Order of the Mystic Shrine.[162] J. R. B. Whitney understood the vital and transformational currency of Black agency and fraternal organizations in the United States and Canada. He also valued the link between military service and the fruits of citizenship, which allowed him and Ada to build a foundation that positioned their children as defenders of the race. As a Tuskegee Airman, Yenwith Whitney personified his parents' commitment to race work, honoring their African North American legacy via his own military service.

As the younger Whitney flew daring sorties in his P-51 Mustang over Italian skies, Canadian-born Sergeant Morrison, now universally seen as an African American, focused on using the *Stars and Stripes* to expose and challenge military segregation on the ground. African American servicemen complained to Morrison that most Black soldiers remained in Jim Crow labor units, seldom participating in combat. "We've been giving a lot of sweat. Now, I think we'll mix some blood with it," one serviceman predicted. The army initiated "the plan of mixing white and colored doughboys in fighting units" principally out of necessity and efficiency but also in response to Black soldiers' constant demands to fight in combat.[163] John C. H. Lee, a three-star general and West Point graduate, played an important role in unofficially desegregating combat units. General Lee felt "irritated and shamed by prejudice in the Army." Activists, such as NAACP executive secretary Walter White, "repeatedly urged him" to make changes. Lee agreed, permitting approximately 2,700 Black GIs to serve in rifle platoons rather than in labor units under his command as they pushed toward Berlin after D-Day.[164]

On 26 December 1944, Lee offered Black GIs with infantry training the opportunity to serve alongside battle-hardened frontline units. "It is planned to assign you without regard to color or race to the units where assistance is most needed," Lee stated. "Your comrades at the front are anxious to share the glory of victory with you. Your relatives and friends everywhere have been urging that you be granted this privilege." Various branches of military leadership, Lee avowed, "are confident that many of you will take advantage of this opportunity and carry on in keeping with the glorious record of our colored troops in our former wars." Thousands applied for a chance to fight Germans on the front lines.[165] One white commanding officer—who led an integrated unit under heavy enemy fire at Honningen, a battlefront near the Rhine—attested, "I was damned glad to get those boys. They fit into our company like any other platoon, and they fight like hell. Maybe that's because they were all volunteers and wanted to get into this."[166]

Despite such advances, racial animus toward African American soldiers continued. Morrison published a piece in which he conveyed the anger of Black servicemen who believed that their fellow white GIs fanned the flames of racial hatred in the manner of their Nazi enemies. "Certain prejudiced white Americans have carried their ideas into Germany and Germans notice. Negroes condemn this as 'fascism in another form.' It is no new experience for them," he wrote. Some white servicemen engaged in a similar behavior in England, France, Belgium, and Italy.[167] Black GIs informed Black newspaper editors of the spread of "American Fascism" in Europe. One Black GI observed, "There are a few members of our own who still are playing the Nazi game of hate-your-fellow-man-because-he's-Black. Sometimes I wonder if we have really defeated Naziism." Others attested to German soldiers' strategy of pointing out the racism of white U.S. servicemen to widen rifts between Black and white soldiers. White GIs, Morrison noted, claimed that they shouldered arms while Black GIs merely performed servile duty on the front lines. Black GIs accused their white counterparts of "betraying the democracy they claim they love" and of being worse than Hitler.[168]

The racism of some U.S. servicemen allowed Germans to see their own country's racial propaganda. "Germans, who once were exhorted to think of themselves as a master race, now gladly wash the clothes of American

Negro soldiers, a racial group the Nazis taught them to despise," Morrison reported. "Children play with Negro soldiers, girls fraternize with them. If the Germans wholly believed Nazi racial theories, the war certainly has put still another complexion on social life in Germany." If a reversal of attitude and policy could occur in Germany, it could occur in the United States, if the government endorsed it vigorously.[169]

The mutual perception between African American GIs and Germans gradually improved. Morrison wrote, "In the larger cities of Germany, the racial myth seems buried beneath the rubble of the Nazi order." Pragmatism triumphed over racism, observed one staff sergeant. "Their hunger has made them very objective on such matters as racial attitude. It didn't take long for them to see that there is no difference between food, chocolate, cigarettes and soap in the hands of" Black or white GIs.[170] For this reason, Morehouse College president Benjamin Mays stated, "If the Nazis can train people for evil in 20 years, America should be able to train them for good" in the same time frame.[171] Morrison used his position as a wartime correspondent to propagate the sacrifices of Black soldiers, their courage under fire, and interracial conflicts and cooperation between Black and white GIs.

The race politics that white servicemen brought with them overseas was truly a product of the domestic climate. When Daniel Grafton Hill III enlisted in the Second World War, like his father had during the Great War, he, too, negotiated segregation in the U.S. Army. The elder Hill, in fact, served as a second lieutenant in the 368th Infantry Division of the U.S. Expeditionary Forces, a segregated fighting unit that resembled a "racial quarantine."[172] Born in Independence, Missouri, on 23 November 1923 to educated African American parents, the impressionable Hill learned from the race politics of the army that his world was a powder keg. During the First and Second World Wars, frustrated African Americans stepped on racial trip wires in civilian and military life.[173] While undergoing his field artillery training under the "blistering hot" Oklahoma sun, Hill asked his mother, "Have you been reading about the race riots that have been fanning the nation[?]" He continued: "The riots are spreading to the army camps now. It's [sic] seems that the Negroes are not going to tolerate anymore prejudice. I am with them and would just as soon clean up on these crackers here as to go overseas."[174] Hill's militancy sprang from the contradictions between the values that his country purported to defend and uphold in Europe and the volatile racial climate that prevailed at home.[175]

Out of three "colored" and one hundred white recruits who took an exam for Officer Candidate School in artillery, Hill and only two others passed. Despite his personal successes, he confided in his mother, "When I first

Autographed postcard of Tuskegee Airman Yenwith Kelly Whitney of the 301st Squadron in his P-51 Mustang, circa 1944. Courtesy of Saundra Curry.

Allan Malcolm Morrison used this naturalization photo on 14 November 1946. Morrison inscribed his new surname as well as his original surname, Moyston. Morrison entered the United States illegally in 1939. Schomburg Center for Research in Black Culture, New York.

came into the army, there were numerous things that I thought about, as to my future and life in general." Hill explained: "It seems that slowly but surely I am completely changing to a total fatalistic viewpoint on life." As an incipient atheist, Hill nonetheless added, "I hope that fate deals me a good hand." Negotiating his precarious place in U.S. society led Hill into an existential crisis. Nevertheless, his unrelenting pursuit of "bars" (military stripes) is indicative of an ambitious young man who desired to distinguish himself from his peers and to match his father's distinction as a second lieutenant. "I want some bars before I turn 20," Hill confessed to his mother. "Lieutenant D. GH III at 19 is my goal."[176]

Officer training at Fort Sill, a U.S. Army installation specializing in field artillery roughly 100 miles southwest of Oklahoma City, completed Hill's transformation into a conscientious advocate of his people. Hill wrote his parents in February 1943, "The army is changing me greatly in one respect. My days of individualism are over, I am beginning to realize that I am part of a group. Living, eating, sleeping, learning to fight side by side with my companions makes me realize that when I do wrong, the group as well as myself suffers." Hill further noted, "When I, and everyone else does right and strives to get ahead, the group advances. Don't get the impression that I am turning communist but take out Hemingway's book, 'For Whom the Bell Tolls,' and you will understand what I feel."[177] In his coming of age, military service and his loyalty to the soldiers in his segregated unit fortified Hill with racial pride. Many other Black World War II veterans learned similar lessons in racial solidarity that they would bring to bear on civil and human rights struggles in their postwar communities.[178]

POSTWAR URGENCY

After the war, Allan Morrison returned to publishing. Working for *Ebony* in 1946, he climbed the ladder to become the editorial bureau chief of Johnson Publishing Company, the largest Black-owned publisher in the United States.[179] Later that year, on 14 November in New York City, Morrison became a naturalized U.S. citizen. His distinguished service in the war effort invariably aided his application.[180] As a Canadian of Jamaican descent, Morrison's immigration to the United States was tantamount to "passing" citizenship. Instead of falling victim to ethnic politics, Morrison embraced the African American struggle, an experience forged in rural and urban areas, in the North and the South, and in the crucible of war. His decision to change his nationality coincided with his decision to change his legal surname from Moyston to Morrison.[181] At the time of his naturalization, he had called himself Morrison for at least seven years. He and his relative Bill Forbes,

Daniel Grafton Hill III in World War
II. Archives of Ontario. Courtesy of
Lawrence Hill.

Gilbert St. Elmo "Gillie" Heron became the
first Black footballer to break the color bar
in the United States and the first to play
for the Celtic Football Club in 1951. Celtic
Football Club.

cofounder of *Negro World Digest*, had entered the United States illegally in 1939, which is the reason he changed his surname to Morrison.[182] It was easily relatable and provided him with a new start. Whether passing across borders or "passing" from one citizenship to another, pan-Africanists like Morrison displayed remarkable dexterity to adapt, evolve, and resist while subtly subverting the hegemony and white supremacy of Canada, the United States, and the British Empire to circumscribe the fate of Black people under racial caste. Their acute understanding of race relations advanced postwar civil and human rights in the United States and Canada, respectively.

In June 1944, Gillie Heron received an honorable discharge from the Royal Canadian Air Force. He returned to Detroit as he had always intended. Although he found work at an auto plant and made $180 per month, he yearned for the pitch. An extraordinary athlete and soccer star, Gillie played in the Detroit District Soccer League, netting a stunning forty-four goals in 1945. By 1946, the Detroit Wolverines, a professional team, issued him a contract. In his debut match against the Chicago Vikings, Gillie disoriented the defense, dazzled fans, and delivered a hat trick. The memorable date, 7 June 1946, at legendary Comiskey Park, was nearly one year before Jackie Robinson broke baseball's color bar. The Black press covered his success. *Ebony*, in a featured piece, called him the "Babe Ruth of Soccer." Without much publicity in the mainstream white press, Gillie—the cross-border cosmopolitan of Jamaican birth who came of age in Great Lakes cities and served in the RCAF—quietly became the first Black soccer player to break that sport's color bar. Yet despite his undeniable merit, subordinate citizenship meant that his profession denied him marketing opportunities. Management paid him $30 a game, compared with the $100 paid to less prolific stars.[183]

Gillie's elder brother Roy chose to make his mark in trade unionism and community mobilization in Canada. He remained with the Royal Canadian Electrical and Mechanical Engineers for two years after the war and worked for nearly three years as an electrician in Montreal. The army examiner who assessed Roy's reintegration prospects and employability anticipated that the discriminatory Canadian labor market would make it harder for him to "sell" his skills to an employer. Notwithstanding his technical training and multilingualism, he noted that Roy would "unfortunately" experience challenges. Although Library and Archives Canada redacted the remainder of the sentence on this military document, it is highly plausible that the army examiner predicated his pessimism of Roy's employability on his race, because there is no indication that he had any personal shortcomings that would limit his success. If anything, the polyglot technician was an exceptional candidate to find work. Nonetheless, the examining officer cautioned, "He will require careful counseling."[184]

The employment discrimination that veterans experienced in Canada compelled them to fight against a broad range of deeply ingrained discriminatory practices. Army veteran Danny Braithwaite participated in the community's efforts to combat discrimination toward the end of the war. Founded in 1944, the Joint Council of Negro Youth harnessed the frustrations of Black people in Toronto. "We figured that the only way that we could get something done is to unify our efforts, [so] the young people [could] see that housing, jobs, education and other fields could be opened to Black youth," recalled Braithwaite, a Garveyite. "So we formed a group of all the young people's groups together. And church groups too and all the young Black organizations. There were representatives from lodges too, just to be observers at the first meeting."[185]

After commissioning the Joint Council, members worked steadily in pursuit of racial justice in housing, jobs, and education—the three areas in which Black folk suffered the most discrimination. Braithwaite and his peers stressed the significance of education for the downtrodden, "because you could speak out against things that are not right and . . . cope with society with the knowledge you have." They emphasized Black history. "That was one of the basics," Braithwaite attested. "Because if you don't know who you are, you are more or less lost; you won't be able to face society."[186]

The persistence of postwar discrimination in Canadian society fueled pan-African consciousness nationwide. In Nova Scotia, for instance, endemic racism positioned African descendants as outcasts. In 1946, Carrie Mae Best, a descendant of Black Loyalists and Black Refugees, enslaved Africans who cast their lot with the British Crown during the U.S. Revolutionary War and the War of 1812, spoke out against racial injustice, demanding dignity for her community. She founded the *Clarion* to challenge her province's de facto racial caste policies. Heartened by Best's intentions, Manuel Zive, a Jewish businessman, gave her fifty dollars in unsolicited seed funding. "You are just a small voice crying in the wilderness, but keep crying," Zive encouraged Best—paraphrasing the ancient Israelite prophet Isaiah's foretelling of John the Baptist.[187] Best used her paper to acknowledge champions of racial justice, including the Nova Scotia Association for the Advancement of Colored People, an independent organization founded in 1945 and modeled after the NAACP. The December 1946 edition of the *Clarion* sounded the alarm for beautician Viola Desmond's campaign to challenge racial segregation at a New Glasgow theater, a legal case that hastened Nova Scotia's postwar trek toward human rights legislation.[188]

In Toronto, Black veterans remained on the offensive, organizing a benevolent association to fight racism. Danny Braithwaite and other servicemen founded the Negro Colored Guards in 1946 for "fraternity reasons" and to combat discrimination. "We had dances. We didn't have any parades at that time. We had a little clubhouse. We had a room where we could go up and talk things over, a social type of thing," said Braithwaite. "The constitution also stated that we would try and eliminate discrimination whenever it was possible, wherever it's found, like in housing or any activity [or] human endeavor."[189] Rella Braithwaite, who had married a Montreal Braithwaite and World War II veteran, helped spearhead the Negro Colored Guard Ladies' Auxiliary. "Discrimination was rampant, but I think we were sort of conditioned to it," she said of the early postwar years.[190] One hopeful indicator was that activists in 1944 had convinced the Ontario government to pass its Racial Discrimination Act, which prohibited proprietors from displaying racist signage.

The Negro Colored Guards and the group's Ladies' Auxiliary had little difficulty finding a just cause to champion. "That's how we became involved with the nursing incident in 1947, where the hospitals didn't permit Black nurses to become trainees—and also some restrictions in regards to nurses in the hospitals," recalled Danny Braithwaite.[191] The group submitted a brief to the provincial health minister, demanding that discriminatory Ontario hospitals forfeit their government funding. The Negro Colored Guards "deplored" Ontario nursing programs that denied Black women training opportunities, while denouncing "the general policy of discrimination against Negroes in hospitals."[192] Petitioning provincial legislators allowed the women and men of the Negro Colored Guards to expose Canada's postwar color line. "It was through our efforts this barrier was broken down because nurses train here and operate in Ontario. That was one of the main issues that we tackled," Danny Braithwaite attested.[193]

In a society that steered Black women and men toward servile work, hospitals and nursing schools, in turn, had few qualms about rebuffing the middle-class, professional aspirations of Black women. Before Black veterans and their women collaborators took on this issue, many Black parents watched helplessly as Canadian institutions refused to allow their daughters opportunities widely available to their white peers. Although most medical institutions denied having a discriminatory policy against Black women, a few flatly admitted having a color bar in place. "I had two daughters who tried for months to get into [nurses' training at] the Toronto and Ontario hospitals and never got it," said a Black father of two in 1947. One daughter acquired her nursing training at Meharry Medical School in Nashville,

Tennessee, while another daughter finally received admission at a school in Nova Scotia and graduated with distinction.[194] The tireless advocacy in 1944, in fact, of Pearleen and William Oliver, an African Nova Scotian couple, helped remove the color bar blocking aspiring Black women nurses.[195]

A 1947 survey on nursing schools revealed systemic racism. The National Council of the Young Women's Christian Association concluded that hospitals and schools displayed "a real tendency to discriminate specifically against Negro girls." Indigenous, Chinese, and Japanese students received better treatment than their Black counterparts. The 178-hospital survey revealed nursing's "anti-Negro discrimination" to be a national phenomenon. The study explained that nursing schools considered teaching hospitals a major "stumbling block" to integration efforts. Initially, hospitals refused to accept Black nurses because of racial stigma, but the University of Toronto "has been endeavoring to alter this attitude" and admit Black nursing students.[196]

Black leaders also attributed Canadian society's shortcomings to systemic anti-Black racism. "The applications of colored girls, with all the qualifications required for training as nurses, have been subtly rejected with unwarranted excuses," argued Rev. W. C. Perry of the British Methodist Episcopal Church. In response to the suggestion of white administrators that Black nurses should leave Canada and train in the United States, the reverend said, "What a reflection on Canadian ideals and our pride as a young and potent democracy."[197] Lawyer B. J. Spencer Pitt, the longtime president of the Toronto UNIA, noted that neither the nursing school at the University of Toronto nor its training hospitals admitted Black women. Pitt also underscored the practice of forcing Canada's Black public health aspirants to the United States, where they eventually naturalized and practiced. "Yet the Rockefeller Foundation sends colored girls to Canada for training in the University of Toronto Nursing School," Pitt said, pointing out Canada's shortcomings vis-à-vis the land of Jim Crow.[198]

Why would a Canadian university admit foreign Black women for nurses' training and not train African Canadians, encouraging instead those who desired training to matriculate at U.S. institutions? Canadian institutions maintained an unofficial policy that African American women and other diasporic Africans who received training would return to their birth country after their fellowship ended. Throughout the 1940s, the Rockefeller Foundation, as part of its global public health mandate, provided fellowships to Black women nurses and the occasional Black faculty, helping facilitate their training at the University of Toronto. Most fellows came from the United States. A few came from the Caribbean and Central America.[199] Although the university's school of nursing made efforts to accommodate a handful of Black nurses on a Rockefeller Fellowship, the director, at least on one occasion, expressed the need to "restrict the number of colored nurses" in teaching and supervision and in public health courses.[200] The rationale for this quota is unclear, but it reveals that racial tolerance, when encouraged by a flush international organization, had its limitations in dismantling systemic Canadian anti-Black racism. By encouraging the best Black minds to pursue professional opportunities across the border and overseas, Canadian society drained the talent pool of future change agents.

Black migration within Canada was a temporary solution to crossing the border into the United States. Central Canada, especially southwestern Ontario, became known to African Canadians as a more racially tolerant region. Metropolitan Montreal held a comparable reputation among Black folk in the Maritimes. Don Carty, an air force serviceman who left his community in New Brunswick for Toronto, said, "Specifically, in Canada, one of the major problems has been one of seeking opportunity, which, out of necessity, meant migration." The veteran recounted community members and extended kin who left the Maritimes for cities in Ontario and Quebec, describing Canadian discrimination, especially in employment, as "a peculiar kind of subterfuge."[201] On his return from Europe after the war, Wilson Brooks, a flying officer and one of Carty's air force comrades, vowed, "I was determined that, no way that [Toronto], where my family had lived for four generations[,] would force me to go across the line to Detroit to earn a living."[202]

Despite Brooks's personal protest, the flow of Black workers from Canada to the United States continued throughout the decade. Another commentator explained that after experiencing marital struggles, she moved to Chicago in 1947: "I went to the States because I did not want to go back to factory work. I felt there was nothing here for me." She quickly found secretarial work with a major retailer, earning a promotion to administrative assistant before returning to Toronto several months later.[203]

After the war, some African American veterans immigrated to Canada, believing that one could escape Jim Crow and McCarthyism. After receiving an honorable discharge, for example, Daniel G. Hill III completed his bachelor's degree, cum laude, in sociology at Howard University in 1948. That summer, Hill traveled to Oslo University in Norway on Howard's International Lucy Moten Fellowship. He enrolled briefly as a graduate student at the University of Michigan from 1948 to 1949 and then served as a social worker in Detroit from 1949 to 1950. In the summer of 1950, he crossed the river into Canada to pursue a master's degree in sociology at the University of Toronto. Hill saw unparalleled opportunity for racial advancement in postwar Canada. "There is one great difference between Toronto and an American city of comparable size and, that is, that discrimination can be fought, and the battle won in Toronto with greater facility," Hill observed.[204]

Meanwhile, veterans who served Crown and country in uniform continued to serve their communities in civvies. They collaborated with Pan-Africanists at home and abroad, advocating on behalf of aspiring nurses and other community members.[205] Danny Braithwaite presided over the Toronto Negro Study Group, a body that helped coordinate the activism of various Black organizations, encouraging "political action" and racial unity. "That was the time [1948] when the emphasis was on human rights in regards to accommodation . . . getting haircuts at different public places, having restaurants where you could eat," he explained. Appreciating the postwar Canadian experience within diasporic and transnational currents, Braithwaite even convinced the study group to join the Pan-African, anti-colonial Council on African Affairs. "Any time that Paul Robeson [council chairman] came here to sing at Massey Hall, I used to get in touch with him," he said. "The study group would sponsor him at the churches. We were the ones that were in contact with him."[206]

While community organizing created opportunities to imagine and realize a Pan-African Atlantic World, collective action and capital deployment allowed others to see beyond borders and create new lives there. From 1949 to 1952, two prominent African American businessmen in the numbers-running industry founded a resort outside of Windsor on the shores of Lake St. Clair. One of the partners, Eddie Cummings, invested $5,000 of his own money and invited nineteen other partners from Detroit. They incorporated the venture as Belle Clair Shores Limited and an accompanying nonprofit entity called the Surf Club. The partners constructed a stately two-story house on one mile of pristine beachfront and a clubhouse for the Surf Club for $250,000. They also gave land to Joe Louis, who trained there briefly. Some Detroiters involved in the venture decided to build homes nearby. Buying homes on the Canadian side of the border was in vogue for upper-middle-class Black Detroiters. Those who owned boats sailed across the river to the resort. The venture provided an economic boost to the local economy.[207]

To obtain full citizenship in the 1930s and 1940s, Black migrants went wherever opportunity abounded. Don Carty believed that Canadian anti-Black racism was "making a last-ditch stand."[208] Carty's air force mate Gillie Heron, like some African Canadians, sought opportunity in the United

States in the late 1940s. After breaking professional soccer's color bar in June 1946, Heron joined the Chicago Maroons in 1947. It was in Chicago where he met Bobbie Scott, a Mississippi-born librarian. In April 1949, the couple had a son whom they named Gil Scott-Heron. By 1951, Gillie's pitch prowess took him full circle to Scotland, birthplace of his ancestor Alexander Heron. In Glasgow, he broke new ground once more, becoming the first Black footballer to play for the Celtic Football Club. Gillie netted a goal in his debut match in front of 50,000 Scotsmen. Referring to Celtic's home turf, the news reported, "He took Parkhead by storm. There is more than Olympic about Heron. There is real football, too."[209] Before long, fans and the press dubbed him the "Black Flash" and "Black Arrow."[210] Despite his pitch prowess and professional promise, though, Gillie had a truncated tenure at Celtic.[211]

Not only did borders symbolize a threshold in the quest for Black social and economic advancement, but crossing borders was also integral to maintaining familial and social ties. After legal woes and clashes with Italian mobsters forced the Jones brothers to relinquish their numbers-running empire in Chicago, they fled to Mexico City. In the late 1940s, Beulah and Earle Cuzzens visited the policy kings. The Windsor couple considered the brothers, who were honored guests at their wedding, kin. The Jones brothers feted their longtime Canadian friends with VIP service and accommodation.[212]

In many instances, crossing borders was more than an economic decision. It was an act of solidarity, intimacy, and survival. Border crossing provided Black men and women in North America with an exit strategy and release valve when the pressures of anti-Black racism and disillusionment proved overwhelming at home. Interspatial citizenship—that is, the cross-border movements, military service, leisure, activism, and labor aspirations of African North Americans—during the 1930s and 1940s reveals the complex factors that influence citizenship and attachment to space and place. Knowing and understanding the racial landscape in North America became a matter of knowing and navigating an unwelcoming home. The postwar surge in human rights activism renewed the hopes of those whose cross-border consciousness would give them new tools to advance postwar Black liberation in North America.

TABLE 2.1 PERMANENT U.S. IMMIGRATION TO CANADA

	U.S. citizens	Other nationals entering Canada from the United States	Total
1935	3,049	5,349	8,398
1936	2,872	5,777	8,649
1937	2,862	6,323	9,185
1938	3,306	6,654	9,960
1939	2,933	6,484	9,417
1940	2,695	6,253	8,948
1941	3,331	4,245	7,576
1942	3,413	3,413	6,826
1943	2,053	3,253	5,306
1944	2,282	4,616	6,898
1945	2,260	3,641	5,901
1946	4,624	4,217	8,841

Source: Statistics Canada, *Canada Year Book*, 1947.

TABLE 2.2 MASSACHUSETTS CENSUS TRACTS 1950*

Total foreign-born population	450,883	
Canada French	24,695	5.5%
Canada Other	95,160	21.1%
England/Wales	22,519	5.0%
Ireland	64,292	14.3%
Italy	74,778	16.6%
Poland	22,540	5.0%
USSR	43,683	9.7%
Other / Not reported	103,216	22.8%
Total population	2,845,729	
Under 20 years	849,539	29.9%
20 to 34 years	665,012	23.4%
35 to 64 years	1,053,850	37.0%
65 and over	277,328**	9.8%
Total population	2,845,729	
White	2,781,572	97.8%
Black	59,735	2.1%
Other	4,422	0.2%
Total population	2,845,729	
Male	1,372,303	48.2%
Female	1,473,426	51.8%

Source: *Social Explorer* 1950 Census Tract.

* Percentages do not always add up to 100.00, likely due to rounded figures in the original data.

** Figure unavailable in the original data set. Added by the author.

TABLE 2.3 FOREIGN-BORN IN ILLINOIS, MICHIGAN, NEW YORK,
AND OHIO CENSUS TRACTS 1950*

Total foreign-born population	3,386,416	
Canada French	22,580	0.7%
Canada Other	178,790	5.3%
Germany	345,751	10.2%
Ireland	207,501	6.1%
Italy	547,690	16.2%
Poland	410,903	12.1%
USSR	428,312	12.6%
Other / Not reported	1,244,889	36.8%
Total population	21,645,535	
Under 20 years	6,196,048	28.6%
20 to 34 years	5,313,141	24.5%
35 to 64 years	8,518,051	39.4%
65 and over	1,458,046	6.7%
Not reported	160,249	0.8%
Total population**	21,645,535	
White	19,473,297	90.0%
Black	2,142,394	9.9%
Other	57,367	0.3%
Total population	21,645,535	
Male	10,586,049	48.9%
Female	11,059,486	51.1%

Source: *Social Explorer* 1950 Census Tract.

* Percentages do not always add up to 100.00, likely due to rounded figures in the original data.

** Inconsistencies in data might be due to unreleased Census figures.

TABLE 2.4 FOREIGN-BORN IN WAYNE COUNTY (MICH.)
CENSUS TRACT 1950*

Total foreign-born population	345,627	
Canada French	9,076	2.6%
Canada Other	71,455	20.7%
England/Wales	22,537	6.5%
Germany	20,658	6.0%
Italy	28,887	8.4%
Poland	58,982	17.1%
USSR	21,645	6.3%
Other / Not reported	112,387	32.4%
Total population	2,373,404	
Under 20 years	730,781	30.8%
20 to 34 years	619,534	26.1%
35 to 64 years	891,934	37.6%
65 and over	131,155	5.5%
Total population	2,373,404	
White	2,037,548	85.9%
Black	332,237	14.0%
Other	3,619	0.2%
Total population	2,373,404	
Male	1,191,748	50.2%
Female	1,181,656	49.8%

Source: *Social Explorer* 1950 Census Tract.
* Percentages do not always add up to 100.00, likely due to rounded figures in the original data.

TABLE 2.5 FOREIGN-BORN IN COOK COUNTY (CHICAGO, ILL.) CENSUS TRACT 1950

Total foreign-born population	613,883	
Canada French	2,576	0.4%
Canada Other	19,103	3.1%
Germany	68,297	11.1%
Ireland	32,265	5.3%
Italy	64,661	10.5%
Poland	102,759	16.7%
USSR	56,035	9.1%
Other / Not reported	268,187	43.8%
Total population	4,489,431	
Under 20 years	1,261,919	28.1%
20 to 34 years	1,108,373	24.7%
35 to 64 years	1,783,294	39.7%
65 and over	335,845	7.5%
Total population	4,489,431	
White	3,949,604	88.0%
Black	521,533	11.6%
Other / Not reported	18,294	0.4%
Total population	4,489,431	
Male	2,204,254	49.1%
Female	2,285,177	50.9%

Source: *Social Explorer* 1950 Census Tract.

TABLE 2.6 FOREIGN-BORN IN OHIO CENSUS TRACTS 1950*

Total foreign-born population	282,517	
Canada French	1,192	0.4%
Canada Other	12,497	4.4%
Czechoslovakia	24,091	8.5%
Germany	33,297	11.8%
Hungary	29,062	10.3%
Italy	30,653	10.8%
Poland	30,832	10.9%
Other / Not reported	120,893	42.9%
Total population	3,649,464	
Under 20 years	1,083,859	29.7%
20 to 34 years	909,430	24.9%
35 to 64 years	1,362,526	37.3%
65 and over	293,649	8.0%
Total population	3,649,464	
White	3,265,272	89.5%
Black	380,460	10.4%
Other	3,732	0.1%
Total population	3,649,464	
Male	1,779,519	48.8%
Female	1,869,945	51.2%

Source: *Social Explorer* 1950 Census Tract.

* Percentages do not always add up to 100.00, likely due to rounded figures in the original data.

TABLE 2.7 FOREIGN-BORN IN NEW YORK COUNTIES:
ERIE, MONROE, NEW YORK, AND ONONDAGA 1950

Total foreign-born population	630,253	
Canada French	3,688	0.6%
Canada Other	32,794	5.2%
Germany	83,671	13.3%
Ireland	55,140	8.7%
Italy	103,723	16.5%
Poland	62,838	10.0%
USSR	59,822	9.5%
Other / Not reported	228,577	36.2%
Total population	3,411,590	
Under 20 years	851,021	24.9%
20 to 34 years	853,297	25.0%
35 to 64 years	1,409,037	41.3%
65 and over	252,241	7.4%
Not reported	45,994	1.4%
Total population*	3,411,590	
White	2,971,980	87.1%
Black	436,841	12.8%
Other	21,789	0.6%
Total population	3,411,590	
Male	1,645,773	48.2%
Female	1,765,817	51.8%

Source: *Social Explorer* 1950 Census Tract.

* Inconsistencies in data might be due to unreleased Census figures.

CHAPTER 3

CIVIL RIGHTS OR HUMAN RIGHTS? 1950–1967

▼ ▼ ▼

So long as lynchings, intractable segregation, and a blatantly unjust legal system cast shadows over African American life, Canada could retain its status as a beacon of hope, notwithstanding its own racial fault lines. In the wake of war against genocide and fascism, however, Canadian society could no longer conceal the racist and discriminatory practices behind a veneer of British civility and fair play. The postwar global climate proved conducive for activists who sought to cement interracial ties. In the Ontario town of Dresden—an iconic terminus of the Underground Railroad and the resting place of the purported protagonist of Harriet Beecher Stowe's *Uncle Tom's Cabin*—anti-Black discrimination strengthened the relationship between Black and Jewish communities. Hugh Burnett, an African Canadian carpenter who had enlisted briefly in the army during the Second World War, helped lead the National Unity Association (NUA), a human rights organization that Black residents from nearby Chatham and North Buxton founded in 1948. In Dresden, one of the most segregated and racist towns north of the Mason-Dixon Line, business owners routinely Jim Crowed Black people.[1]

With support from the Joint Public Relations Committee, the Association for Civil Liberties, and Canada's Jewish Labor Committee, an outgrowth of the U.S. equivalent, the National Unity Association tapped into a wide network of postwar human rights activists who lobbied the provincial government to act in July 1949. Five months later, a town referendum unmasked Canada's worst-kept secret. A secret ballot asked whether residents "approved of the Council passing a by-law licensing restaurants in Dresden and restraining owners from refusing service regardless of race, creed or color." They overwhelmingly rejected the measure, voting 517 in opposition and 108 in favor. This five-to-one margin corresponded with the town's white and Black population, drawing a sharp electoral line through the community. Tapping into Cold War paranoia, Burnett seized on the racial divide: "There are no Communists among the colored people of Dresden, but I don't know how long we can assure that, if the discrimination practiced there is to continue."[2] Despite the resounding setback of the town referendum, Burnett and the National Unity Association maintained their resolve to exorcise the ghost of Jim Crow from Dresden and other parts of Ontario.

Under the umbrella of human rights—not civil rights, which require nationalist political instruments—the protections that Canada afforded racial and ethnic minorities, women, and workers improved gradually in the postwar period.[3] After its distinguished contribution to the Allied and Commonwealth cause in the Second World War, Canada emerged as an aspiring middle power, but it remained in the perpetual shadow of U.S. military and economic might.[4] Nonetheless, Canadian officials hedged the country's postwar national interests by aligning with multilateral institutions, such as the United Nations, which they believed could rein in the imperial ambitions of the United States.[5]

As the global Cold War intensified, Ottawa embraced liberal internationalism, the doctrine that promotes Western liberal policies, and recognized Washington, not London, as the leader of a new world order. In its pursuit of human rights, specifically antidiscrimination legislation, Canada accrued moral authority, which functioned as soft power to counterbalance U.S. influence and as a way for Canada to assert itself in global affairs. Ottawa bureaucrats—and Canadians in general—had long believed that "the problem of the color line" was uniquely an "American dilemma."[6] By 1959, exercising moral authority, especially on matters of racial discrimination and other injustices, positioned Canada to showcase its ascendancy, illustrating the limitations of U.S. hard power. With Canada's fiercely guarded and romanticized abolitionist legacy, the prospect of postwar moral authority through moral suasion appealed to white Canadians.

Black, Jewish, and Asian activists' demands for human rights in the early twentieth century amid the failure of British rights rhetoric provided the initial impetus for officials to address oppression based on race, ethnicity, religion, and gender. As early as 1920, in fact, signatories of the Pan-Africanist Universal Negro Improvement Association at New York City's Madison Square Garden, five of whom were Canadian, codified a Declaration of Rights of the Negro Peoples of the World. Article 52 stipulated that all nations and multilateral organizations must respect the "human rights" of Black people.[7] As a signatory to the 1948 UN Universal Declaration of Human Rights (UDHR), unlike the United States, Canada had a national and international obligation to address racism and other discriminatory practices.[8] Canadian legal scholar John Peters Humphrey, a staunch socialist, served as the UDHR's chief legal architect. Canada's embrace of the UDHR was not inevitable, however. Since preliminary drafts of the Declaration advocated social, political, civil, and economic rights, the mainstream Canadian establishment—particularly business elites, center-right politicians, and conservative lawyers—rejected the UDHR. Despite U.S. former First Lady Eleanor Roosevelt serving as chairperson of the UN Commission on Human Rights, which produced the UDHR, U.S. officials expressed hostility to the Declaration from its inception, mostly because of southern attitudes on "states' rights." Furthermore, Franklin Roosevelt's application of the New Deal's principle of individual security to global security in 1941 did not improve the perception of international human rights in the United States.[9]

Canada's embrace of liberal internationalism meant that it had to address its own human rights violations. Through progressive federal and provincial legislation, Canada tackled, sometimes begrudgingly, matters where it had erred egregiously, such as the formal and informal systems of anti-Black racial subordination and subjugation, dispossession of Indigenous peoples, internment of Japanese Canadians, a moratorium on Chinese immigration and discriminatory treatment of other Asian groups, and enabling widespread anti-Semitism.[10] Ottawa's international ambitions created an opening for domestic social change, one that finally brought African descendants' historic grievances of racial injustice into the national consciousness.[11] In this new and complex social landscape, critiquing U.S. race relations had the effect of signaling white Canadians' acceptance of a multiracial polity while vindicating Canada's domestic racial record toward vulnerable groups.

While Burnett and the National Unity Association provided the early grassroots leadership, African American Daniel Grafton Hill III worked within the state apparatus to enforce human rights legislation, advocating on behalf of marginalized groups, including newly arrived immigrants. The pages that follow uncover the critical role that Hill played in human rights advocacy in postwar Canada. Hill's doctoral research on Black community building in 1950s Toronto and his experience as a U.S. immigrant with intimate knowledge of Jim Crow proved integral to a multiracial Canada in search of moral authority. Canada's gentle pivot toward human rights positioned Hill to leave an indelible mark on his adopted society. Hill's cross-border consciousness is a blueprint of how a U.S. pan-Africanist imagined freedom outside the constraints of McCarthyism to effect change for African North Americans.[12] Moreover, this chapter introduces the "paradox of progress" to illustrate the intractability of "race" in the promising postwar period and the challenges of using human rights to mitigate centuries of racist attitudes and systemic practices. The rights regime allowed states to consolidate power and, with sufficient external pressure, legislate change. For these reasons, one historian of human rights cautioned that historians should avoid arguments predicated on "linear progressivism."[13] The analysis juxtaposes Hill's doctoral research and social advocacy for the pathbreaking Ontario Human Rights Commission (OHRC) with a U.S. human rights case that attracted global attention to reveal tensions, contradictions, and breakthroughs. The geopolitical forces and racial tension that pushed Hill to Toronto in the summer of 1950 are rooted in a pan-African conscious-ness that nineteenth-century African American intellectuals and activists championed. A borderless, hemispheric racial community beckoned the mobile to aid Black freedom struggles wherever they landed.

"SON, YOU ARE NOT MADE FOR THIS COUNTRY"

Born in Independence, Missouri, on 23 November 1923, Daniel G. Hill III was the son of a Lincoln University graduate, Howard University theolo-gian, and ordained minister of the African Methodist Episcopal Church. His mother, May Edwards Hill, was a Howard University alumna and social worker. Despite coming of age in a social milieu where racial subordina-tion and subjugation of African Americans was the law of the land, Daniel Hill III could access social mobility unknown to most Black people of his generation. He inherited a racial calling—a consciousness refined on the battleground of U.S. race relations.

Much of Hill's outlook on racial justice came from his middle-class family, which was committed to civil rights and the Black church. His parents fit the archetype of educated, progressive Race Men and Women in the early twentieth century. The elder Hill, like other Black men in U.S. society at the dawn of the Great War, enlisted because he saw military service as an avenue to full citizenship and manhood. As historians have pointed out, for African Americans, military service and the prospects of valor mitigated the shame of Jim Crow.[14]

When the elder Hill returned home to Washington, D.C., in 1919 from France, he had few economic prospects. A life in ministry became both a spiritual calling and a practical one. The AME Church ordained him. Because of their father's itinerant career as a minister, Daniel Hill III and his sisters, Jean, Margaret, and Doris, lived in several states—Oregon, Colorado, and Kansas—before settling in Washington, D.C. The AME Church sent the family to Portland, Oregon, during the depression, where the city's Black shantytown constituted the senior Hill's parish. "I saw sights there, hovels, shacks, that will never, never let me forget my roots—never let me forget the poor and those who are in need," the younger Hill recalled.[15] Experiencing racism was one form of social injury. However, witnessing both hopeless-ness and economic deprivation, in addition to anti-blackness, was another.

His parents' professions as church minister and social worker shielded him from poverty, meaning he received ample instruction on personal and social responsibility. Although Hill's family described him as an "irrepressible and rambunctious" youth with a "predilection for mischief," he acquired his parents' sense of moral courage in adulthood.[16] His parents also admonished him to become his sisters' keeper, drilling into him the meaning of honor. His mother and father taught their restless son, "The gentlemen always protect the women of the family."[17] In a racially violent society that denied Black men their manhood, Black men's expressions of chivalry and affection for Black women illustrated the ways that working- and middle-class Black families negotiated gender and race. Hill enjoyed an endearing and affectionate relationship with his three sisters.

Hill had the blessing—or burden—of having many "firsts" in his family lineage. His maternal grandfather, Dr. Thomas W. Edwards, was the first Black dentist in Washington, D.C. An aunt became one of the country's first Black women psychiatrists and the first Black woman gynecologist to practice in New Jersey.[18] Hill's mother, May, served on the board of Planned Parenthood in the interwar years. Some parishioners in her husband's congregation misconstrued her progressive views on women's rights as her endorsement of "casual relations."[19]

Two of his forebears purchased their freedom; they also bought their spouses' and children's freedom. Born into slavery in Virginia, Hill's paternal great-grandparents Richard Hill and Demias Crew purchased their freedom and that of their eight children in 1858.[20] Gabriel Coakley, his maternal great-great-grandfather, purchased his entire family's freedom in Maryland for $3,300 in 1862, months before President Lincoln issued the Emancipation Proclamation. Coakley, along with a few other free Black people, with Lincoln's permission, hosted a fundraiser for the District's only Black Catholic church on the White House lawn. President Lincoln and First Lady Mary Todd Lincoln attended and donated money. Because of his adroit networking, Coakley's daughter—Genevieve, Hill's maternal great-grandmother—found work as a seamstress in the White House of General Ulysses S. Grant. An unidentified white laborer who worked at the White House raped sixteen-year-old Genevieve. Her fatherless daughter was Hill's maternal grandmother, Marie Coakley.[21] That which gave Hill pride and resilience also gave him pause—even more as he learned about the ways of U.S. slavery and Jim Crow. After his distinguished service in the Second World War, Hill immigrated to Canada in 1950 to pursue graduate studies at the University of Toronto. Although Hill found Canadian society hospitable upon arrival, geopolitics, specifically the Red Scare sentiments of the Cold War, limited social and economic progress. For example, on 12 May 1952 at Maple Leaf Gardens in Toronto, the leftist, anti-imperialist Canadian Peace Congress sponsored a rally in which they invited W. E. B. Du Bois to speak alongside Canadian peace champion James Endicott. But Canadian immigration officials prevented Du Bois—one of the most famous Black intellectuals and Pan-Africanists of his era and a known leftist—from leaving the Toronto airport. They feared that he would poison the minds of both Black and white Canadians.[22]

Hill understood that he must till the soil of adversity before he could harvest the fruits of racial progress. After returning to the United States to teach at Morgan State College in Baltimore in the summer of 1951, he went back to the University of Toronto, this time for a doctorate in sociology. His relocation and intellectual projects in Canadian society subsequently changed the course of Ontario's and Canada's postwar freedom movement.

In 1952, while visiting a friend in Washington, D.C., he had a chance encounter. He met Donna Bender, a civil rights activist and aide to Democratic senator Herbert Lehman. Bender, who came from a white Republican family in Chicago, had immersed herself in the African American freedom struggle after graduating from Oberlin College. She lived in an interracial co-op, much to the consternation of her family and friends. "Her eyes brimmed with intelligence and fire," Hill recalled of their serendipitous encounter. "She was well acquainted with the black experience in America, and that was a good thing, because I didn't want to have to educate her."[23]

The interracial couple married on 8 June 1953 at the elder Hill's chapel located on the Howard University campus, notwithstanding objections from both families. Because of the prohibition of interracial marriage in some states, the couple decided to live permanently in Toronto, where Hill pursued his Ph.D. Hill's decision to leave his birth country is rooted in a pan-African imaginary of African American women and men who embraced voluntary and often informed immigration as a critique of U.S. citizenship. The elder Hill once admonished his child, "Son, you are not made for this country."[24] And before Hill moved to Toronto, his father reminded him, "You are not blessed with the temperament to live in the U.S. Get out before this country destroys you."[25]

Once in Toronto, the Hills realized that one could not simply escape anti-blackness by emigrating from the United States. Racism permeated Canadian society. When the Hills searched for an apartment, they quickly observed a recurring pattern: landlords drew the color line. Because Ontario did not legally outlaw housing discrimination until 1962, when the government introduced an amendment to the province's Fair Accommodation

Practices Act, the couple enlisted the assistance of a white jazz musician whom Hill had befriended when he first lived in Toronto in 1950. The plan worked. The musician pretended to be Donna's husband, as Hill waited out of sight during apartment viewings. After the landlord discovered that an interracial couple lived in one of his units, Donna Hill recalled that he "watched Dan and me for six weeks or so and decided we weren't going to cause any horrible problems . . . and finally let us sign a lease [in their own names] for about $80 a month plus parking."[26] This first skirmish strengthened the couple's resolve to ensure that racialized peoples acquired the legal mechanisms and institutional backing to rid their society of structural discrimination.

RETRACTING THE "JIM CROW IRON CURTAIN"

In the tradition of W. E. B. Du Bois's *The Philadelphia Negro*, in September 1953 Daniel Hill embarked on a doctoral dissertation on African descendants titled "Negroes in Toronto: A Sociological Study of a Minority Group."[27] This seven-year project was a blueprint on postwar Black activism in Toronto. Because of Hill's unfamiliarity with the racial dynamics and history of Canadian society, his participant observation gave him insight into Black Toronto—a requisite step to redressing racial injustice for the community. Although Hill's study tried to represent sparsely populated Black communities throughout Toronto, much of his ethnography is centered on a neighborhood called "the District" in lower Ward IV—an area comprising Front and Bathurst Streets in the downtown section with small rowhouses and factories, just north of Lake Ontario. Hill described the District, a working-class neighborhood, as "a reception center" for postwar settlement. The District had high poverty and residential density, along with a dearth of recreational space.[28] Municipal demographic data estimated nearly 1,100 Black people of Canadian, Caribbean, and U.S. birth resided in the District in 1951, just 3 percent of the neighborhood's population.[29]

"Negroes in Toronto" uncovered a rich history of Black Toronto. Their demographics and ancestry, employment, and religious life complicated what Hill dismissed as "the myth of a negro community." Hill perceived a lack of racial cohesion, waning organizations, low racial consciousness, and an effort by the Canadian-born middle-class members to integrate into white society in the first half of the twentieth century. His analysis influenced historian Robin Winks to embrace a pessimistic outlook on African Canadians in his seminal study *The Blacks in Canada*.[30] But unlike Winks, Hill did not rule out the possibility of a postwar resurgence for Canadians of African descent. In fact, due to postwar transformations, Hill later urged Winks to reconsider his book's negative conclusions.[31]

In Hill, Canada gained a Black intellectual whose intimate knowledge of U.S. race relations dovetailed with national aspirations for postwar global legitimacy grounded in the liberal internationalist value of human rights. In striving to give African Canadians a platform for civic protest and group solidarity during the 1950s, Hill parlayed his research findings into advocacy and social policy. While he worked on his dissertation from 1955 to 1957, he also served as the research director of the Toronto Welfare Council, as well as the executive secretary of the North York Area Social Planning Council from 1957 to 1960. These administrative roles provided Hill with critical insight into public policy.

Hill's equally committed and resourceful wife resumed her activism in Toronto. Donna Hill's efforts to help Black activists win antidiscrimination legislation and her penchant for racial justice complemented her husband's scholarship. Starting in 1953, she worked as the executive secretary of the Toronto Labor Committee for Human Rights (TLCHR), which investigated racial discrimination, often notifying the media of its findings. This organization was part of a broader strategy by civil society groups to pressure the government to introduce holistic antidiscrimination legislation that had teeth. Donna Hill believed that Ontario's 1951 Fair Employment Practices legislation—a landmark action that forbade job discrimination along ethnic, racial, and religious lines—"existed as a monument to good-hearted hypocrisy."[32]

Although a positive leap, postwar legislation against discrimination required dedicated activists to test the efficacy of the law.[33] As the executive secretary of the TLCHR, Donna Hill worked alongside Bromley Armstrong—a Jamaican immigrant and labor activist. Using test cases to expose prejudiced proprietors, they coordinated massive letter-writing campaigns that exposed rampant segregation in Toronto and other southwestern Ontario communities. The committee sought to recruit individuals who would assist with testing whether businesses and landlords discriminated against Black and other minorities.[34]

Donna Hill's work with the TLCHR had earned her a reputation as a committed ally of racial minorities. When members of the Brotherhood of Sleeping Car Porters invited her in 1953 to speak at their Toronto local about racial discrimination, she had a chance encounter with Harry Gairey, a porter and senior community ambassador in Black Toronto. "Harry Gairey attended that meeting and later asked me to work with the Negro Citizenship Association in its struggle to change Canada's discriminatory immigration policies," she recalled. "He came to my office again with information leading to one of the first federal [Fair Employment Practices] incidents, a case which had nothing to do with Blacks but concerned a Japanese medical student whose application for a summer job as a CPR [Canadian Pacific Railway] cook had been rejected."[35] The Black community's commitment to securing justice for all Canadians encouraged Donna Hill. As a white woman with intimate connections to the Black freedom struggle, she humanized her fellow Black activists, similar to how Black activists validated her sincerity and knowledge of race relations to the dominant society.

Donna Hill reluctantly resigned from the TLCHR right before giving birth to her first child in the spring of 1954.[36] Although Donna enjoyed her grassroots human rights work and looked forward to motherhood, the chauvinist sentiments of the 1960s and her husband's desire to be the sole household breadwinner, notwithstanding his ferocious affection for and devotion to her, is why he asked her to quit her job and become a full-time household manager.[37] But before the demands of childbirth, childcare, and family monopolized most of her time, she assisted the Negro Citizenship Association to draft a monumental report published on 27 April 1954. Don Moore, president and another elder Black statesman, and thirty-four other delegates, with the support of organized labor, clergy, and community groups, presented the report to immigration minister Walter Harris.

During their meeting with the minister, the 1954 delegation asserted that Canada's resistance to the immigration of African descendants directly contravened the spirit of the Universal Declaration of Human Rights. One of the delegation officers told the immigration minister that Canada must retract its "Jim Crow Iron Curtain."[38] This forthrightness sounded a major death knell of the whites-only Canadian immigration policy, which discriminated against not only prospective Black nation-builders but also Jews and Asians, specifically Chinese immigrants.[39] The 1954 meeting, in sum, also signaled that African Canadians had every intention of holding the federal and provincial governments accountable to Canada's commitment to uphold human rights.

The suspicion that Canada, at its core, adhered to the same morally bankrupt racist logic as the United States resurfaced in a most embarrassing episode for Ottawa in 1954, weeks after the Negro Citizenship Association conferred with the immigration minister. Known as the "Adams affair" in confidential British diplomatic cables, a hotel in Montreal denied Barbados premier Grantley Adams lodging on his layover from London to Barbados on 26 October 1954.[40] As Canadian and British diplomats scrambled to ease the fallout, one newspaper apologetically attributed the incident to "a clerk's stupidity."[41]

Secretary of State for External Affairs Lester B. Pearson, a staunch liberal internationalist, wrote a remorseful letter to Adams. Referencing Canada's

Hill family: Daniel G. Hill III, Dan IV, Larry, Karen, and Donna. Archives of Ontario. Courtesy of Lawrence Hill.

commitment to the UDHR, the chief diplomat had to genuflect before the altar of racial atonement. "You are, of course, aware of the position of the Canadian Government on the question of racial discrimination as stated by its representatives at the United Nations and elsewhere," Pearson pleaded.[42] Pearson encouraged Adams not to let the unfortunate incident sully the "friendly relations" between Barbados and Canada.[43] Yet Canada's Immigration Act barred nearly all dark-hued members of the Commonwealth, Barbados included. Although the Adams affair was sensational anti-Black racism, the restriction against Black immigrants was more profound and global in its reach.

Senior officials managed to disarm a potentially explosive situation. The British high commissioner to Canada recommended that his subordinates notify him whenever "West Indian notables" or "V.I.Ps." planned to visit Canada, like the protocol in place for the Bahamas, Bermuda, New York, and Washington, D.C., where U.S. officials refused Adams's entry in June 1952.[44] One cannot overstate the Montreal incident's potential damage, considering Cold War racial politics. An unidentified source on the "Adams affair" stated that Westerners "too often adopt attitudes which are excellent feeding grounds for Communist propaganda."[45] As historians of U.S. foreign relations have observed, the Cold War's strategic bipolarity had to confront global white supremacy.[46] As Daniel and Donna Hill combined scholarship and human rights activism in Toronto, they observed on multiple occasions that Canadian society fell short of a racial utopia. But hope existed, nevertheless.

THE SPIRIT OF THE TIMES
AND THE PARADOX OF PROGRESS

The Canadian public had an insatiable appetite for sensational news of U.S. racism. It fueled the paradox of progress, which made Canadians feel exonerated of their record on racism. Race, in fact, influenced the identity that Canadians wanted to project to a postwar world. Race also shaped Canadians' perceptions of the United States, a society that, they believed, lacked the virtues of British civility concerning the treatment of Black people. For Canadians, the enduring legacies of these historical processes continued to permeate notions of race, justice, and freedom. As such, some white Canadians, especially those of British origin, used race relations in the United States not only as a litmus test of sorts to disavow claims of racism in Canadian society but also as the standard by which they could deny accusations of subtle yet insidious forms of Canadian racism, especially anti-blackness.

The myth of the Canadian refuge point—the North Star—endured, partly because of Canada's proximity to a racist United States. To Canadian citizens and newcomers, such as Daniel and Donna Hill in the postwar years, racial progress constituted a slippery paradox. Sensational coverage of lynchings, segregation, and a two-tiered legal system in the United States allowed Canada and Canadians to project an image of goodwill, masking systemic white supremacy. Herein lies the paradox of progress: social regression in one place erroneously created the *perception* of progress in another. That the nadir of Canadian race relations could not compare to the post-Reconstruction anti-Black racial terrorism in the United States made it difficult for accusations of racism in Canadian society to gain wide traction. The paradox of progress aided Canada's pursuit of moral authority via human rights.

As white Canadians remained adamant that theirs was a tolerant society, many demanded de facto segregation of their neighborhoods and social spaces. This hypocrisy frustrated the pursuit of "Black lebensraum" in Canada.[47] The Hills faced another unfortunate encounter with segregated housing after purchasing their first home in the Toronto suburb of

Newmarket in 1955. With a population under 10,000 and all white, many of Newmarket's residents had emigrated from the British Isles in the wake of the war to work on the Avro Arrow, Canada's groundbreaking Cold War supersonic jet interceptor. Interracial families like the Hills were still unusual in most parts of the country in the postwar period. When their eldest child, Dan Hill IV, started kindergarten, he recalled a peculiar exercise to which his teacher subjected him and his classmates. "Time to check for niggers under your fingernails, children!" his teacher demanded.[48] Within months of living in Newmarket, some residents approached Donna Hill's best friend and the family's next-door neighbor, asking her to sign a petition to oust the interracial family.[49] Newmarket's homogeneity was not exceptional. The few Black people in Toronto (under 5,000) and lack of economic opportunities kept most middle-class residential neighborhoods lily white.[50]

Nonetheless, the paradox of progress enabled Canadians to criticize U.S. racism in the 1950s. When an infamous miscarriage of justice in Alabama aroused Canadian indignation in 1958, the Hills felt puzzled by a society that subscribed to white supremacist ideals yet repudiated it swiftly when it occurred in a "racist" country, such as the United States. The Jimmy Wilson case, a blow to U.S. reputation during the Cold War, revealed how Canadians understood race relations in their own country as human rights norms gained traction.[51]

In August 1958, news of African American Jimmy Wilson's imminent death by electrocution in less than eight days for petty larceny in Alabama shocked Canadians' notions of democracy and the rule of law.[52] Within five days of airing, the death sentence inspired Canadian citizens—homemakers, children and students, business owners, trade unionists, and newly arrived immigrants—to submit over 3,000 letters of petition that played a pivotal role in the governor's decision to grant clemency to the condemned Black man.[53] One white Torontonian, Kay Lines, felt so incensed at the news that she called her personal friend Kwame Nkrumah, Ghana's first prime minister. Lines and her husband had lived and worked in Accra, Ghana (formerly the Gold Coast), from 1951 to 1956. She pleaded for Nkrumah to "investigate and lead a world protest."[54] Other people around the world also expressed outrage. From London to Montevideo to Jamaica, Europeans and racialized peoples peppered U.S. consulates with petitions and published editorials in newspapers deriding the self-appointed leader of the free world for its shameful treatment of African Americans.[55]

Jimmy Wilson, a fifty-four-year-old handyman and occasional transient, worked odd jobs in sparsely populated Marion, Alabama. Estelle Barker, an elderly white widow who occasionally hired Wilson to complete chores around her house and yard, alleged that he had robbed her on 27 July 1957. According to Barker, Wilson became physically and sexually suggestive in his demands. "He threw me on the bed, pulled off my stepins, and attempted to rape me, that is what he did."[56] Barker's testimony painted the stereotypical image of the lascivious Black male who preys on white women.[57] An all-white jury, after hearing Barker's testimony, handed Wilson a swift death sentence not for assault but for robbery.

One white resident of Newmarket, the same subdivision where the Hills faced a town-led eviction and where at least one public school teacher routinely evoked "nigger" as an epithet when addressing her students, issued a swift condemnation of U.S. race relations. "This is a poor example to the world of American democracy," he wrote. "It is little wonder that American prestige has sunk into the gutter in the past few years. . . . Does not the law say that a man on trial shall be tried by an unbiased jury[?]" To substantiate his claim that the United States was losing favor among overseas white people, the petitioner claimed that Canadians "are slowly losing their respect for Americans."[58]

White women made up over two-thirds of the petitioners.[59] Demanding clemency, one petitioner justified her outrage using words that were part and parcel of the Canadian imagination of the United States. "I am a Canadian and a proud one and I know and am proud to say this action will never happen in Canada. And I know if I were living where this Negro man lives in the same State and I being a white woman I would be ashamed." At its core, this self-proclaimed Canadian patriot's indictment of U.S. racism also alluded to the role white women in the South played in lynching culture. "When I heard the story over my Radio," she added, "I just couldn't believe it was true. I feel sorry for this man and his people; maybe I should feel sorry for the White people who are wishing him to receive the death sentence."[60] This significant yet mostly unknown episode in Canadian postwar human rights activism illustrated how white Canadians used gross miscarriages of justice as an opportunity to showcase progressive attitudes. They pointed out the stark divide in the United States between rhetoric and ideals on one hand and blatant racial injustice on the other.

As citizens with a global consciousness, Canadians repeatedly framed their activism in a Cold War discourse that challenged Washington's credibility to lead the free world, arguing that some parts of the United States resembled the communist bloc. The sententious critiques that Canadians leveled at U.S. society were rooted in the Anglo-Atlantic abolitionist legacy that Canada allegedly inherited from Britain. Because the British offered token freedom to enslaved Africans during the U.S. Revolutionary War and

Toronto Woman Calls Ghana in Appeal to Save Negro

12,500-MILE TELEPHONE call to Ghana was made by Mrs. Kay Lines of Toronto, right, to ask Premier Kwame Nkrumah to appeal for life of Alabama Negro Jimmy Wilson, sentenced to die for robbery of $1.95.

"Toronto Woman Calls Ghana in Appeal to Save Negro," Toronto Daily Star, 22 August 1958. Toronto Public Library.

Ghanaian prime minister Kwame Nkrumah meeting Canadian prime minister John Diefenbaker on an official state visit to Canada in July 1959. University of Saskatchewan, Saskatoon, University Archives and Special Collections.

Cabinet of Ghana's first president, Kwame Nkrumah. Nkrumah sent this photo to Inez
Walker-Barker, granddaughter of C. W. French, delegate from Saint Kitts who spoke at the
1900 Pan-African Conference in London. Courtesy of Alphonse Pierpont "Big Al" Barker.

the War of 1812—a geopolitical, military strategy that led to the relocation
of a few thousand Black people to British North America (Canada)—in
addition to the nominal abolition of the slave trade in 1807 and slavery in
1834 and tacit support of the Underground Railroad, white Canadians had
a semblance of moral authority when critiquing U.S. racism and hegemony.

In Canada, this news of another persecuted African American fostered
interracial alliance. The solidarity between Jews and African Canadians had
begun in the interwar years, and it revealed the capacity for ordinary citizens
to redress racism and discrimination. Although interracial cooperation ebbs
and flows in situations where minorities compete for scarce resources in a
racially stratified society, compassion between Jews and African Canadians
persisted. Stanley Grizzle, one of the leading Black labor organizers for the
Brotherhood of Sleeping Car Porters, described Jews and Black folk—who
attended the same schools and resided in the same neighborhoods, with
Jews the only group that consistently rented housing to Black tenants in
Toronto—as a "community of suffering."[61]

It is understandable, then, why fourteen-year-old petitioner Alan Kruger
submitted a letter in Wilson's behalf. His Jewish identity helped him understand a complicated issue. "We all hear great propaganda about the free

U.S.A. where everyone has an equal chance," he wrote. "Isn't this fact a little over emphasized[?]" Kruger recalled, "I have read a lot about the situation in the South and I recall in my mind about a young Negro youth named Till who was attacked and killed by some white men for [allegedly] whistling at a white woman." He continued: "They were all acquitted. A similar incident took place recently. That was in the U.S.A. where everyone has an equal chance."[62]

Kruger's assessment of U.S. racial injustice had much to do with his family's experience with anti-Jewish discrimination in early postwar Toronto.[63] But unlike most Canadian petitioners, Kruger understood, as a minority, that racism also existed in Canadian society. He developed a racial consciousness because of growing "up in a house where everybody felt an obligation to equal rights." He explained, "There was a lot of prejudice in Toronto in the fifties. My father was very aware of it. There were a lot of exclusions. When you went to the beach there were signs that said 'no Dogs or Jews.'" In his youth, Kruger and his family participated in civil rights marches at the University of Toronto in a show of solidarity with the African American freedom struggle. "Canadians hold themselves as superior to the Americans," Kruger acknowledged, "but there was just as much discrimination here as in the United States."[64]

The *Toronto Daily Star* sent Martin Goodman—an affable, up-and-coming twenty-three-year-old Jewish Canadian reporter—to cover the Wilson case in Alabama. He secured an exclusive interview with Wilson. "It wasn't considered major news," Goodman wrote, "until *The Star*, a Chicago magazine and the Associated Press inquired into it."[65] Covering a story about racial injustice that involved an African American accused of robbery and attempted rape in the Deep South, a place hostile to African descendants and Jews, underscored Goodman's conviction in fighting racism.[66] For this Canadian, discrimination against any group was unconscionable. He was "a principled man; a man who stood up for justice," said Goodman's childhood friend.[67]

The *Toronto Daily Star* broke the news in the Canadian print media one week before radio station CKEY informed radio listeners on 28 August 1958 about Jimmy Wilson's looming execution. On 20 August, Goodman published an exclusive interview with Wilson while the accused sat on death row at a state penitentiary. The article made the front page.[68] Goodman painted a bleak image of Wilson, perhaps one of the only descriptive accounts we have of him. "His cheeks sunken, his eyes haggard, he perspired during our hour-long interview, though the warden's office was air-conditioned." As he inquired into the alleged robbery and rape, he noticed Wilson's uneasiness.

"He crossed and uncrossed his arms, patted his shoulders and scratched his short, gray fuzzy hair while puzzling two syllable words." When Goodman probed further, Wilson broke his silence and strung together a response that challenged his conviction and death sentence. "They never asked me anything. The policeman that arrested me . . . he didn't ask. He say 'that's how it happened, wasn't it?' I say 'no.' He cuffed me until I say 'yeah . . . that's how.'"[69]

In Wilson's words, the events that led to his arrest and death sentence began on a Friday evening when he and an acquaintance decided to celebrate after picking and then selling a day's worth of cotton. "That was bad . . . an old man like me . . . but it was only drinking. All of a sudden I didn't have any more money." After spending his earnings, Wilson needed more to get through the weekend. The following day, a Saturday, Wilson thought of a plan that had worked in the past: "I had worked once for Mrs. Barker and she loaned me some money against my wages," Wilson recalled. "So I went back. She refused. I thought about it all day and went back again. She must have been scared because she gave me some, about $1.50." This sum is less than what the county solicitor alleged he had robbed from Barker, a sum that he spent on his return cab fare from Barker's home. Wilson said that when he returned to Barker's home for the second time that Saturday, she "was sitting into a rocker. . . . She told me to come in. I ain't lyin' . . . before God I ain't."[70]

Wilson said that he and Barker exchanged some words before she finally agreed to give him money. "She reached inside her purse," Wilson recounted, "and threw the change on the bed. I asked for more but she said she didn't have no more. I never touched her. I never broke in. I know I shouldn't have been drinking . . . but I didn't do anything wrong. I know there isn't much good to me . . . but I'm telling the truth. I don't want to die." According to Goodman, Wilson "steadfastly denied having made any attempt to assault the woman and added that the police had beaten him to confess that he had."[71]

That Wilson had been alone with a white woman at a private dwelling made him guilty in the court of southern public opinion. For this reason, one petitioner from Toronto noted, "It soon became apparent to me that this man was being executed not for robbery, but for the 'alleged,' mind you, just 'ALLEGED,' assault of a white woman."[72] A Toronto couple pleaded, "It would be a crime to the human race to execute a man on such flimsy grounds, as prejudice is very obvious. . . . The people in the U.S.A. are terrible narrow-minded about the negros."[73]

A Toronto resident expressed her outrage over the South's gender politics: "Why by the looks of things down there it seems to be a crime to walk down the street, talk to a white girl or go to a white school. . . . I'm glad I'm Canadian & not American."[74] Most Canadians would have disavowed that racial segregation and the strict policing and surveillance of Black (male) sexuality existed in Canadian society. The sententious tone with which many Canadians expressed their anger is of import in how postwar European Canadians viewed matters of racial injustice and human rights. Some petitioners spoke with more reason and less emotion. A Ms. Cumming of Gilford, Ontario, about an hour's drive north of Toronto, explained, "As we do not know all the details we feel a suitable jail sentence would be recommendable." Another petitioner wrote, "I can understand the death sentence for murder, but not for robbery and unproven assault."[75]

White Canadians demanded redress for racial oppression in the United States. Meanwhile, some of those same individuals who registered their outrage against the treatment of African Americans had no reservation about demanding the removal of Black and interracial families from all-white neighborhoods. Such was the contradiction and paradox of "race" in postwar Canada. And, although one would never know from the petitions to save Jimmy Wilson, the idea of the ubiquitous Black rapist also occupied a place in the Canadian political imagination.[76] In fact, so entrenched remained this fear that after Britain removed the death penalty from its inventory of capital punishments in cases involving rape, the Dominion of Canada refused in 1868 to follow the metropole's lead. It feared that the absence of the death penalty would embolden Black men to rape white women.[77]

The Wilson case allowed naturalized Canadians to comment on racial injustice in the U.S. South and around the world. When Englishman D. F. Sanderson immigrated in 1955 to Port Credit, Ontario, he understood the racial tensions that hallmarked the postwar period. "I have strong, very strong views regarding the increasing problem of racial discrimination," Sanderson admitted. "Even in London, England, it is becoming increasingly evident that this modern world in which we live no longer has any connection with democracy."[78] As both a British national and new Canadian, Sanderson's perspective, although critical of the metropole, portrayed Canadian society as racially liberal. Sanderson perceived Canada, a former colony with a majority Anglophone population, as a *new* England—one free from racial tensions, overt or subtle. And because the Dominion government adhered to strict white supremacist immigration policies, racial conflict in Canadian society appeared nonexistent or "better managed."

In a clear break from most petitioners, Sanderson prescribed a remedy that would help address the albatross of race. "The solution to the entire affair," he argued, "is surely education; education by some authority like the U.N. Council, after all, the problem is an International one."[79] As a new and proud Canadian, Sanderson's belief that the United Nations was best suited to stop racism aligned with postwar Canadian domestic and foreign policy goals that placed enormous import on multilateralism and liberal internationalism. These same institutions, and particularly Canada's role as an influential member of a multiracial Commonwealth, helped Canadian society implement human rights legislations in the 1950s and 1960s.

But the naturalized Anglo-Canadian's critiques of U.S. racism, while concomitantly recommending that an international institution dominated by Western powers end racism, exposed a blind spot. As an Englishman, Sanderson embodied Canada's most "ideal" immigrant. He critiqued U.S. racial injustice without questioning the structures of white supremacy that facilitated his immigration to Canada when Black people from the Commonwealth could not easily immigrate there. Furthermore, Canadians might have been more forgiving of U.S. race relations had they been competing with Black people for scarce economic resources and residential space on the same scale as white people in the U.S. North. In the 1950s, for example, the African American population was 15 million, or 16 percent of the U.S. Census. This figure alone was larger than Canada's entire population of 14 million, roughly 20,000 of whom were Black.

Most of the petitioners who wrote on Jimmy Wilson's behalf portrayed Canada as a racially egalitarian society. One Torontonian, with the signature "A White Canadian, who speaks for *Justice for all*," declared, "White Southerners practice a cowardly *racial discrimination and visciousness* [sic] much worse than any *Communist* could do, and which is far from civilized" (emphasis in original).[80] Another white Canadian woman stated, "We in Canada feel deep disgust when we hear how Negroes are treated in certain U.S. States; we hope it will soon be over."[81] Signing their petition "Disgusted," two Toronto sisters wrote that it is "disgraceful and outrageous for the United States and the State of Alabama to pass such a sentence on Jimmy Wilson. The whole of Toronto and a good many others feel the same way."[82]

The Cold War exposed U.S. hypocrisy, much of which stemmed from the subordinate citizenship of African Americans. A group of petitioners from a small town north of Toronto linked racism and the spread of communism, a reality that alarmed Washington.[83] "The United States of America by this so called 'trial,'" they opined, "has made a mockery of its constitution & destroyed the faith of peoples who looked upon their country as a living example of freedom & justice. In a true democracy," they continued, "there cannot be laws that apply differently for white than for colored people. In sentencing this man to death on the flimsy evidence presented at the so called 'trial,' the U.S.A has placed itself on the same level as Communist Russia who has shown in *its* 'trials' that it doesn't matter if the man sentenced is really guilty, just so long as his death serves as an example to anyone contemplating a similar act."[84]

Canadians' perceptions of U.S. hypocrisy encouraged their hubristic certainty that whites in the United States should adopt their humane views on race. Another petitioner, Florence Turner, echoed this sentiment: "Here is one of the keys to why America is slowly hated by every country in the world including we neighbors in Canada. This attitude that you are displaying openly for all the world to see and all people to question," she noted, "is just the fuel for communist propaganda that they try to create."[85]

The paradox of progress meant that critiquing racial injustice elsewhere, but especially in the United States, obfuscated anti-blackness in Canada. When Canadians denounced U.S. racism, it allayed fears, even among some African descendants, that Canadian society could be similarly racist, especially in the absence of lynch law. Thus, white Canadians incorporated Jimmy Wilson and the tens of thousands of fugitives from slavery who fled to Canada in the nineteenth century into a benign narrative that celebrated white Canadian paternalism. The paradox of progress persisted.

When radio station CKEY forwarded the petitions to Governor James Folsom's office in Montgomery, Alabama, few Canadians could have predicted the immediate impact that their activism would have on Jimmy Wilson's impending execution. With pressure mounting on U.S. diplomats around the world, the State of Alabama had to pay closer attention to the currents of international affairs. Although the Alabama Supreme Court denied Wilson's appeal following a routine motion in August 1958, the state delayed his execution date to 24 October. But by 13 September, Folsom had received over 3,000 letters from Toronto's CKEY, quipping "he was snowed under with mail from Toronto demanding clemency." He admitted that in his two terms as governor, he had "never seen anything like it." On 30 September 1958, Governor Folsom granted Jimmy Wilson clemency, although he was still subjected to a life sentence.[86]

The Wilson affair compelled Canadians to live up to the rhetoric of British justice and fair play, which, in both theory and praxis, enabled white Canadians to showcase their moral superiority vis-à-vis their counterparts in the United States. The case also helped to create a sense of moral authority and command over racial issues that white Canadians neither possessed nor fully comprehended. As historian Robin Winks observed, Canadians, historically, have believed that "they understand the American political system and that they are uncommonly well-informed on American matters."

According to Winks, who was then touring Canada and researching his book *The Blacks in Canada*, white Canadians "feel free to comment often and at length on America's racial problems." At the core, Winks believed that Canadians spoke glibly about U.S. race relations, because only a handful "are well informed on Canada's own Negro record."[87] His observations of white Canadian attitudes toward the United States amounted to a deft reading of history and the zeitgeist. It became clearer to postwar Canadian officials that interpreting the African North American experience required someone whose history and personal struggles unfolded behind the veil.[88]

DANIEL G. HILL III AND THE CONTINGENCY OF HISTORY

As an African American who had intimate knowledge of Jim Crow, Daniel Hill brought credibility to human rights advocacy and the enforcement of antidiscrimination legislation in 1960s Canada. Hill's U.S. upbringing made him a credible observer on U.S. race relations, unlike most white Canadians who primarily learned about the topic through sensational newspaper headlines. This point could also explain how an African American was more likely to receive a major leadership position on race relations in Canada than an African Canadian. White Canadians simply believed that African Americans knew much more about racial hardship than their northern siblings and thus were more likely to listen to criticisms and recommendations that came from an African American authority. Cross-border solidarity enabled African North Americans to understand that they faced a common foe in white supremacy and subordinate citizenship, which made it easy for Black communities in Ontario to welcome Hill's contributions to Canada's human rights struggle.

Hill's work on Canadian race relations came at a propitious moment. The confluence of events, which later distinguished Hill as one of the foremost statesmen of postwar North American race relations, is integral to our appreciation of how an African American came to help lead Black liberation on Canadian soil. As an interracial couple committed to fighting discrimination, Donna and Daniel Hill found unparalleled opportunities in Canada in the 1950s and 1960s to leverage their interracial partnership in ways inconceivable in U.S. society, even as they encountered racism in Canadian society.

The Hill couple was well situated for this struggle. The senior Hill once gave his son indispensable advice about marriage: "The key to happiness and success in life is to marry a woman smarter than you."[89] In choosing Donna as his wife, Hill had a fiercely loyal life partner and faithful foot soldier with whom he fought racial injustice. But Donna Hill was more than a faithful wife; she was also an adroit strategist. A case in point: after completing his Ph.D. in 1960, Hill lectured briefly at the University of Toronto, until Donna helped engineer a significant post for her husband in human rights advocacy. In the winter of 1962, Donna learned that the Ontario government would hire its first ever full-time director to oversee its new Human Rights Commission. She contacted a friend who knew the deputy minister of labor, Tom Eberle, to recommend her husband.[90] "You tell Tom Eberle," she instructed her friend over the phone, "that no one's better qualified than Dan Hill."[91] When Hill reflected on his appointment, he admitted, "I really didn't want it; I knew it would be a tough, emotionally-laden job, but my friends and my wife persuaded me that I should."[92] After Hill secured the new position, he toasted his wife in front of their friends: "Without this woman I would never have made it through the University of Toronto. And I would never have received my PhD. So let's toast Donna, the smartest, most loving woman in the world."[93] Hill might have envisioned an academic life, but he nonetheless embraced his new job and the challenges that lay ahead.

On 3 April 1962, Ontario premier John P. Robarts—a Progressive Conservative and successor of Leslie M. Frost, a skeptic turned proponent of provincial antidiscrimination legislation—appointed Hill as the inaugural director of the Ontario Human Rights Commission. The first of its kind in Canada and also the Western Hemisphere, the commission had statutory powers. One scholar, describing the pride with which Ontario politicians held Ontario's Human Rights Code, said that it was a justified "expression of provincial narcissism."[94] In his brief speech at Queen's Park, the provincial seat of power, Premier Robarts stated that the legislature "is deeply gratified by [Hill's] decision to accept this task. We feel that Dr. Hill's background and training, together with his rich experience in the field of human relations, make him admirably suited for the post."[95] Hill's appointment symbolized a watershed in postwar Canada. A new era of racial incorporation, however limited, had begun—one that was connected to hard-fought progressive transformations taking place in the U.S. civil rights movement, such as the 1964 Civil Rights Act and the 1965 Voting Rights Act.

After Hill's appointment, Allan Grossman, a cabinet minister sans portfolio, congratulated Hill. Grossman said he had "no doubt at all but that you will be a credit to the Government and to the job which has been assigned to you."[96] This acknowledgment was imbued with notions of solidarity that extended beyond partisan politics. By saluting Hill, Grossman signaled that Hill not only had the support of lawmakers but also the backing of Jewish Canadians, a community that had played a leading role in human rights advocacy, not to mention historic expressions of commonality with African Canadians.

Before Hill started his directorship on 1 June 1962, postwar Canada had witnessed major, sometimes symbolic, human rights legislations. In 1951, at the urging of organized labor and the Jewish Labor Committee, the Fair Employment Practices Act became the first human rights law at the federal level. In 1960, the National Housing Act incorporated an antidiscrimination measure. Individual politicians also took a stance. On 10 August 1960, the majority government of Prime Minister John Diefenbaker pushed through a Canadian Bill of Rights in Parliament, the first such measure at the federal level. Diefenbaker envisioned this victory as early as 1936, four years before he joined Parliament, when he drafted the initial version in the Saskatchewan provincial legislature.[97] By March 1950, the fiery politician delivered a rousing speech in Parliament outlining why Canada needed such a bold legislative step. "A national Bill of Rights would safeguard our freedoms of religion, speech, press, radio, and association," Diefenbaker averred. "It would declare the equality of all Canadians and would take a forthright stand against discrimination based on color, creed, or racial origin. It would deny," Diefenbaker continued, "that there are first- and second-class citizens in our country measured by color, race, or surname. In addition, it would protect us as individuals from the arbitrary orders made by government officials."[98]

More than simple goodwill, Diefenbaker's Bill of Rights contained an element of realpolitik. The prime minister understood that a liberal approach toward racialized peoples, many of whom became full rights-bearing members of the British Commonwealth of Nations in the postwar period, would help Ottawa expand its sphere of influence. A growing and ambitious Canada needed access to foreign markets and untapped natural resources, which meant that Canada had to treat its non-white Commonwealth partners as equals. In fact, when Diefenbaker openly rebuked apartheid South Africa at the Commonwealth Conference in March 1961, he once more signaled his endorsement of anti-racism. Diefenbaker's words also provided an opening through which racialized peoples at home and within the Commonwealth could scrutinize Canada's own record on discrimination.[99] This social milieu helped propel Daniel Hill's career as one of the foremost human rights advocates in Canada.

Diefenbaker hoped that the levers of democracy would provide the necessary checks and balances to keep government accountable to Canadians, so he recommended that the Bill of Rights contain a bicameral standing committee to oversee Parliament. "Publicity is an antiseptic," Diefenbaker asserted, "against bureaucratic and executive orders that deny freedom."[100]

Although admirable in its aims, several factors, specifically around jurisdiction, hamstrung Canada's Bill of Rights. That the federal Bill of Rights was not constitutionally entrenched precluded it from binding the provinces into compliance. This loophole meant that provincial and private entities could violate the rights of Canadians, undermining the Bill of Rights.

Saskatchewan, Diefenbaker's home province, first adopted the Bill of Rights in 1947. Other provinces incorporated features of the federal Bill of Rights. Ontario established a Human Rights Commission and presented its own Human Rights Code on 15 June 1962—two unprecedented legislative steps for a Canadian province. Unlike the federal Bill of Rights, these measures operated on a provincial level, which made them more potent. The Human Rights Code subsumed previous progressive fair practices laws that activists and Ontario legislators had designed to combat inequality. These included the 1944 Racial Discrimination Act, proscribing the display of discriminatory language in establishments; the 1950 Conveyancing Act, rendering restrictive covenants invalid in land sales; the 1951 Fair Employment Practices Act; the 1951 Female Employees' Fair Remuneration Act; the 1954 Fair Accommodations Practices Act; and the 1958 Ontario Anti-discrimination Commission Act.[101] These developments in Ontario acquired traction from the UN Universal Declaration of Human Rights, inspiring similar liberal changes in other provinces such as Quebec, British Columbia, and Nova Scotia. By 1964, Canada had become the fiftieth country to ratify the International Labor Convention concerning Discrimination in the Workplace. This measure vowed to "declare and pursue a national policy designed to promote, by methods appropriate to national conditions and practice, equality of opportunity and treatment in respect of employment and occupation, with a view of eliminating any discrimination in respect thereof."[102]

Canada, unlike the United States, institutionalized human rights legislation and commissions partly because of the United Nations and mostly because of grassroots activists, especially organized labor. Passage of anti-discrimination laws throughout Canada also stemmed from the credibility and import that activists, civic leaders, and politicians accorded the United Nations. In contrast, the United States principally focused on the power and legitimacy that the United Nations accorded it on the world stage. As an African American in Canada, Hill considered the UN's 1948 UDHR the "well-spring of Canadian legislative action against discrimination."[103] It is principally for this reason that "human rights" entered the postwar Canadian lexicon, compared to "civil rights" in the United States. Moreover, the British rights rhetoric of justice and fair play had failed, and activists in

Canada rejected the premise that they had to appeal to a declining empire for human rights.

African American leaders wagered that the postwar period would usher in unprecedented internationally binding human rights that would transform their lives. Black organizations—such as the National Association for the Advancement of Colored People, the National Negro Congress, the National Council of Negro Women, the Civil Rights Congress, and the Council on African Affairs—sought protection from the UN Charter, the UDHR, and the UN Human Rights Commission. Black activists specifically wanted national self-determination—which meant anti-colonialism in Africa and its diaspora and control over institutions in their communities in Canada and the United States—and to uplift all racialized peoples, especially those who suffered political and economic disenfranchisement.[104] Leading Black organizations had the capacity to help transform the freedom struggle. The NAACP, the premier African American organization, mobilized its million-dollar endowment and half-million members and influential allies to make *human rights*—not civil rights—the polestar of the postwar U.S. freedom struggle. However, Dixiecrats and conservative Republicans, as well as "friends" such as President Truman and Eleanor Roosevelt, historian Carol Anderson argues, frustrated such plans by limiting UN influence on and jurisdiction in the United States.[105] Observing the limitations of liberalism, leftist individuals and groups stepped into the fray. In 1946, nearly three years after the announcement of the UDHR, the indefatigable rights activist W. E. B. Du Bois, with the support of Black and white intellectuals, drafted "An Appeal to the World" for the UN Commission on Human Rights. An undersecretary finally accepted the document in 1947. In December 1951, African American William L. Patterson, on behalf of the Communist Party–affiliated Civil Rights Congress, attended the UN assembly meeting in Paris. Patterson and the Civil Rights Congress presented the United Nations with a document titled *We Charge Genocide: The Historic Petition to the United Nations for Relief from a Crime of the United States Government against the Negro People*. In New York, Paul Robeson led a delegation that submitted copies of the report to the UN secretary-general's office. The Civil Rights Congress intended for the document to "arouse the moral conscience of progressive" people. Every facet of U.S. society, the document concluded, had shown "consistent, conscious, unified policies" to destroy in part or whole the African American people.[106]

Because the U.S. government was not a signatory to the UDHR, African Americans used the language of the 1951 UN Genocide Convention, to which the United States *was* a signatory, to make their human rights case.[107]

However, southern opposition and Cold War concerns torpedoed African Americans' pursuit of internationally binding human rights. Canada, too, wanted to contain communism, but the Red Scare there did not nullify the pursuit of racial justice. This betrayal of the African American justice claim led to Black leaders' pursuit of "civil rights" rather than the more holistic "human rights." This compromise fueled a long and limited struggle in the United States and, ultimately, strong white resentment.[108] Furthermore, damage control by the State Department to save face during the Cold War proved futile, because, as Canadians stated repeatedly in their 1958 petitions to save Jimmy Wilson, there existed a wide chasm between U.S. idealism and its commitment to uphold democracy and the rule of law.

During the apex of the U.S. civil rights movement in the mid-1960s, Malcolm X revived the notion of human rights as the original objective. The son of Garveyite parents who organized for the Universal Negro Improvement Association—which, in 1920, issued the Declaration of the Rights of the Negro Peoples of the World demanding "human rights," among other objectives—Malcolm could not have renewed the call for human rights without an internationalist orientation, such as Pan-Africanisms. His founding of the Organization of Afro-American Unity in June 1964 was Malcolm's return to his parents' Garveyite roots, for he believed that organizing African peoples throughout the Americas, like the UNIA had, would precipitate all Black people's fulsome liberation. In his 1964 "Ballot or the Bullet" speech, one of the most important meditations on Black self-determination, Malcolm X evoked a Pan-Africanist vision grounded in human rights. "They keep you wrapped up in civil rights. And you spend so much time barking up the civil-rights tree, you don't even know there's a human-rights tree on the same floor," he stated. "When you expand the civil-rights struggle to the level of human rights," he added, "you can then take the case of the Black man in this country before the nations in the UN. You can take it before the General Assembly. You can take Uncle Sam before a world court." Malcolm continued: "But the only level you can do it on is the level of human rights. Civil rights keeps you under his restrictions, under his jurisdiction. Civil rights keeps you in his pocket. Civil rights means you're asking Uncle Sam to treat you right. Human rights are something you were born with. Human rights are your God-given rights. Human rights are the rights that are recognized by all nations. . . . And any time anyone violates your human rights, you can take them to the world court."[109]

Pan-Africanists' focus on international accountability illustrated a vital dimension of the twentieth-century Black freedom struggle. In Canada, activists' and government officials' reliance on UN values and principles of universal human rights lent the state a source of postwar legitimacy and moral authority. Canada, for better or worse, made a covenant to uphold the spirit of antidiscrimination, unlike its southern neighbor. Civil rights proved a runner-up prize, a conciliation for African Americans, while Black people and other minorities in Canada received the more promising prize: state-sanctioned human rights legislation, the moral cornerstone of the UDHR. If the trajectory and efficacy of Daniel Hill's African American contemporaries in the United States reveal anything about the freedom struggle, it is partly the power of contingency (that is, context and cultural climate) in shaping historical outcomes.

A RACE MAN VS. "GENTLEMAN BIGOTS"

As the first director of the Ontario Human Rights Commission, Hill over-saw an ambitious race relations program in a postwar setting where many Canadians had learned to mask their prejudice with civility. "In Ontario, the racist bigot is not the key enemy. The person who wants to gas Jews and lynch Negroes is an impotent minority," contested Alan Borovoy, a Jewish attorney in Toronto and tireless champion of minorities. Instead, the contagion of racism in Canada, Borovoy commented, existed in the "Gentleman Bigot," or "the employer, proprietor or landlord who acts out of *business* interests. He *likes* minority groups. He simply cannot *hire* or *do business* with them" for fear of stigma. "In his scale of values," wrote Borovoy, "human dignity ranks behind business considerations." Borovoy identified another rights violator: the "apathetic in-betweener"—a "nice guy who dislikes discrimination, but will not risk his social comforts in order to fight it. He is the person," asserted Borovoy, "who will patronize discriminatory institutions, belong to restricted clubs, and refuse to testify as a witness because he prefers not to get 'involved.'"[110]

Overcoming the apparition of Canadian racism required a socially deft human rights champion who could disarm the "gentleman bigot" and reform indifferent spectators whose active and passive complicity denied minorities their rights. Nongovernmental organizations such as the Brotherhood of Sleeping Car Porters, the National Unity Association, the Canadian Labor Congress, the Canadian Jewish Congress, the National Committee on Human Rights, the Toronto Labor Committee for Human Rights, the Canadian Civil Liberties Association, and many others helped democratize and liberalize postwar Canadian society. Given the intersection of labor and human rights, most of the organizations had a labor angle.

In November 1962, seven months after commencing his tenure as the director of the OHRC, Hill updated Premier Robarts's office on the commission's progress and racialized Canadians' demand for its services. Within a few months as director, Hill had convinced over 1,000 business and industry executives to support the Ontario Human Rights Code and display it in their workplace. Academic institutions, religious groups, and community organizations endorsed the commission's work. "No other Canadian province," Hill exclaimed, "begins to compare with Ontario in this field."[111] Despite this headway, there still existed a law authorizing Jim Crow public schools in southern Ontario and Nova Scotia during this time, a legacy of the 1850 Common School Act, which allowed (white) French- and English-speaking children to attend separate schools.[112]

The OHRC's focus on re-education and moderate arbitration became a model for success. When a human rights violation occurred, the commission required complainants to file a formal grievance in writing, after which point a human rights officer investigated and pursued conciliation. Individuals and corporations/trade unions found guilty of violating the Human Rights Code faced fines of $100 and $500, respectively, in 1962.[113] The process placed a great deal of power in the commission, kept the procedure at a relatively local level, and worked speedily. The U.S. Equal Employment Opportunity Commission, established in 1965, functioned similarly.

Despite this penalty, Hill considered the commission's conciliation process "highly flexible and, as a policy, the investigator concentrates rather less on the issue of legal guilt than on the issue of effectuating a satisfactory settlement." Reconciling complainants and respondents involved "a judicious blending of the 'velvet glove' and 'iron fist.'" Moreover, the commission required the respondent to apologize publicly to the complainant and offer any accommodation or service previously denied. Underscoring the public and social merits of re-education, respondents agreed to train others in their workplace about the commission's policies and to issue a "written assurance to the Commission of future compliance with the provisions of the code."[114]

Notwithstanding its noble motives and practicality, Hill had to dispel myths about the OHRC and justify its existence. A Canadian sociologist inferred that Canada could forgo its human rights commission, because racism was a minor issue in the country. Although Hill understood the premise of this academic's statement, he remained resolute, lest he reinforce a common myth that racism in Canadian society was a nonissue. Concerning the state of human rights in Ontario, Hill noted, "I am afraid that we still have a long way to go in Ontario." Hill also used this correspondence to illuminate which ethno-racial constituencies suffered most from discrimination and other forms of bias. According to Hill, 60 percent of complaints came from Black and Jewish people. A growing number of European immigrants,

Asians, and Indigenous peoples also sought assistance from the commission. That Hill considered the public's usage of the commission "healthy and necessary" sheds light on his belief that marginalized Canadians wanted their government to set the standard on equitable race and intergroup relations.[115]

As one of the most visible and influential Black statesmen in postwar Canadian society, Hill's human rights work drew much attention. Black leaders and organizations deferred to Hill for counsel on how they should harness the freedom struggle that swept across U.S. society during the turbulent 1960s. A few weeks before civil rights activists marched on Washington in July 1963, St. Clair Pindar, secretary of the Toronto United Negro Association, a group that strove to unify and consolidate the city's Black organizations, contacted Hill. "In view of the present circumstances surrounding our fellow Negroes in the United States in the life and death struggle for their right and complete acceptance," Pindar wrote, "we feel that the Negro community should be aware of their conditions and needs, and rise to the occasion with aid. We must not in our haste to help, forget that Canada is also guilty of race bias." Pindar expressed his organization's desire to convene churches, fraternities, and social clubs and create a "permanent committee" to "unite the voice of the Negro community into a powerful voice." The various ethnic, cultural, linguistic, and religious divisions among African Canadians in Toronto and nationwide undermined their effectiveness to resist racism. Striking the tocsin of racial injustice, Pindar opined, "We believe that the time has come, the need has arisen, for us to unite our force and strength, don't you?"[116]

Daniel Hill and his office's reputation extended beyond Ontario in the 1960s. In one correspondence, a Philadelphian sent Hill a newspaper clipping that a Wilmington, Delaware–based paper published on the OHRC's intervention on behalf of a racially discriminated patron in Windsor, Ontario.[117] A cheerful Hill sent a packet of human rights brochures to the Philadelphian. The man expressed his enthusiasm that a gust of tolerance and justice was sweeping across Canadian society. "At least, if some ill-advised countryman should aver in my presence that the civil rights of gentlefolk of color are not properly protected in your province, I shall be able to argue persuasively to the contrary."[118]

On one hand, Hill's human rights advocacy in Ontario had the effect of casting Canadian society, especially to race-conscious U.S. onlookers, in a far more progressive light than the actual lived experience of Canada's racial minorities. On the other hand, the OHRC's small victories signaled a shift toward racial justice during the mid-1960s. Hill demonstrated a cross-border awareness of connections among racial identity, the state, and transformative social movements. He was an esteemed state bureaucrat who could advance Black solidarity discreetly.

In the 1960s, the Hills decided to acquire Canadian citizenship, signaling that they would stay in Canada. Their resolve continued when, in November 1965, another friend, Sidney Olyan, a professor of sociology at the University of Washington, recommended Hill for a "major appointment" at the school of social work. Hill responded, "I'd have a minor riot on my hands if I threatened to 'pull up stakes' and head West."[119] In 1963, Sidney Vincent—a friend and the associate director of the Jewish Community Federation in Cleveland—expressed "mingled feelings" over Hill's recent acquisition of Canadian citizenship. Nearly six weeks later, Vincent lamented Hill's absence at a moment in history when U.S. society desperately needed its best thinkers and doers: "Deploring our having lost you, when the need here is becoming ugly and requires the very best brains we can muster." Vincent believed that the United States represented the "major leagues" of race relations, thus relegating Canadian society to the minor leagues. "I shudder to think of what would happen," he admitted, "if [Canada] had anything like our concentration of minority groups."[120]

In fact, Canada did have a concentrated minority group: its Indigenous peoples. By the mid-1960s, Hill's work with them justified his resolve to remain in Canada. Indigenous groups in northern Ontario, including the Cree and Ojibway, felt marginalized, even as the standard of living improved for other minorities. This double standard troubled Hill. A report submitted to the OHRC and signed by Fred Kelly, co-chairman of the Indian-White Committee; eleven chiefs; and delegation consultant Alan Borovoy painted a bleak picture facing Indigenous peoples in the northern Ontario town of Kenora.[121] Despite public misgivings about the new wave of Indigenous militancy, the leaders wrote, "We are here not to beat the drums of war, but rather to smoke the pipe of peace." Evoking the spirit of human rights, they explained, "The peace we seek, unlike the peace we have, is a peace based upon dignity, equality, and justice for the Indian people."[122]

The report documented rampant discrimination against Indigenous groups in Kenora and neighboring towns. It sought to alleviate poverty and end economic exploitation; stimulate infrastructure investment, including telecommunication for remote communities; build adequate housing; and improve health care, especially assistance to combat alcoholism.[123] Having scrutinized Hill's work, the petitioners cited a speech that he delivered to the Indian-White Committee in which he stated that the OHRC assisted "communities and groups of people who are attempting to resolve interracial difficulties."[124]

Hill knew that the OHRC and the Ontario Department of Labor "received numerous complaints" from Indigenous communities "regarding violations of minimum wages, long hours of work with inadequate compensation, and insolent treatment by employers." After the commission recovered back pay for 142 workers on a nearby reserve, others cooperated with the commission, asserted Hill, because they had heard of this success through "moccasin telegraph." Hill believed that the commission must address "bread and butter" matters of Indigenous peoples—concerns that caused "smoldering resentment" among them. Without justice and community empowerment, such conditions, Hill predicted, could push Indigenous groups in Canada to become as rebellious as urban African Americans.[125]

So committed was Hill to the Indigenous cause that he declined an academic appointment at the Yale School of Forestry in 1967 to teach courses on "sociological or psychological aspects of natural resource use." The hiring committee offered him a "free hand in developing" the subject area, since no school of forestry in the United States had a "similar position."[126] Although tempted by the prospect of returning to academe, Hill felt "deeply committed" to a new program that opened regional offices to serve Indigenous peoples in northern Ontario.[127]

In Canada, unlike the United States, Hill realized that he could extend the principle of human rights to all groups. When the standing committee on external affairs invited him to speak about the persistence of hate literature, which could have tarnished the Canadian reputation overseas, Hill acknowledged that the OHRC's six full-time human rights officers could not proselytize those with "twisted minds" or the career "merchants of hate." These racists peddled white supremacist and anti-Semitic literature. Hill concluded his address in a manner that disarmed and inspired moderate Anglo-Canadians. "I am firm in the conviction that the residents of Ontario have not forgotten their legacy and traditions in the human rights field," he said. "They have not forgotten their history and therefore will never permit a group of demented, misguided individuals to jeopardize or endanger human liberty."[128] Ever the tactful statesman, Hill placed the onus of Canada's international reputation and national cohesion in the hands of people whose forebears ostensibly promoted racial tolerance and justice. Their descendants, Hill insisted, must rebuke a small discredited minority who sought to sow racial discord. Pandering, he understood, could at times be more expedient than outright chastisement.

As Hill worked toward a more racially just Ontario, the commission's reputation grew. By the mid-1960s, the U.K. Parliament was monitoring the OHRC's work. British society sought constructive ways to address the embarrassing and sensitive matter of racial discrimination after the influx of racialized persons from the Commonwealth. Ontario provided a successful Commonwealth model of antidiscrimination legislation and postwar racial incorporation.

In 1966, senior British bureaucrat G. H. Roberts sent Hill a copy of the newly created 1965 Race Relations Act, which he described as "a good deal narrower" than the Ontario Human Rights Code. Roberts spoke truthfully. This act represented the United Kingdom's first legislation to curtail ethnic or racial discrimination. Ontario passed such legislation first in 1944. Roberts, secretary of the British Race Relations Board, which served a similar adjudicatory purpose as the OHRC, inquired what Ontario's conciliation process recommended when a complainant accused a respondent of discrimination. He sought clarification on whether the OHRC engaged in shaming of persons or establishments guilty of discrimination. Hill explained that the commission did not publicize matters that the parties resolved informally or through conciliation but that matters requiring boards of inquiry were by nature high profile and thus invariably attracted media attention and scrutiny.[129]

Hill also crossed the Atlantic to enlighten European governments about human rights advocacy. In October and November 1966—after attending a conference sponsored by the United Nations and the International Labor Organization in Geneva, Switzerland—Hill met with Parliamentarians in London to discuss the British Race Relations Board and to share ideas on employment equity, issues on which postwar Canada had acquired some expertise. In 1967, British officials assembled a task force to research antidiscrimination legislation in various countries and consulted with Hill. In April 1968, he spoke with David Ennals, a British human rights champion and under-secretary of state for the Home Department, about "the latest in human rights developments in Britain and Canada."[130] Receiving royal assent on 25 October, the 1968 Race Relations Act became law. It proscribed discrimination based on ethno-racial identity in housing, employment, and public services.[131] True to its postwar aims, the acquisition of moral authority through human rights legislations allowed Canada to assert expertise on matters of liberal internationalism—even in the metropole.

Daniel Grafton Hill III's foundational role in shaping postwar Canadian history from 1962 to 1973 hinged on a grueling schedule that weakened his body. Although Hill nearly succumbed to pneumonia six months into the job, his demanding itinerary, which saw him crisscrossing Ontario in his Volkswagen Beetle, eventually took its full toll on his health. Even after contracting diabetes, Hill remained committed to social change. When he resigned from the commission in 1973, he founded Canada's first human rights firm. "This is the age of specialization and consultants," he said. "Ontario's human rights laws are the best in the country," Hill asserted. "We were the first province to give its commission statutory powers."[132] Hill's diasporic consciousness and commitment to racial justice guided him into the halls of civic power. Aided by his equally competent and committed wife, Donna, he enjoyed a distinguished career as one of Canada's most important postwar statesmen. Although determined and extraordinary, Hill was human and had feet of clay. According to his sons, his "autocratic" nature and use of occasional corporal punishment to control them show that, in some ways, he had not healed as a Black man from the abuses and humiliations that Jim Crow had inflicted on him in the United States and Canada.[133]

Nevertheless, Hill's achievements in Canadian society provide a case study of how a postwar human rights activist in Canada shaped access to employment, housing, and accommodation with the backing of legislation. Human rights, however, could do only so much to overhaul centuries of systemic anti-blackness and transform the material conditions of working-poor Black people. For this reason, Black activists' demands for social revolution would deepen toward the end of the 1960s and into the 1970s. On balance, Hill's experience provides historians a window into understanding transnational history, cross-border racial consciousness, and interspatial citizenship. Although Hill arrived in a country where most white people believed that true racism stemmed from the United States—as Jimmy Wilson's death sentence for alleged robbery indicated in 1958—his struggles as an African American provided him with perspective where Canada's potential was concerned. Hill discerned that, unlike the United States, Canada was redeemable, and he set out to help redeem it, first, with his sociology doctoral research, "Negroes in Toronto," and, second, by institutional reform. His cofounding of the Ontario Black History Society in 1978 with Donna and other friends, which utilized African Canadian history as a vehicle for race pride and Black self-determination, and his monograph *The Freedom Seekers: Blacks in Early Canada* reveal his penchant for scholarship and history as tools of Black liberation.[134]

Hill's emigration from the United States in 1950 and his journey to become one of the leading human rights advocates in Canada provide an alternative perspective of how African North Americans imagined freedom and negotiated identity, race, and diaspora. Before Hill, of course, nineteenth-century Black intellectuals and activists, such as Mary Ann

Shadd Cary and Martin Delany—as well as countless enslaved and free fugitives, speaking with their feet—advocated emigration from the United States as a critique of U.S. citizenship. Daniel and Donna Hill challenged U.S. racial injustice, but their focus on Canada's own injustices changed their adopted country. Because of postwar contributions by activists, such as the Hills, Ontario and by extension Canada as a whole were bound to honor human rights commitments. This culture of social change positioned Canadian society as the alternative site for race relations, a goal that Hill dared not dream in his birth country.

Even so, the paradox of progress meant that, although Canadian society advanced in some regards, it remained regressive in other ways. The enduring problem of race and the rightful claims of Black people—whether native born or emigrants from the British Commonwealth or the United States—unsettled the landscape. One fact remained certain: Black activists had every intention to add new victories to their postwar gains.

PART **TWO**

▼ ▼ ▼

CHAPTER 4

IMMIGRATION, BLACK POWER,
AND DRAFT RESISTERS

Barring revolution, the rights regime requires social change to transpire within the legal framework of the state. And states are reactive entities. This dynamic means that the impetus for change must almost always begin from the outside with grassroots activists, lobbyists, international organizations, or foreign states.

States are also adept at incorporating radical voices into the machinery of state governance, which, over the passage of time, has a moderating effect. A case in point: Anne Cools, the longest-serving member of the Senate of Canada (1984–2018), was a Black woman who had served time behind bars in her early thirties. Cools initially gained national and international notoriety as a student activist and radical feminist turned revolutionary socialist who had visited Cuba as a delegate in 1966 on behalf of her Black comrades. One of her collaborators, dating back to their days of student activism, was Rosie Douglas from Dominica. He spent nearly two years in prison for his student activism. Although the Canadian government deported Douglas, denying him the opportunity of working within the state apparatus, he later became prime minister of his Caribbean island. In the art of revolutionary struggle on one hand and national self-preservation on the other, states, large and small, play a vital role in anointing and appointing leaders.

Hailing from the quaint British Caribbean colony of Barbados, Anne Clare Cools descended from prominent professionals, politicians, and stateswomen. Her father was a pharmacist, and her mother owned a sugar plantation—the crop that was once the linchpin of her island's plantation economy. Other kinfolk held distinguished positions, such as senators, members of Parliament, and the first woman cabinet minister. "We all had servants," recalled Cools of a childhood ensconced within the island bourgeoisie. Family and friends affectionately called her "Dogbones" because of her gaunt features. Make no mistake, however. Cools's family had immense class power.[1]

Empire, for a select few like the Cools family, had its nominal upside. British subjects in the Caribbean could, in theory, immigrate to Canada. In practice, though, Canadian immigration policies tightly controlled access for non-white Caribbean people, except for a small elite and the occasional domestic workers and laborers whom Canadian households and industries needed.[2] In 1957, like many aspiring families in the Caribbean, but unlike many who lacked ways and means to make the transition, Cools's family immigrated to Montreal. She was thirteen.

Born on 12 August 1943, Cools came of age in a world and society undergoing seismic shifts. As a woman of African descent, Cools remembered a hierarchical island society where female relatives had accomplished the improbable as high-ranking public officials. Thus, life in a highly race-conscious Canadian society arguably positioned Cools for a young adulthood of self-assertion and combating injustice.[3]

For Roosevelt Bernard "Rosie" Douglas, Canada was the destination of choice for his postsecondary education. As a restless seventeen-year-old who worked on his father's coconut plantation in 1959, Canada represented the surest way for him to leave his native island of Dominica, a sleepy British colony in the Lesser Antilles. Immigrating to Canada would also help Douglas to escape the austere and authoritarian gaze of his father, Robert Bernard Douglas—or, as his sons called him, RBD—an industrious and wealthy man. "If Rosie had stayed behind instead of going to Canada," recalled Douglas's younger brother Macintyre, "it would have been bend or break for him with RBD."[4] Obtaining that student visa to study in Canada, however, proved difficult for the dark-hued teenager.

Douglas's father had achieved wealth and prestige at a time when colonial and other structural barriers denied most Black people upward class mobility. Serious and regimented, RBD subscribed to the conservative ethos of bootstrap individualism that characterized the orientation of some Caribbean men of his generation. He first cut his teeth working on a Shell refinery in Curaçao as a twenty-three-year-old circa 1928.[5] In two years of hard labor, RBD, a frugal man by all accounts, saved $700.[6] Back in his native Portsmouth, Dominica, he purchased abandoned plantations and opened a grocery store and cinema. He accumulated other assets—such as boats, a hotel, and more land. A shrewd pragmatist, he was twice elected to the legislature on these promises to the proletariat: "I give you a job on my estate, credit at my store, a dress for a christening, and a coffin when you die. All I ask is that you vote for me."[7]

African Caribbean immigrants, rich and poor, sought opportunities in a booming Commonwealth country like Canada. Workers, families, and students became one of the primary beneficiaries of a gradually liberalizing Canadian immigration policy in the postwar period. Change came slowly and often required some additional cajoling from the halls of power. While awaiting his student visa to study agronomics in Canada, Douglas worked on one of his father's coconut plantations near Portsmouth, a verdant, hilly town on the northwestern peninsula of the island, for seventeen months. Growing impatient, Douglas decided to reach out to the most powerful man he could think of: the Canadian prime minister.

One fateful afternoon, the teenager picked up the telephone on his father's estate and asked the operator for Canada. "I said I wanted to speak to the prime minister. I didn't know who that was," admitted Douglas. This unusual display of agency connected him to the office telephone line of John Diefenbaker—the fiery orator and thirteenth prime minister. Douglas left a message with one of the prime minister's secretaries. One month later, the Progressive Conservative leader called RBD's estate to speak with Douglas. "I told him what my problem was. Within a week I got my visa and went to Canada."[8] That Douglas had ready access to a telephone at a time before it had become a ubiquitous household fixture in the Caribbean and the ease with which he paid for his travel fare to Canada are strong indications of his family's class power. In May 1961, he arrived in southwestern Ontario to study at the Ontario Agricultural College, now the University of Guelph. The Department of Immigration "compelled" him to work ten-hour days during the summer months milking cows and shoveling pig manure without compensation. Douglas described this experience as "a distasteful welcome" to Canadian society.[9]

Roosevelt Douglas was born to Robert and Bernadette Douglas on 15 October 1941. His parents named him after the New Deal and wartime president. Of their sixteen children, at least three other sons received names of prominent statesmen: Eisenhower, Atlee, and Adenauer.[10] A member of a dark-hued family, Rosie Douglas's class mobility came from the grit and enterprising spirit of his parents, not a colortocracy inherited from a bygone generation of a European ancestor.

For African descendants who lived in Canada in the two decades after the Second World War, the promise of social change constituted a real paradox. The presence of Black bodies in a postwar Canada that contended with decolonization in the British Commonwealth helped the country acquire international legitimacy and moral authority. Yet, Canadian society remained hostile to Black people from the Caribbean and the United States.

As opposition to the racism, sexism, and imperialism of the Cold War global order intensified, leftists from the Caribbean and Black Panthers and war resisters from the United States sought social and economic refuge in Canada. The racism and latent imperialism of Canadian society compelled these individuals to agitate for social change. This chapter uncovers the struggles of these African Caribbean and Black and white radicals from the United States, as well as Canadian-born activists, who tried to improve the material conditions of vulnerable groups in Canada. They predicated their optimism on the progress that previous generations of Black, Jewish, and Asian activists had achieved in resisting racism and discrimination. Canada's long-standing reputation as a refuge point of sorts for Black people persisted into the 1960s and 1970s, notwithstanding the racial fault lines that existed in Canadian society. It is within this logic that Caribbean immigrants, Black Panthers, and U.S. draft resisters looked north to Canada as a viable alternative to an increasingly repressive U.S. government.

"THE STONE THAT THE BUILDERS REJECTED"

For diasporic Africans in the British West Indies, Canada was a proxy of the Crown. It represented a regional metropole—a place of economic prosperity and modernity.[11] Since the 1870s Canadian courtship of British West Indies islands, such as Barbados and Jamaica, for the purposes of political federation amounted to "flirtation." Canadians had curated "an image of the honest broker"—the interlocutor that could distill the complexities of intergroup relations: Francophones vis-à-vis Anglophones, Britain vis-à-vis the United States, the white Commonwealth vis-à-vis the racialized Commonwealth.[12] As the United States cultivated an empire in the Caribbean Basin, Canadian politicians looked on enviously, hoping to manicure a similar "Canadian backyard in the sun" before their southern neighbor "turned the Caribbean into an American lake." Canada desired to counter growing U.S. hegemony in the hemisphere while strengthening its commercial ties, but the prospects of political union, Robin Winks concluded, "floundered upon the rock of race." In other words, political union with Caribbean colonies invariably meant that Canada would forfeit its right to deny entry to Black immigrants. Although Ottawa wanted a "Canadian colony," in the interwar years the actions of Canadian officials proved that race trumped economics, even though race and capitalism were inextricably linked.[13]

Throughout the early twentieth century as Canada romanced British West Indies colonies with the possibility of political federation, it permitted entry only to a handful of immigrants from these colonies. Even when the Dominion Iron Steel Company felt compelled to recruit Caribbean laborers to toil in the steel plants and coal mines in Sydney, Nova Scotia, during the Great War, Canadian officials discouraged and frustrated the permanent residency aspirations of Black subjects of the British Empire. In fact, British

West Indians who visited Canada and the United States noticed clear racial hierarchies during their sojourn.

In the 1950s when Lascelles "Peabody" Small visited the North American mainland as a seaman aboard freighters that transported bauxite and other iron ores from his native Jamaica, Jim Crow left him "in a trance" after first disembarking in Mobile, Alabama, before his ship entered port in Baltimore and Montreal. The racial hierarchies remained in place in all three cities but with stark and subtle regional and local differences. From 1958 to 1960, Small resided at the Norwegian Seamen's House in New York City. He recalled, "As long as you're Black and you're washing dishes, no one bothers you," adding, "I could disguise my accent and sound like one of the brothers, even from the South. I adapted. I spoke like the [African] Americans." This cultural dexterity resembled how Black people in Great Lakes cities bridged the U.S.-Canadian border during the interwar years, mirroring a form of citizenship passing. When Small crossed the Atlantic to deliver cargo at the Norwegian ports of Bergen, Sunndalsøra, and Oslo, he noticed an attitude of acceptance among the youth. He also observed that Norwegian and other Nordic ships hired women on their crews, despite men holding a near monopoly in the global shipping sector as seafarers. Small's travels as a British sailor reveal not only the importance of waterways—complements of land travel and border crossings—as sites of exchange for Black people but also the power of seafaring or what one scholar called "micro-systems of linguistic and political hybridity" in the Black Atlantic.[14] His travels also illustrate the ways that working-class Black people resisted anti-blackness by leveraging their diasporic identity when interacting with white people. Yet, Small did not seek residency in Canada until the mid-1960s.

Canadian officials' condescending attitudes toward Black members of the Commonwealth was part of the problem. Jamaican-born labor and human rights activist Bromley Armstrong believed that the Crown and Canada perceived African descendants in the Caribbean as "objects rather than subjects."[15] Canadian authorities consistently denied Black immigrants entry by using dubious policies, such as suitability to the climate, fitness, health, and "exceptional merit," that is, those admitted to Canada despite restrictions. No greater obstacle, in fact, hindered Canada's postwar claims to legitimacy and moral authority than its anachronistic and white supremacist immigration policy, which gave nearly unbridled preference to Anglo-Saxons and Nordic peoples while effectively closing Canadian ports to African descendants, Asians, and Jews.[16]

With the 1947 onset of decolonization in the British Empire, Canada had to consider seriously its credibility both as a Commonwealth ally and as a trading partner. Although the 1948 British Nationality Act allowed Caribbean subjects to immigrate to the metropole to mitigate labor shortages in postwar Britain and alleviate economic depression in the Anglophone Caribbean, Canada lacked a comparable olive branch in its immigration policy.[17] Instead, Canadian prime minister Mackenzie King remained obstinate when his Liberal government introduced its immigration platform in 1947. "With regard to the selection of immigrants, much has been said about discrimination. I wish to make quite clear," King stated, "that Canada is perfectly within her rights in selecting the persons whom we regard as desirable future citizens." Reassuring Canadians and the international community, King continued, "It is not a 'fundamental human right' of any alien to enter Canada. It is a privilege. It is a matter of domestic policy." King further asserted that white Canadians did not desire "to make a fundamental alteration in the character of our population."[18] F. C. Blair, King's chief immigration bureaucrat, had made similar remarks in 1923, stating that no one had "a natural right" to enter Canada and that the government had absolute authority to "bar" those it deemed unsuitable "for the good of Canada."[19]

Yet, in the 1950s, the importance of trade—specifically in the Caribbean Basin and generally throughout the Commonwealth, which Canada's trade commissioners conveyed to leaders in Ottawa—meant that Canadian officials could no longer conceive of their borders with absolute hubris. Moreover, antidiscrimination provisions in the Universal Declaration of Human Rights mitigated race-based immigration. Also, postwar reconstruction in Britain and continental Europe, buttressed by the Marshall Plan, fueled Canada's export economy of raw materials and agricultural and manufactured goods. Coupled with domestic consumption, these trends illustrated Canada's labor needs. In 1951, as a show of "goodwill" toward the newly independent countries of India, Pakistan, and Ceylon (Sri Lanka), Canada set its quota of immigrants from these countries, a token gesture that welcomed a few hundred more immigrants each year. This sign of pacification sprang from Canadian bureaucrats' realization that they now had to defend their exclusionary policies toward racialized members of the Commonwealth at a time of rapid decolonization and repudiation of Western imperialism. The evidence was irrefutable; until 1960, Canada managed twenty-seven immigration-processing centers: twenty-four in western Europe, one in Israel, two in Asia, but none in sub-Saharan Africa, the Caribbean, or South America.[20]

South Africa's codification of apartheid in 1948, the same year that the United Nations adopted the Universal Declaration of Human Rights, revealed the moral dissonance in the postwar Commonwealth. South Africa's brutal repression of Indigenous Africans, which culminated in the 1960 Sharpeville massacre, further signaled to an aspiring power broker, such as Canada, that it must take a stance on the race question. John Diefenbaker was prime minister from 1957 to 1963, and his opposition to South Africa's membership at the 1961 Commonwealth Conference in London effectively paved the way for his Progressive Conservative government to introduce reforms to the Immigration Act in 1962. Except for family sponsorship, the 1962 act removed most discrimination along ethno-racial and geographical lines, placing instead emphasis on applicants' skills and merits. This rapprochement constituted a "rethinking" of Canada's place in the world.[21]

By making these concessions in 1962, Canada, according to one historian, "crossed the line" in moving beyond a white supremacist country.[22] On balance, Canadian immigration policy changed partly because of criticisms from the metropole. As a close ally of Britain, Canada came under pressure in the late 1950s and early 1960s, because Britain desired to constrict its Commonwealth immigration pipeline and for Canada to expand its intake. White Britons, in short, feared immigration from the Caribbean, Africa, and South Asia—Commonwealth members who would encroach on their limited economic opportunities.[23]

Nonetheless, the new immigration measures proved incomplete. Immigration officers wielded discretionary power to reject prospective immigrants, and they often did. As a result of persistent agitation, the Liberal government of Lester B. Pearson, Diefenbaker's successor in 1963, introduced the points system on 1 October 1967. This meritocratic measure "capped a 20-year" postwar shift away from racially offensive immigration policies and embraced foreign workers and refugees. It promoted more equitable family reunification. Global events—such as the Holocaust, independence movement in the Global South, and human rights on a worldwide scale—rendered Canada's reliance on a white supremacist immigration policy incongruous with the rights-based postwar world order. Ottawa bureaucrats embraced this social climate of humanitarianism, because they wanted the world to perceive Canada as a credible champion of liberal internationalism.[24]

The implementation of the 1967 points system radically changed Canadian immigration policy.[25] But even as officials disavowed discrimination in immigration selection, they underscored skills and meritocratic standards. The points system privileged education, technical skills, Canadian connections, and competence in English or French, without regard to nationality or ethno-racial heritage. Earning fifty points or higher made a candidate competitive. Obviously, economically underprivileged members of the

Commonwealth stood at a disadvantage. Moreover, the Canadian government found it difficult to root out the culture it had created of empowering immigration officers to discriminate against prospective immigrants based on nationality and corporeal features.[26]

FROM PETTY BOURGEOISIE TO REVOLUTIONARIES

As undergraduate students at Canadian universities, Rosie Douglas and Anne Cools cut their activist teeth as organizers of interracial coalitions and champions of the Black cause for dignity and human rights. Although the two hailed from what was akin to the "Black Bourgeoisie," once in Canada, they squared off against members of their own economic class. For Douglas, his politics and orientation toward racial justice, however, swung from mainstream or even Canadian progressive conservatism to radicalism and Black Power—that is, complete self-determination for African descendants—within a decade as the pendulum of social change in Canada hit a snag. Cools, too, underwent her own radicalism, and she had to leave Canada briefly to spark her political development.

In November 1960, Prime Minister Diefenbaker delivered a poignant address to the Ottawa Canadian Club, a veritable amalgamation of Canadian and global dignitaries. In a speech on the Commonwealth and collective security against Soviet expansionism, Diefenbaker borrowed British prime minister Harold Macmillan's watershed "the wind of change is blowing" rhetoric that the British leader had delivered in Ghana and South Africa earlier in 1960. Diefenbaker warned against Canada's acquisition of nuclear weapons. "We hope that new developments will come ushered in by winds of change rather than gales of destruction," Diefenbaker pleaded. "My message to you is this: that we, as Canadians, set our Canadian sails, follow and steer a course so that those winds will not become gales." He continued: "I hope that Providence and human intelligence will together allow these changes to take place without the storm that hovers over the horizon."[27] Although Diefenbaker specifically referred to the threat of strategic bipolarity and a nuclear arms race, his words were just as apt—even prophetic—in describing Western governments' fear of social revolution.

Ever the quintessential Progressive Conservative statesman, Diefenbaker cautioned against imprudent change but, more importantly, also against the type of haste that masquerades as progress. He was a lawyer by training, and his brand of Canadian conservatism was grounded in populism and moral courage.[28] A man of conviction, Diefenbaker came of age in a Canada that distrusted Germans, which meant that as a Canadian of partly German ancestry, he often experienced discrimination and nativism, particularly during the two world wars. He felt that his political rivals took jabs at him because of his German roots. Diefenbaker confessed in his memoirs that he believed his fellow politicians would have treated him much differently had his surname been his mother's Scottish maiden name. "It distressed me that those who were neither British nor French in origin were not treated with the regard that non-discrimination demands."[29]

Diefenbaker's early experiences in Canada made him a champion of the underdog. Winks described him as a leader who was "sincere in his opposition to discrimination."[30] Unlike most of his contemporaries, for example, Diefenbaker expressed apprehension over Canada's decision to intern Japanese Canadians during World War II, because it would trample the liberties of these law-abiding Canadians. His personal resentment of second-class citizenship and his awareness of others' sense of alienation had fueled his desire to see Canada adopt its own Bill of Rights that would protect Canadians of all stripes, not just the "founding" Anglophone or Francophone "races."[31] Diefenbaker had credibility on the race issue. After all, his government cracked the white supremacist edifice of Canadian immigration policy with amendments to the Immigration Act in 1962.

Rosie Douglas saw in Diefenbaker a Canadian politician who championed relevant social causes and spoke sincerely about issues affecting diasporic Africans and other minorities. Moreover, that Diefenbaker returned Douglas's phone call and facilitated his immigration to Canada seemed unusually magnanimous. Having been socialized in a deeply hierarchical and class-conscious society, Douglas, notwithstanding his upper-class status, understood that it would be a flagrant offense for common folk to exercise such boldness when dealing with an elder or those of a higher social class.

When Douglas left Dominica in 1961, the excitement of adulthood was not the only current passing through his mind. He felt a sense of obligation to his parents, especially his father, RBD, who wanted his son to acquire the technical skills in agronomics. Douglas's father believed that such skills would benefit the family's plantation, allowing their assets to flourish. In three years, Douglas completed his undergraduate degree in agricultural science.

But instead of returning to apply his technical skills to good use on his father's plantations, Douglas "defected," according to his family. By that time, he and Diefenbaker had a solid rapport. He visited the prime minister in Ottawa and even met Olive, his wife. Because of RBD's disappointment that his son chose to extend his Canadian sojourn rather than return home and manage the family plantations, Douglas considered asking Diefenbaker to send a glowing letter of recommendation to his father. His relationship with Diefenbaker pulled him into the orbit of the federal Progressive Conservatives.[32]

Douglas relocated to Montreal in 1964, where he enrolled in another undergraduate program in political economy at Sir George Williams University (now Concordia University). His degree choice indicates that he yearned to learn more about society in general and structures of power in the precarious 1960s. And given his involvement in the Progressive Conservatives' youth wing, it is equally plausible that Douglas, at that critical juncture, began to subordinate a career in agribusiness and capital accumulation in Dominica to politics and public service. The freedom struggle raged in the United States, and Canadians of African descent, too, acquired a heightened racial consciousness, which Douglas tapped into when he arrived in Montreal.[33]

Like Douglas, class power and the fear of mediocrity made Anne Cools chafe. But unlike Douglas, who could assert his radicalism with a modicum of confidence in a heteronormative society (although tempered by his race), Cools had to contend more with the gender norms of her times that tried to constrain her agency. Despite coming from a family of self-assured and accomplished women, gender factored into the ways that Cools negotiated public and private spaces. In 1963, when she traveled to Greece and Turkey as a nineteen-year-old undergraduate, Cools sought exposure and meaning away from the parochialism of life in Montreal. In fact, she pinpointed the pivotal moment when she visited war memorials in Europe as her entry point into radical politics.[34]

As a McGill University undergraduate, Cools eventually settled on social work over medicine, her father's profession. As a budding activist coming into her own, she did not oppose convention per se, but she did place a premium on independence of thought. As a middle-class Caribbean immigrant coming of age in the turbulent 1960s, duty and social convention should have led Cools toward nursing or teaching. After interning at a social agency for young women during her McGill years, she confirmed what she knew intuitively: serving others, specifically women, gave her meaning and purpose. "My mother always used to say that I had somewhat of a bedside nature," she recalled.[35]

In childhood, family tragedy helped Cools develop empathy. By age four, she had lost two siblings to peritonitis, an inflammation within the abdominal wall.[36] "I'm not the sort of person who can see a problem and neglect it," she admitted. When confronted with adversity, Cools knew how to respond. "I'm a very upfront, very candid, very honest person." In fact, she shone brightest when she spoke truth to power, even if this made her lose her cool. Trinidadian Akua Benjamin, a contemporary, recalled a time when the firebrand Cools attended a gathering of Black radicals. Cools "blasted the men" for treating the women like "workhorses" and relegating them to do "grunge work" while the men flexed their leadership muscles. "She challenged us women in the room as to why we were not talking. In those days, I just sat quietly in the back of the room," Benjamin acknowledged. "I would sit there and sweat. I was afraid to speak, afraid that I would get shut down. Anne cursed the men out, saying, 'fucking' this and 'fucking' that." Captivated by this display of mettle, Benjamin admitted, "We had never heard a woman talk like that. She really empowered me. After that I thought, 'I'm going to raise my voice.'"[37]

Having been brought up in a family and social context that valued self-assertion and public leadership, Cools remarked of her youth, "We have to go forth, we have to face issues. Those of us who have additional skills—humanity—whatever they may be, we have a duty to share them."[38] Cools stood out as a confident woman with sympathy for human suffering and a straight-shooting demeanor. As a promising activist, she embodied the invaluable contributions that Black women made to the freedom struggle in Canada, the Caribbean, and the United States.

By 1965, Montreal had become a bona fide lair of Black intellectuals, many of whom subscribed to revolutionary leftist or Marxist ideas. The city represented Canada's heartbeat of political and cultural activism. Black Montreal went from 7,000 people in the early 1960s to 50,000 by decade's end, due in large part to the liberalization of immigration. The influx of Caribbean immigrants and visitors during this period fanned the flames of Black thought and consciousness, which nurtured multiple radical epistemic communities.

The Caribbean Conference Committee (CCC) and the C. L. R. James Study Circle, both founded in 1965, became "profoundly important" to Montreal as hubs for diasporic political activism. These spaces provided Douglas and fellow Montreal-based Canadian and Caribbean students— such as Cools, Leonard "Tim" Hector, Robert Hill, Bridget Joseph, Jean Depradine, and Gloria Simmons—access to intellectuals and revolutionaries. They would form a community that collaborated in North America and the Caribbean in the coming years. The young intellectuals and activists in the CCC yearned for Caribbean self-determination to lift the region "from the bottom up," given that only four islands had acquired independence by the mid-1960s.[39] The political consciousness of these sentinels underscores the meaning of Pan-Africanisms—community building and mobilization of the masses to gain control of the state. It demonstrates the inherently transnational orientation of Black radicalism on the North American mainland.

With the CCC, Cools stood out among her peers. David Austin described her as the "only woman in a prominent position." The respect with which her male colleagues regarded Cools is reflected in the fact that the CCC selected her to visit Cuba on the group's behalf in 1966 to persuade Cuban authorities to translate C. L. R. James's *Black Jacobins* into Spanish. Cools and fellow radical women Bridget Joseph, Gloria Simmons, and Jean Depradine became female vanguards "in the forefront of the movement for a new Caribbean."[40]

Cools remained resolute on questions relating to women in the struggle for Black liberation. Although she published very little during her activist years, she once wrote that Black women endured the "burdensome, back-breaking and stultifying labor" of Canadian society. Moreover, she lamented in an essay titled "Womanhood" that Black women had effectively become "the slave of the slaves."[41] Sexism existed in some pockets of the Black liberation struggle, but the notion that the social relations between Black men and Black women paralleled a class of enslavers and enslaved persons was not grounded in empirical evidence or a serious material analysis.[42] Feminist discourses of the 1960s and 1970s, which propagated the idea that male descendants of enslaved Africans also benefited from or practiced their own patriarchy, obfuscated and disavowed the true nature of white supremacist patriarchy. This hegemonic force was less about controlling females—regardless of race—and principally about the extermination of subordinate males outside of the dominant racial group (that is, Black males), for they posed a perceived existential threat to the social order.[43] Nonetheless, Cools's other point was noteworthy: some Black men needed to appreciate Black women's concerns in movement politics.

Douglas found himself at an ideological crossroads during this period of racial, gender, and intellectual ferment and Black organizing. As a Sir George Williams student, Douglas actively participated in Young Progressive Conservatives initiatives—a farm team of sorts responsible for yielding future crops of progressive-minded conservative politicians, bureaucrats, and citizens. On 19 and 20 February 1965, the gregarious Dominican student showcased his versatile speaking skills to his fellow Young Progressive Conservatives and other members at the annual Model Parliament. The parliamentary simulation, which took place at Douglas's university, pitted him against the Liberal minority government's proposed immigration bill.

To Douglas, Model Parliament meant more than a perfunctory exercise in democracy. This gathering of middle-class university students, the overwhelming majority of whom were white and male, permitted Douglas to participate in a meaningful dialogue. In his opening gambit, he wasted little time in rebuking the minority Liberal government. "This bit of trash defined by the Minister of Citizenship and Immigration as being his Immigration Bill, or in effect his government's Immigration policy, leaves much to be desired and does not meet the needs or contribute any constructive cure to the Immigration ills of this vast-empty country."[44]

Douglas's opposition to and scrutiny of the Liberals' proposed immigration policy stemmed from the simple fact that it still contained what he called "seeds" of discrimination. He believed that partiality toward industrialized countries acted as a "deliberate obstacle," frustrating prospective newcomers from nonindustrialized regions like the Caribbean. For Douglas, Canada could not exercise the moral authority that it desired in the postwar period if it refused to "accept her responsibility" to "incorporate the underdeveloped commonwealth countries into her Immigration policy."[45]

Douglas also interrogated the proposed bill by pointing out that the elimination of quotas in favor of a "saturation point" policy—that is, restricting immigration from a specific source from reaching an undesired level—was effectively a different form of numerus clausus. He averred that such policies were even more harmful when one considered that officials had excessive arbitrary authority to deny entry to certain immigrants. "As long as you place the keys for admitting immigrants into Canada in the discretionary hands of a biased Immigration Department," Douglas stated, "discrimination against the colored countries of the commonwealth will never cease." Douglas called on his fellow parliamentarians not to equivocate in abolishing "all forms of racial discrimination" in Canadian immigration policy. He received a resounding ovation.[46]

Douglas even disclosed his own two-year struggle to immigrate to Canada, illustrating that obtaining a Canadian visa was difficult for Caribbean students. He publicly acknowledged Progressive Conservative Member of Parliament Andrew Robinson of Bruce County, Ontario, for assisting him. He said nothing in his speech, however, about his phone call to Diefenbaker and the role that the prime minister had played. This omission is puzzling, especially given that Douglas delivered his speech to a sea of white students. Had Douglas shared his personal relationship with Diefenbaker, he would have solidified his institutional credibility as an international student. Douglas might have been enjoying a rare moment of modesty.

Douglas saved his most scathing critique for Canada's ongoing domestic servant program as an "unenviable scheme" that recruited only women from racialized countries, thus reinforcing racial, class, and gender hierarchies and splitting families. He considered this policy as a "deliberate attempt to humiliate the colored people of the Commonwealth." Assessing his fellow parliamentarians' commitment to an equitable Canada, he asked rhetorically, "Can't [Black women], in your government's opinion, rise honorably above the level of domestics?" The acting Liberal prime minister disputed Douglas's questioning, but the Speaker quietly reprimanded him for interrupting the charismatic Dominican.[47]

Douglas challenged his fellow parliamentarians once more. If they, as educated university students, failed to grasp the sense of urgency regarding racial discrimination in Canadian public and foreign policy, what future was there for Canada to play a leading role as a power broker in a complex and rapidly changing international system?

While Douglas exploited the Model Parliament platform to underscore Canada's need to hasten its postwar liberalization efforts, he chafed under the Progressive Conservative cloak. Soon, his deft networking skills and nimble political maneuverings gave him real political options, if he were to choose to remain in Canada after securing his second undergraduate degree. Douglas explained that during this period, Diefenbaker encouraged him to run as a Progressive Conservative in a Halifax, Nova Scotia, riding—one of the historic cities of the descendants of Black Loyalists and Black Refugees.[48]

The lure of becoming the first Black Member of Parliament in Canada enticed Douglas, but he determined that the Progressive Conservative Party lacked the racial politics that he could support.[49] The persistence of racial injustice in Canada demanded a radical approach, like the one for which diasporic African intellectuals advocated in 1960s Montreal. Douglas felt a deep sense of urgency to commit full-time to the freedom struggle in Canada and the Black world. "It was really the intensification of the civil-rights movement by the late sixties," he recalled, "that led Diefenbaker and myself to drift apart."[50] His rhetoric of Black radicalism became unintelligible to Diefenbaker, Douglas's onetime mentor who once cautioned Canadians against the "gales of destruction."[51] Douglas's generation would not wait on permission from elders. They would act based on their conscience.

A SURGING TEMPEST "OVERFLOWS THE BORDER"

In the late 1960s, a palpable radical force surfaced in Canadian society. Anti–Vietnam War protesters and Black Power, Red Power, and Woman Power advocates, closely following U.S. developments, demanded greater accountability from the state and resistance to its exploitation. Additionally, a resurging Quebecois nationalist sentiment, which the bellicose Front de libération du Québec (FLQ) led, threatened to torpedo the dream of

Confederation and a unified Canada.[52] While attending Expo 67 in Montreal, French president Charles de Gaulle's "Vive le Québec libre!" speech sounded like a veritable war cry intended to break up Canada.[53] By 1968, Pierre Vallières, an FLQ member and intellectual, published the first edition of his manifesto *White Niggers of America.*[54] Bombings and other insurrectionist acts, including two high-profile kidnappings and the assassination of a Quebec deputy premier, culminated in the October Crisis of 1970. Prime Minister Pierre Trudeau invoked the War Measures Act, which placed a moratorium on civil liberties.

Some Quebec separatists co-opted the African American narrative to illustrate their historical subordination and suffering under Canada's Anglophone population. And some African North American activists and intellectuals in Montreal supported the FLQ. Their Black Power and Pan-African consciousness, coupled with an awareness of having suffered under both of Canada's Anglophone and Francophone "founders," came to a climax at the pivotal Congress of Black Writers Conference. The conference, which took place at McGill University from 11 to 14 October 1968, brought together revolutionaries Walter Rodney, Stokely Carmichael, and C. L. R. James, among others. Notwithstanding that this unprecedented gathering, in the words of one scholar, "romanticized" Africa and boasted a roster of lecturers that snubbed women speakers, it nonetheless "signaled a turning point" of sorts, elevating Montreal to the fore of the Black freedom struggle.[55] Douglas perceived the objective as "bridging the political gap between the two ethnic poles" (native-born African Canadians and African Caribbean peoples).[56] According to one historian, this moment "marked an intriguing Black Power triangulation" of diasporic activists.[57] As a result of this leftist conference, the Jamaican government banned Walter Rodney from returning to his faculty position at the University of the West Indies at Mona. Student uprisings ensued in Jamaica, and demonstrations occurred in North America and England.

Canadian authorities vigilantly monitored this Black Power upheaval because of the urban uprisings in the United States. White Canadians consumed images of raging infernos and billowing smoke in Watts, Chicago, Philadelphia, Rochester, Newark, Detroit, and other U.S. cities in the 1960s and worried about Canada's "fire next time."[58] As one Detroiter phrased it, "The victories and struggles of African and Caribbean nations against colonialism all increased a sense of being part of a revolution that was sweeping through the inner-cities."[59]

The fear that Black revolution would spread to Canadian cities existed in the highest offices. Pierre Trudeau became prime minister in April 1968, a particularly violent moment when urban uprisings destabilized U.S. cities after the assassination of Martin Luther King Jr. on 4 April. Later that year in November at Queen's University in Kingston, Ontario—a small city between Toronto and Montreal—Trudeau gave a speech in which he shared his belief that the United States, in a bipolar, Cold War world, was "more strongly threatened by internal disorders than external pressures." The deep and existential fault lines in U.S. society—the cause of which Trudeau attributed to "problems created by urbanization, created by racial strife, and problems in many sections of the society . . . not only the young and the trade unions, but also the new elite"—were alarming, considering that they "might seriously lead to large rebellions and large disturbances of civil order and of social stability in North America."[60]

Domestic turmoil in the United States, according to the young Canadian leader, could undermine Canadian society. According to Trudeau, "If in the next half dozen years or so there were to be great riots, beginnings of civil war in the United States, I'm quite certain they would overflow the borders and they would perhaps link up with the underprivileged Mexican and the underprivileged Canadian." The imagery of revolutionary violence "overflowing" a porous and demilitarized U.S.-Canadian border spoke to a possibility that Canadians often feared. Trudeau believed that the true threat in the postwar period was not communism, fascism, or even nuclear war but rather "the two-thirds of the world's population that goes to bed hungry every night and large fractions of our own society which do not find fulfillment."[61] Understanding the spirit of the times, he prioritized reforms, such as social welfare and immigration liberalization, to signal a new direction in Canadian domestic and foreign policy, one that remained true to Canada's role as an international diplomat.

As an intellectual turned politician, Trudeau possessed sensibilities and insights that some of his peers lacked. In a November 1968 *New York Times* review of *Federalism and the French Canadians*, Trudeau's important meditation on national reconciliation, the eminent communications theorist Marshall McLuhan wrote, "No American President, past or present, can approximate his range of awareness or his reading of men and affairs." For McLuhan, Trudeau possessed real depth perception because of his bicultural Anglophone and Francophone background. In other words, Trudeau, too, had a double consciousness of sorts. For this reason, McLuhan asserted that the charismatic prime minister "would find no difficulty in coping with the American dilemma of the Negro."[62] But McLuhan grossly underestimated anti-Black racism in Canada, and certainly in the United States.[63]

In a humbling twist of fate, Trudeau witnessed his own Canadian dilemma weeks after McLuhan's commentary when, in December 1968, a serious accusation of racism resurfaced. A few months earlier in April, six Caribbean students at Sir George Williams University alleged that their white biology professor repeatedly gave failing grades to his Black students, regardless of the quality of their work. Administrators at the university agreed to investigate the incident but stalled. After the Congress of Black Writers Conference in October, it became clear to everyone involved that the issue had metastasized into something potentially explosive. University administrators simply refused to take the students' accusations seriously.

By 29 January 1969, Black students and their allies at Sir George squared off against administrators, and 400 student activists occupied the university's computer center for two weeks. Rosie Douglas and Anne Cools were among them. By then a graduate student at McGill University, Douglas had acquired impressive bona fides. In addition to his leadership work for the Young Progressive Conservatives, he had befriended members of the Montreal elite, such as politicians Pierre Trudeau and René Lévesque, as well as relatives of the wealthy Bronfman family.[64] These contacts had helped fund the monumental Congress of Black Writers Conference of 1968.[65] "His self-confidence was innate, natural and native," said his comrade Tim Hector.[66] Douglas also associated with international radicals, served as president of the Association of British West Indian Students, and helped lead the Caribbean Conference Committee along with Cools.

Sensing that the student occupation could unravel quickly, Douglas made a phone call to his mentor, Diefenbaker. The former prime minister was displeased: "If the students occupy any section of the building during winter, they [the administration] should turn the heat off and let them freeze to death."[67] Diefenbaker's response rattled Douglas. His Progressive Conservative sage who, eight years before, declared to the world that an apartheid South Africa was unwelcome in the Commonwealth rebuffed Douglas's concerns. Nonetheless, Douglas believed that leading a student protest against anti-Black racism placed him on the right side of history. "Black people in this country, as in the United States, are victims of an excruciatingly destructive system of oppression and persecution," Douglas recalled. Slavery's "ideological heritage" is "institutional racism."[68]

Douglas told Diefenbaker that the occupation "was a fight for black people to have a stake in the nation." While Diefenbaker likely sympathized with the racism that the six Caribbean students believed they had experienced, he sharply disagreed with their method of protest. The struggle, Douglas countered, had nothing to do with "malice" in the hearts of the protesters but everything to do with effecting racial "justice."[69] Six years after the student occupation, Diefenbaker wrote in his memoirs, "Too often have Conservatives in this country lost sight of the fact that change must take place to meet changing conditions, that the health of the tree is preserved by pruning the withered limbs." It is difficult to ascertain whether the student occupation weighed on Diefenbaker's consciousness when he authored these words.[70]

Instead of turning off the heat, as the former prime minister suggested, the administration colluded with the police, who stormed the computer center without warning. In the ensuing pandemonium, an unidentified person set the computer center ablaze. Students threw the contents of the computer center onto the street, as some passersby gathered and chanted, "Let the niggers burn!"[71] Many Black people in Montreal felt unsafe after the computer center occupation, so members of the C. L. R. James Study Circle discussed mustering a militia to defend Black communities. They eventually abandoned the idea.[72]

After police arrested Douglas, he heard a lawyer representing the university describe him as an "extremely dangerous individual" at his bail hearing. The university counsel accused Douglas of recruiting radicals from Dominica to "set up committees of agitation" on campus, only to recant and admit that Douglas sought the establishment of "committees of financial support."[73] As principal figures in the initial organizing—although unclear that they were present when the fire began—Douglas and Cools received steep fines and jail terms of twenty-four months and four months, respectively.[74] The talented and fearless African Canadian lawyer Juanita Westmoreland represented Douglas, Cools, and other student activists. After posting a $14,000 bail, Douglas toured several Caribbean islands in December 1969 to enlist support. In Jamaica he met with Michael Manley, leftist opposition leader.[75]

Some Black people in Quebec felt Douglas's actions looked suspicious. Others perceived him as arrogant. In fact, moderate voices illustrated rifts in Black communities, dispelling any notion that Pan-Africanisms in North America were Pollyannaish affairs. One Black person from the Montreal suburb Verdun, for example, chastised Douglas for telling the white media that he was the spokesperson for all African Canadians, although he lacked Canadian citizenship. In the national paper of record, the concerned individual asked what Douglas and his government would say if a Canadian-born Black person went to Dominica and "became a Black militant leader to enlighten his people about racism and class distinction. . . . Would I get the same television, radio and newspaper coverage that he enjoys in my country? I think not."[76] Building class consciousness, in other words, necessitated humility and circumspection. Even in an era that witnessed agitation based on Pan-Africanisms, national borders mattered to some people, and distinctions based on national origin served the purpose of chastening those who transgressed boundaries.

Nevertheless, the fear of racial subversion and student radicalism entered Canadian consciousness.[77] At the October 1969 African Heritage Studies Association meeting in Montreal, for example, Black scholars and activists, some of whom had participated in the Congress of Black Writers Conference, protested white control of the organization. Led by the eminent historian John Henrik Clarke, the newly established African Heritage Studies Association provided an alternate vision of a self-determinative, African-centered approach to the study of Black people. Although disruptive, white organizers knew not to call the police, which would have exacerbated the nonviolent confrontation.[78] In many cases, however, Canadian authorities jailed agitators and deported others. Students who participated in the Sir George Williams occupation experienced physical violence and blackballing, which impacted their material well-being, especially Black students and those who did not have Canadian citizenship. When the trial of fourteen Trinidadian students involved in the computer center occupation ended in convictions, deportation orders, and $33,000 in indemnities paid by the Trinidadian government, Caribbean student activists took to the streets to express solidarity with their comrades. They vented their anger at Canada and the acquiescent Trinidadian government for paying a fine for its daughters and sons who stood up against racism.[79]

BLACK POWER 2.0

Meanwhile in Halifax, Nova Scotia, African Canadians experienced a parallel set of daunting racial obstacles. Up until the late 1960s, Africville, arguably the only veritable slum that housed African Canadians, rivaled housing conditions for African Americans in ghettoes in the urban North.[80] African Nova Scotians' geographic isolation from other Black people, particularly in Quebec and Ontario, rendered their centuries-long struggle against racial subordination and subjugation as one that was "out of sight and out of mind."[81] Postwar militance in North America and a new generation of activists portended new possibilities for social change and national and international recognition of African Nova Scotian history and experience.

Burnley "Rocky" Jones, a charismatic and militant young man, emerged as the spokesperson for Black Power in Canada.[82] Born on 26 August 1941 in Truro, Nova Scotia, Jones came from a large family of ten children. He was the descendant of Black Refugees from the War of 1812 and grandson of the steely World War I hero Jeremiah Jones.[83] Although his forebears had served the Crown and Canada with great distinction, they never received their due. This bitter memory of racial scorn shaped Jones's understanding of Canadian society. At age seventeen, he left Nova Scotia to enlist in the Canadian Armed Forces. Jones spent time in British Columbia and Toronto, where he and his wife, Joan, who had been born in Buffalo, New York, worked as civil rights organizers.[84]

Jones attributed his political education to Harry Gairey, a staunch Garveyite and one of the founders of the Toronto local of the Brotherhood of Sleeping Car Porters. He recalled that Gairey, a leader in Toronto's West Indian community, which sometimes experienced friction with the African Nova Scotian community that migrated to the city, taught him the fundamentals of Black self-determination. According to Jones, Gairey "translated the idea of organized labor to organized communities and organized people." Gairey was also the first person who taught him the importance of Black people devising solutions to their liberation. This race-first theology not only sparked Jones's revolutionary transformation but also revealed the meaning of institution building within Black communities. Other elders in Toronto, such as former Brotherhood of Sleeping Car Porters organizer Stan Grizzle and Leonard "Lenny" Johnston—both Canadian-born and of Jamaican extraction—underscored Gairey's message of Pan-Africanisms. "Their politics were Canada and the Diaspora," Jones said of his political idols.[85] This sentiment undermines perceptions that tribalism or cliquishness influenced West Indian politics.

Starting in the 1960s, some in the Canadian press called Jones "Canada's own Stokely Carmichael."[86] The appellation fit. Jones was one of the only African Canadians who spoke at the historic 1968 Congress of Black Writers Conference in Montreal and the activist who brought the term "systemic racism" to the Canadian mainstream.[87] Jones developed a rapport with Carmichael when they met at the pivotal Montreal conference; Jones later invited him to Halifax for two days. Soon after the Montreal conference, FBI assistant director William C. Sullivan said to the *Toronto Daily Star* that Black Power militants "have been crossing the border" to incite revolutionary fervor among Canada's downtrodden. Sullivan suggested that the FBI and its counterpart, the Royal Canadian Mounted Police (RCMP), would cooperate to disrupt Black Power.[88]

When U.S. Black Panthers visited Halifax in November 1968, they implored the community to embrace the Black Power tidal wave cascading over North America.[89] Robert Waddell Smith (better known as George Sams) and T. D. Pawley met with the Nova Scotia Association for the Advancement of Colored People, a moderate, integrationist advocacy organization modeled after the NAACP. At a town hall, Pawley declared, "I'm here to walk and talk with you, I'm telling you that I love you, and I love you because you're black and because you're my brother and you're my sister and I think we should sit down and have a family meeting and talk." Because of the presence of some white Canadians, Pawley requested a "family meeting"—a Black Power euphemism for a social setting where Black people could speak candidly without the hindrance of the white gaze or ears.[90]

On 30 November, 500 community members attended this "family meeting" behind closed doors. The Black United Front (BUF), a canopy organization to unite African Nova Scotians, came out of this meeting. Don Oliver, a young Halifax lawyer from a prominent family, pointed out, "BUF wouldn't have gotten off the ground without the Panthers."[91] Jules Oliver, Don's nephew, who shortly thereafter became executive director of BUF, echoed his uncle's remarks: "The Panthers had a positive effect. They were a catalyst. Before they came, there was little awareness among Black people in the province. Now you can see changes everywhere."[92] One could misconstrue this sentiment of gratitude as portraying African Canadians as a group that needed an exogenous shock, specifically from African American militants, before they could exercise their agency. It is true that African descendants in Canada draw inspiration from their more populous U.S. counterparts, but this was a function of having a small population dispersed across an expansive land mass. One week after the community in Nova Scotia created BUF, it hosted a human rights conference called "The Black Man in Nova Scotia." Similar to the Montreal Congress of Black Writers Conference a few weeks before, this human rights conference paid little attention to women as a separate gender.[93]

Canadian authorities went on high alert, because they expected that the conference would attract a horde of unsavory militants from the United States. The RCMP advised immigration officials to deny entry to all Black border crossers. In total, 200 of the 800 attendees were Black. The conference organizers proposed tougher penalties for human rights violations and mandatory public hearings for discrimination and petitioned the premier—the head of the provincial government—to choose an African Nova Scotian as the director of the human rights commission.[94]

Instead, the premier chose a white former journalist from Toronto, Marvin Schiff. Despite widespread disappointment among African Nova Scotians, Gus Wedderburn, a leader in the Nova Scotia Association for the Advancement of Colored People, concluded that Schiff was "an excellent man for the job." Since Schiff was a Jewish Canadian, Wedderburn felt he would be sensitive to the suffering and needs of African descendants. But most

African Nova Scotians felt disappointed. Don Jones deplored the choice: "The Black man once again has to go to the white man for help. We want to plead our own cause. For too long others have spoken for us." For Jones, Black Nationalism and leftist politics meant self-determination within the confines of Canadian society. "We're not going to be segregating because segregation is when you confine yourself for reasons that you are superior, for reasons that are harmful to another group of people. We're speaking of Black independence," he asserted. "Your white system can function as you wish. Black people will function as we wish."[95]

African Nova Scotians had moved from human rights protests to Black Power in a matter of months. Delaying progress at a moment in history when the rhetoric of Black Power spread rapidly jeopardized social cohesion. It would be a "grave mistake to keep the Negro community powerless," Wedderburn discerned. "The ranks of the malcontents are swelling, racial tensions are on the increase, and it is only a matter of time before the violence in the United States spills into Canada and the Maritimes." African Canadian leaders hoped that such alarmist rhetoric would spur state action.[96]

At the same time, most understood the downside of resorting to violence. When the sojourning Panthers organized their own meeting after the human rights conference, only a dozen people attended. "If we have to kill whitey or if we have to kill cops, we're ready," one Panther said, to galvanize the few attendees. This hyperbolic rhetoric offended some participants. The following day, only two Nova Scotians attended the Panther gathering. Dr. William Pearly Oliver shied away from framing Black agitation in Nova Scotia as strictly operating within the context of Black Power or the Black Panther Party. He proclaimed that BUF's work would be "one of anti-violence, in favor of a new firmness, dignity, aggressiveness, even militance."[97]

Halifax authorities threatened to deport BUF's second-in-command back to the United States for his radical politics. Paul Winn got the job as Jules Oliver's deputy when he responded to an employment ad in *Time* magazine. In the late 1960s, Winn attended a Panthers conference in San Francisco, where he acquired lessons on grassroots organizing, militancy, and political education. When the chief of police said he would deport Winn, the young activist responded, "You do what you have to do and I'll do what I have to do." But there was a logistical problem with this very serious threat of deportation: Paul Winn was Canadian. He had been born in Toronto. Although Winn spent many childhood summers in New York City and briefly attended English High School in Boston in the early 1950s—where he lived and apprenticed under the care of his uncle Laurance Banks, the lawyer and pioneering Republican municipal official—he lived mostly in Toronto and later Vancouver. Furthermore, Winn observed that militancy transcended gender in Nova Scotia: "Some of the women were just as militant as the men." He recalled that the U.S.-born Joan Jones, wife of Rocky Jones, was especially receptive to his contributions to BUF and the African Nova Scotian people, which was high praise, considering how wary these communities were of outsiders.[98]

A stark contrast existed between old guard leaders and young radicals. When Rocky Jones attended a gathering of 500 radicals (of whom 100 were Black) at the University of Toronto a few days after the "Black Man in Nova Scotia" human rights conference, he captivated the attendees with his militancy.[99] Jones delivered this ominous warning to the predominantly white audience: "If you don't get up off me I am going to throw you off and I'm going to stomp you. Whatever you do to us, we will do to you." Jones accused Canadian law enforcement of behaving "up tight" when they discovered that Panthers now prowled on Canadian soil. "This harassment has got to stop—it's got to stop as of now," he declared. Jones alleged that 15,000 African Nova Scotians were "prepared to do anything to control their destiny," ignoring the failure of the Panthers' recruiting efforts there.[100]

At the same rally, Jan Carew—the Guyanese novelist, playwright, and Black Power advocate—underscored African Canadians' frustration with Canada's imperial past. According to Carew, "Racism exists with the monumental hypocrisy which Canadians inherited from the British—a new kind of colonialism—a Canadian cracker mentality."[101] As a British subject, Carew deployed the rhetoric of colonialism and related it broadly to the Panthers' notion that African Canadians, too, were an internal colony. As one of the founders of the Afro-American Progressive Association of Toronto, a militant Marxist organization, Carew chastened Canadian society for its underhanded liberalism. "Don't pat yourself on the back for the beautiful race relations in Canada," he asserted. "You don't have less race prejudice in Canada, you have less Black people."[102]

The marquee event of the Black Power rally at the University of Toronto promised to feature U.S. Olympic sprinters turned Black Power advocates John Carlos and Tommie Smith. They did not appear, but the Detroit chapter of the Panthers attended in full force. Marian Kramer, vice deputy minister of education of the Detroit chapter, stated, "Like Queen Elizabeth, ever since we set foot in Canada, right outside that tunnel, we've had the RCMP escort all the way."[103] Another high-ranking Michigan Panther predicted, "They saw Watts and they saw Detroit, but they haven't seen Toronto yet." This insinuation that Toronto's nearly 20,000 Black residents could lead an uprising dramatized the revolutionary flare of the event. Although militant in his opposition to the oppression of African Canadians, Jones spoke up when a moment called for the voice of reason. He encouraged attendees to consider serious constructive directions in which to "channel" the desires and frustration of Canadian youth.[104]

As a Black Nationalist, Nova Scotia's Rocky Jones, like other militant young men and women of his generation, harbored skepticism of interracial coalitions with white radicals. "The only way to tell is to watch which way their guns are pointed when the shooting starts," suggested Jones, an avid hunter and gun enthusiast. "We haven't reached that point yet." Jones's affiliation with the Black Panthers and his embrace of social revolution put him on the radical fringe in Nova Scotia, but he realized the power his words had to confuse and frighten officials.[105] "The Black people today in North America are revolutionaries, because we are faced with extermination. We are forced to fight," he argued, despite knowing that African Nova Scotians preferred progressive politics to violent outbursts.[106]

Denny Grant, a Caribbean immigrant and comrade in the struggle, pointed out that Jones's logic would not lead to victory. According to Grant, "We will be faced with extermination if we decide to fight for what is right, but there won't be extermination if we decide to go on being slaves. We bring on extermination ourselves, but it is a necessary extermination," he reasoned. On the likelihood of revolution in Canada, Grant explained that very few Black people sought a complete overhaul of the system: "Black people want to live like ordinary human beings. Those who want to overthrow the system are those with international minds, or those who have talked with international figures." Grant favored revolution, but not a "quiet" revolution, such as the one taking place in Quebec with the FLQ. Channeling Frantz Fanon's advocacy of violence as an equalizing force, he concluded, "It's a very sad thing, man, but white people will not listen unless you're violent." Grant, who abhorred white Canadians for patronizing their fellow Black citizens with platitudes, such as "We don't treat Negroes like they do in the States," reminded African Canadians that the struggle for dignity and racial equality must occur with the utmost scrutiny of Canadian society.

Despite Grant's pronouncements, interracialism was a fact of life in Black activist circles. Like Fred Hampton, chairman of the Illinois chapter of the Black Panther Party, Rocky Jones worked with a handful of white leftists, believing there was a place for some of them in the struggle.[107] Moreover, some Black men dated and married white women. Sightings of Black radicals with white partners was a fact of life. Paul Winn, deputy executive director of BUF, recalled walking on the streets of Halifax with his white girlfriend when a group of Black teenage girls trailed and taunted him: "Talk Black, sleep white! Talk Black, sleep white!" Although Winn took no offense and shrugged off the snarky remarks, he appreciated the masculinist limitations and sexual contradictions that the teenage girls observed about Black Power.[108]

Despite ideological inconsistencies, Black militancy continued to gain traction in 1969. The Afro-American Progressive Association, which Carew cofounded, provided an intellectual and activist platform for African descendants to challenge inequality in Canadian society. Cofounder José Garcia, a stocky Aruban who immigrated to Toronto in 1965, served as the group's secretary. Garcia, who accused Canada of being "racist to the core," described the association—which extended membership only to Black people (Garcia's white wife could not attend meetings)—as kindred of the Panthers. "We're part of the same political line, which is a Marxist-Leninist line. Why call it a Black Panther Party? It's a nationalist thing," he declared. "The struggle internationally takes different faces. Like in Vietnam. We identify with the Vietnamese. They're struggling for us." The Afro-American Progressive Association promoted the independence of African Canadians on the one hand and racial solidarity and international class-consciousness on the other.[109]

As pockets of Black communities in Canada embraced radicalism, the Panthers themselves increased their presence in Canadian cities. In fact, a few days before the FBI and Chicago police brazenly assassinated Fred Hampton while he slept in his Chicago apartment, Hampton had traveled north to Regina, Saskatchewan, on 18 November 1969. Although Regina is an unusual destination given its scant population of African descendants, this speaking engagement allowed Hampton to fundraise on behalf of the Black Panther Party. He spread its gospel of social revolution to white student radicals and the populous Indigenous community in Western Canada.[110] On 21 November, the tour ended abruptly for Panthers William Calvin and Jeraldine Eldridge when Canadian officials arrested and deported them. An immigration hearing classified them as prohibited subjects because of their prior criminal convictions. Canadian officials permitted Hampton to return to the United States on his own accord, without formal deportation, however. When Canada's solicitor-general told the press that "the Panthers are infiltrating Western Canada to stir up trouble among Canadian Indians," he was perpetuating the myth that radicalism and agitation came exclusively from non-Canadian sources.[111] In reality, internal and external forces had worked symbiotically throughout the century to produce a system that Black radicals—and Indigenous ones, too—could no longer tolerate.

Black Power in the United States dovetailed with the racial politics in 1960s and 1970s Canada, which created an opening for Black and white draft resisters to influence international discourse. As the United States ramped up its involvement in Vietnam after 1964, anti-war activists became more militant in their opposition to a war steeped in aggression and senseless bloodshed. Social unrest, much of which stemmed from the perceived racial and class inequities of the draft, left few options for those whom military service, especially combat in Asia, constituted an existential moral dilemma. Depending on one's draft status, defection from the United States or outright desertion from a military installation represented two of the few outlets for war resisters. Western European countries—such as Sweden, Germany, and France—welcomed hordes of military-age men and their female partners who chose to quit the United States. But Canada, a perennial refuge point in the U.S. imagination, proved much more strategic for war resisters because of its proximity, ease of entry, cultural resemblance, and potential for economic integration.[112]

The flow of U.S. war resisters across the border into Canadian cities went from a mere trickle in the mid-1960s to a deluge by 1970. Some conservative estimates place the number of draft-age men who immigrated to Canada from 1965 to 1972 at roughly 30,150, 20,230 of whom identified as "dodger" or "deserter."[113] Conversely, the number of U.S. resisters paralleled the number of Canadians who fought for the United States in Vietnam.[114] In 1969, Canada received 22,785 U.S. immigrants, the first time since 1932 that it received more immigrants from the United States than it sent.[115] Most war resisters entered through southwestern Ontario, although Montreal also proved a vital point of entry.

In response to the sudden influx of U.S. radicals, one commentator explained that some Canadians in the Vancouver area felt "uptight," an opinion that had less to do with the immigrants' "draft status or military status" and more with their appearance as "hippies." The countercultural anxieties extended beyond British Columbia. Benevolent groups that aided draft resisters processed an estimated 70 percent of all U.S. expatriates in Toronto and Ottawa, because of southwestern Ontario's strong employment prospects, compared with the West Coast, the Prairies, Quebec, and Eastern Canada.[116] With their government identification, some resisters drove across the border into Canada, while some flew into Canadian airports. An unknown number of draft resisters, of course, entered Canada illegally by walking across the border or by having friends and associates smuggle them into the country.

Leaders in the "refugee" movement established numerous organizations nationwide to assist draft resisters and their families while refraining from declaring Canada a haven for deserters. Such a declaration could have turned public opinion against resisters.[117] Twelve U.S. war resisters founded the Union of American Exiles (UAE) on 4 April 1968. As one of the principal aid groups, the UAE had its own dedicated magazine, the *American Exile in Canada*, or *Amex*.[118] The UAE and *Amex* played a significant role in the immigration, settlement, and integration of war resisters in Canadian society. The American Deserters Committee, the Toronto Anti-Draft Programme, and the group Red, White and Black served U.S. expatriates in the Toronto area.[119] During the war years, between twenty-six and thirty-two organizations supported U.S. refugees.[120] Similar to Caribbean immigrants and Black Panthers, this influx of U.S. radicals further contributed to the subversive climate of Canadian society in the 1960s and early 1970s.

In addition to emphasizing self-help, the Union of American Exiles questioned sociopolitical and economic injustices in Canadian society. The UAE stated its organizational mission: cooperation "with Toronto Anti-Draft *Programme* by acclimating those young men who have already been admitted to *our Canadian way of life*. The Union handles all housing arrangements for the new-Canadian's first hectic days in Toronto. . . . The Union also provides employment *counselling* and a place for the Canadian-American to meet others recently arrived from south of the border."[121] The use of Canadian diction was purposeful; it signified a true breakaway from U.S. folkways on one hand and a willful embrace of Canadian ones on the other.

One of the first major cases that the UAE championed involved Robert Sherwood, an African American radical who fled to Canada. In November 1968, Charles Henry, secretary of the Workers League, sought the UAE's support in establishing a defense committee for Sherwood. He was charged with violating section 50(f) of the Immigration Act, concealing a criminal record upon entering Canada. Sherwood, along with Dick Gregory and Martin Luther King Jr., had participated in a nonviolent protest that denounced segregated schools in Chicago. The U.S. courts fined Sherwood twenty-five dollars for engaging in disorderly conduct and resisting arrest. Henry argued, "If they [Canada] choose to find him guilty, [they] must feel that participation in a demonstration for equal rights for Negroes is immoral." Sherwood's advocates believed that the Canadian government targeted him because he was a "draft resister and a member of the Workers League of Canada, and is actively engaged in working class politics."[122]

Such public defenses brought resisters notoriety, but aid groups focused principally on integration and settlement services, such as acquiring employment and permanent residency. Given that individuals could apply for landed immigrant status (that is, permanent residence) if they entered Canada legally, aid groups channeled draft resisters through this pipeline to attain citizenship. It provided this vulnerable group with a layer of protection from U.S. authorities. As unemployment increased nationally (3–5 percent to 5–7 percent) in 1970, however, many war resisters failed to procure job letters, a prerequisite to become a landed immigrant. Under the points system, prospective landed immigrants had to score at least 50 out of 100 possible points to acquire that coveted status. Immigration officers could award 60 of these points based on an applicant's education and employment skills.[123] Draft resisters from working-class backgrounds with minimal education or technical skills and African Americans in general experienced greater obstacles when applying for landed status. Immigration officers wielded discretionary powers, and many exercised bias.

The radical periodicals of the draft resister community sought to connect with Canadian and U.S. readers. Resisters evoked Canada's past as a haven for enslaved persons to revive Canada's image as a refuge point for the persecuted. To some readers in the late 1960s, overt references to slavery and the Underground Railroad by all-white leftist organizations seeking broad legitimacy in their anti-war struggle might have sounded contrived. However, calculated references to Canadian free soil during the Vietnam War was precisely what the publishers of *Amex* and other underground periodicals believed would sway public opinion to their cause.

A published manual for draft resisters, for example, juxtaposed two letters. In one written in 1853, John H. Hill, an enslaved person, recounted his escape from slavery in Richmond, Virginia, to Toronto. An unidentified draft resister in Toronto wrote the other letter on 10 November 1967. It is difficult to ascertain the race of the draft resister, although it is probable that he was white. Both writers document their escapes from the United States. Both marveled at Toronto's beauty and receptiveness upon their arrival. Both expressed a yearning for distant friends. Moreover, the draft resister, much like the enslaved person a century before him, recalled how FBI agents—or modern slave catchers—nearly apprehended him after his induction date. Had he not hidden under a pile of civvies, the authorities would have foiled his escape.[124]

U.S.-led anti-war organizations in Toronto co-opted the nineteenth-century narrative of a Black transnational freedom struggle to signify the centrality of race and migration in critiques of U.S. citizenship. This observation was particularly accurate during times of social and moral upheaval. The myth of the North Star was at its most potent when a liberal

Canada is contrasted with a repressive United States. One commentator described Canada as an adjacent utopia—an antipode to the imperialist, hawkish United States: "I've been considering splitting to Canada to escape the draft, racism, fear of the police, air pollution, omnipresent freeways and traffic congestions, overpopulation and urban sprawl, and a few more million things I'm not too pleased about down here." He also criticized "the public's general approval of police tactics in Chicago" as additional proof of public intransigence. The writer demonstrated a nuanced understanding of Canadian politics: "I know things aren't perfect in Canada either. The English pretty much control the economy and the French can't get anywhere in their corporations. A lot of French want separatism."[125] To this writer, these uniquely Canadian problems seemed much more manageable than the issues facing the United States.

Sensing the deep disquiet among military-age men because of the draft, *Amex* editors published a full poem that historians often attribute to Sojourner Truth or Harriet Tubman:

I'm on my way to Canada,
That cold but happy land.
The dire effects of slavery
I can no longer stand.

Oh righteous father
Do look down on me,
And help me on to Canada
Where colored folks are free!

The Queen comes down unto the slave
With arms extended wide,
To welcome the poor fugitive
Safe unto freedom's side.[126]

This direct appeal to Black radicals and Black draft resisters to quit the United States romanticized Canada by portraying it as a racially egalitarian society and the United States as the unreformed land of slavery.[127]

Another contributor's verse portrays Canada as the promised land and the flight from the United States as a response to the malevolence of its intelligence and security services in their zealous opposition to domestic and international freedom movements.

We came, a few beginning notes
flute soundings on the wind

but more to follow, building
cadence and movement always northward
out of the fearsounding shifting
uncertain American century we came
always northward always
into Canada singing

behind us J. Edgar fiddled
counterpoint, another key,
sadder, *legato*:
curious CIA, the roving eye
the FBI wondering why
we march always northward
a round sound of tall men
like golden trumpets
wearing conscience like a melody
played to open keys
still coming, northward
begging your pardon, our accents
midwest, southern, startling
Toronto: youse guys
among the cheerios
tea and winter but finally
free.
We slept on trains, singing of free places;
settling here, alive, glad to be living,
breathing free air, we wait.
The north wind blows us clean again.[128]

No discussion of the Underground Railroad can occur without some reference to one of the most porous and fluid points of entry in the U.S.-Canadian
border: Detroit and Windsor, two cities separated by a bridge over and a
tunnel under the Detroit River. The Detroit-Windsor corridor historically
constituted a significant border crossing or point of exchange for migrants
and goods. Windsor, the "way-station for exiles," was the home of a network
that smuggled war resisters into Canada. The "convenience of geography"
made this operation viable. "Past success with Canadian officials at this
location," one observer concluded, "has led to the establishment of an
underground network of Canadians who meet Americans seeking to immigrate at a predetermined location, drive them back into the States and then
again to the Canadian border to [process them] legally." Explaining how

smugglers identified prospective refugees, the article noted, "The intrigue usually involves memorizing color schemes of clothing and bus depot locales. Similar operations exist on either side of the Ontario–New York border."[129]

An underground railroad of sorts, according to an internal FBI memo, existed between the United States and Canada. A former Panther turned FBI informant from Jersey City, New Jersey, confirmed that there was an underground network that helped "political fugitives" escape to Canada and that some proceeded to Africa or majority Black countries in the hemisphere. The informant used false identification to enter Canada, and in some cases morticians who feared the Black Panther Party furnished these false identifications to Panthers. The RCMP suspected that such a network existed but knew little about it and was "most anxious to infiltrate it." Activists initially conceived the plan in 1969 at a Black Panther Party meeting in Nova Scotia to create underground cross-border networks. Ultimately, activists decided that Eastern Canada provided the least barriers to entry from the United States. Black militants, the FBI also alleged, planned to "cache arms in Canada," identifying various villages in Nova Scotia.[130]

There was a real sense of struggle—perhaps revolution—between leftists and the U.S. government. Therefore, showcasing the perspectives of African American war resisters in leftist periodicals allowed white radicals to link the anti-war cause to the Underground Railroad and the Black freedom struggle. Eusi Ndugu, a draft resister from Mississippi who escaped to Toronto in 1969, said he "traded in his slave name. He also traded in countries recently."[131] This notion of Ndugu "exchanging" his "country marks," to borrow historian Michael Gomez's words, illustrates the efforts that some Black Nationalists made to reverse the deracination to which the U.S. ruling class had subjected their forebears.[132] Therefore, name and citizenship, under the oppressive regime of the turbulent 1960s and 1970s, became fungible markers, especially for diasporic Africans.

Ndugu explained that upon arriving in Canada, he "felt like a beautiful black crow who had escaped from the bullet of a farmer." Growing up in the Deep South, Ndugu heard tales about how some of his ancestors "followed the North Star" to Canada. As a draft resister who had obtained permanent residency, Ndugu, on his own accord, embraced the noble task of encouraging African American defection from the United States to Canada. Although he acknowledged the pervasiveness of white supremacy, Ndugu believed that racial hostility in Canada was much less destructive. "I know," he professed, "that someday I will explain to other Blacks who come from the States that my reason for coming to Canada is the same as the run-away slaves who came in the 19th century, but I am a 20th century run-away slave."[133]

Ndugu's declaration of cross-border radicals, specifically African American war resisters, as modern fugitives fleeing despotism marked a watershed in the draft resister movement. Justifying why, as a draft resister, he believed that the appellation "run-away" was more apt, Ndugu stated, "The reason I think of myself as a run-away slave is that I ran away from an oppressive racist, genocidal (educationally, physically, psychologically, and financially) and very imperialistic country." These are the same reasons, Ndugu argued, that led his forebears to follow the North Star to Canada.[134]

At a time when Canadian officials dreaded the influx of foreign radicals, Ndugu proclaimed to his comrades that they should make Canada their new home. He wrote, "We could build a strong community of our own." Ndugu reassured African Americans that Canada, especially English-speaking Toronto, would nurture their sense of Black Nationalism. African Canadians, he explained, acquired periodicals such as *Ebony, Jet*, and *Negro Digest*. He identified Lenny Johnston's radical Third World Bookstore, a well-known Toronto cultural establishment, as a place to procure "African artifacts, dashikis, and everything in the line of Black identity." For Ndugu, the choice between modern bondage and the promised land was self-evident. "We can look better in dashikis or African robes in Canada," he admonished, "than wearing a green army or blue navy outfit in Vietnam." Underscoring the theme of Black self-exile and refuge in North America, he referenced the iconic Toronto soul food restaurant called the Underground Railroad, which opened on 12 February 1969—Abraham Lincoln's birthday.[135]

Although Ndugu admitted that he had yet to visit every part of Canada, he nonetheless attested that for "Black people, especially Black men . . . the air of freedom blows a little better." This gendered statement was deliberate. As an African American with intimate insight into Jim Crow mores, Ndugu believed that his presence in Canada insulated him, to a degree, from U.S. white supremacist patriarchy, a genocidal logic that seeks to vanquish subordinate males. He also endorsed interracial radicalism on Canadian soil, perhaps as a kind gesture to his fellow white draft resisters who offered him a platform to share his story. "Brothers, the white draft-dodgers and deserters are good people, people who know why our race is fighting so damn hard in the States," he pleaded. After urging other African Americans to "come and dig on the scene here," Ndugu repeated his most important appeal: "Do like the 19th century slaves and follow the North Star to Canada."[136]

Some Black war resisters looked at Canada more critically. A 1971 article claimed that the presence of only 1,000 military-age African Americans in the land of the North Star indicated Canadian society's unwelcoming posture toward Black people. The challenge, it seemed, also stemmed from the atomized and fractured experience of African Canadians. According to Mike Vance, an African American who absconded to escape his Wisconsin draft board, "It's just now dawning on the black Canadians that they're black, and they seem to look on blacks from the States—particularly the dodgers and deserters—as troublemakers." African Canadians, Vance noted, lacked a critical mass and thus were not "concentrated" like they are in U.S. cities. Vance further criticized Black people in Canada because they were "not organized" but were "un-together," a view that some in the community shared. Vance had also encountered challenges accessing support from the white-led Toronto Anti-Draft Programme, which he attributed to his race.[137]

Although Vance made some plausible observations about African Canadians, he grossly underestimated their multilayered and extensive tradition of activism. Echoing Vance's sentiments on the obscurity of African Canadian identity to African Americans, deserter Charlie Coates said few Black enlistees knew much about Canada, hence the low numbers who had fled there. "It's the thing of leaving home, of leaving all your people. . . . There are so few Blacks here, and most of them are West Indians, and that's like a different culture."[138] For Coates, the misperception that diasporic Africans, especially those of U.S. origin, were rare in Canada led to his inaccurate conclusion that fleeing to Canada would be equivalent to "leaving your people" behind. Furthermore, the dearth of service providers catering to Black war resisters throughout Canada mystified the presence of Black radicals in the early 1970s. One reporter had trouble contacting the Toronto-based Black Refugee Organization (BRO), one of the only Black-led aid groups for resisters. Because of Canada's scrutiny and hyper-surveillance of Black war resisters and other leftists, some concluded that BRO had gone "underground." Jim Russell, a leading organizer for BRO, said he could not be forthcoming about journalists' inquiries "because we have a policy against discussing [BRO] with journalists from the States."[139]

Black draft resisters operated informally and covertly. In fact, in May 1970, Toronto police claimed that twenty-four draft resisters had found refuge with other Black people in the city who aided and hid them from the RCMP. The Mounties alleged that the U.S. government wanted to apprehend these men for weapons and drug offenses. "It [the clandestine network] is not as sophisticated," according to one detective's assessment. He further added, "Nor is it as effective as any of those wartime organizations," referring to the underground cells that helped Allied prisoners escape occupied France in World War II. Even with their lack of "sophistication" and "effectiveness," some of these draft resisters used the government-issued identification of their friends and sympathizers in Canada and the United States to evade law enforcement.[140]

Integrating into Canadian society proved much more difficult for Black draft resisters than for their white counterparts. After a year in the promised land, for instance, Ndugu sounded more tempered: "The Black thing here is completely different from the whites. A lot of the whites who come here are as racist as whites in the States." European and white U.S. immigrants brought their anti-blackness, which interfaced with white Canadians' own racism. "Whites here are no different," he concluded. "The Canadian Government is putting a quota on Blacks immigrating from the States." Refusing to accept anything short of complete racial equality, Ndugu declared, "I won't take up Canadian citizenship. Africa is my home, and that's where I am going."[141] This common but often futile search for a racial utopia in a white supremacist world is reminiscent of Claude Brown's 1965 *Manchild in the Promised Land*, a literary classic about Great Migration southerners and their disappointing and backbreaking transition to life in Harlem. Brown asked, "For where does one run to when he's already in the promised land?"[142]

Ndugu exercised agency to make Canadian society more hospitable for racialized peoples. In March 1970, he wrote an op-ed criticizing Canadian society for publicly promoting a lily-white appearance, notwithstanding its numerous Indigenous peoples and to a lesser extent Black population. According to him, "Black and native people never appear in the advertising pages of the city's three largest newspapers." Ndugu also observed, "When travelling on street cars, subways, and city buses one rarely sees a black face on the billboard."[143] Three weeks later, the director of information services for the Department of Manpower and Immigration wrote an op-ed in response to Ndugu's. He explained that the federal government had made a concerted effort, starting in February of that year, to showcase different Canadians in its advertisements. The director acknowledged the efforts of his own federal department in "running a student summer employment advertisement in the Toronto daily newspapers . . . with a photograph representing a black, 'native' Canadian, as well as white students." He confirmed that his department had recently begun to advertise on Toronto public transportation the "cultural, economic and social contributions of immigrants." The director appeared to have missed the mark in his rebuttal, however. He failed to appreciate the structural roots of Ndugu's angst. And given the timing of this federal advertisement initiative, one could only wonder if Ndugu's op-ed inspired the department to address the role it played in disavowing the presence of Black, Indigenous, and other non-white bodies from the Canadian mosaic.[144]

Ndugu further highlighted his disaffection with Canadian society. "I can't say how many Blacks have come, but the number is very low because if you leave Watts or Harlem or the Black Bottom in Detroit and get into this, it's like jumping into a pitcher of buttermilk." Like any immigrant group, the pull of vibrant and thriving Black communities played a role in whether African Americans chose to leave their oppressive but familiar racial environs for Canada's sparsely populated Black communities. He added, "Its [sic] all white—the music on the radio, the pictures in the papers and magazines and on television. There's a race problem here, just like in the northern cities of the U.S."[145]

Basil Gray, an African American draft resister in Toronto, reflected on the challenges that Black radicals experienced when they sought employment. According to Gray, "Being from the US seems to conjure visions of 'Activist,' Deserter, Betrayer of Democracy, Shirker, Trouble-maker; and if you happen to be visible, pigmentally speaking, then discrimination on this basis becomes even more subtle." He added, "One may conclude that elements in the system from which we seek refuge up here pursues like a noon day shadow in a land that has not fully realized itself as yet."[146] This cynicism with which some African Americans regarded race relations in Canadian society mirrored the way that many African Canadians viewed Canada.

Lenny Johnston and his wife, Gwendolyn, co-owned Third World Bookstore and Crafts in downtown Toronto, a popular hangout that leftists frequented. He speculated, "They [Black draft resisters] can't trust anyone, and they can't melt into the city like they could in New York or Detroit."[147] The absence of a Black critical mass in Toronto and historically discriminatory immigration limited the numbers of African descendants in Canada, which deterred others from immigrating.

The son of Jamaicans who immigrated to Toronto in 1890, Johnston, like many of his Black male contemporaries in Canada, worked full-time as a porter on the Canadian Pacific Railway in the 1940s. The fifty-two-year-old Canadian-born Johnston believed that Canada and the United States shared much in common in terms of their racist foundations. "The only difference is in degree and percentage," he asserted. "If there were more Blacks here it would be the same. America's racism is raw, it's out of control. Here [in Canada], it's covered up." According to Johnston, the problem for African descendants in Canada stemmed from their numerical marginality, which subjected them, among other forces, to whimsical treatment whenever most Canadians experienced prolonged economic or political challenges. "Sure, there's peace and tranquility here, there's very little in the way of [overt] discrimination," he conceded. "But the situation here is now like pre-war

Germany, where the Jews thought they were Germans. They weren't, and we're not Canadians. If a depression comes, we'll be niggers again. Fascism is the real threat."[148] As the son of Garveyites, Johnston's race consciousness prevented him from committing to Canada's pseudo multiracial nation-building project. He saw himself as a refugee without a permanent home for himself and his people.

Notwithstanding the political asylum that U.S. expatriates found in Canada, one draft resister in Vancouver underscored the transnationalism of white supremacy and the embedded colonialisms of the United States and Canada. "In short, it finally dawns on us that it's the same old shit all over again. We see that we never had an alternative to the pathetic racist culture we left behind." He further explained, "If you don't like what's happening to the Black man down there, dig what's happening to the Red man here."[149] For some war resisters who sought refuge in Canada, racism and imperialism illustrated limitations of the state.

The racism that African North Americans alluded to in Canadian society sometimes appeared overt and unmistakable, showing its face without shame. The Canadian white supremacist organization the Western Guard (formerly the Edmund Burke Society), which one U.S. expatriate described as "a mélange of Eastern European and Canadian-born fascists" who advocate "for the murder of black people and 'white race traitors,'" had acquired a notorious reputation for disrupting anti-war demonstrations. It also committed acts of racism against minorities.[150] On 29 April 1972, it hosted a hate banquet for other white supremacists in Toronto. The KKK and Canadian and U.S. Nazi parties, among others, attended. One participant indicted for bombing school buses in Pontiac, Michigan, to stall that city's court-ordered school integration described Canada as "the last stronghold of white . . . supremacist culture and a place for white Americans to come if . . . the Jewish conspired mongrelization of white and black is allowed to continue."[151] That white supremacists also regarded Canada as their place of refuge further complicated the image of Canada as a haven for persons of African descent. In mid-March, moreover, as Rosie Douglas canvassed Toronto for his Black community center project, the Klan painted a white cross on his car, slashed the tires, and left an ominous note that said, "NIGGER, YOUR TIME IS UP."[152]

Racism was not the only obstacle. In the war resister community, concerns over sexism mobilized some activists. Women's rights advocates voiced their grievances, given the supporting cast and lead roles that they played in the refugee community. Many women helped men publish magazines, wrote articles, and made inquiries on behalf of their loved ones. *Amex*, which made a concerted effort to discuss the organizing efforts of women, ran an article acknowledging the invaluable contributions of three women in the anti-draft struggle in Vancouver and Toronto and their overall efforts in the women's liberation movement.[153] Often the spouses of draft resisters, women formed their own support networks, in addition to their broader contributions to the anti-war movement. In Toronto, white women, such as Sandy Gaetano, Dorothy Jones, Maryann Campbell, Karen Sheehan, and Nancy Goldsberry, spearheaded a committee to procure medical care, specifically prenatal aid and birth control, and baby clothing.[154]

Women shaped the draft resister community. At the May 1970 Pan-Canadian Conference in Montreal, for instance, the women of the Montreal-American Deserters Committee organized a women's caucus. These activists felt that they had been "put down" and tasked with completing "shit work." The lack of gender inclusion created sparks as the broader anti-war and leftist machine mobilized. Women expressed deep frustration that some of their male counterparts discounted their contributions to the struggle because they were technically not draft resisters, which some argued amounted to "blatant male chauvinism." The women's caucus made several policy recommendations. Most notably, they pointed out that the Toronto Anti-Draft Programme should create programming that served all U.S. expatriates, not just men who were subjected to military service. They also requested that the resister publications should signal class consciousness by using simpler language for those who lacked formal education. Furthermore, the aid group Red, White and Black, they recommended, should show sensitivity for "women's problems," such as birth control and childcare.[155]

The women's caucus adopted a militant, assertive tone. In response to the notion that women were not war resisters and therefore did not experience U.S. imperialism firsthand, one participant responded, "Bullshit. Women lose their husbands, sons and brothers to the military machine. As a result, women are often obligated to change their role entirely and take over as family breadwinner." She also noted, "A woman's decision to leave the U.S. is just as political as a man's." The hubris that some men exuded, according to these women, undermined the struggle. Members of the women's caucus believed that they could temper this "ego tripping." Some also took aim at Canada's immigration policy, identifying its blatant white male patriarchy, because married women could not acquire landed immigrant status before their husbands.[156]

With the influx of U.S. war resisters and other radicals in the late 1960s and early 1970s, a recurring and urgent debate on Canadian sovereignty and U.S. imperialism resurfaced. When U.S. radicals made Canada their haven, it complicated and threatened Canadian sovereignty. In 1968, before the uptick in draft resisters, a Canadian intellectual reflected on the complex dynamic of being neighbors with, and close allies of, the United States. "There is a tendency to see Canada as facing a time of deep crisis, trying to find an appropriate place for Quebec and its aspirations, and trying to be independent and yet not lose the good things that American capital and enterprise bring us," he explained. "Our identity in a sense is up for grabs."[157]

The publishers of *Amex* vowed to shape that identity by promoting U.S. "anti-imperialism" and raising awareness of the ways that it impacted Canada.[158] Engaging in diasporic semantics, aid organizations in Canada scrutinized their place and belonging and how it was situated within the dialectics of imperialism.[159] It is partly for this reason that the publisher of *Amex* admitted that U.S. refugees "don't fit into the mosaic very nicely."[160]

One debate interrogated whether the Union of American Exiles should change "Exiles" to "Expatriates."[161] The latter noun, some believed, signified greater commitment and devotion to improving Canadian society, compared with exiles whose primary preoccupation remained the land from whence they came. In other words, did draft resisters leave willingly (expatriates), or did the United States force them out (exiles)?[162] Black Panther Party communications secretary Kathleen Cleaver described exile as "a political response to intolerable conditions."[163] In Canada, draft resisters referred to the tension in nomenclature as "American Exile Politics."[164]

The exile-expatriate divide brought into sharp focus the draft resisters' devotion to liberalizing Canadian society and the method to achieve this. One could distill the semantic battle to this point: "The 'expatriate' claims that it is ridiculous to look across a border, willingly crossed, and ignore the social injustices on your own doorstep." U.S. draft resisters in Canada contemplated two issues: pursue change in a relatively peaceful Canada, or change in the bellicose United States.[165] According to the expatriate camp, "If our attention is south of border, while living north of it, how, they ask, can we possibly be the citizens that Canada wants and so urgently needs?" The exile camp offered an equally plausible response: U.S. refugees "must keep the States in mind as much as possible, they say, as this insures continuing participation in the struggle being waged now in the U.S."[166] Ultimately, the community recognized that refugees perpetuated subtle forms of U.S. imperialism. By the summer of 1969, *Amex* replaced "exile" with "expatriate," becoming the *American Expatriate in Canada*.[167]

U.S. expatriates arrived in Canada believing that Canada was perfectible. One lamented, "We have dropped into Canada ready to build a Canadian society that will be a vast improvement over the American model. We do not want Canada to evolve as another carbon copy of the Coca Cola culture." With gradual enfranchisement for the outspoken expatriates, they challenged Canadian support for U.S. domestic and foreign policy. Subversion of U.S. imperialism seemed possible. "As long as we have anything to say about it," declared a draft resister, "America will increasingly be unable to take Canadian support for granted."[168]

Many Canadian intellectuals disavowed politically active U.S. expatriates. Robin Mathews, a Canadian academic and a member of the leftist Canadian Liberation Movement, asserted that draft resisters were "contemptuous of Canadian citizenship." As "cultural imperialists," they believed in the supremacy of their way of life. Referencing the anxiety in Canadian intellectual history, Mathews declared, "The American has always been recognized as a threat to survival."[169]

Nonetheless, Ron Lambert, another Canadian academic who counseled many draft resisters, tried to bridge the ideological divide between staunch Canadian nationalists, such as Mathews, and the colonial mindset of many U.S. expatriates who used Canada as a staging ground from which to resist U.S. military and economic might. Lambert described both camps as espousing valid but "myopic" views.[170]

Lambert disagreed with Mathews that U.S. expatriates were taking over Canada. "They do not," Lambert noted, "contribute noteworthy inputs to policy making in Parliament, the mass media, industry and commerce, unions, churches, schools, and all the institutions which weigh heavily upon the lives of Canadians." As landed immigrants, Lambert observed, most draft resisters lacked the full "franchise" to make sweeping changes to Canadian society. He encouraged expatriates to learn about Canadian society and "to understand the peculiar thrust of the nationalist movement in Canada." Although Lambert acknowledged the absence of a significant "cultural fifth column in Canada," he conceded a major point: "The threads of Canadian independence and American war-making are very much intertwined."[171] In other words, it was impractical, especially in a Cold War context, to disentangle Canada's sovereignty from U.S. imperialism.

Employing a Marxist analysis in this debate, one University of Toronto doctoral student, who wrote under the pseudonym V. S. Brown, criticized Mathews for championing the aspirations of the Canadian bourgeoisie. Explaining the immateriality of Mathews's Canadian nationalism, Brown wrote, "There is nothing in nationalism for working people and hence they repudiate it." As an aspiring academic, Brown believed that Mathews's only concern was that U.S. professors and graduate students took faculty and other administrative positions that Canadians should occupy. Brown considered Mathews's call for Canadian self-determination questionable, because it was unclear whether he advocated for the masses or for the corporations, most of which U.S. interests controlled. Brown accused Mathews of blaming domestic problems in Canada, "a dependent capitalist state," on the draft resister, the "fall guy."[172]

Delores Broten, student at York University in Toronto and a member of the Canadian Liberation Movement to which Mathews belonged, nuanced the conversation with her deft synthesis of the U.S.-Canadian context. Writing to politically conscious draft resisters in Canada, Broten explained, "You must realize that you're not fighting imperialism in the heartland, but in the colony—a colony that hardly knows its own condition."[173] Broten stressed the importance of cross-border solidarity, especially as Canadians struggled to liberalize their society. In supporting Canadian progressivism, however, Broten cautioned U.S. refugees to refrain from usurping or subordinating the voices of their Canadian allies.

Other Canadians on the opposite end of the debate criticized their newly arrived neighbors from the United States for their moderate and apolitical views. Ken Stone, a member of the Ontario Union of Students, expressed a minority viewpoint: "I can't figure out why American exiles are not the most radical people around or at least people who are in the process of becoming so." Stone surmised that perhaps "the Canadian environment forces immigrants to be withdrawn into themselves or in ghettos where it's hard to develop an analysis." In a gesture of Canadian goodwill, Stone invited all U.S. exiles to work alongside the University of Toronto Student Movement, the Women's Liberation Front, and the Student Labor Committee, all of which contributed to the leftist climate of the period.[174]

As the sovereignty debate waxed, so, too, did the Canadian government's surveillance of draft resisters. Canadian officials conspired with their U.S. counterparts to return refugees, in line with the 1850 Fugitive Slave Act, which had the effect of encouraging widespread use of the Underground Railroad. Unlike the actual 1850 Act, British officials in what was then Canada West, recognizing the draconian nature of U.S. law, refused to abide by extradition requests. During the Vietnam War, however, desertion from U.S. military service put war resisters at risk, because law enforcement in Canada had no qualms about spiriting said individuals back into the awaiting arms of U.S. authorities.

For example, Michael Whalen, a twenty-two-year-old white resister who deserted in June 1969 while training at Fort Dix, New Jersey, arrived in Toronto as a visitor in July. The FBI and U.S. immigration officials, along with the RCMP and Canadian immigration, tracked his movements. After overstaying his visitation, immigration officers approached Whalen and advised him to leave Canada and to apply and reenter legally as a landed immigrant. When Whalen complied, Canadian immigration officers denied him access at the Peace Bridge border crossing in Buffalo, even though he had three letters of employment and $1,000. Instead, immigration officials handed him over to their U.S. counterparts for safekeeping until the FBI arrived and whisked him away to the stockade. "He was a deserter, so we took him," said the district director of U.S. Immigration. "We gave him to the FBI, who charged him with desertion. . . . Sometimes we tell people in Canada [RCMP and immigration] where our deserters are . . . just like sometimes the Canadians tell us where their people are in the U.S. . . . We cooperate."[175]

Such acts of collusion became commonplace. As Charles Campbell, one of the leaders in the draft resister community, concluded, "Canada's national police force likes to enforce U.S. law." He admonished U.S. expatriates to remain cognizant of "repressive forces" during "the best of times" in Canada. Fearing the threat of subversion, the security and intelligence apparatus in both Canada and the United States maintained a heightened level of vigilance. For this reason, Campbell declared that Canadian authorities' "collusion with the F.B.I. is practically the R.C.M.P.'s *raison d'etre*." Campbell concluded, "They [RCMP] slavishly run errands for Washington." He saw the RCMP as the FBI's lackey, spreading misinformation about deserters throughout Canada as the RCMP "harassed" them. Referencing war resisters' perceptions of unjust treatment and the overall pervasiveness of this surveillance, Campbell added, "The R.C.M.P mentality . . . exists in the judiciary as well as the constabulary of Canada." Campbell called the RCMP "the northern arm of American law-enforcement."[176]

As Canada liberalized its immigration policy in the 1960s, it had to contend with the challenges of an increasingly multiracial society. Caribbean immigrants and cross-border radicals, such as draft resisters and Black Panthers, sought refuge and linkages in Canada, notwithstanding its Cold War politics. Canadian authorities clamped down on leftist politics, perceiving the continental scope of Pan-Africanisms as an existential matter. At times, Black and non-Black people considered Canadian society a hospitable extension of the United States. Viewing Canada as a haven, African American and white immigrants believed they could promote revolution in U.S. society while concomitantly advocating for progressive change in Canada.

The 1960s further strengthened connections among U.S., Canadian, and Caribbean actors. For Black Panthers, Black war resisters, and Caribbean immigrants, such as Anne Cools and Rosie Douglas and homegrown African Canadian activist Burnley "Rocky" Jones, social agitation meant ownership of community affairs, economic security, anti-racism, and anti-imperialism. For Cools, Douglas, and other West Indians, Black liberation also meant self-determination in the Caribbean. The Sir George Williams University student occupation in Montreal and the emergence of the Black United Front in Nova Scotia and the Marxist Afro-American Progressive Association of Toronto—in addition to community institutions, such as the Third World Bookstore and the Underground Railroad restaurant—gave diasporic Africans opportunities to practice Pan-Africanisms and to shape Canadian society as they saw fit.

No singular vision of self-determination prevailed. Instead, a plurality of Black actors with different national or ethnic origins shaped diasporic politics concerning Canada, the United States, and the Caribbean. Activist demands for racial justice, anti-imperialism, and anti-colonialism exposed the structural shortcomings of Canadian society. By 1971, the veil of Canada's reputation as the North Star had been torn asunder.[177] Like their forebears, Black people looked to the horizon where real, tangible change always seemed to hover just out of reach.

CHAPTER 5

THE MIND OF THE STATE

▼ ▼ ▼

Deception is a state of mind—and the mind of the state.
—James Jesus Angleton, CIA counterintelligence chief,
1954–75

At the height of the Black Power struggle in 1969, Sam Greenlee, a U.S. Army veteran and one of the first African Americans whom the U.S. Information Agency had stationed overseas as a foreign service officer, published a monumental text. Before Black America embraced the cool, crime-fighting John Shaft as a television cultural icon, *The Spook Who Sat by the Door*, Greenlee's novel, followed the exploits of Dan Freeman, a steely jawed Korean War veteran and Black revolutionary who joined the CIA, becoming the first token Black agent. Freeman underwent weapons and ordnance training, studied guerrilla warfare, and learned counterinsurgency or counter-subversion: the art of neutralizing foes. A cloak-and-dagger freedom fighter behind enemy lines, he maintained an unassuming low profile at the CIA by acting as an Uncle Tom. Freeman's self-effacing nature obscured his brilliance, and his constant grinning and subdued temperament prevented his superiors from entertaining the thought that he was a revolutionary.[1]

After a few years of service, he retired from the CIA, but the drama continued. Returning to inner-city Chicago, he used the deadly arts he learned from the U.S. government to transform Black gang members into a well-trained guerrilla unit that fought the empire from within. Freeman's lieutenants recruited, instructed, and mobilized guerrilla cells in other major cities. The FBI incorporated the novel into instruction manuals on urban counterinsurgency.[2] The government and Black revolutionaries understood counterinsurgency was essential to maintaining or breaking hegemony.

In 1973, producers adapted the novel into a film with financial backing from Black communities. "There is no way that the United States can police the world and keep us on our ass, too," Freeman informed one of his lieutenants in the film, "unless we cooperate." Revolution at home, Freeman asserted, would paralyze the imperial machinery. The FBI suppressed the film shortly after it premiered. Greenlee and others resorted to bootlegging.

Both the novel and the film quickly emerged as cult classics in Black America. By deploying African American agent provocateurs—who mimicked Dan Freeman—to infiltrate and disrupt revolutionary Black organizations, the national security and intelligence apparatus counter-subverted one of the most prominent revolutionary tropes, aspirations, and fantasies in the post–civil rights movement. "Deception," indeed, is "the mind of the state."[3]

Black activists' attempts to subvert the imperial, capitalistic, and racist logics of the United States and Canada in the late 1960s and 1970s set them on a collision course with the state. White resentment accompanied the passage of landmark antidiscrimination measures but did not silence shouts for Pan-Africanisms broadly and self-determination specifically in North America.[4] The pursuit of Black liberation in U.S. and Canadian societies brought activists into the crosshairs of the security and intelligence apparatus.[5] Black activists tested postwar liberalism, exposing the machinations of the state when they organized to expand the boundaries of citizenship. Using declassified intelligence reports obtained under freedom of information provisions in the United States and Canada, this chapter uncovers the only known case of U.S. and Canadian authorities deploying the Black "spook." In so doing, they played on Black people's fantasy that a Dan Freeman would come and liberate their communities. Without thorough organization of the Black masses, of course, a messiah alone could not manifest a Pan-African dream. But messianism resonated with some Black people, making Freeman's archetype alluring.

A BLACK TROJAN HORSE

In 1968, U.S. and Canadian authorities considered cross-border radicalism a grave continental threat. Federal Bureau of Investigation director J. Edgar Hoover believed that the Black Panther Party (BPP) posed the "greatest threat to the internal security" of the United States.[6] Hoover, who authorized the FBI's crackdown on U.S. Black Nationalists, wanted his bureau to thwart "the RISE OF A 'MESSIAH.'" Using assassinations and other forms of violence to intimidate African Americans, Hoover planned to "neutralize" male leaders before they could fully "unify" and "electrify" the masses.[7] In his attempt to eliminate messianic Black men, Hoover was a modern-day King Herod, the Roman official whom Christians believe ordered the killing of the baby Jesus and other infant boys to prevent the rise of a Jewish messiah. Hoover's persona also mirrored Sheriff John Brown, the fictitious infanticidal antagonist who admonished his deputies to "kill them before they grow" in Bob Marley's song "I Shot the Sheriff."[8] Black Power in the late 1960s and anti-colonial resistance movements underscored a Cold War reality: the downtrodden perceived the white man's burden as self-inflicted.

Subversion represented a reasonable response for oppressed Black people, reasoned Eldridge Cleaver, the BPP minister of information. Echoing Dan Freeman, Cleaver posited that subversion would distract Western imperial governments, preventing them from extinguishing the global flames of revolution. "At home there is a Trojan Horse," Cleaver declaimed, "a Black Trojan Horse that has become aware of itself and is now struggling to get on its feet. It, too, demands liberation."[9] This reference is imbued with notions of chattel, frailty, and insurgency. A Trojan horse of sorts also appeared in Canada in the 1960s and 1970s with a renewed commitment to confront anti-Black racism. Although similar in some ways to African American militants, Black activists in Canada were slow to resorting to arms.

The Royal Canadian Mounted Police—the federal police—perceived cross-border activists as Trojan horses. This threat, the RCMP reasoned, warranted Canada's collusion with U.S. intelligence agencies. The 1970 October Crisis in which the Front de libération du Québec kidnapped political officials, bombed landmarks, and assassinated Quebec deputy premier Pierre Laporte heightened the overall threat perception in Canadian society. As racial conflict raged in the United States and other parts of the globe, some Canadian authorities considered Black liberation a threat to national security. "Subversion," as a postwar security concern, broadened widely from communist agitators to most leftist actors, from women's groups to student organizations to civil servants. The national security establishment also targeted gay and lesbian communities, perceiving queer persons not only as subversives but also as individuals acutely prone to Soviet blackmail.[10] This broad definition suggests that RCMP brass lacked a precise vision of—and policies to address—the perceived internal security challenges facing Canadian society.

The RCMP's Security Service, which gathered intelligence and oversaw national security investigations, had a dedicated counter-subversion wing. The FBI's Counterintelligence Program, or COINTELPRO (1956–71), which surveilled, infiltrated, disrupted, and assassinated Black leaders, shared some similarities to Canada's Security Service's counter-subversion program. From 1967 to 1977, the RCMP counter-subversion branch launched the Key Sectors initiative to remain abreast of the evolving subversive landscape within Canadian society. The RCMP assigned some Mounties to investigate potential penetration of different levels of government, media, and universities. In the 1960s, Mounties flagged two subversive elements that they believed posed serious threats to national security: "Black nationalists and student agitators."[11]

To maintain a clear sightline, Key Sectors had a threefold objective: first, determination of the extent to which a sector had been penetrated; second, threat assessment; and third, threat containment or elimination.[12] It was within the third objective that national security personnel in Canada exercised enormous discretion, usually unlawfully, to undermine Black activists. The RCMP collaborated with the FBI to gather intelligence. However, taming a Black Trojan horse in Canada would prove much more complicated than the RCMP anticipated.

A FAUSTIAN BARGAIN

As Black Power in the United States went from a national to a transnational aspiration in the 1960s and 1970s, U.S. security and intelligence officials felt vulnerable on their northern flank. For Canadian officials, Black radicals' migration there in the 1960s and 1970s did not elicit the same reception that nineteenth-century fugitive and free African Americans enjoyed when they crossed the border. Canadian officials perceived these new activists, with their militant Pan-African and Black Nationalist outlook, as carriers of a contagion that could spread and undermine the postwar economic and social order.

Rumblings of Pan-Africanisms in Montreal in 1968 and 1969 and the border crossings of Stokely Carmichael and Fred Hampton heightened fears of radicalism in Canada.[13] But the Black Power era was not the first time that a perceived continental threat encouraged intelligence sharing. The FBI cooperated with the RCMP in the 1930s when J. Edgar Hoover and his Canadian counterpart Commissioner James Howden MacBrien met in Washington, D.C. During the Second World War, the RCMP and the FBI maintained attachés in Washington, D.C., and Ottawa, respectively.[14]

Canadian officials often shared with the FBI their alarm over Black militancy. An October 1970 secret memo from the RCMP to the FBI attaché at the U.S. embassy in Ottawa declared Toronto "the major center of black nationalist activity in Ontario."[15] As the emerging Anglophone bastion, Toronto enjoyed a level of cosmopolitanism and immigration that paralleled Montreal's. With a Black population of 20,000 and growing due to Caribbean immigration, along with U.S. draft resisters, Toronto slowly became a hotbed for Black resistance.[16] Its Black Nationalist–inspired Third World Bookstore, the Marxist-Leninist Afro-American Progressive Association, and the draft resister group Black Refugee Organization elevated the city's reputation as a site of Pan-Africanisms. In fact, Toronto's strategic location in the Great Lakes region ensured easy access to African Americans in search of an international city where they could evade U.S. authorities.

In April 1970, the FBI sent operative Warren Hart to conduct reconnaissance on Black radicalism in Canada. A Baltimore-based African American, Hart attended a weeklong gathering of Black radicals.[17] Hart's reconnaissance of the conference of Black radicals in Toronto was the first leg of what became an extended relationship that saw him serving two masters in the United States and Canada. Hoover admonished his agents in November 1970 to "remain constantly alert for opportunities to send our informants to Canada and give consideration to such action in all instances where warranted."[18] Hoover's suggestion resonated with his deputies and the RCMP.

Both the RCMP and the FBI believed that Black activists in Canada and the United States communicated and collaborated frequently. When violent urban uprisings occurred in cities near the U.S.-Canadian border, such as Detroit in 1967 or Rochester, New York, in 1964, the RCMP had to consider the possibility of a violent uprising in Canada. The RCMP made a counter-subversion pact with the FBI to conduct surveillance on cross-border movement.[19] Canadian officials wanted names of known African American militants who planned to visit Canada or had interests in forging linkages with their Canadian-based counterparts. This quid pro quo arrangement, in turn, incentivized the FBI's cross-border surveillance. The urgency is discernible in a 1970 memo in which Hoover instructed his agents that quick action on their part would "afford RCMP the opportunity of developing valuable information concerning individuals of interest to this Bureau."[20]

In its pursuit of Black radicals, the FBI cast its dragnet far beyond Montreal and Toronto. Black people in other Canadian cities, such as Halifax and Vancouver, came under surveillance. On the West Coast, agents monitored closely the organizing efforts of the Vancouver Black Action Group, a militant cross-border organization with strong links to other subversive groups in San Francisco and throughout the Bay Area. The RCMP informed the FBI that the Vancouver Black Action Group had concocted an elaborate scheme whereby members "interchange personal documentation to allow new Black extremists entry to Canada" for the purposes of fomenting domestic insurrection. Canadian officials suggested that Black Nationalists had discussed this "exchange program" in previous years. "In the past," the RCMP informed the FBI, "we have on occasions received some rather vague reports from your agency on the possible existence of 'safe houses' and 'passports' in Canada for utilization by the Black Panthers."[21] These elaborate, clandestine schemes are indicative of the ways that a transnational consciousness allowed Black people in North America to resist surveillance and assert their right to mobility. Such clandestine networks are reminiscent of the complex systems that aided and abetted fugitives escaping U.S. slavery.

Highly porous and largely undefended, the U.S.-Canadian border provided Black radicals a modicum of cover from detection. The proximity and regional linkages of Great Lakes cities, such as Buffalo-Cleveland-Toronto or Detroit-Windsor, in addition to the San Francisco-Seattle-Vancouver corridor, frustrated the security and intelligence services in Canada and the United States. The RCMP conceded to the FBI that the Detroit-Windsor "border crossing appears to have become one of the focal points for travel of Black nationalists to and from Canada and a loosely knit center of assistance. . . . Refuge for fugitives appears to have been established in the Toronto area as was witnessed at the time of Eldridge Cleaver's escape."[22]

The FBI forged a Great Lakes strategy for surveillance of cross-border activists. The Mounties informed the bureau in 1969 that they had estimated that 100,000 African Americans would visit Windsor for the annual Emancipation Day celebration in August, a major pan-African cultural attraction that commemorates the abolition of slavery throughout the British Empire. Both security forces feared that African American activists would radicalize and then highjack the festivities. When the RCMP informed the bureau that several Black Nationalists had entered Windsor from the United States and likely would be serving on the Emancipation Day committee, the FBI warned its field offices in Chicago, Cincinnati, Cleveland, Detroit, and New York.[23]

The FBI and the RCMP also monitored various activities in the Caribbean because of freedom linkages and migration of African Caribbean people to the North American mainland. Caribbean radicalism nurtured Black revolutionary thought and agitation in the late 1960s and 1970s.[24] The influx of Caribbean students and U.S. radicals into Canada at the time stoked the two agencies' fears. The Congress of Black Writers Conference in 1968 Montreal followed by the student occupation of Sir George Williams University in 1969 had triggered massive protests in the Caribbean, nearly toppling the government of Eric Williams in Trinidad and Tobago. The uprisings indicated the organizing power of Pan-Africanisms to link activists across international boundaries. Then the RCMP informed the FBI that Rosie Douglas enjoyed the backing of "50 strong supporters" and was the "chief" point of contact for revolutionaries in the Caribbean. The Mounties predicted the likelihood of a violent showdown between Pan-Africanists and Caribbean governments.[25]

Security and intelligence officials suspected that finances flowed from the United States and Canada to Caribbean revolutionaries, which they feared would destabilize the region. The RCMP sought assistance from the

FBI to trace the finances of Caribbean nationals in Montreal and Toronto who fundraised from their Black and white allies in North America for the purposes of underwriting, allegedly, "guerrilla activities" in the Caribbean.[26]

Tracing the money that sustained Pan-Africanists uncovered diasporic connections among Black people in Canada, the United States, and the Caribbean. As early as 18 October 1968, the Mounties ascertained through vetted sources and wiretaps that one Reico Cranshaw, or "Brother Reico," a person of interest under investigation by the Chicago Police Department Gang Intelligence Unit, personally couriered to Toronto a package containing approximately $550 for Michael X, the Trinidadian-born, London-based Black revolutionary.[27] Michael X visited Canada around this time, attending the Congress of Black Writers Conference at McGill University in Montreal from 11 to 14 October 1968.[28] The RCMP's sources believed that this money came from artist Sammy Davis Jr. Based on the intelligence gathering of "a highly confidential source," the FBI also alleged that phone calls to Black activists in Toronto came from Davis's suite when he stayed at the Chicago Sherman Hotel in October 1968. The bureau conceded that some of the calls "may in fact be legitimate business calls." However, the bureau cautioned that all telephone contacts must be screened to "ascertain if these individuals are possibly involved in any Black militant movements."[29]

The RCMP expressed doubts about the FBI information that came its way, creating a heightened state of suspense as well as tension between the two agencies. The RCMP conveyed uncertainty over "the many vague and often uncorroborated reports of the existence of guerrilla training camps and the acquisition of firearms by extremist groups in Canada for use by Black revolutionaries in the United States and abroad."[30] Black activists in Canada operated cautiously, of course, but at the same time the authorities had to consider seriously their capacity to shape the Cold War state by mobilizing revolutionary networks in the hemisphere.

The FBI might have deliberately contributed to this air of paranoia in Canada by providing Canadian authorities with misinformation about the BPP and other Pan-Africanists. Moreover, the bureau indirectly placed culpability on the RCMP. If the FBI could convince its Canadian counterpart of sluggish intelligence gathering, the bureau would have greater leverage in coercing the Mounties to feed it information and even to adopt some of the FBI's COINTELPRO tactics.

Considering the RCMP's smaller capacity and scope in comparison to the bureau, Canada's federal police worried about the recklessness of pursuing "negative" FBI leads, which would "merely dissipate [its] efforts in [a] wrong direction."[31] The Mounties feared that they would have to relinquish their autonomy and wanted the FBI to respect them as equals. At a time when Prime Minister Pierre Trudeau believed in cultivating a distinct Canadian identity in national and foreign affairs, officials in Ottawa felt sensitive about the RCMP subordinating its national security duties to the FBI. Notwithstanding the RCMP's concern over the alarmist tone of FBI briefings, the Mounties assured the bureau that they would share without hesitation any "positive" actionable intelligence.[32]

THE MAKING OF AN AGENT PROVOCATEUR

When Warren Hart visited Toronto as an FBI operative in April 1970 to map the Black radical scene in Canada's largest city, nearly one year had passed since he had vanished from the Baltimore BPP. Hart feared that he had blown his cover as an FBI operative. The second of five children born to a blue-collar African American couple in Durham, North Carolina, on 26 July 1928, Hart's first few years of life were an uphill struggle against the Great Depression. His bricklayer father and stay-at-home mother of five imparted unto their eldest son a penchant for work and economic survival. As a result, there was almost no category of work that Hart refused in adulthood, whether it was backbreaking construction labor or rendering military or intelligence services to a government that was callous about the suffering of African Americans at best and murderous or "genocidal" at worst.[33]

Hart worked for the federal government after stints in small businesses. His first occupation with the U.S. government occurred in 1943 when he enlisted in the navy at Raleigh, North Carolina.[34] He served overseas as a machine rigger and cartographer for twenty-three months in the South Pacific. Hart served another four months in Korea from September to December 1945, weeks after the United States had dropped nuclear bombs on the Japanese cities of Hiroshima and Nagasaki, forcing Japan to relinquish control of Korea. After his service, Hart received an honorable discharge. He left Durham a humble teenager and returned a decorated veteran: he received the National Defense Service Medal, the Korean Service Medal, and the navy's American Theater Asiatic-Pacific 1 Star, among others.[35]

Hart struggled to find his footing in civilian life. After a year with the U.S. Merchant Marines from 1946 to 1947, he again returned to Durham and married Sallie McNeal of Lillington, North Carolina. Family life compelled Hart to earn more, which he tried to accomplish in different jobs, from freelance contractor in Durham to storekeeper at a Philadelphia furrier and later as an insurance agent in Baltimore. Poor prospects for occupational advancement, coupled with economic insecurity, encouraged him in 1950 to enroll briefly at the Durham Business School. The G.I. Bill, which provided Hart an opportunity to pursue a college education when most Black southerners lacked access, revealed to him the social benefits and programs available through the federal government. As a veteran, Hart knew that he could leverage his military record for the economic advancement and security that he coveted.

Returning to federal employment posed some unique challenges. In addition to multiple U.S. Civil Service Commission exams and the racial politics that excluded most African Americans from securing employment similar to that which sustained the white middle class, entry-level work with the federal government paid less than what Hart already earned. As a storekeeper in 1951, he had made nearly $2,000, but in 1953, he earned only $1,200 as a clerk for the U.S. Army. Hart processed "201 files"—the documents relating to personnel military and civilian records. Despite the lower salary, Hart joined the federal government on the presumption that he could advance more quickly and have access to a wide range of opportunities unknown to most African Americans of his generation. Moreover, his exposure working on 201 files taught Hart how military personnel and veterans advanced in their careers.

In 1955, Hart resigned from his low-level clerkship in pursuit of other opportunities within the federal government. By January 1956, he found work as a nursing assistant at the Durham VA hospital with the help of his younger brother Alphonza, who was also employed there.[36] Hart's starting salary, which was nearly $3,000, proved that his strategy was succeeding. As a nursing assistant, he performed demanding, labor-intensive tasks, such as carrying patients and providing them bodily care duties. Nursing assistants did significant work; they lessened the brute harshness of nursing. As a veteran, he likely perceived his job as a step above domestic work. Yet Hart's pay increase and job security neither fulfilled him nor provided the occupational prestige that he desired.

Five months into his tour at the VA hospital, Hart received several reprimands for sleeping on the job. One of his supervisors, in a written evaluation, rebuked him for his "increasing lack of interest and concern."[37] A few days later, his supervisor again chastened him for poor performance; she wrote that he "seemed very unconcerned without showing any desire to improve." Hart's supervisor concluded, "His work and his attitude have been very unsatisfactory."[38] On the following day, Hart resigned, perhaps to flex his masculinity. "I feel that I am not happy with the work that I am doing now in the V.A. Hospital," Hart wrote. "I can't adjust myself to my duties."[39] Hart worked odd jobs, experiencing an eight-year hiatus from the federal civil service after he resigned from the VA hospital in mid-1956.

Hart's fortunes would change. In 1964, he attended and graduated from the 29th Division Intelligence School at Fort A. P. Hill, Virginia. Hart had learned of this career-advancing opportunity when he had processed 201 files as an army clerk. The exposure that Hart received to arms training, military intelligence, and explosives—reminiscent of *The Spook Who Sat by the Door*—proved invaluable to his quest for career advancement. In August 1966, Hart worked as an administrative supply technician at the 5th Regiment Armory of the Maryland National Guard in Baltimore. On all objective accounts, he was doing well. His starting yearly salary was almost $7,000.[40]

After exactly two years with the National Guard, in September 1968 the FBI recruited him as an informant. His first assignment was to masquerade as a Black Power activist and establish the Baltimore chapter of the Black Panther Party. This preemptive move by the bureau against the Panthers had much to do with the nine-day violent uprising that shook Baltimore after the assassination of Martin Luther King Jr. Urban rebellions in U.S. cities during the 1960s hamstrung the FBI and the entire federal security apparatus.

At the height of the Black Power movement in the late 1960s, the FBI discovered limitations in its counter-subversion measures. It lacked access to predictive intelligence on urban uprisings, despite the draconian tactics of COINTELPRO. After the violent resistance in Watts, the racial fault lines in the nation's foundations were undeniable. In August 1965, the bureau ramped up its efforts to prevent future urban rebellions. Under COINTELPRO, the FBI spawned the Ghetto Informant Program in 1965 to recruit inner-city residents, such as proprietors and patrons of small businesses. In other words, the bureau deputized inner-city Black men to create counter-subversion sleeper cells.[41]

In exchange for cooperating with the FBI, participants in the Ghetto Informant Program received remuneration. Inner-city Black business owners helped the FBI, because they had much to lose when their neighbors unleashed economic frustration and the pain of racial terror in their own neighborhoods. In Baltimore, for example, the 1968 violence destroyed approximately 1,000 small businesses.[42] Furthermore, the FBI's exploitation of economically disenfranchised inner-city residents underscores the extent to which Black communities appeared spatially removed and impervious to the federal government. That Hart secured a position with the FBI because of the Ghetto Informant Program—with less than glowing recommendations in his federal personnel records—illustrates the bureau's desperation for Black operatives. Nevertheless, Hart's value to the bureau far exceeded the social prestige and economic advancement that the FBI could offer him.

A WOLF IN PANTHER'S CLOTHING

The Washington, D.C., metropolitan area allowed Hart to meet major players in the Black liberation and Pan-African movements. On 3 October 1968, an associate named William "Shotgun" Green introduced Hart to honorary BPP prime minister Stokely Carmichael at the Soul School. Carmichael advised Hart that if he was a loyal Panther, he would replace his "Anglo-Saxon name" with "Kamani," the Kikuyu word for sailor or adventurer. When Carmichael learned that Hart had a military background and had bailed out fellow Panthers after Hart, Shotgun Green, and a couple others had been arrested, Carmichael promised to make Hart chairman of the board of Black Panthers in Baltimore.[43]

As the sole founder of the Baltimore chapter of the BPP via the FBI in autumn 1968, Hart had unbridled access to the internal workings of the organization. In November 1968, he attended the party's National Steering Committee in Oakland for orientation and training and for learning the code of conduct, governance, and rules of engagement.[44] The Oakland retreat also ensured that Hart had access to the party's leadership. As the defense captain, Hart was the highest-ranking Panther in the state of Maryland and one of the highest ranking on the East Coast.[45] Because the FBI founded the Baltimore chapter, the bureau wrote in December 1968, "It is felt that the Black Panther Party can be effectively controlled in the Baltimore area."[46]

Widespread frustration in African American neighborhoods in 1968 ensured that the Panthers' doctrine of self-determination resonated with the disenfranchised. Marshall Conway was one of many Baltimoreans who sought to improve his community and uplift his people by joining the BPP. The social climate of Conway's youth conditioned him to believe, like many women and men of his generation, that racism and oppression in the United States was "government-sanctioned."[47] Reflecting on his childhood in Baltimore, Conway described the late 1950s—his junior high years—as "a turning point" and that Rosa Parks's defiance on a bus in Montgomery, Alabama, provided his peers with a model of resistance. "We weren't going to take any shit from anyone," Conway professed, "or at least so we thought."[48]

Before Conway fought for his community, he enlisted in the army in 1964, ostensibly to fight for his country, because it was one of the only viable outlets for poor African Americans. Stationed in Germany, Conway, a fast learner, rose to sergeant. As an amiable person and one of the only Black officers,

Black privates confided in him that their white peers held Klan meetings at night and that they experienced discrimination when they sought promotions. Conway's exposure to racism in the army sapped his patriotism. While stationed overseas, he recalled seeing newspaper images in July 1967 of National Guardsmen aiming high-caliber machine guns at protesting Black women after police brutality triggered uprisings in Newark. Another Black activist made a similar observation about the 1967 Detroit rebellion: "The children of my neighborhood watched as army jeeps with big machine guns mounted on the back patrolled our streets often pointing their guns at us and while calling us names."[49] The siege on African Americans convinced Conway that he had enlisted in the wrong army.

After his honorable discharge, Conway left Germany and returned to Baltimore, where living conditions had worsened. He found work as a technician at the Johns Hopkins Hospital. There, he witnessed hospital staff inflicting violence on Black patients. On one occasion, a white doctor who performed a mastectomy on a middle-aged Black woman "butchered" her when excising her breasts with an electric scalpel, then a high-tech surgical device. The procedure should have taken three hours, but the doctor completed it in one hour so that he could play his routine round of golf. The woman died and the hospital hid the truth from her family.[50] This incident and other demoralizing experiences further radicalized Conway. He described these pivotal years and his one-man pursuit of justice for the downtrodden as "a study in slow motion."[51] He temporarily found a sense of purpose working for the Congress of Racial Equality. When it came to the conditions of poor African Americans and their dire material circumstances, Conway learned that one could not reconcile the irreconcilable truths about U.S. society, especially not without bravado and militancy.[52]

Racial tension had cast the die long before an assassin's bullet cut down Martin Luther King Jr. in April 1968. Black Power advocates believed in meeting force with force, state violence with quasi-guerrilla resistance, and white supremacy with Black Nationalism and Pan-Africanisms.[53] Conway searched for and found purpose in the Baltimore chapter of the BPP after King's assassination. Warren Hart administered the Baltimore chapter from his home, which enabled the FBI to outfit it with surveillance equipment. He also ran the chapter more like "a social group than a political organization."[54] Under Hart's leadership, the group lacked the constructive community militancy, political education, and revolutionary ethos that would have helped revive a moribund postindustrial city like Baltimore.[55]

Law enforcement increased its surveillance of known Panthers. When the chapter relocated its office from Hart's house, police surveilled the new office twenty-four hours a day. Marked and unmarked cruisers followed Panthers throughout the city. Electricity mysteriously stopped working at the office.[56] Visible and subtle forms of surveillance and disruption indicated to chapter members that the federal government had infiltrated their ranks. Moreover, the success of the Panthers' Free Breakfast Program, which provided nourishing meals to inner-city Black children before school, compelled the bureau to escalate its counter-subversion tactics. The bureau secretly distributed coloring books of Black children shooting and stabbing police to delegitimize the breakfast program, arrested members on trumped up charges when they left the office, and sabotaged their cars. An unidentified arsonist also set the office ablaze. By mid-1969, the Baltimore chapter had put Conway in charge of security.

Unbeknownst to the members, Warren Hart was behind most of these mysterious events.[57] Conway devoted time to vetting everyone who showed interest in joining the chapter and "scrutinized" the existing members. "I soon became aware," Conway recalled, "that we had some serious internal problems, and it was likely that they had existed right from the inception of the Baltimore chapter."[58] Conway reported numerous breaches and "violations" to Hart, but he ignored them. Once during an open house, members observed an unidentified person taking pictures inside the office in a place that was off limits to the public. When Conway confronted Hart, he admitted that he had permitted this violation.[59]

As the highest-ranking Panther in the state of Maryland, Hart's carelessness raised red flags. Conway contacted New Yorker Donald Cox, the regional field marshal who oversaw the Panthers' East Coast operations. During the July 1969 investigation, the regional leadership demoted Hart to a rank-and-file member for "fucking up."[60] In addition to taking police infiltration lightly, Hart had fouled up on other fronts, too. Reeva White, the chapter's first communications secretary, accused Hart of defending another Panther who, she said, had "repeatedly shot up headquarters."[61] Hart also failed to implement the "political education" that would help the party achieve social and political goals. His "over-emphasis of para-military procedures" indicated that Hart had tried to entrap his fellow Panthers by steering them to armed confrontation rather than to political agitation.[62]

Hart's gross negligence made it hard for him to maintain his membership. Shortly after the disciplinary hearing, Cox dismissed Hart from the party. Maintaining protocol for purged members, the 23 August 1969 edition of the official newspaper the *Black Panther* published his picture, along with five other expelled members from the Baltimore chapter. The FBI monitored Hart's national exposé, but his cover as a spy had not yet been blown, which meant he could still conduct counter-subversion operations for the bureau.[63] On 22 September 1969, he traveled to Durham, North Carolina, to meet with Owusu Sadaukai (Howard Fuller), cofounder of the Pan-Africanist Malcolm X Liberation University.[64] Hart took stock of the weapons that Sadaukai's men possessed. He offered to train them, so that he could gather more intelligence. Hart had a history of training militants and disclosing their whereabouts and internal structure to his handlers.[65]

Upon returning to Baltimore, Hart turned his attention back to the Panthers. In December 1969, he conspired with former Panthers Donald Bonds and Charlie Williams to break into party headquarters and steal M-14 and M-16 rifles, as well as handguns. These arms would allegedly aid a new militant organization. When his friend Stokely Carmichael, who had also left the party in 1969, returned to the United States in April 1970 after a West African trip, Hart was his personal security as Carmichael lectured at Baltimore's Douglas Memorial Baptist Church. Up until September 1970, Hart continued to ingratiate himself with Black militants in the eastern United States. In one instance, he tried to procure ten M-16s from a contact in Atlanta.[66] The Baltimore chapter learned a few months later that their onetime defense captain was a federal operative. For this reason, Sadaukai acknowledged that there were "not many mechanisms in place to vet radicals."[67] True to its objective, COINTELPRO, according to Conway, "created a climate of fear and suspicion that left our chapter seriously wounded."[68] And as the Panther whose instincts helped his comrades sniff Hart out, Conway had to pay a price.

On the night of 21 April 1970, authorities alleged that three Panthers, including Conway, shot two Baltimore police officers in their patrol car. One officer died. On the night of the shooting, officers arrested two Panthers near the crime scene; the state charged them with first-degree murder. Authorities later arrested Conway at a U.S. postal office where he worked, charging him as the third accomplice in the homicide, even though investigators lacked any ballistic or forensic evidence.[69] "The alleged murder of police officers," Conway observed of the state's counter-subversion of the Panthers, "would soon take the place of the mythological rape of white women as the basis for the legal lynching of Black men."[70] On 24 April 1970, the State of Maryland sentenced Conway to life in prison.

Conway believed Hart played a role in his unjust imprisonment. To the Panthers, Hart had committed an egregious sin, arguably among the worst concerning diasporic Africans in the Americas. His transgression was akin to enslaved persons who disclosed a plot of insurrection to ingratiate themselves with their enslavers. In this scenario, however, Hart had

Officers of the Baltimore chapter of the Black Panther Party, circa 1968 (left to right)*: Defense Captain Warren Hart, Second Lieutenant Hezekiah Claxton, and Major Charles E. Smith. Permission from Baltimore Sun Media. All Rights Reserved.*

masterminded a potential insurrection, undermining the Panthers' efforts for genuine race- and class-conscious community building in a distraught city.

Paul Coates, a leader in the Baltimore chapter, believed that "infiltration came from many segments of the government."[71] Conway explained the likely fate of an infiltrator: "In most cases when agent provocateurs were discovered, they were put in the front of [the *Black Panther*] newspaper. They were basically exposed around the country, all the chapters were warned about them, their pictures were posted, a rundown on who they were and what they had been doing and who they were operating on behalf of." He added, "That happened in most cases. In some cases, there was actual violence on the ground," alluding to the murder of alleged FBI informant Alex Rackley and the 1970 New Haven Panther trials.[72]

When the bureau discovered through wiretaps that the Panthers had uncovered Hart's identity around 1970, they alerted him immediately.[73] As a fugitive of sorts, the FBI operative journeyed to the most logical place where

Defense Captain Warren Hart serves breakfast to schoolchildren, circa 1969. Permission from Baltimore Sun Media. All Rights Reserved.

Purged members of the Baltimore chapter of the Black Panther Party. The Black Panther, *23 August 1969. Used with permission of Fredrika Newton.*

African American fugitives historically found refuge and, more important, anonymity: Canada.

A FREE AGENT ON LOAN

Canada has become a left-hand lackey of America. They get
together collectively, and they become partners in crime.
— Leonard Brown, Michigan Black Panther Party

In 1971 when Hart arrived in Toronto, his past as an FBI operative impressed his RCMP superiors. As defense captain in Baltimore, Hart had played an instrumental role in the Justice Department's entrapment and subsequent indictment of twenty-one Panthers in an infamous 1969 New York City case. Trial transcripts reveal that Hart had smuggled weapons to New York City and provided explosives to New York Panthers when they visited the Baltimore chapter in early 1969.[74] (One of the indicted Panthers was Afeni Shakur. After the Panthers' acquittal on 12 May 1971, Shakur gave birth one month later to a baby boy named Lesane, whom she subsequently renamed Tupac.) Hart's duplicity and willful provocation of Panthers to engage in domestic terrorism made him lethal, especially to radicals and other activists who desired nothing more than to achieve self-determination. In every way, Hart tried to mimic Dan Freeman, protagonist of *The Spook Who Sat by the Door*.

The 5′8″, 220-pound operative arrived in Toronto brazenly using his own name. Sometimes Hart told people to call him "Clay." The FBI, Hart later admitted, "loaned" him to the Security Service of the RCMP from April 1971 to December 1975 to infiltrate, surveil, and disrupt Black radical organizations in Canada. The bureau and the RCMP also tasked him with undermining radical groups in the Caribbean and South America that had ties to Canadian activists.[75] The security and intelligence services feared the long tentacles of Pan-Africanisms.

Hart's use of the verb "loan"—and it is plausible that the bureau understood its high-level, unprecedented transaction with the RCMP as such—illustrates one of the ways that the imperial machinery exploited blackness and undermined Black liberation. "I was told that I would be the first one in the history of [the United States] loaned to another country," Hart recounted, "and that I was a pioneer in that if I made good it would set up proceedings for sending other people [to Canada] to work." Hart alluded to the opacity of the transaction that brought him to Canada: "Later I learned that the entire transaction had been handled by the State Department and the Minister of External Affairs."[76] The arrangement reveals the way that the state commodified Black labor to maintain systems of racial subordination and subjugation.

As Michigan Black Panther Leonard Brown suggested, when it came to cross-border counter-subversion, Canada acted like the left hand of the United States.[77] However, it would be too simplistic to conclude that Canada had become a U.S. lackey in the counter-subversion of Black activists. The RCMP acted on its own accord and enforced policies that it believed would ensure Canada's national security and discredit Black activists.

Two months before Hart arrived, militants met in Toronto to convene the Black People's Conference at Harbord Collegiate, which they themed "Toward the Political Direction and Liberation of Black People in Canada."[78] Of the approximately 2,000 delegates who attended, some came from the Caribbean and the United States to profess their commitment to the "liberation of Black people in Canada." The gathering, which prohibited access to white journalists, marked a radical—if not revolutionary—reawakening among Black activists in Toronto and throughout Canada. According to Burnley Jones—considered Canada's first Black Panther—the movement had one goal: "to destroy the basis of exploitation and racism." Jones explained, "We recognize that Black people have been living in a white society that is hostile to Blacks. The white society has been warned time and time again that there are minority groups that are not pleased with the way things are going." Anne Cools—a key organizer and one of the leaders of the 1969 Sir George Williams University occupation—told the media that the National Black Action Committee was a brainchild of the conference, although she stopped short of disclosing the group's full intentions.[79]

The RCMP then tried unsuccessfully to recruit a local spy to infiltrate the Black community. As a result, Hart came at a premium. He enjoyed a starting monthly salary of $900, plus expenses, a significant climb from his clerical days as a lowly federal employee. The RCMP believed this investment was necessary, fearing that Black activists in Canada wanted to forge "a very, very radical party like they had . . . in the United States." The Security Service, dreading the transnational connections of Black militants in Canada, tasked Hart with befriending Rosie Douglas and his associate Horace Campbell, a Toronto-based activist of Jamaican descent.[80] An FBI internal memo described Douglas as a "revolutionary Messiah" among his people in Dominica.[81] Canada's federal police also feared the trope of the Black male messiah.

Hart boasted of his ties to the U.S. Black Panthers and underworld connections that kept an endless flow of cash in his pocket and fuel in his fancy cars.[82] He created a facade that allowed him to penetrate Douglas's loose inner circle. Hart first cultivated a relationship with Douglas's friend Campbell. By becoming Douglas's bodyguard and chauffeur, Hart created a cover that allowed him close and prolonged contact with his target. Sometime at the end of 1971, he traveled to the Caribbean with Douglas and Campbell for two weeks to liaise with Black revolutionaries. When they left the Caribbean, Hart rerouted to the Maryland area to brief the Central Intelligence Agency about the Black radical situation before returning to Canada. "The RCMP decided to arrest Rosie Douglas," Hart recalled, presumably for traveling overseas to meet with radicals, "and I was to set it up. Also, I was to be arrested with him," to ward off any suspicion. After his December 1971 arrest, immigration officials conspired with the Security Service to "deport" Hart. This ruse provided Hart with street credibility. After spending five days in the Toronto Don Jail with Douglas, authorities released Hart, who then went "underground" in the back of a Toronto barbershop for two months before resurfacing in the city.[83]

The presence of Black militants in Canada with Caribbean roots and the steady immigration of Caribbean nationals in the late 1960s increased RCMP suspicions of the Caribbean. Hart confirmed that his superiors wanted to determine whether a "working relationship" existed between radicals in Canada and the Caribbean.[84] In fact, undercover Security Service officials occasionally traveled with Hart to Antigua, Barbados, St. Vincent, Dominica, and Guyana when Hart visited to train militants in guerrilla warfare.[85] "They would always come behind me. I would proceed to an island, and we would make arrangements prior to leaving Toronto." While on the ground, Hart "would file reports with [the RCMP] and if no one accompanied me on the trip I had to maintain the reports myself until I returned to Toronto."[86] He provided guerrilla training to leftist revolutionary groups, such as the Antigua Caribbean Liberation Movement, which Douglas's friend Tim Hector founded, and Grenada's New Jewel Movement. When questioned about these allegations, Hart replied, "I saw no better way to infiltrate those organizations. I had something to offer, and they wanted it." Hector dismissed Hart's allegations as "absolutely absurd."[87]

For the RCMP to gain the necessary leverage to halt or discredit postwar immigration liberalization, it needed to create or uncover a revolutionary plot that linked radicals in the Caribbean and Canada.[88] To borrow the phrase of cultural theorist Stuart Hall, the RCMP was "policing the crisis."[89] In essence, diasporic Africans could immigrate to Canada, if they left behind their racial consciousness and accepted a subordinate position in a racially stratified society.

Hart's multiple travels to the Caribbean in behalf of the RCMP illustrate anxieties over hemispheric Black liberation. His briefing of the CIA, and later Britain's MI6, uncovers the Anglo trident that stalked revolutionary Pan-Africanists in the Caribbean Basin.[90] The RCMP also collaborated with the CIA in counter-espionage, known in the Security Service as "B" Branch.[91] Counter-subversion, or "D" Branch, which enabled the Mounties to recruit Hart from the FBI, employed questionable tactics for a liberal, democratic society that purported to uphold the rule of law, while blending domestic and foreign spying.[92]

Hart made serious allegations against Douglas. He claimed that during Douglas's trial in 1971 for his participation in the Sir George Williams University computer center occupation, Douglas had conspired with other radicals to assassinate two racist university professors. According to Hart, Douglas and his coconspirators planned the assassination to coincide with armed insurrection in Dominica, which they hoped would derail Douglas's trial and that of other accused Caribbean students involved in the computer center occupation.[93] In light of such serious allegations—and Hart's surveillance of radicals in the Caribbean—a palpable fear of Black Power remained throughout the Canadian national security apparatus.

In September 1972, eighteen months after the Citizens' Commission to Investigate the FBI exposed COINTELPRO, "D" Branch launched Operation Checkmate.[94] The two-year secret program gave the RCMP's Security Service an offensive edge to undermine organizations that used violence, such as the FLQ and other radical organizations. When it went on the offensive, the Security Service relied heavily on "dirty tricks"—drafting false letters, filing bogus tax returns, making threatening phone calls to subversives, sabotage, unlawful entry, and entrapment by agent provocateurs. For example, in 1972, the Security Service burned a barn in Sainte-Anne-de-la-Rochelle, Quebec, preventing a meeting between Panthers and the FLQ.[95] Except for government assassinations of citizens, Operation Checkmate resembled COINTELPRO.

Entrapping or manipulating unsuspecting Black activists to embrace violent agitation was a preferred method in Operation Checkmate. Those who knew Hart, for instance, commented extensively on his brazen display of a firearm arsenal in his apartment.[96] "I saw them," declared Ainsley Vaughan, a young activist who orbited the same militant social spaces as Hart and Douglas in 1972. "There must have been a hundred of them: sub-machine guns, rifles, pistols—and hand grenades. And he kept them all right there in his bedroom, without even any curtains on the windows."[97] A Black teenager whom Hart had befriended had broken into an armory and stolen the weapons, which he gave to Hart for safekeeping.[98]

This cache of weapons, which the Security Service authorized Hart to store in his apartment, raises many red flags about democratic processes in postwar Canada. That the Security Service wanted Black activists in Toronto—including impressionable boys—to acquire some of these weapons illustrates the RCMP's desperation to discredit anti-racist struggle as a veneer for violence.[99] Crisis manufacturing was central to counter-subversion.[100]

Vaughan made other indicting remarks about Hart. "He offered us guns around the time the Jamaican Canadian Association was burned down in [May] 1972; no one knows who was responsible for that," Vaughan recalled. "When we were going to hold a rally there the General [as Hart styled himself] stockpiled the guns in the back of his car, ready. But we never used them. We never felt the need," he said. "We saw the struggle in a different light from that. And we didn't want to be locked up in some jail."[101]

Vaughan stated that Douglas, in sharp contrast to Hart's dubious form of violent agitation, always spoke with the voice of reason, especially when it came to matters of the police and the Black community. Along with his friends—Vaughan grew up in the racially mixed Alexandra Park housing project in downtown Toronto—he admitted to shouting "oink, oink" whenever the police drove past them. "Rosie always discouraged that kind of thing," Vaughan recalled. "He'd say that wasn't helping the struggle, that we should be educating people about our identity, not getting into trouble with the police." Hart, with his demolition background, preferred a different approach to training the next generation of revolutionaries. Hart encouraged Vaughan and his friends to bomb police stations. "He once suggested blowing up the South African embassy. It was like he was always testing us, seeing how far we'd go. But we never went very far."[102]

Hart used his U.S. Black Panther facade to penetrate different pockets of Toronto's Black community. As he did with Vaughan, Hart befriended poor Black boys who expressed Black Power sympathies. Unlike Vaughan and his peers, however, not all the Black teenagers whom Hart associated with successfully resisted his duplicity. Ricky Atkinson, an aspiring Black Panther, also lived in Alexandra Park with his African Nova Scotian father and Ukrainian Canadian mother. Atkinson's working-poor family experienced racism, much like the other poor families in their neighborhood. As poverty pushed Atkinson away from family life, the streets pulled him into Black Power circles. He stumbled into petty crime, too.[103]

In 1972, at age seventeen, Atkinson experienced his first encounter with the dirty tricks tactics of Operation Checkmate. The Security Service perceived Atkinson and his peers as future national security threats, because the teenagers wanted to become Black Panthers. Atkinson and his friends committed their first of many armed robberies. Their target was a bakery. Hart masterminded this score, according to Atkinson. Hart produced the firearm. Hart drew the entire robbery plot. Hart also told the aspiring Panthers that he would send the proceeds to the Panthers' central leadership in the United States, thus giving the impressionable teenagers a false and misdirected sense of purpose and racial pride. A few days after the robbery, the police arrested Atkinson and his coconspirators. During the trial, Atkinson spent time at Toronto's Don Jail. On his cellblock range, he met Harold Barnes—the brother of African American crime boss Nicky Barnes—and African American militants. Atkinson eventually served four years in prison for the crime, which Hart had informed the RCMP and local law enforcement about.[104] This stiff prison sentence for a minor was partly because Atkinson participated in a violent criminal activity in which he intended to send the proceeds overseas to underwrite revolutionary activities.[105]

Conway's reflection on the agent provocateur and Hart's brand of counter-subversion, which became more predatory when he operated in Canada, is insightful:

A normal informer can work for any police agency or anybody and can come in and basically spy on people, report back what is going on, give information, steal records, take pictures, etc. But an agent provocateur is different. An agent provocateur . . . goes into an organization and . . . creates conspiracies around illegal activities. . . . Now what he [Hart] did was that he initiated certain activities as the [defense] captain among the Panthers—he sent Panthers out to do things that were illegal, and because he was in charge, because most of them were new recruits and a lot of them were being trained directly by him, they didn't know that these were not the things that needed to be done. The consequence of it is that some of them end[ed] up getting arrested; at least one of them end[ed] up getting killed in a robbery attempt; some of them just disappeared with like no real record of whatever happened to them. . . . Agent provocateurs caused groups to run afoul of law-enforcement agencies at the behest of the law-enforcement agencies.[106]

Hart's loose-knit Panther cell consisted of risk-taking teenagers mainly because Hart, their role model, instructed them to commit felonies. "Warren Hart's intention," Atkinson concluded, "was to create a Black radical organization and then rat that organization out to the government to make the government look good that they were doing something to fight radicalism of the late 1960s."[107] For Atkinson and Black people in Canada, these years marked a type of dissonant citizenship: the state's subtle and at times outright disavowal of a Black person's membership in the Canadian polity, even though Canadian society accrued moral authority from Black people's engagement in democratic processes. From age sixteen to seventeen, Atkinson confessed that he "became a victim of Warren Hart's ploy."[108] Masterminding over 100 heists, Canada's most notorious serial bank robber admitted, "It was with Warren Hart's gun that he gave to me that he got from the government that I did the robbery that sent me to the penitentiary at seventeen years old."[109] Hart's exploitation knew no limits. While tape recording Atkinson and his boyhood peers, Hart asked them how they might assassinate Prime Minister Trudeau.[110]

Atkinson returned from prison a hardened criminal. He formed an outfit and named it the Dirty Tricks Gang—the RCMP Security Service's code name for counter-subversion. "We were pissed off at the government," he recalled, "all of us that were affected by Warren Hart's dubious nature. We just said screw the government; [crime] is an easy way to make money."[111] Warren Hart's persona as a gun-toting African American Panther—who could teach activists about demolition, weapons, and guerrilla warfare—exploited the trope of *The Spook Who Sat by the Door* in devastating ways. More important, the U.S. and Canadian governments' use of counter-subversion against Black activists was fundamentally a patriarchal—that is, "gendercidal"—policy meant to discredit, imprison, and exterminate Black boys and men, especially those who embraced revolutionary struggle.

Operation Checkmate did not merely undermine subversive activity; it spawned Black teenage gangsters whom the state could vilify as inherently criminal. A Toronto policeman who trailed Atkinson's gang in the 1970s described the clever strategies that the men deployed: "They had roofing shingles cut in pieces and they put nails in the shingles and if they were chased or followed by the police, they'd throw them on the road, so that's how they got the name Dirty Tricks." According to Atkinson, Hart devised this scheme and others. "The nails on the street, that was his idea. He used to give us books on military tactics and stuff like that," Atkinson recalled. "He taught us demolition and police avoidance and surveillance."[112]

When Hart was recruiting boys to commit armed robbery in 1972 on behalf of the RCMP, Rosie Douglas was still appealing the charge of mischief for leading the 1969 student occupation at Sir George Williams University. By August, when Douglas relocated to Toronto on $14,000 bail, he was also fighting a deportation order as a landed immigrant.[113] Douglas's nonviolent agitation and Pan-African organizing against Canadian racism and Western imperialism in the Caribbean made him an enemy of the postwar state. In May 1972, he cochaired the African Liberation Day Committee in Toronto.[114] Douglas's awareness of the shortcomings of Canadian society and his efforts to address these issues made him anathema to the state. Canada's embrace of multiculturalism, which implied a certain multiracialism of sorts, was a way to secure legitimacy and moral authority on the international stage. As progressive policies and human rights norms gained traction on one hand, authorities had to contend with Black activists who denounced the culminating effects of centuries of anti-blackness in Canada on the other.

In the early 1970s, various politically savvy and goal-oriented groups organized for Black liberation. The National Black Coalition of Canada (NBCC), which community members launched in the wake of the Sir George Williams crisis, was the first of its kind in the country. Politically moderate, the underfunded NBCC navigated a contentious landscape.[115] Vice Chair Kay Livingstone, daughter of James F. Jenkins, founding editor of the *Dawn of Tomorrow* newspaper, believed in political education that fortified Black children and youth with race pride, much like her late father. When the NBCC sponsored an excursion in the rural Ontario town of Parry Sound, she explained, "For the first time these Black children will go to a camp where they will have Black supervisors. They'll be studying Black art and sculpture and African dances. Prominent Black authors will be holding discussion groups on Black literature and poetry." The campers also excavated the area for signs of Black history, since Black pioneers had founded a church in the area decades before.[116]

Toronto's Black Youth Organization, which the RCMP and the FBI monitored closely, had also been in the trenches of community mobilization since 1969. The organization spearheaded, among other initiatives, Black Family Affair, Black Information Service, and Housing and Bail Fund. "The significance of these self-help projects," stated Harold Hoyte, editor of *Contrast*, Toronto's largest Black-owned newspaper, "is that they represent what an increasing number of Blacks in Toronto consider to be the real way to achieve Black Power." Hoyte argued that this radical approach was rooted in a legacy of Black self-help, which had nothing to do with "violence."[117]

Other radical grassroots organizations, such as the Black Education Project, which Douglas's friends Horace Campbell and Marlene Green led, and the Black Heritage Association of the Black People's Movement at York University, empowered the community.[118] Because York University was a site of Black Power sentiments, Hart enrolled in classes there from June to September 1972, presumably for cover as he surveilled Black activists.[119] These activists subscribed to Black Power and self-awareness grounded in a race, class, and gender analysis. Some even acted circumspectly to avoid conflating Pan-Africanisms and Black Power with revolutionary violence. "Too many of us think that Black studies is a subversion of society or a base for the preparation of blood-thirsty revolutionaries," said Dr. Lynherst Pena, a faculty member and volunteer for the Black People's Movement at York University. Dr. Pena's remark was in response to some Black parents' anxieties over teaching their children conscious Black history. "And too many of us feel that all is well because we do not see the Royal Canadian Mounted Police in our homes every day."[120] The reality, of course, was that the RCMP, on whose behalf Hart operated, had entered many Toronto homes and community groups unannounced.

In 1970s Toronto, some young radicals feared that complacency and a false sense of belonging had weakened community agitation. Deborah Clark, a biracial woman who had moved from Montreal to Toronto at sixteen, helped found in the late 1960s the militant Black Student Union, a consortium of college and university student groups in the Toronto Metropolitan Area. As the Black Student Union's spokeswoman, Clark lobbied the University of Toronto for a grant to tutor poor Black children. With a transnational and diasporic outlook, she established a breakfast program modeled after the Black Panthers' wildly popular socialist praxis of redistributive resources that addressed the immediate material needs of the Black working poor. For Clark, a working mother of six children, five of whom lived in state custody, racism and structural inequality in Canada necessitated resistance. "The myth of racial equality is one reason why there are no strong, militant Black organizations in Canada," Clark posited. "But a sufficient number of us now know differently. That's why we must organize."[121] From Clark's vantage point, race constituted a slippery, elusive, and deceptive construct in Canadian society. This conundrum had the effect of disarming Black militancy, which Canadian authorities appreciated, considering the violent urban uprisings unfolding in U.S. cities.

The zeitgeist troubled former prime minister John Diefenbaker, who once described the era as susceptible to the "gales of destruction." Diefenbaker, under whose government the edifice of a white supremacist immigration policy had begun to crumble, averred in a meeting with the Law Society of Upper Canada in 1970 that Canada's immigration laws should exclude "revolutionaries and international gangsters." Visitations by revolution-aries, such as Jerry Rubin of the revolutionary Youth International Party or Black Panther militant Stokely Carmichael and "their like from the U.S.," troubled the former prime minister, the political establishment, and the Security Service. Diefenbaker perceived such actors and their organizations as "half-baked liberators" who spread a false gospel of subversive ideas, denigrating law enforcement as "pigs."[122]

Anti-war groups in Canada appreciated the work of "half-baked liberators" from the United States. In November 1972, students lobbied the minister of immigration for one month to grant BPP cofounder Bobby Seale a special two-day visa to speak about the travesty of the Vietnam War. In his 5 November speech to 500 students at the University of Toronto, Seale explained that Nixon's reelection would amount to "four more years of continuing fascist, racist oppression." Seale encouraged students to protest U.S. imperialism in Canadian streets, a message that Diefenbaker espoused as prime minister when Washington wanted Ottawa to accept nuclear weapons on Canadian soil as part of its Cold War deterrence in the early 1960s.[123]

Diefenbaker's former mentee's ordeals with Canadian authorities continued. In the summer of 1973, after the Quebec Court of Appeals denied Douglas's petitions for redress in the 1969 computer center "riot," the thirty-one-year-old submitted himself to the authorities. Although the court dropped eleven of Douglas's criminal charges, obstructing the use of private property remained. The court sentenced him to two years less a day, which meant a provincial rather than a federal institution would house him. To atone for his sin of exposing to the world the structures of racism in postwar Canadian society, the province imprisoned Douglas at Leclerc Institution, a medium security facility near Montreal. As for the $5,000 fine, the court gave him an option of spending an additional six months behind bars instead of paying this indemnity. He chose a lengthier sentence. By this time, Douglas's father had paid $6,000 of his son's legal fees.[124]

Before starting his prison sentence, Douglas had been laying the groundwork for Black self-defense. An FBI internal memo confirmed that Deborah Clark and her common-law, German-born husband, Jorg Schneider, offered Douglas use of their 350-acre farm in Tweed, Ontario, a two-hour drive east of Toronto. Douglas intended to use the farm as a legal gun club, which would have been fully operational by early 1973. The true purpose, the FBI alleged, was that it would serve as a guerrilla training camp for Black revolutionaries. Militants had transferred a cache of weapons to the camp. Drilling exercises would buttress revolutionary struggle in the Caribbean. Funding would come from U.S., Canadian, and Caribbean revolutionaries who would contribute to the camp's maintenance.[125]

During Douglas's imprisonment, Hart ran amok in Canada, working tirelessly to induce law-abiding citizens to commit serious felonies. "He [Hart] was just a big joke," recalled Roy States, an executive secretary of the National Black Coalition of Canada. "I personally dismissed Warren

Hart—I've never taken him seriously," said Al Hamilton, the publisher of the Toronto-based *Contrast* newspaper. Hart, according to Hamilton, "was not really achieving anything great[,] to walk into the Black community and become an agent," because African Canadian communities accepted newcomers. Ronald Joseph, an NBCC executive and a close friend of Douglas, said the Dominican radical "never had no respect for Hart," who often carried a recording device and sometimes introduced himself to members of the Black community in Toronto and Montreal as "Clay" or "the General." Douglas simply "felt powerful" that Hart, his chauffeur and bodyguard, "was a guy with a revolver." The three men had a legitimate ax to grind. There is a clear sense of resentment that Hart, in his service to the Canadian government, infiltrated law-abiding civic groups and that the Security Service had chosen to target activists who wanted to combat anti-Black racism in Canadian society.[126]

"A SEASON OF SORROW"

On the cold morning of 7 November 1974, Leclerc Institution released Douglas early on parole after sixteen months of his two-and-a-half-year sentence. He had lost almost fifty pounds. "I learned a lot about the injustices in Canadian society," Douglas said of his time behind bars. "I met a lot of ordinary Canadians and I set up a literacy class for prisoners who couldn't read or write."[127] His exposure to the plight of Indigenous peoples and FLQ foot soldiers and the overall harshness of incarceration had further radicalized him. "Before I went into prison," admitted Douglas, "I was working for the rights of Blacks. It was a more narrow vision. But I realized the attempt to solve the Black person's problems is related to the problems of all the other poor in the community." And as if to punctuate and declare his complete radical transformation, Douglas referenced solidarity among the working class as the binding thread—the organizing principle for downtrodden peoples to resist capitalism, neocolonialism, and neoimperialism. "The fundamental problems are economic," he said.[128] Douglas's Pan-Africanisms complemented his new leftist internationalism.

Instead of remaining in Montreal, where his political activism began, Douglas relocated to Toronto, where he had previously set down roots to work on the Brotherhood Community Center Project. This organization mobilized Pan-African protest and community building at home and abroad.[129] "Our only salvation is to work collectively towards building co-operative institutions within our community controlled democratically by ourselves. Through them," Douglas asserted, "we can harness and develop our resources, escalate our support to liberation movements in southern

Africa and the Caribbean, work towards meaningful revolutionary Pan African unification and identify functionally with the global movement against imperialism."[130]

Anne Cools also transitioned to Toronto in 1974. After almost four years of appeals, Cools served four months in jail for her role in leading the computer center occupation. "It was like a cage," Cools recounted of her time behind bars. "I viewed it as a season of sorrow." When she refused to clean toilets one day, she spent two weeks in solitary confinement. "I was alone again. You just sat on that bench and cried and cried and cried." Upon her release, she spent a winter convalescing on a beach in her native Barbados.[131] When she returned to Canada, Cools decided to utilize her McGill University degree in social work. After a brief stint working in Montreal group homes, she moved to Toronto, where she landed a major leadership position. At age thirty, she took over the reins of Women in Transition, Canada's first shelter for battered women and their children. A dynamic activist and manager, Cools transformed the fledgling shelter into a robust institution that championed the needs of abused women and children. These years proved decisive for Cools's transformation into a stateswoman. She received a formal pardon from the Canadian government in the subsequent years. There is no redemption, especially for the criminalized, without public penance.

As Douglas's onetime coconspirator, Cools moved within the frameworks of the establishment to effect change, while Douglas agitated on the periphery because he had yet to renounce his burgeoning Pan-African revolutionary socialism. While transitioning back into his civilian lifestyle in November 1974, he tried to stave off a federal deportation order. Hart, Douglas's bodyguard and chauffeur, went into counter-subversion overdrive when the Security Service discovered that Angela Davis would speak to students and community members at the University of Toronto. When the Student Administrative Council, the Toronto-based Black Student Union, and the Committee in Defense of Black Prisoners met in the basement of a local church to finalize details of Davis's 22 November visit, Hart attended. He insisted at the student-led meeting that the planning committee arm itself with many guns. He offered to provide the weapons. Hart tried to convince students to allow him to retrieve Davis from the airport in his car, which the RCMP had outfitted with recording devices. A van filled with students armed with semiautomatic rifles, he suggested, would trail him and Davis, providing cover. In case another car attempted to smash into his to injure Davis, the van with the semiautomatic-wielding university students could "do them in," Hart proposed.[132]

Hart even suggested that armed shooters stand behind Davis when she gave her speech at the university to deter assassins. "It seemed like he was trying to bully us into something," an executive member of the student committee recalled. Hart told some members of the committee that they "were just middle-class white students trying to tell revolutionary Black Nationalists what to do." The reality, however, was that Hart desperately wanted student radicals to behave like violent thugs to vindicate himself and the RCMP.[133]

Unnerved by Hart's insistence on arming student activists, one of the committee members called Davis's aides in New York. An aide assured the student that Davis would return to the airplane immediately if any of her hosts carried a firearm in her presence. Ultimately, Davis and the other non-violent radicals got their way. They avoided entrapment and the potential powder keg of someone confronting Davis and the armed students. The media reported that the Western Guard, a white supremacist group that harassed racial minorities and draft resisters, might attack Davis's entourage.[134] To ensure her security and that of the other attendees, the planning committee procured 140 security guards and uniformed university and Toronto police officers. Davis delivered her speech without incident and with her usual charismatic charm. She singled out the Canadian government and the minister of immigration for engaging in racial scapegoating. They "can get white people riled up against Black people from the Caribbean and Africa with the idea that they will take jobs away from them. Then they [white people] will forget there's somebody up there exploiting them." The 1,500 guests in attendance roared.[135] In North America, though, race was not always Black and white. Sometimes, it was Black and Red.

BLACK POWER AND RED POWER VS.
UNCLE TOMS AND "UNCLE TOMAHAWKS"

After the Sir George Williams occupation in February 1969, Black activists in Canada and Indigenous peoples explored opportunities for interracial cooperation. At that time, militant Pan-Africanists and their Indigenous counterparts in Toronto met and discussed an interracial coalition. Jan Carew, the Guyanese writer and proud descendant of Amerindians and enslaved Africans, chaired the first meeting of the Toronto Liberation Front. Carew, who grew up upper-middle class in Guyana, anticipated the challenges of organizing some Black people in Toronto because there existed "a higher proportion of Uncle Toms than perhaps anywhere else." Fred Kelly, an Ojibway leader, brought with him a contingent from Kenora, a remote town that the Ontario Human Rights Commission and its leader Daniel Hill III assisted. Kelly lamented that Indigenous communities also suffered from a prevalence of "Uncle Tomahawks."[136]

The social inequities and underlining tensions that brought Black Power and Red Power together in 1969 in Toronto remained the same in 1974 when Douglas set out to rekindle this connection. For Indigenous groups, the early 1970s witnessed an uptick in militant nationalism to redress unfulfilled treaty obligations, sovereignty, racism, and other injustices of which the Canadian government stood directly and indirectly culpable. Describing the racial climate in mid-1970s Canada, a writer for the draft resister magazine *American Expatriate* (*Amex*) labeled Indigenous reserves "ghettos in the woods" that rivaled postindustrial U.S. inner cities. He explained, "Attacks on native, Third World, and Black people are not isolated events. Racism," he argued, "is always encouraged during times of economic crisis to stop working people from understanding their common oppression and achieving the unity they must forge to defeat it."[137]

The dire conditions of many Indigenous communities made the authorities fear linkages between Red and Black Power, and a Pan-Red Power in Canada and the United States.[138] The RCMP perceived the tenacious U.S. American Indian Movement, which the FBI thoroughly infiltrated and counter-subverted, as the mortar that would cement relations between Indigenous groups across the forty-ninth parallel. Skirmishes and violent confrontations in October 1973 at Caughnawaga, a Mohawk reserve near Montreal, and in July 1974 at Anicinabe Park in Ontario, which bordered Manitoba, between Indigenous communities and Canadian authorities, as well as other high-profile incidents, two of which occurred in Ottawa, rattled the RCMP. So, when Douglas and Hart traveled on a Canada-wide speaking tour in Hart's new, RCMP-issued Lincoln Continental, making frequent stops at First Nations communities, the Security Service anticipated that its operative would help facilitate a major takedown that would simultaneously discredit Black Power and Red Power.

Vern Harper, a seasoned Cree activist and a lineal descendant of Big Bear, the prominent Cree leader who resisted nineteenth-century Canadian colonialism, served as Douglas's point person in Indigenous communities. Together, Douglas and Harper represented Canada's two most historically disadvantaged racial groups. The alliance between Black Power and Red Power had the potential to mount an effective campaign against colonialism and institutional racism in Canadian society. According to Harper, the three Indigenous communities that they visited discerned Douglas's sincerity and empathy for their cause.

Near Kenora, Indigenous people at the Grassy Narrows reserve, whose waterways a chemical plant had contaminated by discharging untreated effluent, expressed their acceptance of and gratitude to Douglas by giving him presents and allowing him to smoke their peace pipe.[139] Daniel Hill's advocacy in that region on behalf of the Ontario Human Rights Commission likely generated goodwill concerning Black people. "This wasn't a ceremony like some sellout tribes have, you know," said Harper, "where they give a headdress to Diefenbaker or Prince Charles to get funding. These are real traditional people. This was a very unusual thing for them to do."[140] Furthermore, that Douglas connected enthusiastically and sincerely with Indigenous people indicated a consciousness of his native Dominica's Indigenous Carib population (Kaligano), whom the British had sequestered to a reserve in the northeastern part of the island. As a teenager, Douglas recalled feeling vexed at the sight of Black and Kaligano workers being "exploited" on his father's coconut plantation.[141]

As Hart chauffeured Douglas and Harper, the two comrades met with Indigenous elders to strategize around organizing rallies and combining Indigenous and Black newspapers in Canada. Hart expressed little interest in these constructive and genuine forms of nonviolent, interracial liberation struggle. At opportune moments, however, Hart goaded his Indigenous passenger, Harper, to embrace violence. "He wanted to get a group of us and train us in explosives," Harper recalled. Louie Cameron, another Indigenous activist and an eminent member of the Ojibway Warrior Society, said Hart encouraged them to detonate police cars. "He said that if we place a bomb under a police car, the chemical would eat away at the metal for two or three days, so that when the bomb went off, we wouldn't be there to be identified. We were kind of surprised," admitted Cameron. "We'd never heard of anything like that before." In looking back, Cameron believed that they all should have been more guarded around Hart. Cameron recalled one evening when Douglas and Harper slept contently on the floor of a mosquito-infested boathouse—while Hart drove his Lincoln to a nearby Holiday Inn.[142]

If deception was the mind of the state, Black activists learned quickly. Although Warren Hart's facade was a counter-subversion of *The Spook Who Sat by the Door*, Douglas and his fellow activists in Toronto and Montreal ensured that this cloak-and-dagger affair had a counterpunch. According to one of Douglas's comrades in the C. L. R. James Study Circle, Haitian Philippe Fils-Aimé, who spent a few years in the late 1960s living in New York before fleeing north to Montreal to avoid the draft, they all knew that Hart was a spy.[143]

Douglas decided to turn Hart into "a double agent."[144] Hart served the interests of Black activists, including shuttling Douglas across the country in his work with Indigenous peoples. In exchange for material support, Douglas helped Hart write his intelligence briefings for the RCMP and the FBI. Hart also cooked for Douglas, fetched his dry cleaning, and waited on him as a personal attendant and bodyguard. Fils-Aimé said Hart was Douglas's "*major d'homme*" or butler. Their "relationship was kind of sick," Fils-Aimé acknowledged.[145] There is folly in introducing a spy to a community, because spies are unpredictable. "Rosie had the profound conviction that he was in control" of Hart.[146] When a journalist questioned Douglas about allegations that Hart had made against him, the Dominican activist did not disclose the true nature of his relationship to the RCMP and FBI spy. "Warren Hart came into the Black community, and we met him and at the time there were a number of Black people in the United States that were running away from persecution, and we always greeted them with an open heart," recalled Douglas. "Maybe we were naive. And if we were naive . . . I accept the blame for it."[147]

Douglas's comrades feared neither Hart nor the authorities. Members of the Study Circle had nothing to hide. In fact, they had experience sniffing out government agents. When former Black Panther George Sams—and accused murderer of New Haven Panther Alex Rackley—visited McGill University in Montreal, he presented himself as a professor of African American southern dialects, a ruse that "impressed" some McGill faculty. "Sams also pretended to be a fugitive Afro-American freedom fighter, a hero, who had shot down a helicopter during a riot in Washington [D.C.]. He was a good case study for the C. L. R. James Study Group." Fils-Aimé added, "He called for violent action and played on emotions only, that's how we knew he was an agent. We were learning so fast. Incredible. I remember Alfie [Roberts, the doyen] saying that if that's their best agent we don't have much to worry about."[148]

Ultimately, Douglas turned Hart into an asset. Hart's vehicle made him indispensable to Douglas and his Indigenous comrades. This mutual dependence ensured that neither Hart nor Douglas had overwhelming power at any given time in the RCMP's efforts to entrap Black and Indigenous activists. At every turn, of course, Hart tried to gain an upper hand on his targets. When he drove Douglas and Harper across the country to Vancouver, where Douglas would speak at a rally, Hart deliberately took multiple detours so that the three men would arrive after the crowd had disbanded. Hart later went on the offensive again, encouraging Indigenous activists in British Columbia to embrace domestic terrorism and resist the illegal logging of their forests. Hart offered AK-47 assault rifles to the National

Indian Brotherhood in British Columbia. His insistence on violence would have tarnished, if not effectively torpedoed, Indigenous peoples' demands for state redress. It would have also done irreparable damage to Black people in Canada and Indigenous peoples. "We try to organize democratically, and they send out provocateurs to disrupt us," Harper stated. "No wonder no one has faith in the system."[149] Douglas alerted his Indigenous comrades that Hart was a spy, and his traps failed.

DISSOLVED PACTS AND DEPORTATION ORDERS

After Douglas's Canada-wide tour with First Nations leaders in 1975, he revisited the issue of prison reform, a personal battleground. During his incarceration, he wrote a report on the conditions of prisons and potential solutions that could improve the well-being of inmates. So, when Solicitor General Warren Allmand visited Leclerc Institution in 1974, he recalled a distinct encounter. "When I was walking down the range, I heard: 'Mr. Allmand! Mr. Allmand!'"[150] Douglas told Allmand that he wanted to share his critique of the prison system, emphasizing better rehabilitation and improved training for correction officers.

Facing a deportation order, Douglas clawed for any opportunity that would help him stay and organize in Canada. With only one remaining lifeline and no viable appeals to stave off deportation, he contacted the Liberal cabinet minister who held his fate in his hand—Canada's solicitor general. At the end of November 1974, Douglas and Hart, who was armed with his trademark concealed tape recorder, drove to Montreal. In their meeting, Douglas shared his report with Allmand, who, in turn, offered Douglas a job in his department to draft an official policy memo on prison reform. This olive branch would have placed Douglas within the same federal department that employed the RCMP. Douglas refused to accept Allmand's offer until the solicitor general "removed the certificate against me saying I'm a risk to national security."[151] Allmand was not interested in Douglas's ultimatum, although he recalled that they had "established a good rapport" after their meeting.[152]

Unbeknownst to Douglas and Allmand, Hart recorded the entire conversation. In shadowing Douglas, Hart had effectively surveilled his handlers' superior. Hart maintained emphatically that his handlers gave him the nod to do so, because they suspected from wiretaps of Douglas's phone that their boss—the solicitor general—was prepared to offer the Dominican employment, which would allow him to stay in Canada. Hart's recollection of the clandestine recording portrayed the Security Service in a roguish light. "Well, Mr. Allmand was considered to be an ass by the RCMP officers, simply because of his association with so called Black leaders there—radicals, what have you," said Hart. As the RCMP was vehemently opposed to communism, Hart claimed that the security force considered Allmand a "pinko" and a "red."[153]

In implementing an undemocratic and opaque counter-subversion mandate, the RCMP had bitten its own tail, and the man whom they borrowed from the U.S. Justice Department failed to incriminate any Black or Indigenous leaders. In his pursuit of occupational prestige, Hart had entered a Faustian pact of sorts with the FBI and later the RCMP. His service on behalf of repressive security and intelligence agencies—whose operations seemed fanatical—required Hart to stir up trouble to exacerbate the suffering of a beleaguered people in the United States and Canada. He later acknowledged that the RCMP acted overzealously in its surveillance of Black organizations. When he reflected on his infiltration of the Black Caucus, a rights-based advocacy group, Hart conceded, "I don't think you would find hardly anyone in there with a traffic ticket."[154] The pursuit of Black self-determination in Canada was less about revolutionary violence than racial progress, although some groups embraced militancy and revolutionary Pan-African nationalism, such as the African Liberation Day Committee.

Ultimately, Hart, who enjoyed a $1,300 monthly salary plus expenses in 1975, became a burden on the Security Service's budget. The Mounties gave Hart a two-week notice and a $6,000 severance before they terminated his employment and expelled him from Canada in December 1975.[155] To expel Hart, the Canadian government used his falsification of immigration papers in 1971 after he accompanied Douglas to the Caribbean to train revolutionaries. In their ploy to preserve Hart's cover during that 1971 immigration hearing, his handlers had advised him to declare himself as a U.S. "revolutionary" with a criminal record.[156]

On 30 April 1976, four months after the Canadian government expelled Hart from the country, immigration officials placed Rosie Douglas on a plane bound for the Caribbean. After fifteen years of activism and community building, Douglas's life in Canada, which once held so much promise had he chosen to run for Parliament, as Diefenbaker suggested, came to an end. But instead of returning to Dominica and living with the stigma of deportation on his disgruntled father's estate, Douglas requested that Canadian authorities deport him to Jamaica.[157] As a result, he avoided an oppressive government in Dominica, whose police force had warned him to stay away.[158] For several months, fear of the police and the agony of confronting his family's disapproval kept Douglas at bay. A brief stay in Michael Manley's Jamaica gave Douglas a sense of hope in the possibility of self-determinative socialist governments in the Caribbean that valued Pan-Africanisms.

The Canadian government, in collaboration with the FBI, squandered resources to incite violence among law-abiding activists. Had Douglas and other members of the Black or Indigenous communities complied with Hart's schemes, the Canadian government could then have justifiably discredited their grievances and undermined their work for racial progress. The need for unscrupulous and predatory agent provocateurs as a form of counter-subversion undermined ideas of civility, democracy, and the rule of law in Canada and the United States.

That Hart and the Security Service failed on numerous occasions to entice activists in Canada to use violence is a testament to the Black community's resolve. When Hart went public with his story in 1978, Douglas acknowledged, "His role was to entice me to use violence . . . and he failed. We were not about any violence. We were about the demands of the Black community in terms of their human rights, their civil rights, and their full equality."[159] In an internal FBI memo, Hart tarnished Douglas's credibility by lying that Douglas had directed his predatory actions. He confessed to committing "a series of raids and robberies, minor and major, that he had personally executed in Toronto for Douglas' personal benefit, not for true revolutionary purpose."[160] It is difficult to substantiate these allegations for two reasons. First, Hart had a documented history of instructing and training minors to commit robbery. And second, he was an agent provocateur who placed culpability on Douglas, his target.

Rosie Douglas's deportation provided authorities the surest way to neutralize the impact of his revolutionary Pan-Africanisms on Canadian and U.S. societies. Warren Hart and Douglas tested Canadian society in opposite ways. Hart served not only the RCMP's Security Service but also his original master, the FBI, which exposed the limitations of Canadian sovereignty. Douglas, the immigrant success story, tested the limits of sanctuary and peaceful dissent, ideals on which Canada had long prided itself. In the end, Canadian authorities expelled both men. Each, in his own way, sullied the sanitized image of a racially progressive postwar Canada.

CHAPTER 6

COLD WARS, HOT WARS

▼ ▼ ▼

Incarceration in Quebec and deportation from Canada did not weaken Rosie Douglas's resolve for a Pan-African socialist revolution. It strengthened it. Although Douglas returned to Dominica humbled in early 1977 after spending six months in Jamaica and a few weeks in Cuba, he committed himself fully to proletariat struggle. He organized in Grand Bay, where his enslaved African forebears had waged a successful insurrection in January 1791. While receiving a $100 monthly stipend from a Canadian doctor in Saskatchewan, he also organized the workers on his father's vast banana and coconut plantations, a decision that inflamed tensions between father and son. When a Canadian journalist interrogated Douglas about his status as a beneficiary of the island's bourgeoisie, asking whether he would redistribute his family lands to the workers, he acknowledged the charge but stopped short of radical land redistribution. "I wouldn't give it away [to the workers], but I would try to develop it in a manner which would allow the workers . . . to enjoy a decent standard of living." As long as his father was alive, Douglas had to show deference, especially because his father considered him a communist. Douglas's love for the working poor was more than rhetoric. The Dominica-Cuba Friendship Association that he founded created social programs and scholarship opportunities for the Dominican peasantry.[1]

Douglas's connections to and collaborations with African Caribbean, African Canadian, and African American militants in the 1970s illustrated the urgency of Pan-African struggle against Western imperialism and neocolonialism. In fact, revolutionary struggle in Mozambique, Angola, and other parts of southern Africa during the waning years of the North American Black Power era strengthened transatlantic Pan-Africanisms. As a result of the intelligence community in the United States and Canada counter-subverting Black activists' dream of revolutionary social change, Black revolutionaries in the United States, Canada, and the Eastern Caribbean positioned African liberation as the most important battle front for Black self-determination.[2] The pivot to supporting liberation struggles in Africa symbolized a "back-to-Africa" movement of sorts. Centering Africa was reminiscent of the heyday of the Universal Negro Improvement

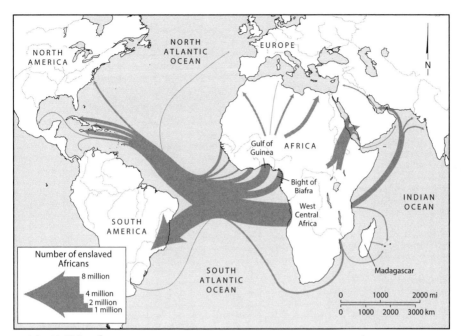

Atlantic Triangle

Association in the 1920s, when Marcus Garvey insisted that the only way diasporic Africans could enjoy true freedom was if all Black people fought to liberate Africa from foreign domination.

Anti-colonial struggle in the Atlantic World heightened Pan-Africanisms' revolutionary spirit. This chapter, which partly relies on declassified sources obtained under freedom of information provisions, uncovers connections between African Liberation Day (ALD) organizing in North America and a U.S.-Canadian arms manufacturer. Working in partnership with the intelligence community, this multinational arms dealer transshipped sophisticated ordnance, cannons, and radar defense systems via the Eastern Caribbean to apartheid South Africa, an action meant to undermine revolutionary Pan-African struggle. The chapter also unearths revolutionary and counterrevolutionary currents in the Caribbean, including the role that U.S. and Canadian white supremacists sought to play in creating an ethno-state paradise in the Eastern Caribbean.

Black liberation, especially when it manifested as a transnational phenomenon that aspired to unify African peoples, encountered unrelenting headwinds not only from the imperial state but also from white paramilitary groups that held notions of Black self-determination in contempt. In the post–Black Power era, when liberalism and integration politics had run its

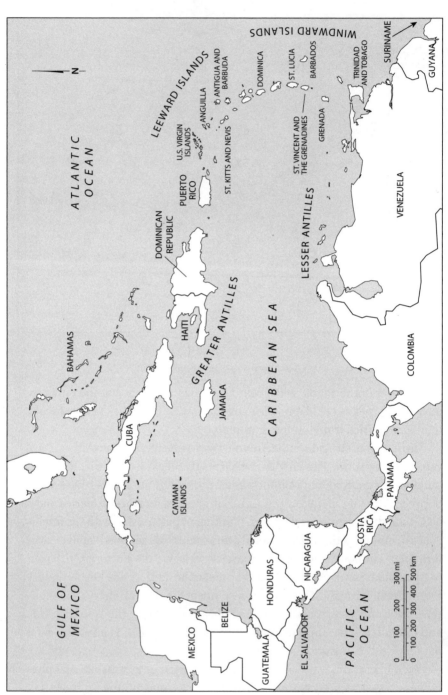

Caribbean Basin

course, Washington and Ottawa continued to perceive the Caribbean as a major geopolitical site, especially because of linkages between activists on the islands and the mainland.[3] Canadian officials feared a convergence of Pan-Africanisms on the home front and deported Caribbean and African American activists in the early 1970s to silence critiques of capitalism and Western imperialism in the Americas and Africa. Washington, with Ottawa's explicit and tacit approval on regional and transatlantic matters, took the initiative in frustrating dreams of global Black liberation.

THE SWORD AND THE SHIELD

Pan-Africanists saw a clear connection between Black liberation in the Americas and Africa. The challenge, according to one of Douglas's African American comrades Owusu Sadaukai, formerly known as Howard Fuller, was that some Black people in the United States and Canada enjoyed the fruits of imperialism, which compromised the struggle for global Black liberation. Resistance would be more effective in the Caribbean or Africa, Sadaukai reasoned, because the masses did not benefit materially from imperialism and neocolonialism. As a cofounder of the experimental Malcolm X Liberation University in Durham and Greensboro, North Carolina, Sadaukai described African Liberation Day as "the nucleus of Pan-African solidarity in the Americas against fascist oppression in southern Africa."[4]

In the summer of 1971, Sadaukai and fellow Black Power advocate Ron Daniels attended the International Black Ministers Conference as consultants in Dar es Salaam, Tanzania. One of the organizers was James Cone, a proponent of Black liberation theology. The conference endeavored to examine the role of white Protestant Christian churches in the anti-colonial struggle and to foster ties between activists in the United States and Africa. The trip was the first time that Sadaukai and Daniels, aspiring Pan-Africanists, had trod African soil. From Tanzania, African American delegates traveled to Kenya and Ethiopia, where they witnessed the economic misery of the masses and the hollowness of nominal political independence. In Addis Ababa, Ethiopia, the delegates met with the secretary-general of the Organization of African Unity, Diallo Telli, a Guinean statesman. Telli explained to his visitors that Pan-Africanism was "sheer romanticism" if its advocates did not help constrain the hard power of the United States, specifically Washington's support for colonialism and neocolonialism in Africa. He stressed the need to provide material aid to revolutionaries and pointed out that Jews and Arabs in the United States remained vociferous supporters of Israel and Palestine, respectively, and that African Americans should learn from these diasporic geopolitics. One of the many lessons imparted to the delegates was that the Organization of African Unity observed African Solidarity Day every 25 May to focus attention on uprooting white settler-colonialism.[5]

After his visit to Ethiopia, the Liberation Front of Mozambique, or FRE-LIMO, invited Sadaukai to the country, where he was embedded with guerrilla forces resisting Portuguese colonialism. "It is hard to tell the civilians from the freedom fighters. FRELIMO is, in fact, the people of Mozambique in arms. . . . Women are total comrades," Sadaukai recalled. "There is no chauvinism. No drinking and promiscuity. No long rhetorical arguments and useless wolf tickets."[6] When Sadaukai asked Mozambican freedom fighters how their distant kindred in North America could support their cause, FRELIMO requested material aid and political demonstrations of Pan-African solidarity. Diasporic support of anti-colonial freedom struggles in Africa was part of a rich Pan-African tradition, including denunciation of German atrocities in East Africa in the early 1900s and mobilization of support for Ethiopia after Fascist Italy's invasion in 1935.[7] "Liberation movements will be isolated and destroyed," Sadaukai concluded, "if we do not develop a continual interest and a support base of African peoples, wherever we may be."[8]

Upon returning to the United States, Sadaukai convened comrades who could assist with Pan-African political organizing. At Malcolm X Liberation University, he debriefed Cleve Sellers, Haki Madhubuti, Jamila Jones, Dowolu Gene Locke, Aleem Mashindi, Nelson Johnson, and Ron Daniels of his time with FRELIMO.[9] This group became founding members of the ALD Coordinating Committee. Inspired by the Organization of African Unity, the ALD Coordinating Committee chose Saturday, 27 May 1972, to observe the first ALD demonstrations in key English-speaking North American locations: Washington, D.C., San Francisco, Toronto, Antigua, Dominica, and Grenada. In Grenada, for example, Maurice Bishop, a rising political star, led ALD organizing on that island. These transnational ties were more than symbolic. With a moribund civil rights movement and retreating Black Power in the United States, disciples of Malcolm X, such as Sadaukai, tried to fulfill X's dream of transforming the African American freedom struggle into a revolutionary Pan-African cause with continental, hemispheric, and transatlantic dimensions. Sadaukai, after all, had participated in the monumental March 1972 National Black Political Convention in Gary, Indiana, where 10,000 delegates made a valiant, although unsuccessful, push to resuscitate a conscientious Black politics that could address the urgent material insecurities of the African American masses.[10]

To ensure successful execution of ALD on the North American mainland, Sadaukai visited Rosie Douglas in Toronto. Douglas was then awaiting sentencing for participating in the 1969 Sir George Williams University student occupation. In the early 1970s, Douglas had become a prominent activist and knew many African Americans in the Black Power scene. One month before the first scheduled ALD protests in 1972, Sadaukai met Douglas and other Caribbean activists in Toronto, where he addressed the importance of triangulating African peoples in the United States and Canada, the Caribbean, and Africa. Before such progress could materialize, Caribbean peoples, Sadaukai argued, would have to resist the forces of neocolonialism and miseducation. "The only thing that has changed is new Black faces in high white places," Sadaukai lamented in his April 1972 speech.[11] As a result of his visit, Douglas agreed to serve as the national co-coordinator of the ALD Coordinating Committee in Canada.[12]

May 1972 proved a historic moment in North American history. With 65,000 Black people marching in six locations, including in Toronto, Washington, D.C., and St. John's, Antigua, ALD allowed the masses to participate in direct political action that impacted liberation struggles in southern Africa. Knowing the significance of the griot—historians and history—to African peoples, their freedom struggles, and the Black radical tradition, the eminent Guyanese historian and Pan-Africanist revolutionary Walter Rodney described ALD as "an act of identification." One of the fiercest critics of African and Caribbean neocolonialism and its petty bourgeoisie, Rodney admonished attendees at the 1972 San Francisco ALD rally to reject Western hegemony and embrace African identity and consciousness as acts of revolution.[13] This message was timely, for in 1972 Rodney published his forceful book *How Europe Underdeveloped Africa*. Harvard Law School graduate Randall Robinson and his dynamic wife, Brenda Randolph Robinson, led a national boycott of Gulf Oil Corporation and subsidiary Holiday Inn for exploiting Angola. Black communities also boycotted Portuguese, South African, and Rhodesian goods. Not since the early 1920s under the leadership of the UNIA had diasporic Africans expressed such militant opposition to Western imperialism and colonialism.[14] The subtext of ALD, of course, was that because the U.S., Canadian, and neocolonial governments in the Caribbean refused to create conditions that would allow the Black masses to enjoy material security, ALD participants had few options other than to help liberate the continent of their ancestors. Indeed, "back to Africa" was more than physical repatriation. It was, as Rodney asserted, "an act of identification" that linked the fates of all African peoples in their pursuit of self-determination and opposition to capitalist exploitation.

The intractable nature of Western colonialism in Africa imbued ALD with urgency and legitimacy. British recognition of the white supremacist

Rhodesian regime in December 1971, in addition to Israel's support for apartheid South Africa, encouraged Pan-Africanists in the United States, Canada, and the Caribbean to champion self-determination not only in southern Africa but also in Palestine.[15] At the 1972 ALD commemoration in Washington, D.C., protesters converged on the Portuguese embassy and the Rhodesian Information Center. Congressman Charles Diggs Jr. highlighted the spirit of the occasion: "Black people in America and Black people in the Caribbean understand that our African past is intimately bound up with our African future." So, too, did luminaries such as Elaine Brown, who became chairwoman of the Black Panther Party in 1974; writer and Black Arts Movement pioneer Amiri Baraka; the celebrated reparations advocate and Pan-African nationalist Queen Mother Audley Moore; and Roy Innis, chairman of the Congress of Racial Equality. As some protesters waved the Garveyite tricolor red, black, and green, Sadaukai concluded an impassioned speech for global African liberation, leading the chant, "We-are-an-African-people! We-are-an-African-people!"[16]

This mobilization in the United States complemented similar efforts in Canada. In 1972, several activists, along with John Saul, the socialist political economist, who had previously taught alongside Walter Rodney at the University of Dar es Salaam, founded the Toronto Committee for the Liberation of Portugal's African Colonies. After the January 1973 assassination of Pan-African revolutionary and intellectual Amílcar Cabral in the Portuguese colony of Guinea-Bissau, the mission of the Toronto Committee and the ALD Support Committee (formerly the ALD Coordinating Committee) gained renewed urgency.[17] In fact, the May 1973 ALD commemoration occurred in twenty-five U.S. cities, in addition to Toronto and Caribbean states. The Carnation Revolution in April 1974, the coup that the Portuguese military launched to topple the authoritarian regime, effectively ended the country's colonial wars in Guinea Bissau, Angola, and Mozambique. As a result, the Toronto Committee for the Liberation of Portugal's African Colonies became the Toronto Committee for the Liberation of Southern Africa. Shedding light on the ways that Canadian and U.S. corporations contributed to the imperial subjugation of southern African states—Angola, Mozambique, Namibia, South Africa, and Zimbabwe—the committee helped bring colonialism in Africa squarely into the public consciousness. It also illustrated the continental and transatlantic dimensions of the liberation struggle in southern Africa.[18]

Activist organizations in general and ALD mobilization specifically generated much excitement and hope for revolutionary Pan-Africanisms in the 1970s. According to Tim Hector, one of the principal activists who helped Sadaukai organize ALD in his native Antigua, the concept of ALD "spread like wildfire, fueling . . . the anti-apartheid movement around the world."[19] By embracing a stance that was "pro-Black people" and "pro-Pan-Africanism" and "pro-African Socialism," ALD's revolutionary fervor encouraged a positive and proactive outlook, not a reactionary movement.[20]

So, when activists planned for the Sixth Pan-African Congress in June 1974 in Tanzania, the first time on African soil and sponsored by a Black government, they believed that the gathering would help topple the neocolonial regimes in the Caribbean and Africa. However, the Sixth Pan-African Congress marginalized the voices of critical intellectuals and activists at the behest of African and Caribbean neocolonial states and the petty bourgeoisie that maintained its power and dominance over workers and peasants, thus thwarting class reconciliation and unity.[21] For this reason, Rodney pointed out that the objective of Pan-Africanisms must focus on cultivating "solidarity between the Caribbean peoples and African peoples. It is not the same question as developing solidarity between African states and the Caribbean states."[22]

Despite this major setback, many people contributed to the Sixth Pan-African Congress, including women, such as Shirley Graham Du Bois and Amy Jacques Garvey, two of the principal conveners. The indefatigable Audley Moore, member of the U.S.-based Universal Association of Ethiopian Women, also attended and affirmed her commitment to Pan-African nationalism.[23] Over 200 delegates from the United States and Canada participated, one of whom was the young Montreal-born activist Brenda Paris, who translated French for African American delegates.[24] In 1973, Paris, as secretary of the ALD Support Committee, outgoing president Sadaukai, and incoming president Gene Locke traveled to Africa on official ALD business. After landing in Ethiopia, the three executives visited Somalia, Tanzania, Zimbabwe, Côte d'Ivoire, and Guinea Bissau, where the respective heads of state received them as a formal delegation.[25]

This type of political organizing during the Cold War generated as much angst for U.S. and Canadian authorities as it did for colonial and neocolonial governments in the Caribbean and Africa. For example, the Maurice Bishop–led New Joint Endeavor for Welfare, Education, and Liberation (New Jewel Movement or NJM), a Marxist-Leninist party in Grenada, gained traction in 1973. His comrade Tim Hector, a rising star in the Caribbean New Left, had presided over the Antigua-Caribbean Liberation Movement (ACLM) for five years when the NJM appeared on the national scene.[26] Bishop, Hector, Sadaukai, Douglas, and Rodney—along with Anne Cools, Brenda Paris, and other men and women—were friends or acquaintances and all belonged or had connections to the influential C. L. R. James Study Circle and leftist political communities in Montreal, Toronto, Washington, D.C., New York City, and London.[27] As a result, when former RCMP and FBI operative Warren Hart visited Antigua in 1978 to "defuse" leftist agitation, fear and suspicion abounded.[28] Hector's critiques of the island's neocolonial politics and Western domination, as well as the ACLM's organizing, made him a despised activist.

Warren Hart had visited Antigua before. In the early 1970s, he traveled to the island with Douglas, alleging to have provided guerrilla training to revolutionaries in Hector's ACLM. When Hart returned to the island in the summer of 1978 as a fixer for Space Research Corporation (SRC), the joint U.S.-Canadian weapons manufacturer and Pentagon contractor, Hector and the ACLM watched his every move. Hart worked with the Antiguan constabulary and funneled SRC money into community projects to improve the company's public image. Hart wrote in his U.S. government personnel file that SRC hired him as a "community organizer" when in fact his job was to discredit islanders in their boycott of the multinational arms dealer.[29] An outspoken critic of SRC, Hector outed Hart as a police informant, undermining his credibility on the tight-knit island. Desperate, Hart attempted to smuggle a sniper rifle onto the island, but customs agents intercepted it. The ACLM, which had members working for Antigua's telephone company, monitored phone calls that Hart made in which he threatened to assassinate Hector.[30]

Hart's employer was public enemy number one. Not only did SRC test its long-range artillery in Antigua, but it had also negotiated a secret agreement with the Antiguan government to bypass various regulations, including immigration. The company brought South African agents to the island at will, despite UN sanctions against such personnel. Some observers began to suspect that SRC used Antigua as a base to ship arms directly and indirectly to the apartheid regime.

PAN-AFRICANISMS AND STRATEGIC BIPOLARITY

In the summer of 1961 at age thirty-four, Dr. Gerald Bull became McGill University's youngest professor. Founder of the arms firm Space Research Corp., Bull was a brilliant ballistics engineer whose goal between 1961 and 1967 was to create a satellite launcher—a supergun of sorts—that could fire projectiles into space. McGill provided $200,000 in seed capital, and the Pentagon funded Bull as well. McGill's existing projects in Barbados provided an opportunity for Bull to use the island as a launch site. Young, ambitious, and networked, Bull spent a decade helping build the Canadian

Armaments and Research Development Establishment, which collaborated with the U.S. Army's Ballistic Research Laboratory. The Canadian Armaments and Research project was an outgrowth of McGill's Space Research Institute after termination of the High Altitude Research Program, a joint U.S. Army and Canadian government venture. It created modified 16-inch guns that launched missiles.[31]

The Caribbean was not only a frontier in the Cold War but also an important site for weapons development.[32] Because of Barbados's proximity to the equator, the island provided favorable launch conditions, whether for satellites or artillery. Scientific probe launchings, missile engineering development flights, and long-range gun performance testing occurred on the southeast coast of Barbados, where crews launched projectiles toward Ascension Island, an archipelago between Brazil and Angola. These various expeditions required a bevy of surveillance radar and workers, including a permanent U.S. and Canadian staff of seventy-five engineers, technicians, and support personnel who managed communications and tracking facilities. In fact, the Barbados Oceanographic and Meteorological Experiment, a joint initiative of seven U.S. departments and agencies, also used the same facilities in 1969. At its official vertical launching site, SRC commissioned over 500 launchings, using a 16-inch 75-caliber vertical firing smooth-bore gun, a 16-inch 50-caliber Mark 7 naval rifle, 5-inch 38- and 54-caliber rifles, 6-inch 80-caliber smooth-bore guns, and 155-mm rifled guns.[33] Under the guise of scientific advancement, Washington and Ottawa turned Barbados into a heavily fortified island that advanced the West's Cold War interests in the Caribbean Basin.

Bull founded SRC as a joint U.S.-Canadian venture to maximize its potential for Cold War strategic funding. Its headquarters was in North Troy, Vermont, and Highwater, Quebec, adjoining border towns. By the early 1970s, SRC had constructed a 172-foot, 16.4-inch smooth-bore cannon, which successfully fired 140-pound projectiles at 10,000 feet per second. It also manufactured advanced, remote-operated long-range cannons. The Canadian government designated SRC a "wartime and peacetime vital point" in April 1976. In other words, SRC's weapons technology had become integral to Canadian officials' formulation of foreign policy and national security. This designation was lucrative, for SRC test-fired almost 1,000 projectiles at its Antigua artillery site from March to May 1977.[34]

Canada and the United States were not the only countries that benefited from SRC's weapons technology. A confidential source living in the United States revealed that a group of white South Africans purchased restored 155-mm cannons from SRC in 1976, despite an arms embargo on the apartheid regime.[35] Explaining the way that SRC facilitated the shipment, he said, "The guns were completely dismantled and placed in large crates and tubes."[36] In April, SRC negotiated the sale of the projectiles under a shell corporation called Paragon Holdings. The South African government purchased these weapons for $3,627,000 via the Liechtenstein-based shell company Colet Trading Establishment. When SRC experienced insolvency throughout 1977, a Netherlands-based South African front company called Space Capitol invested $10,000,000 in Canadian Technical Industries, SRC's holding company. The transaction gave Space Capitol 20 percent of Canadian Technical Industries' shares and nullified the Paragon-Colet agreement.[37]

SRC and South African authorities continued to cooperate illicitly. An unidentified SRC technical expert traveled between Antigua and South Africa on multiple occasions to facilitate the 1976 deal, around the same time that the Canadian government designated SRC a "vital" entity. In January 1977, SRC shipped some weapons components from Montreal's Mirabel Airport to Visco Transgear Industries in Johannesburg. In August, it shipped 560 projectiles, radar, and other equipment from St. John, New Brunswick, to Antigua aboard the *Tugelaland*, a vessel belonging to a German company, which, in fact, was another front for the South African government.[38] But the *Tugelaland* made two stops in Antigua that the captain failed to report in the maritime logbook.[39] During a loading session, a collapsed crane broke open the contents of one of the containers, which alerted longshoremen of the elaborate scheme. They immediately informed Tim Hector, who exposed the plot in his biweekly newspaper, the *Outlet*. Although the authorities tried many times to censor him, Hector printed pictures of checks deposited at a Toronto bank that SRC had paid to senior government officials. One of the most prominent and principled radicals of the Caribbean New Left, Hector broke not only the story of SRC arms smuggling to South Africa but also the story of SRC's parasitic relationship with Antiguan premier V. C. Bird and his son Lester.[40]

The intrigue went beyond Antigua, of course. John Alsop, a McGill University computer science graduate who worked for SRC in North Troy, Vermont, traveled to South Africa in October 1977 to ensure that SRC's weapons system worked properly. Alsop's superiors told him that the trip must be discreet "to avoid adverse publicity."[41] Upon arrival, South African officials escorted Alsop and other SRC personnel through customs without stamping their passports. On 20 October 1977, Joshua Nkomo, head of Zimbabwe's African Peoples Union, stated in a news conference in Ottawa that a Canadian firm had supplied white Rhodesian forces in southern Africa with 900 tons of small arms.[42] This scandal was not the first time that the Canadian government or a proxy had supported the white nationalism of the South African regime in the postwar period.[43]

The U.S.-Canadian arms manufacturer and dealer had many reasons to fear public outcry. By sending weapons and technical experts to the apartheid regime and inviting their officials to Antigua, SRC had violated the UN embargo against South Africa. Although it was a pariah state by the mid-1970s, South Africa's assassination of anti-apartheid freedom fighter Steve Biko in September 1977 had compelled the international community to tighten the embargo. On 4 November 1977, the UN National Security Council adopted Security Council Resolution 418, a binding and mandatory arms embargo against the South African government.[44] The RCMP began investigating SRC in October 1977, pursuing charges under Canada's Export and Import Permits Act, which came with a maximum five-year prison sentence and a $25,000 fine. An internal memo revealed that Canadian authorities worried about SRC fallout and how it would discredit the government in the eyes of African nations.[45]

As Canadian officials tried to manage the public relations and foreign policy embarrassment, so too did U.S. officials. In fact, U.S. intelligence played a direct role in the SRC–South Africa affair. A senior official at the State Department found the arms smuggling "inconceivable" without CIA and Pentagon awareness. They "likely" had "a hand in it," he said.[46] Pretoria happily courted and accepted intelligence cooperation with the CIA. After all, South Africa's expulsion from the British Commonwealth in 1961 meant a decline in British intelligence support for the regime.[47]

The CIA and Pentagon worried over geopolitical rivalry. Beginning in 1975, Cuban authorities sent 3,000 troops and several hundred military advisors to Angola, in addition to Soviet hardware. Jamaican prime minister Michael Manley, an important socialist leader in the region, supported Cuba's military aid to Angola, much to the annoyance of the United States. The battle over the future of southern Africa defined U.S. foreign policy in the region. John Stockwell, CIA officer turned whistleblower, had led the agency's Angolan task force. He confirmed that the South Africans had requested in October 1975 "ammunition for their 155-mm howitzers" to match Cuban contributions to Angolan revolutionaries.[48] On balance, Stockwell acknowledged, "Angola had little plausible importance to American national security and little economic importance." Pentagon officials and Washington political elites, including Secretary of State Henry Kissinger, sought geopolitical redemption after the nation's humiliation in Vietnam, and they promoted a hawkish policy in Angola.[49] On the ground, U.S.

diplomats rejected the South Africans' ordnance request, which would have not only violated the embargo but also generated global uproar.

The CIA's reliance on covert operations, however, circumvented diplomats' decision-making while subordinating concerns over public outcry. Prior to the CIA colluding with SRC to supply the apartheid regime with 155-mm howitzer shells, and before formal independence from Portugal commenced in November 1975, Angola—which had emerged as a significant site of interest for Washington, Havana, Pretoria, London, and Moscow—was mired in a civil war.[50] As a result, the CIA funneled Second World War–era light arms to two factions: the National Liberation Front of Angola and the National Union for the Total Independence of Angola. Because the global arms market was awash in these dated weapons, not new ones, the CIA and the U.S. president could, if questioned, exercise "plausible deniability."[51]

This intervention was not the CIA's first in Angola. In 1962, during President John F. Kennedy's administration, the agency financed rebel leader Holden Roberto's National Liberation Front of Angola, which the CIA considered a "moderate" alternative to the fascist Portuguese colonial regime. U.S. and CIA policy toward Portugal and its colonial administrators in Angola oscillated throughout the 1960s and 1970s. In the context of the Cold War, CIA proxies in southern Africa tried to counter the hot wars that raged in the region. Often, they initiated these wars or granted their tacit approval, such as South Africa's invasion of Angola in August 1975 and the counterinsurgencies within the country, as well as similar struggles in Zaire, Mozambique, and Rhodesia.[52] Wherever revolutionary Pan-Africanists mobilized to resist imperialism and neocolonialism, the West had little appetite for détente.

Revolutionary Pan-Africanisms or Black self-determination lacked better prospects on the other side of the Iron Curtain. Anticipating the challenges of navigating a bipolar world, Trinidadian-born former Comintern trail-blazer turned Pan-African revolutionary Malcolm Nurse, better known by his nom de guerre George Padmore, advised his fellow Pan-African revolutionaries not to seek comfort at Moscow's bosom. Expelled from the Communist Party in 1934, Padmore did not become anti-communist, even though he knew firsthand that the Kremlin desired to exploit Black people to advance its own imperial ambitions. Equally skeptical of the West and a staunch opponent of its imperialism and colonialism, although amenable to socialist African nations accepting foreign direct investment from the West, Padmore did not foresee a meaningful solution in substituting Western colonialism with Soviet communism. In 1956, he outlined the centrality of a race-first, revolutionary Pan-African nationalism that prioritized industrial socialism for the masses.[53] A principal advisor to Kwame Nkrumah, Ghana's first president, who was a staunch Garveyite and pioneering Pan-Africanist in his own right, Padmore proved more influential than CIA covert operations to limit Soviet influence in Africa. Moreover, the resemblance of his Africa policy to Marcus Garvey's original philosophy on revolutionary Pan-African liberation is unmistakable. Padmore called Garvey "one of the greatest Negroes since Emancipation, a visionary."[54]

Strategic bipolarity notwithstanding, U.S. diplomats in the Eastern Caribbean suspected Washington's complicity in the SRC–South Africa affair, because revelation of the arms smuggling generated minimal reaction among U.S. officials. "The boredom in Washington was thundering," one diplomat asserted. "Much too loud." When U.S. diplomats threatened SRC's interests, the company's hired gun, Warren Hart, sent a subtle yet clear message. In July 1978, for example, John Eddy, deputy chief of mission in Barbados, briefed Antiguan premier V. C. Bird on the embassy's findings. A few hours later at the local airport, Hart confronted Eddy and told him to back off, calmly revealing the .38-caliber revolver tucked in his waistband.[55] Hart also engaged in disinformation in Barbados and Antigua, telling locals that SRC planned to abandon its operations in the Caribbean.[56] Authorities on the island, along with SRC, had another firewall in place to keep popular discontent at bay: SRC founder Gerald Bull utilized his high-level contacts at the Pentagon to invite a retired special forces officer to train the Antigua and Barbuda Defense Force. This force became the private army of the premier and SRC.[57]

Despite using deception, intimidation, and brawn to evade scrutiny, SRC and its supporters could not silence critics. A secret diplomatic memo to Ottawa revealed that ACLM leader Tim Hector accused Premier V. C. Bird's son Lester of profiting from the illicit arms shipment from Antigua to South Africa. Lester Bird threatened to sue Hector for defamation. In response, the ACLM lobbied the leaders of Guyana, Jamaica, Trinidad, and Barbados to repudiate Antigua for undermining Pan-African struggle and helping to facilitate crimes against humanity in southern Africa.[58]

The mounting pressure on SRC proved overwhelming. A U.S. customs agent, who investigated the alleged arms smuggling in 1978, described SRC's Antiguan operations as "certainly a cover for something" and that the quantity of shells imported to the island from its headquarters on the U.S.-Canadian border was "far more than necessary for testing." An investigative memo concluded, "Allegations of gun-running to South Africa by Space Research Corp. through its facilities on Barbados and Antigua . . . are in fact true."[59]

The evidence against SRC was incontrovertible. So, too, was the duplicity of the intelligence community. Bull alleged in court filings that senior CIA contacts, including the "Directorate of CIA," played a direct role in facilitating the arms smuggling to South Africa. Between 1976 and 1978, Bull acknowledged that at the same time that SRC transshipped artillery shells to South Africa, U.S. intelligence agencies had known that his company sold shells and other military equipment to Israel, which diverted the hardware to South Africa.[60] Watergate, Vietnam, the Senate's Church Committee, and Congress's Clark Amendment, which proscribed appropriation for covert operations in Angola and Zaire—not to mention a demoralized citizenry—did not stop illicit, covert operations in Africa via the Eastern Caribbean. By recruiting SRC to send technical experts and arms covertly to U.S. proxies in southern Africa, the CIA effectively retraced the same coordinates that the organizers of African Liberation Day had mapped to triangulate their revolutionary efforts in the Atlantic World: U.S.-Canadian mainland, Eastern Caribbean, and southern Africa.

In November 1978, with mounting pressure from Hector's exposé and ACLM protests, Antigua dismissed SRC from the island. On 25 March 1980, Gerald Bull pleaded guilty to providing South Africa with munitions, equipment, and technical expertise. "Everywhere in the Caribbean Sea," said a former Antiguan attorney general, "fellows looked at Antigua with a black eye and blamed us for sending arms to South Africa." Canada, the United States, and the United Kingdom, which were responsible for the island's defense and foreign affairs, had effectively turned a blind eye. The opposition, the Progressive Labor Movement, apologized to African peoples everywhere on behalf of Antiguans while praising Caribbean nationals who provided material and moral support to revolutionary groups in southern Africa.[61] The Caribbean Sea remained in the eye of a proverbial storm. More trouble and destruction loomed on the horizon.

THE "BAYOU OF PIGS"

Cold War machinations and revolutionary and counterrevolutionary currents in the Caribbean kept North America's Pan-Africanists and their adversaries on high alert. When Grenada's New Jewel Movement seized power on 13 March 1979, overthrowing the authoritarian Eric Gairy, the excitement of revolutionary socialism, which derived its moral authority from the masses of poor working people, gripped the island nation. With three people killed, NJM leader and new prime minister Maurice Bishop called the coup "the most humanitarian revolution" in modern history. Rhetoric of national self-determination, dignity for workers, universal health care and literacy, and women's liberation not only endeared the NJM to the masses but also illustrated the dialectical significance of revolutionary movements that spoke specifically to the material conditions of ordinary folk living under neocolonialism.

The People's Revolutionary Government (PRG) promoted women into important positions and clamped down on their sexual exploitation, a social ill that Gairy himself encouraged. "The movement of our women is part of the movement of all our people to extend the rights and the power of all our people in our society," asserted revolutionary Beverley Steele in a speech after the NJM assumed control. Bishop and the NJM also espoused this sentiment. The PRG empowered women to participate actively in the National Women's Organization, the National Youth Organization, trade unions, parish councils, and the people's militia.[62] Hope abounded.

So, too, did festering feelings of uncertainty, alienation, and resentment. Elements of the bourgeoisie, reactionaries within the trade unions, and opposition groups plotted counter-coups. Equally disaffected were the Rastafarians who had initially embraced the revolution and the NJM, lending grassroots credibility to their socialist platform.[63] For subversives operating on an island as small as Grenada, waging consistent and sophisticated acts of counterrevolution, although not impossible, would require outside assistance. Immediately after the NJM overthrew Gairy, the CIA launched counterintelligence and terrorism against the PRG, such as two major acts of arson in the tourist district, followed by Grenadian officials intercepting mercenaries off the coast, which conveniently coincided with a planned power plant strike that would have cut electricity to the entire island.

Dangerous and mysterious events continued. On 19 June 1980, six days after Guyanese officials detonated a device that assassinated Pan-Africanist revolutionary and historian Walter Rodney, another bomb exploded at a PRG rally in Queen's Park, killing three females and injuring dozens more people. Had the explosives been placed in a slightly different location, it could have wiped out the entire PRG leadership. In addition to other acts of subversion, a U.S. naval exercise off the coast of Grenada simulated an invasion, which reminded Bishop and PRG officials of gunboat diplomacy that harked back to the enforcement of the Monroe Doctrine earlier in the twentieth century. There is also the strange case of Cyrus Stanley, a Grenadian-born Howard University professor identified as a CIA asset, who tried to foment insurrection against the PRG under the guise of militant labor organizing.[64]

Washington, in short, feared that a Marxist-Leninist party under the charismatic leadership of Bishop would further undermine U.S. interests in the region. After all, the Grenada Revolution occurred in the wake of the

Counterintelligence Program (COINTELPRO), the most widespread and sophisticated operation in U.S. domestic history designed, in large part, to eliminate revolutionary African American organizations and the rise of a Black messiah. For all intents and purposes, Bishop embodied the archetype of a revolutionary Black messiah. His leadership in a Pan-African revolutionary government on the path toward full-scale socialism was reminiscent of the aspirations of the decapitated Black Panther Party and uncompromising revolutionary leaders, such as Malcolm X, Fred Hampton, and others, all of whom the U.S. national security and intelligence apparatus neutralized. Messianic leadership in Grenada, moreover, was not an overstatement. Despite its small population and relative obscurity in the Americas, an African American revolutionary in 1829 prophesied in *The Ethiopian Manifesto* that the Black Messiah would come from Grenada and would be partly of European ancestry.[65] Malcolm X's mother was born in Grenada to a white father. Bishop, too, had European ancestry. The U.S. government had a history of reading Black revolutionary literature and drawing conclusions that suited its interpretations of the world.[66]

Bishop was not, however, the only member of the PRG whose self-assertion worried the U.S. intelligence community. Grenadian Franklyn Harvey was the architect behind the NJM's manifesto and one of its principal founders. After obtaining a bachelor of science degree in engineering from the University of London, where Bishop had obtained a law degree, Harvey matriculated at McGill University in 1966 to pursue a master's degree in environmental science. In Montreal, Harvey participated in the C. L. R. James Study Circle, contributing to Pan-African organizing and the Black freedom struggle in Canada, the Caribbean, and the United States. This revolutionary organizing brought Harvey under FBI and RCMP surveillance. In July 1972, for example, an FBI memo inaccurately described Harvey as a "Canadian Black extremist" who had helped Rosie Douglas and other comrades establish a guerrilla training camp in rural Ontario. Harvey allegedly planned to finance the camp by soliciting funds from revolutionaries to create "an international pool of money."[67]

The leaders of the Grenada Revolution had cultivated connections throughout North America. In fact, members of the NJM—including Harvey, Bishop, and Deputy Prime Minister Bernard Coard, among others— had studied in Canada and the United States or had established strong linkages to radical leftist organizations in those two countries, illustrating the hemispheric reach of Pan-Africanisms. The Canada-Grenada Friendship Society, for example, sent a delegation in 1980 and 1981 to celebrate the first and second anniversaries of the revolution. Trinidadian-born Lennox Farrell, who immigrated to Canada in 1969 to pursue an undergraduate degree at the University of Toronto, chaired the society.[68]

Regional collaborations also troubled U.S. officials. Jamaican prime minister Michael Manley was an avid proponent of Caribbean interests in the Non-Aligned Movement, the Cold War forum that resisted further polarization along the East-West axis. Manley rejected the premise that Caribbean nations, in pursuit of self-determination, posed a threat to the United States. "I think it is dangerous nonsense to talk about any threat to the security interests in the United States in this hemisphere," he said in August 1980, a few weeks before the UN General Assembly convened. A strong ally of Castro and Bishop, Manley believed that the decolonization wave in the region, the failures of capitalism, and the promise of socialism encouraged new states to "experiment." The headwinds of U.S. propaganda, he acknowledged, created "a devil theory of history, in which all sorts of wild imaginings go on that have nothing to do with reality at all." Post-revolution Grenada was ground zero for such fabrications.[69]

It is therefore not surprising that Washington set out to undermine the Grenada Revolution. Gairy, the ousted authoritarian, did as well. So, when a thirty-year-old Michael Perdue of Houston, Texas, read about the Grenada Revolution and the threat of communism in a mercenary journal in 1979, he found a way to meet Gairy in San Diego. Although incarceration ended Perdue's aspirations to serve in the Marine Corps, the truck driver and aspiring soldier of fortune believed that he could still find riches and notoriety. In his meeting with Gairy, Perdue made him a tantalizing offer: he would assemble a team of mercenaries to invade and overthrow Bishop and reinstall Gairy as prime minister. Gairy agreed. Perdue planned the assault with coconspirators in the United States and Canada, and he dispatched an emissary to Dominica who invested in a coffee firm as cover to procure intelligence and establish a beachhead for storming Grenada. Ultimately, the Grenada plot fell through. Gairy had disagreed with Perdue that he should accompany the mercenaries when they stormed the island.[70]

Social unrest made electoral politics unpredictable in the Cold War Caribbean. So, when a popular uprising forced Dominica's prime minister Patrick John to resign in June 1979, Oliver Seraphin's Labor Party served as the interim government. Rosie Douglas joined the senate and negotiated hundreds of scholarships for Dominican students to pursue their education in Cuba. But in July 1980, voters ousted the Labor Party because Michael Douglas, finance minister and elder brother of Rosie, had been embroiled in a controversy in which Dominica would have furnished exiled Iranian loyalists of the shah with Dominican passports for $10,000 each. As a result,

Eugenia Charles—leader of the Freedom Party, a centrist-leaning conservative platform—came into power. After John's failed electoral bid and Charles's success, Perdue and his coconspirators found another Caribbean client in Dominica. John desperately wanted help to regain power, even by force of arms.[71] It was the season of coups and counter-coups. Indeed, it was a mercenaries' market.[72]

Michael Perdue was a staunch white nationalist who relished an opportunity to establish white supremacist rule on a Caribbean island. On 20 September 1980, John and Perdue signed a contract to reinstall John and provide Perdue's shell corporation, Nortic Enterprises, $150,000 in cash and twenty-year tax-exempt concessions in banking, agriculture, and gambling. The mercenaries also planned to open a cocaine processing plant. They, in fact, wanted to turn Dominica into an Aryan criminal enterprise.[73] Seed capital would flow from sources in Canada, as well as from businessmen in Las Vegas, Houston, Memphis, and Jackson, Mississippi. James McQuirter, Grand Wizard of the Canadian Ku Klux Klan and one of Perdue's coconspirators, said that Dominica needed "white order and white government" and that it would provide an ideal setting to propagate white supremacy throughout the region and hemisphere. He asked, "If we're so fascist and racist, why would we be putting a Negro back in power?" Although McQuirter confessed that using a Black puppet leader was a deliberate strategy to undermine critiques that white supremacists controlled Dominica, he seemed willfully ignorant of neocolonialism as a concept of international relations and governance.[74]

Operation Red Dog, as the conspirators called it, was not as fantastical as it sounds. The mercenaries planned to rendezvous in Dominica with John loyalists, some of whom served in the island's ninety-nine-member army. They also recruited the feared Dreads—Rastafarian outlaws who lived on the margins of island society. Dominica's 1974 Dread Act, which sought to expel Rastafarianism from the conservative, mostly Catholic island, granted immunity to individuals who harmed or killed Rastafarians in civilian homes or on civilian property.[75]

Perdue and his collaborators dispatched two spies to gather intelligence near the end of 1980. The first was Marian McGuire, an Irish-born Canadian woman. She liaised with John's supporters, scouted possible landing points on the island, monitored the frequency of coastal patrols, and observed police readiness. A KKK sympathizer who socialized with far-right and white supremacist groups, McGuire was born in Londonderry, Northern Ireland. Her father admired Adolf Hitler. As a teenager, she allied with the Irish Republican Army to fight the British.[76] McGuire explained why she joined the plot: "I'd been a pretty bad boozer. I'd just been married, and the marriage broke up over alcohol. I was desperate to get out of Toronto."[77] Another participant was Charles "Chuckie" Yanover, a Toronto mobster and international gunrunner. He reconnoitered Dominica, snapping copious photographs of the airport, police station, and other vital installations. Perdue and other leaders of the plot planned to reward Yanover with the position of major in the army and then kill him because he was a Jew.[78]

How did a Canadian Jewish mobster become a coconspirator of a coup with U.S. and Canadian KKK and neo-Nazi mercenaries? Perdue sought assistance for the coup from David Duke, former Grand Wizard of the Knights of the Ku Klux Klan. Duke then connected Perdue with the Canadian coconspirators of the plot: German-born neo-Nazi Wolfgang Droege and Don Andrews, former leader of the Western Guard and Edmund Burke Society, which harassed Douglas and Black activists, along with draft resisters, in Toronto.[79] The Ontario courts convicted Droege in 1975 for painting white power slogans along the ALD route in Toronto.[80] Knowing Yanover's underworld connections and access to financing and firearms, Droege asked him to join the venture as a minority stakeholder. "You know I'm Jewish? If I catch you putting swastikas on synagogues, I'll come after you," Yanover warned.[81]

The Dominica coup had little chance of success, particularly if its plotters and foot soldiers consisted mainly of card-carrying Klan members and neo-Nazis. So, when Perdue attempted on 23 February 1981 to charter a fifty-two-foot boat in Louisiana for the Dominica invasion, he tried to augment his legitimacy by claiming that he was a CIA agent. The marina operator, a Vietnam veteran, sought verification of Perdue's identity with the State Department, which recognized him as an impostor. "This guy said he was with the C.I.A. He sounded hokey," said the marina operator. "I didn't think we were doing covert overthrows anymore." The Intelligence Oversight Act, which Congress approved in September 1980, stipulating that intelligence agencies must report covert activity to oversight committees, did not limit the use of hostile tools or proxy wars in the Americas, Africa, and the Middle East. As a result of Perdue's reported impersonation, the FBI immediately began investigating the Dominica plot. Around the same time, the Ontario Provincial Police learned of the conspiracy as well.[82]

In the late dawn hours of 27 April 1981, the ten-man mercenary team planned to depart a Lake Pontchartrain dock near New Orleans and arrive in Dominica between 1:00 and 3:00 A.M. on 7 May. They brought dozens of assault rifles, handguns, and shotguns; over 5,000 rounds of ammunition; and military grade explosives. They also carried an oversize Nazi flag.

An FBI counterterrorism team intercepted the mercenaries before their departure.[83] Perdue implicated former Texas governor John Connally and Texas representative Ron Paul, informing federal prosecutors that he had appraised the two men of the coup.[84] Toronto radio station CFTR had also been aware of the plot since October 1980 but had chosen not to disclose it for fear of losing the scoop.[85]

Meanwhile in Dominica, the authorities and a key witness who had infiltrated the conspirators exposed the plan. Police intercepted a handwritten letter from a jailed army officer loyal to ousted prime minister Patrick John instructing Perdue to hasten the invasion and attack the police station first, which also housed the island's only jail. The letter read, "Don't PANIC we must make it!!" When Dominican authorities foiled the plot, McGuire, the KKK emissary on the island, sent a cable from her hotel to her employer in Toronto: "Alexander is dead," code to abort the mission. An alarmed hotel staff called the police, who arrested McGuire.[86] Furthermore, Algie Maffei, one of the Dreads whom Perdue and John had recruited to participate in the assault on the government, remained loyal to Rosie Douglas. He acted as Douglas's eyes and ears throughout the planning phase, part of which took place in nearby Antigua. Maffei had previously immigrated to Montreal in 1970, living briefly with Douglas. When the Quebec courts had sentenced Douglas to prison for his role in the 1969 university occupation, Maffei visited him frequently. The Canadian government deported Maffei in 1974 for immigration infractions, which he believed stemmed from information that RCMP operative Warren Hart, Douglas's bodyguard and chauffeur, had provided authorities.[87] In addition to playing a pivotal role in Dominica's pursuit of independence from the United Kingdom in 1978, Douglas considered his role in helping Maffei subvert the white supremacist conspiracy as one of his most important achievements in Dominican politics.[88]

News of the foiled white supremacist coup generated responses of incredulity and ridicule. Dominicans perceived the affair as a "comic-book escapade," while Louisianans called it the "Bayou of Pigs."[89] The KKK and neo-Nazi mercenaries were entirely committed to overthrowing Prime Minister Eugenia Charles and installing Patrick John as their puppet. "If they'd caught us by surprise, they could have walked right in and done what they wanted to do," said Charles. "It may seem farcical, but there might have been a lot of people killed." Charles sacked the entire army. Signaling a desire for closer ties and support from Washington, she acknowledged, "We have no aircraft, limited communications facilities and bad roads. We could be invaded any day of the week at a number of points. To try to defend this island with 99 men was nonsense."[90]

Because of the perceived threat emanating from revolutionary Grenada, as well as Cuba and Nicaragua, officials in Washington moved swiftly to support Dominica.[91] The State Department provided a $60,000 grant, coordinated for Dominican police to receive training in Panama, and rerouted small arms and ammunition via the Jamaican government of Edward Seaga. Barbados, whose army the United States had trained and equipped, agreed to aid Dominica in an event of a security breach. France and Britain, which had maintained semicolonial and neocolonial interests in the region, also agreed to provide security assistance.[92] Moreover, President Ronald Reagan's idea to finance a Caribbean "Marshall Plan" was the reason why Washington, according to one reporter, did not "want to sully the image of conservative anti-communism with petty corruption and gangsterism" in Dominica.[93]

The foiled coup had little to do with justice and the rule of law, for the CIA reserved the right to recruit mercenaries in its illicit wars and covert operations.[94] If, truly, deception is "the mind of the state," it is plausible that, from the outset, the CIA planned the Dominican coup as a false flag operation. In this vein, Perdue was an agent provocateur acting on behalf of the CIA, as he initially claimed to the marina operator. After all, it is not entirely clear how an obscure white supremacist with a long criminal record managed to connect with deposed Dominican leader Patrick John, let alone Grenadian strongman Eric Gairy. If it was a CIA false flag operation, it would have served U.S. interests in two ways. First, it would illustrate the feasibility of recruiting mercenaries to topple a Caribbean government. And second, it would create the coercive pretext for a Caribbean country to seek security guarantees and other aid from Washington. These two objectives would bring the U.S. government closer to its endgame of toppling the Bishop government and initiating regime change.

Dominican authorities handed stiff sentences to the conspirators. McGuire, the only woman prisoner on the island, received three years for her role in the conspiracy, but officials commuted her sentence after eleven months. In an interview with Canada's *Globe and Mail*, she acknowledged her white supremacist beliefs and connections but denied that she ever served as Grand Titan of the Canadian Klan, a lie that she said McQuirter, leader of the Canadian KKK, fabricated to the press to gain notoriety for his organization. McGuire attributed prison in Dominica for curing her alcoholism and anti-Black racism. "Considering what I had done and what I represented to them," she admitted, "I was treated very well. They were unbelievably tolerant and kind to me."[95]

U.S. and Canadian courts also took decisive legal action. Seven out of the ten U.S. and Canadian mercenaries, including Michael Perdue and

Wolfgang Droege, pleaded guilty to a federal conspiracy to finance and execute a military and naval operation against Dominica, in addition to federal charges for weapons and explosives.[96] Perdue, however, struck a deal with the federal government, becoming the principal witness for the prosecution. This leniency and cooperation adds credence to the hypothesis that Perdue may have been a CIA agent provocateur. As for his less fortunate KKK and neo-Nazi comrades, the government charged them for violating the Neutrality Act, which prohibits U.S. citizens from attacking nations that are not at war with the United States. "I don't think it was any kind of K.K.K. thing. I think it was an anti-Communist thing," demurred David Duke in an interview.[97] Canadian authorities also charged KKK leader McQuirter and mobster Chuckie Yanover with conspiracy to assist in a foreign coup. Three months after the coup attempt and before his charges, Yanover traveled to the Philippines on behalf of North and South Korean clients in July 1981 to plan the assassination of South Korean president Chun Doo Hwan. James Choi, businessman and son of retired South Korean general Choi Hong-hi, the reputed father of tae kwon do who was living in exile in Metropolitan Toronto, allegedly hired Yanover for the job.[98] Absurd and ill-fated as the attempted coup may have been, it was emblematic of shadowy efforts to undermine Black nationhood. More serious interventions loomed.

BURYING JEWELS

In the arena of Cold War realpolitik, anything was conceivable. Even after the foiled Dominican plot brought such ignominy to Canada and the United States, the CIA planned a covert intelligence operation in the summer of 1981 to crush Grenada economically and undermine the People's Revolutionary Government. It waged a disinformation campaign about a Cuban-Soviet plot that would turn Grenada into a "virtual surrogate" and about how the new airport under construction was a forward-operating military base to mount attacks against U.S. and allied interests in the region and southern Africa. As a tourist-dependent economy, the PRG considered a modernized airport an urgent economic matter that would accelerate Grenada's self-determination. The existing airport, built in 1943, was too small to accommodate commercial flights, let alone evening flights.

Grenadian, Canadian, French, British, and World Bank studies concluded that a new airport would jump-start the Grenadian economy.[99] The PRG categorically rejected the Reagan administration's assertions about a Cuban-Soviet plot, pointing out that Africa-bound Cuban troops departed from Barbados, a strong U.S. ally. Moreover, financing for the airport came from Libya, Algeria, Iraq, and Syria, which contributed $50 million in cash,

$1.3 million in loans, thousands of barrels of fuel, and a storage facility. Cuba, a staunch regional ally, sent engineers, technicians, and construction equipment. Nonetheless, the PRG awarded $11 million in contracts to U.S. engineering firms.[100]

In the aftermath of the Cuban Revolution, Washington subjected that island nation to unrelenting economic warfare and failed assassination attempts on Fidel Castro's life, planned the Bay of Pigs invasion, and conducted disinformation campaigns. On 6 October 1976, an act of terrorism against the Cuban people occurred when two bombs exploded on Cubana Flight 455, a DC-8 McDonnell Douglas four-engine jet, over the Caribbean Sea after takeoff from Barbados. All passengers perished: fifty-seven Cubans, twenty-four of whom were teenage fencers on the national team; eleven Guyanese medical students who had received scholarships to train in Cuba; and five North Koreans. Several coconspirators played a role, including Luis Posada Carriles, onetime CIA operative and anti-Castro crusader. A declassified report to Secretary of State Henry Kissinger acknowledged that before the bombing, a CIA source overheard Posada say, "We are going to hit a Cuban airliner." An FBI informant admitted that after one of the terrorists planted a bomb on the plane, the terrorist notified coconspirator Orlando Bosch, also Cuban, anti-Castro, and former CIA asset.[101] The dogged resilience of Castro's Cuba and its regional popularity infuriated the U.S. government.

Because of U.S. anti-Cuban hysteria and policies, the Grenadian government's efforts at transparency had no impact on Washington's disinformation campaign against it. The alarm over a new civilian airport was simply a pretext to destabilize a revolutionary Black country.[102] Moreover, race played a central role in Washington's concerns over the geopolitics of the Grenada Revolution. Maurice Bishop paraphrased the concerns of U.S. intelligence at a 5 June 1983 New York City rally that the eminent anti-apartheid activist Randall Robinson and his Pan-African organization TransAfrica sponsored along with the Congressional Black Caucus. Before a packed and raucous crowd, Bishop said, "The people of Grenada and the leadership of Grenada are predominantly Black. . . . And if we have 95 percent of predominantly African origin in our country, then we can have a dangerous appeal to 30 million Black people in the United States."[103] A successful revolutionary socialist government in Grenada would have been exponentially more symbolic than in Cuba.

Nearly four months after Bishop's speech, the Grenadian Revolution self-destructed. Disagreements over power sharing between Bishop and Coard led to the prime minister's house arrest. On 19 October 1983, the masses liberated him. Weakened from his detention, the throngs tried to take him to a nearby hospital before Bishop could formally address them. Fearing an insurrection and a threat to the authority of the NJM Central Committee, soldiers received orders to neutralize the uprising. They killed and wounded dozens of civilians at Grenada's Fort Rupert. Soldiers then apprehended Bishop's common-law partner, Jacqueline Creft, six NJM and PRG senior officials loyal to Bishop, and Bishop—whose father had been executed during Eric Gairy's dictatorship—lined them up against a wall, and strafed them with machine-gun fire.[104] Details of the 19 October massacre remain contested history, but what is certain is that the United States was unwilling to tolerate the first English-speaking revolutionary Pan-African socialist government near its southern flank. Containing revolutionary Pan-Africanisms in Angola, Mozambique, and Zimbabwe was difficult enough. The threat of the PRG under a charismatic and eloquent prime minister, truly, was that it would deepen revolutionary Pan-African, socialist ties between Grenadians and other Black peoples in the Americas and Africa.

Some of Bishop's comrades in the Caribbean New Left foresaw a power grab unfolding in the NJM. Deputy Prime Minister Coard and the NJM Central Committee, of which Coard's Jamaican-born wife, Phyllis, was a member, had placed Bishop under house arrest and authorized his execution. "Bishop sought consensus with the Stalinist tendency represented by Coard. . . . That consensus was not wrong, [but] it lasted too long. Therein lies Maurice Bishop's tragic flaw," Tim Hector pointed out. In a debate in November 1982, Bishop, according to Hector, argued, "We must have a steeled, ideologically-advanced vanguard party, not a mass based party." Hector responded, "Your 'vanguard' isn't s——! It's ideologically confused, and despised by the masses." He believed that Bishop was further left than the Coard faction in the NJM. "But a true left is that which learns from and is led by the masses. The greatest failure of Bishop," Hector concluded, "was his assumption that his critics inside the NJM [shared] his own morality . . . that disagreements between individuals could be resolved peacefully and constructively."[105]

With political upheaval in Grenada, the United States had found the perfect justification to invade and overthrow the government. Even then, it did so under the thin veneer of humanitarianism. In the ensuing firefights between U.S. Marines and Grenadian troops and their Cuban advisors— what writer Dionne Brand called "the five day war"—Western governments squabbled over the evacuation of expats.[106] Amid the pandemonium was Marlene Green, a stalwart of the North American Black liberation movement in the 1960s and 1970s. Born into an elite family in Dominica, Green's activist journey in Toronto sharpened her analyses of power, which interrogated the impact of race and class on Black people's material security. She also understood the ways that capitalism and white power weaponized gender against African peoples. She arrived in revolutionary Grenada in 1979 as the Canadian University Services Overseas regional field officer for the Windward Islands, Jamaica, and Belize. Along with Grenadian partners, she led developmental programs for youth, women, and farmers. Green and other Canadian University Services Overseas staff accused marines of releasing prisoners and inciting them to loot. In late October 1983, the U.S. military eventually airlifted Green and Trinidadian-born Torontonian Dionne Brand—who had spent ten months working in Grenada as an information officer for the Agency for Rural Transformation—along with twenty-one other Canadians and two dozen Britons and West Germans to Barbados.[107] U.S. refusal to grant Canadian military aircraft landing rights to evacuate Canadian nationals conveyed to senior diplomats Washington's contempt for Canada's sovereignty, as did the fact that Canadian officials did not learn about the invasion of a British Commonwealth country until after it happened.[108] Returning to Canada during a diplomatic row, Green soon relocated to Africa, where she worked throughout the continent, supporting the anti-apartheid struggle.

Grenada and Dominica are integral to understanding U.S. imperialism and counterrevolutionary strategies in the Caribbean. That the United States had ostensibly thwarted a coup in Dominica, which saved the government of Eugenia Charles, while subsequently providing that government with aid turned it into Washington's proxy. The Organization of Eastern Caribbean States, which Charles chaired and helped found in June 1981 for collective security, camouflaged U.S. Cold War ambitions in the Caribbean. When Charles accompanied President Reagan to announce the U.S. invasion of Grenada at a White House press conference on 25 October 1983, the optics evoked images of a manipulated, neocolonial Black leader. Reflecting on that joint press conference, an African American congressman derided the Dominican prime minister as "this puppet of our President" who "represents 'Aunt Jemimaism' in geopolitics."[109] Charles's collaboration with the United States not only cemented her political future but also ensured a major windfall from CIA coffers.[110]

BACK TO AFRICA

Such political intrigue in the mid-1980s illustrated that nominal decolonization alone—or what Owusu Sadaukai called "Black faces in high white places"—could not liberate the Black masses. Neocolonialism as a phenomenon of plunder, exploitation, and anti-blackness thrived. At the 1984 ALD commemoration in Washington, D.C., Kwame Turé (formerly Stokely Carmichael), head of the All-African People's Revolutionary Party, instructed his U.S.-based spokesman, Bob Brown, to emphasize why Pan-African socialism was the only revolutionary framework that could improve the material conditions of Black people.[111] According to the thirty-five-year-old Brown, "We, as descendants of slaves, still are not free because the masses of our people are poor and oppressed. In order to achieve freedom, we must have Pan-Africanism and socialism. Africa must be unified and free." Brown stressed the need to establish "a united front" of African American and African leaders. "We want Blacks of all persuasions to sit at the same table and discuss how we can help each other help the masses of our people." The All-African People's Revolutionary Party, which derived its name and mission from Ghanaian president Kwame Nkrumah's 1958 All-African People's Conference in Accra, continued to beat the drum of African unity at home and abroad. Other honored speakers who received a platform at the 1984 ALD include Native Americans, Iranians, and Salvadorean guerrillas, in addition to African liberation groups.[112]

Like his comrade Kwame Turé, Rosie Douglas still yearned for revolutionary change. In his native Dominica, leftist groups on the island agitated under the umbrella of the Dominica Liberation Movement, in which Rosie and his brother Michael temporarily held membership. They protested the Charles government's crackdowns on civil liberties and economic austerity. In the grand struggle for Pan-African liberation, Dominica was simply too small a battlefield. In the 1980s, Douglas became more involved with brokering, coordinating, and securing financing for liberation movements throughout Africa. He befriended Chris Hani of the African National Congress. Hani served as commander of uMkhonto we Sizwe, the African National Congress's guerrilla branch, which oversaw liberation fighters in South Africa. A devotee of Winnie Mandela, Douglas "single-handedly" secured Libyan support for the African National Congress, shuttling from Libya to Zambia to Tanzania to meet its leaders and foot soldiers.[113]

Douglas was an admirer and comrade of Muammar Gaddafi, not to mention a principal interlocutor to the Libyan regime on matters of revolutionary struggle in southern Africa. In 1982, when Gaddafi launched the Center to Resist Imperialism, Racism, and Fascism, or "Mathaba" in Arabic—Africa's first Socialist International—he appointed Douglas as its director. So vital was this work that from 1980 to 1987, Douglas spent considerable time living in and working from Tripoli. Douglas attempted to convince Turé on the merits of mustering an African Liberation Army that Gaddafi would fund. But Turé, having already spent over fifteen years by the early 1980s living in West Africa and studying under his Pan-African heroes Kwame Nkrumah and Guinean president Sekou Touré, understood the challenges of unifying factions in Africa. Moreover, he remembered the difficulties that Ernesto "Che" Guevara had encountered in the mid-1960s when he tried to rally and unify rebel groups in the Congo. Nevertheless, Douglas admonished Turé that he had to mobilize troops as soon as possible and enter the bush, which was the only way to rally various African warlords. For this reason, Douglas traveled to Mozambique, where he met rebel leaders and guerrilla fighters from southern African territories.[114]

Douglas had no regrets about his revolutionary activities from 1980 to 1987. "Overseeing and assisting the activity of liberation movements throughout the world" was his mission. Pan-African liberation was a costly affair, not an abstract, romantic, or bloodless endeavor. "All Dominicans supported the freedom of [Nelson] Mandela. And the freedom of Mandela wasn't a cakewalk on a Sunday morning—it was a revolutionary struggle in which people fought, died, and killed," Douglas recalled of his material support to the African National Congress.[115] In the words of his long-time Antiguan comrade Tim Hector, Douglas was "a Pan-Africanist Extraordinaire, not in theory, but . . . praxis."[116]

The 1986 World Mathaba Conference in Tripoli further solidified Douglas's reputation as a revolutionary. Many leaders attended, including Nation of Islam minister Louis Farrakhan, who sought stronger ties to the *ummah* and African Diaspora. U.S. authorities charged two African Americans with terrorism for attending and allegedly accepting $2.5 million from Gaddafi to carry out attacks in the United States.[117] Douglas's political ambitions in Dominica, which the Libyans appreciated, having bankrolled his successful election to the legislature in 1985, led to his resignation from directorship of the Mathaba in 1987. In 1988 and 1989, respectively, Western intelligence agencies connected the Mathaba to the bombings of Lockerbie Pan Am Flight 103 and French Airlines UTA Flight 772 over the Niger desert.[118] Despite the Mathaba's aspirations to represent a leftist, internationalist, socialist vanguard, its activists and members, according to one political scientist, overlooked Gaddafi's "monarchical dreams."[119] Nonetheless, the Mathaba did an effective job of bringing Black people together. African Canadian Dawn Roach, daughter of the eminent Trinidadian-born civil rights lawyer Charles Roach, traveled to Libya in 1989 for the Mathaba Conference as part of a Black student contingent. Douglas and Turé welcomed the students and shared words of inspiration.[120] The struggle for

Black liberation in the Atlantic World had no end in sight, so seasoned foot soldiers inculcated a younger generation with lessons of self-love and mass mobilization.

Pan-African liberation movements during the Cold War often became hot wars against U.S., Canadian, and other Western proxies. Activists, such as Douglas and Sadaukai, established themselves as true revolutionary Pan-African socialists with deep connections throughout Africa, including with heads of state and rebel leaders. Influenced by the Pan-African teachings, fortitude, and racial martyrdom of Malcolm X, African North American revolutionaries in the 1970s and 1980s appreciated the import of hemispheric and transatlantic linkages. The act of returning "back to Africa" as revolutionaries when U.S. and Canadian officials counter-subverted the Black freedom struggle in the 1960s and 1970s illustrated the centrality of continental African liberation to global Black liberation. In this vein, revolutionaries in the post–Black Power era embraced one of the central tenets of revolutionary Garveyite Pan-Africanisms. However, Africa's significance, warned Walter Rodney, did not mean it must become the sole battlefront in the struggle against imperialism, colonialism, and neocolonialism. "The vast majority of our people will, in fact, not be able to go [to Africa], and struggle takes place where people live and work," Rodney explained. "Black struggle must be universalized wherever Black people happen to be."[121] African Liberation Day celebrations throughout the United States, Canada, and the Caribbean revived the moral urgency for Black liberation in the Americas.

Cold War machinations, whether in the form of arms smuggling or coups and counter-coups, demonstrated the West's fears over the possibilities of Pan-African liberation. That SRC, a U.S.-Canadian arms manufacturer and dealer under the direction of the CIA, furnished apartheid South Africa with sophisticated weaponry via Antigua underscored the geopolitical stakes. Neocolonialism in the Caribbean Basin and Africa was vital to Western hegemony. This geopolitical competition and domination, of course, transcended the Caribbean and Africa. In March 1990, for example, Dr. Gerald Bull, the ballistics genius and founder of SRC who helped mastermind the arms smuggling to South Africa with CIA help, was assassinated at his apartment in Brussels. Bull was developing Project Babylon, a supergun and missiles for the Iraqi army. Mossad suspected that this long-range gun could rain nuclear ordnance on Israel.

National security was also the pretext that allowed Washington to undermine the self-determination of countries in the Americas. The triangulation of Black Power on the North American mainland, in the Caribbean, and in southern Africa in the 1980s threatened U.S. preponderance. U.S. intelligence subverted the Grenada Revolution not because of a valid Cuban-Soviet plot to enlist Grenada as a proxy to attack the United States, but because Washington dreaded the symbolism of the first English-speaking Black country to wage a successful revolution for socialism. In essence, revolutionary Pan-African socialism—a manifestation of uncompromising Black Power for the masses—provided a shield against the omnipresent danger stemming from imperialism and neocolonialism. However, as Walter Rodney eloquently pointed out regarding the Sixth Pan-African Congress in Dar es Salaam in 1974, neocolonial governments in Africa and the Caribbean, with backing from the national bourgeoisie, sabotaged efforts to transform the material conditions of Caribbean and African workers and peasants while paying lip service to supporting the liberation of southern Africa.[122]

A full appreciation of the contours of Pan-Africanisms and an emphasis on the liberation of all African peoples in the United States, Canada, the Caribbean, and Africa demands an account of the ways of white power and white nationalism as articulated by the U.S. imperial project. In other words, it becomes difficult to disentangle non-state actors, such as KKK and neo-Nazi mercenaries, from the U.S. government and its intelligence agencies. White supremacist paramilitaries that felt emboldened to invade and install puppet regimes in two Black countries, Grenada and Dominica, were the fruits of empire. Resistance from African North Americans in the United States, Canada, and the Caribbean sprang from the same tree.

CONCLUSION

▼ ▼ ▼

Despite his resignation from directorship of the Mathaba in 1987 due to political commitments in Dominica, Rosie Douglas remained committed and drawn to liberation struggles in Africa. By 1992, the Mathaba had disbanded and various branches within the Libyan regime had incorporated its commitment to resist imperialism, racism, and fascism. That same year, his elder brother Michael, terminally ill with cancer, beckoned Rosie to return home to Dominica and take up leadership of the Labor Party. Michael died in April and Rosie won his seat in a by-election. Three years later, the Labor Party became the official opposition.[1]

For the remainder of the decade, Douglas forged stronger linkages across the African Diaspora for his underdeveloped island nation of 75,000 people, roughly 2,000 of whom descended from the original Indigenous Carib inhabitants. His critics, however, accused him of being a blowhard. "I think he's a great talker, but I don't think he's a great doer," said former prime minister Eugenia Charles, whose government Douglas had helped save from a KKK–neo-Nazi coup attempt in 1981. "I told him, 'You talk too much. I'm sick of seeing your white teeth on television.' . . . He likes to pretend," she added, "he's the only person who can do anything—he's the most important politician in the world in his own eyes."[2]

Douglas had ample reason to feel important. He had a track record of improving the material conditions of the most vulnerable Dominicans, which endeared him to the masses. Severin McKenzie, a Cuban scholarship recipient who trained in Cuba as an architect in the 1980s, attributed his education and class mobility to Douglas's courage and vision in forging linkages with the Castro regime in the 1970s, an act that many politicians considered heretical in the Americas. "Once the Dominican people truly get to know him," McKenzie asserted, "they'll realize that he is definitely not the type of individual that [his adversaries] portray him to be . . . a selfish . . . tyrant."[3] It was the 1990s, and viable Black leaders were in short supply throughout the Americas.

On the North American mainland, cross-border connections continued. African Liberation Day commemorations every May inspired thousands of

Black protesters to march on streets and assemble at parks in the United States and Canada. Carnival brought hordes of Black people to Miami, New York City, and Toronto. The Toronto carnival, popularly called Caribana, which first began as part of Canada's centennial celebrations in 1967, became the largest attraction of its kind in the United States and Canada by the 1990s. It showcased Caribbean rhythms while retaining its subversiveness. Since its inception, Caribana included a group of queer Black activists called "Zami," Creole for "friend." Lesbians of Caribbean origin adopted this word as an identifier. Carnival and other pan-African celebrations, such as Detroit's annual African World Festival, strengthened cross-border, cultural ties among diasporic Africans.[4]

In the 1980s and 1990s, activists in Toronto ensured that Pan-Africanisms retained the political education and emphasis on Black history that made this worldview a potent force for good at the turn of the twentieth century. After voters in east Toronto elected a Jamaican Canadian to the provincial legislature in 1985, Harry Gairey, founding member of the Toronto UNIA in 1919 and community stalwart, asked the politician in a meeting, "What have you done for Marcus Garvey who helped you get your position?"[5] In addition to long-serving community sentinels, various organizations also resisted apartheid across the United States and Canada using nonviolent, direct action. Some underscored the importance of maintaining cross-border connections from generations past. Dawn Roach, a Pan-Africanist and anti-apartheid activist, for instance, organized "freedom rides" to various U.S. destinations for community members. She recalled a "genderized" division of labor in which women, such as her Trinidadian-born mother and notable activist, Hettie, along with her sisters, performed mostly logistical tasks. Her father, Charles Roach, the prominent civil rights attorney who later represented defendants at the International Criminal Tribunal for Rwanda, acted as chief strategist. Both divisions of labor proved invaluable, for without her mother's contributions, Dawn acknowledged, her father would not have been able to engage in civil rights activism. Dawn planned the itinerary for the freedom rides and, on the buses, led activities where passengers sang freedom songs and discussed educational topics.[6]

Indeed, the freedom rides amounted to nothing less than political education on wheels. Dawn explained that the freedom rides symbolized "movement as in crossing borders and not being restricted to a geographical place and mental space."[7] The freedom rides continued the tradition of the Underground Railroad and the fight against segregation during the civil rights movement, reflecting the importance of a global African community whose peoples transcended national borders. When a large contingent went on a freedom ride to the District of Columbia for the twenty-fifth anniversary of Martin Luther King Jr.'s August 1963 March on Washington, Lennox Farrell, one of the participants, observed, "Today, we, the heirs of Martin and of Malcolm must defeat attempts by the genteel racists at home and abroad to tell us who we should honor and who we should ignore." The Trinidadian-born Farrell continued, "If they succeed in this, they will continue to ignore our just claims for compensation and equality! We have travelled too far, suffered too long, and fought too hard to allow Jim Crow to turn us around!"[8]

Two shocking events of police brutality in the early 1990s illustrated the enduring cross-border consciousness of African North Americans. In 1992, the police beating of African American motorist Rodney King unleashed uprisings in Los Angeles and Toronto, where the Yonge Street "riot" illustrated how Black peoples' struggles fostered transnational freedom movements. On 4 May, Toronto's militant Black Action Defense Committee organized a peaceful march in front of the U.S. Consulate on University Avenue to express African Canadians' solidarity with African Americans in Los Angeles. Protesters also demonstrated their outrage at the local fatal police shooting of Black twenty-two-year-old Raymond Lawrence two days before. Wolfgang Droege, the neo-Nazi who plotted to invade Dominica with other white supremacists in 1981, led a neo-Nazi organization called the Heritage Front, which confronted protesters. Bedlam ensued.

These "deteriorating race relations," according to historian and curator Sheldon Taylor, made Canadian officials receptive to collaborations with Black organizations.[9] From 1992 to 1994, Taylor's exhibition, *Many Rivers to Cross: The African-Canadian Experience*, which borrowed its title from Jamaican musician Jimmy Cliff's song, toured Canada, South Africa, Georgia, and New York City, where it was mounted at the Schomburg Center for Research in Black Culture. African Canadian journalist, researcher, broadcaster, novelist, and diplomat Mairuth Sarsfield provided strategic support. Sarsfield, who was born in the Black Montreal neighborhood in 1925 to Garveyite mother Anne Packwood (née DeShield), studied at Sir George Williams University and then McGill before earning a journalism degree from Columbia University and an M.A. from the University of Ghana, Legon. An organizer during the civil rights movement, she founded Harambee, which advanced Black community development in Ottawa. Because of her pathbreaking work at the United Nations Environmental Program in the early 1980s and development of a global initiative called "For Every Child a Tree," the City of Cleveland observes Mairuth Sarsfield Day every 22 October, a testament to the enduring legacy of Black people and communities across the U.S.-Canadian border.[10] To mitigate anti-Black racism and violence, the state called on Black people who, in turn, mobilized the tenets of cross-border Pan-Africanisms, the same framework that the Canadian and U.S. governments tried to discredit in previous decades.

These linkages continued throughout the 1990s. In 1995, busloads of African Canadians crossed the border to attend the Million Man March in Washington, D.C.[11] Although the diasporic and internationalist National Council of Negro Women—the largest African American women's organization—endorsed the Million Man March, the organizer's missive that women should "stay home and pray" troubled some activists who misinterpreted the march as a sexist affair. According to Dawn Roach—whose father, Charles, along with other men and youth from Toronto bused to Washington—the march was "something our men were doing for themselves and for their own healing."[12] On the National Mall, featured speakers, far from propagating misogyny, admonished Black men to take some responsibility for the ways that their actions and inactions contributed to social disorganization in Black communities.

Critiques about accountability and personal responsibility gained traction in Black liberation discourse as the crack cocaine epidemic and gang violence of the 1980s and 1990s devastated Black communities. Although understandable, such discourse often lacked gendered assessments of the material conditions of inner-city Black boys and men who lived under postindustrialism and mass incarceration, not to mention the ways that the Central Intelligence Agency flooded Black communities with drugs as part of its illicit wars to fund the right-wing Contras of Nicaragua.[13] Despite these headwinds, one of the organizers of the Million Man March pointed out weeks before the 1998 African Liberation Day that this hallowed event symbolized "our oneness as a people with a common past, common set of problems, and a common future."[14] Throughout the twentieth century, mass Black political mobilization often started on the U.S.-Canadian borderlands, gained traction on the North American continent, and reverberated in the hemisphere, while some actors revitalized these movements in Africa and distant parts of the African Diaspora.

Back in Dominica, Rosie Douglas kept his sights on electoral politics. A snap election in January 2000 presented Labor with a golden opportunity to unseat the United Workers' Party and form a new government. Douglas emphasized the ruling government's incessant corruption, pointing out, for example, that it had sold over 1,000 Dominican passports to suspected criminals from Russia, China, western Europe, and the United States for $50,000 each. The price had increased fivefold since 1980, when the opposition accused Douglas's late brother Michael of having done similarly for Iranian exiles when he served as finance minister. Douglas charged his opponents with turning Dominica into a "center for international crime."[15]

In the January 2000 election, the man whom Canada had labeled a national security threat and deported in 1976 became prime minister. "We shifted ideological lines from the hard-left to the center-left," said Douglas. "I was able, really, to tune my policies and persuade the Labor Party that the future is rich if we shift a little."[16] Douglas's coalition government inherited an empty treasury, a $200 million national debt, and a gross domestic product under a quarter billion dollars. Banana cultivation, the island's principal export, contributed to a 60 percent youth unemployment. Compounding the new prime minister's troubles, critics worried whether Dominica, like revolutionary Cuba and Grenada, would receive Washington's ire for posing a threat to U.S. regional interests. "The Caribbean has gone past that stage. We want peace and development," Douglas signaled.[17] Douglas's supporters appreciated his humility and leadership. "Since he has become prime minister, he has kept calm and he has gained much more support," Severin McKenzie attested.[18]

Throughout the twentieth century, transnationalism remained integral to the self-determination of African North Americans, shaping the ways that they imagined freedom within the context of empires, states, and colonies. Since the 1900 Pan-African Conference in London, England—a brainchild of Black intellectuals who navigated the U.S.-Canadian borderlands—Pan-Africanisms articulated borderless Black communities, national self-determination, militant resistance, and shared destinies. Anti-Black racial terrorism after Reconstruction, coupled with Black scholars' reflections on ancient African civilizations, created conditions for a racial renaissance in the wake of the Great War. The psalmist's prophecy that "Ethiopia shall soon stretch out her hands unto God" lent divine credibility to this messianic moment. For those who sought a pragmatic and fearless revolutionary Black messiah to lead the way to racial redemption and a liberated and united Africa, Marcus Mosiah Garvey and his revanchist program of the Universal Negro Improvement Association, from 1919 to the mid-1920s, instilled euphoric hope in Black people in the Atlantic World. Garveyism was the first sustained movement toward twentieth-century Pan-Africanisms in North America, strengthening cross-border and transatlantic linkages and providing a vocabulary and political education for diasporic Africans in the United States, Canada, the Caribbean, and Africa to imagine race unity.

Garvey revitalized a nineteenth-century worldview, which outlived him, of course. When the Western powers undermined Garvey and the UNIA, the borderless Black communities that strengthened his organization persisted. Capitalizing on the vision of a global Black community inspired Black men and women in Great Lakes cities. They migrated across the U.S.-Canadian border to pursue work, leisure, military service, and family reunification. Their mobility contributed to grassroots Black cosmopolitanism and self-determination. Daniel Hill's immigration to Toronto in 1950, his doctoral research, and his pioneering work in human rights advocacy in the 1960s with his wife, Donna, expanded the boundaries of postwar citizenship. Student activists, such as Anne Cools and Rosie Douglas, in addition to African American Black Power militants and Vietnam draft resisters, tested the limits of racial incorporation and progressivism. Fearful of revolutionary Pan-Africanisms, the Royal Canadian Mounted Police and the FBI colluded and subverted the Black freedom struggle.

Black activists, in turn, embraced and supported revolution in southern Africa. The CIA's arms smuggling, illicit wars, coups, and counter-coups weakened revolutionary Pan-Africanisms in the Caribbean and linkages with southern Africa, although not entirely. Rosie Douglas secured Libyan financing in support of anti-colonial revolutionaries in southern Africa. The African National Congress's decades-long quest to defeat apartheid is part of Douglas's illustrious legacy.

Since the Garvey movement's heyday in 1919 and 1920, the establishment perceived expressions of universal Black solidarity and revolutionary self-determination as serious threats to Western hegemony. The U.S. and Canadian governments' role in curtailing Black freedom struggles speaks to the potency and geopolitical implications of Pan-Africanisms. Absent of rigorous democratic oversight, the intelligence and national security apparatus repeatedly violated activists' rights and the rule of law.

In Canada, RCMP misconduct surfaced multiple times in the mid- to late 1970s.[19] In 1978, former FBI operative turned RCMP asset Warren Hart went public, accusing his Canadian employer of surveilling the solicitor general and a Member of Parliament three years earlier.[20] Prime Minister Pierre Trudeau tasked a Royal Commission to investigate alleged RCMP misconduct and "dirty tricks."[21] The U.S. Senate's Church Committee in 1975—which investigated CIA, FBI, NSA, and IRS abuses—provided a useful template. Hart later received $56,000 from the Canadian government for unpaid severance and wrongful termination.[22]

The Royal Commission, also known as the McDonald Commission, recruited a University of Chicago law professor named Antonin Scalia as a consultant to write an addendum to the commission's report. His 1979 trea-tise, titled "United States Intelligence Law," explained how U.S. law governs intelligence gathering.[23] He cautioned, "The unit which regularly performs warrantless electronic surveillance and warrantless physical searches for the purpose of gathering foreign intelligence is likely to develop a more cavalier attitude towards such practices in its ordinary police work, if that is also part of its responsibility."[24]

The McDonald Commission and the Scalia report both underscored the importance of striking a balance between security and civil liberties. Because the RCMP's Security Service performed elements of police work, it blurred the line between intelligence and law enforcement. Deputy Attorney General Robert Tassé, who assisted in the drafting of the 1982 Canadian Charter of Rights and Freedoms, supported Scalia's findings.[25] As per the commission's recommendation, Parliament ended the RCMP's dual mandate of procur-ing foreign and domestic intelligence and policing. On 21 June 1984, an Act of Parliament established the Canadian Security Intelligence Service, or CSIS, which it authorized with covert collection and analysis of threats to Canada's national security. In 1984, Trudeau appointed former student radical activist Anne Cools to the Canadian Senate, the first Black person to serve in its history. Two years later, President Ronald Reagan appointed Antonin Scalia to the U.S. Supreme Court.

Cools's onetime comrade Rosie Douglas never received absolution for his leadership in the 1969 Sir George Williams University student occupa-tion. Even when Douglas became prime minister of Dominica and visited Canada in May 2000 on an official state trip, the Canadian government did not receive him as a Commonwealth dignitary. Having denied Douglas a pardon, the twenty-five-year-old court order that designated him a threat to national security remained valid. "I don't see a pardon as telling the Canadians that I'm sorry for standing up for what I believe in terms of civil rights and human rights for the Black people on this continent," Douglas reflected.[26] Douglas believed what he "contributed" to Canadian society far exceeded the property damage that arose from the computer center occu-pation and destruction. Canadians became "more enlightened . . . [about] human rights and ethnic respect," he asserted.[27]

Canada was not the only official visit on Douglas's itinerary in 2000. He traveled to Australia, Taiwan, and Libya, where he reconvened the World Mathaba to Resist Imperialism, Racism, and Fascism. Dignitaries who spoke included Robert Mugabe of Zimbabwe, Blaise Compaoré of Burkina Faso, Idriss Déby of Chad, Yahya Jammeh of Gambia, Alpha Oumar Konaré of Mali, Abdoulaye Wade of Senegal, Daniel Ortega of the Sandinista

Liberation Front in Nicaragua, and Louis Farrakhan of the Nation of Islam. In fact, Douglas was scheduled to speak at the Nation of Islam's Million Man March in October. He did not get the chance, for Douglas died on 1 October after returning from overseas.

The year 2000 ushered in a denouement of sorts in African North American history. On 28 September, three days before a seemingly healthy and athletic Douglas died of a massive heart attack, Pierre Trudeau also died. Trudeau was the most prominent Canadian prime minister of the twentieth century and a former acquaintance of Douglas. Under his leadership, Canada and the United States strengthened intelligence cooperation to disrupt continental and transatlantic Pan-Africanisms. And on 12 December, a few weeks after Trudeau's death, law enforcement in Florida arrested Warren Hart, along with officers of the Miami-Dade Police Department, for trafficking a large quantity of cocaine using police vehicles. After decades of ignoble service undermining transnational Black organizing at the behest of the U.S. and Canadian governments, Warren Hart, the FBI and RCMP operative who founded the Baltimore chapter of the Black Panther Party in 1969, was engaging in criminal activity in retirement to ensure his material security. Authorities convicted Hart, sentencing him to seven years in prison, where he eventually died.

Long before globalization and cosmopolitanism became buzzwords, diasporic Africans saw advantages in borderless communities and nations. Despite its somewhat Sisyphean rhythms, twentieth-century Pan-Africanisms in North America showed the power of a race-first paradigm to the liberation movements of African peoples living under systems of racist domination and exploitation. The absence of effective firewalls allowed infiltration, counter-subversion, and counterintelligence measures to undermine Black liberation. Like in previous centuries, a race-conscious global Black cosmos remains incompatible with imperialism and neocolonialism. So long as these geopolitical forces continue to subjugate the Black masses and disembowel the African continent, Pan-Africanisms will live. The past offers many lessons for those who continue to dream and organize.

NOTES

ABBREVIATIONS

Archival collections frequently cited have been identified by the following abbreviations:

ADA Alabama Department of Archives, Montgomery
AO Archives of Ontario, Toronto
DBP W. E. B. Du Bois Papers, Special Collections and University Archives, University of Massachusetts Amherst Libraries
FOIA Freedom of Information Act
GIPC Wisconsin Historical Society G.I. Press Collection, Madison
LAC Library and Archives Canada, Ottawa
LOC Library of Congress, Washington, D.C.
MHSO Multicultural History Society of Ontario, Toronto
OPF Official Personnel Folder
SRC Space Research Corporation
STPC Sheldon Taylor's Private Collection

INTRODUCTION

1. Juanita Corinne DeShield, "All for Art," *Challenge* 1, no. 4 (January 1936): 3–11, box 9, folder 23, Papers of Dorothy West, ca. 1890–1998 (inclusive), 1926–95, MC 676, Schlesinger Library, Radcliffe Institute for Advanced Study, Harvard University. Black beauticians Madame C. J. Walker and Madame Sarah Spencer Washington invented the "Anti-kink Walker System" and "Apex News and Hair Company," respectively. See Patricia Carter Sluby, *The Entrepreneurial Spirit of African American Inventors* (Santa Barbara, Calif.: Praeger, 2011), 57–59; and Lynn M. Thomas, *Beneath the Surface: A Transnational History of Skin Lighteners* (Durham, N.C.: Duke University Press, 2020).

2. On racial capitalism, see Cedric J. Robinson, *Black Marxism: The Making of the Black Radical Tradition* (Chapel Hill: University of North Carolina Press, 2000). I use "Black," "diasporic African," "African descendant," and "African peoples" interchangeably to illustrate continuity between "New" World Africans in the Atlantic World and Old World Africans on the continent, as well as in the "Middle East" and on the Indian subcontinent.

3. Like some organizations in that period, the Colored Women's Club evolved and changed names. Minutes of Womans Art Club, 1903, STPC. The preamble of the 1903 Constitution of the Womans Art Club noted the goals: "to become more united in spirit; to eradicate the idiosyncrancy [*sic*] heretofore prevailing; to establish a higher standard of life and for general improvement that necessarily comes from organized association do hereby join themselves for the above purpose."

269

4. DeShield, "All for Art"; pamphlet for Afro-Canadian League, The "Free Lance" Medical Aid to Ethiopia Fund, 27 February 1936, STPC. DeShield, who performed at this Pan-African charity gala to resist Italian aggression and fascism, is described on the program as having "studied dramatic art at the Masters Institute of Roerich Museum" in New York City. On DeShield's activism against anti-Black racism and fascism, see "Canadian Youth Congress Hears of Race Problem: Montreal Girl Says Unfortunate Situation Is Same Everywhere," Baltimore Afro-American, 27 June 1936. Some African Americans knew of her cross-border activism and interest in Black history, literature, and politics. Juanita C. DeShield, Montreal, Quebec, Youth Council letter to NAACP, January 1937, NAACP Papers, box I-G221, folder 13, 1913–1924, LOC. While living in Harlem in 1934, DeShield's uncle designated her the local agent of his Montreal-based periodical the Free Lance, a newspaper for "Afro-Canadians." See chapter 2. On her creative writing, see Juanita De Shield, "Black Velvet," The Crisis 41 (1934): 130. DeShield's surname has no space, but it is spelled with a space in this article. On the Montreal Black community fortifying their children and youth, see Dorothy W. Williams, The Road to Now: A History of Blacks in Montreal (Montreal: Véhicule Press, 1997), 61–62.

5. On repatriation, see James T. Campbell, Middle Passages: African American Journeys to Africa, 1787–2005 (New York: Penguin, 2006); Kenneth C. Barnes, Journey of Hope: The Back-to-Africa Movement in Arkansas in the Late 1800s (Chapel Hill: University of North Carolina Press, 2004); Emma Lapsansky-Werner and Margaret Bacon, eds., Back to Africa: Benjamin Coates and the Colonization Movement in America, 1848–1880 (Philadelphia: University of Pennsylvania Press, 2005); David Jenkins, Black Zion: The Return of Afro-Americans and West Indians to Africa (London: Wildwood House, 1975); and Monique Bedasse, Jah Kingdom: Rastafarians, Tanzania, and Pan-Africanism in the Age of Decolonization (Chapel Hill: University of North Carolina Press, 2017). See also Nemata A. Blyden, African Americans and Africa: A New History (New Haven, Conn.: Yale University Press, 2019). In 1914, African Americans from Texas and other southern states immigrated to the Gold Coast at the request of "Chief" Sam, a flawed Pan-Africanist who promoted a repatriation scheme. Many of the settlers fell on hard times, petitioning the colonial governor to help them return to the United States. Pioneering African American newspaperman in Toronto J. R. B. Whitney wrote about the debacle. "Dreams of Wealth Faded, Wants to Return Home," Canadian Observer (Toronto), 9 June 1917. See also William E. Bittle and Gilbert Geis, The Longest Way Home: Chief Alfred C. Sam's Back-to-Africa Movement (Detroit: Wayne State University Press, 1964); and Robert A. Hill, ed., The Marcus Garvey and Universal Negro Improvement Association Papers, Vol. I: 1826–August 1919 (Berkeley: University of California Press, 1983), 536–46.

6. Although Black people in other parts of the Americas are technically "African American," I reserve this appellation for Black people in the United States, specifically those whose ancestors endured bondage there. I also refer to Black people who are native-born or those who have spent considerable time in Canada as "African Canadians." Given the limited scope of chattel enslavement in the territories that became Canada, many African Canadians, especially in the Maritime provinces and southwestern Ontario, in fact, descended from enslaved and free Black people

from the United States. I use "African Caribbean" or "West Indian" to describe Black people from the Caribbean. Furthermore, I deliberately use "African American" and "African Canadian" to illustrate an incongruity of African peoples living under European systems that exploited Black people and the African continent. W. E. B. Du Bois called this contradiction "double consciousness." See W. E. B. Du Bois, *The Souls of Black Folk* (1903; repr., Gorham, Maine: Myers Education Press, 2018).

7. Toyin Falola and Kevin D. Roberts, *The Atlantic World: 1450–2000* (Bloomington: Indiana University Press, 2008), xiii. The phenomenon of placing the micro into the macro mirrors what one scholar of global history called "the history of connections" or history predicated on "integration." See Sebastian Conrad, *What Is Global History?* (Princeton, N.J.: Princeton University Press, 2016), 6. See also John K. Thornton, *Africa and Africans in the Making of the Atlantic World, 1400–1800*, 2nd ed. (New York: Cambridge University Press, 1998).

8. On DeShield's ancestry, see "Meeting at Church Led to 47-Year Union," *Montreal Gazette*, 6 March 1988; and Wini Rider, "Montreal Women's Club Reminisces," *Montreal Gazette*, 29 December 1977. On African Canadians constructing rail networks, see Sarah-Jane Mathieu, *North of the Color Line: Migration and Black Resistance in Canada, 1870–1955* (Chapel Hill: University of North Carolina Press, 2010), 5. On "Atlantic creoles," see Ira Berlin, *Many Thousands Gone: The First Two Centuries of Slavery in North America* (Cambridge: Belknap Press of Harvard University Press, 1998), 24.

9. Robin D. G. Kelley, "'But a Local Phase of a World Problem': Black History's Global Vision, 1883–1950," *Journal of American History* 86, no. 3 (1999): 1050–51.

10. I use "African North American" to illustrate that Black people are inextricably linked to the continent. This racial-continental framing differs from notions of French North America, British North America, and Spanish North America, all of which were imperial projects that plundered and displaced Indigenous peoples and enslaved Africans and subjugated their descendants. On linkages among various white French-speaking groups—such as French Canadians, Québécois, Cajuns, and Acadians—and their pursuit of cultural and linguistic retention in North America, see Ryan André Brasseaux, *French North America in the Shadows of Conquest* (New York: Routledge, 2021); and Robert Englebert and Andrew N. Wegmann, eds., *French Connections: Cultural Mobility in North America and the Atlantic World, 1600–1875* (Baton Rouge: Louisiana State University Press, 2020). On French North America's direct impact on Manifest Destiny, see Jay Gitlin, *The Bourgeois Frontier: French Towns, French Traders, and American Expansion* (New Haven, Conn.: Yale University Press, 2009).

11. Historical silences concerning African civilizations are vital to understanding the genesis of Pan-Africanisms, which "is about the restoration of African people to their proper place in world history." Although nationhood was integral, so, too, was "respect." John Henrik Clarke, "Pan-Africanism: A Brief History of an Idea in the African World," *Présence Africaine*, no. 145 (1988): 28. See also Michael O. Eze, "Pan-Africanism: A Brief Intellectual History," *History Compass* 11, no. 9 (2013): 663–74.

12. Black studies doyen Molefi Kete Asante called this Black or African consciousness and political education—a theoretical imperative that must first orient

African peoples toward Pan-Africanisms — "Afrocentricity." See Molefi Kete Asante, *An Afrocentric Pan African Vision: Afrocentric Essays* (London: Rowman and Littlefield, 2021).

13. George Shepperson, "Pan-Africanism and 'Pan-Africanism': Some Historical Notes," *Phylon* 23, no. 4 (1962): 346. On "diasporas," see Winston James, "The Caribbean Diaspora and Black Internationalism," in *Dimensions of African and Other Diaspora*, ed. Franklin W. Knight and Ruth Iyob (Kingston, Jam.: University of the West Indies Press, 2014), 256–57. On African peoples in the Atlantic and Indian Ocean Worlds and Mediterranean Sea region, see Patrick Manning, *The African Diaspora: A History through Culture* (New York: Columbia University Press, 2010).

14. Kwame Nantambu, "Pan-Africanism versus Pan-African Nationalism: An Afrocentric Analysis," *Journal of Black Studies* 28, no. 5 (1998): 561–74. On the coming together of Pan-Africanism and Black Nationalism in the 1960s, see Russell Rickford, *We Are an African People: Independent Education, Black Power, and the Radical Imagination* (New York: Oxford University Press, 2016), 132–68.

15. On the origins of the international system and the Westphalian model, see David Armitage, *Foundations of Modern International Thought* (Cambridge: Cambridge University Press, 2013), 1–45, 59–74.

16. On sovereignty or "non-interference," colonial borders, and Pan-Africanism, see Elenga M'buyinga, *Pan-Africanism or Neo-Colonialism? The Bankruptcy of the O.A.U.* (London: Zed Press, 1982), 58. Rodney acknowledged that the radical political party Union des Populations du Cameroun rejected African colonial borders. See Walter Rodney, "Towards the Sixth Pan-African Congress: Aspects of the International Class Struggle in Africa, the Caribbean, and America," in *African Intellectual Heritage: A Book of Sources*, ed. Molefi Kete Asante and Abu S. Abarry (Philadelphia: Temple University Press, 1996), 730.

17. Kwame Nkrumah, Sékou Touré, and Gamal Abdel-Nasser aspired to create a federated Africa—or, put differently, a United States of Africa—which Garvey envisioned in the 1920s. Nkrumah believed that a federated Africa needed an African army to rid the continent of colonialism and to safeguard the freedom of the people, another Garveyite vision. Those who sought a federated African country belonged to the Casablanca Group. The Monrovia Group represented the interests of statesmen who favored national borders.

18. Shepperson, "Pan-Africanism and 'Pan-Africanism'"; Edmund Cronon, *Black Moses: The Story of Marcus Garvey and the Universal Negro Improvement Association* (1955; repr. Madison: University of Wisconsin Press, 1969); Theodore Draper, *The Rediscovery of Black Nationalism* (New York: Viking Press, 1970).

19. Walter Rodney, "The Black Scholar Interviews: Walter Rodney," *Black Scholar* 6, no. 3 (1974): 46.

20. Pan-Africanism "is the cultural and political attempt to take humanhood, nationhood, and culture" in the diaspora and Africa. Aminah Wallace, "Pan-Africanism and Slave Rebellions: The Interconnections," in *Pan-Africanism, and the Politics of African Citizenship and Identity*, ed. Toyin Falola and Kwame Essien (New York: Routledge, 2014), 71. Another historian defined Pan-Africanisms as a fourfold process: African ancestry; a history of subjugation by foreign powers; commitment to a national ethic; and the importance of "solidarity" with

all African peoples. W. James, "Caribbean Diaspora and Black Internationalism," 255–56. The core belief stipulated that African peoples the world over "constitute a common cultural and political community by virtue of our origin in Africa and our common racial, social and economic oppression." Robert Chrisman, "Aspects of Pan-Africanism," *Black Scholar* 4, no. 10 (1973): 2. See also Colin Legum, "The Roots of Pan-Africanism," in *Africa: A Handbook to the Continent*, ed. Colin Legum (London: Anthony Blond, 1965), 413–23; P. Olisanwuche Esedebe, *Pan-Africanism: The Idea and Movement, 1776–1991* (Washington, D.C.: Howard University Press, 1994); and Sidney J. Lemelle, *Pan-Africanism for Beginners* (New York: Writers and Readers Publishing).

21. For the most authoritative work on Garvey and the UNIA, see Tony Martin, *Race First: The Ideological and Organizational Struggles of Marcus Garvey and the Universal Negro Improvement Association* (Westport, Conn.: Greenwood Press, 1976). North African countries posed theoretical and practical challenges to the race-first paradigm of orthodox Pan-Africanisms, partly because the racial enslavement of Black people by non-Black people persisted there. Pan-Africanisms, on balance, sought common ground with non-Black peoples who expressed a commitment to mutual respect and Black liberation.

22. Not every action by a Black person entailed Pan-Africanisms. It would be a methodological folly to categorize Pan-Africanisms as encompassing everything.

23. As one of the leaders of the Republic of New Afrika—which demanded that the U.S. government transfer the states of Louisiana, Mississippi, Alabama, Georgia, and South Carolina to this republic for the creation of a Black nation-state—Moore believed in the necessity of sovereign borders. For her quote, see Sharon Harley, "'I Don't Pay Those Borders No Mind At All': Audley E. Moore ('Queen Mother' Moore)—Grassroots Global Traveler and Activist," in *Women and Migration: Responses in Art and History*, ed. Deborah Willis, Ellyn Toscano, and Kalia Brooks Nelson (Cambridge: Open Book Publishers, 2019), 439–51.

24. Shepperson, "Pan-Africanism and 'Pan-Africanism,'" 350–51; William Scott, "'And Ethiopia Shall Stretch Forth Its Hands': The Origins of Ethiopianism in Afro-American Thought, 1767–1896," *Umoja* 2 (1978): 1–14.

25. See Donald Moore, *Don Moore: An Autobiography* (Toronto: Williams-Wallace, 1985), 32.

26. Whether formal or informal, Black Nationalisms meant that Black people should exercise ownership over communal and national resources and affairs. It speaks to the importance of sovereignty or independence. Not all Black Nationalisms, however, centered African consciousness. The organizing principle in the Nation of Islam was religion and culture (Arabic), not an African or diasporic African worldview. Black Internationalisms, which can also be formal and informal, denote Black actors' engagement with the global community along shared interests. Some historians, on one hand, posit that "Black Internationalism" is less restrictive than Pan-Africanisms, because it concerns Black actors' collaborations with all peoples, unlike the race-first ethos of orthodox Pan-Africanisms. See Michael West, William G. Martin, and Fanon Che Wilkins, eds., *From Toussaint to Tupac: The Black International since the Age of Revolution* (Chapel Hill: University of North Carolina Press, 2009); Keisha Blain and Tiffany Gill, eds., *To Turn the Whole World Over:*

Black Women and Internationalism (Urbana: University of Illinois Press, 2019); and Monique Bedasse, Kim D. Butler, Carlos Fernandes, Dennis Laumann, Tejasvi Nagaraja, Benjamin Talton, and Kira Thurman, "AHR Conversations: Black Internationalism," *American Historical Review* 125, no. 5 (2020): 1699–739. On the other hand, another historian pointed out that the "highest level" of Pan-Africanisms is "Black Internationalism." See W. James, "Caribbean Diaspora and Black Internationalism," 256. See also Minkah Makalani, *In the Cause of Freedom: Radical Black Internationalism from Harlem to London, 1917–1939* (Chapel Hill: University of North Carolina Press, 2011). Other scholars describe Black Internationalism as the "trans-territorial leftwing insurgencies" of Pan-Africanism. See Charisse Burden-Stelly and Gerald Horne, "From Pan-Africanism to Black Internationalism," in *The Routledge Handbook of Pan-Africanism*, ed. Reiland Rabaka (London: Routledge, Taylor & Francis Group, 2020), 69–86. On Black Internationalism and the Far East, see Gerald Horne, *Facing the Rising Sun: African Americans, Japan, and the Rise of Afro-Asian Solidarity* (New York: New York University Press, 2018); Marc S. Gallicchio, *The African American Encounter with Japan and China: Black Internationalism in Asia, 1895–1945* (Chapel Hill: University of North Carolina Press, 2003); and Nico Slate, *Colored Cosmopolitanism: The Shared Struggle for Freedom in the United States and India* (Cambridge, Mass.: Harvard University Press, 2012).

27. For British subjects and other diasporic Africans, Canada, as a Commonwealth country and in juxtaposition to a hostile United States, retained its reputation as a "Promised Land," notwithstanding its deep-seated anti-blackness. Williams immigrated there for these reasons. See James R. Hooker, *Henry Sylvester Williams: Imperial Pan-Africanist* (London: Collings, 1975); Owen C. Mathurin, *Henry Sylvester Williams and the Origins of the Pan-African Movement, 1869–1911* (Westport, Conn.: Greenwood Press, 1976); David Killingray, "Rights, Land, and Labour: Black British Critics of South African Policies before 1948," *Journal of Southern African Studies* 35, no. 2 (2009): 375–98; and J. Barry Cahill, "Constructing an 'Imperial Pan-Africanist': Henry Sylvester Williams as a University Law Student in Canada," in *The African Canadian Legal Odyssey: Historical Essays*, ed. Barrington Walker (Toronto: University of Toronto Press, 2012), 84–98. Conference vice president Reverend Brown shared the same name as the famed Henry "Box" Brown, the African American who shipped himself in a crate from bondage in Virginia to freedom in Philadelphia. The original Box Brown later settled in southwestern Ontario, where he died in 1897. On Reverend Brown, see Imanuel Geiss, *The Pan-African Movement: A History of Pan-Africanism in America, Europe and Africa* (New York: Africana Publishing Co., 1974), 182; Tony Martin, *The Pan-African Connection: From Slavery to Garvey and Beyond* (Dover, Mass.: Majority Press, 1983), 210; and Themon Djaksam, "Conflict and Unity: Towards an Intellectual History of the Forbears of the OAU," *India Quarterly* 46, no. 4 (1990): 41–90. Brown served as minister of the African Methodist Episcopal Zion Church in Nova Scotia. See Marika Sherwood, *Origins of Pan-Africanism: Henry Sylvester Williams, Africa, and the African Diaspora* (New York: Routledge, 2011), 235. See also Milfred C. Fierce, *The Pan-African Idea in the United States, 1900–1919: African-American Interest in Africa and Interaction with West Africa* (New York: Garland, 1993); and Hakim Adi, *Pan-Africanism: A History* (London: Bloomsbury Academic, 2018).

28. For Anna Jones, see Sherwood, *Origins of Pan-Africanism*, 82; and Roland M. Baumann, *Constructing Black Education at Oberlin College: A Documentary History* (Athens: Ohio University Press, 2010), 66. On her father's revolutionary abolitionism, see Steven Lubet, *The "Colored Hero" of Harper's Ferry: John Anthony Copeland and the War against Slavery* (New York: Cambridge University Press, 2015), 38–39. See also Karen Paton-Evans, "Gunsmith James Jones: Canada's First Black Gunsmith, His Part in the Underground Railroad, and His Rifle," *Miller and Miller*, 24 September 2021, https://millerandmillerauctions.squarespace.com/stories/2021/9/23/james-jones-gunsmith (accessed 2 December 2021).

29. Sherwood, *Origins of Pan-Africanism*, 75–97. French might have been born in the Eastern Caribbean island of Saint Lucia. Martin, *Pan-African Connection*, 202.

30. Sherwood, *Origins of Pan-Africanism*, 75–97; Martin, *Pan-African Connection*, 201–16. On the Italo-Ethiopian War, see Raymond Jonas, *The Battle of Adwa: African Victory in the Age of Empire* (Cambridge, Mass.: Belknap Press of Harvard University Press, 2011), 282–84.

31. On Pan-Negroism, see W. E. B. Du Bois, "The Conservation of Races," *American Negro Academy Occasional Papers*, no. 2 (1897): 9. On Du Bois and the color line, see Martin, *Pan-African Connection*, 208–10. See also Marilyn Lake and Henry Reynolds, *Drawing the Global Colour Line: White Men's Countries and the International Challenge of Racial Equality* (Cambridge, U.K.: Cambridge University Press, 2008).

32. Raymond L. Buell, *International Relations* (New York: Henry Holt, 1929), 72–95; Shepperson, "Pan-Africanism and 'Pan-Africanism,'" 353.

33. Isidore Okpewho, Carole Boyce Davies, and Ali A. Mazrui, eds., *The African Diaspora: African Origins and New World Identities* (Bloomington: Indiana University Press, 1999), xiii.

34. Rayford Logan, *Negro in American Life and Thought: The Nadir, 1877–1901* (New York: Collier Books, 1965), 19.

35. The National Afro-American Council, founded in 1898 in Rochester, New York, provided a model for the NAACP. On the NAACP's "Pan-African Department," see Elliott M. Rudwick, *W. E. B. Du Bois: Propagandist of the Negro Protest* (Philadelphia: University of Pennsylvania Press, 1968), 210. No African Canadian participated in the Fort Erie meeting. It would be conjecture, however, to conclude that Du Bois and his peers rejected African Canadians. Widespread racial terrorism and disenfranchisement against African Americans lacked a Canadian equivalent, which reinforced the Promised Land myth.

36. See Benito Sylvain to W. E. B. Du Bois, 24 June 1908 (emphasis in original); Du Bois to Sylvain, 24 January 1907, DBP (MS 312). See also Martin, *Pan-African Connection*, 201–16; and Jonas, *Battle of Adwa*, 282–84.

37. Ida Gibbs Hunt's transnational upbringing shaped her activism. Her father, Mifflin Wistar Gibbs, fled anti-Black racial terror in California along with almost 600 Black migrants, relocating to British Columbia in 1858. There, Mifflin Gibbs became a statesman and wealthy businessman. After his family returned to the United States during Reconstruction, he became a lawyer, the first African American municipal judge, and diplomat. See Mifflin Wistar Gibbs, *Shadow and Light: An Autobiography* (New York: Arno Press and the New York Times, 1968); and Adele

Logan Alexander, *Parallel Worlds: The Remarkable Gibbs-Hunt and the Enduring (In)significance of Melanin* (Charlottesville: University of Virginia Press, 2010); Mona L. Siegel, *Peace on Our Terms: The Global Battle for Women's Rights After the First World War* (New York: Columbia University Press, 2020), 51–90. J. R. B. Whitney's newspaper covered the inaugural Pan-African Congress. "Pan-African Congress to Safe-Guard Race Interest," *Canadian Observer*, 22 February 1919.

38. R. L. Fairbairn, general passenger agent of the Canadian National Railways, wrote a letter of reference for Whitney in which he acknowledged having known him for eight years and indicated that another colleague had known him for ten years. R. L. Fairbairn to J. R. B. Whitney, 20 September 1919, STPC. Census data revealed that Whitney had first been married in Ohio to Joy Wadkins (or Watkins) on 8 May 1903 with whom he had a son named Joseph Whitney III on 28 October 1905. It is unclear whether Joseph Whitney III lived to adulthood. On 23 July 1913, he married Anna Bush (née Vanderhoof or Vanderhoff), a white divorcée, in Lucas, Ohio, less than seventy miles from Detroit. One cannot say definitively if they annulled the marriage or divorced, but his immigration to Canada circa 1909 implies that he sought a new beginning, even though he visited Ohio occasionally. See *Cuyahoga County, Ohio, Marriage Records, 1810-1973*, Cuyahoga County Archive, Cleveland, Ohio, vol. 54–55, 1902 May–1903 May, Ohio, U.S., Births and Christenings Index, 1774–1973, p. 470 (database online), Ancestry.com, http://www.ancestry.com (accessed 2 December 2021); Tenth Census of the United States, 1880 (NARA microfilm publication T9, 1,454 rolls), Records of the Bureau of the Census, Record Group 29, LOC.

39. Whitney owned a home at 154 Jones Street. See Fonds 200, series 612, file 951, City of Toronto Assessment Roll, Ward No. 1, Div. No. 2, 1915 Assessment for Taxation in 1916. I credit Sheldon Taylor and City of Toronto archivists for assisting me in tracking down this source.

40. The *Observer* covered news pertinent to African Canadians and the global Black community. When leaders of Halifax, Nova Scotia's historic Black community, boycotted the film *The Birth of a Nation*, which compelled the province to ban its viewing, Whitney's paper acknowledged this modest group achievement. "*Birth of a Nation* Picture Has Been Banned in Halifax," *Canadian Observer*, 15 April 1916.

41. Whitney to Hughes, 24 November 1915, RG 24, vol. 1206 HQ 297-1-21; and Hughes to Whitney, 3 December 1915, RG 24, vol. 1206, file HQ 297-1-21, Department of National Defense, LAC. During the Great War, an estimated 165 African Americans—or Black people who had emigrated from the United States to Canada—fought in the Canadian military. Ohioan Ulysses Theodore Mays, who relocated to Canada in 1899, enlisted in the Canadian Expeditionary Forces on 22 September 1914 at Valcartier, Quebec. Before and after the war, Mays lived in Sarnia, Ontario, a Great Lake city near the Michigan-Ontario border on the southernmost point of Lake Huron. Others, such as British subjects and Jamaican-born brothers Herbert and Harold Bell, left Massachusetts in 1918 to enlist in a New Brunswick regiment. Harold had worked as an expert mechanic in Boston, so he tried to enlist in the Royal Canadian Air Force, which excluded Black men. See "Colored Men Are Barred from the Royal Air Force," *Canadian Observer*, 7 September 1918; Ulysses Theodore Mays, RG 150, Accession 1992–1993/166, box 6080–47, *Census of Canada, 1901,*

Ottawa, Ontario, Canada, LAC, 2004; series RG 31-C-1, Statistics Canada Fonds, microfilm reels: T-6428 to T-6556, *Sixth Census of Canada, 1921*, Ottawa, Ontario, Canada, LAC, 2013; series RG 31, Statistics Canada Fonds; Sheldon Taylor, "Nobody Is Gonna Keep Us Back: Black Survival in Toronto, 1914–1950" (unpublished book manuscript in Taylor's possession), chap. 1, 2; Fred Gaffen, *Cross-Border Warriors: Canadians in American Forces, Americans in Canadian Forces, from the Civil War to the Gulf* (Toronto: Dundurn Press, 1995).

42. On middle-class African Americans acting as "ambassadors to the white power structure," see Glenda E. Gilmore, *Gender and Jim Crow: Women and the Politics of White Supremacy in North Carolina, 1896–1920* (Chapel Hill: University of North Carolina Press, 1996), xxv.

43. Whitney came from a cultural tradition in which African American men sought to exchange their military service for full citizenship rights. William C. Nell, William Wells Brown, and George Washington Williams, three pioneering nineteenth-century African American historians, were among the first to connect African Americans' pursuit of citizenship and claims of manhood to the military service that Black soldiers rendered to the United States. White historians largely disavowed this interpretation, often evoking some blind patriotism as Black soldiers' main motivation. Benjamin Quarles's seminal study of the U.S. Revolutionary War revised this inaccuracy. See William C. Nell, *The Colored Patriots of the American Revolution with Sketches of Several Distinguished Colored Persons: To Which Is Added a Brief Survey of the Condition and Prospects of Colored Americans* (Boston: Robert F. Wallcut, 1855); William Wells Brown, *The Negro in the American Rebellion: His Heroism and Fidelity* (Boston: Lee and Shepard, 1867); George Washington Williams, *History of the Negro Race in America from 1619 to 1880: Negros as Slaves, as Soldiers, and as Citizens* (New York: G. P. Putnam's Sons, 1883); and Benjamin Quarles, *The Negro in the American Revolution* (Williamsburg, Va.: Institute of Early American History and Culture, 1961).

44. On race and nationalism, see James W. St. G. Walker, "Race and Recruitment in World War I: Enlistment of Visible Minorities in the Canadian Expeditionary Force," *Canadian Historical Review* 70, no. 1 (1989): 1–26.

45. Walker belonged to the Grand Lodge of Canada in the Province of Ontario AF and AM (Ancient Free and Accepted Masons). Prince Hall Masons had no intercourse with white Masons from the Grand Lodge of Canada. Had the Grand Lodge formally or informally recognized the Prince Hall Masons, U.S. lodges, specifically southern ones, would have severed ties with the Grand Lodge of Canada. Author's interview with C. Arthur Downes, Past Grand Master, Grand Chancellor, and Dean, 13 September 2021, notes in author's possession.

46. "Organ of Colored Folk Has First Anniversary," *Globe and Mail* (Toronto), 14 December 1915. Walker acknowledged learning about the fabled Underground Railroad in his youth.

47. Another honored guest present was Whitney's employer, W. H. Moore, secretary of the Canadian Northern Railway. He praised Whitney's enterprising spirit. *Canadian Observer*, 18 December 1915.

48. Edmund Walker to Carter G. Woodson, 26 June 1923, box 6, reel 3–4, Carter G. Woodson Collection of Negro Papers and Related Documents, LOC.

49. Edmund Walker, *Address of Sir Edmund Walker, C.V.O., President of the Canadian Bank of Commerce, Toronto* (New York, s.n., 1912), 4.

50. See also Robin Winks, *The Blacks in Canada: A History*, 2nd ed. (Montreal: McGill-Queen's University Press, 1997), 316, 419; and Richard Hofstadter, *Social Darwinism in American Thought, 1860–1915* (Philadelphia: University of Philadelphia Press, 2016).

51. J. R. B. Whitney, "We Want a Revolution of Thought by Our People," *Canadian Observer*, 23 October 1915. During the war years, the *Observer* ran headlines such as "Be Loyal to Your God, Race and Country." Also, there are many examples of intercourse between Black people in Great Lakes cities in the United States and Canada.

52. On first Black teacher in Windsor, see Ada Ellen Whitney, obituary, 16 March 1972, STPC. On Whitney's letters of recommendation, see William H. Hearst to J. R. B. Whitney, 22 September 1919, and Edmund Walker to Whitney, 19 September 1919, STPC.

53. Alexandre Popovic, *The Revolt of African Slaves in Iraq in the 3rd/9th Century* (Princeton, N.J.: Marcus Wiener, 1999). Black consciousness or "race" pride or proto-Pan-Africanisms were evident in Iraq and other Islamic jurisdictions where enslaved Africans endured bondage. A few months before the Zanj Rebellion began, for example, the prolific African Iraqi intellectual named Al-Jahiz, who was born in Basra, died. His views on proto-Pan-Africanisms in the Middle Ages is evident in one of his works. See Al-Jahiz, *Book of the Glory of the Black Race* (Los Angeles: Preston Publishing Company, [1981]).

54. James C. Scott, *Domination and the Arts of Resistance: Hidden Transcripts* (New Haven, Conn.: Yale University Press, 1992). Africans in the Atlantic World, especially those enslaved, sought absolute secrecy when plotting revolts, often employing blood oaths and other protocols to conceal sacred and forbidden knowledge. One historian acknowledged that scholars cannot know what participants at the Pan-African Conference "discussed in private." Sherwood, *Origins of Pan-Africanism*, 79.

55. Sherwood, *Origins of Pan-Africanism*, 83.

56. Despite their circumspection, Henry Sylvester Williams and his fellow Pan-Africanists understood that Black people would never achieve their inalienable right to dignity and self-determination under systems of imperialism and colonialism. Williams and his peers wanted to end European domination and exploitation of African peoples, not merely reform these systems. The conservative politics of the Victorian period tempered their rhetoric of anti-imperialism and anti-colonialism. I caution for reading against the grain when analyzing the writings of Black people praising European monarchs, empires, and metropoles. There is a long history of enslaved Africans and their descendants using favorable language to petition European monarchs for manumission and other human rights. Scholarship, for example, that portrays Williams as a mere reformer of the barbarism and, in some instances, genocide of European exploitation ignores the context in which Black people lived and the subversive ways that they interacted with power. See Hooker, *Henry Sylvester Williams*; and Susan D. Pennybacker, "The Universal Races Congress, London Political Culture, and Imperial Dissent, 1900–1939," *Radical History*

Review 52 (2005): 103–17. After 1903, when Williams became South Africa's first Black lawyer, he gained greater appreciation for the natives' conditions and urgency to overcome imperialism and colonialism. His legal advocacy laid the groundwork for the founding of the African National Congress in 1912. See Henry S. Williams, *The British Negro: A Factor in the Empire; "The Ethiopian Eunuch." Two Lectures Delivered before Many Distinguished Clubs and Associations in the United Kingdom of Great Britain, at the Request of Several British Friends, Interested in the Progress of the "Negro Race"* (Brighton, U.K.: W. T. Moulton, 1902).

57. C. L. R. James, *The Black Jacobins: Toussaint L'Ouverture and the San Domingo Revolution* (1938; repr., London: Penguin, 2001); Carolyn Fick, *The Making of Haiti: The Saint Domingue Revolution from Below* (Knoxville: University of Tennessee Press, 1990); Laurent Dubois, *Avengers of the New World: The Story of the Haitian Revolution* (Cambridge, Mass.: Belknap Press of Harvard University Press, 2004); James Alexander Dun, *Dangerous Neighbors: Making the Haitian Revolution in Early America* (Philadelphia: University of Pennsylvania Press, 2016); Sarah Fanning, *Caribbean Crossing: African Americans and the Emigration Project* (New York: New York University Press, 2015); West, Martin, and Wilkins, *From Toussaint to Tupac*. On invasion of Ethiopia, see S. K. B. Asante, *Pan-African Protest: West Africa and the Italo-Ethiopian Crisis, 1934–1941* (London: Longman, 1977). On the perils of European humanism, see Eric R. Wolf, *Europe and the People without History* (Berkeley: University of California Press, 1982); and Susan Buck-Morss, *Hegel, Haiti, and Universal History* (Pittsburgh: University of Pittsburgh Press, 2009). Before the Haitian Revolution, the Seven Years' War (1756–63) between Britain and France and their European allies provided enslaved Africans in Jamaica an opening to initiate one of the largest slave revolts in the Atlantic World. See Vincent Brown, *Tacky's Revolt: The Story of an Atlantic Slave War* (Cambridge, Mass.: Belknap Press of Harvard University Press, 2020).

58. C. L. R. James, *Black Jacobins*; C. L. R. James, *A History of Negro Revolt* (London: Fact Ltd., 1938); Kelley, "'But a Local Phase of a World Problem,'" 1069, 1071, 1073.

59. For a skillful example of how to approach a broad and complex subject or "a selection, rather than the sum," see Adam Ewing, *The Age of Garvey: How a Jamaican Activist Created a Mass Movement and Changed Global Black Politics* (Princeton, N.J.: Princeton University Press, 2017), 10. Researching this book required conventional primary sources from the United States, Canada, the English-speaking Caribbean, and the United Kingdom, such as archived and uncatalogued private papers, organizational minutes, newspapers, oral history, military personnel files, autobiographies and diaries, documentaries, ephemera, census data, and other government records. Hard-to-obtain primary sources, such as classified intelligence reports, which I secured under freedom of information provisions in the United States and Canada, provide the historian with a vital, although limited, peek into the inner workings of state power where race is concerned. Given the scarcity of analyses on North American history from the perspectives of Pan-Africanisms, the secondary literature plays an important role in highlighting the visible, recurring—yet often unspoken—central theme of Black struggle, identity formations, and desire from slavery to quasi-freedom.

60. James W. St. G. Walker, *The Black Loyalists: The Search for a Promised Land in Nova Scotia and Sierra Leone, 1783–1870* (Toronto: University of Toronto Press, 1992); Simon Schama, *Rough Crossings: Britain, the Slaves, and the American Revolution* (London: BBC, 2005); Harvey Amani Whitfield, *Blacks on the Border: The Black Refugees in British North America, 1815–1860* (Burlington: University of Vermont Press, 2006); Harvey Amani Whitfield, *North to Bondage: Loyalist Slavery in the Maritimes* (Vancouver: University of British Columbia Press, 2016); Maya Jasanoff, *Liberty's Exiles: American Loyalists in the Revolutionary World* (New York: Alfred A. Knopf, 2011); Afua Cooper, "Acts of Resistance: Black Men and Women Engage Slavery in Upper Canada, 1793–1903," *Ontario History* 99, no. 1 (Spring 2007): 5–17. During the U.S. Revolutionary War and War of 1812, the British incited servile insurrection as a method of counterinsurgency. Legal historian John Fabian Witt considered this controversial issue as "tensions that have been internal to the law of war in American history from the Revolution to the present." Abraham Lincoln borrowed from the British military strategy when the Union recruited enslaved Africans behind Confederate lines as part of its war effort. See John Fabian Witt, *Lincoln's Code: The Laws of War in American History* (New York: Free Press, 2012), 4; and Gerald Horne, *Negro Comrades of the Crown: African Americans and the British Empire Fight the U.S. before Emancipation* (New York: New York University Press, 2012). After the War of 1812, geopolitics remained a major source of tension between the British and the United States. Colonel Charles P. Stacey, historian for the Canadian Army, dismantled the "century of peace" paradigm. Historian Robin Winks added to this revisionism, critiquing the paradigm as selective historical memory. "From 1815 until 1871," wrote Winks, "the British North American provinces felt themselves open to attack from an America that many provincials considered to be emotional, untrustworthy, and grasping." Although Britain and the United States avoided armed confrontation after 1815, the two powers existed in a state of brinkmanship, or what a Canadian newspaper described as "a war in anticipation." See Winks, *The Civil War Years: Canada and the United States* (Montreal: McGill-Queen's University Press, 1998), xvii, 3; and Charles P. Stacey, "The Myth of the Unguarded Frontier, 1815–1871," *American Historical Review* 56, no. 1 (1950): 1–18. See also J. L. Granatstein, *Yankee Go Home? Canadians and Anti-Americanism* (Toronto: HarperCollins, 1996).

61. Concerning the Underground Railroad, James Walker called "the North Star myth" a "liability" that obstructed efforts to scrutinize anti-Black racism. See James St. G. Walker, *Racial Discrimination in Canada: The Black Experience* (Ottawa: Canadian Historical Association, 1985), 6–7. Despite the prevailing narrative of British justice, during the U.S. Civil War, thousands of freedom seekers chose not to remain in Upper Canada—that is, the land of the North Star, the Promised Land—but returned to a precarious "homeland" to fight in the Union army, find kinfolk, and contribute to Reconstruction. The precipitating Antebellum push factors were threefold: westward expansion of slavery and mounting hostility toward free Black people, which culminated in the Fugitive Slave Act of 1850, fueled debates that African Americans had on emigration from the United States. Before British North America gained notoriety for providing refuge to fugitives from slavery from the United States, some enslaved Africans in Upper Canada traveled south on the

Underground Railroad into the northern United States. Because Article VI of the 1787 Northwest Ordinance outlawed slavery in the Northwest Territory—the lands west of the Appalachian Mountains encompassing the Great Lakes, south of British North America, and north of the Ohio River—enslaved persons who fled from their British or Indigenous captors in Upper Canada found refuge in this region of the early republic. See Frederick D. Williams, ed., *The Northwest Ordinance: Essays on Its Formulation, Provisions, and Legacy* (East Lansing: Michigan State University Press, 1989); Wilbur Henry Siebert, *The Underground Railroad from Slavery to Freedom* (New York: Macmillan, 1898), 190; Samuel G. Howe, *The Refugees from Slavery in Canada West: Report to the Freedman's Inquiry Commission* (Boston: Wright and Potter, 1864), 8–9. Robin Winks wrote that "an ambivalent anti-Americanism" encouraged British North Americans to welcome African American fugitives. "To accept the runaway slave," he observed, "was one way to demonstrate the superiority of British liberties and to strike at the Republic, economically as well as morally." See Winks, *Blacks in Canada*, 149; and Winks, *Civil War Years*. See also Christopher L. Brown, *Moral Capital: Foundations of British Abolitionism* (Chapel Hill: University of North Carolina Press, 2006); Richard Blackett, *Making Freedom: The Underground Railroad and the Politics of Slavery* (Chapel Hill: University of North Carolina Press, 2013); Jason Silverman, *Unwelcome Guests: Canada West's Response to American Fugitive Slaves, 1800–1865* (Millwood, N.Y.: Associated Faculty Press, 1985); Karolyn Smardz Frost and Veta Tucker, eds., *A Fluid Frontier: Slavery, Resistance, and the Underground Railroad in the Detroit River Borderland* (Detroit: Wayne State University Press, 2016); and Jane Rhodes, "The Contestation over National Identity: Nineteenth-Century Black Americans in Canada," *Canadian Review of American Studies* 30, no. 2 (2000): 175–86. For nineteenth-century repatriation of "African North Americans" during Reconstruction, see Adam Arenson, "Experience rather than Imagination: Researching the Return Migration of African North Americans during the American Civil War and Reconstruction," *Journal of American Ethnic History* 32, no. 2 (Winter 2013): 73–77. A notable example of this return migration during Reconstruction was Ferdinand Lee Barnett, husband to anti-lynching activist and pioneering investigative journalist Ida B. Wells. Barnett moved as an infant with his family from Nashville, Tennessee, to Windsor, Ontario, circa 1860. The Barnetts left Windsor in 1870 for Chicago, where he blossomed as a journalist and civil rights attorney. See F. L. Barnett, "Golden Wedding of Colored Couple: First Event of the Kind in Local History Celebrated by Mr. and Mrs. F. L. Barnett," *Chicago Daily Tribune*, 28 June 1897, 5; and St. Clair Drake and Horace Cayton, *Black Metropolis: A Study of Negro Life in a Northern City* (Chicago: University of Chicago Press, 1945), 398–99.

62. The Emigration Convention to the Association for the Promotion of the Interest of the Colored People of Canada and the United States in 1858 commissioned Delany's Niger expedition, which Delany understood as promoting the political interests of African descendants in the United States and Canada. See Martin R. Delany and Robert Campbell, *Search for a Place: Black Separatism and Africa, 1860* (Ann Arbor: University of Michigan Press, 1969); Martin R. Delany, *The Condition, Elevation, Emigration, and Destiny of the Colored People of the United States* (New York: Arno Press, 1968); Victor Ullman, *Martin R. Delany: The Beginnings of Black*

Nationalism (Boston: Beacon Press, 1971); Mary Ann Shadd, *A Plea for Emigration; or, Notes of Canada West, in Its Moral, Social, and Political Aspect: with Suggestions respecting Mexico, W. Indies and Vancouver Island, for the Information of Colored Emigrants* (Detroit: George W. Pattison, 1852); Cyril E. Griffith, *The African Dream: Martin R. Delany and the Emergence of Pan-African Thought* (University Park: Pennsylvania State University Press, 1975); Edwin S. Redkey, *Black Exodus: Black Nationalist and Back-to-Africa Movements, 1890–1910* (New Haven, Conn.: Yale University Press, 1969); August Meier, *Negro Thought in America, 1880–1915: Racial Ideologies in the Age of Booker T. Washington* (Ann Arbor: University of Michigan Press, 1966); and Winston James, *The Struggles of John Brown Russwurm: The Life and Writings of a Pan-Africanist Pioneer, 1799–1851* (New York: New York University Press, 2016). On Maroon communities as Pan-Africanist projects, see Tolagbe Ogunleye, "The Self-Emancipated Africans of Florida: Pan-African Nationalists in the 'New World,'" *Journal of Black Studies* 27, no. 1 (1996): 24–27.

63. Sterling Stuckey, *Slave Culture: Nationalist Theory and the Foundations of Black America* (1987; repr., New York: Oxford University Press, 2013); Michael Gomez, *Exchanging Our Country Marks: The Transformation of African Identities in the Colonial and Antebellum South* (Chapel Hill: University of North Carolina Press, 1998); Steven Hahn, *A Nation under Our Feet: Black Political Struggles in the Rural South from Slavery to the Great Migration* (Cambridge, Mass.: Harvard University Press, 2003); Mathieu, *North of the Color Line*; Winston James, *Holding Aloft the Banner of Ethiopia: Caribbean Radicalism in Early Twentieth-Century America* (New York: Verso, 1998); Paul Gilroy, *The Black Atlantic: Modernity and Double Consciousness* (Cambridge, Mass.: Harvard University Press, 1993); Kelley, "'But a Local Phase of a World Problem.'" Also influential are historians Robert Hill and Tony Martin. See Martin, *Race First*; and Robert A. Hill, ed., *The Marcus Garvey and Universal Negro Improvement Association Papers*, 12 vols. (Berkeley: University of California Press, 1983–2011).

64. The concept of "interactional history" is "an attempt to go beyond the national story and get at some of the fragments without losing coherence in the telling of the tale." See Peter van der Veer, *Imperial Encounters: Religion and Modernity in India and Britain* (Princeton, N.J.: Princeton University Press, 2001), 8. See also Slate, *Colored Cosmopolitanism*, 3.

65. As chapters 5 and 6 prove, Black Power in the 1960s and 1970s encouraged collaboration between Washington and Ottawa. See also Quito Swan, *Black Power in Bermuda: The Struggle for Decolonization* (New York: Palgrave Macmillan, 2009), 1–9, 53–75.

66. Carl C. Berger, *The Writing of Canadian History: Aspects of English-Canadian Historical Writing since 1900* (Toronto: University of Toronto Press, 1986), 137–59. See also Thomas Bender, ed., *Rethinking American History in a Global Age* (Berkeley: University of California Press, 2002).

67. Edmund Walker, *Address: Delivered by Sir Edmund Walker, C.V.O., L.L.D., D.C.L., before the International Convention of Life Underwriters* (New York, s.n., 1918), 28.

68. Berger, *Writing of Canadian History*, 137–59. See also Robert S. Bothwell, *Your Country, My Country: A Unified History of the United States and Canada* (New

York: Oxford University Press, 2015); and Benjamin Hoy, *A Line of Blood and Dirt: Creating the Canada-United States Border across Indigenous Lands* (New York: Oxford University Press, 2021). For an anthology that examined the Black experience in the British, French, and Spanish Caribbean and Brazil and Haiti, as well as Black history in the United States and Canada, see Charles H. Wesley, ed., *The Negro in the Americas* (Washington, D.C.: Howard University Press, 1940).

69. See Herbert E. Bolton, "The Epic of Greater America," *American Historical Review* 38, no. 3 (1933): 448–74; Lewis Hanke, ed., *Do the Americas Have a Common History? A Critique of the Bolton Theory* (New York: Alfred A. Knopf, 1964); J. H. Elliott, *Do the Americas Have a Common History? An Address* (Providence, R.I.: John Carter Brown Library, 1996). See also Eric Rutkow, *The Longest Line on the Map: The United States, the Pan-American Highway, and the Quest to Link the Americas* (New York: Simon and Schuster, 2019).

70. Most African Canadians in pre- and post-Confederation Canada lived in Central and Eastern Canada. In Canada, one historian pointed out, "any historical study is limited by this unequal population distribution." See Leo Bertley, *Canada and Its People of African Descent* (Pierrefonds, Que.: Bilongo Publishers, 1977), x. In Nova Scotia, where transplanted enslaved Africans from the United States lobbied for full equality after the Revolutionary War and War of 1812, the British mobilized Jamaican Maroons to oppress the local Black population, which, understandably, left the latter embittered and distrustful of outsiders. See Whitfield, *North to Bondage*; Whitfield, *Blacks on the Border*; Brian D. Tennyson, ed., *Canada and the Commonwealth Caribbean* (Lanham, Md.: University Press of America, 1988); James Lockett, "The Deportation of the Maroons of Trelawny Town to Nova Scotia, then Back to Africa," *Journal of Black Studies* 30, no. 1 (1999): 5–14; and John N. Grant, "Black Immigrants into Nova Scotia, 1776–1815," *Journal of Negro History* 58, no. 3 (1973): 253–70. On enslaved and free Black people and their descendants in Prince Edward Island, see Jim Hornby, *Prince Edward Island's Historical Black Community* (Charlottetown, P.E.I.: Institute of Island Studies, 1991). See also W. A. Spray, *The Blacks in New Brunswick* (Fredericton: N.B.: Brunswick Press, 1972); Elizabeth Beaton, "An African-American Community in Cape Breton, 1901–1904," *Acadiensis* 24, no. 32 (1995): 65–97. Twentieth-century Caribbean immigrants who moved to Nova Scotia maintained a cross-border, cosmopolitan outlook, despite living on the eastern edge of the North American continent. Prior to arriving on the North American mainland, some had traveled from English-speaking islands to Cuba, where they learned Spanish fluently. They immigrated to New York City and later relocated to Nova Scotia. Family and social networks in the eastern United States, Nova Scotia and Ontario, and the Caribbean encouraged serial border crossings. See Mayann Francis, *Mayann Francis: An Honorable Life* (Halifax, N.S.: Nimbus Publishing, 2019), 8–20.

71. Edward Blyden, Marcus Garvey, W. E. B. Du Bois, Amy Ashwood Garvey, Amy Jacques Garvey, George Padmore, C. L. R. James, and countless other Caribbean and U.S. intellectuals and revolutionaries helped awaken the political imagination and racial consciousness of African statesmen in the years leading up to the independence struggle. Many African statesmen from Kwame Nkrumah to Nnamdi Azikiwe studied in the United States and at historically Black colleges and universities. See

Kevin Gaines, *American Africans in Ghana: Black Expatriates and the Civil Rights Era* (Chapel Hill: University of North Carolina Press, 2006); James C. Parker, "'Made-in-America Revolutions'? The 'Black University' and the American Role in the Decolonization of the Black Atlantic," *Journal of American History* 96, no. 3 (2009): 727–50; W. James, *Holding Aloft the Banner of Ethiopia*; and W. James, "Caribbean Diaspora and Black Internationalism," 255, 261. On the "persistence of the West Indian factor," see Shepperson, "Pan-Africanism and 'Pan-Africanism,'" 356. Two important works illuminate the genealogies of Pan-Africanisms in Africa. See J. Ayodele Langley, *Pan-Africanism and Nationalism in West Africa, 1900–1945* (Oxford, U.K.: Clarendon Press, 1973); and Robert W. July, *The Origins of Modern African Thought: Its Development in West Africa during the Nineteenth and Twentieth Centuries* (New York: F. A. Praeger, 1967).

72. Ras Makonnen, *Pan-Africanism from Within*, recorded and ed. Kenneth King (Nairobi: Oxford University Press, 1973), 280–82.

73. Rodney, "Towards the Sixth Pan-African Congress," 729–39.

74. Rickford, *We Are an African People*, 132.

75. Marcus Garvey, "Address at Newport News (1919)," in *Classical Black Nationalism: From the American Revolution to Marcus Garvey*, ed. Wilson Jeremiah Moses (New York: New York University Press, 1996), 248–249.

76. Wilson Jeremiah Moses, *The Golden Age of Black Nationalism, 1850–1925* (Hamden, Conn.: Archon Books, 1978), 17, 30.

77. The UNIA's organization of the masses differed from the ways that Black elites maneuvered colonialism at the turn of the twentieth century. Garveyites sought capital accumulation to improve the material conditions and physical security of the masses. Some—although not all—elites promoted a type of Pan-Africanism based on capital accumulation for the few. See Judith Stein, *The World of Marcus Garvey: Race and Class in Modern Society* (Baton Rouge: Louisiana State University Press, 1991), 7–23.

78. Before the seismically disruptive and genocidal transatlantic slave trade, the Arab slave trade had "shattered the foundations of African nations and cultures." This "catastrophe would scatter African people to the four corners of the earth." Clarke, "Pan-Africanism," 28. See also Michael Gomez, *African Dominion: A New History of Empire in Early and Medieval West Africa* (Princeton, N.J.: Princeton University Press, 2018).

79. See Wilson J. Moses, *Alexander Crummell: A Study of Civilization and Discontent* (Oxford: Oxford University Press, 1989); Delany and Campbell, *Search for a Place*; and Tunde Adeleke, *UnAfrican Americans: Nineteenth-Century Black Nationalists and the Civilizing Mission* (Lexington: University of Kentucky Press, 1998). The Christianizing or civilizing mission did not begin with African Americans or West Indian missionaries. A few eighteenth-century Europeanized Africans propagated the idea that Christianity was compatible with slavery. See Jacobus Capitein and Grant R. Parker, eds., *The Agony of Asar: A Thesis on Slavery by the Former Slave, Jacobus Elisa Johannes Capitein, 1717–1747* (Princeton, N.J.: Marcus Wiener, 2001). This "cultural assimilationism," which amounted to elitism and excessive emulation of European systems, hamstrung Pan-Africanisms' ability to liberate the African masses. See Basil Davidson, *The Black Man's Burden: Africa and the Curse of the Nation-State* (London: James Currey, 1992).

80. M'buyinga, *Pan-Africanism or Neo-Colonialism?*

81. Stein, *World of Marcus Garvey*, 272.

82. "Balkanization" of African Canadians obscures ethnic, regional, and cultural differences. George E. Clarke, *Odysseys Home: Mapping African-Canadian Literature* (Toronto: University of Toronto Press, 2002), 28.

83. Generic applications of patriarchy to Pan-Africanisms and other forms of Black liberation are empirically inaccurate, lack rigor, and imply that Black men seek not only to mimic their oppressors but also to possess similar power. Patriarchy is principally about the conquest, subordination, and extermination of boys and men from undesired groups. In no instance have Black men in Pan-Africanist liberation struggles sought to carry out this pattern of "gendercide." Male chauvinism existed within some pockets of Black liberation movements, but these ideas were never representative of larger social movements. Male chauvinism alone, moreover, lacked the genocidal imperative of patriarchy. See Tommy J. Curry, *The Man-Not: Race, Class, Genre, and the Dilemmas of Black Manhood* (Philadelphia: Temple University Press, 2017); Errol Miller, *Men at Risk* (Kingston, Jam.: Jamaican Publishing House, 1991), 342; Adam Jones, "Gender and Gendercide," *Journal of Genocide Research* 2, no. 2 (June 2000): 185–211; Augusta C. Del Zotto, "Gendercide in a Historical-Structural Context: The Case of Black Male Gendercide in the United States," in *Gendercide and Genocide*, ed. Adam Jones (Nashville: Vanderbilt University Press, 2004), 157–71; and Amy E. Randall, "Introduction: Gendering Genocide Studies," in *Genocide and Gender in the Twentieth Century: A Comparative Study*, ed. Amy E. Randall (New York: Bloomsbury), 1–34. On women and Pan-Africanisms, see Gerald Horne, *Race Woman: The Lives of Shirley Graham Du Bois* (New York: New York University Press, 2000); Ula Y. Taylor, *The Veiled Garvey: The Life and Times of Amy Jacques Garvey* (Chapel Hill: University of North Carolina Press, 2002); Yevette Richards, *Maida Springer: Pan-Africanist and International Labor Leader* (Pittsburgh: University of Pittsburgh Press, 2004); Keisha N. Blain, *Set the World on Fire: Black Nationalist Women and the Global Struggle for Freedom* (Philadelphia: University of Pennsylvania Press, 2018); E. Frances White, "Africa on My Mind: Gender, Counter Discourse and African-American Nationalism," *Journal of Women's History* 2, no. 1 (Spring 1990): 73–97; Keisha N. Blain, Asia Leeds, and Ula Y. Taylor, "Women, Gender Politics, and Pan-Africanism," *Women, Gender, and Families of Color* 4, no. 2 (Fall 2016): 139–45; and Ashley D. Farmer, "Mothers of Pan-Africanism: Audley Moore and Dara Abubakari," *Women, Gender, and Families of Color* 4, no. 2 (Fall 2016): 274–95.

84. On Garveyism, see Theodore G. Vincent, *Black Power and the Garvey Movement* (Berkeley: Ramparts Press, 1971); Martin, *Race First*; Hill, *Marcus Garvey and Universal Negro Improvement Association Papers*; Stein, *World of Marcus Garvey*; Taylor, *Veiled Garvey*; and Robert Trent Vinson, *The Americans Are Coming! Dreams of African American Liberation in Segregationist South Africa* (Athens: Ohio University Press, 2012). For a gendered analysis on diasporic Black collectivism, see Craig Steven Wilder, *In the Company of Black Men: The African Influence on African American Culture in New York City* (New York: New York University Press, 2001). See also St. Clair Drake, "The Black Diaspora in Pan-African Perspective," *Black Scholar* 7, no. 1 (September 1975): 2–13; and St. Clair Drake, "Pan-Africanism

and Diaspora," in *Global Dimensions of the African Diaspora*, ed. Joseph E. Harris, 2nd ed. (Washington, D.C.: Howard University Press, 1993), 451–514. Although racial essentialism can permeate Garveyism or notions of Africanity or blackness, Pan-Africanisms are more complex and multidimensional. Critics often point to the essentialist and romantic nature of Pan-Africanisms and note that creating a movement based on race, a European concept, is regressive. Such critiques seem to overlook the fact that proponents of Pan-Africanisms in the Atlantic World had endured genocidal exploitation in the Americas, not to mention that African peoples, for centuries, had cultivated a "racial" consciousness to resist anti-blackness and bondage under non-European systems—Maghrebi, Ottoman, Levantine, Arabian, and Indian. Diasporic Africans understood their ethnic differences yet willingly chose to organize themselves based on the principal marker that enslavers who sought to exploit their labor could not erase—their blackness or African origin. On critiques of Pan-Africanisms, see Kwame Anthony Appiah, *In My Father's House: Africa in the Philosophy of Culture* (New York: Oxford University Press, 1992), 28–46, 73–84; Gilroy, *Black Atlantic*; and Tunde Adeleke, *The Case against Afrocentrism* (Jackson: University of Mississippi Press, 2009).

85. Arleigh M. Holder interview with Ralph Budd, 2 August 1978, BLA-5123-BUD, MHSO.

86. Philip D. Curtin, *The Atlantic Slave Trade: A Census* (Madison: University of Wisconsin Press, 1969).

87. Some African Americans and West Indians expressed admiration and scorn for each other. See Clarence E. Walker, *Deromanticizing Black History: Critical Essays and Reappraisals* (Knoxville: University of Tennessee Press, 1991), 41–42. Some elite African Americans referred to the UNIA as "Ugly Negroes in America." Author's interview with Ato Seitu (former Ainsley Vaughan), 10 May 2021, notes in author's possession.

88. Holder interview with Budd, BLA-5123-BUD, MHSO. See also W. James, *Holding Aloft the Banner of Ethiopia*; Irma Watkins-Owens, *Blood Relations: Caribbean Immigrants and the Harlem Community, 1900–1930* (Bloomington: Indiana University Press, 1996); James W. St. G. Walker, *The West Indians in Canada* (Ottawa: Canadian Historical Association, 1984); Lara Putnam, "Borderlands and Border-Crossers: Migrants and Boundaries in the Greater Caribbean, 1840–1940," *Small Axe* 42 (2014): 7–21; Jared Toney, "Locating Diaspora: Afro-Caribbean Narratives of Migration and Settlement in Toronto, 1914–1929," *Urban History Review* 38, no. 2 (2010): 75–87; Sheldon Taylor, "Darkening the Complexion of Canadian Society: Black Activism, Policy-Making, and Black Immigration from the Caribbean to Canada, 1940s–1960s" (Ph.D. diss., University of Toronto, 1994); and Yaa Amoaba Gooden, "'Betta Must Come': African Caribbean Migrants in Canada: Migration, Community Building and Cultural Legacies" (Ph.D. diss., Temple University, 2005).

89. I credit Sheldon Taylor for alerting me to the plural "Middle Passages." Historians have documented Africans' initial horrific traversing of the Atlantic but place less emphasis on crossings in the Americas when enslavers bought and resold African peoples. See also J. Campbell, *Middle Passages*. Campbell's book details African American repatriation to Africa, which was integral to Pan-Africanisms.

90. On the vagueness of Woodrow Wilson's notion of self-determination, see Margaret MacMillan, *Paris 1919: Six Months That Changed the World* (New York: Random House, 2001), 11. On the reinvention of self-determination, see Adom Getachew, *Worldmaking after Empire: The Rise and Fall of Self-Determination* (Princeton, N.J.: Princeton University Press, 2019), 74.

91. Ronald W. Walters, *Pan Africanism in the African Diaspora: An Analysis of Modern Afrocentric Political Movements* (Detroit: Wayne State University Press, 1997), 41.

92. G. Williams, *History of the Negro Race in America from 1619 to 1880*, 19.

93. One scholar pointed out that "Black cosmopolitanism" is a world where, for diasporic Africans, "borders are rendered invisible by the power of hybridity and syncretism." See Babacar M'Baye, "Richard Wright and African Francophone Intellectuals: A Reassessment of the 1956 Congress of Black Writers in Paris," *African and Black Diaspora: An International Journal* 2, no. 1 (January 2009): 31. See also W. Jeffrey Bolster, *Black Jacks: African American Seamen in the Age of Sail* (Cambridge, Mass.: Harvard University Press, 1997); and Alexander Byrd, *Captives and Voyagers: Black Migrants across the Eighteenth-Century British Atlantic World* (Baton Rouge: Louisiana State University Press, 2008). On cultural retentions, see Melville Herskovits, *The Myth of the Negro Past* (Boston: Beacon Press, 1958); Paul E. Lovejoy, ed., *Trans-Atlantic Dimensions of Ethnicity in the African Diaspora* (New York: Continuum, 2003); and Jacoby Adeshei Carter, ed., *African American Contributions to the Americas' Cultures: A Critical Edition of Lectures by Alain Locke* (New York: Palgrave Macmillan, 2016) where Locke discussed the "Negro in the Three Americas."

94. For a recent and riveting account, see Lisa A. Lindsay, *Atlantic Bonds: A Nineteenth-Century Odyssey from America to Africa* (Chapel Hill: University of North Carolina Press, 2019).

95. Pan-Africanisms, specifically Garveyism and Ethiopianism, included a Black intelligentsia that leveraged icons of national sentiment, the construction of myths to instill pride in a transnational racial community, the role of elites in credentialing these myths and racial sentiments, and the importance of culture and landmarks as tools of propaganda. On the making of an ethnic national consciousness, see John E. Zucchi, *Italians in Toronto: Development of a National Identity, 1875–1935* (Montreal: McGill-Queens's University Press, 1988), 7–8. See also Benedict Anderson, *Imagined Communities: Reflections on the Origins and Spread of Nationalism*, rev. ed. (London: Verso, 1991); and W. James, "Caribbean Diaspora and Black Internationalism," 256.

96. Winston James, "Harlem's Difference," in *Race Capital? Harlem as Setting and Symbol*, ed. Andrew M. Fearnley and Daniel Matlin (New York: Columbia University Press, 2018), 133–34. Recent emphasis on a race-blind or race-neutral Afropolitanism is problematic at best and dangerous at worst, because it trivializes the persistence—millennia-old struggle, to be precise—of anti-blackness in non-Black peoples' interactions with Black peoples. Equally problematic are analyses on Afropolitanism that perpetuate the myth that African peoples and cultures would achieve liberation from anti-blackness, imperialism, and neocolonialism by embracing modernity. This notion of a cosmopolitan modernity overlooks the fact

that cosmopolitanism has deep roots in multiethnic, multicultural, multilingual, and spiritually syncretic African societies. See Sarah Balakrishnan, "Afropolitanism and the End of Black Nationalism," in *Routledge International Handbook of Cosmopolitanism Studies*, ed. Gerard Delanty, 2nd ed. (London: Routledge, 2018), 575–85.

97. See Ifeoma Nwankwo, *Black Cosmopolitanism: Racial Consciousness and Transnational Identity in the Nineteenth-Century Americas* (Philadelphia: University of Pennsylvania Press, 2005). On cosmopolitanism, see Kwame A. Appiah, *Cosmopolitanism: Ethics in a World of Strangers* (New York: W. W. Norton, 2006); and Achille Mbembe and Sarah Balakrishnan, "Pan-African Legacies, Afropolitan Futures," *Transition* 120, no. 4 (2016): 28–37. See also Joseph E. Harris, ed., *Global Dimensions of the African Diaspora*, 2nd ed. (Washington, D.C.: Howard University Press, 1993); Darlene Clark Hine and Jacqueline McLeod, eds., *Crossing Boundaries: Comparative History of Black People in Diaspora* (Bloomington: Indiana University Press, 1999); Okpewho, Davies, and Mazrui, *The African Diaspora*; Sidney J. Lemelle and Robin D. G. Kelley, eds., *Imagining Home: Class, Culture, and Nationalism in the African Diaspora* (New York: Verso, 1994); Michael Gomez, *Reversing Sail: A History of the African Diaspora* (New York: Cambridge University Press, 2005); Brent Hayes Edwards, *The Practice of Diaspora: Literature, Translation, and the Rise of Black Internationalism* (Cambridge, Mass.: Harvard University Press, 2003); Michelle Ann Stephens, *Black Empire: The Masculine Global Imaginary of Caribbean Intellectuals in the United States, 1914–1962* (Durham, N.C.: Duke University Press, 2005); Tiffany R. Patterson and Robin D. G. Kelley, "Unfinished Migrations: Reflections on the African Diaspora and the Making of the Modern World," *African Studies Review* 43, no. 1 (April 2000): 11–45; Jopi Nyman, ed., *Post-National Enquiries: Essays on Ethnic and Racial Border Crossing* (Newcastle upon Tyne, U.K.: Cambridge Scholars Publishing, 2009); and Alexa Weik von Mossner, *Cosmopolitan Minds: Literature, Emotion, and the Transnational Imagination* (Austin: University of Texas Press, 2014).

98. Julius K. Nyerere, "Julius K. Nyerere's Speech to the Congress," *Black Scholar* 5, no. 10 (1974): 19.

99. In 1937, Garvey explained in an interview, "We were the first Fascists. We had disciplined men, women, and children in training for the liberation of Africa. The Black masses saw that in this extreme nationalism lay their only hope and readily supported it. Mussolini copied fascism from me, but the Negro reactionaries sabotaged it." Garvey's remarks not only preceded the Holocaust, but he had also denounced Nazi Germany's persecution of Jews and Mussolini's invasion of Ethiopia. Garvey died in June 1940, so he did not witness the horrors that Italian and German fascism unleashed on the world and the subsequent hyper taboo that people would associate with the word "fascism." One must underscore, regardless, that never did Garvey endorse anti-labour, genocide, ethnic cleansing, or population displacement of any racial group. His obsessive preoccupation was the complete liberation of African peoples from systems of anti-Black subordination and subjugation at home and abroad. Garvey even publicly denounced Ethiopian emperor Haile Selassie for enslaving Black people in his country in the 1930s. For Garvey quote, see Paul Gilroy, "Black Fascism," *Transition*, no. 8 (2000): 70. Racial nationalism, even among Black people, as Nyerere asserted, was limiting. When deployed critically and as a

defensive mechanism, however, it was the most radical option for Black people who had suffered global anti-Black exploitation for millennia.

100. English has been the principal language of Pan-Africanisms. See W. James, "Caribbean Diaspora and Black Internationalism," 254–55.

101. On diasporic Africans and cross-border U.S.-Mexico connections, see Alice L. Baumgartner, *South to Freedom: Runaway Slaves to Mexico and the Road to the Civil War* (New York: Basic Books, 2020); Gerald Horne, *Black and Brown: African Americans and the Mexican Revolution, 1910–1920* (New York: New York University Press, 2005); Bruce A. Glasrud and Cary D. Wintz, *African Americans in South Texas History* (College Station: Texas A&M University Press, 2011); Debra L. Shutika, *Beyond the Borderlands: Migration and Belonging in the United States and Mexico* (Berkeley: University of California Press, 2011); George H. Junne, *Blacks in the American West and Beyond: America, Canada, and Mexico: A Selectively Annotated Bibliography* (Westport, Conn.: Greenwood Press, 2000); and Julian Lim, *Porous Borders: Multiracial Migrations and the Law in the U.S.-Mexico Borderlands* (Chapel Hill: University of North Carolina Press, 2017). See also Herman L. Bennett, *Colonial Blackness: A History of Afro-Mexico* (Bloomington: Indiana University Press, 2009); and Alicia Schmidt Camacho, *Migrant Imaginaries: Latino Cultural Politics in the U.S.-Mexico Borderlands* (New York: New York University Press, 2008).

102. See Holly M. Karibo and George T. Díaz, *Border Policing: A History of Enforcement and Evasion in North America* (Austin: University of Texas Press, 2020); Kelly Little Hernandez, *Migra!: A History of the U.S. Border Patrol* (Berkeley: University of California Press, 2010). Considering scholars' overwhelming focus on the U.S.-Mexican border, the Great Lakes offer specialists of U.S. borderlands history new possibilities of inquiry. See also John J. Bukowczyk et al., eds., *Permeable Border: The Great Lakes Basin as a Transnational Region, 1650–1990* (Pittsburgh: University of Pittsburgh Press, 2005); and Benjamin Bryce and Alexander Freund, eds., *Entangling Migration History: Borderlands and Transnationalism in the United States and Canada* (Gainesville: University of Florida Press, 2015).

103. The UNIA was thoroughly organized in Latin America. Jamaican expatriates elevated Garveyism. See Marc C. McLeod, "'Sin dejar de ser cubanos': Cuban Blacks and the Challenges of Garveyism in Cuba," *Caribbean Studies* 31, no. 1 (2003): 75–105; Frank Andre Guridy, *Forging Diaspora: Afro-Cubans and African Americans in a World of Empire and Jim Crow* (Chapel Hill: University of North Carolina Press, 2010), 61–106; and W. James, *Holding Aloft the Banner of Ethiopia*, 195–257. Cuba served as a haven for African American revolutionaries. See Assata Shakur, *Assata: An Autobiography* (Chicago: Lawrence Hill Books, 2001); and Timothy B. Tyson, *Radio Free Dixie: Robert F. Williams and Roots of Black Power* (Chapel Hill: University of North Carolina Press, 1999). See also Jorge Duany, *Blurred Borders: Transnational Migration between the Hispanic Caribbean and the United States* (Chapel Hill: University of North Carolina Press, 2011); and Nwankwo, *Black Cosmopolitanism*. Nwankwo examines racial consciousness in the United States, Cuba, and the British West Indies. See also Rayford W. Logan, *Haiti and the Dominican Republic* (New York: Oxford University Press, 1968). On U.S. imperialism and Haiti, see Hans P. Schmidt, *The United States Occupation of Haiti, 1915–1934* (New Brunswick: Rutgers University Press, 1995); Brenda Gayle Plummer, *Haiti and the Great*

Powers, 1902–1915 (Baton Rouge: Louisiana State University, 1988); Millery Polyné, *From Douglass to Duvalier: U.S. African Americans, Haiti, and Pan Americanism, 1870–1964* (Gainesville: University of Florida Press, 2010); Sean Mills, *A Place in the Sun: Haiti, Haitians, and the Remaking of Quebec* (Montreal: McGill-Queen's University Press, 2016); and Christina C. Davidson, "Disruptive Silences: The AME Church and Dominican-Haitian Relations," *Journal of Africana Religions* 5, no. 1 (2017): 1–25.

104. Rodney, "Towards the Sixth Pan-African Congress"; Robert Hill, "Walter Rodney and the Restatement of Pan-Africanism in Theory and Practice," *Ufahamu: A Journal of African Studies* 38, no. 3 (1995): 146. See also A. James Arnold, *Modernism and Negritude: The Poetry and Poetics of Aimé Césaire* (Cambridge, Mass.: Harvard University Press, 1981); and Edwards, *Practice of Diaspora*. Some works of Négritude had a more radical, class-conscious, and structural analysis. See Franz Fanon, *Black Skin, White Masks* (London: Pluto, 2008); Aimé Césaire, *Discourse on Colonialism* (1955; repr., New York: Monthly Review Press, 2000); and Aimé Césaire, *Return to My Native Land* (Baltimore: Penguin Books, 1969).

105. See Elisa Larkin Nascimento, *Pan-Africanism and South America: Emergence of a Black Rebellion* (Buffalo, N.Y.: Afrodiaspora, 1980); Abdias do Nascimento and Elisa Larkin Nascimento, *Africans in Brazil: A Pan-African Perspective* (Trenton, N.J.: Africa World Press, 1992); and Anthony Ratcliff, "'Black Writers of the World, Unite!' Negotiating Pan-African Politics of Cultural Struggle in Afro-Latin America," *Black Scholar* 37, no. 4 (2008): 27–38. On gender and Black racial consciousness, see John Burdick, *Blessed Anastacia: Women, Race and Popular Christianity in Brazil* (New York: Routledge, 2013). On the ways that the Brazilian government uses Lusophone countries to subvert Pan-Africanisms, see W. E. Hewitt, Sean Burges, and Inês Gomes, "The Comunidade dos Países de Língua Portuguesa at 20 Years: An Impact Assessment," *South African Journal of International Affairs* 24, no. 3 (2017): 291–309.

106. Robert Farris Thompson's work on Africanisms in the Americas is a constructive template. One of his works refers to "African Americas." Thompson, in fact, coined the phrase "Black Atlantic," which his scholarship over several decades illuminated. See Robert Farris Thompson, *Face of the Gods: Art and Altars of Africa and the African Americas* (New York: Museum for African Art, 1993).

107. Canada's proximity to the United States and status as a Commonwealth jewel in the Americas gave it broad appeal among diasporic Africans. Although Gilroy's "Black Atlantic" formulation mostly overlooks Canada, he cites African American musician Donald Byrd's sentiments about Canada while growing up in Detroit. See Gilroy, *Black Atlantic*, 18; and George Elliott Clarke, "Must All Blackness Be American? Locating Canada in Borden's 'Tightrope Time,' or Nationalizing Gilroy's *The Black Atlantic*," *Canadian Ethnic Studies* 28, no. 3 (1996): 56–71. For an important intervention on diasporic Africans in Canada, see Mathieu, *North of the Color Line*. See also Karen Flynn, *Moving beyond Borders: A History of Black Canadian and Caribbean Women in the Diaspora* (Toronto: University of Toronto Press, 2011). Robin Winks's study on African Canadians was foundational; however, Winks was less interested in the borderland, diasporic experiences than in what occurred within the fixed boundaries of pre- and post-Confederation Canada. See Winks, *Blacks*

in Canada. See also Peggy Bristow et al., eds., *We're Rooted Here and They Can't Pull Us Up: Essays in African Canadian Women's History* (Toronto: University of Toronto Press, 1994); Dione Brand, *No Burden to Carry: Narratives of Black Working Women in Ontario, 1920s–1950s* (Toronto: Women's Press, 1991); Barrington Walker, *Race on Trial: Black Defendants in Ontario's Criminal Courts, 1858–1958* (Toronto: University of Toronto Press, 2010); Constance Backhouse, *Colour-Coded: A Legal History of Racism in Canada, 1900–1950* (Toronto: University of Toronto Press, 1999); James W. St. G. Walker, *"Race," Rights and the Law in the Supreme Court of Canada: Historical Case Studies* (Waterloo, Ont.: Wilfrid Laurier University Press, 1997); Mills, *Place in the Sun*; David Austin, *Fear of a Black Nation: Race, Sex, and Security in Sixties Montreal* (Toronto: Between the Lines, 2013); Peter James Hudson and Aaron Kamugisha, "On Black Canadian Thought," *CLR James Journal* 20, no. 1/2 (2014): 3–20; Paula Hastings, "Territorial Spoils, Transnational Black Resistance, and Canada's Evolving Autonomy during the First World War," *Social History* 47, no. 94 (2014): 443–70; Charmaine A. Nelson, ed., *Ebony Roots, Northern Soil: Perspectives on Blackness in Canada* (Newcastle upon Tyne, U.K.: Cambridge Scholars Publishing, 2010); Laura Madokoro, Francine McKenzie, and David Meren, eds., *Dominion of Race: Rethinking Canada's International* (Vancouver: University of British Columbia Press, 2017); and Karen Dubinsky, Adele Perry, and Henry Yu, eds., *Within and without the Nation: Canadian History as Transnational History* (Toronto: University of Toronto Press, 2015).

108. On gendercide, see Jones, "Gender and Gendercide"; Del Zotto, "Gendercide in a Historical-Structural Context"; and Randall, "Introduction: Gendering Genocide Studies."

109. See Philip Jenkins, *Mystics and Messiahs: Cults and New Religions in American History* (New York: Oxford University Press, 2000).

110. Logan, *Negro in American Life and Thought*.

111. The paradox of progress draws conceptual inspiration from the interplay between freedom and slavery. Edmund Morgan, reflecting on the intimacy between chattel slavery and freedom, expounded this contradiction authoritatively. Morgan argued that the plantocracy and founding fathers predicated the freedom of white people in the colonial period and early republic on the enslavement of Black people. "The rights of Englishmen," Morgan wrote, "were preserved by destroying the rights of Africans." This fundamental premise enabled U.S. republicanism. See "Slavery and Freedom: The American Paradox," *Journal of American History* 59, no. 1 (1977): 24. See also Morgan, *American Slavery, American Freedom: The Ordeal of Colonial Virginia* (New York: Norton, 1975). Pre-Confederation Canada had its own paradox of progress, such as the resettlement of "Black Loyalists" in Upper Canada and the Maritimes after the U.S. Revolutionary War, on one hand, and the enslaved Africans who accompanied their Loyalist masters from the thirteen colonies, on the other. Whether nominally free or enslaved, racial caste denied African descendants their humanity in British North America. See J. Barry Cahill, "The Black Loyalist Myth in Atlantic Canada," *Acadiensis* 29, no. 1 (1999): 76–87; Whitfield, *North to Bondage* and *Blacks on the Border*; J. Walker, *Black Loyalists*; Wallace Brown, "Negroes and the American Revolution," *History Today* 14, no. 8 (August 1964): 556–63; George Elliott Clarke, "White Niggers, Black Slaves: Slavery, Race and Class in

T. C. Haliburton's *The Clockmaker*," *Nova Scotia Historical Review* 14, no. 1 (1994): 13–40; Barry Cahill, "Slavery and the Judges of Loyalist Nova Scotia," *University of New Brunswick Law Journal* 43 (1994): 73–125; and D. G. Bell, J. Barry Cahill, and Harvey Amani Whitfield, "Slavery and Slave Law in the Maritimes," in *The African Canadian Legal Odyssey: Historical Essays*, ed. Barrington Walker (Toronto: University of Toronto Press, 2012), 363–420.

112. Du Bois, "Conservation of Races," 4.

113. For "stillborn citizenship," see Adriane Lentz-Smith, *Freedom Struggles: African Americans and World War I* (Cambridge, Mass.: Harvard University Press, 2009), 11. The author refers to citizenship constrained by racial caste as subordinate citizenship, not second-class citizenship. Native-born Black citizens were multiple rungs below white citizens, because "ethnic" groups—such as Italians, Irish, and Jews—were a buffer between Black and white citizens. Not all European immigrants and their descendants enjoyed immediate preferential racial treatment in the United States and Canada. Racial stratification among European immigrants persisted in the nineteenth and early twentieth centuries. "Ethnic" Europeans jockeyed for position and status based on North America's racial logic of Anglo and Nordic supremacy on one hand and the subordination of Black and Indigenous peoples on the other. See Noel Ignatiev, *How the Irish Became White* (London: Routledge, 2008); Thomas A. Guglielmo, *White on Arrival: Italians, Race, Color, and Power in Chicago, 1890–1945* (Oxford: Oxford University Press, 2003); Matthew Jacobson, *Whiteness of a Different Color: European Immigrants and the Alchemy of Race* (Cambridge, Mass.: Harvard University Press, 1998); Neil Foley, *The White Scourge: Mexicans, Blacks, and Poor Whites in Texas Cotton Culture* (Berkley: University of California Press, 1997); Pierre Vallières, *White Niggers of America: The Precocious Autobiography of a Québec "Terrorist,"* trans. Joan Pink (New York: Monthly Review Press, 1971); John A. Porter, *The Vertical Mosaic: An Analysis of Social Class and Power in Canada* (Toronto: University of Toronto Press, 1965); and Joseph Costisella, *The Scandal of Canadian Racism: Quebec, a Ghetto for French Canadians* (Ottawa, Ont.: Comité Canadien Français de Vigilance, 1963).

CHAPTER 1

1. Questions over Christianity's liberating power have endured throughout the African American experience. See Mark L. Chapman, *Christianity on Trial: African-American Religious Thought before and after Black Power* (Maryknoll, N.Y.: Orbis Books, 1996).

2. Henry Louis Gates Jr. and Gene Andrew Jarrett, *The New Negro: Readings on Race, Representation, and African American Culture, 1892–1938* (Princeton, N.J.: Princeton University Press, 2007), 4.

3. African American socialists placed the mob violence to which white society subjected them in broader historical context, drawing similarities to and differences from pogroms in Eastern Europe. See "Jewish Pogroms," *The Messenger*, July 1919; and Charles L. Lumpkins, *American Pogrom: The East St. Louis Race Riot and Black Politics* (Athens: Ohio University Press, 2008). On racial violence in 1919, see also William M. Tuttle Jr., *Race Riot: Chicago in the Red Summer of 1919* (Chicago: Atheneum, 1970); Barbara Foley, *Spectres of 1919: Class and Nation in the Making*

of the New Negro (Urbana: University of Illinois Press, 2008); David F. Krugler, *1919, the Year of Racial Violence: How African Americans Fought Back* (New York: Cambridge University Press, 2015); Simon Balto, *Occupied Territory: Policing Black Chicago from Red Summer to Black Power* (Chapel Hill: University of North Carolina Press, 2020); and Jonathan S. Coit, "'Our Changed Attitude': Armed Defense and the New Negro in the 1919 Chicago Race Riot," *Journal of the Gilded Age and Progressive Era* 11, no. 2 (2012): 225–56.

4. W. E. Hawkins, "When Negroes Shot a Lynching Bee into Perdition," *The Messenger*, September 1919. See also Delia Cunningham Mellis, "'The Monsters We Defy': Washington, D.C. in the Red Summer of 1919" (Ph.D. diss., City University of New York, 2008), 348–51. On vigilance groups and vigilantism in 1919, see Christopher Capozzola, *Uncle Sam Wants You: World War I and the Making of the Modern American Citizen* (New York: Oxford University Press, 2008), 118–43.

5. James E. Kennell to W. E. B. Du Bois, 28 July 1919, DBP (MS 312).

6. "Fatal Race Riot: Negro Is Killed," *The Globe* (Toronto), 3 September 1918.

7. "Minutes of the Coloured Literary Association," April 1919, Universal African Improvement Association Toronto Records 1929–1977, reel 376, MHSO. At an event in Newport News, Virginia, on 25 October 1919, Marcus Garvey acknowledged that the Great War provided invaluable military training to millions of Black men, which could serve the cause of African liberation. Robert A. Hill, ed., *The Marcus Garvey and Universal Negro Improvement Association Papers, Vol. II, 27 August 1919 to 31 August 1920* (Berkeley: University of California Press, 1983), 112–20.

8. Claude McKay, "If We Must Die," *Liberator*, July 1919.

9. Recent migrants from the South denounced a wealthy Black lawyer who had arrived in Chicago by way of Georgia and Canada in 1893 as an "Uncle Tom" for blaming the violence on Black men who "have been taught they must act on the policy of an eye for an eye and a tooth for a tooth." See "Lawyer Warns Negroes Here to Arm Selves" in St. Clair Drake and Horace R. Cayton, *Black Metropolis: A Study of Negro Life in a Northern City* (Chicago: University of Chicago Press, 1945), 65–67.

10. "Chicago Rebellion: Free Black Men Fight Free White Men," *The Messenger*, September 1919. Some African American veterans embedded in the Black Belt had fought valiantly in the 370th Regiment in France. In Grandvillars, where French civilians praised their heroism, they clashed with white U.S. soldiers who resented their notoriety and friendliness with French civilians. See William Pickens, *The Vengeance of the Gods: And Three Other Stories of Real American Color Line Life* (Philadelphia: A.M.E. Book Concern, 1922), 117–21; Emmet J. Scott, *Scott's Official History of the American Negro in the World War* (Chicago: Homewood Press, 1919).

11. "A Report on the Chicago Riot by an Eye-Witness," *The Crusader*, September 1919.

12. "Report on the Chicago Riot by an Eye-Witness." The racial violence, which coincided with the "Spanish" flu of 1918 and 1919, might have been a factor in the white death toll. For incidents relating to African Americans shooting or sniping at police officers, see Chicago Commission on Race Relation, *The Negro in Chicago: A Study of Race Relations and a Race Riot* (Chicago: University of Chicago Press, 1923). The commission debunked some of the salacious rumors and misinformation

on which the Chicago and national media reported. See also Tuttle, *Race Riot*, 40; and Coit, "'Our Changed Attitude,'" 240, 246.

13. Wilfred A. Domingo, "If We Must Die," *The Messenger*, September 1919.

14. See W. E. B. Du Bois, "Returning Soldiers," *The Crisis* 18 (May 1919): 13; Adriane Lentz-Smith, *Freedom Struggles: African Americans and World War I* (Cambridge, Mass.: Harvard University Press, 2009); Chad L. Williams, *Torchbearers of Democracy: African American Soldiers in the World War I Era* (Chapel Hill: University of North Carolina Press, 2010); and Davarian L. Baldwin and Minkah Makalani, *Escape from New York: The New Negro Renaissance beyond Harlem* (Minneapolis: University of Minnesota Press, 2013).

15. Dr. Cary Grayson Diary, 10 March 1919, *Papers of Woodrow Wilson*, 55:471, Woodrow Wilson Presidential Library and Museum, Staunton, Virginia. There were approximately fifty Black communists in the United States after the war. See Glenda E. Gilmore, *Defying Dixie: The Radical Roots of Civil Rights, 1919–1950* (New York: W. W. Norton, 2009).

16. On waning racial essentialism, see Mia Bay, *The White Image in the Black Mind: African-American Ideas about White People, 1830–1925* (New York: Oxford University Press, 2000), 187–218.

17. Benjamin E. Mays, *The Negro's God: As Reflected in His Literature* (1938; repr., Eugene, Ore.: Wipf and Stock, 2010), 16.

18. Melissa N. Shaw, "'Most Anxious to Serve Their King and Country': Black Canadians Fight to Enlist in WWI and Emerging Race Consciousness in Ontario, 1914–1919," *Social History* 49, no. 100 (2016): 543–80; Paula Hastings, "Territorial Spoils, Transnational Black Resistance, and Canada's Evolving Autonomy during the First World War," *Social History* 47, no. 94 (2014): 443–70. See also Lentz-Smith, *Freedom Struggles*; and C. Williams, *Torchbearers of Democracy*.

19. "Minutes of the Coloured Literary Association," April 1919, MHSO.

20. See pamphlet of Eureka Association, a self-help Black organization founded in 1917 Montreal to help its members become homeowners. Wilfred E. Israel, "The Montreal Negro Community," (M.A. thesis, McGill University, 1928), 218.

21. Ignatius D. Louisy et al., "The Colored Political and Protective Association of Montreal," 2, NAACP Papers, box I-G221, folder 11, 1913–1924, LOC. In December 1919, Mr. R. A. Valentine wrote to James Weldon Johnson, NAACP field secretary. Valentine enclosed a money order for fifty-six dollars representing the fifty-six founding members of the Montreal branch, which was formerly the Colored Political and Protective Association of Montreal. R. A. Valentine to James Weldon Johnson, 12 December 1919, NAACP Papers, box I-G221, folder 12, 1913–1924, LOC. J. W. Johnson acknowledged the initial success of the Windsor, Ontario, branch and the failure of the Toronto branch. Johnson to Valentine, 23 September 1919, NAACP Papers, box I-G221, folder 12, 1913–1924, LOC. See also Shaw, "'Most Anxious to Serve Their King and Country,'" 576.

22. On "the nadir," see Rayford Logan, *Negro in American Life and Thought: The Nadir, 1877–1901* (New York: Collier Books, 1965). One could point to 1865 to 1930 as the low point of Canadian race relations. See Robin Winks, *The Blacks in Canada: A History*, 2nd ed. (Montreal: McGill-Queen's University Press, 1997), 288–336. This period also inspired significant Black mobilization. See Steven Hahn,

A Nation under Our Feet: Black Political Struggles in the Rural South from Slavery to the Great Migration (Cambridge, Mass.: Harvard University Press, 2005).

23. Jeannette Smith-Irvin, *Footsoldiers of the Universal Negro Improvement Association: Their Own Words* (Trenton, N.J.: Africa World Press, 1989), 3. See also Tony Martin, *Race First: The Ideological and Organizational Struggles of Marcus Garvey and the Universal Negro Improvement Association* (Westport, Conn.: Greenwood Press, 1976), 68. Martin's rigorous and nuanced analysis of Garvey and the UNIA stands in stark contradistinction to other analyses that perceived Garvey and the UNIA dismissively and derisively. See Clarence E. Walker, *Deromanticizing Black History: Critical Essays and Reappraisals* (Knoxville: University of Tennessee Press, 1991), 34–55.

24. Edmund Cronon, *Black Moses: The Story of Marcus Garvey and the Universal Negro Improvement Association* (1955; repr., Madison: University of Wisconsin Press, 1969); Martin, *Race First*; Rupert Lewis, *Marcus Garvey: Anti-Colonial Champion* (Trenton, N.J.: Africa World Press, 1988); Adam Ewing, *The Age of Garvey: How a Jamaican Activist Created a Mass Movement and Changed Global Black Politics* (Princeton, N.J.: Princeton University Press, 2017).

25. Logan, *Negro in American Life and Thought*, 11.

26. See Philip Jenkins, *Mystics and Messiahs: Cults and New Religions in American History* (New York: Oxford University Press, 2000).

27. Despite Woodrow Wilson's racism toward African Americans and disdain for colonized peoples, his rhetoric of self-determination galvanized Egyptian, Indian, Chinese, Kurdish, Jewish, and Indo-Chinese leaders, among others, to demand the liberation of their people. On the ambiguities of "self-determination" and inherent limitations as it pertained to the Paris Peace Conference and a new world order, see Margaret MacMillan, *Paris 1919: Six Months That Changed the World* (New York: Random House, 2001); and Erez Manela, *The Wilsonian Moment: Self-Determination and the International Origins of Anticolonial Nationalism* (New York: Oxford University Press, 2007). See also Marilyn Lake and Henry Reynolds, *Drawing the Global Colour Line: White Men's Countries and the International Challenge of Racial Equality* (Cambridge: Cambridge University Press, 2008); and Susan Pedersen, "Settler Colonialism at the Bar of the League of Nations," in *Settler Colonialism in the Twentieth Century: Projects, Practices, Legacies*, ed. Caroline Elkins and Susan Pederson (New York: Routledge, 2005), 113–34.

28. Ethiopianism here is concerned with North America, not separatist church movements in nineteenth- and twentieth-century Africa.

29. Wilson Jeremiah Moses, *Black Messiahs and Uncle Toms: Social and Religious Manipulations of a Religious Myth* (University Park: Pennsylvania State University Press, 1993), 4.

30. There are parallels between Pan-Africanism and Pan-Islamism. See M. Naeem Qureshi, *Pan-Islamism in British Indian Politics: A Study of the Khilafat Movement, 1918–1924* (Boston: Brill, 1999); and Lorenz M. Lüthi, *Cold Wars: Asia, the Middle East, Europe* (New York: Cambridge University Press, 2020), 307–28.

31. On "Black Zion," see William Scott, "'And Ethiopia Shall Stretch Forth Its Hands': The Origins of Ethiopianism in Afro-American Thought, 1767–1896," *Umoja* 2 (1978): 1. In their quest to imagine freedom and dignity from abject oppression,

diasporic Africans believed their messianic prophecies and quasi-spiritualism as plausible, not baseless superstition. On Black messianism, see Moses, *Black Messiahs and Uncle Toms.*

32. W. E. B. Du Bois, *The Negro* (1915; repr. New York: Cosimo Classics, 2010), 5. See also Daniel 7:9–10 (New King James Version).

33. The UNIA's invocation of Ethiopia parallels the diasporic Jewish prayer "Next year in Jerusalem!" As two archetypes of diasporic peoples who endured forced migration from an ancient homeland, Ethiopia and Jerusalem, both iconic sites with spiritual import, served as a rallying cry for descendants to remember their past as a starting point to imagining a future in exile. These references stipulated not only physical relocation to Ethiopia or Jerusalem but also the act of steadfast remembrance, which is an assertion of a diasporic people's right to self-determination. The redemptive power of the two sites rejuvenated the hopes of these diasporic peoples.

34. Alexander Crummell, a leading Pan-Africanist and theologian, aspired in his teenage years to study Greek and the classics (which he later accomplished at Cambridge University), because John C. Calhoun claimed that Black people were incapable of such advanced learning. See Wilson Jeremiah Moses, *The Wings of Ethiopia: Studies in African-American Life and Letters* (Ames: Iowa State University Press, 1990), 209. Conversely, Hubert Harrison, a prominent Pan-Africanist in the 1920s and an intellectual who was well versed in the Western classics, advocated in 1919 for Black colleges to teach less Greek and Latin and more Hausa and other native African languages. See Winston James, *Holding Aloft the Banner of Ethiopia: Caribbean Radicalism in Early Twentieth-Century America* (New York: Verso, 1998), 130. See also Robbie Shilliam, "'Ethiopia Shall Stretch Forth Her Hands unto God': Garveyism, Rastafari, and Antiquity," in *African Athena: New Agendas*, ed. Daniel Orrells, Gurminder K. Bhambra, and Tessa Roynon (New York: Oxford University Press, 2011), 107–21.

35. Although there are strong theoretical and methodological similarities, this chapter does not automatically interpret nineteenth- and early twentieth-century Black scholars' reflection on or invocation of Ethiopia (or Egypt) as "Afrocentric." Not only is this tendency anachronistic, but it also overlooks the fact that the political, intellectual, and cultural movement known as "Afrocentricity" is a phenomenon of the post-Black Power era as Black academics sought to legitimize African-centered epistemologies (i.e., Black studies). Conflation of Afrocentricity with Black scholars' ruminations on the "Africanity" or "blackness" of ancient Nilotic peoples implies that anyone whose writings affirmed African achievement—including Lucian, Homer, Diodorus, Aeschylus, and others—was "Afrocentric" whose endgame was a romanticized golden era of Black civilization. Mary Maclean, the white managing editor of the *Crisis*, wrote an article in 1911 arguing that Black Africans founded ancient Egyptian civilization. One historian subsequently described Maclean's article as an "astonishing Afro-centric essay." See David Levering Lewis, *W. E. B. Du Bois: Biography of a Race, 1868–1919* (New York: H. Holt, 1993), 416. On misuses of Afrocentricity, see Wilson Jeremiah Moses, *Afrotopia: The Roots of African American Popular History* (New York: Cambridge University Press, 1998). On Du Bois as an "Afro-centric, Pan-Africanist race man," see Wilson J. Moses, "W. E. B. Du Bois's 'The Conservation of Races' and Its Context: Idealism, Conservatism,

and Hero Worship," *Massachusetts Review* 34, no. 2 (Summer 1993): 290. On Afrocentricity, see Molefi K. Asante, *Afrocentricity: The Theory of Social Change* (Chicago: African American Images, 2003). On Africanity, see Sterling Stuckey, *Slave Culture: Nationalist Theory and the Foundations of Black America* (New York: Oxford University Press, 2013).

36. Marcus Garvey and Amy Jacques Garvey, eds. *The Philosophy and Opinions of Marcus Garvey, Part I* (Paterson, N.J.: Frank Cass and Company Limited, 1923), 1.

37. See Raphael Patai, *The Messiah Texts: Jewish Legends of Three Thousand Years* (Detroit: Wayne State University Press, 1979), 37–41.

38. Tony Martin, ed., *African Fundamentalism: A Literary and Cultural Anthology of Garvey's Harlem Renaissance* (Dover, Mass.: Majority Press, 1991), 4. See also Barbara Bair and Robert A. Hill, eds., *Marcus Garvey Life and Lessons: A Centennial Companion to the Marcus Garvey and Universal Negro Improvement Association Papers* (Berkeley: University of California Press, 1987).

39. On radical Black organizations and periodicals—such as the *Voice*, the *Messenger*, the *Crusader*, *Negro World*, the *Challenge*, the *Emancipator*, and so on—in the early 1900s, see W. James, *Holding Aloft the Banner of Ethiopia*; Jeffrey B. Perry, *Hubert Harrison: The Voice of Harlem Radicalism, 1883–1918* (New York: Columbia University Press, 2009); Gilmore, *Defying Dixie*; and Irma Watkins-Owens, *Blood Relations: Caribbean Immigrants and the Harlem Community, 1900–1930* (Bloomington: Indiana University Press, 1996). See also Hubert Harrison, *When Africa Awakes* (1920; repr., Baltimore: Black Classic Press, 1997); Jeffrey B. Perry, *Hubert Harrison: The Struggle for Equality, 1918–1927* (New York: Columbia University Press, 2020); Minkah Makalani, *In the Cause of Freedom: Radical Black Internationalism from Harlem to London, 1917–1939* (Chapel Hill: University of North Carolina Press, 2011); and Marc Matera, *Black London: The Imperial Metropolis and Decolonization in the Twentieth Century* (Oakland: University of California Press, 2015).

40. William Wells Brown, *The Rising Son; or, The Antecedents and Advancement of the Colored Race* (Boston: A. G. Brown, 1874), 536–39. See also Richard Newman, "'Warrior Mother of Africa's Warriors of the Most High God': Laura Adorkor Kofey and the African Universal Church," in *This Far by Faith: Readings in African-American Women's Religious Biography*, ed. Judith Weisenfeld and Richard Newman (New York: Routledge, 1996), 110–23.

41. See Timothy E. Fulop, "'The Future Golden Day of the Race': Millennialism and Black Americans in the Nadir, 1877–1901," *Harvard Theological Review* 84, no. 1 (1991): 75–99. See also Bret E. Carroll, *Spiritualism in Antebellum America* (Bloomington: Indiana University Press, 1997); and Catherine L. Albanese, *A Republic of Mind and Spirit: A Cultural History of American Metaphysical Religion* (New Haven, Conn.: Yale University Press, 2007).

42. On the Ghost Dance, see Michael Hittman, *Wovoka and the Ghost Dance*, expanded ed. (Lincoln: University of Nebraska Press, 1990); James Mooney, *The Ghost Dance Religion and the Sioux Outbreak of 1890* (Lincoln: University of Nebraska Press, 1991); Alice Beck Kehoe, *The Ghost Dance: Ethnohistory and Revitalization* (Long Grove, Ill.: Waveland Press, 2006); Cora Du Bois and Thomas Buckley, *The 1870 Ghost Dance* (Lincoln: University of Nebraska Press, 2007); and

Louis S. Warren, *God's Red Son: The Ghost Dance Religion and the Making of Modern America* (New York: Basic Books, 2017).

43. Franklin L. Baumer, "Intellectual History and Its Problems," *Journal of Modern History* 21, no. 3 (September 1949): 192. See also August Meier and Elliott Rudwick, *Black History and the Historical Profession, 1915–1980* (Urbana: University of Illinois Press, 1986), 1–71.

44. Du Bois, *The Negro*, vii, 6–7.

45. George Wells Parker, *Children of the Sun* (Omaha: Hamitic League of the World, 1918), 5. African Americans have a complex history of embracing the achievements of ancient Nilotic Africans while rejecting their enslavement of the ancient Israelites, with whom they identified, despite the anti-Black Hamitic myth's origins in Judaism. See David Walker, *An Appeal in Four Articles; Together with a Preamble to the Colored Citizens of the World, but in Particular, and Very Expressly, to Those of the United States of America* (Boston: David Walker, 1830). The Exodus mythology and migration broadly, therefore, took on messianic and sometimes millennial dimensions. See Scott Trafton, *Egypt Land: Race and Nine-teenth-Century American Egyptomania* (Durham, N.C.: Duke University Press, 2004), 222–61; Eddie S. Glaude Jr., *Exodus! Religion, Race, and Nation in Early Nineteenth-Century Black America* (Chicago: University of Chicago Press, 2000), 46; Claude Brown, *Manchild in the Promised Land* (New York: Macmillan, 1965); Nell Irvin Painter, *Exodusters: Black Migration to Kansas after Reconstruction* (New York: Knopf, 1977); James R. Grossman, *Land of Hope: Chicago, Black Southerners, and the Great Migration* (Chicago: University of Chicago Press, 1989); Milton C. Sernett, *Bound for the Promised Land: African American Religion and the Great Migration* (Durham, N.C.: Duke University Press, 1997); and Joe William Trotter Jr., *River Jordan: African American Urban Life in the Ohio Valley* (Lexington: University Press of Kentucky, 1998).

46. G. Parker, *Children of the Sun*. On the African Blood Brotherhood and Pan-Africanism, see Makalani, *In the Cause of Freedom*, 45–69.

47. A recent scholarly intervention, which traces the historiography of feminism to the ethnological debates of the nineteenth century, exposes the empirical limitations of white and Black feminisms and gender studies, specifically analyses on Black manhood. Systems of patriarchy, which white and Black feminists ascribed to African American men, was a thesis devoid of empirical evidence, for the U.S. racial order was predicated on denying Black men structural power while portraying them as brutes. See Tommy J. Curry, *The Man-Not: Race, Class, Genre, and the Dilemmas of Black Manhood* (Philadelphia: Temple University Press, 2017).

48. G. Parker, *Children of the Sun*, 7.

49. Moses, *Afrotopia*, 27.

50. Buried deep in the book, Jefferson did not redact this assertion, however: Ethiopia, "the first learned nation was a nation of blacks; for it is incontrovertible, that, by the term Ethiopians, the ancients meant to represent a people of black complexion, thick lips, and woolly hair." Constantin-François de Volney, *The Ruins, or, Meditations on the Revolutions of Empires: And the Law of Nature*, trans. Peter Eckler (New York: Twentieth Century Pub. Co., 1890), 6, 89–90. In response to Herodotus's and Aeschylus's observations that the ancient Egyptians were Black,

Du Bois wrote that it was a "particularly significant statement" for those "used to the brunette Mediterranean type." Du Bois, *The Negro*, 18.

51. "From Thomas Jefferson to Volney, 17 March 1801," in *The Papers of Thomas Jefferson*, vol. 33, *17 February–30 April 1801*, ed. Barbara B. Oberg (Princeton, N.J.: Princeton University Press, 2006), 341–42. Moses classified Volney as a white Afrocentrist whose phantasmagorical sightings undermined his credibility as a historian. See Moses, *Afrotopia*, 55–56.

52. George Wells Parker, "The African Origin of the Grecian Civilization," *Journal of Negro History* 2, no. 3 (1917): 334–44. Many Black scholars accused white scholars of misinformation. One scholar believed that white pseudo-scholars had "egregiously falsified the true history of the Cushites, or the Hamitic branch of the human family." See Rufus Lewis Perry, *The Cushite; or, The Descendants of Ham: As Found in the Sacred Scriptures and in the Writings of Ancient Historians and Poets from Noah to the Christian Era* (Springfield, Mass.: Wiley and Co., 1893), 12.

53. G. Parker, *Children of the Sun*, 31.

54. W. Scott, "'And Ethiopia Shall Stretch Forth Its Hands,'" 4. For one of the most prominent examples of a diasporic African using Ethiopia in a revolutionary, messianic context in the nineteenth century, see Robert Alexander Young, *The Ethiopian Manifesto: Issued in Defence of the Black Man's Rights in the Scale of Universal Freedom* (New York: Robert Alexander Young, 1829); and D. Walker, *Appeal in Four Articles*.

55. St. Clair Drake, *The Redemption of Africa and Black Religion* (Chicago: Third World Press, 1970), 11.

56. See St. Clair Drake, *Black Folk Here and There: An Essay in History and Anthropology* (Los Angeles: University of California Press, 1987).

57. E. Franklin Frazier, "Garvey: A Mass Leader," in *Marcus Garvey and the Vision of Africa*, ed. John Henrik Clarke (New York: Vintage Books, 1974), 236.

58. Perry, *Cushite*, viii, 12, 161. In 1890, another African Canadian published a notable work that underscored the important contributions of ancient Nilotic Africans.

59. W. Brown, *Rising Son*, 43–44.

60. Mario H. Beatty, "Martin Delany and Egyptology," *ANKH* 14, no. 15 (2005–6): 78–99. See also Samuel G. Morton, *Crania Ægyptiaca: Observations on Egyptian Ethnography, Derived Anatomy, History and the Monuments* (Philadelphia: John Penington, 1844); and Josiah C. Nott and George R. Gliddon, *Types of Mankind* (Philadelphia: Lippincott, 1868).

61. Martin R. Delany, *Principia of Ethnology: The Origin of Races and Color, with an Archaeological Compendium of Ethiopian and Egyptian Civilization, from Years of Careful Examination and Inquiry* (Philadelphia: Harper and Brother, 1880), 59–60.

62. Delany, 79.

63. Cyril E. Griffith, *The African Dream: Martin R. Delany and the Emergence of Pan-African Thought* (University Park: Pennsylvania State University Press, 1975); Martin R. Delany, *Official Report of the Niger Valley Exploring Party* (New York: T. Hamilton, 1861). Delany's race pride was unmatched. According to his friend Frederick Douglass, "I thank God for making me a man simply, but Delany always

thanks him for making him a *black man* [emphasis in original]." See Frances Rollin Whipper, *Life and Public Services of Martin R. Delany, Sub-assistant Commissioner, Bureau Relief of Refugees, Freedmen, and of Abandoned Lands, and Late Major 104th U.S. Colored Troops* (Boston: Lee and Shepard, 1883), 19.

64. Delany, *Principia of Ethnology*, 88–89, 16–17. On nineteenth-century African American leaders' reflection on Christian redemption, see Alexander Crummell and Wilson Jeremiah Moses, eds., *Destiny and Race: Selected Writings, 1840–1898* (Amherst: University of Massachusetts Press, 1992); and Henry Highland Garnet, *The Past and the Present Condition, and the Destiny, of the Colored Race* (Troy, N.Y.: Steam Press of J. C. Kneeland and Co., 1848).

65. Edward Wilmot Blyden, *The Aims and Methods of a Liberal Education for Africans: Inaugural Address* (Cambridge, Mass.: John Wilson and Son, 1882), 21. On Galenus and how Arab writers instrumentalized his quasi-racist remarks, see Alexandre Popovic, *The Revolt of African Slaves in Iraq in the 3rd/9th Century* (Princeton, N.J.: Marcus Wiener, 1999), 16–20; and Michael Gomez, *African Dominion: A New History of Empire in Early and Medieval West Africa* (Princeton, N.J.: Princeton University Press, 2018), 52. See also Frank M. Snowden, *Before Color Prejudice: The Ancient View of Blacks* (Cambridge, Mass.: Harvard University Press, 1983).

66. George Washington Williams, *History of the Negro Race in America from 1619 to 1880: Negroes as Slaves, as Soldiers, and as Citizens* (New York: G. P. Putnam's Sons, 1883), 19.

67. G. Williams, vi. See also Pero Gaglo Dagbovie, *The Early Black History Movement, Carter G. Woodson, and Lorenzo Johnston Greene* (Urbana: University of Illinois Press, 2007).

68. Pauline E. Hopkins, *A Primer of Facts Pertaining to the Early Greatness of the African Race and the Possibility of Restoration by Its Descendants, with Epilogue: Compiled and Arranged from the Works of the Best Known Ethnologists and Historians* (Cambridge, Mass.: P. E. Hopkins, 1905). See also Hannah Wallinger, *Pauline E. Hopkins: A Literary Biography* (Athens: University of Georgia Press, 2005). For other examples of African Americans recovering a lost history in the early twentieth century, see John William Norris, *The Ethiopian's Place in History and His Contributions to the World's Civilizations* (Baltimore: Afro-American Company, 1916); and James M. Webb, *The Black Man: The Father of Civilization, Proven by Biblical History* (Chicago: Fraternal Press, 1919).

69. Like African Americans, some African Canadian intellectuals expressed interest in ethnology, ancient Nilotic peoples, and African colonization. In 1903 and 1904, Abraham Beverley Walker, the first African-Canadian-born lawyer, published a magazine called *Neith*, the name of the ancient Egyptian goddess of the universe. Walker, whose forebears were Black Loyalists, trained as a lawyer in the United States but returned to New Brunswick (Canada), where he published *Neith*. The magazine covered race relations and the humanities. See Winks, *Blacks in Canada*, 400–401; and Abraham Beverley Walker, *The Negro Problem; or, The Philosophy of Race Development from a Canadian Standpoint* (Atlanta: Constitution Publishing Company, 1890). On Black history as a liberating force, see Dagbovie, *The Early Black History Movement*.

70. "Minutes of the Coloured Literary Association," April 1919, MHSO.

71. Eric Ashley Hairston, *The Ebony Column: Classics, Civilization, and the African American Reclamation of the West* (Knoxville: University of Tennessee Press, 2013), 25–64. See also Michele Valerie Ronnick, ed., *The Works of William Sanders Scarborough: Black Classicist and Race Leader* (New York: Oxford University Press, 2006); Tracey L. Walters, *African American Literature and the Classicist Tradition: Black Women Writers from Wheatley to Morrison* (New York: Palgrave Macmillan, 2007); and William W. Cook and James Tatum, *African American Writers and Classical Tradition* (Chicago: University of Chicago Press, 2010).

72. David W. Blight, *Frederick Douglass: Prophet of Freedom* (New York: Simon and Schuster, 2018), 389.

73. W. E. B. Du Bois, *Darkwater: Voices from within the Veil* (New York: Harcourt, Brace and Howe, 1920), 26–28. See also Mays, *Negro's God*.

74. Edward J. Blum, *W. E. B. Du Bois, American Prophet* (Philadelphia: University of Pennsylvania Press, 2013), 134–80. In 1898, Bishop Henry McNeal Turner declared that "God is a Negro." See Andre E. Johnson, "God Is a Negro: The (Rhetorical) Black Theology of Bishop Henry McNeal Turner," *Black Theology* 13, no. 1 (2015): 29–40.

75. Andre E. Johnson, *The Forgotten Prophet: Bishop Henry McNeal Turner and the African American Prophetic Tradition* (Lanham, Md.: Lexington Books, 2012).

76. Michael Russell, *Nubia and Abyssinia: Comprehending Their Civil History, Antiquities, Arts, Religion, Literature, and Natural History* (New York: Harper and Brothers, 1845), 93; Hiob Ludolf, *A New History of Ethiopia: Being a Full and Accurate Description of the Kingdom of Abessinia, Vulgarly, Though Erroneously, Called the Empire of Prester John, in Four Books* (London: J. P. Gent, 1684), 71–72. Emphasis in original.

77. Ludolf, *New History of Ethiopia*, 71–72. Like the Ethiopians, the Gã people in Ghana depicted the devil as white-complected. In fact, the ancestors of the Gã consider the Nile Valley as an important point of departure. See Ludewig Ferdinand Rømer and Selena Axelrod Winsnes, *A Reliable Account of the Gold Coast of Guinea* (1760; repr., New York: Oxford University Press, 2000), 80.

78. Russell, *Nubia and Abyssinia*, 275.

79. Du Bois was unequivocally aware that Nilotic Africans imagined and depicted God and Christ according to their subjective phenotype. He cited Ludolf in his seminal work on African history. See Du Bois, *The Negro*, 62.

80. Du Bois, *Darkwater*, 54.

81. Christopher Z. Hobson, *The Mount of Vision: African American Prophetic Tradition, 1800–1950* (Oxford: Oxford University Press, 2012), 31.

82. A. Johnson, *Forgotten Prophet*, 17.

83. David Levering Lewis, *W. E. B. Du Bois: The Fight for Equality and the American Century, 1919–1963* (New York: Henry Holt, 2000), 2.

84. Arthur G. King to Du Bois, 23 February 1918, DBP (MS 312).

85. *The Crusader*, November 1920, 15.

86. Frazier, "Garvey: A Mass Leader," 237.

87. Chandler Owen, "The Failure of the Negro Leader," *The Messenger*, January 1918, 24.

88. Owen, 24.

89. See Martin, *Race First*, 12. George Tyler, a former employee, walked into the UNIA Harlem office and fired multiple rounds at Garvey. One grazed his head and two struck him in the leg. Tyler jumped to his death a few days later in jail, raising suspicion that either he was killed or he committed suicide to prevent the truth from surfacing. See also Hill, ed., *The Marcus Garvey and Universal Negro Improvement Association Papers, Vol. II, 27 August 1919 to 31 August 1920* (Berkeley: University of California Press, 1983), 78–80.

90. See Hill, ed., *Marcus Garvey and Universal Negro Improvement Association Papers, Vol. II*.

91. Randall Burkett, *Black Redemption: Churchmen Speak for the Garvey Movement* (Philadelphia: Temple University Press, 1978), 25.

92. C. L. R. James and Robin D. G. Kelley, *A History of Pan-African Revolt* (Oakland, Calif.: PM Press, 2012), 92.

93. John Henrik Clarke, ed., *Marcus Garvey and the Vision of Africa* (New York: Vintage Books, 1974), xvi.

94. Roi Ottley, *"New World A-Coming": Inside Black America* (New York: Third World, 1945), 69.

95. See Randall Burkett, *Garveyism as a Religious Movement: The Institutionalization of a Black Civil Religion* (Metuchen, N.J.: Scarecrow Press, 1978), xxiv–xxv. In 1916, the U.S. government sentenced to prison Callie House, a leader of a popular grassroots movement to secure reparations for formerly enslaved people. Some of Garvey's early followers belonged to House's organization, the National Ex-Slave Mutual Relief, Bounty and Pension Association. See Mary Frances Berry, *My Face Is Black Is True: Callie House and the Struggle for Ex-Slave Reparations* (New York: Vintage Books, 2006).

96. Drake as cited in Burkett, *Garveyism as a Religious Movement*, xx.

97. Marcus Garvey and Amy Jacques Garvey, eds., *The Philosophy and Opinions of Marcus Garvey, Part II* (Paterson, N.J.: Frank Cass and Company, 1925), 127. Garvey believed that conservation of the race was paramount to liberation efforts. See Martin, *Race First*, 6.

98. See Robert Trent Vinson, *The Americans Are Coming! Dreams of African American Liberation in Segregationist South Africa* (Athens: Ohio University Press, 2012); Ewing, *Age of Garvey*, 77; and Tilman Dedering, "Petitioning Geneva: Transnational Aspects of Protest and Resistance in South West Africa/Namibia after the First World War," *Journal of African Studies* 35, no. 4 (2009): 793.

99. Garvey also credited the following white officials in Jamaica for helping him launch the UNIA in 1914: "a Catholic Bishop, the Governor, Sir John Pringle, the Rev. William Graham, a Scottish clergyman, and several other white friends." Black Jamaicans, especially the upper class, many of whom passed for white, wanted nothing to do with his new organization. See Cary D. Wintz, ed., *African American Political Thought, 1890–1930: Washington, Du Bois, Garvey, and Randolph* (Armonk, N.Y.: M. E. Sharpe), 173.

100. Hill, ed., *Marcus Garvey and Universal Negro Improvement Association Papers, Vol. II*, li, 205.

101. Leo W. Bertley, "The Universal Negro Improvement Association of Montreal, 1917–1979" (Ph.D. diss., Concordia University, 1980).

102. After marrying, Louise and Earl left Montreal to organize full-time for the UNIA initially in Philadelphia and then Omaha. See Jan Carew, *Ghosts in Our Blood: With Malcolm X in Africa, England, and the Caribbean* (Chicago: Lawrence Hill Books, 1994), 131; and Erik S. McDuffie, "The Diasporic Journeys of Louise Little: Grassroots Garveyism, the Midwest, and Community Feminism," *Women, Gender, and Families of Color* 4 (2016): 146–70. The UNIA's forerunner, the Association of Universal Loyal Negroes, had been founded in Panama during the First World War to promote self-determination and nation building in German East Africa. Caribbean immigrants subsequently brought the organization to Montreal in 1918. In November 1918, Dillon C. Govin, secretary of the Association of Universal Loyal Negroes, wrote Du Bois from Montreal, seeking support for the organization. Govin informed Du Bois that he was in touch with the African League in England and Duse Mohammed Ali, African-born editor of the *African Times and Orient Review*, the London-based Pan-African newspaper for which Garvey had worked briefly in 1912. See Dillon C. Govin to Du Bois and letter of endorsement advertisement, 19 November 1918, DBP (MS 312); Bertley, "Universal Negro Improvement Association of Montreal," 40–42; and Robert A. Hill, ed., *The Marcus Garvey and Universal Negro Improvement Association Papers, Vol. XI: The Caribbean Diaspora, 1910–1920* (Durham, N.C.: Duke University Press, 2011), 101.

103. Carla Marano, "'Rising Strongly and Rapidly': The Universal Negro Improvement Association in Canada, 1919–1940," *Canadian Historical Review* 91 (2010): 234.

104. Martin, *Race First*, 13–16.

105. See Smith-Irvin, *Footsoldiers of the Universal Negro Improvement Association*, 57.

106. Letter from Harry Corwin Nixon, 9 December 1920, "Minutes of the Coloured Literary Association," April 1919, MHSO. For a similar example of a global community, see Cemil Aydin, *The Idea of a Muslim World: A Global Intellectual History* (Cambridge, Mass.: Harvard University Press, 2017).

107. Richard D. Riley and George D. Creese of Nova Scotia also signed the Declaration, which highlighted many issues, from Black "human rights" to Black men's sacred commitment to defending the "honor" and "virtue" of Black females. Robert A. Hill et al., eds., *The Marcus Garvey and Universal Negro Improvement Association Papers, Vol. XII: The Caribbean Diaspora, 1920–1921* (Durham, N.C.: Duke University Press, 2014), 32–48. Garvey and other Black leaders connected self-determination for Africans and their diasporic counterparts to Woodrow Wilson's "Fourteen Points" postwar peace strategy. The UNIA also drew attention to nationalist uproar in India and Ireland and to the 1917 Balfour Declaration endorsing the creation of a Jewish state.

108. Dudley Marshall spoke eloquently about journeying from Barbados to Glace Bay, Nova Scotia, to work in the coal mines. See Arleigh M. Holder interview with Dudley Marshall, 19 July 1978, BLA-7176-MAR, MHSO; and Arleigh M. Holder interview with Daniel Braithwaite, 17 August 1978, BLA-7181-BRA, MHSO. The city of Hamilton in southwestern Ontario also had Caribbean influence. Harry Gairey recalled when he and his friends "motored to Hamilton" to socialize and party. "You got a steel mill there and a lot of West Indians work there. . . . I would imagine a lot

of West Indians work there in the steel mill and various industries along with the steel company. I'm sure of that. This boy lives in Hamilton, Lincoln [Alexander]." Born in Toronto to Jamaican and Grenadian parents, Alexander was the first African Canadian member of federal Parliament and a decorated statesman. See Kenneth Amoroso interview with Harry Gairey, 9 July 1977, BLA-1446-GAI, MHSO.

109. W. D. Scott to W. J. Black, 14 November 1914; L. Fortier to Scott, 30 June 1914, Immigration Branch Records, RG 76, vol. 566, file 810666, LAC. See also Agnes Calliste, "Race, Gender and Canadian Immigration Policy: Blacks from the Caribbean, 1900–1932," *Journal of Canadian Studies* 28, no. 4 (1993–94): 135–36. In 1911, the immigration minister issued an Order-in-Council (executive order) prohibiting "any immigrants belonging to the Negro race, which is deemed unsuitable to the climate and requirements of Canada." It was never implemented. See "Orders-in-Council," 12 August 1911, RG 76, vol. 1021, PC 1911–1324, LAC. African Americans explored various opportunities to homestead in the Canadian Prairies, which officials often thwarted. See Constitution of the Lake View Benevolent Association (Calgary), 27 November 1922, DBP. As editor of the *Crisis*, Du Bois often fielded questions and counseled Black people on race relations. After hearing about Canada's anti-Black immigration policy, he sought clarification from officials in Ottawa. Du Bois exposed the Canadian government's racism in the *Crisis*. See Sarah-Jane Mathieu, *North of the Color Line: Migration and Black Resistance in Canada, 1870–1955* (Chapel Hill: University of North Carolina Press, 2010), 39–40. See also Harold Troper, *Only Farmers Need Apply: Official Canadian Government Encouragement of Immigration from the United States, 1896–1911* (Toronto: Griffin House, 1972); R. Bruce Shepard, "Diplomatic Racism: Canadian Government and Black Migration from Oklahoma, 1905–1912," in *African Americans on the Great Plains: An Anthology*, ed. Bruce A. Glasrud (Lincoln: University of Nebraska Press, 2009), 162–83; and Rachel Wolters, "As Migrants and as Immigrants: African Americans Search for Land and Liberty in the Great Plains, 1890–1912," *Great Plains Quarterly* 35, no. 4 (Fall 2015): 333–55.

110. Stanley Frost, "A Nation That Shops for New Neighbors," *Outlook*, 12 December 1923, 639. Frost's brother served as the U.S. consul general in Montreal from 1928 to 1935, working primarily on immigration and population issues.

111. *The Crusader*, March 1921, 9. Du Bois wrote the Canadian government on behalf of African Americans who wanted more information about Canada's immigration policy concerning Black immigrants. See F. C. Blair to W. E. B. Du Bois, 7 March 1911, Immigration Branch, RG 76-192-7552-2, LAC. See also Troper, *Only Farmers Need Apply*.

112. Marano, "'Rising Strongly and Rapidly,'" 257. On Caribbean immigrants and mutual aid in New York City, see also Tyesha Maddox, "From Invisible to Immigrants: Political Activism and the Construction of Caribbean American Identity, 1890–1940" (Ph.D. diss., New York University, 2016).

113. Origins of the Canadian People, Report of the Dominion Bureau of Statistics, 1929, in Ida Greaves, *The Negro in Canada* (Orillia, Ont.: Packet-Times Press, 1929), 45. On Black Loyalists and Black Refugees, respectively, see James W. St. G. Walker, *The Black Loyalists: The Search for a Promised Land in Nova Scotia and Sierra Leone, 1783–1870* (Toronto: University of Toronto Press, 1992); and Harvey Amani Whitfield, *Blacks on the Border: The Refugees in British North America,*

1815–1860 (Burlington: University of Vermont Press, 2006). See also Elizabeth Beaton, "An African-American Community in Cape Breton, 1901–1904," *Acadiensis* 24, no. 32 (1995): 65–97.

114. Given its universalist appeal, the UNIA had class dynamics, which included a bourgeois element. See Judith Stein, *The World of Marcus Garvey: Race and Class in Modern Society* (Baton Rouge: Louisiana State University Press, 1991).

115. Robert A. Hill et al., eds., *The Marcus Garvey and Universal Negro Improvement Association Papers, Vol. XI: The Caribbean Diaspora, 1910–1920* (Durham, N.C.: Duke University Press, 2011), lxxxix.

116. Huguette Casimir interview with Leonard Johnston, 3 August 1978, BLA-5119-JOH, MHSO. African Americans who endured racial terrorism saw African repatriation as a practical goal, not a metaphoric one. Garvey believed white people would not treat Black people fairly in majority-white societies. But because enslaved Africans and their descendants built the Americas and Africa's raw materials sustained the West, he conceded that Black people have every right to enjoy the fruits of the West. See Marcus Garvey and Amy Jacques Garvey, eds., *The Philosophy and Opinions of Marcus Garvey, Part I* (Paterson, N.J.: Frank Cass and Company, 1923); and Garvey and Garvey, eds., *Philosophy and Opinions of Marcus Garvey, Part II*.

117. Establishing a sovereign state in Liberia, for example, to which members of the diaspora could be repatriated would have been challenging for several reasons, including ethnic and class tensions. See Ibrahim Sundiata, *Brothers and Strangers: Black Zion, Black Slavery, 1914–1940* (Durham, N.C.: Duke University Press, 2003).

118. Dionne Brand, *No Burden to Carry: Narratives of Black Working Women in Ontario, 1920s–1950s* (Toronto: Women's Press, 1991), 74.

119. The irony is that African American colonization schemes influenced Garvey. See Edwin S. Redkey, *Black Exodus: Black Nationalist and Back-to-Africa Movements, 1890–1910* (New Haven, Conn.: Yale University Press, 1969). See also James T. Campbell, *Middle Passages: African American Journeys to Africa, 1787–2005* (New York: Penguin, 2006).

120. Holder interview with Marshall, BLA-7176-MAR, MHSO.

121. Brand, *No Burden to Carry*, 39–40.

122. For recent studies on Garveyism and gender, see Ula Y. Taylor, *The Veiled Garvey: The Life and Times of Amy Jacques Garvey* (Chapel Hill: University of North Carolina Press, 2002); Keisha N. Blain, *Set the World on Fire: Black Nationalist Women and the Global Struggle for Freedom* (Philadelphia: University of Pennsylvania Press, 2018); Carla Marano, "'The Splendid Work Our Women Have Done': African-Canadian Women in the UNIA," in *Women in the "Promised Land": Essays in African Canadian History*, ed. Nina Reid-Maroney et al. (Toronto: Women's Press, 2018), 136–60; McDuffie, "Diasporic Journeys of Louise Little"; Rhoda Reddock, "The First Mrs. Garvey: Pan-Africanism and Feminism in the Early Twentieth Century British Colonial Caribbean," *Feminist Africa* 19 (2014): 58–77; Asia Leeds, "Toward the 'Higher Type of Womanhood': The Gendered Contours of Garveyism and the Making of Redemptive Geographies in Costa Rica, 1922–1941," *Palimpsest: A Journal on Women, Gender, and the Black International* 2, no. 1 (2013): 1–27; Newman, "'Warrior Mother of Africa's Warriors of the Most High God'"; Barbara Bair, "True Women, Real Men: Gender, Ideology, and Social Roles in the Garvey

Movement," in *Gendered Domains: Rethinking Public and Private in Women's History*, ed. Dorothy O. Helly and Susan M. Reverby (Ithaca, N.Y.: Cornell University Press, 1992), 154–66; and Karen S. Adler, "'Always Leading Our Men in Service and Sacrifice': Amy Jacques Garvey, Feminist Black Nationalist," *Gender and Society* 6, no. 3 (1992): 346–75.

123. "Article 5 Jurisdiction and Charters," section 5, "Minutes of the Coloured Literary Association and UNIA," Toronto Records, MHSO.

124. Brand, *No Burden to Carry*, 41.

125. Marano, "'Splendid Work Our Women Have Done,'" 149.

126. Historians must reconsider facile attributions of "chauvinism" or "patriarchy" to the UNIA. Such assertions are inaccurate and lack nuance, portraying Black men and Black institutions as mere mimicry of white men and white institutions.

127. On "white man's war," see James W. St. G. Walker, "Race and Recruitment in World War I: Enlistment of Visible Minorities in the Canadian Expeditionary Force," *Canadian Historical Review* 70, no. 1 (1989): 1–26.

128. Donald Moore, *Don Moore: An Autobiography* (Toronto: Williams-Wallace, 1985), 33–34. Balm in Gilead is biblical (spiritual) medicine.

129. Letter from Harry Corwin Nixon, 9 December 1920, "Reprint of the Universal Negro Improvement Association," Toronto Records, MHSO.

130. See Holder interview with Marshall, BLA-7176-MAR, MHSO.

131. Hill, ed., *Marcus Garvey and Universal Negro Improvement Association Papers, Vol. II*, 205.

132. M. Franklin Peters, "The Passing of 'Uncle Tom,'" *The Crusader*, September 1920, 6.

133. During the war, some Nova Scotians embraced their "Ethiopian forefathers." See "The Urgent Demand of the Present Day," *Atlantic Advocate*, May 1917.

134. Holder interview with Marshall, BLA-7176-MAR, MHSO. The reference to "refuge" in Egypt is based on King Herod's massacre of the innocents, the infanticidal decree meant to nullify the alleged birth of a Jewish messiah. See Matthew 2:13–23 (KJV). For a rendition of Arnold Josiah Ford's "Ethiopia, Thou Land of Our Fathers," see Hill et al. eds., *Marcus Garvey and Universal Negro Improvement Association Papers, Vol. XII*, 36–37. The UNIA anthem likely drew inspiration from Abyssinia (Empire of Ethiopia) Menelik II's army, which routed an invading Italian army in 1896. This feat breathed life into Ethiopianism. W. Scott, "'And Ethiopia Shall Stretch Forth Its Hands.'"

135. See Bonnie MacLachlan, "Feasting with Ethiopians: Life on the Fringe," *Quaderni Urbinati di Cultura Classica* 40, no. 1 (1992): 15–33; Homer, *Iliad*, book 1.

136. Theodore G. Vincent, *Black Power and the Garvey Movement* (Berkeley: Ramparts Press, 1971), 153–54.

137. Garvey and Garvey, eds., *Philosophy and Opinions of Marcus Garvey, Part II*, 225.

138. See Hubert Fauntleroy Julian and John Bulloch, *Black Eagle: Colonel Hubert Julian* (London: Adventurers Club, 1965); and Drusilla Dunjee Houston, *Wonderful Ethiopians of the Ancient Cushite Empire, Book I* (1926; repr., Baltimore: Black Classic Press, 1985). As a Black woman historian, Houston did not receive her due;

see Amy Kirschke, "Du Bois, *The Crisis*, and Images of Africa and the Diaspora," in *African Diasporas in the New and Old Worlds: Consciousness and Imagination*, ed. Geneviève Fabre and Klaus Benesch (New York: Rodopi, 2004), 239–62.

139. George Shepperson, "Ethiopianism: Past and Present," in *Christianity in Tropical Africa: Studies Presented and Discussed at the Seventh International African Seminar, University of Ghana, April 1968*, ed. C. G. Baëta (London: Oxford University Press, 1968), 250.

140. Wilson Jeremiah Moses, *The Golden Age of Black Nationalism, 1850–1925* (Hamden, Conn.: Archon Books, 1978), 20.

141. Moses, 11.

142. Matthew 24:37–39 (NKJV). Bob Marley, who frequently wove scripture into his music, sang these words. See Bob Marley and the Wailers, "One Love," *Exodus*, Tuff Gong, 1977.

143. Moses, *Golden Age of Black Nationalism*, 24.

144. Garvey and Garvey, eds., *Philosophy and Opinions of Marcus Garvey, Part I*, 34.

145. Garvey and Garvey, eds., 45.

146. Du Bois to Canada Department of Corporations, 16 November 1920, and Du Bois to Canadian Secretary of State, 10 November 1921, DBP.

147. David Levering Lewis, *When Harlem Was in Vogue* (New York: Penguin Books, 1997), 39. In August 1919, a newly minted law school graduate named John Edgar Hoover became head of the General Intelligence Division of the Bureau of Investigation. Garvey was his assignment. Under Hoover's leadership, the Bureau of Investigation tried as early as October 1919 to frame Garvey for a crime for which he could be deported. See Hill, ed., *Marcus Garvey and Universal Negro Improvement Association Papers, Vol. II*, 72. Garvey specialist Tony Martin observed, "There was nothing inevitable about the failure of the Black Star Line and allied ventures." Martin, *Race First*, 167. Some of Garvey's subordinates were guilty of mismanagement and outright theft. Numerous events suggest that the Black Star Line was sabotaged from within and without. Martin, 151–73; Cronon, *Black Moses*, 39–72.

148. Burkett, *Garveyism as a Religious Movement*; and Burkett, *Black Redemption*.

149. Diana Braithwaite interview with William Aylestock, 13 May 1982, BLA-8997-AYL, MHSO. When Garvey visited the Toronto UNIA in 1920, Dudley Marshall remembered that at least one member of the community objected to Garvey's presence, accusing him of sowing discord. Plain and uniformed police officers attended Garvey's talk, presumably to monitor or silence him. According to Marshall, Garvey said, "There's a speech I'm making here tonight. I've made it in England, made it in France, I've made it in Germany, I've made it in the United States of America, and I want to see the man or set of men that will be able to prevent me making it here tonight." Holder interview with Marshall, BLA-7176-MAR, MHSO. Some Caribbean Pan-Africanists attributed their Canadian-born counterparts' opposition to Garvey as a symptom of "Uncle Tomism." See Winks, *Blacks in Canada*, 416.

150. Jane Rhodes, *Mary Ann Shadd Cary: The Black Press and Protest in the Nineteenth Century* (Bloomington: Indiana University Press, 1998), 70–99. Robert S.

Abbott, founder and publisher of the *Chicago Defender*, became known among African Americans in Chicago as "Modern Moses." See Ethan Michaeli, *The Defender: How the Legendary Black Newspaper Changed America* (Boston: Houghton Mifflin Harcourt, 2016).

151. J. F. Jenkins to W. E. B. Du Bois, 12 June 1923, DBP. Du Bois cautioned Jenkins that Canada's small population might not be able to sustain a race paper. See Du Bois to Jenkins, 14 June 1923, DBP.

152. The Associated Negro Press became the first African American press service in the United States.

153. W. E. B. Du Bois, "The Conservation of Races," *American Negro Academy Occasional Papers*, no. 2 (1897): 4.

154. The U.S. government used the same dubious lie in 1916 to imprison Callie House and undermine the movement for reparations. See Berry, *My Face Is Black Is True.*

155. "Ontario, Canada, Deaths, 1869–1938, 1943–1944, and Deaths Overseas, 1939–1947 for James F. Jenkins," Ancestry.com, http://www.ancestry.com (accessed 2 November 2016). Original data from *Registrations of Deaths, 1869–1938*, MS 935, reels 1–615, Archives of Ontario, Toronto. For his degree, see "Catalogue of the Officers and Students of Atlanta University, 1904–1905" (1905), Atlanta University Catalogs, book 36, http://digitalcommons.auctr.edu/aucatalogs/36; and "Catalogue of the Officers and Students of Atlanta University, 1897–98" (1898), Atlanta University Catalogs, book 29, http://digitalcommons.auctr.edu/aucatalogs/29.

156. Elliott Rudwick, "W. E. B. Du Bois and the Atlanta University Studies on the Negro," *Journal of Negro Education* 26, no. 4 (1957): 466.

157. Du Bois and his coconspirators believed in the unifying power of Pan-Africanisms. The Niagara Movement had a "Pan-African Department." See Elliott M. Rudwick, *W. E. B. Du Bois: Propagandist of the Negro Protest* (Philadelphia: University of Pennsylvania Press, 1968), 210. They neither ignored nor rejected African Canadians. See Rinaldo Walcott, *Black Like Who? Writing Black Canada*, 2nd rev. ed. (Toronto: Insomniac Press, 2003), 32.

158. In response to the violence, Du Bois purchased a double-barreled shotgun. "If a white mob had stepped on the campus where I lived I would without hesitation have sprayed their guts over the grass," said Du Bois. See Nicholas Johnson, *Negroes and the Gun: The Black Tradition of Arms* (New York: Prometheus Books, 2014), 151–57. See also Rebecca Burns, *Rage in the Gate City: The Story of the 1906 Atlanta Race Riot* (Athens: University of Georgia Press, 2009); David Godshalk, *Veiled Visions: The 1906 Atlanta Race Riot and the Reshaping of American Race Relations* (Chapel Hill: University of North Carolina Press, 2005); Gregory Mixon, *Atlanta Riot: Race, Class, and Violence in a New South City* (Gainesville: University of Florida Press, 2005); and Mark Bauerlein, *Negrophobia: A Race Riot in Atlanta, 1906* (San Francisco: Encounter Books, 2001). White supremacy gained traction in the United States seven years after the massacre when President Woodrow Wilson segregated the federal government. See Glenda Elizabeth Gilmore and Thomas J. Sugrue, *These United States: A Nation in the Making, 1890 to the Present* (New York: W. W. Norton, 2015), 82–121.

159. *Telegram* (Toronto), 18 January 1922.

160. See Michele Mitchell, *Righteous Propagation: African Americans and the Politics of Racial Destiny after Reconstruction* (Chapel Hill: University of North Carolina Press, 2004).

161. After arriving in Toronto, Edwards cofounded the Coleridge-Taylor Chorus in honor of the brilliant Sierra Leonean–British composer, conductor, and Pan-Africanist Samuel Coleridge-Taylor. See "Curriculum Vitae," Robert Paris Edwards Scrapbook, circa 1906–36, Stuart A. Rose Manuscript, Archives, and Rare Book Library, Emory University, Atlanta.

162. *Negro World*, 19 February 1921, 1; *The Crisis* (November 1910): 1. The *Atlantic Advocate*, which the Black residents of Halifax, Nova Scotia, founded in April 1915, had a similar motto: "Devoted to the Interests of the Colored People." The *Advocate* went defunct before the war ended. The *Dawn* was concerned almost exclusively with Black life, even though its motto used the plural "Races."

163. "'Dawn of To-Morrow' Makes Initial Bow on Saturday: Devoted to News of Interest to Colored Race," *Dawn of Tomorrow*, 14 July 1923, microfilm vol. 1 and 2, MHSO. See also See also Cheryl Thompson, "Cultivating Narratives of Race, Faith, and Community: *The Dawn of Tomorrow*, 1923–1971," *Canadian Journal of History* 50, no. 1 (2015): 30–67.

164. G. Parker, "African Origin of the Grecian Civilization," 344.

165. "The Dawn of Tomorrow," *Dawn of Tomorrow*, 14 July 1923. There are copious examples of classical Western writers commenting on the reverence of Ethiopia and on Greek gods feasting there. See MacLachlan, "Feasting with Ethiopians."

166. "Dawn of Tomorrow."

167. Casely Hayford, *Ethiopia Unbound: Studies in Race Emancipation* (London: C. M. Phillips, 1911), 165.

168. Carew, *Ghosts in Our Blood*.

169. See Drake, *Redemption of Africa and Black Religion*, 19; Alton B. Pollard III, *Mysticism and Social Change: The Social Witness of Howard Thurman* (New York: Peter Lang, 1992); Yvonne P. Chireau, *Black Magic: Religion and the African American Conjuring Tradition* (Berkeley: University of California Press, 2003); and Joy R. Bostic, *African American Female Mysticism: Nineteenth-Century Religious Activism* (New York: Palgrave Macmillan, 2013). Not even the literary style of the Harlem Renaissance encapsulated Jenkins and Edward's literary flare, which is more complementary to what Martin called "literary Garveyism" or the "Garvey aesthetic." See Tony Martin, *Literary Garveyism: Garvey, Black, Arts, and the Harlem Renaissance* (Dover, Mass.: Majority Press, 1983).

170. Melville Herskovits, *The Myth of the Negro Past* (Boston: Beacon Press, 1958), 207.

171. Arthur Fauset, *Black Gods of the Metropolis: Negro Religious Cults of the Urban North* (Philadelphia: University of Pennsylvania Press, 2002), 3. All religious beliefs are "superstitious," not simply African ones.

172. Garvey's poem "If I Die in Atlanta," in Martin, *Literary Garveyism*, 141–42. See also Vincent Brown, *The Reaper's Garden: Death and Power in the World of Atlantic Slavery* (Cambridge, Mass.: Harvard University Press, 2008).

173. Henry Highland Garnet, "Garnet's Call to Rebellion, 1843," in *A Documentary History of the Negro People in the United States*, ed. Herbert Aptheker (New York: Citadel Press, 1951), 232–34; Stuckey, *Slave Culture*, 157–217.

174. Garvey and Garvey, eds., *The Philosophy and Opinions of Marcus Garvey, Part I*, 182.

175. Kelly Miller, "After Marcus Garvey—What of the Negro?," in J. Clarke, *Marcus Garvey and the Vision of Africa*, 243.

176. Vincent, *Black Power and the Garvey Movement*, 154.

177. "Dawn of Tomorrow."

178. See J. L. Granatstein et al., *Mackenzie King: His Life and World* (Toronto: McGraw-Hill Ryerson, 1977), 80; and Christopher Dummitt, *Unbuttoned: A History of Mackenzie King's Secret Life* (Montreal: McGill-Queen's University Press, 2017).

179. George Elliott Clarke, *Directions Home: Approaches to African-Canadian Literature* (Toronto: University of Toronto Press, 2012), 9; George Elliott Clarke, *Odysseys Home: Mapping African-Canadian Literature* (Toronto: University of Toronto Press, 2002), 11.

180. When Du Bois launched the *Moon*, a magazine in which he illustrated his penchant for the mystical, Du Bois recruited four of his best students, one of whom was Jenkins. In fact, during Jenkins's years at Atlanta University, Du Bois utilized the trope of Ethiopianism as part of his pedagogy of race pride. He inherited this literary tradition in the late nineteenth century from his intellectual mentor and Pan-Africanist Alexander Crummell. Du Bois propagated Ethiopianism into the 1920s as editor of the *Crisis* and the *Moon*. See Moses, *Golden Age of Black Nationalism*, 156–69; Paul G. Partington, *The Moon Illustrated Weekly: Black America's First Weekly Magazine* (Thornton, Colo.: C&M Press, 1985); and "Colored Editor Mourned by Many," *Dawn of Tomorrow*, 18 May 1931.

181. See W. E. B. Du Bois, *The Quest of the Silver Fleece* (1911; repr., Philadelphia: Pine Street Books, 2004); and Du Bois, *Darkwater*.

182. Mathieu, *North of the Color Line*, 147. See also Theodore Kornweibel, *Seeing Red: Federal Campaigns against Black Militancy, 1919-1925* (Bloomington: Indiana University Press, 1998); and William Maxwell, *F. B. Eyes: How J. Edgar Hoover's Ghostreaders Framed African American Literature* (Princeton, N.J.: Princeton University Press, 2015).

183. "Dawn of Tomorrow."

184. While Jenkins and Edwards at times used "Black" as an adjective, some readers still criticized them for referring to Black people as "Negro." They countered, citing that great thinkers and leaders—such as Du Bois, Paul Dunbar, and Booker T. Washington—"unequivocally sanctioned the use of the word 'Negro.'" Those who objected to the use of the term were very likely individuals who did not hold membership in the UNIA. These members of the Black community were upwardly mobile and preferred not to emphasize their racial origin. See "Editorial," *Dawn of Tomorrow*, 11 August 1923. Marcus Garvey called the Negro press "venal" and "ignorant" for treating the noun "Negro" as offensive. See Garvey and Garvey, eds., *Philosophy and Opinions of Marcus Garvey, Part II*, 77–80.

185. "Dawn of Tomorrow." On the biblical reference to the handwriting on the wall, see Daniel 5:1–30 (NKJV).

186. "Why the Dawn of Tomorrow?," *Dawn of Tomorrow*, 14 July 1923. See also Du Bois to Jenkins, 14 June 1923, DBP.

187. Keith S. Henry, *Black Politics in Toronto since World War I* (Toronto: Multicultural History Society of Ontario, 1981).

188. See Kevin Gaines, *Uplifting the Race: Black Leadership, Politics, and Culture during the Twentieth Century* (Chapel Hill: University of North Carolina Press, 1996).

189. A. M. Alberga to Du Bois, 2 October 1925, DBP.

190. Henry, *Black Politics in Toronto since World War I*, 8. Winks considered the *Dawn of Tomorrow* "nonsensational" and "dull." Winks, *Blacks in Canada*, 402. On balance, Mathieu credited the *Dawn* for "fostering a deeply rooted sense of pride." And communications scholar Cheryl Thompson pointed out that the *Dawn* "transcended space and time." See Mathieu, *North of the Color Line*, 148; and Thompson, "Cultivating Narratives of Race, Faith, and Community," 66.

191. On hidden transcripts, see James C. Scott, *Domination and the Arts of Resistance: Hidden Transcripts* (New Haven, Conn.: Yale University Press, 1992).

192. "Colored People Organize for Advancement of Race in General," *Dawn of Tomorrow*, 16 August 1924. Support for the CLACP and the *Dawn* came from notable white patrons, such as Fred Landon, onetime head of the London Public Library and a CLACP advisory board member. Landon earned his doctorate under the tutelage of U. B. Phillips, the sympathetic historian of antebellum slavery at the University of Michigan and became a specialist on nineteenth-century African Canadian history. The *Dawn* occasionally reprinted Landon's articles, some of which he published first in the *Journal of Negro History*. William Renwick Riddell—lawyer, jurist, and historian—also sat on the advisory board of the CLACP. As white Canadians of British "stock," Landon and Riddell subscribed to the racial theories that privileged Anglo-Saxon supremacy. See Winks, *Blacks in Canada*, 402–3; Constance Backhouse, *Colour-Coded: A Legal History of Racism in Canada, 1900–1950* (Toronto: University of Toronto Press, 1999), 340; and Barrington Walker, review of *Ontario's African-Canadian Heritage: Collected Writings by Fred Landon, 1918–1967*, *Canadian Historical Review* 91, no. 1 (2010): 155–57.

193. Mathieu, *North of the Color Line*, 154. Jenkins and Edwards disagreed with Garvey's racialization of God as a Black entity, although they understood the source of Garvey's motivation, since "the present color scheme of North America . . . is calculated to humiliate and degrade the spirit of all black people." Jenkins and Edwards acknowledged, "When a race begins to visualize God in its own color it then begins to worship idols." See "Garvey's Black God," *Dawn of Tomorrow*, 20 September 1924. By the 1920s, the idea that God is Black was no longer novel, for Bishop Henry McNeal Turner and Du Bois had advocated it years before. Du Bois wrote short stories about the Black Christ.

194. "The U.N.I.A. Convention at Montreal," *Dawn of Tomorrow*, 25 August 1924.

195. Winks, *Blacks in Canada*, 402.

196. "Education," *Dawn of Tomorrow*, 21 July 1923. On River Jordan as the "Promised Land," see Trotter, *River Jordan*. See also John A. Arthur, Joseph Takougang, and Thomas Owusu, eds., *Africans in Global Migration: Searching for Promised Lands* (New York: Lexington Books, 2012).

197. Greaves, *Negro in Canada*, 60.

198. "Education," *Dawn of Tomorrow*, 21 July 1923.

199. Blyden, *Aims and Methods of a Liberal Education for Africans*, 27. See also Alexander Crummell, *The Black Woman of the South: Her Neglects and Her Needs* (Cincinnati: Woman's Home Missionary Society of the Methodist, 1883).

200. "The Wrong View Point," *Dawn of Tomorrow*, 18 August 1923.

201. "100 Per Cent Canadians," *Dawn of Tomorrow*, 1 September 1923.

202. "To Africa—Why Not?," *Dawn of Tomorrow*, 1 May 1926. Reaping that which their enslaved forebears had sowed resonated with many African Americans and acted as a bulwark against emigrationist/colonization schemes and anti-Black racism. "The American Negro has a share in the New World. He need not rush out of the land which he bought with two hundred and fifty years of servitude to find his destiny in Africa." See J. Augustus Cole quoted in Fulop, "'Future Golden Day of the Race,'" 81. "Since the Negro has aided in the development of this country, he should remain here to enjoy its splendid civilization." See I. Garland Penn and John W. E. Bowen, eds., *The United Negro: His Problems and His Progress* (Atlanta: D. E. Luther, 1902), 593. "All of the wealth and splendor of this republic are largely due to the sweat of his brow. He came to a wilderness and made it a garden; he found a forest and turned it into cities, and for three hundred years he has filled the coffers of his white masters." See Peters, "Passing of 'Uncle Tom,'" 5.

> This land is ours by right of birth
> This land is ours by right of soil
> We helped to turn its virgin earth
> Our sweat is in its fruitful soil.

See James Weldon Johnson's "Address Delivered at a Dinner for Congressman La Guardia, March 10, 1923," in Carter G. Woodson, *Negro Orators and the Orations* (New York: Russell and Russell), 670.

203. Robert A. Hill et al., eds., *The Marcus Garvey and Universal Negro Improvement Association Papers, Vol. VII: November 1927–August 1940* (Berkeley: University of California Press, 1991), 288; Winks, *Blacks in Canada*, 415.

204. "Again Marcus Garvey," *Dawn of Tomorrow*, 30 November 1928.

205. In the 1910s and 1920s, Prophet Noble Drew Ali's Moorish Science Temple of America had a modest following in Chicago. Noble Ali was friends with Dr. Oscar Brewton and Madame Leona Brewton, two of the most successful and highly regarded members of Toronto's Black community, who had emigrated from Chicago to Toronto around 1919. The Brewtons knew Noble Ali from their time in Chicago and invited him to the city in 1928, where he delivered several lectures. See Azeem Hopkins-Bey, *Prophet Noble Drew Ali: Saviour of Humanity* (Morrisville, N.C.: Lulu Press, 2014), 48. Other charismatic/cult figures arose. Grover Cleveland Redding, leader of the Abyssinians, a breakaway sect of the UNIA, planned to smuggle arms to the South and liberate African Americans from Jim Crow. In the summer of 1920, Redding and a few of his followers led an armed insurrection in Chicago. He was later prosecuted and executed for murder. There was also Father Divine, who claimed to be God. He started the International Peace Mission Movement in New York City, which had some success in the 1930s during the decline of the UNIA. W. D. Fard, who mentored Elijah Muhammad, told his followers that he

was the Mahdi (Muslim messiah). And Elijah Muhammad's followers considered Muhammad a prophet in the 1930s. The Nation of Islam adopted the separatist ideology of the UNIA. None of these charismatic leaders rivaled Garvey's messianic appeal, and none of their movements organized Black people on the same scale as the UNIA. See Vincent, *Black Power and the Garvey Movement*, 85–87, 221–28. Black messianism can resemble "charismatic charlatanry" See Moses, *Black Messiahs and Uncle Toms*, 11.

206. See Newman, "'Warrior Mother of Africa's Warriors of the Most High God'"; Blain, *Set the World on Fire*.

207. See Fauset, *Black Gods of the Metropolis*. In 1928, Du Bois wrote a novel in which his African American protagonist fathered a son with an East Indian princess. This son, according to Du Bois, was destined to become the messiah of the colored peoples of the colonized world. See W. E. B. Du Bois, *Dark Princess: A Romance* (Millwood, N.Y.: Kraus-Thomson Organization, 1928); Nico Slate, *Colored Cosmopolitanism: The Shared Struggle for Freedom in the United States and India* (Cambridge, Mass.: Harvard University Press, 2012), 75.

208. "Curriculum Vitae," Robert Paris Edwards Scrapbook. Robin Winks wrote, "To find opportunity, [Black people] often had to go to the land of segregation." Winks, *Blacks in Canada*, 414.

209. "The Future of the Canadian Negro," *Dawn of Tomorrow*, 1 October 1930.

210. John Barnhill, "Back to Africa Movement," in *Encyclopedia of African American Society, Volume 1*, ed. Gerald D. Jaynes (London: Sage, 2005), 73.

211. Jenkins's widow, Christina, a descendant of free Black communities in the Windsor-Chatham area, continued publishing the *Dawn* after his death, in addition to raising eight children. The *Dawn*'s editorials lost the references to Ethiopianism after Jenkins died.

212. Cronon, *Black Moses*. Like Cronon, John Hope Franklin, in his foreword to *Black Moses*, portrayed Garvey as a tragic historical figure who had few redeemable qualities. See also Theodore Draper, *The Rediscovery of Black Nationalism* (New York: Viking Press, 1970); and Stein, *World of Marcus Garvey*.

213. J. Edgar Hoover, "Memorandum for Mr. Ridgely," 11 October 1919, RG 60, 198940, Department of Justice, LOC.

214. Tony Martin, Theodore Vincent, Robert Hill, and others catalyzed a gradual change in how historians understand and appreciate Garveyism and the UNIA. Recent scholarship continues this trend. See Ronald J. Stephens and Adam Ewing, eds., *Global Garveyism* (Gainesville: University Press of Florida, 2019).

215. Garvey believed that most white people were white supremacists, including liberals and conservatives, who feigned interest in the welfare of Black people. As a result, he respected white supremacists for their candor about their beliefs and disdain of race mixing. On African Americans cooperating with white supremacists, see Reena N. Goldthree, "Amy Jacques Garvey, Theodore Bilbo, and the Paradoxes of Black Nationalism," in *Global Circuits of Blackness: Interrogating the African Diaspora*, ed. Jean Muteba Rahier, Percy C. Hintzen, and Felipe Smith (Urbana: University of Illinois Press, 2010), 152–73.

216. E. Franklin Frazier, *Black Bourgeoisie* (Glencoe, Ill.: Free Press, 1957), 21, 121.

217. Alain Locke quoted in Martin, *Literary Garveyism*, 159. See also Jeffrey C. Stewart, *The New Negro: The Life of Alain Locke* (New York: Oxford University Press, 2018); D. Lewis, *When Harlem Was in Vogue*; and Martin, *African Fundamentalism*.

218. Vincent, *Black Power and the Garvey Movement*, 226. See also Robert A. Parker, *The Incredible Messiah: The Deification of Father Divine* (Boston: Little, Brown, 1937); and Fauset, *Black Gods of the Metropolis*.

CHAPTER 2

1. Gil Scott-Heron, "Home Is Where the Hatred Is," *Pieces of a Man*, Flying Dutchman, 1971.

2. On oikophobia, see Catherine Lu, "Reconciliation as Non-alienation: The Politics of Being at Home in the World," in *Reconciliation and Repair*, ed. Melissa Schwartzberg and Eric Beerbohm (New York: New York University Press, forthcoming).

3. Amiri Baraka, *Blues People: Negro Music in White America* (New York: W. Morrow, 1963).

4. For natal alienation, see Orlando Patterson, *Slavery and Social Death: A Comparative Study* (Cambridge, Mass.: Harvard University Press, 1982).

5. See Wendell Nii Laryea Adjetey, "In Search of Ethiopia: Messianic Pan-Africanism and the Problem of the Promised Land, 1919–1931," *Canadian Historical Review* 102, no. 1 (2021): 53–78.

6. Robin D. G. Kelley, "'But a Local Phase of a World Problem': Black History's Global Vision, 1883–1950," *Journal of American History* 86, no. 3 (1999): 1050, 1077.

7. See Marian L. Smith, "The Immigration and Naturalization Service (INS) at the U.S.-Canadian Border, 1893–1993," *Michigan Historical Review* 26, no. 2 (Fall 2000): 139.

8. See David R. Roediger, *Working toward Whiteness: How America's Immigrants Became White: The Strange Journey from Ellis Island to the Suburbs* (New York: Basic Books, 2005). Another historian argues that some white immigrants attained the status and benefits of whiteness much faster than historians believe. See Thomas A. Guglielmo, *White on Arrival: Italians, Race, Color, and Power in Chicago, 1890–1945* (New York: Oxford University Press, 2003). Unlike African North Americans, for example, French Canadians in New England and other parts of the United States had a welcoming "home," to which officials in Quebec hoped some would return and nation-build. In 1895, as a response to the French Canadian exodus, French Canadian authorities founded the Société Générale de Colonisation et de Rapatriement de la Province de Québec to stop further emigration from the province to the United States and to encourage immigrants to return. See "Report on French Canadian Repatriation," 1890 23, no. 5, Sessional Papers of the Dominion of Canada, LAC.

9. Despite the persistence of ethnic prejudice in North America, white people, or those who looked white, enjoyed social mobility and could wield power over Black and non-white people—hence, passing as white appealed to those whose phenotype facilitated this transition. See definition of racial caste in the introduction.

10. See Ira De A. Reid, *The Negro Immigrant: His Background, Characteristics and Social Adjustment, 1899–1937* (New York: Columbia University Press, 1939);

Winston James, *Holding Aloft the Banner of Ethiopia: Caribbean Radicalism in Early Twentieth-Century America* (New York: Verso, 1998); Irma Watkins-Owens, *Blood Relations: Caribbean Immigrants and the Harlem Community, 1900–1930* (Bloomington: Indiana University Press, 1996); and Lara Putnam, "Borderlands and Border-Crossers: Migrants and Boundaries in the Greater Caribbean, 1840–1940," *Small Axe* 42 (2014): 7–21.

11. Allyson Hobbs, *A Chosen Exile: A History of Racial Passing in American Life* (Cambridge, Mass.: Harvard University Press, 2014).

12. U.S. deportation policy had a relatively mild effect on Canadians, because immigration regulations did not subject Canadians to a similar definition of "illegal alien." See Mae Ngai, *Impossible Subjects: Illegal Aliens and the Making of Modern America*, rev. ed. (Princeton, N.J.: Princeton University Press, 2014), 58.

13. Karolyn Smardz Frost and Veta Tucker, eds., *A Fluid Frontier: Slavery, Resistance, and the Underground Railroad in the Detroit River Borderland* (Detroit: Wayne State University Press, 2016). See also Greg Wigmore, "Before the Railroad: From Slavery to Freedom in the Canadian-American Borderland," *Journal of American History* 98, no. 2 (2011): 437–54.

14. John Bukowczyk, "The Production of History, the Becoming of Place," in *Permeable Border: The Great Lakes Basin as a Transnational Region, 1650–1990*, ed. John Bukowczyk et al. (Pittsburgh: University of Pittsburgh Press, 2005), 7. The recent trend toward borderland and transnational history in North America generally elides the African North American experience. See Bruno Ramirez, *Crossing the 49th Parallel: Migration from Canada to the United States, 1900–1930* (Ithaca: Cornell University Press, 2001); Benjamin Bryce and Alexander Freund, eds., *Entangling Migration History: Borderlands and Transnationalism in the United States and Canada* (Gainesville: University of Florida Press, 2015); and Marc S. Rodriguez, *Repositioning North American Migration History: New Directions in Modern Continental Migration, Citizenship, and Community* (Rochester: University of Rochester Press, 2004). See also Jopi Nyman, ed., *Post-National Enquiries: Essays on Ethnic and Racial Border Crossing* (Newcastle upon Tyne, U.K.: Cambridge Scholars Publishing, 2009), 8–63. On industrialism and postindustrialism in the U.S.-Canadian borderlands, see Tracy Neumann, *Remaking the Rust Belt: The Postindustrial Transformation of North America* (Philadelphia: University of Pennsylvania Press, 2016).

15. Marcus Hansen and John Brebner, *The Mingling of the Canadian and American Peoples* (New Haven. Conn.: Yale University Press, 1940), v, x. See also Fred Gaffen, *Cross-Border Warriors: Canadians in American Forces, Americans in Canadian Forces, from the Civil War to the Gulf* (Toronto: Dundurn Press, 1995); Randy Widdis, *With Scarcely a Ripple: Anglo-Canadian Migration into the United States and Western Canada, 1880–1920* (Montreal: McGill-Queen's University Press, 2014); and Brandon R. Dimmel, *Engaging the Line: Great War Experiences along the Canada-US Border* (Vancouver: University of British Columbia Press, 2016).

16. See Carl C. Berger, *The Writing of Canadian History: Aspects of English-Canadian Historical Writing since 1900* (Toronto: University of Toronto Press, 1986), 142.

17. Bruno Ramirez, "Through the Northern Borderlands: Canada-U.S. Migrations in the Nineteenth and Twentieth Centuries," in *Migrants and Migration in*

Modern North America: Cross-Border Lives, Labor Markets, and Politics, ed. Nora Faires and Dirk Hoerder (Durham, N.C.: Duke University Press, 2011), 82–83.

18. See Gilbert Osofsky, *Harlem, the Making of a Ghetto: Negro New York, 1890–1930* (New York: Harper and Row, 1966); Allan Spear, *Black Chicago: The Making of a Negro Ghetto, 1890–1920* (Chicago: University of Chicago Press, 1967); Kenneth Kusmer, *A Ghetto Takes Shape: Black Cleveland, 1870–1930* (Urbana: University of Illinois Press, 1976); Nell Irvin Painter, *Exodusters: Black Migration to Kansas after Reconstruction* (New York: Knopf, 1977); Joe W. Trotter Jr., *Black Milwaukee: The Making of an Industrial Proletariat, 1915–1945* (Urbana: University of Illinois, Press, 1985); James R. Grossman, *Land of Hope: Chicago, Black Southerners, and the Great Migration* (Chicago: University of Chicago Press, 1989); Joe W. Trotter, ed., *The Great Migration in Historical Perspective: New Dimensions of Race, Class, and Gender* (Bloomington: Indiana University Press, 1991); Milton C. Sernett, *Bound for the Promised Land: African American Religion and the Great Migration* (Durham, N.C.: Duke University Press, 1997); Davarian L. Baldwin, *Chicago's New Negroes: Modernity, the Great Migration, and Black Urban Life* (Chapel Hill: University of North Carolina Press, 2007); and Marcia Chatelain, *South Side Girls: Growing Up in the Great Migration* (Durham, N.C.: Duke University Press, 2015).

19. Grossman references and cites an "influx" of Black southerners into Canadian cities during the Great Migrations. See Grossman, *Land of Hope*, 99. After the 1919 Chicago race "riots," Florida-born Oscar Brewton and Ohio-born Leona Brewton left Chicago for Toronto. They eventually became the most prominent Black business couple in the city. Oscar and Leona operated a podiatry clinic and hair salon, respectively, out of the same building on Toronto's famous artery Yonge Street. Another prominent Black businessman was Nathaniel Redmon, who, in 1913, emigrated from Chicago with his wife and child to Toronto, where he founded and operated a haulage company for several decades. Both Oscar and Nathaniel worked as sleeping car porters in Canada before they became entrepreneurs. See Diana Braithwaite interview with Oscar Brewton, 25 July 1978, BLA-7183-BRE, MHSO; "Elder Citizen's Memoirs: Toronto from the Year 1919," *Contrast*, 15 November 1969; and Ron Fanfair, "Freemon Redmon Built His Scarborough Home 70 Years Ago," Ron Fanfair, 29 April 2020, https://www.ronfanfair.com/home/2020/4/29/ryfxogkokbc1wu0s6m1akbfeyri3zt (accessed 25 May 2021).

20. Hansen and Brebner, *Mingling of the Canadian and American Peoples*, 253–54.

21. Leon Truesdell, *The Canadian Born in the United States: An Analysis of the Statistics of the Canadian Element in the Population of the United States, 1850–1930* (New Haven, Conn.: Yale University Press, 1943), 38.

22. Anderson Ruffin Abbott quoted in Daniel G. Hill, "The Blacks in Toronto," in *Gathering Place: Peoples and Neighbourhoods of Toronto, 1834–1945*, ed. Robert Harney (Toronto: Multicultural History Society of Ontario, 1985), 102–3. Abbott counted Abraham Lincoln and his wife, Mary Todd Lincoln, among his friends. See "Anderson Ruffin Abbott: First Black Canadian Doctor and Graduate," Great Past, http://www.greatpast.utoronto.ca/GreatMinds/ShowBanner.asp?ID=17 (accessed 7 November 2016, site discontinued).

23. Ngai, *Impossible Subjects*, 64–67; M. Smith, "Immigration and Naturalization Service (INS) at the U.S.-Canadian Border," 129–30. See also Holly M. Karibo and George T. Díaz, *Border Policing: A History of Enforcement and Evasion in North America* (Austin: University of Texas Press, 2020).

24. African American immigration into Western Canada at the turn of the century alarmed the Canadian public and authorities. See also Harold Troper, *Only Farmers Need Apply: Official Canadian Government Encouragement of Immigration from the United States, 1896–1911* (Toronto: Griffin House, 1972); D. Chongo Mundende, "The Undesirable Oklahomans: Black Immigration to Western Canada," *Chronicles of Oklahoma* 76, no. 3 (1998): 282–297; R. Bruce Shepard, "Diplomatic Racism: Canadian Government and Black Migration from Oklahoma, 190–1912," in *African Americans on the Great Plains: An Anthology*, ed. Bruce A. Glasrud (Lincoln: University of Nebraska Press, 2009), 162–83; and Edward Dunsworth, "Race, Exclusion, and Archival Silences in the Seasonal Migration of Tobacco Workers from the Southern United States to Ontario," *Canadian Historical Review* 99, no. 4 (December 2018): 563–93.

25. Agnes Calliste, "Race, Gender and Canadian Immigration Policy: Blacks from the Caribbean, 1900–1932," *Journal of Canadian Studies* 28, no. 4 (1993–94): 135–36. In 1911, the immigration minister issued an Order-in-Council (executive order), prohibiting "any immigrants belonging to the Negro race, which is deemed unsuitable to the climate and requirements of Canada." It was never implemented. See "Orders-in-Council," 12 August 1911, RG 76, vol. 1021, PC 1911–1324, LAC.

26. Keith S. Henry, *Black Politics in Toronto since World War I* (Toronto: Multicultural History Society of Ontario, 1981), 13. See also Debra Thompson, *The Schematic State: Race, Transnationalism, and the Politics of the Census* (Cambridge: Cambridge University Press, 2016). Canada and the United States disclose census data fully after ninety-two and seventy-two years, respectively. U.S. population statistics from Great Lakes states in 1950 are the newest and most reliable for the 1940s. These population statistics differentiated between Francophone and Anglophone Canadians residing in the United States. Approximately 900,000 French Canadians from Quebec and New Brunswick immigrated to New England and New York from the 1840s to the 1930s to work in the mills. See Mark Paul Richard, *Loyal but French: The Negotiation of Identity by French-Canadian Descendants in the United States* (East Lansing: Michigan State University Press, 2008); Alice R. Stewart, "The Franco-Americans of Maine: A Historiographical Essay," *Maine Historical Society Quarterly* 26, no. 3 (1987): 160–79; and Gerard Brault, *French-Canadian Heritage in New England* (Hanover: University Press of New England, 1986).

27. Hansen and Brebner, *Mingling of the Canadian and American Peoples*, 246, 260. The seasonal tobacco workers program, which recruited only white southerners to work on Ontario farms starting in the 1920s, contributed to the phenomenon of return migration or serial border crossing. See Dunsworth, "Race, Exclusion, and Archival Silences," 563–93.

28. Hansen and Brebner, *Mingling of the Canadian and American Peoples*, 263.

29. Truesdell, *Canadian Born in the United States*, 35.

30. Truesdell, 42.

31. Dudley Marshall and Daniel Braithwaite both alluded to the westward and southward migration of African descendants from the Maritimes in the early twentieth century. See Arleigh M. Holder interview with Dudley Marshall, 19 July 1978, BLA-7176-MAR, MHSO; and Arleigh M. Holder interview with Daniel Braithwaite, 17 August 1978, BLA-7181-BRA, MHSO. Boston-born Constance Belfon moved to New Liskeard, Ontario, with her Jamaican-born parents likely in the 1910s. See Roy Thompson interview with Constance Belfon, 8 February 1983, BLA-9718-BEL, MHSO. See also John Franklin Belfon, "Lives Lived: Constance Lenora Giscomb Belfon," *Globe and Mail*, 29 January 1999, A20.

32. Truesdell, *Canadian Born in the United States*, 38, 41, 108. See also Charles E. Hall and Charles W. White, *Negroes in the United States, 1920–1932* (New York: Arno Press, 1969), 21.

33. Thomas A. Klug, "Residents by Day, Visitors by Night: The Origins of the Alien Commuter on the US-Canadian Border during the 1920s," *Michigan Historical Review* 34, no. 2 (2008): 79; Thomas A. Klug, "The Immigration and Naturalization Service (INS) and the Making of a Border-Crossing Culture on the US-Canada Border, 1891–1941," *American Review of Canadian Studies* 40, no. 3 (2010): 395–415.

34. Klug, "Immigration and Naturalization Service (INS) and the Making of a Border-Crossing Culture," 403; M. Smith, "Immigration and Naturalization Service (INS) at the U.S.-Canadian Border," 133–35; Donald H. Avery, "Canadian Workers and American Immigration Restriction: A Case Study of the Windsor Commuters, 1924–1931," *Mid-America* 80 (1998): 235–63.

35. Craig Robertson, *The Passport in America: The History of a Document* (New York: Oxford University Press, 2015), 208; Klug, "Residents by Day, Visitors by Night."

36. Robertson, *Passport in America*, 209. See also John Torpey, *The Invention of the Passport: Surveillance, Citizenship, and the State* (Cambridge: Cambridge University Press, 1999).

37. "Orders in Council—Décrets-du-Conseil," 21 March 1931, RG 2-A-1-a, vol. 1479, PC 1931–695, LAC.

38. Ras Makonnen, *Pan-Africanism from Within*, recorded and ed. Kenneth King (Nairobi: Oxford University Press, 1973), ix–x.

39. See Irving Abella and Harold Troper, *None Is Too Many: Canada and the Jews of Europe, 1933–1948* (Toronto: Lester and Orpen Dennys, 1982).

40. Vivian Chavis interview with Beulah Cuzzens, 3 November 1980, BLA-8586-CUZ, MHSO. On the role of the AME Church in the Atlantic World, see Dennis C. Dickerson, *The African Methodist Episcopal Church: A History* (New York: Cambridge University Press, 2020).

41. "Andrew Harding in the Michigan, Marriage Records, 1867–1952," Ancestry.com, http://www.ancestry.com (accessed 2 November 2016). Original data from Lansing, Michigan, Department of Community Health, Division for Vital Records and Health Statistics.

42. Chavis interview with Cuzzens, BLA-8586-CUZ, MHSO.

43. Chavis interview with Cuzzens.

44. Archibald Alexander Alleyne and Sheldon Taylor, *Colour Me Jazz: The Archie Alleyne Story* (Toronto: Archibald Alexander Alleyne, 2015), 3.

45. Chavis interview with Cuzzens, BLA-8586-CUZ, MHSO.

46. Adjetey, "In Search of Ethiopia."

47. Chavis interview with Cuzzens, BLA-8586-CUZ, MHSO.

48. Chavis interview with Cuzzens.

49. Chavis interview with Cuzzens.

50. Albert Barnett, "Canada Towns Recall 'Underground Railroad,'" *Chicago Defender*, 1 December 1945.

51. Vivian Chavis interview with Hilda Watkins, 19 October 1980, BLA-8538-WAT, MHSO.

52. Chavis interview with Cuzzens, BLA-8586-CUZ, MHSO.

53. Chavis interview with Cuzzens. For references on the Jones brothers, see "Arrest Minister's Sons as Policy Racketeers: Preachers Kin Back Number Game, Jones Brothers are Taken in Custody by Stege's Squad," *Chicago Defender*, 26 September 1931, 1; "Allege Jones Brothers Lose Haul to Bandits," *Baltimore Afro-American*, 14 January 1939, 5; "Uncle Sam Gives $850,000 Back to Policy Kings: 3 Negroes Regain Cash in Tax Case Compromise," *Chicago Daily Tribune*, 12 November 1940, 6; and "Millionaire Policy King Given 28 Months in Prison: Mississippian-Born Edward Jones Takes Rap for Two Brothers," *Atlanta Daily World*, 2 February 1941.

54. Chavis interview with Cuzzens, BLA-8586-CUZ, MHSO.

55. Chavis interview with Watkins, BLA-8538-WAT, MHSO.

56. Diana Braithwaite-Spence interview with Rella Braithwaite, 26 July 1981, BLA-5619-BRA, MHSO.

57. Barbara D. Savage, "Professor Merze Tate: Diplomatic Historian, Cosmopolitan Woman," in *Toward an Intellectual History of Black Women*, ed. Mia Bay et al. (Chapel Hill: University of North Carolina Press, 2015), 252–69.

58. See Mark Miller, *Such Melodious Racket: The Lost History of Jazz in Canada* (Toronto: Mercury Press, 1997); and Robin Winks, *The Blacks in Canada: A History*, 2nd ed. (Montreal: McGill-Queen's University Press, 1997), 333. On the enterprising spirit of Black porters who became entrepreneurs, including Rufus Rockhead, see Sarah-Jane Mathieu, *North of the Color Line: Migration and Black Resistance in Canada, 1870–1955* (Chapel Hill: University of North Carolina Press, 2010), 71–72. Paul Winn's father founded the Harlem Aces. Author's interview with Paul Winn, 22 May 2021, notes in author's possession. See also Gene Lees, *Oscar Peterson: The Will to Swing* (Toronto: Prospero Books, 2008); John Gilmore, *Swinging in Paradise: The Story of Jazz in Montreal* (Montreal: Véhicule Press, 1988); and Dorothy W. Williams, *The Road to Now: A History of Blacks in Montreal* (Montreal: Véhicule Press, 1997).

59. See "Pioneer 1930s Tabloid Served Montreal Black," *Montreal Star*, 19 July 1974; "Launch New Paper in Canada," *Philadelphia Tribune*, 9 August 1934; *Some Missing Pages: The Black Community in the History of Québec and Canada, Primary and Secondary Source Materials* (Quebec: Gouvernement du Québec), 130; and Almeta Speaks and Sylvia Sweeney, *In Hymn to Freedom: The History of Blacks in Canada* (New York: Academic Video Online, 1994), digitized film.

60. Holder interview with D. Braithwaite, BLA-7181-BRA, MHSO.

61. See "Curriculum Vitae," Robert Paris Edwards Scrapbook, circa 1906–1936, Stuart A. Rose Manuscript, Archives, and Rare Book Library , Emory University, Atlanta.

62. Holder interview with Daniel Braithwaite, BLA-7181-BRA, MHSO. Mauby is a drink made of tree bark extract, and souse is made from animal by-products—such as pig ears or feet, chicken feet, and the like. See also Lara Putnam, *Radical Moves: Caribbean Migrants and the Politics of Race in the Jazz Age* (Chapel Hill: University of North Carolina Press, 2013).

63. Natasha Henry, *Emancipation Day: Celebrating Freedom in Canada* (Toronto: Natural Heritage Books, 2010), 9–10. See also J. R. Kerr-Ritchie, *Rites of August First: Emancipation Day in the Black Atlantic World* (Baton Rouge: Louisiana State University, 2011).

64. Chavis interview with Cuzzens, BLA-8586-CUZ, MHSO.

65. On the Great Depression, see Victor Hoar, ed., *The Great Depression: Essays and Memoirs from Canada and the United States* (Vancouver, B.C.: Copp Clark Publishing, 1969); Michiel Horn, *The Great Depression of the 1930s in Canada* (Ottawa, Ont.: Canadian Historical Association, 1984); Lara Campbell, *Respectable Citizens: Gender, Family, and Unemployment in Ontario's Great Depression* (Toronto: University of Toronto Press, 2009); and D. Williams, *Road to Now*, 74–82.

66. Chavis interview with Cuzzens, BLA-8586-CUZ, MHSO. Segregated schools, a legacy of colonialism and slavery in British North America, restricted teaching opportunities for most Black educators and students. In 1964, Ontario lawmakers repealed Chapter 368 of the 1850 Separate Schools Act, which permitted the segregation of not only Catholic and Protestant children but also Black and white pupils. In Essex County, a community adjacent to where Cuzzens taught, the segregation of Black students persisted into the 1960s. In the postwar period, a few Black educators found employment in predominantly white public schools. Jamaican-born Denham wrote about his experience teaching at an affluent Toronto high school starting in 1963. See B. Denham Jolly, *In the Black: My Life* (Toronto: ECW Press, 2017), 101–17. See also Charles L. Glenn, *African-American/Afro-Caribbean Schooling: From the Colonial Period to the Present* (New York: Palgrave Macmillan, 2011); and Funké Aladejebi, *Schooling the System: A History of Black Women Teachers* (Montreal: McGill-Queen's University Press, 2021).

67. Chavis interview with Cuzzens, BLA-8586-CUZ, MHSO.

68. Chavis interview with Cuzzens; Richard Bak, *Turkey Stearnes and the Detroit Stars: The Negro Leagues in Detroit, 1919–1933* (Detroit: Wayne State University Press, 1994), 56. On Louis's gloves, see "Windsor Man Donates Boxing Gloves Worn in Famous Fight to Smithsonian," CBC, 26 January 2007, https://www.cbc.ca/news/canada/toronto/windsor-man-donates-boxing-gloves-worn-in-famous-fight-to-smithsonian-1.691242 (accessed 20 May 2019); "National Museum of American History Receives Joe Louis' Boxing Gloves from Historic 1936 Fight," Smithsonian, 1 February 2007, https://americanhistory.si.edu/press/releases/national-museum-american-history-receives-joe-louis%E2%80%80%99-boxing-gloves-historic-1936 (accessed 20 May 2019); and Marty Gervais, "Joe Louis' Gloves Go the Final Round," *Windsor Star*, 26 January 2007.

69. John Cohassey and Sunnie Wilson, *Toast of the Town: The Life and Times of Sunnie Wilson* (Detroit: Wayne State University Press, 2018), 66–67.

70. George Edmund Haynes, *Negro New-Comers in Detroit, Michigan: A Challenge to Christian Statesmanship: A Preliminary Survey* (New York: Home Missions

Council, 1918), 8. See also Holly M. Karibo, *Sin City North: Sex, Drugs, and Citizenship in the Detroit-Windsor Borderland* (Chapel Hill: University of North Carolina Press, 2015).

71. Haynes, *Negro New-Comers in Detroit, Michigan*, 8.

72. See Elaine Latzman Moon, *Untold Tales, Unsung Heroes: An Oral History of Detroit's African American Community, 1918–1967* (Detroit: Wayne State University Press, 1994), 46.

73. Stanley Grizzle with John Cooper, *My Name's Not George: The Story of the Brotherhood of Sleeping Car Porters in Canada; Personal Reminiscences of Stanley G. Grizzle* (Toronto: Umbrella Press, 1998), 36.

74. *Torontonensis* (Toronto: Students' Administrative Council of the University of Toronto, 1937), 35.

75. Edith McGruder, "Canada News: Toronto," *Chicago Defender*, 4 December 1937, 11.

76. Stanley Grizzle, "Canada: Toronto, Ont.," *Chicago Defender*, 17 February 1940, 10.

77. Edith McGruder, "The Change of a Case Work Agency to a Community Center" (M.A. thesis, Atlanta University, 1942).

78. Author's interview with Dr. James Kenneth Echols (Edith McGruder's son), 7 June 2017, notes in author's possession. Jamaican immigrant Harry Gairey recalled working on the Grand Trunk circa 1919 as a second chef alongside a first chef named "MacGregor," who was in fact McGruder. See Harry Gairey, *A Black Man's Toronto, 1914–1980: The Reminiscences of Harry Gairey*, ed. Donna Hill (Toronto: Multicultural History Society of Ontario, 1981), 8.

79. Sleeping car porters played an integral role in bringing information to communities, especially Canada's dispersed population. See Mathieu, *North of the Color Line*, 105.

80. See M. Smith, "Immigration and Naturalization Service (INS) at the U.S.-Canadian Border," 139.

81. "Edna Mae McGregor Obituary," *Detroit News*, 30 December 2012. On the history of Idlewild, see Ronald Jemal Stephen, *Idlewild: The Rise, Decline, and Rebirth of a Unique African American Resort Town* (Ann Arbor: University of Michigan Press, 2013).

82. "Edna Mae McGregor Obituary."

83. "Edna Mae McGregor Obituary."

84. "Robert Lewis Bradby in the Michigan, Federal Naturalization Records, 1887–1931," Ancestry.com, http://www.ancestry.com (accessed 20 April 2017). Original data from National Archives at Chicago (ARC title: *Naturalization Petitions and Records, 1906–1991*; NAI number: 1137682; Record Group title: *Records of District Courts of the United States, 1685–2009*; Record Group number: RG 21). Nora Faires explored African Canadian labor migration into Detroit from Reconstruction to the turn of the century. She referred to the frequent border crossings of African North Americans as "intergenerational return migration." See "Going across the River: Black Canadians and Detroit before the Great Migration," *Citizenship Studies* 10, no. 1 (2006): 117–34.

85. Elisha Anderson, "175 Fruitful, Fateful Years, Second Baptist Church Builds on Long History of Activism," *Detroit Free Press*, 7 February 2011; Second Baptist

Church of Detroit website, http://www.secondbaptistdetroit.org/about (accessed 20 April 2017).

86. Julia Marie Robinson, *Race, Religion, and the Pulpit: Rev. Robert L. Bradby and the Making of Urban Detroit* (Detroit: Wayne State University Press, 2015), 19–26.

87. Robinson, 26.

88. "Detroit Baptist Church Holds Centennial Exercises," *Pittsburgh Courier*, 4 April 1936, A10. See also "Detroit Church, 100, Recalls Its 13 Ex-slave Organizers," *Baltimore Afro-American*, 28 March 1936; and Cara Shelly, "Bradby's Baptists: Second Baptist Church of Detroit, 1910–1946," *Michigan Historical Review* 17, no. 1 (1991): 1–33.

89. Robert Crump, "Dr. R. L. Bradby Celebrates 20 Years' Service," *Philadelphia Tribune*, 6 November 1930, 16.

90. U. S. Poston, "'Bradby Saved Negro in Detroit,' Says U. S. Poston," *Pittsburgh Courier*, 19 November 1927.

91. David Allan Levine, *Internal Combustion: The Races in Detroit, 1915–1926* (Westport, Conn.: Greenwood Press, 1976), 15.

92. August Meier and Elliott Rudwick, *Black Detroit and the Rise of the UAW* (Ann Arbor: University of Michigan Press, 2007), 9–10.

93. For Bradby's economic and political clout, see Beth Tompkins Bates, *The Making of Black Detroit in the Age of Henry Ford* (Chapel Hill: University of North Carolina Press, 2012).

94. Bates, *Making of Black Detroit in the Age of Henry Ford*. See Kevin Boyle, *Arc of Justice: A Saga of Race, Civil Rights, and Murder in the Jazz Age* (New York: Henry Holt, 2004).

95. U. S. Poston, "'Bradby Saved Negro in Detroit.'"

96. "Toronto, Ont.," *Chicago Defender*, 2 November 1935, 23.

97. Sheldon Taylor, "Nobody Is Gonna Keep Us Back: Black Survival in Toronto, 1914–1950" (unpublished book manuscript in Taylor's possession), chaps. 7, 11, 13; K. Henry, *Black Politics in Toronto since World War I*, 15, 25.

98. "Meeting at Church Led to 47-Year Union," *Montreal Gazette*, 6 March 1988. See also William R. Scott, *The Sons of Sheba's Race: African-Americans and the Italo-Ethiopian War, 1935–1941* (Bloomington: Indiana University Press, 1993); and Joseph E. Harris, *African-American Reactions to War in Ethiopia, 1936–1941* (Baton Rouge: Louisiana State University Press, 1994).

99. Pamphlet for Afro-Canadian League, *The "Free Lance" Medical Aid to Ethiopia Fund*, 27 February 1936, STPC.

100. William R. Scott, "Black Nationalism and the Italo-Ethiopian Conflict 1934–1936," *Journal of Negro History* 63, no. 2 (1978): 129–31. In Toronto, Italians began to denounce Mussolini's aggressions when Italy invaded Ethiopia for the second time in December 1934. See John Zucchi, *Italians in Toronto: Development of a National Identity, 1875–1935* (Montreal: McGill-Queen's University Press, 1988), 170, 192.

101. James W. St. G. Walker, *"Race," Rights and the Law in the Supreme Court of Canada: Historical Case Studies* (Waterloo, Ont.: Wilfred Laurier University Press, 1997), 122–81; Eric M. Adams, "Errors of Fact and Law: Race, Space, and Hockey

in *Christie v. York*," in *The African Canadian Legal Odyssey: Historical Essays*, ed. Barrington Walker (Toronto: University of Toronto Press, 2012), 324–60. See also Constance Backhouse, *Colour-Coded: A Legal History of Racism in Canada, 1900–1950* (Toronto: University of Toronto Press, 1999).

102. Robert A. Hill et al., eds., *The Marcus Garvey and Universal Negro Improvement Association Papers, Vol. X: Africa and the Africans, 1923–1945* (Berkeley: University of California Press, 2006), clxv–clxvii.

103. Tony Martin, *Race First: The Ideological and Organizational Struggles of Marcus Garvey and the Universal Negro Improvement Association* (Westport, Conn.: Greenwood Press, 1976), 19.

104. Leo Bertley, "The Universal Negro Improvement Association of Montreal, 1917–1979" (Ph.D. diss., Concordia University, 1980), 352–53.

105. Marano, "'We All Used to Meet at the Hall': Assessing the Significance of the Universal Negro Improvement Association in Toronto, 1900–1950," *Journal of Canadian Historical Association* 25 (2014), 164.

106. Holder interview with D. Braithwaite, BLA-7181-BRA, MHSO.

107. Huguette Casimir interview with Leonard Johnston, 3 August 1978, BLA-5119-JOH, MHSO.

108. Bertley, "Universal Negro Improvement Association of Montreal," 38.

109. Reprinted in *Black Man*, 10 July 1938.

110. Hill et al., eds., *Marcus Garvey and Universal Negro Improvement Association Papers, Vol. X*, 789.

111. Hill et al., 790.

112. White authorities have long held suspicion about arming enslaved and free African peoples. Legal historian John Fabian Witt considered this controversial issue reflective of "tensions that have been internal to the law of war in American history from the Revolution to the present." Abraham Lincoln borrowed from the British military strategy when the Union recruited enslaved Africans behind Confederate lines as part of its war effort. John Fabian Witt, *Lincoln's Code: The Laws of War in American History* (New York: Free Press, 2012), 4; Gerald Horne, *Negro Comrades of the Crown: African Americans and the British Empire Fight the U.S. before Emancipation* (New York: New York University Press, 2012). During World War I, white authorities described the conflict as "a white man's war." James W. St. G. Walker, "Race and Recruitment in World War I: Enlistment of Visible Minorities in the Canadian Expeditionary Force," *Canadian Historical Review* 70, no. 1 (1989): 1. See also Glenford D. Howe, *West Indians and World War One: A Social History of the British West Indies Regiment* (London: University of London Press, 1994); Adriane Lentz-Smith, *Freedom Struggles: African Americans and World War I* (Cambridge, Mass.: Harvard University Press, 2009); Chad L. Williams, *Torchbearers of Democracy: African American Soldiers in the World War I Era* (Chapel Hill: University of North Carolina Press, 2010); Keith L. Nelson, "The 'Black Horror on the Rhine': Race as a Factor in Post–World War I Diplomacy," *Journal of Modern History* 42, no. 4 (1970): 606–27; and Melissa Shaw, "'Most Anxious to Serve Their King and Country': Black Canadians Fight to Enlist in WWI and Emerging Race Consciousness in Ontario, 1914–1919," *Social History* 49, no. 100 (2016): 543–80.

113. See Robin Winks, *The Civil War Years: Canada and the United States* (Montreal: McGill-Queen's University Press, 1998); and Josiah Henson, *An Autobiography of the Rev. Josiah Henson ("Uncle Tom") from 1789–1881* (London, Ont.: Schuyler, Smith and Co., 1881), 262–63.

114. Barbadian-born Donald Moore recalled that his childhood friend Stephen S. Springer—who had immigrated to Montreal and was the person responsible for encouraging Moore to abandon New York City for Montreal in the winter of 1913—wrote him letters while serving on a U.S. battleship during the Great War. Springer remained in the United States after the war, where he died in Chicago. See Donald Moore, *Don Moore: An Autobiography* (Toronto: Williams-Wallace, 1985), 26–28.

115. On wartime discrimination in Canada, see Simon James Theobald, "A False Sense of Equality: The Black Canadian Experience of the Second World War" (M.A. thesis, University of Ottawa, 2008); and Winks, *Blacks in Canada*, 405.

116. "Confrontation at the Palais Royale," *Toronto Star*, 9 April 1992.

117. Taylor, "Nobody Is Gonna Keep Us Back," chap. 9a, 14–15. See also Philip Mascoll, "Canada's First Black Surgeon 'Role Model and Inspiration'; Dr. Douglas Salmon Known for His Courage, Humility, Compassion, Fought for the Rights of Blacks to See Jazz Greats at Palais," *Toronto Star*, 27 September 2005. After marrying Beverly Bell in 1956, the couple moved to Detroit, where Doug and Bev practiced as a surgeon and nurse, respectively. They returned to Canada in the 1960s.

118. See Shaw, "'Most Anxious to Serve Their King and Country'"; Taylor, "Nobody Is Gonna Keep Us Back"; McGruder, "Change of a Case Work Agency to a Community Center," 28.

119. The British Commonwealth Air Training Plan facilitated this movement of Caribbean servicemen to Canada. See Sheldon Taylor, "Darkening the Complexion of Canadian Society: Black Activism, Policy-Making, and Black Immigration from the Caribbean to Canada, 1940s–1960s" (Ph.D. diss., University of Toronto, 1994), 98–99.

120. Gaffen, *Cross-Border Warriors*, 51.

121. Gaffen, 50, 217.

122. See Jon Meacham, *Destiny and Power: The American Odyssey of George Herbert Walker Bush* (New York: Random House, 2015), 39; "Canada's Yanks: Air Force, Part 16," *Legion Magazine*, 7 September 2020, https://legionmagazine.com/en/2006/07/canadas-yanks/. By 1940, Canada had waived its requirement for foreign nationals, such as U.S. citizens, to take the Oath of Allegiance to King George VI. As a result, U.S. nationals did not jeopardize their citizenship or violate the United States' Neutrality Act when enlisting in the Canadian armed forces. Instead, Canada required U.S. nationals to take an Oath of Obedience. Barbadian Owen Rowe recalled leaving home on 14 May 1942 for Canada by way of New York Harbor. As a British subject, Rowe served in the Canadian Army and RCAF, ultimately rising to Flying Officer during the war. "Veteran Stories: Owen Rowe," The Memory Project, http://www.thememoryproject.com/stories/1157:owen-rowe/, (accessed 7 September 2020). See also Gaffen, *Cross-Border Warriors*, 43–150.

123. A117586 and R295543, Heron, Gilbert St. Elmo, 06–97139, Military Personnel file (obtained under Access to Information and Privacy), LAC.

124. Marcus Baram, *Gil Scott-Heron: Pieces of a Man* (New York: St. Martin's Press, 2014), 6.

125. See Thomas C. Holt, *The Problem of Freedom: Race, Labor, and Politics in Jamaica and Britain, 1832–1938* (Baltimore: Johns Hopkins University Press, 1992).

126. A117586 and R295543, Heron, Gilbert St. Elmo, LAC.

127. Notwithstanding the color bar, more than a handful of African Canadians served in the RCAF. See Theobald, "False Sense of Equality," 53.

128. A117586 and R295543, Heron, Gilbert St. Elmo, LAC.

129. "Trooper Heron Inspires Team," *Globe and Mail*, 20 July 1943, 14.

130. "Negro Becomes First U.S. Soccer Player to Win Place on Famous Glasgow Squad," *New York Times*, 18 August 1951.

131. "One Man Gang Active in Army Meet Today," *Globe and Mail*, 24 July 1943.

132. D116521, Heron, Roy Trevor, 06–97165, Military Personnel file (obtained under Access to Information and Privacy), LAC.

133. Lorne Foster, "At 85, Roy Heron Is a Leader," *Share*, 22 December 2004.

134. D116521, Heron, Roy Trevor, LAC.

135. "Job Opportunities with the Signal Corp," Veterans Affairs Canada, http://www.veterans.gc.ca/eng/video-gallery/video/8928 (accessed 19 April 2017).

136. "Veteran Stories: Roy Trevor Gilbert Heron," The Memory Project, http://www.thememoryproject.com/stories/16:roy-trevor-gilbert-heron/ (accessed 19 April 2017).

137. "Veteran Stories: Leonard Braithwaite, Air Force," The Memory Project, http://www.thememoryproject.com/stories/2530:leonard-braithwaite/ (accessed 19 June 2017).

138. Holder interview with D. Braithwaite, BLA-7181-BRA, MHSO.

139. Holder interview with D. Braithwaite.

140. Lincoln M. Alexander, *"Go to School, You're a Little Black Boy": The Honourable Lincoln M. Alexander: A Memoir* (Toronto: Dundurn Press, 2010), 35.

141. See Birte Timm, *Nationalists Abroad: The Jamaica Progressive League and the Foundations of Jamaican Independence* (Kingston, Jam.: Ian Randle Publishers, 2016). See also Steven High, *Base Colonies in the Western Hemisphere, 1940–1967* (Basingstoke, Eng.: Palgrave Macmillan, 2009). On return migration from the United States to the Caribbean after 1924 immigration restriction (1924–45), see W. James, *Holding Aloft the Banner of Ethiopia*, 8.

142. "Malcolm M. Moyston," *Globe and Mail*, 7 September 1951, 24.

143. Allan Morrison Papers, 1940–1968, Folder MG 632, Schomburg Center for Research in Black Culture, New York.

144. DeShield was an outspoken leader against anti-Black racism and fascism. See "Canadian Youth Congress Hears of Race Problem: Montreal Girl Says Unfortunate Situation Is Same Everywhere," *Baltimore Afro-American*, 27 June 1936; and "Housing Refused," *Montreal Gazette*, 15 March 1941. For Helen Redmon, see Fanfair, "Freemon Redmon Built His Scarborough Home 70 Years Ago."

145. Constance Troy to W. E. B. Du Bois, 17 July 1936, DBP. See also Taylor, "Nobody Is Gonna Keep Us Back," chap. 7, 15–16.

146. Edward Toles, "Stars-Stripes Scribe Wins Plaudits of GIs, Generals," *Chicago Defender*, 25 November 1944, 5. See also Maggi Morehouse, "Military Service, Governance, and the African Diaspora," *African and Black Diaspora: An International Journal* 4, no. 1 (January 2011): 41–55.

147. "8 Negro Scribes Now Covering French Invasion," *Chicago Defender*, 26 August 1944, 18.

148. "Race Gunners Down 'Master Race' Theory," *New Journal and Guide* (Norfolk), 15 July 1944, B2.

149. "The 'Lucky Seven,'" *Chicago Defender*, 15 July 1944.

150. "Black White Fighter Pilots from WWII Reunion in Dania Beach," *Westside Gazette (Fort Lauderdale)*, 19 October 2006, 8A; "Ex-Pilot Missionary," *Baltimore Afro-American*, 19 January 1957, 13.

151. Tracie Reddick, "Tuskegee Airman Yenwith Whitney Soared above Barriers," *Bradenton (Fla.) Herald*, 27 July 2000.

152. See Hubert Fauntleroy Julian and John Bulloch, *Black Eagle: Colonel Hubert Julian* (London: Adventurers Club, 1965).

153. "Archives of Ontario; Toronto, Ontario Canada; Registrations of Marriages, 1869–1928; Series: MS932; Reel: 486," Ancestry.com, http://www.ancestry.com (accessed 12 June 2017). Original data from Ontario, Canada, Select Marriages, AO.

154. "Organ of Colored Folk Has First Anniversary," *Globe and Mail*, 14 December 1915.

155. See J. Walker, "Race and Recruitment in World War I"; and Shaw, "'Most Anxious to Serve Their King and Country.'"

156. "Canadian Editor Visits Defender," *Chicago Defender*, 28 August 1915, 1; "Railway Men Hold 4th Annual Convention," *Chicago Defender*, 13 October 1917, 6.

157. *The Detroit Educational Bulletin, Volume 4* (Detroit: Julius Mack and Company, 1920), 11, 61.

158. "1920; Census Place: Bronx Assembly District 8, Bronx, New York; Roll: T625_1143; Page 7A; Enumeration District: 461; Image: 396," Ancestry.com, http://www.ancestry.com (accessed 12 June 2017). Original data from Fourteenth Census of the United States, 1920.

159. It is not entirely clear why the enumerator listed the family as white. There is no indication in the Whitney family's background that suggested a desire to pass for white. "U.S., Social Security Death Index, 1935–2014," Ancestry.com, http://www.ancestry.com (accessed 12 June 2017). Original data from Social Security Administration.

160. Frederick German Detweiler, *The Negro Press in the United States* (Chicago: University of Chicago Press, 1922), 29, 30, 124.

161. Gerald Horne, *The Rise and Fall of the Associated Negro Press: Claude Albert Barnett's Pan-African News and the Jim Crow Paradox* (Champaign: University of Illinois Press, 2017).

162. "Lodge and Fraternal Notes," *Pittsburgh Courier*, 29 March 1924, 13.

163. Morrison's article "Negroes Fight at Side of West Front Whites" reprinted in Rudolph Dunbar, "Army Paper Lauds Mixed Infantry: Stars, Stripes Asserts Change Was Necessary," *Atlanta Daily World*, 5 April 1945, 1.

164. "Gen. Lee, Now Rapped, Mixed Troops in War," *Chicago Defender*, 6 September 1947, 6.

165. General Lee as quoted in Dunbar, "Army Paper Lauds Mixed Infantry."

166. Allan Morrison, "Negro Doughs Join First Army's Eastward Big Drive," *Stars and Stripes*, 6 April 1945.

167. Allan Morrison, "The Negro GI in Germany," *Stars and Stripes*, 12 August 1945.

168. Morrison, "Negro GI in Germany"; "'Worse Than Hitler,' White Americans Chief Source of Race Bigotry in Germany," *Pittsburgh Courier*, 1 September 1945.

169. Morrison, "Negro GI in Germany."

170. Morrison, "Negro GI in Germany."

171. "Nazism in Reverse Can Reform America—Mays: Morehouse President Tells," *Baltimore Afro-American*, 16 June 1945, 47.

172. On segregation of the 368th Infantry Division of the U.S. Expeditionary Forces, see Lentz-Smith, *Freedom Struggles*, 100.

173. Jonathan Holloway used the metaphor of racial trip wires in his spring 2013 lectures at Yale University.

174. Hill to mother, 21 June 1943, F 2130-1-0-2, Daniel G. Hill (DGH) fonds, AO.

175. See Christine Knauer, *Let Us Fight as Free Men: Black Soldiers and Civil Rights* (Philadelphia: University of Pennsylvania Press, 2014); Jennifer E. Brooks, *Defining the Peace: World War II Veterans, Race, and the Remaking of Southern Political Tradition* (Chapel Hill: University of North Carolina Press, 2004); Phillip McGuire, ed., *Taps for a Jim Crow Army: Letters from Black Soldiers in World War Two* (Santa Barbara, Calif.: ABC-CLIO, 1983); Richard Dalfiume, *Desegregation of the U.S. Armed Forces: Fighting on Two Fronts, 1939–1953* (Columbia: University of Missouri Press, 1969); Lawrence P. Scott, *Double V: The Civil Rights Struggle of the Tuskegee Airmen* (East Lansing: Michigan State University Press, 2012); and Julian M. Pleasants, *Home Front: North Carolina during World War II* (Gainesville: University of Florida Press, 2017).

176. Hill to mother, 9 May 1943, F 2130-1-0-2, DGH fonds, AO.

177. Hill to his father and mother, 28 February 1943, F 2130-1-0-2, DGH fonds, AO.

178. See Knauer, *Let Us Fight as Free Men*; Brooks, *Defining the Peace*; L. Scott, *Double V*; McGuire, *Taps for a Jim Crow Army*; and Dalfiume, *Desegregation of the U.S. Armed Forces*.

179. See Ben Burns, *Nitty Gritty: A White Editor in Black Journalism* (Jackson: University of Mississippi Press, 1996), 76, 97. See also Gerald D. Jaynes and Robin M. Williams Jr., *A Common Destiny: Blacks and American Society* (Washington, D.C.: National Academies Press, 1989), xx.

180. Allan Malcolm Morrison Papers, SCM 77-62 (MG 33), box 1, folder 1, Schomburg Center for Research in Black Culture, New York.

181. "Name changed by decree of Court from Allan Malcolm Moyston to Allan Malcolm Morrison, as part of the Naturalization," read the notation on the back of the naturalization certificate. Allan Malcolm Morrison Papers, SCM 77-62 (MG 33), box 1, folder 1.

182. Wendy Forbes to Sheldon Taylor, 29 January 2009, STPC.

183. Baram, *Gil Scott-Heron*, 7–9.

184. D116521, Heron, Roy Trevor, LAC.

185. Holder interview with D. Braithwaite, BLA-7181-BRA, MHSO.

186. Holder interview with D. Braithwaite.

187. "Transcript of presentation to the Donald Marshall Inquiry, Halifax, N.S. Chairman, Mr. Thomas R. Berger, Nov. 1988," Carrie M. Best/A Digital Archive, http://www.parl.ns.ca/carriebest/marshall.html (accessed 19 April 2017).

188. "Takes Action," *Clarion* (New Glasgow), December 1946; "The NSCAAP," *Clarion* (New Glasgow), December 1946. On Desmond's case, see also "Negress Charges Discrimination after Ejection from Theatre in N.S.," *Globe and Mail*, 30 November 1946, 17; "Negro Fined in Segregation Dispute Sues Theater Man," *St. Louis Post-Dispatch*, 1 December 1946, 31; "Canadians Fight Color Bar in Bridge Tournaments: Action Follows Ban on Member," *Chicago Defender*, 14 December 1946, 13; and "Negress' Ejection Case Writ Application Heard," *Globe and Mail*, 11 January 1947, 15.

189. Holder interview with D. Braithwaite, BLA-7181-BRA, MHSO.

190. Diana Braithwaite interview with Rella Braithwaite, 26 July 1981, BLA-5619-BRA, MHSO.

191. Holder interview with D. Braithwaite, BLA-7181-BRA, MHSO. An Ontario Parliamentarian rebuked the racist practice of compelling aspiring African Canadian nurses to move to the United States. See J. B. Salsberg letter to Home Service Association, 13 March 1947, STPC. For a case study of Black women nurses in postwar Canada, see Karen Flynn, *Moving beyond Borders: A History of Black Canadian and Caribbean Women in the Diaspora* (Toronto: University of Toronto Press, 2011).

192. "Veterans Ask Province Act on Negro Ban," *Globe and Mail*, 4 October 1947.

193. Holder interview with D. Braithwaite, BLA-7181-BRA, MHSO.

194. "Negro Reports Hospitals Refused His 2 Daughters," *Toronto Daily Star*, 18 October 1947; "Give High Award to Negro Nurse," *Globe and Mail*, 6 October 1948.

195. Cathy MacDonald, "50 Years Ago, Oliver Campaigned to Get Blacks into Nursing School," *Daily News* (Nova Scotia), 4 March 1994; "Pearleen Oliver, a Long-Time Leader in N.S. Black Community, Dies at 91," *Canadian Press*, 25 July 2008.

196. "Negro Girls as Nurses Are Found 'Unwelcome' YWCA Survey Reveals," *Globe and Mail*, 26 September 1947; "Negro Nurses Asked to Leave, Roadhouse Keeper Rapped," *Globe and Mail*, 15 June 1950.

197. "'Emancipation' Day: Bar to Negro Applicants for Training as Nurses Cited as Example of Discrimination," *Globe and Mail*, 2 August 1946.

198. "'Emancipation' Day: Bar to Negro Applicants."

199. Box 1, folder 4, A1977-0017; box 2, folders 1 and 2, University of Toronto Archives.

200. Letter from University of Toronto Director of Nursing Kathleen Russell to Mary Tennant, 14 May 1942, A77-0017, box 1, folder 4, University of Toronto Archives.

201. Diana Braithwaite interview with Donald Carty, 25 May 1982, BLA-7984-STR, MHSO.

202. Taylor, "Nobody Is Gonna Keep Us Back," chap. 9a, 19.

203. Quoted in Lawrence Hill, *Women of Vision: The Story of the Canadian Negro Women's Association, 1951–1976* (Toronto: Umbrella Press, 1996), 25.

204. Dan Hill, *I Am My Father's Son: A Memoir of Love and Forgiveness* (Toronto: HarperCollins Publishers, 2009), 131.

205. The Negro Citizenship Association in Toronto helped Caribbean nurses find placements in Ontario hospitals. See Moore, *Don Moore*, 139–50.

206. Holder interview with D. Braithwaite, BLA-7181-BRA, MHSO. Robeson participated in U.S.-Canadian cross-border activism. In 1946, for example, he crossed the border from Detroit to support striking Chrysler workers in Windsor. "Paul

Robeson, Negro Baritone, Aids Windsor Chrysler Pickets," *Globe and Mail*, 18 July 1946. See also Laurel Sefton MacDowell, "Paul Robeson in Canada: A Border Story," *Labor* 51 (Spring 2003): 177–221; and Hollis R. Lynch, *Black American Radicals and the Liberation of Africa: The Council on African Affairs, 1937–1955* (Ithaca: Cornell University Press, 1978). In 1944, the social service organization Home Service Association, where Edith McGruder had served as a caseworker, welcomed luminaries, such as Robeson, his friend and fellow cofounder of the Pan-Africanist Council on African Affairs Max Yergan, writer Langston Hughes, and pioneering social worker Forrester Washington. See Home Service Association of Toronto Report, January 1944, STPC.

207. Cohassey and Wilson, *Toast of the Town*, 155.

208. Don Carty, "Discrimination Is Making Last-Ditch Stand in Canada," *Pittsburgh Courier*, 29 July 1950, 26. Carty believed in the power of journalism to ameliorate the conditions of Black people. From 1953 to 1956, Carty and Roy Greenidge founded and edited the *Canadian Negro*. Joe Louis provided financial assistance. See Winks, *Blacks in Canada*, 406.

209. "Glasgow Celtic: New Player Takes Scots by Storm," *South China Morning Post*, 5 September 1951, 2; "Negro Becomes First U.S. Soccer Player to Win Place on Famous Glasgow Squad"; "First Negro Signed with Scotland Soccer Team," *Philadelphia Tribune*, 21 August 1951, 10.

210. See Leslie Gordon Goffe, *Gil Scott-Heron: A Father and Son Story* (Kingston, Jam.: LMH Publishing, 2012); and Baram, *Gil Scott-Heron*, 11.

211. Paul Dimeo and Gerry P. T. Finn, "Racism, National Identity, and Scottish Football," in *"Race," Sport, and British Society*, ed. Ben Carrington and Ian McDonald (London: Routledge), 29–48.

212. Chavis interview with Cuzzens, BLA-8586-CUZ, MHSO.

CHAPTER 3

1. On Black and Jewish relations, see Arleigh M. Holder interview with Dudley Marshall, 19 July 1978, BLA-7176-MAR, MHSO. As consumers and renters, Black residents often lived alongside Jewish immigrants who frequently accommodated them. Gwendolyn Johnston, a Toronto-born resident, who lived on Lippincott Street, a short residential artery in the heart of immigrant Toronto, described Black-Jewish relations in these words: "There were no problems where the Jewish people and Black people were concerned. Black people are, I think, the world's greatest consumers, and Jewish people always have something to sell, so on that basis, we remain pretty good friends." See also Ruth Lewis interview with Gwendolyn Johnston, 22 February 1979, BLAH-6901-JOH, MHSO. On Black tenants leasing rental property from Jewish landlords in Ontario, see Kenneth Amoroso interview with Harry Gairey, 9 July 1977, BLA-1446-GAI, MHSO; Stanley Grizzle with John Cooper, *My Name's Not George: The Story of the Brotherhood of Sleeping Car Porters in Canada; Personal Reminiscences of Stanley G. Grizzle* (Toronto: Umbrella Press, 1998), 32; and Donald Moore, *Don Moore: An Autobiography* (Toronto: Williams-Wallace, 1985), 32. On a critical analysis of Black-Jewish relations, see Jack Salzman and Cornel West, eds., *Struggles in the Promised Land: Towards a History of Black-Jewish Relations in the United States* (New York: Oxford University Press, 1997). On Uncle Tom, see

Josiah Henson and John Lobb, *Uncle Tom's Story of His Life: An Autobiography of the Rev. Josiah Henson, from 1789-1876* (Chapel Hill: University of North Carolina Press, 2011).

2. Kenneth Kidd, "Amid Sweeping Change, Pivotal Anniversary Goes Unremarked; with the Province's Dramatic Revamp of Human Rights System, Events Rooted in 1948 Deserve New Attention," *Toronto Star*, 6 July 2008; Ross Lambertson, "'The Dresden Story': Racism, Human Rights, and the Jewish Labour Committee of Canada," *Labour* 47 (2001): 43–82; James W. St. G. Walker, "The 'Jewish Phase' in the Movement for Racial Equality in Canada," *Canadian Ethnic Studies* 34, no. 1 (2002): 1–29; Sidney Katz, "Jim Crow Lives in Dresden," *Maclean's*, 1 November 1949. See also Kate A. Baldwin, *Beyond the Color Line and the Iron Curtain: Reading Encounters between Black and Red, 1922-1963* (Durham, N.C.: Duke University Press, 2002).

3. See Carmela Patrias and Ruth A. Frager, "'This Is Our Country, These Are Our Rights': Minorities and the Origins of Ontario's Human Rights Campaigns," *Canadian Historical Review* 82, no. 1 (2001): 1–35.

4. Although the 1931 Statute of Westminster made Canada a sovereign nation, Canada continued to look to Great Britain as its principal ally. On the postwar decline of the British Empire and Canada's rise as an aspiring middle power, see Norman Hillmer and J. L. Granatstein, *Empire to Umpire: Canada and the World to the 1990s* (Toronto: Copp Clark Longman, 1994).

5. John Wendell Holmes, *Life with Uncle: The Canadian-American Relationship* (Toronto: University of Toronto Press, 1981).

6. On "the problem of the color line" in the twentieth century, see W. E. B. Du Bois, *The Souls of Black Folk*, with an introduction by Jonathan Holloway (New Haven, Conn.: Yale University Press, 2015). On the "American dilemma," see Gunnar Myrdal, *An American Dilemma* (New Brunswick, N.J.: Transaction Publishers, 2009). At least since Confederation, Canadian officials feared that African American immigrants would bring the "Negro problem" to Canada. See Sarah-Jane Mathieu, *North of the Color Line: Migration and Black Resistance in Canada, 1870-1955* (Chapel Hill: University of North Carolina Press, 2010), 24–26.

7. See Robert A. Hill et al., eds., *The Marcus Garvey and Universal Negro Improvement Association Papers, Vol. XII: The Caribbean Diaspora, 1920-1921* (Durham, N.C.: Duke University Press, 2014), 32–48.

8. In addition to legislating domestic public policies, the liberalization of postwar Canadian immigration policy was indicative of Canada's global aspirations. See Triadafilos Triadafilopoulos, "Dismantling White Canada: Race, Rights, and the Origins of the Points System," in *Wanted and Welcome? Policies for Highly Skilled Immigrants in Comparative Perspective*, ed. Triadafilos Triadafilopoulos (New York: Springer, 2013), 15–37. For a detailed social scientific account of how postwar states internalized human rights norms, see Thomas Risse, Stephen Ropp, and Kathryn Sikkink, eds., *The Power of Human Rights: International Norms and Domestic Change* (New York: Cambridge University Press, 1999). For an account on the evolution of rights in Canada, see Ross Lambertson, *Repression and Resistance: Canadian Human Rights Activists, 1930-1960* (Toronto: University of Toronto Press, 2005).

9. See A. John Hobbins, "Eleanor Roosevelt, John Humphrey, and Canadian Opposition to the Universal Declaration," *International Journal* 53, no. 2 (Spring 1998): 325–42; Dominique Clément, "Human Rights in Canadian Domestic and Foreign Politics: From 'Niggardly Acceptance' to Enthusiastic Embrace," *Human Rights Quarterly* 34, no. 3 (2012): 751–78; Jennifer Tunnicliffe, "A Limited Vision: Canadian Participation in the Adoption of the International Covenants on Human Rights," in *Taking Liberties: A History of Human Rights in Canada*, ed. David Goutor and Stephen Heathorn (Toronto: Oxford University Press, 2013), 166–89; George Egerton, "Entering the Age of Human Rights: Religion, Politics, and Canadian Liberalism, 1945–50," *Canadian Historical Review* 85, no. 3 (2004): 451–79; Cathal Nolan, "Reluctant Liberal: Canada, Human Rights, and the United Nations, 1944–65," *Diplomacy and Statecraft* 2, no. 3 (1991): 281–305; and William Schabas, "Canada and the Adoption of the Universal Declaration," *McGill Law Journal* 43, no. 2 (1998): 403–41. See also A. John Hobbins, ed., *On the Edge of Greatness: The Diaries of John Humphrey, First Director of the United Nations Division of Human Rights* (Montreal: McGill-Queen's University Press, 1994). On FDR and the role that the United States played in the establishment of the UDHR, see Elizabeth Borgwardt, *A New Deal for the World: America's Vision for Human Rights* (Cambridge, Mass.: Belknap Press of Harvard University Press, 2005). Because of the racial question, the U.S. government resisted human rights for African Americans. See Carol Anderson, *Eyes Off the Prize: The United Nations and the African American Struggle for Human Rights, 1944–1955* (New York: Cambridge University Press, 2003).

10. The persistence of Canada's mistreatment of Indigenous peoples throughout the twentieth century remains a glaring exception. This blight underscores the intractability of Canadian colonialism and epitomizes the dissonance between social progress and racialized oppression of an "invisible" people.

11. After 1945, African Canadians increased their commitment to dismantle the vestiges of ethno-racial preferences in Canadian immigration policy and to confront domestic racial discrimination. These stalwarts—often operating through organized labor and community organizations, chiefly the Negro Citizenship Association—demanded that Ottawa bureaucrats liberalize Black immigration. Black activists shone light on Ottawa's trading partnerships with Commonwealth territories, especially in the Caribbean Basin, to denounce Canadian hypocrisy and hubris—while borrowing from the discourse of liberal internationalism. Harry Gairey, a senior statesman in Toronto's Black community, critiqued this double standard. See Harry Gairey, *A Black Man's Toronto, 1914–1980: The Reminiscences of Harry Gairey*, ed. Donna Hill (Toronto: Multicultural History Society of Ontario, 1981), 32. See Sheldon Taylor, "Darkening the Complexion of Canadian Society: Black Activism, Policy-Making, and Black Immigration from the Caribbean to Canada, 1940s-1960s" (Ph.D. diss., University of Toronto, 1994); and Adrienne Shadd, *The Journey from Tollgate to Parkway: African Canadians in Hamilton* (Toronto: Dundurn Press, 2010), 252–54. At the 1966 Canada–West Indies Conference in Ottawa, Canadian officials hoped that decolonization would provide them with greater access into Caribbean markets. See Vic Satzewich, "Racism and Canadian Immigration Policy: The Government's View of Caribbean Migration, 1962–1966," *Canadian Ethnic Studies* 21, no. 1 (1989): 80.

12. On cross-pollination between Black activists in the United States and Canada, see Rosanne Waters, "African Canadian Anti-discrimination Activism and the Transnational Civil Rights Movement, 1945–1965," *Journal of the Canadian Historical Association* 24, no. 2 (2013): 386–424; and Agnes Calliste, "The Influence of the Civil Rights and Black Power Movement in Canada," *Race, Gender and Class* 2, no. 3 (Spring 1995): 123–39.

13. Bonny Ibhawoh, *Imperialism and Human Rights: Colonial Discourses of Rights and Liberties in African History* (Albany: State University of New York Press, 2007), 2.

14. See Adrian Lentz-Smith, *Freedom Struggles: African Americans and World War I* (Cambridge, Mass.: Harvard University Press, 2009). See Chad L. Williams, *Torchbearers of Democracy: African American Soldiers in the World War I Era* (Chapel Hill: University of North Carolina Press, 2010); and Mark Whalan, *The Great War and the Culture of the New Negro* (Gainesville: University Press of Florida, 2008). See William C. Nell, *The Colored Patriots of the American Revolution with Sketches of Several Distinguished Colored Persons: To Which Is Added a Brief Survey of the Condition and Prospects of Colored Americans* (Boston: Robert F. Wallcut, 1855); William Wells Brown, *The Negro in the American Rebellion: His Heroism and Fidelity* (Boston: Lee and Shepard, 1867); George Washington Williams, *History of the Negro Race in America from 1619 to 1880: Negros as Slaves, as Soldiers, and as Citizens* (New York: G. P. Putnam's Sons, 1883); and Benjamin Quarles, *The Negro in the American Revolution* (Williamsburg, Va.: Institute of Early American History and Culture, 1961).

15. Trish Crawford, "Key to Ombudsman in His Own Roots," *Toronto Star*, 15 July 1984.

16. Dan Hill, *I Am My Father's Son: A Memoir of Love and Forgiveness* (Toronto: HarperCollins Publishers, 2009), 34, 37.

17. D. Hill, 33.

18. D. Hill, 63.

19. D. Hill, 34.

20. Lawrence Hill, "Dad Will Always 'Live within Us'; A Son Remembers Daniel Hill III; Activist, Storyteller, Champion, Inspirer," *Toronto Star*, 6 July 2003.

21. D. Hill, *I Am My Father's Son*, 26–27.

22. See "Dr. Du Bois to Speak at Gardens Sunday," *Toronto Daily Star*, 6 May 1952.

23. L. Hill, "Dad Will Always 'Live within Us.'"

24. "The War Years," F 2130-8-0-3, DGH fonds, AO.

25. D. Hill, *I Am My Father's Son*, 130–31.

26. "Coming to Canada," F 2130-8-0-3, DGH fonds, AO.

27. W. E. B. Du Bois, *The Philadelphia Negro: A Social Study* (New York: Oxford University Press, 2007).

28. Daniel G. Hill, "Negroes in Toronto: A Sociological Study of a Minority Group" (Ph.D. diss., University of Toronto, 1960).

29. D. Hill, 82.

30. See Robin Winks, *The Blacks in Canada: A History* (Montreal: McGill-Queen's University Press, 1997).

31. After reading an October 1968 article that Winks had published on African Canadian history in the *Journal of Negro History*, Hill sent Winks a letter at Yale University, where he taught. Hill believed that the situation of African Canadians no longer looked as bleak as it once did, especially in Toronto, "which is a 'major point of entry' for blacks and a new history as well as a new sociology may have to be written," Hill explained. Acknowledging the meaningful changes that had taken place since 1960, Hill admitted to Winks, "Your material and my Ph.D. thesis are rather out of date." Hill to Robin Winks, December 1968, F 2130-2-1-1 to F 2130-2-1-8, DGH fonds, AO.

32. Gairey, *Black Man's Toronto*, 2.

33. The act provided no protections to domestic workers, nonprofit organizations (parochial, fraternal, charitable, or social), or small businesses with fewer than five employees. See Fair Employment Practices Act, 1951.

34. Bromley Armstrong and Sheldon Taylor, *Bromley, Tireless Champion for Just Causes: Memoirs of Bromley L. Armstrong* (Pickering, Ont.: Vitabu Publications, 2000), 79. Armstrong, Chinese Canadian activist Ruth Lor, and Sid Blum, director of the Joint Labour Committee on Human Rights, helped integrate Dresden, Ontario, in 1954. For an account of the role that Jewish Canadian activists played in this struggle, see J. Walker, "'Jewish Phase' in the Movement for Racial Equality in Canada"; and Lambertson, "'Dresden Story.'"

35. Gairey, *Black Man's Toronto*, 2.

36. Despite an empty maternity ward, doctors waited nearly two hours before attending to Donna and her husband in the emergency room. Describing the incident to their son years later, Donna and Daniel Hill recalled sensing a silent hostility toward them from the medical staff. The image of a pregnant, petite white woman with a six-foot-two Black husband who weighed over 200 pounds infuriated the senior white male doctor who eventually came to Donna Hill's aide with two junior colleagues. Although Donna was clearly in labor, the senior doctor attributed her pain to an "appendicitis attack" for which he had to "operate for appendicitis." After the hospital staff sent Daniel Hill home, the senior doctor performed the appendectomy, before allowing a laboring Donna Hill to give birth to her baby boy. After the nightmarish evening, Daniel Hill returned to the hospital to greet his wife and newborn son only to have one of the junior doctors confide in him, "I witnessed your wife's operation and read the report. Her appendix was perfectly normal." The junior doctor confirmed what the Hills knew intuitively: the ranking obstetrician made the Hills, especially Donna, pay an excruciating price for their interracial union and biracial child that evening. See D. Hill, *I Am My Father's Son*, chap. 1, "Mom's Pregnant Appendix."

37. See Lawrence Hill, "Lawrence Hill Reflects on His Relationship with His Father and with His Own Children," *CBC Books*, 18 January 2020. See also Lawrence Hill, *Black Berry, Sweet Juice: On Being Black and White in Canada* (Toronto: HarperCollins, 2010).

38. Moore, *Don Moore*, 111, 114.

39. On anti-Asian racism, see W. Peter Ward, *White Canada Forever: Popular Attitudes and Public Policy towards Orientals in British Columbia* (Montreal: McGill-Queen's University Press, 2002); and Ken Adachi, *The Enemy That Never Was: A History of Japanese Canadians* (Toronto: McClelland and Steward, 1976).

40. Quebec avoided fair accommodation legislation when most provinces moved in this direction. The Quebec Hotels Act of 1963 helped remedy discrimination.

41. "Clerk Bars Coloured Premier," *Ottawa Journal*, 5 November 1954.

42. "From the Secretary of State for the Colonies," 18 November 1954, CO 1031/1464, U.K. National Archives, Kew; "Insult to Barbados," *Barbados Advocate*, 2 November 1954.

43. "From the Secretary of State for the Colonies."

44. "From the Secretary of State for the Colonies."

45. "Insult to Barbados." See K. Baldwin, *Beyond the Color Line and the Iron Curtain*.

46. See Thomas Borstelmann, *The Cold War and the Color Line: American Race Relations in the Global Arena* (Cambridge, Mass.: Harvard University Press, 2001); and Mary L. Dudziak, *Cold War Civil Rights: Race and the Image of American Democracy* (Princeton, N.J.: Princeton University Press, 2000).

47. See St. Clair Drake and Horace Cayton, *Black Metropolis: A Study of Negro Life in a Northern City* (Chicago: University of Chicago Press, 1945), 61.

48. D. Hill, *I Am My Father's Son*, 55.

49. D. Hill, 49.

50. The population statistics for African descendants before the 1970s are unreliable because of under-reporting. See Keith S. Henry, *Black Politics in Toronto since World War I* (Toronto: Multicultural History Society of Ontario, 1981), 13. When Romain Pitt, nephew of prominent Toronto lawyer and long-time UNIA president B. J. Spencer-Pitt, arrived in Toronto from Grenada in December 1954, he observed that "Black people were scarce as gold." Lance Talbot interview with Romain Pitt, 16 May 1990, BLA-10794-PIT, MHSO.

51. Mary L. Dudziak, "The Case of 'Death for a Dollar Ninety-Five': Miscarriages of Justice and Constructions of American Identity," in *When Law Fails: Making Sense of Miscarriages of Justice*, ed. Charles J. Ogletree Jr. and Austin Sarat (New York: New York University Press, 2009), 25–49.

52. For an analysis of postwar U.S. media consumption in Canada, see Adam J. Green, "Images of Americans: The United States in Canadian Newspapers during the 1960s" (Ph.D. diss., University of Ottawa, 2006).

53. 1955-1959, "Correspondence Re: Jimmy Wilson, 1958—Letters to Canada's Station CKEY," container SG 13823, folders 1 and 2, J. Folsom Governor of Alabama, ADA.

54. "Toronto Woman Asks Nkrumah to Help Avert $1.95 Execution," *Toronto Star*, 22 August 1958.

55. Dudziak, *Cold War Civil Rights*, 3–46.

56. Dudziak, "Case of 'Death for a Dollar Ninety-Five,'" 28.

57. On southern constructs of Black masculinity, see Crystal Feimster, *Southern Horrors: Women and the Politics of Rape and Lynching* (Cambridge, Mass.: Harvard University Press, 2009). See also Stewart Tolnay and E. M. Beck, *A Festival of Violence: An Analysis of Southern Lynchings, 1882-1930* (Champaign: University of Illinois Press, 1995).

58. 1955-1959, container SG 13823, folder 1, CKEY letters to Folsom, ADA.

59. African Canadian voices constitute a glaring absence in the petitions. Either these men or women chose not to disclose their racial identity in their letters, which is, in and of itself, counterintuitive to the ideals of Black Internationalisms and post-war African diasporic solidarity—that is, the unity and political agitation of persons of African descent to combat global white supremacy—or perhaps these men and women exercised other forms of protest through their churches, communities, and other social organizations that are not registered in this particular archive. For others, a lack of access to circuits of information (that is, radios and "white" or mainstream newspapers) and poor literacy skills might have been another contributing factor as to why Black voices were silent in this civil rights case.

60. 1955–1959, container SG 13823, folder 1, CKEY letters to Folsom, ADA.

61. Grizzle with Cooper, *My Name's Not George*, 32.

62. 1955–1959, container SG 13823, folder 2, CKEY letters to Folsom, ADA.

63. On anti-Semitism in Canadian society, see Irving Abella and Harold Troper, *None Is Too Many: Canada and the Jews of Europe, 1933–1948* (Toronto: Lester and Orpen Dennys, 1982); and Alan Davies, ed., *Antisemitism in Canada: History and Interpretation* (Waterloo, Ont.: Wilfrid Laurier University Press, 1992).

64. Author's telephone interview with Alan Kruger, 10 April 2013, notes in author's possession.

65. Marty Goodman, "Robs White Widow, Can't Read, Write, Aware He'll Die," *Toronto Daily Star*, 20 August 1958, 4.

66. On civil rights and intergroup relations, see Cheryl Greenberg, "The Southern Jewish Community and the Struggle for Civil Rights," in *African Americans and Jews in the Twentieth Century*, ed. V. P. Franklin et al. (Columbia: University of Missouri Press, 1998), 123–64; and Maurianne Adams and John Bracey, eds., *Strangers and Neighbors: Relations between Blacks and Jews in the United States* (Amherst: University of Massachusetts Press, 1999), 476–640.

67. Phone interview with Marvin Goldsmith, 4 April 2013, notes in the author's possession.

68. Goodman, "Robs White Widow, Can't Read, Write, Aware He'll Die," 1.

69. Goodman, 1, 4.

70. Goodman.

71. Goodman.

72. 1955–1959, container SG 13823, folder 2, CKEY letters to Folsom, ADA.

73. 1955–1959, container SG 13823, folder 2.

74. 1955–1959, container SG 13823, folder 1.

75. 1955–1959, container SG 13823, folder 1.

76. See Barrington Walker, *Race on Trial: Black Defendants in Ontario's Criminal Courts, 1858–1958* (Toronto: University of Toronto Press, 2010), 116–82; and Mathieu, *North of the Color Line*, 15, 25, 52–54.

77. B. Walker, *Race on Trial*, 184.

78. 1955–1959, container SG 13823, folder 1, CKEY letters to Folsom, ADA.

79. 1955–1959, container SG 13823, folder 1.

80. 1955–1959, container SG 13823, folder 1.

81. 1955–1959, container SG 13823, folder 1.

82. 1955–1959, container SG 13823, folder 2.

83. See Borstelmann, *Cold War and the Color Line*, 85–250; and Dudziak, *Cold War Civil Rights*, 3–114.

84. 1955–1959, container SG 13823, folder 1, CKEY letters to Folsom, ADA.

85. 1955–1959, container SG 13823, folder 1.

86. See Dudziak, "Case of 'Death for a Dollar Ninety-Five,'" 36.

87. Robin Winks, "The Canadian Negro: A Historical Assessment," *Journal of Negro History* 53, no. 4 (1968): 289–90.

88. W. E. B. Du Bois, "Strivings of the Negro People," *The Atlantic*, August 1897.

89. D. Hill, *I Am My Father's Son*, 158.

90. The commission is similar in name and mission to the United Nations Commission on Human Rights founded in 1946.

91. D. Hill, *I Am My Father's Son*, 162.

92. Elaine Carey, "Cult Study Brings Dan Hill Senior Back to Centre-Stage," *Toronto Star*, 28 October 1928.

93. D. Hill, *I Am My Father's Son*, 158.

94. Ian A. Hunter, "The Development of the Ontario Human Rights Code: A Decade in Retrospect," *University of Toronto Law Journal* 22, no. 4 (1972): 237–57. On conservatives and social change, see John Bagnall, "The Ontario Conservatives and the Development of Anti-discrimination Policy" (Ph.D. diss., Queen's University, 1984).

95. Statement to legislative assembly, John P. Robarts speeches and statements, 3 April 1962, RG 3–103, AO.

96. Allan Grossman to Hill, 24 April 1962, F 2130-8-0-3, DGH fonds, AO.

97. On post-war Canadian diplomats and the U.N. Bill of Rights, see Jennifer Tunnicliffe, *Resisting Rights: Canada and the International Bill of Rights, 1947–76* (Vancouver: University of British Columbia Press, 2019).

98. "John Diefenbaker and the Canadian Bill of Rights," *Citizen's Forum*, CBC Radio, 16 March 1950.

99. Rhetorically, Diefenbaker sided with the racialized countries of the Commonwealth to expel apartheid South Africa because the African and Asian countries threatened to leave the Commonwealth. Diefenbaker's stance toward South Africa was not purely on moral grounds. Like other Western countries, Canada had a complex relationship with South Africa where national interests often superseded moral imperatives. South African delegates visited residential schools and Indigenous reservations in Canada to learn about Canada's apartheid policy. Indian Affairs and External Affairs, federal departments, facilitated the visits. See Linda Freeman, *The Ambiguous Champion: Canada and South Africa in the Trudeau and Mulroney Years* (Toronto: University of Toronto Press, 1997), 16. On race and multilateralism, see Dan Gorman, "Race, the Commonwealth, and the United Nations: From Imperialism to Internationalism in Canada, 1940–1960," in *Dominion of Race: Rethinking Canada's International*, ed. Laura Madokoro, Francine McKenzie, and David Meren (Vancouver: University of British Columbia Press, 2017), 139–59.

100. "John Diefenbaker and the Canadian Bill of Rights."

101. Two years after Ontario, Parliament legislated a federal Fair Employment Practices Act in 1953, a measure that made discrimination based on race, national

origin, color, and religion in the workplace and trade union illegal. See also Michelle Johnson and Frank Luce, eds., *Daniel Grafton Hill: His Life and Work* (Toronto: Harriet Tubman Institute, 2016); R. Brian Howe, "The Evolution of Human Rights Policy in Ontario," *Canadian Journal of Political Science* 24, no. 4 (1991): 783–802; and R. Brian Howe, "Incrementalism and Human Rights Reform," *Journal of Canadian Studies* 28, no. 3 (1993): 29–44.

102. See Canada Fair Employment Practices Branch, *Human Rights in Canada: Related to Employment* (Ottawa: Queen's Printer, 1967), 2.

103. Daniel G. Hill, *Human Rights in Canada: A Focus on Racism* (Ottawa: Canadian Labour Congress, 1977), 2.

104. C. Anderson, *Eyes Off the Prize*.

105. C. Anderson, 180–99. See also C. Anderson, *Bourgeois Radicals* (New York: Cambridge University Press, 2015).

106. See Philip S. Foner, ed., *W. E. B. Du Bois Speaks: Speeches and Addresses, 1920–1963* (New York: Pathfinder Press, 1970), 179–91, 202–21; and Civil Rights Congress, *We Charge Genocide: The Historic Petition to the United Nations for Relief from a Crime of the United States Government against the Negro People* (1951; repr., New York: International Publishers, 1970), vii, xiv.

107. Civil Rights Congress, *We Charge Genocide*; C. Anderson, *Eyes Off the Prize*. See also Brenda Gayle Plummer, *Rising Wind: Black Americans and U.S. Foreign Affairs, 1935–1960* (Chapel Hill: University of North Carolina Press, 1996); Azza Salama Layton, *International Politics and Civil Rights Policies in the United States, 1941–1960* (New York: Cambridge University Press, 2000); and Gerald Horne, *Black and Red: W. E. B. Du Bois and the Afro-American Response to the Cold War, 1944–1963* (Albany: State University of New York Press, 1986).

108. Civil rights, on balance, is a historically apt construct that has informed the enfranchisement (that is, citizenship) of African Americans. The Reconstruction Congress enacted the first national Civil Rights Act in 1866, although limited in scope.

109. Malcolm X, *Malcolm X Speaks: Selected Speeches and Statements*, ed. George Breitman (New York: Grove Press, 1965), 23–44.

110. Alan Borovoy to Lloyd Lockhart, F 2130-2-1-1 to F 2130-2-1-8, DGH fonds, AO. Emphasis in original.

111. Hill to William Kinmond, John P. Robarts Office, F 2130-2-1-1 to F 2130-2-1-8, DGH fonds, AO.

112. On 4 February 1964, in his maiden speech as the first African Canadian Parliamentarian, Leonard Braithwaite—a veteran of the Second World War, class of 1952 graduate of Harvard Business School, and a trained lawyer—reminded the Ontario legislature of Chapter 368 of the 1850 Common Schools Act that permitted the segregation of not only Catholic and Protestant children but also Black and white pupils. In Essex County, an Underground Railroad terminus in southwestern Ontario, the segregation of Black students persisted into the 1960s. Less than six weeks after Braithwaite's reminder, the minister of education introduced a bill that repealed the 114-year-old provision. Two years later, Braithwaite, a progressive man who understood the shame of racial discrimination, convinced lawmakers to allow young women also to serve as pages in the legislature. See Barrington Morrison,

"Repeal of the Common School Act of 1850," *Share*, 25 March 2015; "Leonard Braithwaite: Canada's First Black Parliamentarian, Dead at 88," *Globe and Mail*, 20 April 2012; and Stanley Lartey, *My Visit with Leonard A. Braithwaite, C.M., O.Ont., Q.C.* (Toronto: Ontario Black History Society, 2009). See also Charles L. Glenn, *African-American/Afro-Canadian Schooling: From the Colonial Period to the Present* (New York: Palgrave Macmillan, 2011); Funké Aladejebi, *Schooling the System: A History of Black Women Teachers* (Montreal: McGill-Queen's University Press, 2021); and Wilson A. Head and Jeri Lee, "The Black Presence in the Canadian Mosaic: Discrimination in Education," *Interchange* 9, no. 1 (1978): 85–93.

113. By 1968, the penalty for individuals and corporations/trade unions increased to $500 and $2,000, respectively. Hunter, "Development of the Ontario Human Rights Code," 240.

114. Daniel G. Hill, "The Role of a Human Rights Commission: The Ontario Experience," *University of Toronto Law Journal* 19, no. 3 (1969): 392–94.

115. Hill to Harold H. Potter, 11 September 1963, F F 2130-2-1-2, DGH fonds, AO. For studies on anti-blackness and the OHRC, see Franklin Henry, *Perception of Discrimination among Negroes and Japanese-Canadians: A Report Submitted to the Ontario Human Rights Commission* (Toronto: Ontario Human Rights Commission, 1965); Rudolph Helling, *The Position of Negroes, Chinese and Italians in the Social Structure of Windsor, Ontario: A Report Submitted to the Ontario Human Rights Commission* (Windsor: University of Windsor Press, 1965); and William Morton, "Fair Accommodation Practices in Ontario: A Study of the Negro Complainants' and Leaders' Knowledge of, and Attitudes towards, the Ontario Human Rights Code and Commission" (M.S.W. thesis, University of Toronto, 1966).

116. St. Clair Pindar to Hill, 9 July 1963, F F 2130-2-1-2, DGH fonds, AO.

117. Clipping from the *Morning News* (Wilmington, Del.), 9 July 1964, F F 2130-2-1-3, DGH fonds, AO.

118. Wagner D. Jackson to Hill, 24 August 1964, F F 2130-2-1-2, DGH fonds, AO.

119. Hill to Sidney Olyan, 10 November 1965, F F 2130-2-1-2, DGH fonds, AO.

120. Sidney Vincent to Hill, 12 April 1963 and 21 May 1963, F F 2130-2-1-2, DGH fonds, AO. Hill received goodwill from non-Black Ontarians. His outreach to Ontario's Jewish communities, particularly its clergy and politicians, and the receptiveness with which said individuals embraced both him and his office are noteworthy. These interracial linkages show, in part, the ways in which postwar Ontarians leveraged their subaltern status. In February 1965, for example, the Toronto Lodge of B'nai B'rith welcomed Hill as an honored guest at an organizational meeting. Toronto Lodge of B'nai B'rith open meeting, 8 February 1965, F 2130-8-0-2, DGH fonds, AO.

121. Borovoy also penned a memorandum to the Jewish Labor Committee in which he expressed concern over the impoverishment of Indigenous peoples. According to Borovoy, "What is required is not merely [the] absence of discrimination but the presence of some special programme" that could facilitate sustained economic growth and prosperity. "A New Emphasis in Human Rights Activity," 1965, F 2130-2-1-1, DGH fonds, AO.

122. "New Emphasis in Human Rights Activity."

123. Indian-White Committee, "Submissions to Kenora Town Council Re: Indian and Non-Indian Relations," November 1965, F 2130-2-1-1, DGH fonds, AO. The

petitioners explained that federal regulations contributed to their poverty. Historically, trapping in the winter months and fishing in the summer sustained many Native families. Elders requested the federal government to extend trapping season by one week beyond the annual April 15 deadline, but the federal Department of Lands and Forests refused on account of the poor quality of pelts in the latter end of the trapping season. See also Anastasia Shkilnyk, *A Poison Stronger Than Love: The Destruction of an Ojibway Community* (New Haven, Conn.: Yale University Press, 1985).

124. Indian-White Committee, "Submissions to Kenora Town Council Re: Indian and Non-Indian Relations."

125. D. Hill, "Role of a Human Rights Commission," 400–401.

126. Albert Worrell to Hill, 20 November 1967, F 2130-8-0-3, DGH fonds, AO.

127. Hill to Worrell, 8 December 1967, F 2130-8-0-3, DGH fonds, AO.

128. "The Problem of Hate in Ontario," 25 February 1965, F 2130-8-0-3, DGH fonds, AO.

129. G. H. Roberts to Hill, 22 March 1966, CK 2/33, U.K. National Archives.

130. Hill to Ella Bannister, 28 October 1966, F 2130-8-0-3, DGH fonds, AO; John Lyttle to Daniel Hill, 21 March 1967, and David Ennals to Daniel Hill, April 1968, CK 2/33, U.K. National Archives.

131. David Ennals to Daniel Hill, April 1968, CK 2/33, U.K. National Archives.

132. Clipping from the *Ottawa Citizen*, "Human Rights Expert Own Boss," February 1974, F 2130-8-0-3, DGH fonds, AO.

133. See L. Hill, "Lawrence Hill Reflects on His Relationship with His Father and with His Own Children"; L. Hill *Black Berry, Sweet Juice*; and D. Hill, *I Am My Father's Son*.

134. See Daniel G. Hill, *The Freedom Seekers: Blacks in Early Canada* (1981; repr., Toronto: Stoddart, 1992).

CHAPTER 4

1. Jackie Smith, "Anne Cools Down and Joins the Establishment," *Montreal Gazette*, 24 March 1984.

2. See Agnes Calliste, "Canada's Immigration Policy and Domestics from the Caribbean: The Second Domestic Scheme," *Socialist Studies* 5 (1991): 136–68.

3. Calliste, 136–68; Smith, "Anne Cools Down and Joins the Establishment."

4. Eric Siblin, "Rosie the Red Stops Smashing the State," *Saturday Night* 115, no. 5 (May 2000): 27.

5. "Douglas Family a Study in Caribbean Politics," *Reading Eagle*, 11 September 1977.

6. Adrienne Clarkson, *From Activist to Head of State* (Toronto: CBC Fifth Estate, 1978), digitized film.

7. Clarkson, *From Activist to Head of State*.

8. Siblin, "Rosie the Red Stops Smashing the State." It is plausible that before Douglas called Diefenbaker's office from his father's plantation, he might have met Diefenbaker when he visited Dominica as prime minister or as a Parliamentarian. It is also plausible that Diefenbaker and Douglas's father had met on one of these occasions, given that the latter served in Dominica's legislature and was one of

the wealthiest men on the island. Even if Douglas did not meet Diefenbaker, he still could have had access to the prime minister through his father, which could explain, in part, why a Canadian prime minister would personally return an obscure seventeen-year-old Dominican's phone call about a student visa. See also Tim Hector, "Pan-Caribbean and Pan-African Extraordinaire," *The Outlet*, 6 October 2000, https://web.archive.org/web/20120416011318/http://www.candw.ag/~jardinea /fanflame.htm (accessed 10 April 2021). Historian James W. St. G. Walker shared an anecdote confirming Diefenbaker's reputation for directly advocating for those whom Canadian immigration had treated unfairly, such as Trinidadian visitor Harry Singh. Author's interview with Walker, 14 May 2021, notes in author's possession. For Singh's 1955 Supreme Court case, see James W. St. G. Walker, *"Race," Rights and the Law in the Supreme Court of Canada: Historical Case Studies* (Waterloo, Ont.: Wilfred Laurier University Press, 1997), 246–300.

9. Headley Tulloch, *Black Canadians: A Long Line of Fighters* (Toronto: NC Press, 1975), 135; Hector, "Pan-Caribbean and Pan-African Extraordinaire."

10. Robert Bernard Douglas bore other children out of wedlock.

11. See Kennetta Hammond Perry, *London Is the Place for Me: Black Britons, Citizenship, and the Politics of Race* (New York: Oxford University Press, 2015); and Joshua B. Guild, "You Can't Go Home Again: Migration, Citizenship, and Black Community in Postwar New York and London" (Ph.D. diss., Yale University Press, 2007).

12. Robin Winks, *Canadian-West Indian Union: A Forty-Year Flirtation* (Oxford: Rhodes House, 1966). See also Paula Pears Hastings, "Dreams of a Tropical Canada: Race, Nation, and Canadian Aspirations in the Caribbean Basin, 1883–1919" (Ph.D. diss., Duke University Press, 2010); and Brian D. Tennyson, ed., *Canada and the Commonwealth Caribbean* (Lanham, Md.: University Press of America, 1988).

13. Winks, *Canadian-West Indian Union*, 12–15.

14. Author's interview with Lascelles Small, 7 May 2021, notes in author's possession. Another diasporic African recounted a positive experience of Scandinavia in the 1930s, although Danish economic ties to Fascist Italy exposed deeper problems of European domination. See Ras Makonnen, *Pan-Africanism from Within*, recorded and ed. Kenneth King (Nairobi: Oxford University Press, 1973), 110–11. On seafaring and the Black Atlantic, see Paul Gilroy, *The Black Atlantic: Modernity and Double Consciousness* (Cambridge, Mass.: Harvard University Press, 1995), 12–13.

15. Author's interview with Bromley Armstrong, 8 October 2014, notes in author's possession.

16. Agnes Calliste, "Race, Gender and Canadian Immigration Policy: Blacks from the Caribbean, 1900–1932," *Journal of Canadian Studies* 28, no. 4 (1993–94): 131–48; Vic Satzewich, "Racism and Canadian Immigration Policy: The Government's View of Caribbean Migration, 1962–1966," *Canadian Ethnic Studies* 21, no. 1 (1989): 77–97; Sarah-Jane Mathieu, *North of the Color Line: Migration and Black Resistance in Canada, 1870–1955* (Chapel Hill: University of North Carolina Press, 2010), 3–60; R. Bruce Shepard, *Deemed Unsuitable: Blacks from Oklahoma Move to the Canadian Prairies in Search of Equality in the Early 20th Century, Only to Find Racism in Their New Home* (Toronto: Umbrella Press, 1997); Harold Troper, *Only Famers Need Apply: Official Canadian Government Encouragement of Immigration*

from the United States, 1896–1911 (Toronto: Griffin House, 1972). By 1946, Chinese Canadians and non-Chinese Canadians lobbied the repeal of the 1923 Chinese Immigration Act (or Chinese Exclusion Act). See Stephanie D. Bangarth, "'We Are Not Asking You to Open Wide the Gates for Chinese Immigration': The Committee for the Repeal of the Chinese Immigration Act and Early Human Rights Activism in Canada," *Canadian Historical Review* 84, no. 3 (2003): 395–422. On anti-Asian racism, see also W. Peter Ward, *White Canada Forever: Popular Attitudes and Public Policy towards Orientals in British Columbia* (Montreal: McGill-Queen's University Press, 2002); and Ken Adachi, *The Enemy That Never Was: A History of Japanese Canadians* (Toronto: McClelland and Steward, 1976).

17. For a detailed account of how African Canadians shaped the immigration discourse and policy in postwar Canada, see Sheldon Taylor, "Darkening the Complexion of Canadian Society: Black Activism, Policy-Making, and Black Immigration from the Caribbean to Canada, 1940s–1960s" (Ph.D. diss., University of Toronto, 1994).

18. House of Commons, *Debates*, 1 May 1947, 2644–546, LAC.

19. Blair asserted that it was Canada's right to admit "suitable and desirable" immigrants. See Stanley Frost, "A Nation That Shops for New Neighbors," *Observer*, 12 December 1923, 638.

20. Canada opened its first immigration office in the Caribbean in 1967. See Harold Troper, "Canada's Immigration Policy since 1945," *International Journal* 48, no. 2 (1993): 255–81; and L. W. St. John-Jones, "Canadian Immigration Trends and Policies in the 1960s," *International Migration* 11, no. 4 (1973): 141–70.

21. Taylor, "Darkening the Complexion of Canadian Society," 2–3. See also Satzewich, "Racism and Canadian Immigration Policy."

22. Taylor, "Darkening the Complexion of Canadian Society," 3.

23. Taylor, "Darkening the Complexion of Canadian Society." For a detailed account of the 1962 immigration reforms and Canada's international reputation and membership in the Commonwealth, see Triadafilos Triadafilopoulos, "Dismantling White Canada: Race, Rights, and the Origins of the Points System," in *Wanted and Welcome? Policies for Highly Skilled Immigrants in Comparative Perspective*, ed. Triadafilos Triadafilopoulos (New York: Springer, 2013), 15–37.

24. Triadafilopoulos, "Dismantling White Canada," 16. Triadafilopoulos shows the importance of bridging the scholarly gap between economic imperatives and liberal internationalist objectives. On Canada's response to Jewish refugees and the Holocaust, see Irving Abella and Harold Troper, *None Is Too Many: Canada and the Jews of Europe, 1933–1948* (Toronto: Lester and Orpen Dennys, 2000).

25. Triadafilopoulos, "Dismantling White Canada," 27.

26. Triadafilopoulos, 27. On the evolution of postwar Canadian immigration policy, specifically the points system, see Ninette Kelley and Michael Trebilcock, *The Making of the Mosaic: A History of Canadian Immigration Policy* (Toronto: University of Toronto Press, 2000); Alan Green, *Immigration and the Postwar Canadian Economy* (Toronto: Macmillan-Hunter Press, 1976); and Peter Li, *Destination Canada: Immigration Debates and Issues* (Toronto: Oxford University Press, 2003).

27. John G. Diefenbaker, *Address by the Rt. Hon. John G. Diefenbaker, Prime Minister of Canada, to the Canadian Club of Ottawa* (Ottawa: Office of the Prime Minister, 1960), 10.

28. The Progressive Conservative Party of Canada was the center-right party (that is, conservative) and the main rival of the Liberal Party. On a political spectrum, the Progressive Conservatives would stand right of the Liberals and slightly left of the Republican Party.

29. John. G. Diefenbaker, *One Canada: Memoirs of the Right Honourable John G. Diefenbaker; The Crusading Years, 1895–1956* (Toronto: Macmillan Canada, 1975), 253.

30. Robin Winks, *The Blacks in Canada: A History*, 2nd ed. (Montreal: McGill-Queen's University Press, 1997), 447.

31. Diefenbaker, *One Canada*, 16–20.

32. Siblin, "Rosie the Red Stops Smashing the State."

33. See Rosanne Waters, "African Canadian Anti-discrimination Activism and the Transnational Civil Rights Movement, 1945–1965," *Journal of the Canadian Historical Association* 24, no. 2 (2013): 386–424; and Agnes Calliste, "The Influence of the Civil Rights and Black Power Movement in Canada," *Race, Gender and Class* 2, no. 3 (Spring 1995): 123–39.

34. J. Smith, "Anne Cools Down and Joins the Establishment."

35. Jim Robb, "From Student Radical to Senator," *Ottawa Citizen*, 28 January 1984.

36. J. Smith, "Anne Cools Down and Joins the Establishment."

37. Judy Rebick, *Ten Thousand Roses: The Making of a Feminist Revolution* (Toronto: Penguin Canada, 2005), 9–10.

38. Robb, "From Student Radical to Senator."

39. David Austin writes that these activists had a passion for Caribbean history and its impact on Western civilization and the development of the Americas. He identifies three pivotal conferences held in Montreal from 1965 to 1967 that championed these ideas: "Shaping the Future of the West Indies," "The Making of the Caribbean Peoples," and "The West Indian Nation in Exile." These focal events featured George Lamming, C. L. R. James, Orlando Patterson, Jan Carew, and Austin Clarke, among others. See David Austin, *Fear of a Black Nation: Race, Sex, and Security in Sixties Montreal* (Toronto: Between the Lines, 2013), 6, 75. On the radical climate in 1960s Canada, see M. Althena Palaeologu, ed., *The Sixties in Canada: A Turbulent and Creative Decade* (Montreal: Black Rose Press, 2009), 65–350.

40. Austin, *Fear of a Black Nation*, 81–83.

41. Cools wrote this essay in 1971. Austin, *Fear of a Black Nation*, 81–83.

42. For a more nuanced analysis of gender, sexism, and sexuality by Black revolutionary women, see Safiya Bukhari, *The War Before: The True Life Story of Becoming a Black Panther, Keeping the Faith in Prison, and Fighting for Those Left Behind* (New York: Feminist Press at CUNY, 2010), 52–61; Elaine Brown, *Speech on Feminism* (Greenwood, Ind.: Educational Video Group, 2007); Assata Shakur, *Assata: An Autobiography* (Chicago: Lawrence Hill Books, 2001), 116; and Ashley D. Farmer, *Remaking Black Power: How Black Women Transformed an Era* (Chapel Hill: University of North Carolina Press, 2017).

43. On the empirical limitations of intersectionality and (Black) feminisms to explain the conditions of Black males, and for explanations of Black male "gendercide" under white supremacist patriarchy, see Tommy J. Curry, *The Man-Not: Race,*

Class, Genre, and the Dilemmas of Black Manhood (Philadelphia: Temple University Press, 2017); Errol Miller, *Men at Risk* (Kingston, Jam.: Jamaican Publishing House, 1991), 342; Adam Jones, "Gender and Gendercide," *Journal of Genocide Research* 2, no. 2 (June 2000): 185–211; Augusta C. Del Zotto, "Gendercide in a Historical-Structural Context: The Case of Black Male Gendercide in the United States," in *Gendercide and Genocide*, ed. Adam Jones (Nashville: Vanderbilt University Press, 2004), 157–71; and Amy E. Randall, "Introduction: Gendering Genocide Studies," in *Genocide and Gender in the Twentieth Century: A Comparative Study*, ed. Amy E. Randall (New York: Bloomsbury, 2021), 1–34. Because patriarchy is a system of hegemonic domination of subordinate or conquered males, the assertion that "Black men enjoyed a residual but fragile form of patriarchal power" is not only inaccurate but problematic, for this conclusion is devoid of empirical evidence and material analysis. See Barrington Walker, *Race on Trial: Black Defendants in Ontario's Criminal Courts, 1858–1958* (Toronto: University of Toronto Press, 2010), 90.

44. "Roosevelt Douglas Speech at Model Parliament," MG01, VII, A, 831, John Diefenbaker Archival Collections, University of Saskatchewan, Saskatoon.

45. "Roosevelt Douglas Speech at Model Parliament."

46. "Roosevelt Douglas Speech at Model Parliament."

47. "Roosevelt Douglas Speech at Model Parliament." For first-person accounts of the experiences of Black domestic workers, see Makeda Silvera, *Silenced: Talks with Working Class Caribbean Women about Their Lives and Struggles as Domestic Workers in Canada* (Toronto: Sister Vision Press, 1989).

48. Siblin, "Rosie the Red Stops Smashing the State."

49. Douglas disagreed with Joe Clark, the student leader of the Progressive Conservatives, for not addressing racism on a national level. See Cabral Douglas, "From Prisoner to Prime Minister," *Montreal Community Contact*, 27 October 2016, 23.

50. Siblin, "Rosie the Red Stops Smashing the State."

51. Diefenbaker, *Address by the Rt. Hon. John G. Diefenbaker.*

52. See William Tetley, *The October Crisis, 1970: An Insider's View* (Montreal: McGill-Queen's University Press, 2006); and Louis Fournier, *F.L.Q.: The Anatomy of an Underground Movement*, trans. Edward Baxter (Toronto: NC Press, 1984).

53. See Jay Walz, "'Vive Quebec Libre!' De Gaulle Cries Out to Montreal Crowd," *New York Times*, 25 July 1967.

54. Pierre Vallières, *White Niggers of America: The Precocious Autobiography of a Québec "Terrorist,"* trans. Joan Pink (New York: Monthly Review Press, 1971).

55. Austin, *Fear of a Black Nation*, 17, 24; David Austin, *Moving against the System: The 1968 Congress of Black Writers and the Making of Global Consciousness* (London: Pluto Press, 2018).

56. Tulloch, *Black Canadians*, 137.

57. Brenda Gayle Plummer, *In Search of Power: African Americans in the Era of Decolonization, 1956–1974* (New York: Cambridge University Press, 2013), 228.

58. For a class analysis of the U.S. urban upheaval, see Gerald Horne, *Fire This Time: The Watts Uprisings and the 1960s* (Charlottesville: University of Virginia Press, 1995). Canadian newspapers closely reported violence in U.S. cities during the 1967 uprisings, which further reinforced the notion that Canada was a perennial haven for Black refugees from the United States. See "Windsor Links Sealed as

Curfew Clamped On," *Globe and Mail*, 24 July 1967, 9; "Windsor Alarm Grows as across the River Detroit Havoc Spreads," *Globe and Mail*, 25 July 1967, 27; "Negroes Flee Detroit, Seek Windsor Refuge," *Globe and Mail*, 26 July 1967, 9; Peter Lisagor, "Fury in Detroit Has Washington Stunned," *Toronto Star*, 25 July 1967, 11; and "Teenage Race Rioters Beat Policeman to Death," *Toronto Star*, 17 July 1967, A1.

59. Michael Simanga, *Amiri Baraka and the Congress of African People: History and Memory* (New York: Palgrave Macmillan, 2015), 20.

60. "Trudeau Fears Spread of Strife into Canada," *Spokane Daily Chronicle*, 9 November 1968.

61. Bruce Grant, "Trudeau Stirs a Country—and Canada's New Image Emerges," *The Age* (Melbourne), 2 December 1968.

62. "McLuhan Analysis: Trudeau's Writing," *Ottawa Citizen*, 23 November 1968; Marshall McLuhan, "Federalism and the French-Canadians," *New York Times*, 17 November 1968. See also Bryan D. Palmer, *Canada's 1960s: The Ironies of Identity in a Rebellious Era* (Toronto: University of Toronto Press, 2009), 139–77.

63. For personal accounts of postwar Canadian racism, see J. Ashton Brathwaite, *Niggers, This Is Canada* (New York: Deep Root Books, 2000); and Austin Clarke, "Race Prejudice in White Canada: Seeking Dignity, in 1963," *Maclean's*, 20 April 1963.

64. Hector, "Pan-Caribbean and Pan-African Extraordinaire."

65. Tim Hector, "What I Said and What Rosie Said," *The Outlet*, 20 October 2000, https://web.archive.org/web/20120416011318/http://www.candw.ag/~jardinea/fanflame.htm (accessed 10 April 2021).

66. Hector, "Pan-Caribbean and Pan-African Extraordinaire."

67. Clarkson, *From Activist to Head of State*. Months before the uprising at Sir George Williams, Douglas made speeches in Halifax to university students, highlighting important human rights issues such as safe and affordable housing and interracial cooperation between Black and white citizens. When the police charged and arrested the young activist for "loitering," Diefenbaker came to his defense. Douglas chose jail instead of paying a five dollar fine because of his principles. After speaking with police officials and the press, he paid the fine. Douglas was campaigning for the Progressive Conservatives during the 1968 federal elections. See "Rosie Douglas Refused Bail: Diefenbaker, King Invoked Here," *Montreal Gazette*, 27 February 1969; and Dulcie Conrad, "The Negro in Nova Scotia: A Ray of Hope Filters through a Clouded Issue," *Globe and Mail*, 9 December 1968, 7. According to James Walker, a native Nova Scotian who had befriended Black activists, including Rocky Jones, "The day after [Douglas's] arrest the word 'in the street' was that the Mayor of Halifax paid Rosie's fine because of a fear that the brothers were going to break him out of jail." Author's email exchange with Walker, 15 May 2021.

68. Tulloch, *Black Canadians*, 140.

69. Jane Shulman, "Rosie Douglas Returns a Mellower Man," Concordia's *Thursday Report Online*, 28 September 2000, http://ctr.concordia.ca/2000–01/Sept_28/17-Rosie/ (accessed 6 October 2015).

70. See Diefenbaker, *One Canada*, 140.

71. Dennis Forsythe, ed., *Let the Niggers Burn! The Sir George Williams University Affair and Its Caribbean Aftermath* (Montreal: Our Generation Press, 1971); Dorothy Eber, *The Computer Centre Party: Canada Meets Black Power* (Montreal:

Tundra Books, 1969); Dorothy W. Williams, *The Road to Now: A History of Blacks in Montreal* (Montreal: Véhicule Press, 1997), 118–38. For an excellent documentary that features some of the activists—such as Anne Cools, Rodney John, and Terrence Ballantyne, among others—and original still and motion footage, see Mina Shum, dir., *Ninth Floor*, producer Selwyn Jacob, writer Mina Shum (Ottawa: National Film Board of Canada, 2015), digitized film. Before this crisis, students at Columbia University occupied parts of the campus in response to revelations that their institution was supporting the defense industry and the Vietnam War. See Roger Kahn, *The Battle for Morningside Heights: Why Students Rebel* (New York: William Morrow, 1970); Jerry L. Avorn et al., *Up Against the Ivy Wall: A History of the Columbia Crisis* (New York: Atheneum Press, 1969); Martha Biondi, *Black Revolution on Campus* (Berkeley: University of California Press, 2014); and James Kunen, *The Strawberry Statement: Notes of a College Revolutionary* (New York: Random House, 1969).

72. Author's interview with Philippe Fils-Aimé, 28 November 2019, notes in author's possession.

73. "Rosie Douglas Court Record Corrected," *Montreal Gazette*, 22 February 1969.

74. "Sir George Sit-In Sentences Upheld," *Montreal Gazette*, 12 April 1973. Several accounts state that the courts sentenced Cools to six months in jail. This reporting is accurate; Cools came out in four months. See Greg Weston, "Five Liberals Go to Senate," *Ottawa Citizen*, 14 January 1984.

75. "Canada Is as Racist as the U.S., Student from West Indies Says," *Globe and Mail*, 30 December 1969.

76. E. Ferguson, "Who Speaks for Blacks," *Globe and Mail*, 10 March 1970. African Canadian opinion in the 1960s and 1970s ranged from conservative (*Africa Speaks*) to militant (*Black Liberation News*). Carl H. Woodbeck, the publisher of *Africa Speaks*, favored Christian, nonconfrontational preachers like Martin Luther King Jr. but denounced revolutionary leaders like Malcolm X and Stokely Carmichael. The short-lived *Black Liberation News* sought the complete eradication of anti-Black racism and capitalist exploitation. *Africa Speaks*, 1965–75, microfilm no. 1052, MHSO; *Black Liberation News*, July 1969–February 1970, microfilm no. 933, MHSO.

77. For an encyclopedic account of the Royal Canadian Mounted Police's surveillance of subversive activities at Canadian academic institutions, see Steve Hewitt, *Spying 101: The RCMP's Secret Activities at Canadian Universities, 1917–1997* (Toronto: University of Toronto Press, 2002).

78. Jane Banfield Haynes, "ASA Meeting Disrupted by Crisis," *Africa Report* 14, no. 8 (December 1969): 16. See also Austin, *Fear of a Black Nation*, xxxii.

79. As the February Revolution raged in Trinidad, Douglas and Cools and two other co-accused traveled to Ottawa in hopes of meeting with Prime Minister Trudeau to convince him to launch a federal investigation of the computer center fiasco. Trudeau refused to meet with the four activists. "Negro Defendants Fail to See PM," *Montreal Gazette*, 27 February 1970. On Trinidad's February Revolution, see Ivar Oxaal, *Race and Revolutionary Consciousness: A Documentary Interpretation of the 1970s Black Power Revolt in Trinidad* (Cambridge, Mass.: Schenkman, 1971); Alfie Roberts, *A View from Freedom: Alfie Roberts Speaks on the Caribbean, Cricket,*

Montreal and C. L. R. James (Montreal: Alfie Roberts Institute, 2005); Kate Quinn, ed., *Black Power in the Caribbean* (Gainesville: University of Florida Press, 2014); Forsythe, *Let the Niggers Burn!*; "Computer Trial Demonstrators Invade Bank," *Montreal Gazette*, 27 February 1970; and "'Issue Was Basically Racism': Sir George Sit-In Fire of 15 Years Ago Left Lasting Marks," *Montreal Gazette*, 24 March 1984.

80. Ted Rutland, *Displacing Blackness: Planning, Power, and Race in Twentieth-Century Halifax* (Toronto: University of Toronto Press, 2018).

81. James W. St. G. Walker, "Black Confrontation in 1960s Halifax," in *Debating Dissent: Canada and the Sixties*, ed. Greg Kealey et al. (Toronto: University of Toronto Press, 2012), 174.

82. See Burnley "Rocky" Jones and James W. St. G. Walker, *Burnley "Rocky" Jones: Revolutionary: An Autobiography* (Halifax, N.S.: Fernwood Books, 2016).

83. Jeremiah Jones enlisted in the Nova Scotian 106th Battalion during World War I. He performed one of the most daring acts of valor and gallantry in Canadian military history. Private Jones saved many Canadian troops bogged down by German machine gun fire at the Battle of Vimy Ridge. Volunteering to attack a machine gun nest, Private Jones sprang into action and tossed a hand grenade in the German bunker, killing several soldiers. Private Jones then marched his prisoners and the machine gun across the battlefield to Canadian lines. A comrade recommended him for the Distinguished Conduct Medal, the highest honor for gallantry in the British Empire, but the Canadian government snubbed Private Jones. See Calvin Ruck, *The Black Battalion: Canada's Best Kept Military Secret* (Halifax, N.S.: Nimbus Publishers, 1987).

84. J. Walker, "Black Confrontation in 1960s Halifax," 179–80.

85. Jones and Walker, *Burnley "Rocky" Jones*, 50–51.

86. "In the Panthers' Wake," *Globe and Mail*, 15 February 1969.

87. Jones and Walker, *Burnley "Rocky" Jones*.

88. "Black Power Active Here, FBI Says," *Toronto Daily Star*, 14 December 1968.

89. Don Oliver's brother, Dr. W. P. Oliver, served as the chairman of a committee that explored the need for a united front organization. See "Agent of Black Panthers Appeals to N.S. Negroes," *Toronto Daily Star*, 25 November 1968. One Panther's observation of race relations in Nova Scotia is illustrative. As an Alabamian, he marveled at the ease with which he moved in public spaces. In less than two weeks, though, he felt an acute level of disquiet, because, unlike in the U.S. South, he could not anticipate how white Canadians perceived him, even though he knew they likely despised him. In other words, there was solace in knowing where one stood vis-à-vis racist neighbors, unlike the unsettling element of surprise that one could stumble into in a society that concealed its racism. See "In the Panthers' Wake."

90. "In the Panthers' Wake." Pan-Africanist revolutionary Walter Rodney described this form of racial intimacy as "family discussions." See Walter Rodney, *The Groundings with My Brothers* (London: Bogle-L'Ouverture Publications, 1969), 64.

91. "In the Panthers' Wake."

92. "N.S. Human Rights Officer: Black Participation in Betterment Programs Urged," *Globe and Mail*, 23 January 1970. See also J. Walker, "Black Confrontation in 1960s Halifax."

93. On the agency of Black women in Nova Scotia, see Susan Marion-Jean Precious, "The Women of Africville: Race and Gender in Postwar Halifax" (M.A. thesis, Queen's University, 1998).

94. "N.S. Human Rights Officer: Black Participation in Betterment Programs Urged," 9.

95. "N.S. Human Rights Officer: Black Participation in Betterment Programs Urged," 9.

96. Conrad, "Negro in Nova Scotia," 7.

97. Conrad, 7. Ross Kinney, committee member and moderator of the African United Baptist Association of Nova Scotia, implied that his constituents favored integration to the Black Panthers or the Black United Front.

98. Author's interview with Paul Winn, 22 May 2021, notes in author's possession.

99. The event was a fundraiser for Huey Newton and Clifford Watkins, brother of the late Canadian Football League star Ted Watkins. Ted was the founding chairman of the Afro-American Progressive Association, a militant human rights group in Toronto. On 2 June 1968, the manager and a clerk of a liquor store wounded Clifford and killed Ted in a confrontation in Stockton, California. See John Oliver, "Man Who Shot Ti-Cat Ted Watkins Is Grilled on 'Anti-Negro Prejudices,'" *Ottawa Citizen*, 27 February 1969. Shortly after the incident, Constance Belfon, an active member of Toronto's Black community, dispatched her son John and his friend to investigate Ted Watkins's death. They discovered that it was not robbery, as the store owner alleged, but that he had mistakenly murdered Watkins, thinking he was a robber. The police later exonerated Ted posthumously. See John Franklin Belfon, "Lives Lived: Constance Lenora Giscomb Belfon," *Globe and Mail*, 29 January 1999.

100. "Time to Get Off Our Backs, Black Panther Tells Canadians," *Toronto Daily Star*, 14 December 1968.

101. "Time to Get Off Our Backs, Black Panther Tells Canadians."

102. "Called Racist by Black, White Radicals Cheer," *Globe and Mail*, 14 December 1968. Carew's expressed views on the ways in which Canadians masked their racism parallels a statement his mother made. As British subjects, Carew's family, especially his mother, struggled with the dynamics of race relations in the United States after living for a few years in Harlem in the 1920s. "Whereas the Yankee people are crude and there's no mistaking where you stand with them," Carew recalled his mother saying, "the English are perfidious and they're good at hiding their true feelings behind a façade of politeness." Carew's angst with Canadian race relations mirrored his mother's. See Jan Carew, *Potaro Dreams: My Youth in Guyana* (Hertford, U.K.: Hansib, 2014), 29–30.

103. "Time to Get Off Our Backs, Black Panther Tells Canadians."

104. "Called Racist by Black, White Radicals Cheer."

105. Jones's contemporaries considered him "affectionate," while they regarded George Sams as "a real killer." See "In the Panthers' Wake."

106. "In the Panthers' Wake."

107. "In the Panthers' Wake." Jones cofounded the Transition Year Program, a university bridging initiative, with James Walker and several other white friends. Author's email with Walker, 15 May 2021.

108. Author's interview with Paul Winn, 24 May 2021, notes in author's possession.

109. Martin Omalley, "A Tolerant People? Nice to Believe. We're Really Just Polite Racists," *Globe and Mail*, 15 February 1969.

110. Dawn Rae Flood, "A Black Panther in the Great White North: Fred Hampton Visits Saskatchewan, 1969," *Journal for the Study of Radicalism* 8, no. 2 (2014): 21–50. The Panthers received support from some white Canadian radicals. U.S. Treasury agents, on 2 October 1969, arrested thirty-five-year-old Shirley Jean Sutherland, daughter of T. C. Douglas, leader of the New Democratic Party, for procuring hand grenades from an undercover Los Angeles police officer, which the LAPD alleged Sutherland and her accomplice intended to provide the Panthers. The state freed Sutherland after she paid a $15,000 bond. Law enforcement also alleged Sutherland held membership in the Friends of the Black Panthers and that her coconspirator headed the John Brown Brigade, a splinter cell of the Panthers. See "Grand Jury Indicts Daughter of Douglas," *Globe and Mail*, 16 October 1969, 4; and "Shirley Douglas Charged in L.A. over Grenades," *Globe and Mail*, 4 October 1969, 1.

111. "2 Black Panthers on Prairie Tour Deported to U.S.," *Toronto Daily Star*, 22 November 1969, B5.

112. Although conscientious objectors used "deserter" and "dodger" interchangeably, even though they had different legal ramifications, I will use "resister" to convey the resentment and righteous indignation that U.S. expatriates in Canada felt toward U.S. imperialism in Vietnam. On draft resisters, see Bruce Dancis, *Resister: A Story of Protest and Prison during the Vietnam War* (Ithaca: Cornell University Press, 2014); Michael Foley, *Confronting the War Machine: Draft Resisting during the Vietnam War* (Chapel Hill: University of North Carolina Press, 2007); Jerry Ellmer, *Felon for Peace: The Memoir of a Vietnam-Era Draft Resister* (Nashville: Vanderbilt University Press, 2005); Sherry Gershon Gottlieb, *Hell No, We Won't Go! Resisting the Draft during the Vietnam War* (New York: Viking, 1991); Renée G. Kasinsky, *Refugees from Militarism: Draft-Age Americans in Canada* (New Brunswick, N.J.: Transaction Books, 1976); Laurence M. Baskir and William A. Strauss, *Chance and Circumstance: The Draft, the War, and the Vietnam Generation* (New York: Knopf, 1978); Kenneth Fred Emerick, *War Resisters Canada: The World of the American Military-Political Refugees* (Knox: Pennsylvania Free Press, 1972); and Jim Christy, *The New Refugees: American Voices in Canada* (Toronto: Martin, 1972). There are records of U.S. and Canadian draft resisters in the Immigration and Naturalization Service files dating back to the First World War. See Marian L. Smith, "The Immigration and Naturalization Service (INS) at the U.S.-Canadian Border, 1893–1993," *Michigan Review* 26, no. 2 (Fall 2000): 1141–42. See also Eric L. Muller, *Free to Die for Their Country: The Story of the Japanese American Draft Resisters in World War II* (Chicago: University of Chicago Press, 2001).

113. Kasinsky, *Refugees from Militarism*, 79.

114. Fred Gaffen, *Unknown Warriors: Canadians in Vietnam* (Toronto: Dundurn Press, 1990).

115. "1969 Figures Are Released," *Amex: The American Expatriate in Canada* 2, no. 19 (1970): 33, GIPC.

116. *Amex: The American Expatriate in Canada* 2, no. 17 (1969): 7, GIPC.

117. Kasinsky, *Refugees from Militarism*, 110. The Canadian government supported a "gentlemen's agreement" that allowed aid groups to operate unencumbered, as long as they did not advertise that Canada "welcomed deserters," an action that would create friction between Washington and Ottawa. See Kasinsky, 111. It also behooved resisters in Canada to maintain a low profile. See Terrance Wills, "Pentagon Orders Files Be Kept on Deserters Now Living in Canada," *Globe and Mail*, 16 September 1970, 1.

118. *Amex* was arguably the longest-circulating magazine for draft resisters in Canada and the United States. It addressed issues of critical importance such as immigration, race, imperialism, radicalism, and gender. Therefore, it captured the zeitgeist of the period in a detailed way that similar periodicals that catered to the Canadian-U.S. radical/anti-war community did not.

119. One article described Red, White, and Black as "a loose association of Americans of varying political, creative and religious persuasions." See "Radio Free America or Just about Anything Else," *Amex: American Expatriate in Canada* 2, no. 19 (1970): 24, GIPC.

120. Kasinsky, *Refugees from Militarism*, 80.

121. *American Exile in Canada* 1, no. 6 (1968): 22, GIPC. (Added emphasis.)

122. *American Exile in Canada*, 4.

123. The Ministry of Manpower and Immigration issued a memo in 1968 granting immigration officers greater authority to award "personal assessment" points. Aid organizations exposed this new policy and how it unfairly discriminated against deserters. Students from Glendon College in Toronto raised awareness of the deserter crisis when five of them attempted unsuccessfully to enter Canada as a deserter named William John Heintzelman. The Canadian press highlighted the closing of the border, and Canadians expressed disappointment in their government for subordinating its sovereignty to U.S. imperialism. By May 1969, Canada had reopened its borders to deserters. See Kasinsky, *Refugees from Militarism*, 119–21.

124. *Manual for Draft-Age Immigrants to Canada*, 2nd ed., Toronto Anti-Draft Programme, 1968, GIPC.

125. *American Exile in Canada* 1, no. 10 (1969): 5, GIPC.

126. For attribution of this poem, see Carleton Mabee and Susan Mabee Newhouse, *Sojourner Truth: Slave, Prophet, Legend* (New York: New York University Press, 1993), 105; and *Amex: The American Expatriate in Canada* 1, no. 16 (1969): 11, GIPC.

127. This volume also described British Columbia as "merely a way-station in the underground railway." *Amex-Canada: The American Expatriate in Canada* 1, no. 16 (1969): 15, GIPC.

128. Barry Hale, "Immigrant's Song," *Amex: The American Expatriate in Canada* 2, no. 17 (1969): 25, GIPC.

129. *Amex: The American Expatriate in Canada* 2, no. 18 (1970): 16–17, GIPC. In this issue, the publishers invoke Loyalists from the U.S. Revolutionary War as also heirs to the Canadian haven narrative. See also p. 19.

130. "Underground Railroad System in Canada," FBI Case File 157-BA-7664. RD 46209 obtained under FOIA provisions.

131. "Black Draft Dodger Speaks Out on Canada," *Amex-Canada* 2, no. 18 (1970): 21.

132. See Michael Gomez, *Exchanging Our Country Marks: The Transformation of African Identities in the Colonial and Antebellum South* (Chapel Hill: University of North Carolina Press, 1998).

133. "Black Draft Dodger Speaks Out on Canada," 21.

134. "Black Draft Dodger Speaks Out on Canada," 21.

135. "Black Draft Dodger Speaks Out on Canada," 21. In 1960, Georgia native John Henry Jackson arrived in Toronto to quarterback the Argonauts, the local Canadian Football League team. Jackson's yearning for the comforts of home inspired him to pursue this venture.

136. "Black Draft Dodger Speaks Out on Canada," 21.

137. John Egerton, "Why So Few U.S. Blacks Come Here," *Amex-Canada: The American Expatriate in Canada* 2, no. 23 (1971): 13–15, GIPC.

138. This "othering" of Caribbean immigrants in Canada on the surface disrupts notions of Black solidarity in Canadian society. Upon closer scrutiny, however, one discerns that diasporic Black folk in Canada subordinated ethnicity and culture to race, because race was more effective in binding Canada's loosely knit, small Black community together.

139. Egerton, "Why So Few U.S. Blacks Come Here," *Amex-Canada: The American Expatriate in Canada* 2, no. 23 (1971): 13–15, GIPC.

140. "Blacks Flee U.S. Free, Militant and Organizing," *Amex-Canada: The American Expatriate in Canada* 2, no. 3 (1970): 29, GIPC. The same article referenced a 1969 incident where three Black militants evaded police in Toronto and Ottawa. The police later found bombs in their hideout. Law enforcement sought the trio for the shooting of three U.S. agents at the Champlain, New York, border crossing; police recovered smoke bombs, improvised explosives, and shotguns from their hideout. See "3 Fugitive Panthers Could Be in Metro," *Toronto Daily Star*, 2 October 1969. It was a common occurrence for Black fugitives to seek refuge in Canada during this period. Joseph Pannell is unique in that he not only had been arrested in November 1970 for shooting a Chicago police officer but also had been AWOL from the U.S. Navy since 3 October 1968. After June 1972, he fled to Montreal, where he adopted the alias Douglas Gary Freeman. See Gabrielle Giroday, "'Gentle and Shy,' Fugitive Lived a Quiet Family Life in Canada," *Globe and Mail*, 31 July 2004.

141. Egerton, "Why So Few U.S. Blacks Come Here," 14.

142. Claude Brown, *Manchild in the Promised Land* (New York: Macmillan, 1965), 8.

143. See Gilles E. Chiasson, "Black Faces in Ads," *Toronto Daily Star*, 4 April 1970; Eusi Ndugu, "Blacks and Native People Never Appear in Toronto Ads," *Toronto Daily Star*, 14 March 1970.

144. Chiasson, "Black Faces in Ads."

145. Egerton, "Why So Few U.S. Blacks Come Here," 14.

146. *Amex: The American Expatriate in Canada* 1, no. 10 (1969): 9, GIPC.

147. Egerton, "Why So Few U.S. Blacks Come Here," 13–15.

148. Egerton, 13–15.

149. This reference came from the *Yankee Refugee*, a draft resister magazine published in Vancouver. See "To Dodge or Not to Dodge," *Amex: The American Expatriate in Canada* 1, no. 12 (1969): 9, GIPC.

150. Charlie Stimac, "Racism in Toronto on the Rise in a Deepening Economic Crisis," *Amex: The American Expatriate in Canada* 5, no. 43 (1975): 9, 17, GIPC.

151. "U.S. Right-Wing Extremists in Canada," *Amex: The American Expatriate in Canada* 3, no. 29 (1972): 15, GIPC. See also "School Buses Set Ablaze in Color Row," *The Age* (Melbourne), 1 September 1971; and "10 Buses Blown Up in Michigan," *Tuscaloosa News*, 31 August 1971.

152. "Man Threatened," *Globe and Mail*, 5 May 1972, 5.

153. For most of its circulation, *Amex* had at least one senior female publisher. For an article on women leaders in the draft resister community, see "Where Are They Now?," *Amex: The American Expatriate in Canada* 1, no. 17 (1969): 28, GIPC.

154. "Women Exiles Organize Group," *Amex: The American Expatriate in Canada* 2, no. 18 (1970): 31, GIPC.

155. Sandy Stevens and Mora Gregg, "The Parley in Montreal," *Amex: The American Expatriate in Canada* 2, no. 20 (1970): 8–9, GIPC.

156. Stevens and Gregg, 8–9. Black women were invisible in this movement, although some journeyed to Canada with their mates.

157. *Manual for Draft-Age Immigrants to Canada*, 3. The Waffle, or the Movement for an Independent Socialist Canada, the radical arm of Canada's New Democratic Party, cautioned against the "Americanization" of Canada. It even published a "Waffle Manifesto." See Stanley McDowell, "Labor Pains in NDP over the Waffle," *Globe and Mail*, 1 August 1972, 7; and Graham Fraser, "Expelled Waffle Group Made Lasting Impact on Canadian Politics: The Left: Which Way to Turn?," *Globe and Mail*, 21 November 1989, A3.

158. *American Exile in Canada* 1, no. 5 (1968): 10, GIPC.

159. Matthew Jacobson discusses this subject deftly in *Special Sorrows: The Diasporic Imagination of Irish, Polish, and Jewish Immigrants in the United States* (Cambridge, Mass.: Harvard University Press, 1995).

160. While U.S. society took pride in its melting pot assimilation, Canadian society had a mosaic. On U.S. refugees' difficulty integrating into the mosaic, see Stan Pietlock, "Editorial," *Amex: The American Expatriate in Canada* 2, no. 23 (1971): 7, GIPC.

161. John Levy of the Toronto Anti-Draft Programme first made this suggestion as a motion to change the UAE to Union of American Expatriates.

162. The movement of African North Americans, especially across the Canadian-U.S. border, is also emblematic of this debate.

163. Kathleen Cleaver, "Why Eldridge Cleaver Has Come Home," *Los Angeles Times*, 1 December 1975, A7.

164. The inauguration of Eldridge Cleaver as the first U.S. president in exile in January 1969 signaled the beginning of "American Exile Politics." Ernest Fusco Jr., "For a Government in Exile," *American Exile in Canada* 1, no. 10 (1969): 14–15, GIPC.

165. "Are We Exiles or Expatriates?," *American Exile in Canada* 1, no. 15 (1969): 12–13, GIPC.

166. "Are We Exiles or Expatriates?," 12–13.

167. "Are We Exiles or Expatriates?," 12–13. On draft resister community building and political engagement in Canada, see David S. Churchill, "American Expatriates and the Building of Alternative Social Space in Toronto, 1965–1977," *Urban History*

Review 39, no. 1 (2010): 31–44; David S. Churchill, "Draft Resisters, Left Nationalism, and the Politics of Anti-Imperialism," *Canadian Historical Review* 93, no. 2 (2012), 227–60.

168. *Amex: The American Expatriate in Canada* 1, no. 16 (1969): 7, GIPC.

169. Robin Mathews, "The U.S. Draft Dodger in Canada Is Part of U.S. Imperialism," *Amex: The American Expatriate in Canada* 2, no. 20 (1970): 24–25, GIPC. On 26 January 1971, police arrested Robin Mathews, George Haggar (a Lebanese Canadian active in student protests in Canada and the United States, and anti-Zionist), two other professors, and University of Toronto students for a sit-in at the immigration office on University Avenue in downtown Toronto. Mathews and the other activists protested the department for admitting draft resisters and the department's preference for selecting U.S. immigrants and how that implicated Canada in U.S. imperialism. This demonstration occurred under the auspices of the Canadian Liberation Movement, a leftist organization committed to Canadian sovereignty and nationalism by protecting Canadian institutions from U.S. imperialism.

170. Ron Lambert, "Answering Mr. Mathews," *Amex: The American Expatriate in Canada* 2, no. 21 (1970): 8–9, GIPC.

171. Lambert, 8–9.

172. V. S. Brown, "Robin Mathew Is a Foe of the American Exile Community and an Enemy of the Canadian Working Class," *Amex: The American Expatriate in Canada* 2, no. 21 (1970): 23–24, GIPC.

173. Delores Broten, "Platform," *Amex: The American Expatriate in Canada* 2, no. 22 (1970): 22, GIPC.

174. "A Letter from Our Neighbour Upstairs," *American Exile in Canada* 1, no. 10 (1969): 14, GIPC.

175. "U.S. Deserter Doublecrossed, Student Claims," *Globe and Mail*, 1 April 1970, 5. On RCMP-FBI cooperation, see Reg Whitaker and Gary Marcuse, *Cold War Canada: The Making of a National Insecurity State* (Toronto: University of Toronto Press, 1994). See also Ross Munro, "Files Show Canada Is Giving U.S. Data on Army Deserters," *Globe and Mail*, 26 March 1975, 1. Educator and entrepreneur Denham Jolly recalled FBI agents visiting him in the late 1960s to inquire if his rooming houses had sheltered draft resisters. See B. Denham Jolly, *In the Black: My Life* (Toronto: ECW Press, 2017), 109–10.

176. Charles Campbell, "R.C.M.P. Harassment of U.S. Deserters a Three-Year History," *Amex-Canada: The American Expatriate in Canada* 2, no. 22 (1970): 18–19, GIPC.

177. On the demands of Black activists in 1970s Toronto, see Malgorzata Kieryło, "'Equality Now!': Race, Racism, and Resistance in 1970s Toronto" (Ph.D. diss., Queen's University, 2012).

CHAPTER 5

1. For James Jesus Angleton's quote, see the opening epigraph in Edward Jay Epstein, *Deception: The Invisible War between the KGB and the CIA* (New York: Simon and Schuster, 1989). Angleton's mother was white Mexican. He pronounced his middle name with a Spanish accent (Jesús). For a biography on Angleton and his leading role theorizing and implementing counterintelligence policy in the Office of

Strategic Services and later the CIA, see Robin Winks, *Cloak and Gown: Scholars in the Secret War, 1939–1961* (New York: William Morrow, 1987), 322–438; Jefferson Morley, *The Ghost: The Secret Life of CIA Spymaster James Jesus Angleton* (New York: St. Martin's Press, 2017). See also Sam Greenlee, *The Spook Who Sat by the Door* (Detroit: Wayne State University Press, 1969).

2. As a required text at FBI training schools, see Gregg Reese, "Radical Novelist Sam Greenlee Dies at 83," *Our Weekly,* 22 May 2014.

3. Ivan Dixon, dir., *The Spook Who Sat by the Door,* produced by Ivan Dixon and Sam Greenlee (Hollywood: United Artists, 1973). On FBI suppression, see Matt Schudel, "Sam Greenlee, Whose Movie 'The Spook Who Sat by the Door' Became a Cult Classic, Dies," *Washington Post,* 20 May 2014. See also Marilyn Yaquinto, "Cinema as Political Activism: Contemporary Meanings in *The Spook Who Sat by the Door,*" *Black Camera: An International Film Journal* 6, no. 1 (Fall 2014): 5–33; and William Maxwell, *F. B. Eyes: How J. Edgar Hoover's Ghostreaders Framed African American Literature* (Princeton, N.J.: Princeton University Press, 2015). Despite its satire, *The Spook Who Sat by the Door* was astute political analysis. See Richard Iton, *In Search of the Black Fantastic: Politics and Popular Culture in the Post–Civil Rights Era* (New York: Oxford University Press, 2008). Counter-subversion, counter-intelligence, and other types of state-sponsored disinformation are forms of psyops (psychological operations). See Peter Watson, *War on the Mind: The Military Uses and Abuses of Psychology* (London: Hutchinson and Co., 1978).

4. See Manning Marable, *Race, Reform, and Rebellion: The Second Reconstruction in Black America, 1945–1990* (Jackson: University of Mississippi Press, 1991).

5. David J. Garrow, *The FBI and Martin Luther King, Jr: From "Solo" to Memphis* (New York: W. W. Norton, 1981); Clayborne Carson and David Gallen, *Malcolm X: The FBI File* (New York: Graf, 1991); Alexander Charns, *Cloak and Gavel: FBI Wiretaps, Bugs, Informers, and the Supreme Court* (Urbana: University of Illinois Press, 1992); U.S. Federal Bureau of Investigation, *Federal Surveillance of African Americans, 1920–1984* (Farmington Hills, Mich.: Gale, 2010); Richard G. Powers, *Secrecy and Power: The Life of J. Edgar Hoover* (New York: Free Press, 1987).

6. Henry Hampton, *Voices of Freedom: An Oral History of the Civil Rights Movement from the 1950s through the 1960s* (New York: Bantam Books, 1990), 512.

7. Hoover issued the directive on 4 March 1968. See J. Edgar Hoover, "The FBI Sets Goals for COINTELPRO," HERB: Resources for Teachers, https://herb.ashp .cuny.edu/items/show/814 (accessed 9 February 2018).

8. Bob Marley, "I Shot the Sheriff," *Burnin',* Tuff Gong, 1973.

9. *Counter Attack,* May 1970, p. 6, GIPC. On the revolutionary spirit of the BPP and the group's resistance against U.S. domestic aggression and overseas imperialism, see Joshua Bloom and Waldo E. Martin Jr., *Black against Empire: The History and Politics of the Black Panther Party* (Berkeley: University of California Press, 2013).

10. Steve Hewitt, "Reforming the Canadian Security State: Royal Canadian Mounted Police Security Service and the 'Key Sectors' Program," *Intelligence and National Security* 7, no. 4 (2002): 165–84. See also Gary Kinsman, Dieter K. Buse, and Mercedes Steedman, eds., *Whose National Security: Canadian State Surveillance and the Creation of Enemies* (Toronto: Between the Lines, 2000); Gary Kinsman

and Patrizia Gentile, *The Canadian War on Queers: National Security as Sexual Regulation* (Vancouver: University of British Columbia Press, 2010).

11. Hewitt, "Reforming the Canadian Security State." On assassinations and political violence against Black activists, including Fred Hampton, Martin Luther King Jr., and Malcolm X, see Ward Churchill and Jim Vander Wall, *Agents of Repression: The FBI's Secret Wars against the Black Panther Party and the American Indian Movement* (Cambridge, Mass.: South End Press, 2002); Anna Stubblefield, *Ethics along the Color Line* (Ithaca: Cornell University Press, 2005), 60–61; Bryan Burroughs, *Days of Rage: America's Radical Underground, the FBI, and the Forgotten Age of Revolutionary Violence* (New York: Penguin, 2015); and Sydney Trent, "Malcolm X's Family Reveals Letter They Say Shows NYPD, FBI Assassination Involvement," *Washington Post*, 22 February 2021.

12. Hewitt, "Reforming the Canadian Security State," 170.

13. Dawn Rae Flood, "A Black Panther in the Great White North: Fred Hampton Visits Saskatchewan, 1969," *Journal for the Study of Radicalism* 8, no. 2 (2014): 21–50. See also David Austin, *Fear of a Black Nation: Race, Sex, and Security in Sixties Montreal* (Toronto: Between the Lines, 2013); and Sean Mills, *The Empire Within: Postcolonial Thought and Political Activism in Sixties Montreal* (Montreal: McGill-Queen's University Press, 2010).

14. Steve Hewitt, *Spying 101: The RCMP's Secret Activities at Canadian Universities, 1917–1997* (Toronto: University of Toronto Press, 2002), 159. On RCMP-FBI cooperation, see Reg Whitaker and Gary Marcuse, *Cold War Canada: The Making of a National Insecurity State* (Toronto: University of Toronto Press, 1994).

15. "Black Nationalist Movement–Canada Racial Matters," letter to Moss Innes— U.S. Embassy, 19 October 1970, FOIA Case Number RD 46549, FBI Case File 157-NY-3836, box 136, RG 65, Class 157. Cited as RD 46549 hereafter.

16. See Christopher Harris, "Canadian Black Power, Organic Intellectuals, and the War of Position in Toronto, 1967–1975," *CLR James Journal* 20, no. 1–2 (2014): 139–58.

17. John Sawatsky, "Inside Informers Snugger Than Bugs," *Montreal Gazette*, 18 March 1980; John Sawatsky, *Men in the Shadows: The RCMP Security Service* (Toronto: Doubleday Canada, 1980), 43.

18. Black Nationalist Movement–Canada Racial Matters, Hoover Memo, 3 November 1970, FBI Case File 157-11206, Jackson, Miss., obtained under FOIA provisions.

19. For a recent study of the surveillance of blackness in North America, see Simone Browne, *Dark Matters: On the Surveillance of Blackness* (Durham, N.C.: Duke University Press, 2015).

20. Memo from Hoover to Special Agent in Charge, Albany, 31 July 1970, FBI Case File 157-11206.

21. Memo, 19 October 1970, RD 46549.

22. Memo, 19 October 1970, RD 46549. Imprisoned for parole violation, the authorities released Cleaver in June 1968. He fled the country in November for Canada, where he found temporary refuge in Montreal. He might have gone there to participate in a conference of anti-war militants before flying to Cuba. See Kathleen Cleaver, "Why Eldridge Cleaver Has Come Home," *Los Angeles Times*, 1 December

1975, A7; Henry Mitchell, "Eldridge Cleaver at Exile's End: 'I Wanted to Be Free,'" *Washington Post*, 1 September 1976; Earl Caldwell, "Cleaver Search Turns to Montreal," *New York Times*, 1 December 1968, 70; William Drummond, "Speculation Grows That Cleaver Is in Montreal for Parley," *Los Angeles Times*, 1 December 1968.

23. Urgent memo, "Windsor Emancipation Day Celebration," 29 July 1969, RD 46549. Informants in the Chicago area failed to uncover any Black Nationalists who planned to visit Windsor for the Emancipation Day celebration.

24. Kate Quinn, ed., *Black Power in the Caribbean* (Gainesville: University of Florida Press, 2014); Nico Slate, ed., *Black Power beyond Borders: The Global Dimensions of the Black Power Movement* (New York: Palgrave Macmillan, 2012).

25. Memo, 19 October 1970, RD 46549. Warren Hart tried to goad Douglas into leading an armed revolution in Dominica because of the Sir George Williams University incident and the island's repressive government.

26. Memo, 19 October 1970, RD 46549. Warren Hart traveled to the Caribbean to train guerrillas. For an analysis of the surveillance of Black Power in the Caribbean, see W. Chris Johnson, "Guerrilla Ganja Gun Girls: Policing Black Revolutionaries from Notting Hill to Laventille," *Gender and History* 26, no. 3 (2014): 661–87.

27. In 1987, the federal government sentenced Cranshaw to sixty-three years in prison for conspiring to receive $2.5 million from Libya in exchange for committing terrorist acts in the United States. His codefendants included Jeff Fort, leader of the El-Rukn Gang (formerly the Blackstone Rangers and Black P. Stone Nation), Alan Knox, Leon McAnderson, and Roosevelt Hawkins.

28. Mills, *Empire Within*, 102.

29. Memo from Special Agent in Charge, Chicago, re: Reico Cranshaw, RD 46549. An article in the *Atlantic* confirmed that Sammy Davis Jr. had given his stake in a local liquor store to the Blackstone Rangers. See James McPherson, "Chicago's Blackstone Rangers (II)," *The Atlantic*, June 1969. Another article stated that Davis refused to refinance the liquor store, to which the Blackstone Rangers took offense. See "Report Fear of Gang by Sammy Davis Jr.," *Chicago Tribune*, 6 March 1970.

30. Memo, 19 October 1970, RD 46549.

31. Memo, 19 October 1970, RD 46549.

32. Memo, 19 October 1970, RD 46549.

33. Civil Rights Congress, *We Charge Genocide: The Historic Petition to the United Nations for Relief from a Crime of the United States Government against the Negro People* (1951; repr., New York: International Publishers, 1970).

34. This enlistment date meant Hart joined the navy at age fifteen. His Official Personnel Folder has two conflicting birth years: 1926 and 1928. Hart used 1928 frequently.

35. Hart also received the Victory–World War II, Navy Combat Infantry Brigade, and Navy of Occupation medals. Warren Hart, OPF, National Personnel Records Center, St. Louis, Mo. Obtained under FOIA provisions on 23 April 2015.

36. Before he could draw his first paycheck, Hart had to swear an appointment affidavit, which the federal government required of all civil servants, because of the paranoia that undergirded McCarthyism: "I will support and defend the Constitution of the United States against all enemies, foreign and domestic." Due to heightened Cold War anxieties in the 1950s, the affidavit required Hart to affirm that he was

"not a Communist or Fascist" and that he was not an "advocate" or "a member of any organization that advocates the overthrow of the Government of the United States by force or violence or other unconstitutional means or seeking by force or violence to deny other persons their rights under the Constitution of the United States." Furthermore, Hart swore not to "become a member of such organization during the period that [he is] an employee of the Federal Government." Hart OPF.

37. Commentary from Acting Night Supervisor Mary L. Johnson, 27 May 1956, Hart OPF.

38. Commentary from Johnson, 7 June 1956. Hart OPF.

39. Letter of resignation, 8 June 1956, Hart OPF.

40. Hart OPF.

41. See George Lardner Jr., "Detailed Report: Panel Details Abuses on Domestic Spying," *Washington Post*, 29 April 1976.

42. Leon Neyfakh, "The Riots of '68: What the Violence in the Wake of the King Assassination Can, and Can't, Teach Us about Baltimore Today," *Slate*, 27 April 2015.

43. FBI Case File 157-BA-3365, vol. 1, 5. RD 46213 obtained under FOIA provisions. Cited as Case File 157-BA-3365 hereafter.

44. FBI Case File 157-BA-3365, vol. 1, 9–10.

45. Hart became defense captain by virtue of winning a coin toss between him and fellow Panther Elijah Boyd during a leadership vote.

46. Jean Marbella and Justin Fenton, "Release of Black Panther Leader Renews Decades-Old Debate," *Baltimore Sun*, 13 March 2014.

47. Marshall E. Conway and Dominique Stevenson, *Marshall Law: The Life and Times of a Baltimore Black Panther* (Oakland: AK Press, 2011), 24. On Black Power in Oakland, see Robert O. Self, *American Babylon: Race and the Struggle for Postwar Oakland* (Princeton, N.J.: Princeton University Press, 2003); and Robyn C. Spencer, *The Revolution Has Come: Black Power, Gender, and the Black Panther Party in Oakland* (Durham, N.C.: Duke University Press, 2016).

48. Conway and Stevenson, *Marshall Law*, 12.

49. Michael Simanga, *Amiri Baraka and the Congress of African People: History and Memory* (New York: Palgrave Macmillan, 2015), 22.

50. Conway and Stevenson, *Marshall Law*, 33–34. See also Harriet A. Washington, *Medical Apartheid: The Dark History of Medical Experimentation on Black Americans from Colonial Times to the Present* (New York: Doubleday, 2006); and John M. Hoberman, *Black and Blue: The Origins and Consequences of Medical Racism* (Berkeley: University of California Press, 2012).

51. Conway and Stevenson, *Marshall Law*, 35.

52. See Rhonda Y. Williams, *Concrete Demands: The Search for Black Power in the 20th Century* (New York: Taylor and Francis, 2015).

53. See Curtis J. Austin, *Up Against the Wall: Violence in the Making and Unmaking of the Black Panther Party* (Fayetteville, Ark.: University of Arkansas Press, 2006).

54. Conway and Stevenson, *Marshall Law*, 39.

55. On the dilemmas of the post–civil rights era, see Robin D. G. Kelley, *Into the Fire: African Americans since 1970* (New York: Oxford University Press, 1996).

56. Conway and Stevenson, *Marshall Law*, 43. See also "Lights Cut Off at Black Panthers' Baltimore Home," *Baltimore Afro-American*, 13 December 1969, 20.

57. Other police and security informants had infiltrated the Panthers, but Hart remained the most senior-ranking member.

58. Conway and Stevenson, *Marshall Law*, 47.

59. Conway and Stevenson, 47.

60. Hart petitioned his demotion. Steve McCutchen, the lieutenant of information for the Baltimore chapter, chronicled these events in his diary. See Steve McCutchen, "Selections from a Panther Diary," in *The Black Panther Party (Reconsidered)*, ed. Charles E. Jones (Baltimore: Black Classic Press, 1998), 115–33.

61. Case File 157-BA-3365, vol. 2, 24.

62. Stephen Lynton, "Head of Baltimore Panthers Resigns Following Demotion," *Baltimore Sun*, 13 July 1969, 20.

63. See Case File 157-BA-3365, vol. 3, 24; *The Black Panther*, 23 August 1969, 27.

64. Russell Rickford, *We Are an African People: Independent Education, Black Power, and the Radical Imagination* (New York: Oxford University Press, 2016), 169–218.

65. Case File 157-BA-3365, vol. 3, 5–10.

66. Case File 157-BA-3365, vol. 4.

67. Author's interview with Howard Fuller, 14 October 2020, notes in author's possession.

68. Conway and Stevenson, *Marshall Law*, 48.

69. The FBI framed Conway because he exposed Hart. Conway's sheer competence and commitment to liberation might also have condemned him. The state of Maryland sentenced Conway to life in prison. He spent forty-four years in the penitentiary before the state acquitted and released him. Michelle D. Brown, "Marshall 'Eddie' Conway Awareness Weekend," *Baltimore Afro-American*, 4 May 2001.

70. Conway and Stevenson, *Marshall Law*, 43.

71. Sandra Crockett, "25 Years into Sentence, Ex-Panther Maintains Authorities Set Him Up: Cop Killer or Victim?," *Baltimore Sun*, 13 May 1995, 2.

72. Marshall Eddie Conway, "Domestic Warfare: A Dialogue," in *Warfare in the American Homeland: Policing and Prison in a Penal Democracy*, ed., Joy James (Durham, N.C.: Duke University Press, 2007), 100.

73. Conway and Stevenson, *Marshall Law*, 100.

74. Hart is directly and indirectly implicated in the Alex Rackley murder and the New Haven Panther trial. Rackley was a New York Panther who allegedly performed the same infiltration/agent provocateur work for the FBI. George Sams, who befriended Rocky Jones when he stayed in Nova Scotia, was one of the alleged murderers. The U.S. Justice Department spirited Hart to Canada, believing that he could have suffered a similar fate as Rackley. See Hugh Pearson, *The Shadow of the Panther: Huey Newton and the Price of Black Power in America* (Reading, Mass.: Addison-Wesley, 1994). On Hart's entrapment of the New York Panthers, see Stephen Chaberski, "The Strategy of Defense in a Political Trial: The Trial of the 'Panther 21'" (Ph.D. diss., Columbia University, 1975), 223–54.

75. Work history memo, Hart OPF.

76. "Mounties Went with Him, CTV Told: Spied on Blacks in Caribbean for RCMP, Hart Says," *Globe and Mail*, 27 February 1978.

77. Martin O'Malley, "A Tolerant People? Nice to Believe. We're Really Just Polite Racists," *Globe and Mail*, 15 February 1969, A7.

78. "There Are Other Voices," *Globe and Mail*, 24 February 1971, 6.

79. "No More Warnings: Canada's Black Revolution Under Way, Says Militant," *Toronto Star*, 22 February 1971, 27.

80. "Mounties Went with Him, CTV Told." Perhaps because of the gender dynamics, the Mounties did not task Hart with surveilling Cools.

81. Case File 157-BA-3365, vol. 4.

82. The RCMP allowed Hart to smuggle immigrants into Canada so that he could maintain his spurious connections to organized crime and justify his flashy lifestyle. See "'Cover' Job: Informer Smuggled Immigrants," *Ottawa Citizen*, 27 February 1978.

83. It appears that the RCMP arrested Douglas temporarily to interrogate him. They did not charge him with committing a crime. See Andrew Szende, "U.S. Informer Says He Bugged Allmand and MP for Mounties," *Toronto Star*, 23 February 1978. Douglas said the fact that Hart left the jail after five days and was deported, only to resurface in Toronto a few days later, raised his suspicion that Hart had police connections. It is also unclear whether the Security Service physically escorted Hart to the U.S. border only to "smuggle" him back into Canada with tacit approval from immigration officials. See Jon Ferry, "'We Used to Laugh in His Face': Avowed RCMP Agent 'a Joker,' Blacks Say," *Globe and Mail*, 24 February 1978; John Sawatsky, "The Seamy Business of Recruiting Informers," *Toronto Star*, 17 March 1980; and *Certain R.C.M.P. Activities and the Question of Governmental Knowledge: Third Report* (Ottawa: Commission of Inquiry concerning Certain Activities of the Royal Canadian Mounted Police, Canadian Government Publishing Centre, 1981), 485.

84. "Mounties Went with Him, CTV Told," 5.

85. Hart likely met these individuals through Douglas, Campbell, and other Canadian-based activists. And as an agent provocateur with a track record of inciting activists to use violence, Hart likely offered to train his contacts in armed struggle. See "American Claims Communist Threat to Antigua," *Virgin Island Daily News*, 8 January 1979.

86. "Mounties Went with Him, CTV Told."

87. See "American Claims Communist Threat to Antigua."

88. See "Black Leader's Denial 'Hogwash,'" *Ottawa Citizen*, 9 March 1978.

89. See Stuart Hall, *Policing the Crisis: Mugging, the State, and Law and Order* (New York: Holmes and Meier, 1978).

90. As an RCMP operative, Hart briefed the CIA and British MI6 when he visited the Caribbean to train radicals in guerrilla warfare. The three intelligence agencies worried about the spread of radicalism in the Caribbean and South America. See Hart OPF. See also Sawatsky, "Seamy Business of Recruiting Informers." Furthermore, the postwar immigration of Caribbean nationals to North America and Britain signaled to the intelligence communities of the three countries the need to deny subversives entry or monitor those who had already entered. The onset of the Cold War helped create the Anglo intelligence pact that brought U.K., U.S., Canadian, New Zealand, and Australian intelligence into cooperation. See Hewitt,

Spying 101, 159. Although Bermuda is not in the Caribbean, U.S., Canadian, and British officials tried to undermine Black militancy on the island. See Quito Swan, *Black Power in Bermuda: The Struggle for Decolonization* (New York: Palgrave Macmillan, 2009), 53–73.

91. The CIA was active in Canada. The CBC's *The Fifth Estate*, a documentary series, aired on 9 January 1974 an exposé that alleged the Communications Branch of the National Research Council (CBNRC), "one of Canada's major spying agencies," was a CIA front, overseeing communications between diplomatic installations in Ottawa and foreign countries to contain communism. *The Fifth Estate* also accused the CIA of operating throughout Canada. *The Fifth Estate* interviewed a U.S. intelligence analyst who admitted that Canada is "merely an extension of the United States in a northward direction." A former deputy commissioner of the RCMP also conceded that it is "rather stupid of any Canadian authority to think that if the NSA covers the rest of the world, that they would make an exception of this country." See "The CIA Lives in Canada," *Amex: The American Expatriate in Canada* 4, no. 38 (1974): 34–35, GIPC; and Bill Macadam and James R. Dubro, "How the CIA Has Us Spooked," *Maclean's*, 1 July 1974, 20.

92. For a detailed breakdown of RCMP covert activities, see Robert Sheppard, "Greater Parliamentary Scrutiny of RCMP to Be Urged: McDonald to Release Final Report," *Globe and Mail*, 24 August 1981.

93. Hart did not testify at the trial. See "Black Leader's Denial 'Hogwash.'"

94. On 8 March 1971, radicals broke into an FBI field office in Media, Pennsylvania, where they obtained a trove of classified documents that outlined the bureau's elaborate domestic surveillance and counter-subversion. They mailed the documents to journalists around the country, and the media scrutiny helped trigger in 1975 the Church Committee (formally the United States Senate Select Committee to Study Governmental Operations with Respect to Intelligence Activities). See Mark Mazzetti, "Burglars Who Took on FBI Abandon Shadows," *New York Times*, 7 January 2014; and Betty Medsger, *The Burglary: The Discovery of J. Edgar Hoover's Secret F.B.I.* (New York: Vintage Books, 2014).

95. Jonathan Fowlie and Timothy Appleby, "Former Black Panther Extradition Case Opens," *Globe and Mail*, 30 July 2004.

96. For other media references to Hart's firearm arsenal, see "Indians Got Guns from RCMP Spy," *Toronto Star*, 23 April 1980.

97. Linda McQuaig, "The Man with the Guns," *Montreal Gazette*, 13 January 1981.

98. Richard Atkinson and Joe Fiorito, *The Life Crimes and Hard Times of Ricky Atkinson: Leader of the Dirty Tricks Gang; A True Story* (Toronto: Exile Editions, 2017), 181.

99. McQuaig, "Man with the Guns."

100. See S. Hall, *Policing the Crisis*.

101. McQuaig, "Man with the Guns."

102. McQuaig, "Man with the Guns."

103. Rob Tripp, "Last Chance for Aged Thief," *National Post* (Toronto), 9 April 2011.

104. Hart stated in a work history memo that he "investigated organized crime, fugitives, and bank *robbery*" (my emphasis on his use of the singular rather than

plural form). Moreover, Hart's job profile for the RCMP had less to do with crimes that regular police investigated, yet he initiated and planned several. See Hart OPF.

105. Tripp, "Last Chance for Aged Thief." See also Atkinson and Fiorito, *Life Crimes and Hard Times of Ricky Atkinson*, 129.

106. Conway and Stevenson, *Marshall Law*, 99.

107. Atkinson and Fiorito, *Life Crimes and Hard Times of Ricky Atkinson*, 320–21.

108. Atkinson and Fiorito, 320–21.

109. His gang robbed over 100 banks. When Atkinson was in his early forties, he had already racked up nearly fifty years of prison time for bank robberies and other felonies.

110. Atkinson and Fiorito, 320–21.

111. Rob Tripp, "Dirty Tricks Bank Robbing Gang Leader Richard Atkinson," Skype interview, https://www.youtube.com/watch?v=39mXnOK4G5w (accessed 14 October 2015). In 1995, while serving time at Frontenac Institution, Atkinson participated in media productions called Prison TV in which he interviewed Warren Allmand, the solicitor general of Canada at the time when Hart entrapped Atkinson and his peers to commit robbery. See "Black Panthers, Warren Hart & the Dirty Tricks Gang," YouTube, https://www.youtube.com/watch?v=nCDwQzW-WHU (accessed 14 October 2015).

112. Tripp, "Last Chance for Aged Thief."

113. "Rosie's Stalling Bid Defeated: Douglas Deportation Case to Go On," *Montreal Gazette*, 5 August 1972.

114. "Blacks Get Together May 27 for African Liberation Day," *Amex: The American Expatriate in Canada* 3, no. 30 (1972): 15, GIPC. Owusu Sadaukai (Howard Fuller) of Malcolm X Liberation University oversaw the international coordination of efforts in San Francisco and D.C. and throughout the Caribbean. The mission of African Liberation Day was "to demonstrate solidarity with our African brothers and sisters and to pinpoint Canadian and European involvement in southern Africa." The mission further stated, "Such a protest demonstration would heighten international publicity and attention around the struggles in southern Africa and would aid in educating our people to the nature and magnitude of Canadian imperialism."

115. The short-lived Black Liberation Front of Canada accused the NBCC of serving a counterrevolutionary purpose for the state. Although suspicion ran high and the Black Liberation Front of Canada incorrectly attributed a counter-subversion motive to the NBCC, it was a moderate force of working-class and middle-class people. It lacked a revolutionary ethos. "National Black Coalition: Whose Baby Is It Really?" *Black Liberation News* 1, no. 5 (November 1969), microfilm no. 933, MHSO. See also Barrington Walker, "The National Black Coalition of Canada: 'Race' and Social Equality in the Age of Multiculturalism," *CLR James Journal* 20, vol. 1/2 (Fall 2014): 159–78.

116. "Summer Camp to Offer Courses in Black History, Drama, Crafts," *Toronto Star*, 9 June 1971.

117. Harold Hoyte, "Black Power in Toronto: Self-Help Projects Chart the Way," *Toronto Star*, 19 January 1972.

118. On the importance of schooling and self-determination during the freedom struggle, see Rickford, *We Are an African People.*

119. Memo on educational history, Hart OPF.

120. Hoyte, "Black Power in Toronto."

121. Sidney Katz, "A Tough-Talking Bunny Girl Seeks a Better Deal for Black Children," *Toronto Daily Star*, 31 October 1970, C18.

122. "Probe Urged to Block 'Liberators' from U.S.," *Globe and Mail*, 14 March 1970.

123. Sheila Gormley, "Take to Streets, Students Urged," *Toronto Star*, 6 November 1972.

124. Adrienne Clarkson, *From Activist to Head of State* (Toronto: CBC Fifth Estate, 1978), digitized film.

125. See "Establishment of a Guerrilla Training Camp, Tweed, Ontario, Canada, by Black Extremists," FBI Case File 157-BA-7664. RD 46209 obtained under FOIA provisions. The memo referred to "Debra Clarke," but it is certain that figure is the same Black activist who worked for the Black Student Union.

126. Ferry, "'We Used to Laugh in His Face': Avowed RCMP Agent 'a Joker,' Blacks Say."

127. Isabel Vincent, "Premier's Politics Forged in Montreal Riot: Jailed in Canada: Leader of Dominica Says World Has Come Around to His Views," *National Post*, 23 February 2000.

128. Angela Ferrante, "Paroled Rosie Will Help Poor," *The Montreal Gazette*, 8 November 1974. On racial capitalism, see Cedric J. Robinson, *Black Marxism: The Making of the Black Radical Tradition* (Chapel Hill: University of North Carolina Press, 2000).

129. Ferrante, "Paroled Rosie Will Help Poor." Douglas's prison sentence was the longest of all the student agitators involved in the Sir George Williams occupation. Douglas suspected that Hart was an undercover operative because Hart visited him in prison, which is against all protocol. At the time, only relatives of inmates could visit.

130. Headley Tulloch, *Black Canadians: A Long Line of Fighters* (Toronto: NC Press, 1975), 140.

131. John Hay, "Cools Still Waiting in Liberal Wings," *Ottawa Citizen*, 18 October 1978.

132. McQuaig, "Man with the Guns."

133. McQuaig, "Man with the Guns."

134. "Angela Davis Attacks Ottawa 'Racist' Policy," *Toronto Star*, 23 November 1974.

135. "Angela Davis Attacks Ottawa 'Racist' Policy."

136. "Negro, Indian Assail Toronto's Uncle Toms," *Globe and Mail*, 22 February 1969.

137. Charlie Stimac, "Racism in Toronto on the Rise in a Deepening Economic Crisis," *Amex-Canada: The American Expatriate in Canada* 5, no. 43 (1975): 9, 17, GIPC.

138. See Scott Rutherford, *Canada's Other Red Scare: Indigenous Protest and Colonial Encounters during the Global Sixties* (Montreal: McGill-Queen's University Press, 2020); Churchill and Vander Wall, *Agents of Repression*; and Bryan D. Palmer,

"'Indians of All Tribes': The Birth of Red Power," in *Debating Dissent: Canada and the Sixties*, ed. Greg Kealey et al. (Toronto: University of Toronto Press, 2012), 193–210.

139. On the pollution of Kenora, see Anastasia Shkilnyk, *A Poison Stronger Than Love: The Destruction of an Ojibway Community* (New Haven, Conn.: Yale University Press, 1985).

140. Harper's observation is noteworthy: except for the Caribbean, Douglas was not widely known in Canadian politics. See McQuaig, "Man with the Guns." Harper's comment on Diefenbaker is in reference to a 1959 ceremony when Chief Little Crow of the Sioux Indian Tribe crowned the prime minister with a headdress, thereby naming him Chief Standing Buffalo. Diefenbaker's government took modest strides to improve relations between Indigenous communities and the Canadian government. In 1960, his government amended the Canada Elections Act, which, starting in 1962, gave Indigenous peoples the franchise without requiring them to forfeit their federal status. See Wendy Moss and Elaine Gardner-O'Toole, "Aboriginal People: History of Discriminatory Laws," Government of Canada, http://publications .gc.ca/Collection-R/LoPBdP/BP/bp175-e.htm#(6)txt (accessed 18 February 2018).

141. Tim Hector, "What I Said and What Rosie Said," *The Outlet*, 20 October 2000, https://web.archive.org/web/20120416011318/http://www.candw.ag/~jardinea /fanflame.htm (accessed 10 April 2021).

142. McQuaig, "Man with the Guns."

143. "Suspected Hart Was Agent, Douglas Says," *Globe and Mail*, 23 February 1978. Author's interview with Philippe Fils-Aimé, 28 November 2019, notes in author's possession.

144. Author's interview with Philippe Fils-Aimé.

145. Author's interview with Philippe Fils-Aimé.

146. Author's interview with Philippe Fils-Aimé, 14 October 2020, notes in author's possession.

147. Clarkson, *From Activist to Head of State*.

148. Author's interview with Fils-Aimé, 28 November 2019.

149. McQuaig, "Man with the Guns."

150. Author's telephone interview with Warren Allmand, 5 November 2014, notes in author's possession.

151. "Suspected Hart was Agent, Douglas Says."

152. Author's interview with Allmand.

153. "Mounties Went with Him, CTV Told."

154. "Mounties Went with Him, CTV Told."

155. "Black Radicals Plotted to Murder Montreal Professors, Probe Told," *Montreal Gazette*, 10 January 1980.

156. "Victim of Vendetta, Claims Ex-Undercover Agent," *Ottawa Citizen*, 9 January 1980. The Security Service, according to Hart, reneged on its promise to provide him with the posh civilian job and permanent residency that he desired in Canada, where his wife and son lived. Feeling dejected and disgruntled, Hart came out three years later and announced that as an undercover operative for the Security Service, he had secretly recorded the solicitor general and a federal Member of Parliament who expressed interest in assisting Douglas in fighting his deportation order. This revelation became a public relations crisis for the sitting Liberal government and

the Security Service. It triggered a federal inquiry into RCMP misconduct, and the multiyear investigations produced in 1981 the "Royal Commission of Inquiry into Certain Activities of the RCMP" or the McDonald Commission, which led to the federal government splitting the Security Service from the RCMP and subsequently creating the Canadian Security Intelligence Service in 1984.

157. "Rosie Douglas Leaves for Jamaica," *Montreal Gazette*, 1 May 1976.

158. "Deportation Fight by Black Militant," *Ottawa Citizen*, 2 December 1975.

159. Eric Siblin, "Rosie the Red Stops Smashing the State," *Saturday Night* 115, no. 5 (May 2000): 27.

160. Case File 157-BA-3365, vol. 4.

CHAPTER 6

1. Adrienne Clarkson, *From Activist to Head of State* (Toronto: CBC Fifth Estate, 1978), digitized film.

2. In the 1960s, some African American activists pivoted from Black Nationalism to Pan-African nationalism. See Russell Rickford, *We Are an African People: Independent Education, Black Power, and the Radical Imagination* (New York: Oxford University Press, 2016). See also Robin D. G. Kelley, *Into the Fire: African American since 1970* (New York: Oxford University Press, 1996); Nikhil P. Singh, *Black Is a Country: Race and the Unfinished Struggle for Democracy* (Cambridge, Mass.: Harvard University Press, 2005); and Manning Marable, *Race, Reform, and Rebellion: The Second Reconstruction in Black America, 1945–1990* (Jackson: University of Mississippi Press, 1991). On the decline of Black Power, see Peniel E. Joseph, *Waiting 'til the Midnight Hour: A Narrative History of Black Power in America* (New York: Henry Holt, 2006).

3. On the liberal order in the 1960s, see Allen J. Matusow, *The Unraveling of America: A History of Liberalism in the 1960s* (New York: Harper and Row, 1984); Todd Gitlin, *The Sixties: Years of Hope, Days of Rage* (New York: Bantam Books, 1987); William L. Van Deburg, *New Day in Babylon: Black Power and American Culture, 1965–1975* (Chicago: University of Chicago Press, 1992); and Maurice Isserman and Michael Kazin, *America Divided: The Civil War of the 1960s* (New York: Oxford University Press, 2000).

4. Rosie Douglas, *Chains or Change: Focus on Dominica* (self-pub., 1975), v.

5. Ron Daniels, "30 Years since the First African Liberation Day USA: Vantage Point," *New Pittsburgh Courier*, 22 June 2002; Ron Daniels, "The Race and Class Dimensions of the Black Freedom Struggle in the United States" (Ph.D. diss., Union Institute Graduate College, 2000). See also Benjamin Talton, *In This Land of Plenty: Mickey Leland and Africa in American Politics* (Philadelphia: University of Pennsylvania Press, 2019).

6. Roy Campanella Jr. and Henry Johnson, dirs., *Black Unity: Breaking the Chains of Oppression*, narrated by Fred Thomas (n.p., ALD Documentary, 1972), digitized film.

7. See William R. Scott, *The Sons of Sheba's Race: African-Americans and the Italo-Ethiopian War, 1935–1941* (Bloomington: Indiana University Press, 1993); and Joseph E. Harris, *African-American Reactions to War in Ethiopia, 1936–1941* (Baton Rouge: Louisiana State University Press, 1994). On ALD and the 1935 Ethiopian

invasion, see Cedric Johnson, *From Revolutionaries to Race Leaders: Black Power and the Making of African American Politics* (Minneapolis: University of Minnesota Press, 2007), 132. The UNIA's forerunner, the Association of Universal Loyal Negroes, had been founded in Panama during the First World War to expose German atrocities against the Indigenous population while promoting self-determination and nation building in East Africa. In November 1918, Dillon C. Govin, secretary of the Association of Universal Loyal Negroes, wrote Du Bois from Montreal, seeking support for the organization. Govin informed Du Bois that he was in touch with the African League in England and Duse Mohammed Ali, Egyptian-born editor of the *African Times and Orient Review*, the London-based Pan-African newspaper. See Dillon C. Govin to Du Bois and letter of endorsement advertisement, 19 November 1918, DBP (MS 312); Leo Bertley, "The Universal Negro Improvement Association of Montreal, 1917–1979" (Ph.D. diss., Concordia University, 1980), 40–42; and Robert A. Hill et al., eds., *The Marcus Garvey and Universal Negro Improvement Association Papers, Vol. XI: The Caribbean Diaspora, 1910–1920* (Durham, N.C.: Duke University Press, 2011), 101.

8. Campanella and Johnson, *Black Unity*; Owusu Sadaukai, "Political and Material Support for the Liberation Movements," in *Pan-Africanism: The Struggle against Imperialism and Neo-Colonialism*, ed. Horace Campbell (Toronto: Afro-Carib Publications, 1975), 103–13. For analyses on African anti-colonialism and the African American freedom struggle, see Brenda Gayle Plummer, *Rising Wind: Black Americans and U.S. Foreign Affairs, 1935–1960* (Chapel Hill: University of North Carolina Press, 1996); Penny Von Eschen, *Race against Empire: Black Americans and Anti-colonialism, 1937–1957* (Ithaca: Cornell University Press, 1997); Kevin Gaines, *American Africans in Ghana: Black Expatriates and the Civil Rights Era* (Chapel Hill: University of North Carolina Press, 2006); and James Meriwether, *Proudly We Can Be Africans: Black Americans and Africa, 1935–1961* (Chapel Hill: University of North Carolina Press, 2009). On postwar linkages in the Americas, see Jason C. Parker, *Brother's Keeper: The United States, Race, and Empire in the British Caribbean, 1938–1962* (New York: Oxford University Press, 2008).

9. Daniels, "30 Years since the First African Liberation Day USA"; Edward O. Erhagbe, "The African-American Contribution to the Liberation Struggle in Southern Africa: The Case of the African Liberation Support Committee, 1972–1979," *Journal of Pan African Studies* 4, no. 5 (2011): 26–56.

10. Leonard N. Moore, *The Defeat of Black Power: Civil Rights and the National Black Political Convention of 1972* (Baton Rouge: Louisiana State University Press, 2017); Daniels, "Race and Class Dimensions of the Black Freedom Struggle in the United States."

11. Douglas, *Chains or Change*, ii.

12. Headley Tulloch, *Black Canadians: A Long Line of Fighters* (Toronto: NC Press, 1975), 140–41.

13. Campanella and Johnson, *Black Unity*. See also Walter Rodney, "African History in the Service of the Black Liberation," in *Moving against the System: The 1968 Congress of Black Writers and the Making of Global Consciousness*, ed. David Austin (London: Pluto Press, 2018), 127–42; Walter Rodney, "Towards the Sixth Pan-African Congress: Aspects of the International Class Struggle in Africa, the

Caribbean, and America," in *African Intellectual Heritage: A Book of Sources*, ed. Molefi Kete Asante and Abu S. Abarry (Philadelphia: Temple University Press, 1996), 729–39; and Robert Hill, "Walter Rodney and the Restatement of Pan-Africanism in Theory and Practice," *Ufahamu: A Journal of African Studies* 38, no. 3 (1995): 135–58.

14. R. Joseph Parrott, "Boycott Gulf! Angolan Oil and the Black Power Roots of American Anti-apartheid Organizing," *Modern American History* 1, no. 2 (2018): 195–220; "The Reasons behind African Liberation Day," *Sun Reporter* (San Francisco), 20 May 1972; Daniels, "30 Years since the First African Liberation Day USA."

15. Ilan Pappé, *Israel and South Africa: The Many Faces of Apartheid* (London: Zed Books, 2015); Michael W. Williams, "Pan-Africanism and Zionism: The Delusion of Comparability," *Journal of Black Studies* 21, no. 3 (1991): 348–71; Russell Rickford, "'To Build a New World': Black American Internationalism and Palestine Solidarity," *Journal of Palestine Studies* 48, no. 4 (2019): 52–68. Despite public disapproval, some Canadian corporations tried to exploit opportunities in Rhodesia and South Africa. See Stephanie Bangarth, "'Vocal but Not Particularly Strong'? Air Canada's Ill-Fated Vacation Package to Rhodesia and South Africa and the Anti-apartheid Movement in Canada," *International Journal* 71, no. 3 (2016): 488–97; and Linda Freeman, *The Ambiguous Champion: Canada and South Africa in the Trudeau and Mulroney Years* (Toronto: University of Toronto Press, 1997).

16. Campanella and Johnson, *Black Unity*. Author's interview with Howard Fuller, 14 October 2020, notes in author's possession. See also Howard Fuller with Lisa Frazier Page, *No Struggle, No Progress: A Warrior's Life from Black Power to Education Reform* (Milwaukee: Marquette University Press, 2014).

17. According to Howard Fuller (Sadaukai), the ALD Support Committee succeeded the provisional ALD Coordinating Committee after the first successful commemoration in May 1972. Author's email exchange with Fuller, 3 June 2021.

18. Toronto Committee for the Liberation of Southern Africa, *Words and Deeds: Canada, Portugal, and Africa* (Toronto: TCLSAC, 1976); John S. Saul, *On Building a Social Movement: The North American Campaign for Southern African Liberation Revisited* (Trenton, N.J.: Africa World Press, 2017).

19. Tim Hector, "War and Peace in Our Time, Part I," *The Outlet*, 8 March 2002, https://web.archive.org/web/20110911172642/http://www.candw.ag/~jardinea/ffhtm/ff020308.htm (accessed 10 April 2021).

20. Don L. Lee, "African Liberation Day: Thousands of Black Americans March to Support African Freedom Fighters," *Ebony*, July 1973, 42.

21. See Rodney, "Towards the Sixth Pan-African Congress"; and Horace Campbell, ed., *Pan-Africanism: The Struggle against Imperialism and Neo-Colonialism* (Toronto: Afro-Carib Publications, 1975).

22. Walter Rodney, "The Black Scholar Interviews: Walter Rodney," *Black Scholar* 6, no. 3 (1974): 40. See also Robert Carr, *Black Nationalism in the New World: Reading the African-American and West Indian Experience* (Durham, N.C.: Duke University Press, 2002).

23. Ashley D. Farmer, "Mothers of Pan-Africanism: Audley Moore and Dara Abubakari," *Women, Gender, and Families of Color* 4, no. 2 (Fall 2016): 283–84.

24. See La TaSha Levy, "Remembering Sixth-PAC: Interviews with Sylvia Hill and Judy Claude, Organizers of the Sixth Pan-African Congress," *Black Scholar* 37,

no. 4 (Winter 2008): 39–47; and author's interview with Brenda Paris, 13 November 2020, notes in author's possession.

25. Author's interview with Brenda Paris, 28 April 2021, notes in author's possession.

26. Paul Buhle, *Tim Hector: A Caribbean Radical's Story* (Jackson: University of Mississippi Press, 2006).

27. Author's interview with Philippe Fils-Aimé, 14 October 2020, notes in author's possession. See also David Austin, *Fear of a Black Nation: Race, Sex, and Security in Sixties Montreal* (Toronto: Between the Lines, 2013).

28. "Man Named as Informer for RCMP Employed by Arms Firm in Antigua," *Globe and Mail*, 30 November 1978.

29. Before SRC, Hart worked as an officer in the Naval Air Service Command Police Division from 12 September 1977 to 19 June 1978, when he resigned due to "family personal affairs." He had, in fact, received a better offer from SRC. Warren Hart, Official Personnel Folder, National Personnel Records Center, St. Louis, Mo. Obtained under FOIA provisions on 23 April 2015. See document "Police Officer," Naval Air Service Command Police Division, Patuxent River, Md.

30. Peter Moon, "Bitterness Remains on Caribbean Island after Canadian Arms Company Forced Out," *Globe and Mail*, 10 March 1980.

31. Space Research Corporation, vol. 1, 7C-102-100-1-1. Obtained under the Access to Information and Privacy Act, LAC.

32. On the Cold War and the Caribbean, see Timothy Ashby, *The Bear in the Back Yard: Moscow's Caribbean Strategy* (Lexington, Mass.: Lexington Books, 1987); Robert A. Pastor, *Whirlpool: U.S. Foreign Policy toward Latin America and the Caribbean* (Princeton, N.J.: Princeton University Press, 1992); Parker, *Brother's Keeper*; and Rachel A. May, Alejandro Schneider, and Roberto G. Arana, *Caribbean Revolutions: Cold War Armed Movements* (Cambridge: Cambridge University Press, 2018). On the Cold War as a multipolar, multisited phenomenon, see Lorenz M. Lüthi, *Cold Wars: Asia, the Middle East, Europe* (New York: Cambridge University Press, 2020).

33. SRC, vol. 1.

34. SRC, vol. 1, 17, 336.

35. When SRC partnered with Israel to help it meet its procurement orders of 155-mm shells, the Israelis allegedly withdrew when they discovered that the shells would end up in South Africa. SRC, vol. 3, 1036.

36. SRC, vol. 1, "Resident of the U.S.A. Interviewed, 78-08-08."

37. SRC, vol. 1, 337. This transaction occurred on 7 July 1977.

38. SRC, vol. 1.

39. SRC, vol. 2, 662. See also "Arms for South Africa: The American Connection," *A Journal of Opinion* 9, no. 1/2 (1979): 52–55.

40. See Robert Coram, *Caribbean Time Bomb: The United States' Complicity in the Corruption of Antigua* (New York: Morrow, 1993), 46–47. Volumes of *The Outlet* from May to December 1978, the same time when Hector and the ACLM mounted an aggressive campaign against Premier Bird and SRC, are mysteriously missing from the Antigua and Barbuda National Archives.

41. SRC, vol. 1, "Statement of John Alsop." He resigned in early 1978.

42. SRC, vol. 2, 785, 801. It is imperative that historians conceptualize Africa as a constitutive part of Cold War killing fields. See Paul T. Chamberlain, *The Cold War's Killing Fields: Rethinking the Long Peace* (New York: Harper, 2018).

43. South African delegates visited residential schools and Indigenous reservations in Canada to learn about Canada's apartheid policy. Indian Affairs and External Affairs, federal departments, facilitated the visits. See Freeman, *Ambiguous Champion*, 16.

44. S.C. Res. 418, 32 U.N. SCOR Res. & Decs. at 5, U.N. Doc. S/INF/33 (1977).

45. SRC, vol. 2, 720, 722, 785, 965.

46. David C. Martin and John Walcott, "Smuggling Arms to South Africa," *Washington Post*, 5 August 1979.

47. Thomas Borstelmann, *The Cold War and the Color Line: American Race Relations in the Global Arena* (Cambridge, Mass.: Harvard University Press, 2001), 156–57.

48. Martin and Walcott, "Smuggling Arms to South Africa." See Christine Hatzky, *Cubans in Angola: South-South Cooperation and Transfer of Knowledge, 1976–1991* (Madison: University of Wisconsin Press, 2015); Piero Gleijeses, *Conflicting Missions: Havana, Washington, and Africa, 1959–1976* (Chapel Hill: University of North Carolina Press, 2002); Carlos Moore, *Castro, the Blacks, and Africa* (Los Angeles: Center for Afro-American Studies, 1988); and Harry Villegas, *Cuba and Angola: The War for Freedom* (London: Pathfinder Press, 2017).

49. John Stockwell, *In Search of Enemies: A CIA Story* (New York: Norton, 1978), 43. See also Michael T. Klare et al., *Supplying Repression: U.S. Support for Authoritarian Regimes Abroad* (Washington, D.C.: Institute for Policy Studies, 1981).

50. See Piero Gleijeses, *Visions of Freedom: Havana, Washington, Pretoria, and the Struggle for Southern Africa, 1976–1991* (Chapel Hill: University of North Carolina Press, 2013); Ellen Ray et al., eds., *Dirty Work 2: The CIA in Africa* (London: Zed Press, 1980); James P. Hubbard, *The United States and the End of British Colonial Rule in Africa, 1941–1968* (Jefferson, N.C.: McFarland, 2010); Vladimir Shubin, *The Hot "Cold War": The USSR in Southern Africa* (London: Pluto Press, 2008).

51. James Dingeman, "Covert Operations in Central and Southern Africa," in *U.S. Military Involvement in Southern Africa*, ed. Western Massachusetts Association of Concerned African Scholars (Boston: South End Press, 1978), 87.

52. Dingeman, 82–108. See also Western Massachusetts Association of Concerned African Scholars, ed., *U.S. Military Involvement in Southern Africa* (Boston: South End Press, 1978); Thomas J. Noer, *Cold War and Black Liberation: The United States and White Rule in Africa, 1948–1968* (Columbia: University of Missouri Press, 1985); Thomas Borstelmann, *Apartheid's Reluctant Uncle: The United States and Southern Africa in the Early Cold War* (New York: Oxford University Press, 1993); Abiodun Alao, *Brothers at War: Dissidence and Rebellion in Southern Africa* (New York: St. Martin's Press, 1994); Sue Onslow, ed., *The Cold War in Southern Africa: White Power, Black Liberation* (New York: Routledge, 2009); Nancy Mitchell, *Jimmy Carter in Africa: Race and the Cold War* (Stanford: Stanford University Press, 2016); and Susan Williams, *White Malice: The CIA and the Neocolonization of Africa* (London: C. Hurst Publishers, 2019); James Meriwether, *Tears, Fire, and*

Blood: The United States and the Decolonization of Africa (Chapel Hill: University of North Carolina Press, 2021).

53. George Padmore, *Pan-Africanism or Communism? The Coming Struggle for Africa* (London: Dobson, 1956); George Padmore, *How Britain Rules Africa* (New York: Lothrop, Lee and Shepard, 1936); Leslie James, *George Padmore and Decolonization from Below: Pan-Africanism, the Cold War, and the End of Empire* (Houndmills, U.K.: Palgrave Macmillan, 2014). On the Soviet Union's unwillingness to support Ethiopia in the face of Fascist Italy's aggression, see Christian Høgsbjerg, *C. L. R. James in Imperial England* (Durham, N.C.: Duke University Press, 2014), 101–2; and Hakim Adi, "Pan-Africanism and Communism: The Comintern, the 'Negro Question' and the First International Conference of Negro Workers, Hamburg 1930," *African and Black Diaspora: An International Journal* 1, no. 2 (2008): 237–54; Jan Carew, *Moscow is Not My Mecca* (London: Secker & Warburg, 1964). On African self-determination, see Kwame Nkrumah, *Neo-Colonialism: The Last Stage of Imperialism* (London: Nelson, 1965). On Padmore, W. E. B. Du Bois, and Pan-Africanism in Ghana, see Gaines, *American Africans in Ghana*, 148–50.

54. Padmore, *Pan Africanism or Communism?*, 104.

55. Martin and Walcott, "Smuggling Arms to South Africa."

56. SRC, vol. 2, 696.

57. Coram, *Caribbean Time Bomb*, 45.

58. SRC, vol. 2, 770.

59. Martin and Walcott, "Smuggling Arms to South Africa."

60. Memorandum, CIA, 3 December 1979, declassified 27 November 2006, https://www.cia.gov/readingroom/docs/CIA-RDP81M01032R000700020001-3 .pdf (accessed 1 November 2019). There has been a long-standing relationship between scientists and other academics at universities on one hand and the CIA on the other. See Alfred McCoy, *A Question of Torture: CIA Interrogation, from the Cold War to the War on Terror* (New York: Henry Holt, 2007); and Arthur S. Hulnick, "CIA's Relations with Academia: Symbiosis not Psychosis," *International Journal of Intelligence and CounterIntelligence* 1, no. 4 (1986): 41–50.

61. Moon, "Bitterness Remains on Caribbean Island after Canadian Arms Company Forced Out." See also "Progressive Labor Movement Resolution on the Space Research Issue in Antigua Adopted by the Executive Committee on 9 November 1978 and Published on Saturday 11 November 1978" and "Resolution: Re: Activities of Space Research Corporation to Be Moved by the Honorable Leader of the Opposition in the House of Representative," Antigua Space Research 1978, Loc. no. L01843, Antigua and Barbuda National Archives, Saint John's.

62. Bruce Paddington, dir., *Forward Ever: The Killing of a Revolution*, co-director Luke Paddington, producers Grenada Operations and Princess Donelan (New York: Third World Newsreel, 2013), digitized film. The PRG and Bishop were champions for women's rights. Maurice Bishop and Chris Searle, *In Nobody's Backyard: Maurice Bishop's Speeches, 1979–1983; A Memorial Volume* (Totowa, N.J.: Biblio Distribution Center, 1984). Beverley A. Steele, *Grenada: A History of Its People* (Oxford: Macmillan Caribbean, 2003); Laurie R. Lambert, *Comrade Sister: Caribbean Feminist Revisions of the Grenada Revolution* (Charlottesville: University of Virginia Press, 2020).

63. Arthur Newland, "Rastafari in the Grenada Revolution," *Social and Economic Studies* 62, no. 3/4 (September/December 2013): 205–26. See also Walter Rodney, *The Groundings with My Brothers* (London: Bogle-L'Ouverture Publications, 1969); Ikael Tafari, *Rastafari in Transition: The Politics of Cultural Confrontation in Africa and the Caribbean, 1966–1988* (Chicago: Research Associates School Timers Publications, 2001); and Monique Bedasse, *Jah Kingdom: Rastafarians, Tanzania, and Pan-Africanism in the Age of Decolonization* (Chapel Hill: University of North Carolina Press, 2017).

64. See Ellen Ray and Bill Schaap, "U.S. Crushes Caribbean Jewel," *CovertAction* 20 (Winter 1984): 3–20; Bob Woodward, *Veil: The Secret Wars of the CIA, 1981–1987* (New York: Simon and Schuster, 1987); Joachim Mark, "1979–1983: Grenada-Cuba Relations," *Everybody's* 22, vol. 8 (September 1998): 11; and "C.I.A.'s Role to be Discussed," *New York Times*, 28 October 1983.

65. See Robert Alexander Young, *The Ethiopian Manifesto: Issued in Defence of the Black Man's Rights in the Scale of Universal Freedom* (New York: Robert Alexander Young, 1829); Wilson J. Moses, ed., *Classical Black Nationalism: From the American Revolution to Marcus Garvey* (New York: New York University Press, 1996), 60–67.

66. See William Maxwell, *F. B. Eyes: How J. Edgar Hoover's Ghostreaders Framed African American Literature* (Princeton, N.J.: Princeton University Press, 2015).

67. "Establishment of a Guerrilla Training Camp, Tweed, Ontario, Canada, by Black Extremists," FBI Case File 157-BA-7664. RD 46209 obtained under FOIA provisions.

68. Author's interview with Lennox Farrell, 26 May 2021, notes in author's possession.

69. Karen De Young, "Jamaica's Manley Is Pivotal Leader," *Washington Post*, 28 September 1980. On the Non-Aligned Movement in Latin America and the Caribbean, see also Thomas C. Field Jr., ed., *Latin America and the Global Cold War* (Chapel Hill: University of North Carolina Press, 2020), 148–73; and Sue Onslow, "The Commonwealth and the Cold War, Neutralism, and Non-alignment," *International History Review* 37, no. 5 (2015): 1059–82.

70. Ken Lawrence, "Behind the Klan's Karibbean Koup Attempt, Part II," *CovertAction* 16 (March 1982): 44–50, 21.

71. Lawrence, 44–50, 21.

72. Hundreds, maybe a couple thousand, anti-communist, white supremacist mercenaries from the United States fought for the white minority government of Rhodesia in the late 1970s. See Gerald Horne, *From the Barrel of a Gun: The United States and the War against Zimbabwe, 1965–1980* (Chapel Hill: University of North Carolina Press, 2001).

73. Lawrence, "Behind the Klan's Karibbean Koup Attempt, Part II," 44–50, 21.

74. "Many Backers of Dominican Plot Unknown," *Globe and Mail*, 13 May 1981.

75. Richard C. Salter, "Shooting Dreads on Sight: Violence, Persecution, Millennialism, and Dominica's Dread Act," in *Millennialism, Persecution, and Violence: Historical Cases*, ed. Catherine Wessinger (Syracuse, N.Y.: Syracuse University Press, 2000), 101–18; Tafari, *Rastafari in Transition*.

76. "Plotted Dominica Coup Canadian Nurse Gets 3 Years," *Globe and Mail*, 18 September 1981.

77. Dial Torgerson, "'Comic' Coup Effort No Joke to Dominica," *Los Angeles Times*, 13 December 1981.

78. Lawrence, "Behind the Klan's Karibbean Koup Attempt, Part II"; Les Whittington, "Canadian Sentenced for Bilking N. Korean in Plot to Kill Rival," *Washington Post*, 18 February 1984.

79. See "Dominica Coup Plot Described in Court," *New York Times*, 18 June 1981; and Stewart Bell, *Bayou of Pigs: The True Story of an Audacious Plot to Turn a Tropical Island into a Criminal Paradise* (Mississauga, Ont.: John Wiley and Sons, 2008).

80. Michael Tenszen, "Convicted Criminal Wolfgang Droege, of Scarborough and Prison," *Toronto Star*, 21 February 1993.

81. Bell, *Bayou of Pigs*, 135.

82. Jo Thomas, "Dominica Unsettled in Wake of Thwarted Invasion," *New York Times*, 7 June 1981.

83. Thomas, "Dominica Unsettled in Wake of Thwarted Invasion."

84. "Judge Denies Connally Subpoena in Trial of 3 Alleged Mercenaries," *New York Times*, 14 June 1981.

85. Peter Moon, "Designs on Dominica: The Ku Klux Klan, a Mobster's Money and a Foiled Coup," *Globe and Mail*, 13 May 1981.

86. Thomas, "Dominica Unsettled in Wake of Thwarted Invasion"; Torgerson, "'Comic' Coup Effort No Joke to Dominica."

87. Bell, *Bayou of Pigs*, 28–29.

88. Tim Hector, "Pan-Caribbean and Pan-African Extraordinaire: Rosie Douglas, Brother Friend and Extraordinary International Activist," *The Outlet*, 6 October 2000, https://web.archive.org/web/20120416011318/http://www.candw.ag/~jardinea/fanflame.htm (accessed 10 April 2021). On Dominican history, see Lennox Honeychurch, *The Dominica Story: A History of the Island* (Roseau: Dominica Institute, 1984); and Patrick L. Baker, *Centering the Periphery: Chaos, Order, and the Ethnohistory of Dominica* (Montreal: McGill-Queen's University, 1994).

89. Thomas, "Dominica Unsettled in Wake of Thwarted Invasion."

90. Torgerson, "'Comic' Coup Effort No Joke to Dominica."

91. See Fred Landis, "CIA Media Operations in Chile, Jamaica, and Nicaragua," *CovertAction* 16 (March 1982): 32–43.

92. Lawrence, "Behind the Klan's Karibbean Koup Attempt, Part II."

93. Lawrence, "Behind the Klan's Karibbean Koup Attempt, Part II"; "Behind the Klan's Karibbean Koup Attempt," *CovertAction* 13 (July–August 1981): 28–29.

94. Lawrence, "Behind the Klan's Karibbean Koup Attempt, Part II"; "Behind the Klan's Karibbean Koup Attempt."

95. Peter Moon, "Alcoholism and Racism Cured by Dominica Jail, Woman Says," *Globe and Mail*, 13 April 1982.

96. "Dominica Coup Plot Described in Court."

97. "Klansmen Are among 10 Indicted in Plot on Caribbean Island Nation," *New York Times*, 8 May 1981.

98. Whittington, "Canadian Sentenced for Bilking N. Korean in Plot to Kill Rival"; Jackie Carlos, "The Plot to Murder a President," *Maclean's*, 27 February 1984.

99. Patrick E. Tyler, "U.S. Tracks Cuban Aid to Grenada: In '81, Senate Unit Nixed CIA Plan to Destabilize Isle," *Washington Post*, 27 February 1983.

100. Clarence Lusane, "Grenada, Airport '83: Reagan's Big Lie," *CovertAction* 19 (Spring–Summer 1983): 39–43.

101. See "Document 02. State Department, Bureau of Intelligence and Research, Memorandum, Castro's Allegations," 18 October 1975, https://nsarchive.gwu.edu/dc .html?doc=3214332-Document-02-State-Department-Bureau-of (accessed 28 May 2021); and "Luis Posada Carriles, the Declassified Record, CIA and FBI Documents Detail Career in International Terrorism; Connection to U.S. National Security Archive Electronic Briefing Book No. 153," 10 May 2005, https://nsarchive2.gwu .edu/NSAEBB/NSAEBB153/ (accessed 28 May 2021). See also Kevin B. Blackistone, "1976 Bombing That Killed Cuban Fencing Team Requires Painful Reflection," *Washington Post*, 4 December 2016; Peter Kornbluh, *Back Channel to Cuba: The Hidden History of Negotiations between Washington and Havana* (Chapel Hill: University of North Carolina Press, 2014); and Peter Kornbluh, "Former CIA Asset Luis Posada Goes to Trial," *The Nation*, 5 January 2011, https://www.thenation.com /article/archive/former-cia-asset-luis-posada-goes-trial/ (accessed 28 May 2021).

102. On Bishop's own views about CIA machinations to destabilize Grenada, see Bishop and Searle, *In Nobody's Backyard*.

103. Paddington, *Forward Ever*.

104. Paddington, *Forward Ever*; Hugh O'Shaughnessy, *Grenada: An Eyewitness Account of the U.S. Invasion and the Caribbean History That Provoked It* (New York: Dodd, Mead, 1984). See Kai P. Schoenhals and Richard A. Melanson, *Revolution and Intervention in Grenada: The New Jewel Movement, the United States, and the Caribbean* (London: Routledge, 2019).

105. See Manning Marable, *African and Caribbean Politics: From Kwame Nkrumah to the Grenada Revolution* (London: Verso, 1987), 303 (endnotes 110 and 116). Another comrade of Bishop and Hector also observed serious conflict before the October 1983 countercoup and assassination. He called Hector an "ideologue." Author's interview with Fils-Aimé, 14 October 2020.

106. Dionne Brand, *Bread Out of Stone: Recollections, Sex, Recognitions, Race, Dreaming, Politics* (Toronto: Vintage Books, 2019), 100.

107. Oakland Ross, "'Incredible' Attack on Beach Recalled by Rescued Canadian," *Globe and Mail*, 29 October 1983; Jeff Sallot, "The Grenada Invasion: U.S. Unleashed Chaos, Workers Say," *Globe and Mail*, 1 November 1983; Ashante Infantry, "Marlene Green Devoted Life to Social Equality; Civil Rights Champion Pioneered Programs in Black Education with CUSO, She Aided Development in Caribbean and Africa," *Toronto Star*, 26 November 2002. See also Dionne Brand, "Marlene Green 1940–2002," *Now Magazine*, 7 November 2002; and "Women in Our History," *Our Lives* 2, no. 1 (March–April 1987): 7.

108. Ross Laver, "Gotlieb Protests Plane Ban," *Globe and Mail*, 27 October 1983.

109. Ray and Schaap, "U.S. Crushes Caribbean Jewel," 5.

110. Woodward, *Veil*, 290–300.

111. Edward D. Sargent, "700 Celebrate African Liberation Day," *The Washington Post*, 27 May 1984. See also Stokely Carmichael and Mumia Abu-Jamal, *Stokely Speaks: From Black Power to Pan-Africanism* (Chicago: Chicago Review Press, 2007).

112. Sargent, "700 Celebrate African Liberation Day."

113. See Hector, "Pan-Caribbean and Pan-African Extraordinaire"; and Tim Hector, "What I Said and What Rosie Said," *The Outlet*, 20 October 2000, https://web.archive .org/web/20120416011318/http://www.candw.ag/~jardinea/fanflame.htm (accessed 10 April 2021). On the apartheid regime's military intelligence and infiltration of the African National Congress, see Daniel L. Douek, *Insurgency and Counterinsurgency in South Africa* (New York: Oxford University Press, 2020).

114. Author's interview with Fils-Aimé, 14 October 2020.

115. Eric Siblin, "Rosie the Red Stops Smashing the State," *Saturday Night* 115, no. 5 (May 2000): 27.

116. Hector, "Pan-Caribbean and Pan-African Extraordinaire."

117. The RCMP and FBI placed Reico Cranshaw under surveillance in 1968, because he traveled from Chicago to Toronto, delivering cash to Michael X, one of the participants of the Congress of Black Writers Conference at McGill University. It is highly plausible that Cranshaw and Douglas knew of each other as early as 1968. In 1987, the U.S. government sentenced him to sixty-three years in prison for conspiring to receive $2.5 million from Libya in exchange for committing terrorist acts in the United States. See Memo from Special Agent in Charge, Chicago, re: Reico Cranshaw, RD 46549. See also Liz Sly, "Witness: Gadhafi and Fort Chatted Gang Member Tells of Phone Hookup," *Chicago Tribune*, 28 October 1987. See also chap. 5, note 27 of this volume.

118. See Siblin, "Rosie the Red Stops Smashing the State"; and Dirk Vandewalle, *A History of Modern Libya*, 2nd ed. (Cambridge: Cambridge University Press, 2012).

119. See Horace Campbell, *Global NATO and the Catastrophic Failure in Libya: Lessons for Africa in the Forging of African Unity* (New York: Monthly Review Press, 2013), 53–54. For a critique of the ways that Arab leaders weaponized the Arab world and Islam against Pan-Africanism, see Elenga M'buyinga, *Pan-Africanism or Neo-Colonialism? The Bankruptcy of the O.A.U.* (London: Zed Press, 1982), 22–23, 148, 194, 209.

120. Author's interview with Dawn Roach Bowen, 30 May 2021, notes in author's possession.

121. Rodney, "Black Scholar Interviews," 39.

122. Rodney, "Towards the Sixth Pan-African Congress."

CONCLUSION

1. Eric Siblin, "Rosie the Red Stops Smashing the State," *Saturday Night* 115, no. 5 (May 2000): 27.

2. Don Butler, "Waiting for Rosie, Part II: From Pariah to PM, a 30-Year Quest for Absolution Has Taken Rosie Douglas from Canada to Dominica—and Back," *Ottawa Citizen*, 16 July 2000.

3. Butler, "Waiting for Rosie, Part II."

4. Regarding Caribana, see author's interview with Sheldon Taylor, 11 May 2021, notes in author's possession. See also El-Ra Adair Radney, "Pan African Agency and the Cultural Political Economy of the Black City: The Case of the African World Festival in Detroit" (Ph.D. diss., Michigan State University, 2019); and author's interview with Dawn Roach Bowen, 30 May 2021, notes in author's possession.

5. Author's interview with Sheldon Taylor, 11 November 2021. Notes in author's possession.

6. Author's interview with Bowen.

7. Author's interview with Bowen.

8. Lennox Farrell, "Canadians March on Washington: 25th Anniversary (1989) of Dr. King's Historic March," African Canadian Web Active, https://lenxfarl.tripod .com/page7.html (accessed 30 May 2021).

9. In 1989–90, the Royal Ontario Museum mounted a racist exhibition titled *Into the Heart of Africa*, which generated vitriol among African Canadians. And from 1993 to 1994, Canadian entrepreneur Garth Drabinsky reproduced the U.S. play *Show Boat* in Toronto and New York City. Based on Edna Ferber's 1927 book, and with anti-Black lyrics by Jerome Kern and Oscar Hammerstein II, *Show Boat* depicted life on a Mississippi steamboat from the 1880s to the 1920s, the height of anti-Black terrorism—a by-product of anti-Black sentiments. Paul Robeson received acclaim for his rendition of "Ol' Man River" in the 1936 film. Black activists boycotted the play in Toronto, accusing some Jewish people of complicity in white supremacy and anti-Black racism. Clyde H. Farnsworth, "Blacks Accuse Jews in 'Show Boat' Revival: Blacks and Jews at Odds over 'Show Boat' in Toronto," *New York Times*, 1 May 1993.

10. At the Canadian Museum of Civilization, Anne Packwood received honor as a "Wazee," Swahili for an esteemed elder who is a bulwark of his or her community. See Mohammed Adam, "'A Very Giving Woman': Sarsfield Was Honoured Worldwide for Environmental Work," *Ottawa Citizen*, 1 June 2013; Sheldon Taylor, *Many Rivers to Cross: The African-Canadian Experience*, National Tour 1992–1994, mounted by The Canadian Museum of Civilization, curated by Sheldon Taylor (Toronto: Multicultural History Society of Ontario); Sheldon Taylor, "Many Rivers to Cross: The African-Canadian Experience," *Precinct Reporter*, 22 February 2001; and Jeannine Amber, "Sheldon Taylor: Afro-Canadian Scholar," *Essence* 25, no. 1 (May 1994): 62.

11. "March Strikes Chord Here (Million Man March)," *Share*, 19 October 1995. On other cross-border connections in the late twentieth century, see D. Alissa Trotz, "Bustling Across the Canada-US Border: Gender and the Remapping of the Caribbean Across Place," Small Axe 15, no. 2 (2011), 59–77. See also Eddie S. Glaude Jr., ed., *Is It Nation Time? Contemporary Essays on Black Power and Black Nationalism* (Chicago: University of Chicago Press, 2002).

12. Author's interview with Bowen.

13. See Carol Anderson, *White Rage: The Unspoken Truth of Our Racial Divide* (New York: Bloomsbury USA, 2016).

14. Conrad W. Worrill, "Entering Season of African Liberation Day," *Los Angeles Sentinel*, 7 May 1998.

15. Don Butler, "Waiting for Rosie, Part I," *Ottawa Citizen*, 16 July 2000.

16. Butler, "Waiting for Rosie, Part II."

17. Mark Fineman, "Rosie Douglas: Dominica's Radical Son, and PM," *Montreal Gazette*, 7 March 2000.

18. Butler, "Waiting for Rosie, Part II."

19. Jeff Sallot, "Ottawa vs RCMP: Cabinet Lawyers Fighting to Suppress Papers on Ministers' Knowledge of Mountie Activities," *Globe and Mail*, 27 October 1978,

1; James Jefferson, "Fox Reverses His Stand: Ottawa Orders Probe of RCMP after Unlawful Actions Alleged," *Globe and Mail*, 7 July 1977, 1.

20. Hart broke his silence with an affidavit that he sent to opposition Member of Parliament Elmer McKay. Andrew Szende, "U.S. Informer Says He Bugged Allmand and MP for Mounties," *Toronto Star*, 23 February 1978.

21. Warren Hart provided multiple testimonies to the commissions in January and April 1980. *Security and Information: First Report* (Ottawa: Commission of Inquiry concerning Certain Activities of the Royal Canadian Mounted Police, Canadian Government Publishing Centre, 1979); *Freedom and Security under the Law: Second Report* (Ottawa: Commission of Inquiry concerning Certain Activities of the Royal Canadian Mounted Police, Canadian Government Publishing Centre, [January] 1981); *Certain R.C.M.P. Activities and the Question of Governmental Knowledge: Third Report* (Ottawa: Commission of Inquiry concerning Certain Activities of the Royal Canadian Mounted Police, Canadian Government Publishing Centre, 1981).

22. "Ex-RCMP Spy to Get $56,000 Compensation for '75 Firing," *Toronto Star*, 6 May 1987.

23. Antonin Scalia, "United States Intelligence Law," obtained by *Globe and Mail* under the Access to Information and Privacy Act, https://www.scribd.com/document/336455920/The-Scalia-file#from_embed (accessed 9 February 2018).

24. Scalia, 2.

25. Sean Fine, "The Untold Story of How Antonin Scalia's 'Gift to Canada' Shaped Our Spy Services," *Globe and Mail*, 13 January 2017.

26. Lynn Moore, "Dominican PM 'Humiliated' Canada Won't Grant Him Pardon: Former Student Activist Deported in 1960s after Violent Protest," *Ottawa Citizen*, 28 May 2000.

27. Fineman, "Rosie Douglas."

INDEX

Page numbers in italics refer to illustrations.

Chicago, 70; foreign-born population in, *114*; interracial violence in, 34–35. *See also* Great Lakes region
Chicago Defender (newspaper), 81, 92, 95
Chicago Police Department, 201
Children of the Sun (Parker), 39
Chinese immigration, 119, 125
Choi, James, 252
Choi Hong-hi, 252
Christ, Black, 44
Christianity, 42, 44, 57
Christie, Fred, 85
Christie v. York, 85
Chun Doo Hwan, 252
churches, 233
Churchill, Winston, 94
CIA. *See* Central Intelligence Agency
Citizens' Commission to Investigate the FBI, 214
citizenship, 67, 69, 97; Black, 26; Canadian, 146; dissonant, 217; as fungible marker, 183; military service and, 89–94, 97, 120; passing, 69–70, 83, 101, 103, 157; stillborn, 29; subordinate, 29. *See also* dignity
citizenship, interspatial, 69, 70, 82, 109, 149. *See also* border crossing; Great Lakes region
citizenship, U.S.: criticism of, 180; emigration as critique of, 122; naturalized, 101
civil liberties, moratorium on, 167
civil rights, 9, 26; vs. human rights, 118, 140–44. *See also* freedom struggle, Black; race relations, British; race relations, Canadian; race relations, U.S.
Civil Rights Act (1964), 138
Civil Rights Congress, 141
civil rights movement, U.S., 138, 261
Civil War, U.S., 9, 38
CLACP (Canadian League for the Advancement of Colored People), 60
Clarion, The (newspaper), 104
Clark, Deborah, 219, 220
Clark Amendment, 244
Clarke, John Henrik, 46, 171
class: mobility, 120, 154, 155; consciousness, 170; power, 162

Claxton, Hezekiah, *209*
Cleaver, Eldridge, 197, 200
Cleaver, Kathleen, 190
Cleveland, 70. *See also* Great Lakes region
Cliff, Jimmy, 262
Coakley, Gabriel, 121
Coakley, Genevieve, 121
Coakley, Marie, 121
coal miners, 71, 72, 74, 156. *See also* jobs, in Canada
Coard, Bernard, 246, 253, 254
Coard, Phyllis, 254
Coates, Charlie, 185
Coates, Paul, 209
cocaine, 267
COINTELPRO. *See* Counterintelligence Program
Cold War, 26, 117, 118, 121–22, 128, 197, 258; Africa and, 242; Caribbean and, 239; Non-Aligned Movement, 247; racial politics and, 126–27; U.S. credibility and, 129, 142; U.S. hypocrisy and, 135–36. *See also* communism; moral authority, Canada's
colonialism, 28, 67, 188, 224; in Africa, 5, 9, 22, 62, 233, 234, 235; resistance to, 2, 5, 7, 8, 9, 17, 27, 28, 230–31, 234, 235; terror inflicted by, 46; Washington's support for, 233. *See also* imperialism
Colored Literary Association of Toronto, 43
Colored Political and Protective Association, 36
Colored Women's Club (Montreal), 1, 79
Common School Act, 144
Commonwealth: immigration and, 154–55; moral dissonance in, 159; 1961 conference, 159; non-white partners, 51, 139, 148, 156–57, 158, 159 (*see also* African Caribbean peoples); South Africa's expulsion from, 241
communism, 117, 127, 141, 142, 242; Dominican coup attempt and, 252; exploitation of Black people, 242; racism linked to, 135; threat of in Caribbean, 247; Young Communist League, 91. *See also* Cold War

communities, cosmopolitan, 23
community institutions, 79
commuter permits, 73
complacency, 219
condemnation, 129
Cone, James, 233
Congo Free State, 22
Congressional Black Caucus, 253
Congress of Black Writers Conference,
 167, 169, 171, 172, 200, 201
Congress of Racial Equality (CORE),
 206, 236
Connally, John, 250
consciousness, cross-border, 67, 74,
 109, 119, 149
Contrast (newspaper), 218
Conway, Marshall, 205–6, 207, 216
Cook County, foreign-born population
 in, *114*
Cools, Anne, 27, 160, 194, 212, 237,
 265, 266; gender norms and,
 162–63; immigration to Canada,
 153; pardon, 222; prison sentence,
 222; Sir George Williams University
 occupation and, 170; student activism of, 169; "Womanhood," 164
Cooper, Anna Julia, 20
cosmopolitanism, 21, 22–23, 35, 78
Council on African Affairs, 108
Counterintelligence Program, 197, 201,
 204, 208, 214, 246. *See also* Federal
 Bureau of Investigation
counterrevolutionary tactics, 28–29;
 Garvey and, 62–63. *See also* intelligence gathering; U.S.-Canadian
 relations
counter-subversion, 27–28, 195,
 cross-border, 212. *See also* Hart,
 Warren; *and names of individual
 intelligence agencies*
counterterrorism, 250
Couzens, James, 83–84
Cox, Donald, 207
crack cocaine, 263
Cranshaw, Reico, 201
"Credit to My Race, A" (Edwards), *32*,
 56
Creft, Jacqueline, 254
Crew, Demias, 121
Crisis, The (journal), 45, 53, 55, 56, 61

crisis manufacturing, 215
Cronon, Edmund, 64; *Black Moses*, 64
cross-border connections, 25–26, 145.
 See also borderlands; Great Lakes
 region; transnationalism
cross-border consciousness, 67, 74,
 109, 119, 149
cross-border migrations. *See* border
 crossing; Great Lakes region
Crummell, Alexander, 20
CSIS (Canadian Security Intelligence
 Service), 266
Cuba, 164, 230, 241, 251, 252–53, 260
Cummings, Eddie, 108
Curse of Ham (or Curse of Canaan),
 19, 39
Cushite, The (Perry), 41
Cuzzens, Beulah Harding, 4, 20, 26,
 69, 74–77, 80, 85, *88*, 109
Cuzzens, Earle A., 80, 85, *88*, 109

Daniels, Ron, 233
Darkwater (Du Bois), 43–44, 45
Davis, Angela, 222–23
Davis, Sammy, Jr., 201
Dawn of Tomorrow (newspaper), 37,
 55, 56, 61, 63, 79, 96, 218; ancestor-
 focused spirituality and, 58; revolution and, 59, 60; as sedition, 60. *See
 also* messianism
"D" Branch, 214
death penalty, 134
deception, 196, 225
Declaration of the Rights of the Negro
 Peoples of the World, 48, 118, 142
decolonization, 51, 157, 158. *See also*
 Africa; Caribbean; Commonwealth:
 non-white partners
de Gaulle, Charles, 167
dehumanization, 29
Delany, Martin, 15, 20, 42, 150
deportation: of Douglas, 217, 222, 227,
 228, 229; of Hart, 228; of radicals,
 171, 174, 177
Depradine, Jean, 163
Depression. *See* Great Depression
deracination, 29
deserters, 193. *See also* draft resisters
DeShield, Juanita Corinne, 1–2, 3–4,
 20, 78, 85, *88*, 95

Desmond, Viola, 104
destiny, shared, 36. *See also* Ethiopia
Detroit, 70; African World Festival, 261; Bradby, 82–84; Canadian-born persons in, 72; entertainment in, 76–77; gambling in, 80. *See also* Great Lakes region
Detroit and Cleveland Navigation Company, 79
Detroit-Windsor corridor, 72–73, 76–77, *87*, 182–83, 200
diasporic communities, 2
Diefenbaker, John, *130*, 139, 155, 159, 160–62, 165, 166, 169–70, 219–20, 228
Diggs, Charles, Jr., 236
dignity, 67, 89, 143. *See also* citizenship
Dirty Tricks Gang, 217
discrimination: Great Depression and, 77; in military, 89–94; seeds of, 165. *See also* antidiscrimination legislation; human rights
disinheritance, 29
divine intervention, 38
domestic workers, 71, 74, 79, 154, 165–66. *See also* jobs, in Canada
Domingo, Wilfred, 35, 94
Dominica, 28, 153, 154, 214, 228, 247–52, 259, 263–64; African Liberation Day organizing in, 234; army of, 248; attempted coup in, 247, 248–52; Douglas's return to, 230; Dread Act, 248; Indigenous population, 225; U.S. support for, 251. *See also* Douglas, Roosevelt Bernard "Rosie"
Dominica-Cuba Friendship Association, 230
Dominica Liberation Movement, 256
double consciousness, 83; Trudeau's, 168
Douglas, Bernadette, 155
Douglas, Macintyre, 154
Douglas, Michael, 247, 256, 260, 264
Douglas, Robert Bernard (RBD), 154, 155, 161
Douglas, Roosevelt Bernard "Rosie," 4, 27, 153, 160, 164, 167, 194, 200, 212, 217–18, 237, 246, 247, 256, 265; accusations against, 170, 214; African

Liberation Day and, 234–35; African liberation movements and, 256; arrest of, 213; attempted coup and, 250; background, 154–55; Brotherhood Community Center Project, 221; criticisms of, 260; deportation order, 217, 222, 227, 228, 229; Diefenbaker and, 161–62; Dominica Liberation Movement, 256; in Dominican politics, 257, 260, 263–64, 266–67; Hart and, 212, 214, 221, 222, 224, 225–27; Indigenous Canadians and, 227; Maffei and, 250; at Model Parliament, 164–66; in Montreal, 162; Pan-African socialism and, 230, 258; as prime minister, 266–67; prison reform and, 227; prison sentence, 220, 221; student activism of, 169; threatened by Klan, 188; in Toronto, 221–22; Vaughan on, 215. *See also* Dominica; Sir George Williams University, student occupation
draft resisters, 27, 156, 178–94, 225, 265; aid for, 179–80, 185; in Canada, 155; Canadian intellectuals on, 191–92; Canadian surveillance of, 192; employment and, 187; entry points, 182–83; exile-expatriate divide and, 190; racism experienced by, 184–85, 186–87, 188; Royal Canadian Mounted Police and, 185–86; as run-away slaves, 184; sexism and, 188–89. *See also* refuge, Canada's reputation as
Drake, St. Clair, 41, 46, 57
Dread Act, 248
Dreads, 245, 248, 250
Dresden, Ont., 117–18
Droege, Wolfgang, 249, 252, 262
Du Bois, Shirley Graham, 237
Du Bois, W. E. B., 8, 9, 28, 37, 39, 43–44, 49, 60, 64; "An Appeal to the World," 141; Christianity and, 44; *The Crisis* and, 55; *Darkwater*, 43–44, 45; distrust of Garvey, 54, 61; lack of mass following, 45; "A Litany at Atlanta," 43–44; literary mysticism and, 59; *The Moon*, 59; *The Negro*, 39; Pan-African Congresses, 9; *The Philadelphia Negro*, 123;

human rights, 9, 26, 117, 124, 137; African Americans and, 141; "The Black Man in Nova Scotia" conference, 173, 175; in Britain, 148; Canada and, 118, 119, 129, 139–40; vs. civil rights, 118, 140–44; immigration policy and, 125, 126, 158; lack of linear progressivism in, 120; legal framework for, 153; Universal Declaration of Human Rights, 118–19, 125, 126, 140, 141, 158; in United States, 119. *See also* antidiscrimination legislation; freedom struggle, Black; Hill, Daniel Grafton, III; Ontario Human Rights Commission; race relations

Human Rights Code (Ontario), 138, 140, 144, 148

Human Rights Commission. *See* Ontario Human Rights Commission

human rights legislation, 139; in Nova Scotia, 104; provincial vs. federal, 140

Humphrey, John Peters, 118

Hunt, Ida Gibbs, 9, 20

hypocrisy, U.S., 135

identity: Black, 69; Canadian, 202; subgroup, 20

"If We Must Die" (McKay), 34

Illinois, 72; foreign-born population in, *112*. *See also* Chicago

immigration, 73; Commonwealth and, 154–55; competition for resources and, 159; quotas, 165

Immigration and Naturalization Service, U.S., 69

immigration policy, Canadian, 24, 27, 48, 71, 124; African Americans prohibited from entering Canada, 10, 173; African Caribbean peoples and, 153–56, 158; amendments to Immigration Act, 161; anti-Black, 24; change in, 159–60; claims to moral authority and, 157; criminal records and, 177, 179; defense of, 158; domestic servant program, 165–66; Douglas on, 165; Du Bois and, 122; exclusion of revolutionaries, 219; human rights and,

126; Immigration Act, 48, 71, 159; Jewish refugees and, 74; jobs and, 71, 165–66; labor needs and, 154; liberalization of, 154–55, 163, 193; non-white Commonwealth partners and, 156–57; Order-in-Council PC 695, 73–74; points system, 159–60; sexism in, 189; Universal Declaration of Human Rights and, 125

immigration policy, U.S., 73

immigration status, in Canada, 180, 189

immigration to Canada: by African American veterans, 107–8 (*see also* Hill, Daniel Grafton, III); white, 135

imperialism, 28, 67; resistance to, 9, 233, 235. *See also* anti-colonialism; colonialism; neocolonialism

imperialism, European, 85. *See also* Africa

imperialism, in Canada, 155

imperialism, U.S., 191, 259; Canadian sovereignty and, 189–92; in Caribbean, 255; women and, 189

Indian-White Committee, 146

Indigenous Canadians, 27, 119, 146–47, 177, 221, 223–24; activism of, 224; conditions of, 224; Douglas and, 224, 227; Hart and, 226–27, 229; invisibility of, 186; Red Power, 27, 166, 224

Indigenous reserves, 224

indignity, 67

industry, Black, 47–48. *See also* capitalism, Black

informants: Sams, 226. *See also* Hart, Warren

Innis, Roy, 236

INS (U.S. Immigration and Naturalization Service), 69

integration, racial, 56, 71

intellectual climate, 37

intellectuals, Black, 163; Garvey and, 53–54

intellectuals, Canadian, 191–92

intelligence gathering, 27–28, 196, 198–202, 266. *See also* U.S.-Canadian relations; *and names of individual intelligence agencies*

Marxist Afro-American Progressive Association, 194
Massachusetts, 72, *111*
Mathaba (Center to Resist Imperialism, Racism, and Fascism), 256, 257, 260
Mathews, Robin, 191
Mathieu, Sarah-Jane, 16; *North of the Color Line*, 16
Mays, Benjamin, 35, 99
M'buyinga, Elenga, 20
McCarthyism, 26, 119
McDonald Commission, 265–66
McGill University, 167, 238, 240, 246
McGruder, Edith Gertrude, 69, 81–82
McGruder, Edna Mae, 69, 82
McGruder, James Louis, 82
McGruder family, 81
McGuire, Marian, 248–49, 250, 251
McKay, Claude, 34; "If We Must Die," 34
McKenley, Herb, 91
McKenzie, Severin, 260, 264
McLuhan, Marshall, 168
McNeal, Sallie, 202
McQuirter, James, 248, 251, 252
means of production, Black ownership of, 50. *See also* capitalism, Black
mediocrity, fear of, 162
mercenaries, 245, 247, 248, 249, 251, 259
messiah, described, 37
messianic Black men: attempts to eliminate, 196; fear of, 246
messianism, 25–26, 36, 37, 60, 63, 64, 196; defined, 37; Du Bois and, 44–45; gender and, 38; revelation and, 46; self-remaking and, 38; Wells, 54. *See also* Black Panther Party; *Dawn of Tomorrow* (newspaper); Ethiopianism; Garvey, Marcus Mosiah; Garveyism
metropole, Canada as, 156
Mexico, 24
Miami-Dade Police Department, 267
Michigan: Canadian-born Black people in, 72; foreign-born population in, *112, 113. See also* Detroit
middle-class, Black, 45, 49

migration, 22; within Canada, 107. *See also* mobility; travel
militancy, 171, 176, 177, 198; Black People's Conference, 212; gender and, 175. *See also* Black Panther Party; Black Power; revolution; social change
military, Canadian: Black men in, 10, 90–94; in Great War, 10; segregation of, 10; systemic discrimination in, 92, 93; U.S. citizens in, 90. *See also* Great War; Second World War; veterans, Black
military, U.S.: African Canadians in, 94–95; Ballistic Research Laboratory, 239; Conway in, 205–6; racism in, 98–101; segregation of, 10, 92, 97–101; Tuskegee Airmen, 95–97. *See also* draft resisters; Great War; Second World War; veterans, Black
military service: citizenship and, 89–94, 97, 120; Hart's, 202. *See also* draft resisters; Great War; Second World War; veterans, Black
millennialism, Ethiopian, 38
Miller, Kelly, 58
Million Man March, 263
mobility, 3, 26, 265. *See also* migration; movement
mobility rights, 22
Model Parliament, 164–66
Mondlane, Eduardo Chivambo, 25
Monroe Doctrine, 9
Montreal: Black freedom struggle and, 167; Black intellectuals in, 163; Black population of, 78, 163; Black veterans in, 36; C. L. R. James Study Circle, 163, 170, 225, 226, 238, 246; Colored Political and Protective Association, 36; Colored Women's Club, 1, 79; discrimination in, 125–26; jazz in, 78; Pan-Africanisms in, 198; reputation for racial tolerance, 107; tourism in, 78–79; Universal Negro Improvement Association in, 61, 79, 84, 85
Montreal-American Deserters Committee, 189
Moore, Audley "Queen Mother," 6, 20, 236, 237

Railway Men's International Benevolent and Industrial Association, 96
rape, death penalty for, 134
Rastafarians, 245, 248, 250
RCAF (Royal Canadian Air Force), 90, 91. *See also* military, Canadian
RCMP. *See* Royal Canadian Mounted Police
Reagan, Ronald, 251, 252, 255, 266
Reconstruction, 9, 33
Redmon, Helen, 95
Redmon, Nathaniel, 95
Red Power, 27, 166, 224. *See also* Indigenous Canadians
Red Scare, 121, 142
Red Summer (1919), 11, 33–35
refuge, Canada's reputation as, 156, 178, 180, 181–82, 193, 211. *See also* draft resisters; North Star; Underground Railroad
refugees, U.S. *See* Black Refugees; draft resisters
Regina, Saskatchewan, 177
religion, 54
repatriation, African, 63. *See also* back-to-Africa philosophy
Republic of New Afrika, 6
resources, competition for, 223
respectability politics, 56
responsibility, personal, 263
revelation, messianism and, 46
revolts. *See* Haitian Revolution
revolution, 176, 177, 195; Black activists' demands for, 149; *Dawn of Tomorrow* and, 59, 60; efforts to undermine, 28–29; fear of, 167–68, 171, 173; Western governments' fear of, 160. *See also* Black Panther Party; Black Power; militancy; social change; violence
Revolutionary War, U.S., 15, 89, 104, 129
Rhodesia, 236, 240
riots, 99, 167–68
Rising Son, The (Brown), 42
Rivers, Mary Catherine, 83
Roach, Charles, 257, 261, 263
Roach, Dawn, 257, 261, 263
Roach, Hettie, 261
Robarts, John P., 138, 143

Roberto, Holden, 242
Roberts, G. H., 148
Roberts, Kevin D., 2
Robeson, Paul, 108, 141
Robinson, Andrew, 165
Robinson, Brenda Randolph, 235
Robinson, Cedric, 1
Robinson, Randall, 235, 253
Rockefeller Foundation, 106–7
Rockhead, Rufus, 78
Rodney, Walter, 6, 18, 24, 167, 235, 236, 237, 245, 258, 259
Roosevelt, Eleanor, 119
Roosevelt, Franklin D., 94, 119
Roxborough, John, 80
Royal Canadian Air Force, 90, 91. *See also* military, Canadian
Royal Canadian Electrical and Mechanical Engineers, 91, 103
Royal Canadian Mounted Police, 172, 173, 183, 192–93, 197, 238, 241, 265, 267; Allmand and, 227–28; Central Intelligence Agency and, 214; cooperation with Federal Bureau of Investigation, 198–202; "D" Branch, 214; draft resisters and, 185–86; Hart and, 211–17, 223; Indigenous activism and, 224; Key Sectors initiative, 197–98; Operation Checkmate, 214; perceived internal security challenges, 197–98; Security Service, 197, 266; surveillance of Harvey, 246. *See also* counter-subversion; Hart, Warren; intelligence gathering; security, national; U.S.-Canadian relations
Rubin, Jerry, 219
Ruins of Empires (Volney), 40
Russell, Jim, 185

Sadaukai, Owusu (Howard Fuller), 4, 28, 208, 233, 234, 235, 236, 237, 255–56, 258
Saint-Domingue. *See* Haiti
Salmon, Doug, 89
Sams, George (Robert Waddell Smith), 172, 226
Sanderson, D. F., 134–35
San Francisco-Seattle-Vancouver corridor, 200

Winn, Paul, 174–75, 176–77
womanism, anti-Black, 40
Woman Power, 166
women, 20, 50, 76, 121; anti-Black womanism and, 40; Cools on, 164; domestic servant program, 165–66; gender norms and, 162–63; in Grenada, 245; human rights and, 173; in messianic moment, 63; in Montreal, 1, 79; Parker on, 40; professional opportunities denied to, 105; at Sixth Pan-African Congress, 237; Universal Negro Improvement Association and, 50–51; U.S. imperialism and, 189
women, Southern white, 129, 132, 133–34, 208
women, white, 40
Women in Transition, 222
women's rights, 51, 121, 188
women's shelter, 222
Wonderful Ethiopians of the Ancient Cushite Empire (Houston), 53
Woodson, Carter G., 11
workers, industrial, 19, 83, 84. *See also* jobs, in Canada
Workers League of Canada, 179

working class: pan-African ethic and, 84; solidarity among, 221. *See also* jobs, in Canada
worldmaking, 21. *See also* self-determination, Black
World War I. *See* Great War
World War II. *See* Second World War
writers, Black, 54, 94

X, Malcolm, 25, 28, 47, 142, 234, 246, 258; "Ballot or the Bullet," 142
X, Michael, 201

Yanover, Charles "Chuckie," 249, 252
Yonge Street "riot," 262
York University, 218–19
Young Communist League, 91
Young Progressive Conservatives, 164
Young Women's Christian Association, 106
Youth International Party, 219

Zaire, 244
Zami, 261
Zanj Rebellion, 12
Zimbabwe, 240, 254
Zive, Manuel, 104